REASON IS

On the Nature of Consciousness and how
Everything is Connected

Roar Mikalsen

To the Sons and Daughters of the Universe

MAN IS ONLY FALLEN UNTIL HE PICKS
HIMSELF UP AGAIN

CONTENTS

PART 3
HOW EVERYTHING IS CONNECTED

PART 4
CONSCIOUSNESS RESEARCH

PART 5

THE TROUBLE WITH THE WORLD TODAY

PART 6
THE ROAD AHEAD

Introduction

"Everything must be based on a simple idea. Once we have finally discovered it, [it] will be so compelling, so beautiful, that we will say to one another, yes, how could it have been any different?" (11.37)[1]

—John Wheeler, Physicist—

WHO AM I? What am I doing here? Where did I come from? What is right and what is wrong? And where do our moral codes come from? Can we say that our existence has some sort of meaning—a purpose? Could there be a plan involved—and hence an Architect? Or is every-thing just the result of a series of insignificant coincidences? Are we alone in the Universe? And where do our thoughts about this come from? *What exactly is consciousness, this mystery that cannot be grasped but exists behind and beyond everything we, with our under-standing, can comprehend*? Is it a result of the brain's electro-chemical impulses, of inanimate atoms' random cooperation, or could it be due to something else? To put it bluntly, have we, with our thoughts, created the world or has it created us out of dead matter?

This is, briefly summarized, the big question. It is the enigma that people for thousands of years have concerned themselves with, but the answers to the questions above have remained vague. Indeed, they have been so many, so conflicting, and their paradoxes so difficult to resolve, that most have taken it for granted that these are riddles humanity can never satisfactorily resolve. More than a few, therefore, have considered it nonsensical to waste too much time on these issues, and they have from

---

[1] Source references to quotes are numbered as follows: The first number refers to a list of books that is found in the appendix, the second refers to the page where the quote is found.

birth to death, from generation to generation, lived life as fate would have it.

Still, no matter how marginally people have dealt with these issues, they have never been untouched. In short, these queries have been the underlying basis for (and the drive behind) all their joys and sorrows, and the assumptions regarding these questions have informed every minute aspect of their lives. Hence, everyone, whether we are talking about history's greatest sages or fools, have lived their lives in the shadow of these questions. They inform everything we think and do, and when we look at history there has been a wonderful but confusing number of ways to approach them. After all, innumerable philosophical, scientific, and religious traditions have contradicted and condemned each other, and for an unbiased observer it can seem as if there is little more than a matter of taste (or cultural preferences) whichever way one prefers to look at it.

Thus, it may seem like a difficult task to get to the bottom of Being. However, when it comes to existence theory, people who have thought long and hard tend to think that it really boils down to one question and based on how this is answered much will follow. This question was alluded to above and can be formulated thus: *Is consciousness an epiphenomenon of matter, or is matter instead an epiphenomenon of consciousness?* If the former is the case, if life is the result of dead matter and has evolved as a result of blind chance, the logical implication would seem to be that we can eliminate God, a creative force, a meaningful universe, all values, and any qualitative observation from the calculation—as many evolutionary theorists do. On the other hand, if consciousness has its origins independent of matter, it would, with all that it implies, be reasonable to draw the opposite conclusion.

This issue, therefore, is the crux of the matter. And according to what we think about it, people have spun their worldview throughout the ages. From the earliest of times until well into the 1800s, most have intuitively taken for granted that the latter must be the case. But those who believed in a creator could never agree on much else; from this starting point, they have moved on in all kinds of directions and we see the result reflected in today's world with more than 10.000 different religions. Nearly 150 have more than a million followers, with Islam, Christianity, Hinduism, and Buddhism being the most popular. One would think that these creeds provided enough choice, but this does not even come close to describing the versatility of contemporary religious movements; within all the major religions there are a vast number of smaller factions and Christianity alone has nearly 40.000 branches.

One could argue that such a diversity of interpretations—not to mention all the religious wars that have been fought—reveal an inner discord that only serves to undermine these traditions' credibility. After all, from an empirical perspective, the absolute truth they claim to convey present itself as quite relative. And as a result of the Church's vulnerability to reason, with the advance of the 19th century, a more "rational" counterforce gained momentum. By then, science was becoming more and more a discipline of its own and as it strengthened its influence it became increasingly difficult for the Church to defend certified truths. The idea that the world was no more than 6.000 years old was in poor compliance with scientific discoveries such as fossil findings and the geological record, and with Charles Darwin's theory of natural selection an alternative—and to many people a more credible—creation story was put forward.

Confronted with emerging scientific findings, the authorities of the Church defended old dogmas so feebly that they fought a losing battle throughout the 19th and 20th century. Dethroned by "reason", it was difficult not to see that organized religion had become a powerhouse itself, one more eager to protect its position than to look for a meaningful connection between the world of matter and the world of spirit. And as the Church's refusal to reconsider traditionally accepted truisms has continued to this day, many people take for granted that the first option, that our consciousness is the result of dead matter and a play of random chance spanning some 14 billion years, must be the correct answer.

Seen in this light, it may seem as if the case is closed when it comes to the relationship between matter and consciousness. This, however, is not so, for while the traditional interpretation of evolutionary theory consolidated its position, a body of research was produced which could not be reconciled with this depressing view on man and his place in the world. These findings, which we shall go into later, indicate that it is the other way around. They suggest not only that consciousness *is not* created from matter, but that consciousness exists independently of matter and has a direct impact on the world around us. Stanislav Grof, a psychiatrist with more than fifty years of experience in consciousness research, summarizes the findings:

> "The observations from consciousness research dispel the current myth of materialistic science that consciousness is an epiphenomenon of matter, a product of neuro-physiological processes in the brain. They show that consciousness is a primary attribute of existence and that it is capable of many activities that the brain could not possibly perform. According to the new findings . . . the deepest nature of humanity is not bestial, but divine. The universe is imbued with creative intelligence and consciousness is inextricably woven into its fabric. Our identification with the separate ego is an illusion and our true identity is the totality of existence."(48.xi,300)

We shall soon see what this means. But with this research at hand, it is possible to put forward a new theory of existence which is both more credible and encouraging than the old. More credible, because the new theory (which is not "new" at all) not only synthesizes the insights produced by science into a coherent and meaningful whole—a grand unified theory of *everything*—but because this picture is consistent with the essence of all the religious traditions. It is also more encouraging, because this modern theory of everything is deeply interwoven and consistent with humanity's wisdom traditions—and because what this entails is far better news than most can possibly imagine.

As shall be seen, contemporary humans have the privilege of being born into a time where we finally have enough information about the world to do away with all those misconceptions which have caused us so much suffering. The nature of these delusions, and how dealing with them will help us overcome challenges, shall soon be elaborated upon. Even so, as we merge humanity's ancient wisdom teachings with findings from disciplines as seemingly diverse as philosophy, modern science, psychology, and religion, it follows that we must challenge some well-established "truths". For instance, many believe that religion is contrary to science and vice versa. However, at their core, both are intimately concerned with the laws of nature and the study of reality, and the increasing gulf between them (now some 400 years in the making) is an artificially contrived separation.

Indeed, if we think about it, it is not only obvious that any self-respecting existence theory *must include both*, but that a theory which is able to reconcile the seemingly fundamental contradictions will be able to take the material that is viable within each tradition and separate it from that which is redundant. A slight trimming of all the irrelevant and misleading material which has accumulated within each tradition must therefore be made. And in that respect, we must do away with some "truths" that many people cling on to. Yet, such a pruning will be of great benefit, for it will not only elevate the scientific and spiritual traditions to a level way beyond ours but it will provide a context that is much needed.

A look around us speaks volumes as most people build their lives on the worldview provided by established science or organized religion. Most scientists have taken the theory of evolution to mean that the Universe is an accidental and meaningless quantity; they believe that we are born into a hostile world ruled by chance and the survival of the fittest; that we exist and live our lives on this planet only for a very short time; and that neither life nor existence itself has any inherent value. Based on this belief, "common-sense" tells us that we, whatever the cost, will do wisely in grabbing as much power and wealth as possible in the time we are here so that we can secure for ourselves and our loved ones an easier life. In other words, moral ground—guiding by the ideals, values, and principles that follow from the Wholeness— becomes not a priority.

Science, then, has proven a curse as much as a blessing. In the realm of value, it has taught us that life has no meaning, whereas organized religion, for its part, has tried to convince us that we are separate from God, that "He" has created us with a wealth of depraved inclinations, and that he will punish everyone who gives in to this sinful nature with the eternal damnation of hell. Seen as such, neither science nor religion provides us with reason to feel good about God, ourselves, or our fellowmen, and we see the fruits of these beliefs in the current state of affairs: We live in a hierarchical, competitive world where the have-nots are becoming poorer and more plentiful, while the haves are amassing evermore wealth and power. As a result of their control of the political process, class divisions are steadily increasing and so is the control apparatus that the elites rely on to continue their plunder.

It is, however, a class struggle only by appearances as everyone is fighting more for him/herself than the grouping he or she identifies with. The situation, therefore, can more accurately be described as a dog-eat-dog world: a giant rat race where the rich fight a battle amongst themselves for control of ever-dwindling natural resources and to stay on top, whereas the poor are busy fighting to survive or get ahead in the world. This, of course, is a simplification as throughout all walks of life we find people with a greater perspective who are more compassionate. Yet, the logic of fear has a solid grasp on inhabitants, and shortsighted ambitions have not only brought us into a vicious circle where the consequences of our reasoning—violence, exploitation, and war—increasingly wreak havoc on our interpersonal relationships but is threatening to destroy our common livelihood, the planet.

All the problems we are struggling with, whether they be social, political, mental, environmental, or economical, are in other words the result of our fundamental beliefs about the world. And as Einstein pointed out, no problem can be solved at the same level of consciousness at which it was created. Thus, we need a new way of looking at things if we are to solve looming problems. We need a new understanding, *a cognitive revolution,* which allows us to see the world through a whole new set of eyes—and it is provided, in the nick of time, by the new theory of existence.

So then, what does this new paradigm, this new way of looking at things entail? We all know how the world is put together as seen from the old perspective, but what does the new worldview tell us about the world and our place?

We will spend the rest of the book elaborating. Even so, a synopsis may be of assistance, and briefly summarized the new existence theory can be outlined as follows:

• *To begin with consciousness is all there is.* Einstein showed us a 100 years ago, with the theory of relativity, that matter and energy were two sides of the same coin. And thanks to new research, we can add another variable to Einstein's calculation and say that matter, energy, *and* consciousness are all basically expressions of the same thing!

• Despite the impression presented by our five senses, therefore, *we are not separate from our surroundings*. What is "outside" can more accurately be seen as an energetic extension of ourselves (of our mind's reality) and the most sensible way to think of the world is as if we exist in a collectively shared dream where our environment is a part of us.

• Everything, in other words, is connected and we are part of a unified Whole: a superintelligent, self-conscious, and multi-dimensional webwork which we may call God, the Absolute, All-That-Is, the Force of Foreverness, Intelligent Infinity, or whatever. Thus, consciousness is not separated, limited to the brain. Instead, we are all fragments of God, long-lost wanderers who from our point of view, through the illusion of separation and the potential for experience this brings, contribute to an adventure far grander than you and I can comprehend.

• As seen from the cosmic consciousness, however, there is a bigger play, and by dividing into innumerable fragments, the Totality makes possible a dynamic in which neither God/the Wholeness nor we could otherwise partake. Hence, we are on earth to experience life under those terms provided for by Consciousness in the context of duality.

• This implies quite a bit of hardship seen from our point of view. Even so, without gravity there could be no weight and everything that happens, good or bad, must be judged on the basis of how it affects us in the long run and not on how it feels in the present moment. Looking back, we find that adversity, more than anything, helped us mature as individuals—and so we should be equally grateful for our enemies as our friends.

• Now, most people will agree that a certain hardship may be of benefit. Even so, how can this yet-vaguely defined theory account for events such as war, rape, and young children's death and disease? If there is a God, why would "he" allow such terrible things?

• This is a very good question which we shall return to later. But to comprehend the meaning behind suffering on this scale, we must understand that we do not exist as part of the Whole in the same way as a fish when eaten by a bigger fish. In fact, we are part of a *highly personal* multidimensional Universe. A Universe which in the depths of its being (where we slowly but surely, as we evolve, are on our way), in its purest essence, vibrates with such unconditional love for everything/everyone that only direct experience can comprehend its magnificence and repercussions.

• This Universe, whose fundamental nature is Absolute love, protects and honors all its fragments' inherent integrity, even though we forget. Hence, while we may lose our ways in despair, there is, just outside reach of ordinary consciousness, a Wake Frequency that arranges things according to a greater understanding. Behind this wake frequency, we find the blueprint of a Divine Plan, but to realize what it means we must first consider the reincarnation- and karma principle.

• No more did awareness, our sense of self, begin with birth than it will disappear with death. In reality, just like the Universe, we are multidimensional beings and only a small part of our personality/psyche/soul is embodied in this dimension—which means here on earth.

• The reincarnation concept, therefore, is valid, although oversimplified and incorrectly portrayed in religious traditions. Valid is also karma, the idea that every action has a consequence and that whatever we put out into the universe sooner or later returns. However, neither the karma- nor the reincarnation principle should be seen as punishment. Instead, they are a necessary and inherent consequence of living in a Universe where everything is most appropriately arranged for personal progress.

• The earth, in this sense, can be seen as a school where we choose time and place for our incarnation based on a greater overall assessment of what type of experiences we need to accumulate for our soul's progress. And thanks to the abovementioned concepts (as well as a few others, which are universal and simple to understand) even more inexperienced souls, after having been around a few times, will discover that they have a certain influence over their lives and destiny.

• Speaking of these energy laws, they bring us to the core of the new existence theory as they help us understand how we, with our thoughts, can affect matter. According to the old worldview, this was impossible, but we must remember that the starting point for the new paradigm is that matter and consciousness are the same. As we observe the world it is easy to forget this since matter, from our perspective, looks as real as the environment appears separate. Nonetheless, as we shall see, matter is only energy which is pressed down to a slow vibration—and energy is nothing more than an expression of consciousness.

• In other words, everything manifested is the result of idea-vibrations, and thoughts are not insignificant reflections—mirages. Instead, *every thought* has a certain vibration which reflects its quality. And whether we like it, we send this thought/vibration into the world where it not only (as a result of the law of attraction) affects what kind of experience we draw to ourselves, but also has an impact on our planet's collective consciousness.

• If this is difficult to conceive, we will go into details later. However, everything becomes easier to understand if we remember that *there are no boundaries and that everything is connected*. Just forget about the idea that you are separated and try to see yourself (your perspective) as an energetic focal point which is a minor but unique part of a boundless field; an energy field to which humanity, with our thoughts, contribute positively or negatively.

• It follows that the world, more properly, can be seen as a mirage of our minds than the other way around. This is completely opposite of how we are used to thinking about things. Nevertheless, as soon as a sufficient percentage of the population understand what this means, we will begin to arrange for ourselves much more constructively, both on a personal and global level. Not only is it scientifically documented that thoughts affect habitat, but the energy laws at the heart of this process are simple to understand and provide the basis for a new discipline—constructive social engineering.

• Indeed, ultimately two basic motivating impulses stimulate and shape thought patterns, and on the basis of these variables all calculations and actions follow. *These two fundamental forces are fear and love,* and to the extent that we allow the former to influence us our thoughts will have a qualitatively poor (low) vibration, while the latter ensures a higher, more profound. These two, then, are polar opposites. And if we wonder to what extent our thought-process are motivated by one or the other it is obvious, as even the most insensitive cannot avoid registering the impact of these vibrations.

• To explain: bitterness, hatred, anger, envy, contempt, control urges, and so on, are created by the logic of fear. It is derived from fragmented thinking, and to the degree we feed off its energy we will experience how it makes us feel less than we truly are by reinforcing the illusion of separation and our sense of disconnect. Conversely, it is the other way around with joy, trust, forgiveness, patience, understanding, altruism, compassion, and so on. These emotions and the belief systems behind them are derived from the logic of love. They are intimately connected to the Wholeness concept and undermine the illusion of separation; they make us feel *more whole*, more as one with the world, and in so doing they make us experience ourselves as "more" than what we apparently are.

• Thus, each way of thinking has its own energetic signature, and those who understand a thing or two aspire to thought patterns that have the highest possible vibration. This is what is called *self-actualization*, and it is not only because of the immediate emotional rewards this quest brings that people make it their primary objective. As mentioned, the law of attraction will ensure that our thoughts attract an answer, and because of this and the law of resonance (which we shall speak about later) we constantly reap what we sow. Enlightened people know this full well—

and they also know that the higher vibration they can hold, the better off they and the world are.

• Hence, as *every* thought affects our relationship with the world in one way or another, we have a choice whether to arrange our lives in a more or less constructive manner. This is true not only at the individual but at the collective level. Simply put, while we are here on earth, we give our contribution to a field of consciousness—a global psyche—which at any given time reflects our modes of thinking. And to the extent that we embrace the logic of fear, we will see war, violence, abuse, and exploitation become a more and more prominent part of our lives. The opposite, however, is equally true and to the extent that we allow the logic of love to thrive, we will witness the coming-into-being of peaceful, cooperative-oriented, and viable communities.

This, briefly summarized, is the basis for the new existence theory. For many people this will confirm what they already either intellectually or intuitively knew, while for others it is hard to take seriously. Indeed, to see the world as a thought, as a dream we can manipulate in whatever direction we want, is such a foreign concept that many will not even consider the possibility. For hundreds of years, the "rational" approach has been to rely on what our five senses tell us, and because scientists can only study matter in their microscopes and telescopes—and not the spirit, which builds it—they have long considered it unscientific to read between the lines.

Still, this worldview, which we have just outlined, has been gaining momentum for quite some time. The evidence, for those who consider it, is so impressive that even if we must rethink some fundamental assumptions about reality more and more are doing so. Consequently, within all disciplines of science, people are coming around and the trend within the major religions is also the same.

This itself is an indication of the new paradigm's superiority to the old as radical changes in the thought pattern do not come easily.

I remember the difficulties I had myself in coming to grips with this new perspective. It probably took me five years from the time I realized that the old worldview was misleading until, after much reading and reflection, I began to understand how the world worked. Looking back, it seems kind of strange that it could be so difficult to put it all together because all it took was to realize that the map was upside down—and turning it on its head was all it took to connect the dots to where everything made sense. Still, that is the way with belief systems. They are stubborn things and for years I went around trying to get the terrain to agree with the map. As soon as I turned the map, however, and really looked at the terrain, everything fit perfectly. And if you are one of many who have yet to step into the new paradigm, I can promise that doing so is the beginning of a continuous to-and-fro dynamic (between you and habitat) that will elevate your Being to greater and greater levels of knowledge, understanding, and happiness.

In fact, when we understand what the consciousness-comes-first perspective implies; when we begin to guide by those values, ideals, and principles that follow from Wholeness, we step out of the circle of daily motion, knee-jerk autopilot functioning that describes most of the population's relationship to habitat. We are released from Nietzsche's Hell and move into a spiral-like dynamic which each day brings us closer to the heart of the Universe and the realization of what it fully means that all is *one*. As we progress, we develop a more and more intimate personal relationship with God. We will never ever again feel alone (at least, not like before) and we will increasingly, as our inner-senses evolve and our brain develops a new kind of functioning, not only transcend the dualistic, ego-bound worldview but access higher and higher analytical knowledge and perspectives. This expansion and recalibration of Mind will in turn make us experience more directly the Wholeness. Our sense of boundary dissolves as we realize what it means that the world is a journey *through ourselves* and that everything we encounter is there to help us realize inner potential.

That it is possible to develop consciousness in such a direction may come as a surprise. Nevertheless, as shall be seen, our brain is greatly undeveloped and those who embark on this process will reconfigure the mind in a way that provides access to perspectives, perceptions, and insights hidden to a "normal" brain.

I have no idea whether this seems obvious or absurd. If you are a skeptic, you may think that only knowledge arrived at from the normal state of awareness should be considered credible and that those who talk about different states are talking about pathological conditions such as delirium or schizophrenia. Moreover, talk of a personal, caring, and superconscious Universe, perfectly tailored to (and attending) each person's growth process will sound like the ravings of lunatics. Even so, I beg to differ, and all this will be confirmed by professionals and their research.

As we shall see, the typical adult brain is like a child's compared to the potential that awaits and the possibilities of this expansion is not reserved for an intellectual elite. On the contrary, compared to today's standards you do not have to be "intellectual" or "smart" to embark on this process. As our world is built on the old paradigm, "authorities" in all areas—law, education, politics, church, health care, etc.—have a perceived vested interest in the status quo. It is the old paradigm that has brought them their power and position and the most likely to rise to the top are those who adapt to the demands of this worldview.

Thus, people in positions of authority have never been too keen on change and the status quo itself has always been reactionary. Excelling at school (or being "smart"), therefore, basically means that we soak up the old worldview like a good sponge and those who want to get ahead will discover that they must do so at the expense of integrity. In fact, because identity and morality are intimately entwined, to succeed in the system is equal to a pact with the devil; we must ignore the implications of Wholeness, which can only diminish our sense of self and connection with others, and so, if self-actualization is our objective, the first thing we need to reevaluate is our reverence for self-proclaimed authorities.

Hence, being equipped with a healthy dose of skepticism is a good start. And if we add an open mind—a willingness to question every-thing, mixed with humility—we will be well on our way. We will, then, easily break free from old, disempowering patterns of thought. And as we embark on that journey which day-by-day brings us out of duality and closer toward innate potentials, we find that boundaries are illusory; that they are a product of fallacious belief systems which serve to limit and confuse—and that nothing ever happens by chance.

As already mentioned, more and more embark on this quest. This is no coincidence for the more who do, the easier it will be for others to follow. Remember that mind and matter ultimately are one. As a result, just like matter is subjected to the laws of gravity, so are thoughts—and just as an object, the greater its weight, carry more attraction so an idea, the more widespread it becomes, will have greater pull. It is also no coincidence that more and more people are becoming interested in this process; that they start thinking for themselves; that they evolve out of the old group-consciousness and into another; and that they begin to see a larger picture which previously escaped them. It is a natural result of living in a meticulously ordered, perfectly structured, and purpose-built Universe and that we are approaching a preordained point—the Egregor —where the global psyche will recalibrate into a vibration of such quality that it will enable awe-inspiring changes.

I shall, however, not reveal too much. I can only ensure that there is much to look forward to, and the purpose of this book is to prepare for the transformation ahead by taking the reader on a journey through himself/herself. In part one, we shall take a look at expanded states of consciousness and what they have to say about our relationship to the Universe. In part two, we shall examine history and how the evolution of man, as it relates to religion and science, confirms the worldview and insights of expanded states of consciousness. In part three, we shall go into detail and see how the knowledge derived from experiential spirituality (i.e., mystics) is consistent with understandings offered by disciplines as diverse as physics, psychology, biology, and medicine. In part four, we continue to explore the findings of consciousness research and how it ties together with everything we have discussed. In part five, the reader will be presented with an overview of our constitutional heritage; we shall see how the morality of the prophets and the founders are one and the same, that the values, ideals, and principles that follow from Wholeness have always been our guiding lights, but that the power of fear made us too weak to honor the responsibilities that come with being adults. This resulted in political structures far beneath human potential. Indeed, psychopaths are as plentiful in powerful positions as in prisons; they are only more successful in covering up their crimes, and while this is not officially accepted, the result is a gap between constitutional ground and reality—a void not unlike Nietzsche's abyss, so painful that we are psychologically predisposed to look the other way.

Nevertheless, if we are to improve our ways, we better understand our problems, and in chapter five we shall see how the logic of fear has corrupted society.

In part six, we shall look at solutions to this condition. We shall have more to say on the logic of love, integrity building at the personal and national level, and its implications for social engineering. We shall see how the new theory of existence is compatible with findings from social sciences, and how—if we apply this knowledge—we can remedy the problems previously discussed and create a new and better world.

Such a project might seem ambitious. Nonetheless, considering the timing, the findings and conclusions of this book are neither unique nor controversial. On the contrary, the sum of all knowledge mankind has produced fits together in an interconnected and overlapping whole. And we have today, within each discipline of human endeavor, more than enough professionals on hand whose research confirms the worldview we are about to become familiar with.

When it comes to modern existence theory, then, this is nothing more than a primary course, a basic walk-through of how the "inner" and "outer" world is connected and why everything is as it is. It builds on the insights of people who together know far more about the world than I, and the only thing I have done is (hopefully) to put it together and present it in a way that makes the new worldview easily accessible to any student of life.

That said, I do not want you to embrace these findings uncritically. The wise reader knows that anyone can go wrong at any time and common-sense dictates that one should be skeptical of an author who claims to present an overview of consciousness and how it is connected to everything. Before we begin this journey, therefore, I stress that this is *nothing more than my interpretation of how the world is put together as seen from the cosmic perspective*. No writer/thinker can present any truth but his/her own and although I will do my best to move forward tongue in check, it should be obvious that I would rather this be read as a fairy tale than prophecy. All I do is present the book that I, myself, would like to have found 25 years ago. And I hope that every reader, whether you are a 20-year-old who has just begun to explore the big questions, a professor wanting to build a bridge to other disciplines, or a mystic already well versed in the ways of the world, will find something of interest.

Before we go on, perhaps I should add that a book exploring such a considerable topic cannot possibly satisfy every reader's skepticism or curiosity. This, of course, is not its purpose. What's offered is a framework that can be used as a basis for further exploration and I leave it to the reader to find your own way in a direction of your choosing. Among its pages, therefore, the reader will find references to books that elaborate on details and in the afterword you will find a list consisting of books which provide a basis for further investigations.

That said, the reader should be prepared for the road ahead. So let us now begin this adventure, this quest which is the timeless story of our journey through the Universe—a journey that is multidimensional, which goes through ourselves, and where we and the Universe end up as one.

From one traveler to another,
Godspeed

Roar A. Mikalsen,
Ullersmo 2014

PART 1

THE NATURE OF CONSCIOUSNESS

1

EGO AND OTHER
FORMS OF CONSCIOUSNESS

"The main problem in life is Ego, and nobody knows it better than I."

—*Swami Rama*—

NOW THAT WE have a general idea of where we are going, let us begin with discussing consciousness as perceived from the consciousness-comes-first perspective. As already mentioned, this perspective builds on the premise that consciousness is the nature of all things and it follows that the Universe is not a stillborn, lifeless, or pointless creation but a vibrant, exuberant and superintelligent organism.

This is completely opposed to the old way of seeing things. Our scientists have been investigating this subject for centuries and the majority work from the hypothesis that the world is made of dead matter and that consciousness has arisen as a by-product. Yet, nothing can be reduced to dead matter. When we look into the matter, we find that there isn't any real substance present at all, only energy that takes on different forms and which to us appears as skin, hair, glass, stone, fire, wood, water, and so on, as a result of our sense-apparatus.

This may sound strange, but it is a scientific fact we shall return to later. Everything, in other words, consists of energy and since all energy is a manifestation of consciousness, everything we see—from the cells in our body to the stars in the sky—can be considered living beings.

This does not mean that their form of consciousness is similar to ours. GodForce assumes such a diversity as consciousness manifests throughout the physical and non-physical dimensions that it is beyond any individual fragment's ability to fully appreciate what it means. And just as a stone cannot comprehend what it means to be a man, we cannot possibly, with our ordinary consciousness, imagine what it means to experience a cat's consciousness or the Universe's.

Notice that I said *ordinary* consciousness. By this, I mean the type of awareness which the vast majority believe is the only wholesome state of consciousness. However, to quote psychologist C.D. King "we all convince one another that the waking condition is the healthy and proper one, for no other reason than that we are all its common victims."(27.41) "Victims", because the ego believes that it knows best, when in reality it is impotent. To properly understand its place in the world, it needs a greater reference, and fortunately, to quote William James, the father of American psychology, it is "but one special type of consciousness, whilst all about it, parted from it by the flimsiest of screens, there lie potential forms of consciousness entirely different." (61.335)

James himself had some experience with expanded states due to his experiments with nitrous oxide, a gas which at the end of the 19th century was not only used as an anesthetic but was also in demand for its ability to alter consciousness. In today's world, psychoactive drugs such as LSD, psilocybin (magic mushrooms), and ayahuasca are more popular and probably have a better effect.

Speaking of these substances, it is well-known that many people, while knowing very little, are highly skeptical. Although shamans and wisdom seekers for thousands of years have hailed such substances as doorways to the numinous and used them to reach insights not obtainable from the normal state, they are currently endowed with a bad reputation because of our drug policies. As we shall see, however, the real problem is drug policy and not these drugs—but there are not too many who realize this. Quite a few, therefore, suppose that the intoxication caused by these substances represents an unhealthy and psychosis-like state of consciousness and they dismiss the knowledge derived from such use as nonsense.

This is, of course, a pity. But like most who have interacted with these substances, James himself was grateful for the insights offered by the drug-experience. He claimed that his experiences revealed an understanding that, although strange and unfamiliar to the normal consciousness, transcended its reasoning and concluded that although "We may go through life without suspecting their existence, . . . no account of the universe in its totality can be final which leaves these other forms of consciousness quite disregarded."(61.335)

We shall therefore, throughout this book, become acquainted with the alternative states of consciousness and the insights they convey. As James points out, they are an essential part of the Universe's, as well as our nature, and to build an existence theory based on the world as seen from the perspective of ego-consciousness alone is doomed to fail. The simple reason for this is that our Universe—just as we are—is a multi-dimensional ocean of consciousness and compared to this greater wholeness our ego is nothing more than a ripple on the surface.

Seen from this greater perspective it is obvious why we, with our five senses and ordinary reason alone, never will get to the bottom of things. To do so, would be as difficult as to meaningfully describe the contents of a book based on a single sentence, but still this is what the majority of theologians, philosophers, and scientists have tried to do.

Now, it is not my intention to scorn the ego. As we shall see, it plays a significant role in humanity's evolutionary process and it has made possible a grand play of consciousness which otherwise could not take place. The point, therefore, is not to criticize the ego. It is just to emphasize that it tends to see itself as everything that is—and this is not the case. If we are to learn something worthwhile about the world, therefore, we must either transcend the limited boundaries of our ego-consciousness or listen to others.

Finding such people is not difficult, for throughout millennia there have always been people around who have devoted their lives to know the workings of consciousness. Guided by their efforts and the rewards brought about, they have found a road to the inner-universe and together they have mapped out its basic landscape. This book presents an outline of the experiences and realizations that they have come back with. And although it is impossible to present a detailed picture of the inner land-scape, it is my objective to provide a proper overview.

Now, as mentioned, many are skeptical of these findings because they believe that the only real landscape is the one we are familiar with at the surface. They therefore presume that this inner landscape must be an imaginary product of the psyche. Even so, virtually everyone who has had the full-blown mystical experience come back to tell the same story as people from other times and cultures have done, and the landscape they describe both overlap and coincide. It is this fact that makes it possible to put their experiences into a meaningful and coherent context, and so we should treat their accounts with the same reverence as earlier generations demonstrated towards the explorers of high seas and foreign continents.

Another thing we should consider is that people who have had such experiences describe them as being far more real and convincing than anything they have experienced with normal consciousness. To them, experiencing this new state of consciousness is like waking from a dream because the new, expanded type of awareness surpasses and transcends the old in the same way as our everyday awareness surpasses and transcends our dream consciousness.

We also do not have to rely on the narratives of "dopeheads" when it comes to gathering accounts of this inner landscape. As we shall see, there are several ways to bring about these states of consciousness, and throughout history many have obtained them through meditation, hypnosis, a near-death experience, spontaneously, or in other ways.

These experiences have been given many names, differing from culture to culture. Common to all, however, is the way people describe them and for those who have experienced these states, they tend to make such an impression that it turns everything they took for granted on its ear. Before the experience, everything they "knew" was derived from the ego's understanding, and because this tells us that we are separate from habitat they viewed life through the traditional dualistic model of interpretation. Hence, it seemed that self-interest and public interest were two different things, they saw good and evil as opposites, and they viewed life and death as fundamentally conflicting variables. Having experienced the new state, however, they saw clearly—as the illusion of separation dissolved—how they were a part of a greater, unified, and divine Whole. And because the old consciousness felt like a flimsy, pathological state compared to this new and more advanced expression of being, it was no doubt that the visions from expanded states were the most credible.

To understand the difference between the ordinary and expanded states of consciousness, a proper way to describe it would be to imagine the world as an enormous billion-piece jigsaw puzzle without its box: all we are left with to figure out the big picture is a million colorful pieces and there is no way to know wherein the greater picture the different chips belong. After all, the chips themselves are way too small and insignificant to make sense on their own—and the box being gone, we have not got a clue what we are looking at. All we can do is patiently use logic and intuition and systematically work our way forward. As we go through life, we constantly try to put two and two together, and as time goes by more and more pieces seem to fall into place. After a while, we get an idea of what the greater picture must look like—or, at least, so we think. Nevertheless, from time to time we find that the chips do not fit where we thought. Perhaps, at first, the blue chips looked like they were part of a sky and then, as more pictures fall into place, we find that they belong to a woman's dress, or possibly a sea.

Point is: without having seen the big picture it is a most confusing and challenging endeavor. And considering that we are dealing with a multidimensional puzzle, one where most of the pieces are not possible to see from the normal perspective, it is easy to understand why we have not yet grasped the bigger picture. As seen from the expanded states of consciousness, however, life looks very different. I am not saying that every piece of the puzzle is immediately accounted for, but the overall picture is and from there the rest follows.

An example of what such an experience entails and how it effects lives is found in Richard Maurice Bucke, one of the great pioneers of psychiatry. He had such an experience spontaneously when he was 36 years old and afterward described it thus:

> "[There came] upon me a sense of exultation of immense
> joyousness accompanied . . . by an intellectual illumination
> quite impossible to describe. Into my brain streamed one
> momentary lightning—[a] flash of Brahmic[2] Splendour

---

[2] With "Brahmic" Bucke refers to the word *Brahman* which in Indian/Vedic philosophy represents the Universe as seen from the standpoint of the Absolute. I.e.,

which has ever since lightened my life; upon my heart fell one drop of Brahmic Bliss, leaving thence forward for always an aftertaste of heaven. Among other things . . . I saw and knew that the Cosmos is not dead matter but a living Presence, that the soul of man is immortal, that the Universe is so built and ordered that without any peradventure all things work together for the good of each and all, that the foundation principle for the world is what we call love and that the happiness of everyone is in the long run absolutely certain.

. . . I learned more within the few seconds during which the illumination lasted than in previous months or even years of study, and I learned much that no study could ever have thought. . . . Especially [I] obtained such a conception of THE WHOLE . . . as dwarfs all conception, imagination or speculation, springing from and belonging to ordinary self consciousness, such a conception as makes the old attempts to mentally grasp the Universe and its meaning petty and even ridiculous. . . . A great deal of this is, of course, from the point of view of self conscious-ness, absurd—[but] it is nevertheless undoubtedly true." (17.8,14)

As Bucke himself points out, much of this appears absurd. Seen from our perspective, it seems obvious that evil, separation, loss, and death are real. We always take them into account, and consequently we walk through life with the conviction that darkness, damnation, loneliness, and annihilation are real and present dangers. Nothing threatens the ego more. And as a result, life to most people presents itself as a continuous survival strategy, an endless fight whereby our ideals give way to more "practical" considerations.

---

one sees the world from a perspective where everything is blissful, unbounded ecstasy and where the separation, fragmentation, and relativity we are so familiar with (as a result of our limited perspective on things) is lost to a consciousness that includes all. From this point of view, we experience ourselves as *all that is*.

Still, those who have had mystical experiences claim that all the ego's worries are delusions. They are convinced that they, with the new consciousness, see the world as it really is; that they pierce through the foggy, fearful, and confusing landscape constructed by the surface-consciousness and into a deeper, more profound reality—and as already mentioned, the insights they come back with are the same. To give the reader an example, I will introduce the Indian freedom activist, mystic, and philosopher Sri Aurobindo. Not only did his integrity threaten an Empire. As a result of his meditation practice, he was familiar with the expanded states of consciousness and described them as follows:

> "States of consciousness there are in which Death is only a change in immortal life, pain a violent backwash of the waters of Universal delight, limitation a turning of the infinite upon itself, evil a circling of the good around its own perfection; and this is not in abstract conception only, but in actual vision and in constant and substantial experience. To arrive at such states of consciousness may, for the individual, be one of the most important and indispensable steps of his progress towards self perfection."(9.52)

As we can gather from Aurobindo's report, it is only at the surface that the dualistic model of interpretation has power to convince. And as soon as we gain access to the greater perspective—as soon as we see the Wholeness that unites and transcends the apparent duality—we understand how life, while subjugated to the ego's trancelike state, is part of a larger divine play.

Now, it is not easy to picture what a perspective that transcends the world of duality implies. Our ego-consciousness always defines itself in opposition to something "other" and so it must "die" before we can access the perspective of the greater Whole. Consequently, ordinary people have great difficulties understanding how it could be possible for consciousness to include *all* while at the same time preserving identity, and they cannot really imagine what it means to see the world from a perspective that reveals (and brings together) the totality.

It must also be noted that those who have had such encounters claim to take part of a state so profoundly different that words cannot convey the experience. This can be a point of frustration, being that the insights they have encountered are so deep, so overwhelming, that they are impossible to impart without direct experience. To normal people, for instance, it will sound like a crazy person's rambling when told that everything—as seen from this greater perspective—is perfect and that everything is as it should be. From the ego's point of view, it seems obvious that this is not the case, and so a "realist" is much more likely to dismiss such experiences than take them seriously.

To do the latter, they must cast aside everything their ego has told them and it goes without saying that good reasons, for a skeptic, is hard to find. Most, therefore, choose to deal with the "grueling realities" of life rather than examine their preconvictions. Yet, they do themselves a great disservice, for just as people 500 years ago refused to accept the findings of explorers because they had to accept that the earth was round, modern skeptics reject information which would bring human understanding an important step forward.

Now, I myself am familiar with these states of consciousness. I know how difficult it is to convey the experience and how challenging it is to open a closed mind to the possibility that there is more to this world and so I will present a few more descriptions of the realizations offered by these expanded states, while I emphasize that it is not just the naive and gullible who find such insights convincing. Stanislav Grof, the psychiatrist who has done the most research into this field, confirms:

"In my experience, everyone who has reached these levels [of consciousness] develops convincing insights into the utmost relevance of the spiritual and religious dimensions in the universal scheme of things. Even hardcore materialists, positivistically oriented scientists, sceptics and cynics, and uncompromising atheists and antireligious crusaders such as the Marxist philosophers suddenly become interested in a spiritual search after they [are] confronted [with] these levels in themselves."(49.95)

Grof, himself, started out as a committed Freudian psychologist, meaning that he was convinced that consciousness was a phenomenon limited to the patient's head and had its origins in matter. His extensive experience with LSD therapy from the mid-1950's to the early 1970's, however, made it clear that Freud's psychology was too limited. The more research he did, the more vibrant the inner landscape appeared. And it became obvious that consciousness was not confined to the physical body, but that it existed independently of the brain and would continue after physical death.

As his quote above makes clear, many of his subjects were initially skeptics and one, a psychiatrist, recounts his transformative experience:

> "[During my trip] I became the entire universe; I was witnessing the spectacle of the macrocosm with countless pulsating and vibrating galaxies and *was* it as the same time. These radiant and breathtaking cosmic vistas were intermingled with experiences of the equally miraculous microcosm—from the dance of atoms and molecules to the origins of life and the biochemical world of individual cells. For the first time, I was experiencing the universe for what it really is—an unfathomable mystery, a divine play of energy. Everything in this universe appeared to be conscious.
>
> . . . I was confronted with a . . . startling discovery: consciousness might actually pervade all existence. My scientific mind was heavily tested by this possibility until I realized that although many of these experiences were incompatible with our common sense, they were not necessarily out of the realm of science. These revelations were certainly not more baffling than the implications of Einstein's theory of relativity, quantum mechanics, various astronomical concepts, and modern cosmogenic theories. Pantheistic religions, Spinoza's philosophy, the teachings of the Buddha, the Hindu concepts of Atman-Brahman, *maya* and *lila*—all these suddenly came alive and were illuminated with new meaning. . . . I suddenly understood

the message of so many spiritual teachers that the only revolution that can work is the inner transformation of every human being."(49.113)

Another reformed skeptic (also a psychiatrist) had this to say:

> "I was preoccupied with the problems of time and space and the insoluble paradoxes of infinity and eternity that baffle our reason in the usual state of consciousness. I could not understand how I could have let myself be "brainwashed" into accepting the simple-minded concept of one-dimensional time and three-dimensional space as being mandatory and existing in objective reality. It appeared to me rather obvious that there are no limits in the realm of spirit and that time and space are arbitrary constructs of the mind."(49.187)

As we can see, there is indication that the expanded states help us access a perspective where it is possible to see how the world is put together. While the ego-consciousness concerns itself with the surface and only perceives things as they appear from the outside, we hereby experience directly the depth which underlie everything—we experience their "insides." Seen from this perspective, therefore, the world looks entirely different. The Whole permeates all perception and as we understand how sedated the surface-consciousness is, we realize how incredibly limited its cognition must be.

That is why this new perspective seems so much more convincing. For the first time, we recognize the depth behind that which our surface-consciousness can barely touch; we immerse ourselves more directly in the cosmic fabric and we begin to understand the deeper, more profound implications of words like "me", "you", "being", "non-being", "integrity," "dishonesty", "justice"—terms that we may use, but fail to comprehend.

One way to compare the difference between the normal and the expanded states of consciousness is if we sat on the beach and tried to understand the ocean by observing its surface. It goes without saying how inadequate such an approach is when we consider that those who explore the expanded states exit the beach, enter the sea, and suddenly become one with the water and everything in it. *Only then will we be able to say something worthwhile about the substance we are dealing with* and as a result we see the world in a whole new way; we go beyond appearances to experience things as they really are—and the deeper into these states we go, the more overwhelming their beauty and terror becomes.

I add terror, not only because there are also demonic realms, but because the Divine can be so overpowering, so ripe with majesty and awe, that bliss and terror merge. The deeper into these states we travel, therefore, the more likely we will reach a point where disintegration seems imminent. Aldous Huxley, one of the great authors of the 20th century, came close. He wrote *The Doors of Perception* about his experience with mescaline, a psychedelic substance, and in this book, he conveys capably how the ordinary appeared completely different. It should be noted that Huxley was almost blind from an eye-disease (he was occasionally guided by a dog), but as he sits in his house in Los Angeles and the mescaline starts working, he describes how everything began to change. He depicts the furniture as being permeated by an inner, divine light and even the fabric of his pants as a source of deep reflection. Beside him stood a vase with some flowers and what he saw took his breath away:

> "I was seeing what Adam had seen on the morning of his creation—the miracle, moment by moment, of naked existence. . . . Flowers shining with their own inner light and all but quivering under the pressure of the significance with which they were charged.
>
> . . . What rose and iris and carnation so intensely signified was nothing more, and nothing less, than what they were— a transience that was yet eternal life, a perpetual perishing that was at the same time pure Being, a bundle of minute, unique particulars in which, by some unspeakable and yet self-evident paradox, was to be seen the divine source of all existence.

. . . [Everything in the room] shone with the Inner Light, and was infinite in its significance. The legs, for example of that chair—how miraculous their tubularity, how supernatural their polished smoothness! I spent several minutes—or was it several centuries?—not merely gazing at those bamboo legs, but actually being myself in them; or, to be more accurate (for "I" was not involved in the case, nor in a certain sense were "they") being my Not-self in the Not-self which was the chair."(43.10, 11)

The experience of fusing with everything—of becoming one with all there is—which Huxley describes, is essential to how the world is seen from the expanded states of consciousness. So is the experience of seeing the Divine manifest in ordinary things, and the deeper we pierce into this consciousness the stronger the experience becomes. At some point it will become overwhelming; it will be perceived as an increasing pressure whereby the experience of Divinity, Beauty, Responsibility, and Significance is imposed with such energy that annihilation seems due, and to Huxley it presented itself as follows: He went out of his house, to the garden, and the sight of a garden chair threatened to consume him:

"Confronted by a chair which looked like the Last Judgement—or, to be more accurate, by a Last Judgement which, after a long time and with considerable difficulty, I recognized as a chair—I found myself all at once on the brink of panic. This, I suddenly felt, was going too far. Too far, even though the going was into intenser beauty, deeper significance. The fear, as I analyze it in retrospect, was of being overwhelmed, of disintegrating under a pressure of reality greater than a mind, accustomed to living most of the time in a cosy world of symbols, could possibly bear."(43.52)

This was the peak experience for Huxley, and after this immersion in his own (and the Universe's) psyche he came to his senses, enriched by the encounter. Still, despite its overwhelming nature, it is possible to go beyond. Both Bucke and Aurobindo did, and we shall have more to say on the experiential picture associated with what LSD therapy calls the "Ego-death" experience. The point here is to provide an idea of the expanded states of consciousness and their relationship to the one that we know so well. And we can see from this why those who have experienced these states tend to describe the normal consciousness as a very confined, subdued, and reduced entity whose purpose is to make it possible to live life here on earth without becoming too overwhelmed by the nature of reality. Huxley put it like this:

> "Each one of us is potentially Mind at Large. But in so far as we are animals, our business is at all costs to survive. To make biological survival possible, Mind at Large has to be funnelled through the reducing valve of the brain and nervous system. What comes out at the other end is a measly trickle of the kind of consciousness which will help us to stay alive on the surface of this particular planet."(43.12)

In addition, there is another reason why the expanded states are not normally available. As we shall see, the cognitive limitations associated with the reduced consciousness have a purpose, for through the illusion of separation it enables the divine play—a play which we are only now beginning to comprehend.

When it comes to this play, the expanded states of consciousness help us understand what it is about, because they provide a perspective from which it is revealed. Hence, Bucke called the most exalted state "cosmic consciousness", as it surpassed the old and revealed an order and meaning which was hidden from the surface-consciousness. As he said:

> "Along with the consciousness of the Cosmos there occurs an intellectual enlightenment . . . which alone would place the individual on a new plane of existence—[that, in fact,] would make him almost a member of a new species."(17.2)

Bucke suspected that this consciousness represented the next step in human development and wrote a couple of books on the subject. As he speculates in *Cosmic Consciousness: A Study in the Evolution of the Human Mind*, evolution progresses in fits and starts, and even if such awareness is an inherent potential some will have a taste before it manifests in the population at large. To support this thesis, Bucke produced numerous examples of personalities whom he considered to be representatives of this consciousness. Besides prophets such as Jesus, Buddha, and Mohammed, he mentioned Dante, St. John of the Cross, Shakespeare, William Blake, Henry David Thoreau, Alfred Tennyson, Walt Whitman, and more. He wrote at the end of the 19th century and as he noticed that the connection became more frequent he expected that, at a given point, *everybody* would get to experience it.

Personally, I think that he is correct and that the time Bucke looked forward to is drawing near. Why I think so will be made clear by the rest of the book. Not only is this the logical outcome of evolution, but more people than before are becoming familiar with this consciousness. Already, millions have attained states similar to those that paved the way for organized religion, and a growing number of those who have yet to experience these states are questioning the status quo.

As is to be expected, powerful forces are doing what they can to keep the old paradigm in place. But even if they are fighting against the new perspective, they are losing ground. The reason for this is that the more we know, the more obvious it becomes that the old way of thinking does not add up. With the progression of time, humanity have gathered more and more data that fail to comply with the demands of the old paradigm, and we now have amassed such knowledge that the dam of ignorance which has kept the old paradigm in place is about to burst.

We shall later explore these data, these anomalies. The point here is to acquaint the reader with the nature of consciousness and to make it clear that there are other states which are superior to the ones we know so well. This more advanced consciousness, which we can call cosmic consciousness, is not only potentially available to all; in part six, we shall see how it represents the next logical step in the evolution of mankind and that we must act on its implications if we are to escape our predicament.

Indeed, looking at things, the problems we are struggling with are a reflection and a result of the ego-consciousness' inadequate worldview. The neo-Darwinian, political-realist, existentialist, positivist—not to forget organized religion's—view of the world, are only some examples which illustrate its limited capacity to comprehend what from the expanded states is the simplest of truths. And it is only because people fail to put two and two together that such models of interpretation continue to wreak havoc.

As we shall see, these belief systems build on false premises as they expand from the matter-comes-first perspective. Hence, they miss the point entirely, and the basic lessons which are so obvious to more evolved minds—that Consciousness is all there is and that everything is one Supreme Being—escape them. Even so, everything is All-That-Is, the Omnipresent Being, manifesting, sensing, and experiencing itself in different shapes and forms, and we are here to experience the world from the perspective of our sense-apparatus and ego-consciousness. Just as the Universe, however, we are multi-dimensional beings, and even though we may seem separate we are indelibly connected.

It is because of this: because the Universe and we are one, that the cosmic consciousness is available. And as we escape the narrow mind-set provided by ego-consciousness, we experience an evolutionary leap and a whole new perspective. Then, all those conundrums that the normal consciousness had difficulty coming to grips with—the nature of the Universe, its order, the divine plan, evil, and the meaning behind everything—make infinite sense. From the perspective of Wholeness, we see that significance and beauty pervade all Being, no matter how horrible events may be on the ground. And even if such an experience rarely lasts long (as measured in conventional time), we bring the insights conveyed by the expanded states back to the physical and integrate them into the surface-consciousness.

Such experiences, in other words, reshape the ego into more than it was. The ego not only glimpses the larger reality of which it is part but interacts with analytical knowledge which, until then, was beyond its comprehension. As it learns to see itself in a larger context, it begins to understand its place in the grander scheme and it also becomes more proficient in applying insights derived from the greater perspective into its own calculations. All this results in an ego-consciousness more sure of itself, more rounded and dissolved, more attuned to Wholeness. The ego now knows that it stands on the shoulders of giants; that not only is there a divine plan, but that it is safe to trust this plan, and so it no longer comes out as such an arrogant, fearful, narrowly-defined and superficially-oriented quantity.

At the time, however, relatively few have experienced this cosmic consciousness. It is impossible to estimate how many millions, not only because there are degrees and levels of these expanded states but also because we live in an age where talking about them remains taboo. True, it has been years since men of power openly tortured and killed all who disagreed with certified truths. Even so, as we shall see, the system depends upon unconsciousness to survive and there are many with a perceived vested interest in the status quo who are threatened by these experiences and the insights they convey. Thus, the subject is hardly ever discussed in public and if someone brings it up, the defenders of the old paradigm join ranks to ridicule those who think it a serious topic of research. Accordingly, people who have had such experiences often keep it to themselves. And while one reason is that they are ineffable, quite a few remain silent because they are afraid that the response will be an uneasy stare and the suspicion that they have become delusional.

Now, in addition to the cosmic consciousness and the healthy stages leading up to it, there are several other states. As our mental hospitals are a testimony to, there are also several sickly conditions and so it is understandable that people fail to differentiate. The pathological conditions, however, are different only in that they arise from confused self-images and belief systems which the individual for various reasons cling on to. When it comes to the nature of consciousness, *our ideas about reality are all there is,* and so distorted and unhealthy ideas are reflected/ results in distorted and unhealthy self-images/worldviews.

We will later, especially in part three, have more to say on the difference between the sick and the healthy mind. Even so, talking of pathological states, our civilization's understanding is no less confused than when it comes to healthy conditions. For this reason, psychiatry has established a habit of pacifying patients with pharmaceutical drugs and to the extent that they keep symptoms at bay, doctors tend to be satisfied with the treatment. However, as science advances, progressive psychiatrists claim that in doing so, we do the mentally ill a great disservice. Instead of seeing their cognitive state as a disease, these psychiatrists understand it to be a spiritual crisis, and provided the right treatment they believe that there is healing potential inherent in the condition—unless blocked with out of place medication. Stanislav Grof speaks to it thus:

> "Over the years we have come to the conclusion that many of the conditions that are currently diagnosed as psychotic and indiscriminately treated by suppressive medication are actually difficult stages of a radical personality trans-formation and of spiritual opening. If they are correctly understood and supported, these psychospiritual crises can result in emotional and psychosomatic healing, remarkable psychological changes, and consciousness evolution." (50.302)

These professionals, in other words, believe that there is a potential for transformation in the pathological states and that they can be a catalyst for personal development *if they are seen for what they are* and treated accordingly.[3] This, unfortunately, requires that society evolves to a point where we stop using the "normal" consciousness as a touchstone for a wholesome mind. And as soon as we have put in place a psychology built on the new paradigm, this is precisely what will happen. We will then understand that the ego-bound consciousness is only an *intermediate* stage in our evolutionary process. And we will not only realize that the cosmic consciousness represents a higher potential, one we would do well to take seriously, but that to the extent we do we will create a heaven on earth. John C. Lilly, a neuroscientist who spent much time exploring the inner landscape, spoke to it thus:

---

[3] For a better understanding of these issues, see STANLEY DEAN, *PSYCHIATRY & MYSTICISM;* WALSH & VAUGHAN, *BEYOND EGO;* AND STANISLAV GROF, *PSYCHOLOGY OF THE FUTURE.*

"It is my firm belief that the experience of higher states of consciousness is necessary for survival of the human species. If we can each experience at least the lower levels of Satori[4], there is hope that we won't blow up the planet or otherwise eliminate life as we know it. If every person on the planet, especially those in power in the establishments, can eventually reach higher levels or states regularly, the planet will be run with relative simple efficiency and joy. Problems such as pollution, slaughter of other species, overpopulation, misuse of natural resources, overproduction, famine, disease, and war will then be solved by the rational application of realizable means."(66.3)

Now, we could ask why mankind earlier—and to a greater extent—hasn't been acquainted with the cosmic consciousness? If the awareness it conveys is so important and if our Universe is a living, caring, and hyper-intelligent organism, isn't this something God should have taken care of long ago? To the ego, it would seem as if God had compassion with our plight, he could have sent humanity shedloads of prophets—or, for that matter, made us all prophets—as it would have ended problems before they began.

If "he" has any sense of decency, then, why is it in our time that the greater reality begins to make its presence felt? Why now, after so much war, violence, and misfortune which could have been avoided? If the Universe is a Being whose fundamental nature is unconditional love, how is this scenario compatible with all the suffering and grief? What could be the meaning of this calamity?

These are all good questions. And to respond, we shall look at how we are connected with the Universe and how the project of history is associated with us; we shall see how the ego connects with everything

---

[4] Satori: A Zen Buddhist word indicating the more advanced states of expanded consciousness.

and how we and the world are components of one Supreme Being, as seen from the perspective of cosmic consciousness.

2

THE NATURE OF OUR UNIVERSE
AND THE
SIGNIFICANCE OF HISTORY

"History is the narrative of man's relationship to his own deepest nature [spirit] played out in time, but grounded in eternity."(123.11)

—*Ken Wilber*—

WHAT IS THE Universe and what is our connection to this enigma? Is our being the result of a random or a purpose-filled process? In other words, *what is history*? What is the driving force? Is there an overall plan—and if there is, what can it be?

These are questions philosophers have been pondering for millennia and that they have not yet reached consensus is explained by the fact that the answers are impossible to grasp for the surface-consciousness. As we have seen, only through the expanded states is the nature of reality revealed, and because we, from the ego perspective, know neither heads from tails on one (us) or the other (the Universe), the answer to the questions above must remain a mystery.

What is clear, however, is that these concerns are deeply related; we cannot know ourselves without knowing history and vice versa. Hence, our identity is not only entwined with morality but our sense of history, and the way we look at history is closely associated with how we see ourselves. If we, for example, construe history to be a meaningless process governed by chance, we will see ourselves (and the world) as pointless beings—which again does not inspire to greatness.

The reason why people accept this view is that they think of the world as consisting of dead matter and that consciousness is a mere byproduct.

And since it is difficult from this point of departure to see the Universe as having an intelligent mind, moving in a conscious direction, their calculations make sense no matter how wide off the mark.

If, however, we turn this equation on its head, accepting the premise that consciousness comes first, everything appears different. And we shall now look at what it means to live in an organized and meaningful Universe, what our role within the framework of this larger context is, and why we have chosen to take part in the challenges and events offered by our play with duality. We shall, in other words, see how everything is connected and how we, the Universe, and history are aspects of the same, namely a Supreme Being's play and realization. It is a truly grand project, so let us start where everything does, at the beginning.

2.1 THE BEGINNING

"With power and skill did we construct the firmament: For it is we who create the vastness of space."

—*The Koran, Sure 51:47*—

Before the Universe, before duality arose and anything that came to be started, there was a "time" when the Force of Foreverness existed but its fragments (we) were not. What this means and what kind of existence it was, we can only imagine. But according to the energy-personality Seth it was

> "a state in which probabilities and possibilities [were] known and anticipated but blocked from expression. . . . It was a state of agony in which the powers of creativity and existence were known, but the ways to produce them were not known."(88.264)

This awakening Life-form, this nascent Wholeness, is probably the greatest mystery of all. Apparently, it's a mystery even to All That Is and not even highly evolved, non-physical energy personalities can say much about this "time" or what it entailed. In other words, figuring out how our own Universe began is a walk in the park compared to the problem of coming to grips with the puzzle of this time before time before time. We only know that it was a "time" before anything existed; that All That Is slowly came to its senses; that it noticed a stirring in its mind, and that it became aware of the ramifications and immenseness of its Being. Then, in the process of waking up, All That Is realized the contours of further potentials and opportunities for existence which could not be fulfilled within the framework presently available. As a solution to this dilemma, All That Is dreamed up new forms of being. Seth[5] describes the process as follows:

> "Desire, wish and expectation rule all actions and are the basis for all realities. Within *All That Is*, therefore, the wish, desire and expectation of creativity existed before all other actuality. The strength and vitality of these desires and expectations then became in your terms so insupportable that *All That Is* was driven to find the means to produce them.
>
> In other words, *All That Is* existed in a state of being, but without the means to find expression for its being. This was the state of agony of which I spoke. Yet it is doubtful that without this 'period' of contracted yearning, *All That Is* could concentrate Its energy sufficiently enough to create the realities that existed in probable suspension within It.
>
> The agony and the desire to create represented Its proof of its own reality. The feelings, in other words, were adequate proof to *All That Is* that It was.

---

[5] As no humans were around, we must turn to more advanced energy gestalts for information. In this sense, the Seth (channelled by Jane Roberts) and the Ra material (channelled by Carla L. Rueckert) is unique. These entities were allegedly, together with other primary gestalts, instrumental in the early formation of energy into physical form and Seth describes himself/his perspective as "one infinite cell, consisting of energy so highly concentrated that it exists in endless dimensions at once and reaches out from its own reality to all others."(88.253)

At first, in your terms, all of probable reality existed as nebulous dreams within the consciousness of *All That Is*. Later, the unspecific nature of these 'dreams' grew more particular and vivid. The dreams became recognizable one from the other until they drew the conscious notice of *All That Is*. And with curiosity and yearning, *All That Is* paid more attention to Its own dreams.

Potential individuals, in your terms, had consciousness before the beginning or any beginning as you know it, then. They clamored to be released into actuality, and *All That Is*, in unspeakable sympathy, sought within itself for the means.

In Its massive imagination, It understood the cosmic multiplication of consciousness that could not occur within that framework. Actuality was necessary if these probabilities were to be given birth. *All That Is* saw, then, an infinity of probable, conscious individuals, and foresaw all possible developments, but they were locked within It until It found the means.

This was in your terms a primary cosmic dilemma, and one with which It wrestled until *All That Was* was completely involved and enveloped within that cosmic problem.

Had It not solved it, *All That Is* would have faced insanity, and there would have been, literally, a reality without reason and a universe run wild."(88.266, 267)

It is from this perspective we must see our world: All That Is could not have realized the diversity of experiences/understanding which emerged as a possibility without dividing into an infinity of fragments. And in doing so, by gracing each fragment with individual awareness and distributing us throughout a Universe consisting of many places and planes of existence, this Force made possible a dynamic that could not otherwise have taken place.

Think about it! If this Supreme Being would have remained in its original condition, completely aware of its fullness and oneness at all times, it would imply an infinity of possibilities that could never be realized; nothing terrible, nothing strenuous, nothing dark and gloomy, nothing less than the optimum—the One in its Perfect form—would ever exist.

At first glance this may not seem too bad. As we find ourselves immersed in duality, we long for perfection and deliverance from our troubles. Yet, if we think about it, we realize that all our striving, misery, and shortcomings (real or imagined) not only provide us with meaningful and important experiences *but that the dualistic model of interpretation creates all other values.*

Again, think about it! Alive on earth we have a unique opportunity to decide for ourselves *who* we want to be and *what* we want to represent. Due to the illusion of separation and the framework offered by duality, we can experience what it is like to be heroic or spineless, proud or ashamed, wise or foolish, altruistic or selfish, merciful or unforgiving, deceitful or loyal, and so on, and so on. In the course of a lifetime, we encounter endless opportunities to experience one or the other. *Every* day offers a choice, and we cannot *not* choose; whether we act or refrain from doing so, there is always a choice—and by our preferences we create ourselves. *Our sense of identity and our actions, therefore, are two sides of the same coin and for any of these options/actions to be realized it must be within a dualistic context.* For us to be forgiving, there must be something to forgive; for us to be brave, there must be something worth fighting for, some cost of effort; and for us to experience shame, there must be also a lesser option.

Hence, for us to experience ourselves as anything at all, and for us to be able to create ourselves in the image of who we want to be, some-one/something must represent what we are not. At this level of being *nothing can exist without its opposite*, and so for All That Is to fully recognize itself as what it is—eternal, absolute, one, and perfect in its light and fullness—it had to facilitate darkness, separateness, imper-manence, and imperfection as conditions of existence—or to be more specific, *the illusion* of these possibilities.

This was accomplished when All That Is dissolved into an infinite number of fragments which again, to different degrees, forgot who they were and where they came from. While the fragments began their own experience, however, GodForce instilled within them a connection—an inner road map—so that they all, sooner or later, would find their way to merge as one with the Totality. And by placing each fragment within the kind of environment that offered the most favorable conditions for growth, this Supreme Being created a highly organized, inviolable, and meaningful Universe.

As seen from the perspective of cosmic consciousness, this is how existence came into being: We have burst from Center—broken into a thousand pieces—to experience the world of duality and feel what it implies to be less than we are. Nevertheless, we have within us a component which has never left the Whole and it whispers to us who we are and where we have come from. This inner voice, which speaks through our conscience, our ideals, values, and intuition, is so low that it is easily ignored by the ego. But it is always there for those who will listen—and the more we listen, the more easily it is heard.

Listening to this inner voice, the one which encourages us to look past our ego's fear and delusion and at all times endeavor to make the highest choice, is the essence of the self-actualization process. To the extent we honor the ideals, values, and principles of Wholeness, we become more than we were, and we shall have much to say on this process. It sums up the point of existence in the physical, but before we explore this maturation process and how history is its reflection, we must discuss the Universe.

2.2 THE STRUCTURE OF OUR UNIVERSE

"The Idea is the Absolute, and all that is real is but the realization of the idea." (68.158)

—*G. W. Hegel*—

We have seen how GodForce/we divided into fragments to take part in a wealth of experience which would not otherwise have been available. For our part, it was only by disentangling from the Wholeness/Center and forgetting who we were that we could recreate ourselves as who we wanted to be, while for All That Is it became possible, through our lives, to experience itself as all things instead of one. We have also seen that the Universe is a multidimensional entity and that its fragments, through an inner connection, is forever linked as one with God/each other in the depths of the multidimensional universe.

So far so good. However, there are important features regarding the nature of our Universe that we have not yet brought into the equation and one is that time and space—as it presents itself to us—is an illusion. We shall have more to say on this in part two, when we discuss the theory of relativity and quantum physics. Even so, we must already at this point take into consideration that our five senses' impression of the world is greatly misleading. While it looks as if all things are separate; that events in our inner-world, for instance, are unrelated to events in the outer and that what happens at one place has no causal relationship to what happens in another, this is simply not true. Instead, we live in a Universe where no boundaries exist: everything affects everything else, and everything is an interconnected Whole.

This may be difficult for our consciousness to understand, but from the expanded states we can see that it is so and that we are living in a holographic Universe—a Universe where the Totality has split in such a way *that each part contains the whole.*

This has huge implications which we shall elaborate upon later. But to contextualize ramifications, this does not only mean that the Universe is so structured that our environment reflects our inner world and that we, by changing our thoughts and belief systems, also directly affect the world around us; it also means that the inner change/thought does not travel in space with any speed but instead is *everywhere all the time* and affects everything immediately.

The idea you are thinking right now, in other words, is a quality that most definitely (whether you like it or not) has an impact on your surroundings, and it influences All That Is to one degree or another. Joseph Chilton Pearce describes this relationship as follows:

"We live in an environment of feedback or mirroring in which creator and created give rise to each other both within us and outside of us. . . . Indeed, we live in fields within fields of a holographic electro-magnetic display where all information is somehow present within every minute part of any particular frequency. Each part is thus representative of the whole, with our human heart somehow the genesis of our personal yet uniquely shared living world."(81.66,60)

Later, we shall elaborate more thoroughly, so do not be discouraged if it does not appear obvious how we are connected. Our purpose here is simply to present a brief outline of the grand design, and when it comes to the physical system's relationship to the multidimensional Universe Gregg Braden summarizes:

"We are part of a much greater system of many realities, within realities, within other realities. In this system our world could be considered a shadow or a projection of events that are happening in a deeper, underlying reality. What we see as our universe is really us—our individual and collective minds—transforming the possibilities of the deeper realms into physical reality."(14.113)

So, the world becomes "real". And another variable we must add to this equation is that time, as we experience it, is an illusion; it is only from our perspective that "past" and "future" have any meaning and seen from the ultimate perspective everything happens *simultaneously*. The whole arrangement then, from the Universe's beginning to end (as we think of it), is an eternal NOW, a vast multidimensional webwork of space-time consisting of an infinite number of variables/threads which are all connected and are constantly being calibrated in relation to each other.

What this means is difficult to comprehend. However, it implies that all that exists is the present moment and that our thoughts and intentions in the Here and Now spread ripples in time and space which again affect possibilities/potentials not only in the "future" (which of course is quite obvious) but also in the "past".

No matter how strange this may sound it is supported by science and consciousness research. And for our part, as well as the Universe, it has some seemingly absurd implications. For instance, it implies that we are living all our reincarnations now, and for the Universe it implies that "beginning" and "end" are one. This, in other words, is a concept which stretches the imagination. It is impossible to fully fathom, and yet, in a way, it helps us understand how it can be that even if we live our lives here and now in the outskirts of the Universe, apparently lightyears away from our inherent potential and godlike-status, we are there already (and always) in the depths of the inner-universe/ourselves.

The idea of time and space, therefore, is only a concept fashioned by Consciousness as a means to ensure a wide range of experience; one that makes it possible to divide Entirety into smaller, more comprehensible packages and to experience an expansive process/totality in an orderly and appropriate fashion. Quantum physicist David Bohm puts it like this:

> "What unfolds or comes into being in any present moment is simply a projection of the whole. That is, some aspect of the whole is unfolded into that moment and that moment is just that aspect. Likewise, the next moment is simply another aspect of the whole."(97.251)

Thus, to see history as a linear process with a beginning and an end, separated by an infinite distance, is incorrect. It is merely because our brain works as it does that it looks this way, and the Universe must be understood as a *total creation process* which at all times, in all parts and directions, changes shape and expands towards greater levels of value fulfillment.

As we can gather from this, to think of the world as an objective and independent thing-in-itself, consisting of fixed and permanent matter, confuses more than it clarifies. What we think of as matter is nothing more than mind-stuff, and the nature of the Universe is easier to grasp if we look at it as a vast play of dreams.

This may seem strange because we are born into a culture which tends to see dreams and reality as diametrically opposed. Despite this, our dreams are highly creative forces of expression and the thought-forms we produce can also be said to have a certain life of their own.

Even so, the Universe is a dream in a completely different order of magnitude than our dreams, being that we as energy personalities incorporate only a fraction of the powers that greater energy gestalts—those who have dreamed us—command. We are nowhere near able to filter, control, transform, and contain the amounts of energy that they do and consequently our personal reality and imagination is more limited. Nonetheless, even though we, when we compare ourselves to the gigantic forces at play in the Universe, may feel small and insignificant, it is important to understand that we are of no less importance. To GodForce *every fragment is of equal value* and so the idea of more and less, better or worse, as we tend to think of things, is the result of biased perception.

We humans, however, have a hard time grasping this because we are burdened with a poor self-image. And if we look closer, we find that our low self-esteem results from erroneous belief systems about our fundamental nature. Not only are psychologists and scientists telling us that there is no soul and no afterlife, but the doctrines of organized religion keep people in chains of stupidity and because we are born into a culture that builds on these misconceptions, we are troubled by feelings of inferiority. Consequently, we become hierarchical-oriented. We think in terms of one being better than the other, and we measure our worth on the basis of a self/culturally defined hierarchical view of the world.

In our mind's eye, therefore, we imagine ourselves less worthy than people we admire, be it rock stars, war heroes, athletes, professors, millionaires, or religious figures. And to cope with this trait, we comfort ourselves with the idea that although we may be less valuable than these people, we are at least worth more than certain others.

This hierarchical mindset is such an elemental part of thinking that we seldom reflect. Even so, whether we look down on gays, criminals, prostitutes, millionaires, colored people, junkies, or the neighbor, such thinking only reflects how we judge our own self-worth. The reason for this is that for us to live, we need to feel that we have a minimum of inherent value and that our lives have a certain legitimacy. Organized religion and the theory of evolution have quite effectively deprived us of any such basis and consequently we do whatever we can to establish a sense of self-worth by measuring ourselves in relation to others.

This hierarchical mindset, in other words, is a survival mechanism, for as long as we find someone to look down on we can at least feel that we are worth *something*. Thus, the more profound we imagine our own shortcomings, the stronger we will feel the urge to put others down. Still, this thinking is the result of a deluded mind, and when we take the greater reality into consideration we find that not only *every single* representative of humanity—from Hitler to Mother Theresa—are of equal value, but *all other* life.

That our greatest villains are as valuable and important to All That Is as our greatest heroes, is a tenet that our ego is likely to oppose. Nevertheless, this thinking in terms of "more and less worth" is only the result of our limited understanding. We see this clearly when we consider that every lifeform is GodForce's fragmented existence and that each fragment offers its unique contribution to the whole—a whole which must be seen in a larger context than a single life.

Even if we must overcome some cherished delusions before the implications sink in, it is a recognition that everyone sooner or later will accept. It is a fundamental part of the world's wisdom traditions and the Indian philosopher/mystic Sri Aurobindo put it this way:

> "The Lord is there equally in all beings. We have to make no essential distinctions between ourself and others, the wise and the ignorant, friend and enemy, man and animal, the saint and the sinner. We must hate none, despise none, be repelled by none; for in all we have to see the One disguised or manifested at his pleasure. He is a little revealed in one or more revealed in another. [In some he is] concealed [and in others] wholly distorted, [but always] according to his will and his knowledge of what is best for that which he intends to become in form in them and to do in works in their nature. All is ourself, one self that has taken many shapes."(10.255)

Although we must admit that this argument is logically sound (that if God exists—and the god-concept shall have meaning—then God must be everything, and we also God), it will oppose the value-neutral worldview this message pretends to convey. Because when someone says "God is everything and everything has its place within the framework of a larger existence", it seems to the ego that what he is saying is that everything—no matter how bad—is just fine, and that it doesn't matter if we are compassionate or cruel, since "it's all just experiences anyway".

This, however, is not what they mean. No one has a more affectionate relationship to the world of ideals, values, and principles than people like Aurobindo, and that your actions are *irrelevant* is the last thing they would suggest. When they say that we must acknowledge the equal worth of all people, no matter how unsympathetic they may appear, because they are an aspect God, they therefore do not mean that we should praise their transgressions or do as them. What they mean is that we must *differentiate between the person and his actions* and have in mind the larger context in which everything takes place. For although it's obvious that child-murdering pedophiles and self-absorbed psychopaths provide a far less appealing contribution to the world than saints and altruistically-oriented people, we must never forget that they also carry the light within and have their place within the framework of a larger plan. We must remember that they (like us) are God who has forgotten Himself and is trying to find Himself. And even if they (like us), in their forgetfulness, can do horrid stuff—from deceiving others to robbing, raping, and murdering—they are a necessary part of all that is.

We have already seen how nothing can exist without its opposite; if everyone were heroic, loving, and forgiving all the time, there would be nothing to be heroic, loving, and forgiving in relation to. We therefore need a standard of reference—and that is what psychopaths and wrong-doers provide.

When we meet people like this, therefore, we should remember that they, with their behavior, not only give all the things we strive for their value but that they, in doing so, present us with an opportunity to show our qualities. If we think about it, even the least of us can love our friends, be grateful and honor the light in them. Even so, it takes a highly evolved soul to do the same with enemies, and when they meet one of life's many nuisances the wisest will see them as a gift from God bestowed so that they have the opportunity to work with concepts such as forgiveness, integrity building, and unconditional love.

It is, indeed, quite difficult to remember that when someone yells at us, betrays us, or otherwise makes our life miserable. Yet, *that is why we need all the practice we can get*, and to the degree we excel at these challenges we realize our inherent divinity.

Seen within the context of a single life, these people therefore assist us this way. Furthermore, we must also perceive their actions in a larger frame and understand that they, like us, are part of a greater process. This process, which we call the Universe's exhalation and inhalation process, will soon be elaborated upon. But before we do, we need to say more about the ways we and the Universe connects, so that we have a better grasp on the greater reality.

When it comes to this, keep in mind that death is an illusion; as shall be substantiated, it is a transition to another plane of existence, a natural continuation of life from our plane. While this may be another dubious claim from the ego's point of view, it is as plain as day for those who have had a taste of cosmic consciousness. Hence, only to the surface-consciousness does death pose a threat. In fact, for those who have glimpsed the bigger picture, death is seen as a relief, because it frees us from the ego's limited expression and allows us to partake in a form of existence which is more boundless, more in sync with the essence of our being.

We shall have more to say on this when we take a closer look at the near-death experience. My purpose here is to point out that "death" is a natural part of existence and that our personality will not perish. On the contrary, when we die, we become far more "ourselves" than we are on earth; we reconnect with the greater part of us, that which was not embodied in the physical, and we get access to a perspective that is foreign to the ego, more aligned with the cosmic range.

Remember that we are multidimensional beings. This not only means that our personality is far vaster than seen from our point of view; that it connects with the inner-universe, and that our ego merely represents the part of our personality which meets the surface and makes physical experience possible. It also means that this life is a tiny part of our energy-personality's reality because, while we are here, the greater part of us also has "sensors" elsewhere.

These are equivalent to past and future lives, and if this is difficult to understand remember that time and space is an illusion and imagine as if earth was the entire Universe. From this analogy, our core being—our energy-essence—springs from the core of the earth. This is where we and God merge: Here we find no separation, no defects, no shortcomings, none of the doom and gloom we're so familiar with. Here there is no relativity, only the Absolute, and everything vibrates as One Harmonious Whole with such a degree of perfection and unconditional love that the highest expressions of love and feelings of ecstasy on earth do not come close.

I believe those who travel in consciousness from our plane rarely—if ever—reach this destination, because the core's vibration is so intense that it would be grueling for a personality at our level to endure. As we remember, everything is energy; if we imagine Center to be an extremely powerful high-voltage unit, a series of gradual reductions is needed before it results in the energy and vibration level we are accustomed to. And given that we are only able to filter and transform more modest amounts of energy, we would, if we tried to reach this core, short-circuit before we came close (much like if we were trying to reach the sun).

Now, it is my impression that the Universe is so ordered that this is not much of a problem and that we will never be able to reach and embody these amazing levels of energy if we are not equipped to handle them. I mention it briefly to emphasize that we are talking about energy levels—and qualities of existence—which we cannot comprehend, and from this Center springs our Soul-essence; it downgrades its vibrational level until it results in us here on the surface, and along the way it is divided into smaller and smaller units of being.

These de-escalations are, supposedly, orderly arranged and some claim that they are based on the number twelve. That they are orderly fashioned is indeed (seen from the larger perspective) self-evident, but whether they have to do with twelve is difficult to say. At any rate, it does not matter much whether they do, but let us for arguments sake use it as an example. In doing so, (to continue the analogy) imagine that our sense of individuality starts as a larger energy-gestalt connected to the earth's core. From here it divides into twelve smaller personalities and if each of these essences again split into twelve, and they in turn divide twelve times, we see that our soul-essence, through four gradual reductions, has distributed its energy into what results in 1728 "individual" fragments located on the surface.

Again, numbers are of little importance. The point is the principle and based on this example we can see ourselves as one of the 1728 fragments. If we stick to our analogy, we can picture these fragments as islands: Seen from our perspective, these islands look as if they are separate but are all, beneath the sea's surface, connected to the oceanic crust and the earth's core. So also with us; we're all connected and our sense of separation is an illusion only the ego finds convincing. We therefore live on the surface of things, unaware that we have 1727 other versions of ourselves hanging out in space-time and accumulating experience.

Nevertheless, while we live as islands under the impression that we are separate, we are part a of a larger Whole which our essence has thrown out from the core of being—and our essence, again, is one with the energy, the live-Webwork which encompasses, contains, and transcends everything. Seen as such, we are all part of God while God is more than the sum of its parts; and so is the hierarchy of energy put together in the multi-dimensional Universe.

Admittedly, there are nuances which we have not touched upon, but as an oversimplified representation of how we are connected to the Universe the analogy is good enough. From this sketch we also have a better understanding of what the reincarnation concept is about, as we in a single lifetime only get to experience a tiny taste of the potential available. We therefore need many lifetimes to explore the physical and each century offers a unique context for experience.

It is for this reason that our energy-essence has "sensors" placed in every century it deems fit, from the most primitive of times to advanced future ages. It also follows that we all have a variety of life-experiences where we have done stupid things, no matter how "holy" we think we are now. We are here to experience *all aspects* of existence and just knowing one side of the equation would be unthinkable. Hence, as we take part in the cycle of life, we get to experience being *both* male and female, black and white, weak and strong, victim and aggressor, ostracized and praised, and so on; every time we enter the physical, we get to experience life from a different point of view, and *every type of experience* is unique and precious as it results in growth and understanding.

Thus, as seen from the larger perspective, it matters not whether the experience is "good" or "bad". These labels derive meaning only from the ego's perspective, and within the framework of a larger existence *everything* has its place and *all experiences* are welcome.

To the ego, this is another dubious claim. But although we have a certain idea about what constitutes a successful life, it would be wise to remember that every experience is valuable and that we are only speaking of our limited understanding when we judge a person based on how he or she appears in this life; what we see is only a tiny part of the personality, and even though somebody may act as a bastard in this life, he may have saved our life in another.

It is *therefore* wise ones distinguish between action and person, for they know that to judge a person's contribution to the Whole based on one single life is no wiser than to judge an apple tree on the basis of one rotten apple. They know, in other words, that what they see does not reflect the person's true nature but the process he/she is in. And even if they do not like the image that is presented, they respect it as a part of all that is because they know enough about God and the order of things to feel confident that everything is as it should be. As Aurobindo says:

> "All things express or disguise, develop or distort, as best they can or with whatever defect they must, under the circumstances intended for them, in the way possible to the immediate status or function or evolution of their nature."(10.256)

The reason for the mystics' poise is that no matter how bad things may seem, they have no doubt that God has a purpose with every existence and that we all fit in perfectly within the framework of a larger context. To the untrained ego, obviously, this sounds outlandishly naïve: It trusts itself only, and its main occupation is to categorize everything according to its own accepted wisdom. Yet, these people have seen the world as it appears beyond the confines of the surface-consciousness. And the more they know about the "machinery" behind the veil, the less reason they see to doubt GodForce's organizational skill and wisdom.

I would agree, however, that from what we have said every lifetime may seem like a game of dice at the soul level. We have not seen much to the "order" and "plan" of which I speak. Hence, we shall now look at the larger context and the overall organization, so that we understand the process we are in.

2.3 THE UNIVERSE'S EXHALATION AND INHALATION PROCESS

"From Delight all these beings are born, by Delight they exist and grow, to Delight they return."

—Taittiriya Upanishad, 111.6—

We have discussed how GodForce split into fragments to enable a level/scale of experience which otherwise would not have been possible and we've also got an idea of how we are connected to the inner-universe. We have seen that we are part of a personality which is far greater than our physical appearance, and we shall now see how all this is related to the Universe's exhalation and inhalation process.

Our Oversoul, before we are born, does not stand by idly and leave it to chance whether we end up as male, female, nun, soldier, serial killer or mentally retarded. Before we incarnate, there is a comprehensive set of consultants and aides available, and this corps not only ensures that our personal interests and needs are attended to but that our incarnation fits into a greater design. The reason for this is that, in addition to earth being a school where not-so-advanced consciousnesses can learn a thing or two, there is a larger plan that plays out and this apparatus ensures that it comes to fruition.

This plan, which has been hinted at several times, works on two levels: the individual and the collective. If we are to summarize it in one word *self-actualization* is appropriate, and we shall now see how our actualization-process is part of the Universe's. We have already seen how all that exists in the physical can be said to be sensory-devices from the inner-universe, sent to take part in the play of consciousness. This part of the process is called out-breath because essences from the Center, which were fused with Entirety, are sent on a voyage of self-rediscovery to the outskirts of the Universe. Out here we are gods playing hide and seek, and because we have forgotten who we are, we get to rediscover it through our play with duality.

Here, we can create ourselves anew; we can decide who we want to be and what kind of ideas we aspire to represent; and even though we are initially so gripped by oblivion that we can do the most appalling things to each other, we will step by step, day by day, lifetime by lifetime, find our way back to god-in-ourselves. The laws of the Universe make it so, for it is in the nature of Consciousness to expand its scope of knowledge and understanding, and thanks to our connection to Center we always find our way back home.

As seen from the cosmic consciousness' perspective it is only here on the surface that we seem left behind, alone and abandoned. It is an indispensable part of the set and setting and the illusion of separation is just as compelling as it ought to be. Nevertheless, GodForce is no less present here than in the Center, and so the Wholeness knows how to organize and facilitate so that everyone's blissful salvation is assured. Energy regulations such as the law of attraction and the law of resonance ensure this result, because they ensure that our thoughts not only attract an answer compatible to the frequency they hold but that the higher, more advanced vibrations uplift the lower. Thus, we reap what we sow—and the higher the frequency we can hold, the more we will help others rise to ours.

In addition to these fundamental laws, karma does its part. This is what binds our lives together into a meaningful mosaic, making the Universe a highly ordered set of circumstances. Ensuring that every action has a consequence, it puts everything in its place, and what we do to others in one life will decide what we experience in another. As already mentioned, there is an extensive apparatus available to assist before we are born. This provides the best possible starting point and time and place is not coincidental. Hence, whether we are born in a cave 20.000 years ago, a Roman town 2000 years ago, the Australian steppes 1000 years ago, Japan 200 years ago, Germany in the 1920's, or the United States today, it's always the result of a choice that was done before we were born as the setting seemed most compatible with our life-project.

Another logical consequence of karma is that we meet people who for various reasons were important in previous lives. The Universe ensures that everything is most appropriately laid out for growth, and so souls tend to follow each other from lifetime to lifetime. Thus, victims and aggressors sometimes switch roles, so that they not only get to expand upon an important aspect of duality but learn to empathize with others.

Based on what I have said, one might wonder to what extent events are predestined, for if victims and perpetrators exchange roles and we in the course of a lifespan meet people we have met before, the question of free will apparently becomes problematic. To this I will say that we have free will. It is a fundamental principle underlying existence in our system and you can for example, here and now, choose whether you want to put down this book; whether you want to end the relationship with your partner; or whether you want to jump off a bridge. That said, the ego does not make this decision all by itself. As we know, it is part of a much larger energy-complex and depending on how well the different aspects of our multi-dimensional personality are attuned—and what the situation is— our soul's aspirations will to a greater or lesser extent shine through.

There are, of course, several nuances regarding this issue of which we shall not go into detail. My point is that although we can *do* what we want we cannot always *want* what we want, and even if our ego can accept or reject whatever stimulus it receives from the deeper parts of our being the choices we make are ideally (to the degree we are in touch with our inner-self) in accordance with the soul's overall ambitions.

Seen in context with the examples mentioned above, then, chances are that you will not put down this book if it resonates with your being and you sense that getting to the bottom of this is important. If your soul, however, has another plan for this lifetime than to dabble with self-actualization, then chances are that you will put it away—but then again, chances are small that you would have had any interest to begin with. Similarly, you are not likely to divorce your partner if the relationship has more to offer, and neither will you jump off a bridge if you listen to your inner voice and life has more to offer.

When it comes to the relationship between soul and ego, certain people are more in touch with their inner reality than others. And if you are wondering to what extent you are living your soul's desire, a simple test is to ask yourself if you think life is meaningful. If the answer is "yes": if your life feels significant and every day you have a sense of purpose despite adversities that come your way, chances are that you and your soul are reasonably matched and that you take part in the "program" agreed upon before you were born. If the answer, however, is "no" and you experience life as a pointless and uninspiring event, chances are that your life is astray and not in resonance with your soul's aspirations.

The reason is that our soul's desire functions as a compass we carry throughout life. Hence, to the extent that we do what brings joy and fills our life with meaning, we stick to the path staked out and we realize our life plan. If we, however, do not follow this internal compass we will give in to baseless desires and life will increasingly present itself as a bleak and miserable event. If this is the case, there is only one thing to do: we must deal with the current set of conditions, with the habits we have acquired or whatever aspects of our life we are not happy with, and we must start focusing on what *feels* right—no matter how inconvenient it may seem to the ego.

This is rarely a simple matter. Nevertheless, it is the only way if we want to feel better—and those who have the courage to reinvent themselves will find the rewards to be proportional to their confidence in the life process. Our soul, after all, knows way better than the ego what is best for us. It does not only see the world from a higher perspective (and takes more variables into account) but its ability to open doors is one of a kind. Consequently, to the extent that we do not let the ego's fears and delusions get in our way, we will provide this creative intelligence with free reins and we will attract optimal experiences for continued growth.

There is much more that could be said about this and we will have more to say later. But to continue where we left off, we were talking about how we, before we are born, have a general idea of what kind of life we are about to experience. Together with the apparatus behind the veil, therefore, we see to it that a program is in place which puts on the menu certain features that we, with great probability, will encounter in life. Except for the choosing of time and place, this menu may consist of items such as lifestyle preferences, career opportunities, and life partners, not to forget certain events and challenges. When it comes to these posts, our past lives and our karmic ties are important factors which determine their arrangement. The Universe, after all, will not only fashion the most appropriate learning curve; its arc bends towards justice and so it will naturally calibrate all variables and balance everything out. Consequently, karmic relations bind our lives together in the most appropriate manner, and one of the primary results is the family that we are born into.

In other words, *chance never comes into play*, and we choose our family based on several variables. These are too many to elaborate on, but the most obvious is what we intend to learn from the dynamic between family members, as well as the opportunities provided for growth. An example of the latter would be if we have a latent genius for playing the piano, for if cultivating this talent is important we will choose a family of sufficient resources.

As it pertains to dynamics within family, karmic ties often manifest in that we are born into a family consisting of personalities with which we previously had a strained relationship. This is a great way to build understanding because it allows us to experience more favorably a personality for whom we previously only knew hatred or contempt. And speaking of contempt, the more we despise a certain group of people, be it gays, Jews, Palestinians, Blacks, women—whoever—the greater is the probability that our next life-experience will be as a member of this group. Again, none of this has to do with punishment. Rather, it is a consequence of being part of a superintelligent organism, an organism who ensures that all fragments attract to themselves the most opportune experiences for their advancement—and the law of karma, in this respect, provides us with exactly what we need.

When it comes to this, remember that death is nothing more than a transition from one plane of existence to another. And even though most will want to live as long and comfortable as possible, such thinking is the result of the ego's shortsighted perspective. As a matter of fact, from our soul's point of view, this is of no priority at all, because as seen from an overall perspective the easiest lives tend to offer the least in return. For instance, chances are that we will learn far more about existential concepts and ourselves through a shorter life as physically or mentally retarded than from a more fortunate life as measured by the ego's standards, and we must take this into account whenever we see destinies that to us seem incomprehensible.

After all, few things have been more difficult to reconcile with the idea of a benevolent God than little children's suffering and death. From the ego perspective, this is truly intolerable. Even so, when we take the larger picture into account, we discover the potential for growth contained within such an experience. Hence, it is often more mature souls who choose such challenges, because at some point in one's development there comes a time to move beyond the more superficial experiential frame offered by "normal" lives. That is when the more difficult life experiences become interesting. They offer opportunities to deal with deeper existential issues, and we see on the children who are born with leukemia and similar afflictions to what extent they grow: By the time they are seven, these brave souls have matured way beyond their years, and in addition they provide others—their parents, not least—with opportunities for life-lessons which they otherwise would have missed.

This alone can be good enough reason for a soul to incarnate as a sick child, for in the reincarnation literature there are examples of souls who do this as a service to their parents (seen in relation to a larger karmic pattern). Among other things, it forces parents who would otherwise have lived more superficial lives to reflect upon issues they normally would not have been concerned with. And although most parents would have done anything to be spared from having to deal with such an experience, they are nonetheless (seen in a greater context) enriched by it.

I am aware of the cultural taboo associated with issues such as these. The topic of little children's death and disease is an immensely sore point and we have a long way to go before parents can look back on such episodes with any degree of gratitude. For that to happen, we need to build an understanding of life that goes *beyond* death and in our culture, this is not the case.

At any rate, life without death is unthinkable, and as we shall see there is more than enough research to dispel the myth of death as the end. Indeed, if we are to live life fully, nothing is more important than to overcome the fear of death and even if the topic is controversial *no death has ever come uninvited*. It comes to each and all exactly when it should, and all things considered it should be seen as a gift and not a curse.

Our soul, after all, did not come here to live forever. It came here to experience a variety of joys and hardships—and to assist a greater plan—and when time has come to move on, it is our ticket out. We should therefore, despite the chaos of emotions that often describes our lives, remember that the lessons are eternal while life and death are only temporary measures. In fact, from the greater perspective, life and death are notes in a grander symphony. We see then, each life as a flower in a bouquet of many that our soul brings back from the physical and that *our experiences are the key to everything*.

It is from this perspective that we must see the suffering and death of mankind. And although our grief may seem unbearable we will, as we wise up, find that the joy of self-*re*discovery and *re*union is always greater than the sorrow generated by illusion of separation. Moreover, we should not forget that the pain and distress have inherent value, for although humanity has inflicted upon itself an unspeakable amount of misfortune this part of the equation only represents the unconscious (dark) aspect of our play with duality—and it has also enabled all our greatness. Just think of the brotherhood in the trenches; the countless accounts of heroism in history's besieged cities; and the possibilities for greatness in opposing totalitarian regimes. *It is only when darkness surrounds us that we have an opportunity to shine*, and the more potent the darkness, the stronger the light has fought back.

Now, some might consider me to be a romantic when it comes to war and misery but this is not the case. From the higher perspective, militaristic moral codes are clearly ridiculous and war is the ultimate admission of failure. If it were up to me, therefore, mendacious military recruiting campaigns would have been prohibited and we would have removed from the curriculum all glorification of war. Hence, nothing I have said should be interpreted as a tribute to war or unconsciousness. I only pointed out that no matter how immense the pressure of darkness, the light has always been stronger—always more instrumental.

Proof can be found in history, for despite everything we have done under the influence of darkness it has only served the light. We shall go into detail on this important aspect later. But from a brief glance at history, we see how humanity is learning from its mistakes and how the ideals, values, and principles derived from Wholeness (i.e., the logic of love) have strengthened their position, becoming ever more influential.

The levels of compassion and comprehension, in other words, have increased as our interpersonal ties have strengthened, and this is due to karma and other laws. Thanks to these forces, our stupidities—as well as our better ideas—bounce back, and so *experience is transformed into understanding*. Hence, as time passes, it becomes a little more obvious what does and does not serve a good cause. And the fact that human nature basically is good, and that our follies result from ignorance not evil doing, ensures that we increasingly choose the better options.

Surely, we have a way to go before we become consistent at embracing better solutions, but as this book hopes to show we are not that far away. Indeed, we have reached times foretold, as humanity has awakened sufficiently that the source of all our problems and errors—the logic of fear—will become obvious to most. Dealing with its impact is essential to integrity-building at the nation level, and so the epoch of constructive social engineering can now begin.

For those who want to know more about how some 30 previous cultures and civilizations have looked forward to this age, Graham Hancock, *Fingerprints of the Gods* and David Wilcock, *The Source Field Investigations* are recommended reading. It shall not be elaborated upon here, but the puzzle of how people thousands of years ago could predict anything about our age is explained by the fact that their understanding of the Universe was not as off the mark as ours. To them astronomy and astrology were two aspects of the same as they knew the Universe to be a living, breathing, and purposeful entity. Knowing this, they saw history as a process where the major evolutionary trends could be predicted with the same accuracy as the planets' orbits.

This, of course, seems strange. These last ten thousand years, the illusion of separation has become more powerful, and so we have forgotten much that was known. The people back then, however, had a less restricted relationship to concepts such as self and other, spirit and matter, present and eternity. To them, spirit was in everything and their ego was not sufficiently honed to perceive duality like we do. Their shamans and seers, therefore, could access inner worlds and they knew that history represented a larger, divine play. These were insights they were familiar with either as a result of their own inner journeys or from folklore and creation myths handed down from ancestors.

Humans had not yet developed the written language. As a result, it is hard to define their knowledge, but we still find remnants of this wisdom contained in some of the earliest writings, especially the Vedas of the Indian culture. They were written between 800 and 200 B.C, but scholars agree that their origin is older. The Upanishads are the part that contains the most interesting philosophical and metaphysical material, and the essence of these scriptures is the same as this book. In other words, we are talking about timeless perspectives, and they communicate that the Universe is a living and superintelligent organism, that consciousness is everything there is, and that we and the Universe are one. They tell us that the Universe is a dream (Vishnu's dream) and that we have created this dream to experience ourselves as less than what we are. Michael Talbot, an eminent consciousness researcher, summarized it this way:

> "There is a Hindu myth about the Self of the universe that perceives all of the existence as a form of play. However, since the Self is what there is, and is all that there is, it has no one separate to play with. Thus, according to the Hindu tradition, it plays a cosmic game of hide-and-seek with itself. It assumes a kaleidoscope of faces and facades—a dazzling infinity of masks and forms until it has become the living substance of the entire universe. In this game of hide-and-seek it can experience ten billion lifetimes, see through ten billion eyes, live and die ten billion times. Eventually, however, the Self awakens from its many dreams and

remembers its true identity. It is the one and eternal Self of the cosmos. The game begins. The game ends."(107.160)

It was this divine play I referred to when I noted that the self-actualization process takes place on two levels, the individual and collective. Throughout this book we shall become more familiar with both as they explain our current predicament. For now, however, we are discussing humanity's ancient wisdom traditions, and when we delve deeper into the oldest scriptures we find—whether we study the Hindu, Buddhist, Christian[6], Jewish, or Islamic texts—that they more or less explicitly talk about the same process we shall be discussing here.

To continue with Hinduism, the Vedas call the fragmented part of our being for *Atman*. Its authors were familiar with the expanded states of consciousness and claim that we (Atman) in our inner world merge with the Universe/the Absolute (Brahman). They profess that we all, through expanded states, can experience this melting-togetherness and that when we do, we will understand what the mystics mean when they describe creation as *Sat-Chit-Ananda*—Being-Consciousness-Bliss.

The Indian culture has fostered numerous meditators who have succeeded in finding this fusion point. And when I described their insights as timeless, it was because the experiential knowledge they have brought back overlap with the realizations brought back by modern westerners. Even though many of these westerners knew nothing about ancient scriptures or Yogic traditions, all who have experienced the cosmic consciousness return with the same basic understanding. And it is obvious, after having experienced the Universe's hidden order and structure, that the essence of all religions is the same; that it was these insights prophets have tried to pass on, but that organized religion has made a mess of things.

The latter comes as no surprise. After all, these insights seem so outlandish to the surface-consciousness that people who have not had direct dealings with the expanded states often dismiss or misunderstand them. History speaks volumes, as we see how the representatives of

---

[6] As it pertains to the Christian tradition, see GEORGE WASHINGTON CAREY, *GOD-MAN: THE WORD MADE FLESH*. More examples will be presented in part three.

organized religion have taken the message of the prophets, twisted it beyond recognition, and adapted it to the ego's limited understanding. This is unfortunate. But no matter how difficult it may be for the ego to understand the insights from a perspective that exists beyond its reach, the altered states of consciousness have revealed the Universe's divine order and grand design.

Those who have seen the world from this perspective, therefore, realize that life on earth is but a small part of a much larger game. They know that everything strives towards its own fulfillment; they know that this process takes place on the collective as well as the individual level and that everything is the Universe in the process of remembering itself; they recognize that history represents the maturation of this Greater Consciousness, and that this process takes place within the framework of a larger context where the major characteristics have always been known as a logical consequence of the process.

Seen from our point of view, it might appear as if the dark side has had a more powerful influence than the light. It may seem as if our development has been at the mercy of chance and that it is only a matter of time before we self-destruct as everything seems to go from bad to worse. Nevertheless, from the greater perspective, one can see that there has been an organizing Force behind this grand project called history and that it has made sure that the powers unfolding in the Universe not only have balanced out but that they have swayed evolution towards the light.

As mentioned, it is only from our point of view that the dualistic way of thinking (life vs. death and good vs. evil) makes any sense. And seen in a larger context these aspects of existence, just like everything else in the physical, are simply means to self-fulfillment. Consequently, what we have interpreted as darkness is a tool used by the light to raise awareness and to assist in the realization of itself. Yes, there have been forces afoot which have cultivated self-interest; who put themselves before others, who violate autonomy rights, and who use the logic of fear to strengthen themselves at the expense of others. Yes, there have been entities that know no other way than to feed off the negative polarity. Even so, this approach has only been the result of limited understanding, and when we see the Universe from the ultimate point of view we understand, as Bucke did, that "death is an absurdity, that everyone and everything has eternal life, that the Universe is God and that God is the Universe, and that no evil ever did or ever will enter into it."(17.14)

What we have interpreted as "evil", in other words, has been the result of the illusion of separation. But since the Totality is all that is—and the Universe is a living, breathing, superintelligent organism—it follows that the ideas borne out of this illusion could never win. Instead, they could only, the more widespread they became, to a greater degree come back to haunt us—and thus make it increasingly clear that the totality was one united Whole. Consequently, throughout history, the dark forces have had room to play—more than enough to be convincing opponents—but they have only helped us progress to a more profound state of understanding.

So it is that, beyond the dynamics of light and dark, the Universe's transcendental order has manifested in a unifying Force which has silently played its part, patiently corrected our ways, and guided everything along. We have already seen how the karma principle and other energy laws reflect its hidden hand and another way it manifests is the Law of ONE. All principles are its subordinate, including the law of self-sacrifice which Aurobindo describes thus:

> "The law of sacrifice is the common divine action that was thrown out into the world in its beginning as a symbol of the solidarity of the universe. It is by the attraction of this law that a divinising, a saving power descends to limit and correct and gradually to eliminate the errors of an egoistic and self-divided creation."(10.120)

The issue, of course, is highly controversial. But if we take this into account, it will not only become possible to see all the world's misery in a whole new light, but to understand why the people who were killed in the Second World War or the terror attacks of 9/11, on a deeper level, were aware of their fate and accepted it[7]. No matter how uncomfortable

---

[7] See BONNIE MCENEANEY, *MESSAGES: SIGNS, VISITS, AND PREMONITIONS FROM LOVED ONES LOST ON 9/11*. Bonnie is a widower after 9/11 who presents accounts regarding loved ones before and after their demise. Also, consider that the crashed planes had 30 percent less passenger load than usual (i.e., some sensed it was a bad idea to fly

this idea sits with the ego, enlightened people all claim that it is so and that GodForce has put together a Universe in which all fragments, from the depths of their being, give one another a helping hand.

Considering that it may result in the shape of our arch-nemesis as well as our best friend this hand is not easy to see. However, we should remember that the Universe's (and our) nature is without the limits defined by the surface-consciousness. If we look more closely, all that exists is a pattern of energy which continuously calibrates on the basis of an infinity of variables, and the ego's idea of itself as an independent and fixed entity reflects only its limited worldview.

Think about it! Every molecule is part of an energetic dance that has been going on for billions of years. It is the air we breathe, the food we eat, and the water we drink which provides energy to keep the body alive but our cells are not fixed quantities. Skin cells are replaced every few weeks and even if bone cells are more resilient, in approximately five years nothing remains—all our physical being has been replaced. *Thus, physically nothing can be defined as ourselves*. Even if we lose an arm or a leg our sense of self remains undiminished, and as we shall see it is entirely independent of the body.

Likewise, there is nothing that we can point to as delineated from others or which over time presents itself as a definable and fixed entity. Again, think about it! The person who you think of as yourself is quite different from the one you thought of as yourself 20 years ago, 5 years ago, or a week ago; due to our experiences, we continually develop new perspectives, we see the world through ever new eyes and our inner world is in a constant state of flux. When it comes to this inner world, we also see how others are an intrinsic part: at all times we hold friends, enemies, relatives and strangers in mind; their world (as it presents itself to us) is very much a part of our own inner world, and their existence and contribution to our life is an inseparable part of our own identity—they

---

these planes and chose not to) and that this phenomenon is a regular find at accident sites. The American parapsychologist William Cox, for instance, did a statistical study on 28 U.S. railroad accidents that confirmed this, and it is also known that at least 19 people had similar premonitions concerning the Titanic.

give us a measure of things, a comparison without which we would not have been ourselves.

Thus, we cannot find anything that we can point to, hold for our own, and say is *me*. And so, as we take a step back and review the overall picture, we discover that when all is said and done, we are part of a larger energy pattern; we find that our sense of identity is the result of a knot in this pattern—and from this focal point, GodForce looks back upon itself *through our eyes*.

Now, from the cosmic perspective, this energy pattern is a vital, vibrant, and finely tuned intelligence. It is a highly sensitive self-aware entity in which each "self" is a sensory device used to experience itself from the fragments' point of view, and through their interaction it assembles a vast array of experience. This experience is little by little transformed into knowledge and understanding as the fragments wake up to the Wholeness of which they are a part—and as we have seen, this is the essence of the self-actualization process.

As the reader has gathered, this is also the essence of the Universe's exhalation and inhalation process and we will soon elaborate on what this process means for the Wholeness. For our part, however, in-breath involves two phases—the unconscious and the conscious. The unconscious is the one we have witnessed, for we live many lives before we have amassed enough understanding to see beyond the veil of illusion. When that happens, when the ego begins to expand beyond its previously defined limits, we have evolved to where the conscious part of the process begins. From there, we access more elevated perceptions and higher analytical knowledge; we begin to walk the mystical path, the one that grants access to greater understanding, which aligns us with our surroundings, and brings us ever closer to Unity with all that is.

Remember that in the depths of our being we are absolutely one with everything and we experience unconditional love for all that is. This, however, is not the case here and now, and so to realize our inner potential we need to move beyond the ego's present boundaries and limiting understanding; we need to expand our horizons until our understanding encompasses everything. This is what we are here for, but to grow in understanding and become more than we are we must face resistance. Without it, we are at a standstill and that is precisely why we can thank God for our enemies as well as our friends, as without them our greatest lessons could not have been learned.

No matter how outlandish it may seem to the ego, she/he who understands everything also forgives everything. The more we learn, the more obvious the implications of this truth becomes, and if we are to realize our inner potential—our true nature—we must grow in understanding to get a grip on this concept.

The way things work, our ego places a number of requirements and conditions on other people (and even animals) and we have difficulty in accepting them as they are. Hence, while we know *conditional* love, the concept of *unconditional love* is extremely hard to fathom. The reason for this is that we ourselves never have experienced what this concept means. Through our upbringing and our lives, we learn to be ashamed for things both within and outside our powers of influence, and we realize that we deserve love only if we conform to others' expectations. These ideas are fed to us through mother's milk and we again pass them on to our children. To most, this practice is so firmly rooted that we do not even reflect on it. Even so, this way of thinking has several adverse consequences which, in turn, come back to haunt us.

We shall see more of that later. The point here is to make it clear that *God does not judge anyone*. In the eyes of Creator, we are just as perfect and just as beloved *no matter what we do*, and if we want to realize our inherent potential—if we want to actualize the divine powers within—then we need to understand this concept and learn to practice unconditional love.

Again, I sense revolting, and if the reader has not yet come to terms with its implications, do not worry. We all fail every day, but even though unconditional love remains a concept too grand for most to grasp it will become obvious as we proceed *why working towards this ideal* is a good idea.

The important thing is to recognize that humanity cannot be considered a fully developed species. Instead, we should see ourselves as a *relatively* developed but unfinished expression of consciousness; behind us we have the animal form which we have outgrown, while before of us we have the godlike consciousness that we are striving for.

We shall shortly see how our consciousness has evolved and is different from the animals'. We shall then expand on how the ego's emergence was a necessary step in the Universe's striving toward self-actualization and how evolution is not a haphazard process. But before we go into detail about our fulfillment process and how we, by realizing the Divine within, also help the Universe become something more than it apparently is, there is more to say about the framework of all things.

Remember that the secret to existence is that the Universe realizes itself *through us*. As the Hindu myth of Vishnu's dream reminds us, we are here to gather certain experiences and then, once we have collected, we are to transcend the dualistic worldview so that we can see ourselves as the One we have always been. This is the Great Play and even if we do our share of stupid stuff, we learn from our experiences.

The progress of evolution, therefore, is always moving in the right direction and we can imagine that the Universe is one giant balloon of existence which, since day one, has filled with experience. As a result of the creative and organizing Force behind everything, life has evolved from less to more advanced forms of being. And if we look at evolution from the larger point of view, we see how consciousness, through all the different expressions of the Life-force's drive towards self-expansion, gains new ground and closes in on its potential.

Seen from the ego's perspective, the Universe and its history may appear meaningless and coincidental. But evolution itself is evidence of this goal-oriented process, and for those who have experienced the cosmic consciousness this process—the divine play—appears in plain sight. Through cosmic consciousness, we gain access to a perspective where we see this universal balloon from the "outside", and from this point of view the divine play reveals its true form. Seen from this perspective, we not only grasp the greater truth behind existence—how all that exists is good and that the fragments' eternal bliss and fulfillment is guaranteed by GodForce's skillful supervision—but we also see how evolution is a result of self-actualization and *what the next step in this process involves*.

We see from this perspective how the framework for everything is woven and how the progress of evolution is determined in the same way as other parameters of existence. I am thinking of the speed of light, the weak and the strong nuclear force, gravity, the electro-magnetic field, and so on—all the laws of nature which make life possible. For just as GodForce stabilizes 15 universal constants, it has balanced the influence of light and darkness on the evolutionary process.

I have mentioned that the darkness never can escape its service to the light and seen from the ultimate perspective it is as if God has put together a perfectly tailored recipe for the Wholeness' realization of itself through the pressure of duality. It is as if the Great Architect thought for Himself "a little more light here, a bit more darkness there, a little more of this kind of awareness now, a bit more of that at this time", and voila! By mixing all the ingredients perfectly, this great architect has prepared for a process that results in the self-actualization of all life forms.

As previously mentioned, along the way we have all had free will and the opportunity to create ourselves in our image. However, we have also lived our lives under the influence of dominant variables, such as the quality of the collective consciousness and our soul's aspirations. This means that if for example Graham Bell was born 100 years earlier, he would never have invented the telephone, and if we were born in Germany in the 1920s, we would have grown up within a context of dynamics that, most likely, would have turned us into Nazis by the time we reached adulthood. We are, in other words, all children of our time. And although most people today, in hindsight, like to think that they would have had the integrity to steer away from Nazism, the vast majority of today's populace—just as easily as the Germans did—fall prey to their leaders' lies and the enemy images of our time.

We shall explore this controversial topic later. The point is that we are all, to a high degree, influenced by the moral climate offered by the collective consciousness. This climate is not only the result of all the experiences which until this point in time has taken place but also of *all the experience that ever will take place*. Those who have seen the world from the perspective of cosmic consciousness have some knowledge of this process and we shall now take a closer look at the overall dynamics associated with the progress of history—as well as what we are heading towards.

2.4 A BRIEF INTRODUCTION
TO THE PROJECT OF HISTORY

*"All life here is a stage or a circumstance in an unfolding
progressive evolution of a Spirit that has involved itself in
Matter and is laboring to manifest itself in that reluctant
substance. This is the whole secret of earthly existence."*
(8.111)

—Sri Aurobindo—

Now that we are ready to get into specifics on the conscious evolution of
our Universe, a good place to begin is with our surroundings. As already
mentioned, everything we observe is a manifestation of energy which, to
some degree, is self-conscious. This even applies to the book you are
reading. Having said that, it must be added that the fundamental energy
contained in this book—the atoms—is the energy that is *the least* self-
conscious.

Atoms, in other words, are the manifestation of GodForce's *least*
wakeful expression in the physical. Yet, they are the building blocks of
everything else and thanks to them Consciousness (with a capital C) can
take on new, more complex, and more conscious forms. We see the result
of this process around us: From the atomic level Consciousness takes a
step above itself, arrives at an increased level of complexity, and forms
molecules. From the molecular level Consciousness rises another step,
takes on new forms, and creates minerals. Life begins when
Consciousness evolves from the molecular level to form single-celled
organisms and from this level it performs another quantum leap, creating
multicellular organisms.

As such, there is a certain hierarchical structure of consciousness but
its complexity does not stop there. After all, it is when we have arrived at
the multicellular level that we see Consciousness in the process of *really*
waking up to itself; on the more unconscious side we have plants, in the
middle we have animals (who between them represent a diverse range of
beings, extending from less to more self-conscious species), and on the
most self-conscious we find humans.

Hence, we represent evolution's most advanced state, being that Consciousness, with us, has taken another step and brought *Mind* into the equation. However, even if we from this line of thinking can put ourselves above other life-forms in the hierarchy, we must remember that thinking in terms of *above and below* (as well as *more or less value*) is nothing but the result of our delusions. Instead of thinking this way, therefore, it is more appropriate to see *every step of the way as perfect in itself*, since every form of existence is GodForce experiencing itself through each fragment's unique perspective. Thus, everything has its place within the framework of a larger whole, and so the evolutionary ladder more properly can be described as *holarchical* rather than hierarchical.

In the final analysis, we are all just preliminary expressions of a much larger process, and the idea that a cat is worth more than a mouse and that we again are more valuable than the animals belong to the garbage pail of history. To think in these terms is no less absurd than to suppose an adult person to be worth more than a child, just because the child is not as cognitively developed. We should also not forget that we too, in many ways, are underdeveloped. There is life in the Universe with far greater emotional and intellectual capacity than us, and from their perspective we come out as a rather primitive race. A quick glance at the current state of affairs says all about why, for there is no creature with a more unbalanced relationship to the environment.

One reason for this is that we are born into a sick world—a world ruled by seriously flawed ideas regarding the Universe and our true nature—and that we, instead of listening to our inner voice and holding these belief systems to account, integrate, polish, and maintain them from generation to generation. We do this automatically because the pressure from culture, the expectation that we must adapt to a sick society's crazed norms, are so overwhelming that it is nigh impossible not to be swayed. From the moment we are born, society instills in us the belief that our inner nature is a dubious one. And as soon as we accept this idea, we will ignore its voice.

Rather than looking within to find truth, therefore, we embrace the collective's established beliefs. Even so, it is no measure of health to be well-adjusted to a sick society. The ideas we hold still create reality, and so false beliefs will come back to haunt us full force. Whether we realize it or not our environment is an extension of ourselves; it mirrors what we collectively think, and as long as we have a fearful and unbalanced relationship to our inner world it will manifest.

Had we known better we would have looked within, understood this, and contemplated our way out. But because we on the one hand believe that our thought process is a mirage of the outer world (and do not know it is vice versa), while we on the other believe that our inner nature is flawed, we neither go within nor see the point in further self-examination. Instead of confronting fears, therefore, we project them on the environment—and this again is the source of all our problems: In doing so, we will never understand our predicament, and consequently we have spent our energy fighting demons in the outside world.

It goes without saying that this is a fight against shadows we can never win, but so far we are none the wiser. Hence, it is no exaggeration to say that all animals—indeed most life forms, including our cells— display a more balanced and constructively oriented relationship to their environment. However, to our consolation, we have a greater challenge, as we have reached a point in our development where we not only see ourselves as detached from creation but are filled with those thought-forms that come with accepting the impulses of a fear-filled ego. As the philosopher Ken Wilber describes our predicament:

> "Nature is unconscious imperfection, God is conscious perfection, but poor humanity is conscious imperfection."
> (120.2)

It is therefore not easy being human. Over thousands of years, our ego has matured into the phenomenon we know so well, and it has positioned itself so strongly that it has forgotten its origin. Thus, it has convinced itself that it is alone in the world, and in its play of hide-and-seek it has lost its way to such an extent that the fact which remain obvious to the animals—that we are one with everything—is hard to recognize. In fact, the ego has evolved into a thing so out of touch with the greater part of creation that the bridge to our inner life, the one that connects us with everything, seems completely blocked. And looking at the world today, we see the result of the ego's fears and loneliness.

Seen in this light it may seem as if God, after creating nature, took a wrong turn when He crafted the ego, lifted it up from the Ground of Being and molded us in such extreme opposition to everything else. But luckily it is not so. Indeed, seen from the larger perspective, the ego is an indispensable part of GodForce's quest for self-actualization, as it could not complete itself at nature's level. To experience consummation, the energy in the Universe had to awaken to the degree that its fragments, through a growing sense of self-awareness, eventually could perceive themselves as the Whole again—and for that to take place the Universe made man. *Thus, the ego is a bridge Consciousness utilizes to transform unconsciousness into super-consciousness, and through our maturation the Universe prepares for another evolutionary leap.*

To understand this process, we can compare the Universe to an all-encompassing supercomputer: In this analogy, we, the fragments, are subprograms who take part in and contribute to a more advanced trial-and-error superprogram. Our experiences constantly increase the information load available to the system and as the input volume increases we will reach a point where the total amount of information becomes so substantial that its processing generates a quantum leap in the program's operational function. What happens then is that the subprograms—us—not only become aware of our role within the larger system, but we gain access to the superprogram's overall perspective so that the entirety becomes an optimally functioning unit.

So, we take part in an evolutionary process which is *anything but* accidental, haphazard, and meaningless. It is the snake biting its tail—the ouroboros—and throughout history many thinkers have seen the writing on the wall. To mystics, it has always been known that consciousness is all there is and that history represents a purposeful script. The wisdom traditions of different indigenous people have also mirrored these assumptions, and even among the philosophers there have been those who came close to figuring it out.

Looking at the history of philosophy, we find that the idea was not unheard of among the ancient Greeks and that it was carried on by the idealists in the 1700s and 1800s. One of them was the German philosopher Hegel. As other idealists, he believed that the *idea* was everything, and he saw history as a result of the Universe/Spirit's efforts towards self-realization. As he put it:

> "Morality . . . is . . . intimately connected with the consciousness of Freedom. Universal history . . . shows the development of the consciousness of Freedom on the part of Spirit and the consequent realization of that Freedom."(53.70, 63)

Another great thinker who concerned himself with this idea was the French scientist Teilhard de Chardin, one of the leading paleontologists of the 20th century. He wrote several books on how evolution was driven by purpose and believed that one day it would take us to a point where the universal force had accumulated enough experience for consciousness to expand beyond its current position and re-enter the perspective of the Totality. He referred to this point as *the Omega Point*, and described it this way:

> "This will be the end and the fulfilment of the spirit of the Earth . . . The end of the World: The overthrow of equilibrium, detaching the mind, fulfilled at last, from its material matrix, so that it will henceforth rest with all its weight on God-Omega."(11.201)

It is hard to envision what this transformation entails, as it requires an understanding of existential qualities and other aspects of existence which are essentially different from the ego's experience and imagination. Nevertheless, through the expanded states, some claim to have had a glimpse of what this point—the end of history (as we know it)—implies. And although it is difficult to place anything within the framework of time when one is outside, quite a few believe that it is not that far away.

We shall expand on this issue later, especially in part six. What we can say, however, is that this point, when the world will turn inside out and the Cosmos will remember itself *through us* as full and complete, lies ahead as a pending reality. *How far* into the future is tuff to say, but from a certain perspective one can see how time is like a great river. We see how this river-of-life consists of a divine Webwork, a sensework of exceedingly fine-tuned threads of existence; how all the fragments of the Universe make up their own thread; and how this river, this miracle of existence, is an awe-inspiring creation process flowing towards the Omega point in the same way as it springs from Origin.

In a way, "beginning" and "end" are problematic concepts, not truly fit for a process that is expanding all at once. And yet, another way to see this process is like a lava lamp, as souls (and universes) are born and evolve much in the same way as the bubbles that pop up at one end only to merge with the totality at the other. The spark of creation seems to be inherent in the basic stuff, consciousness, who organizes, experiences, and reclaims itself on a journey where the idea of "self" and "time" only make sense from a fragmented perspective.

One can question these visionaries' judgment. But the reality of the ascension process and an Omega point follows as a logical consequence when we take into consideration that Consciousness/Spirit is all there is; that we are dealing with a purposeful evolutionary process; and that value fulfillment and self-actualization is the guiding principle behind all being.

Whether this point lies 5 or 500.000 years ahead is something the ego would like to clarify. Also, if the Omega Point and the Egregor represent the same phenomenon is of interest. The latter, indicating the upliftment of Humanity into a higher, collective state of consciousness, could be a prelude to an even more intriguing finish—i.e., the Omega Point. Even so, this question is hardly relevant. Considering that the "time" needed for this process to complete itself is a flexible variable which depends on our own growth, what is important is the present: It is witnessing and taking part in the process *here and now* that is crucial, for only to the extent that we excel at this shall we cross the finish line.

In other words, how much "time" it takes before we experience the Omega Point depends on how quickly we can bring our inner nature to the surface. It is a matter of building integrity by sticking with the ideals, values, and principles that follow from the Wholeness. And when it comes to the self-actualization process, this book will elaborate on basics. In today's world, there is also more than enough information available elsewhere, and so it only remains to be seen how long it will take before we translate what we know into practice.

The Omega Point, therefore, does not have to be far away. Even so, as the wise ones know, the journey itself is the goal and when it comes to the road ahead, we can describe its essence. It follows as a logical consequence of the voyage so far—and while we shall have a look at the road ahead in part six, we shall now explore the distance traveled.

PART 2

THE ROAD UNTIL TODAY

3

THE EMERGENCE OF EGO CONSCIOUSNESS AND THE RISE OF DUALITY

"The ego-feeling we are aware of now is only a shrunken vestige of a far more extensive feeling—a feeling that embraced the universe and expressed an inseparable connection of the ego with the external world."(118.123)

—*Sigmund Freud*—

IN THE FIRST part, we were acquainted with the nature of consciousness and we saw how evolution is a goal-oriented process whose purpose it is to realize inherent potential: We saw how the Totality before the morning of time split into an infinity of fragments and how these, from the Center, were sent to different places of the Universe while they forgot about their origins. We saw how this made possible a dynamic of existence (as well as a potential for experience) which otherwise would not have been achievable and how history represents our gradual recollection of our origin and true nature. We also saw how the ego's emergence was a built-in, necessary evolutionary step towards our/the Universe's self-actualization and how we only appear to be separate. In addition, we saw how the Cosmos is multidimensional; how we, in the depths of our being, forever are one with GodForce, and how there is a built-in mechanism which, through the pressure of duality, ensures that we find our way Home again.

In other words, we got some insight into the Universe's basic nature and modus operandi—in what we summarized as its exhalation and inhalation process—and so we now have a sense of why everything is as it is.

In this part, we shall approach these issues from a more down-to-earth perspective and we shall see how everything we have discussed applies to history, as well as our current worldview: We shall see how the dualistic model of interpretation reflects our level of understanding; how the division between the outer and the inner world, spirit and matter, science and religion, and so on, is the result of the ego's emergence, and how these distinctions do not communicate the nature of reality—just our way of perception.

To shed light on this, we begin by showing how the ego, since the Stone Age, has separated from the Ground of Being; how this has created our dualistic worldview, and how this in turn has led to the current separation between science and religion. We shall also see how these two, in our day and age, are coming together, and how this is a natural consequence of our ego maturing to overcome its strained relationship with the environment.

That said, we shall again start at the beginning, which for the earth was between four and five billion years ago. By this time, stardust and the forces of the Universe had molded it into shape, and although it took several billion years before life could evolve, evolution has moved forward the last 500 million years; plant life was established some 400 million years ago, and some 30 million years later animals appeared. Since then, the wildlife has assumed ever-new forms and some 200.000 years ago (according to our scientists' estimates) humans arrived.

Looking back, evolution has progressed faster and faster and then, approximately 50.000 years ago, evolution went into overdrive. There is not much known about the life of humans at this time. But we have found burial grounds where the dead were laid to rest with flowers, tools, and other things which suggest that rituals and ideas about the afterlife were part of their culture. What seems clear, however, is that people at this time and over the next 40.000 years lived their lives without the kind of consciousness we now take for granted. At this time, the ego was not yet developed to see itself in opposition to the world. Consequently, people lived in harmony with nature; they saw the circle of life as not only interconnected but animated by spirit and took part in hunter-gatherer societies where men and women were of equal worth, experiencing themselves as a living extension of nature.

Even so, we need only fast-forward to 6000 years ago to find that changes had taken place. For thousands of years, people had been cultivating the earth and with the more organized labor society took on a different form. As it became more organized, the social structure became more hierarchical, war became more common, and men strengthened their position at the expense of women.

Looking back, then, it is at this time we see the ego waking up. With the new type of awareness people became more alienated and eventually they lost contact with their environment. The world, as a result, became *externalized* and we see how this change in mindset was reflected in the image of the gods.[8]

Prior to the ego's advance, people saw God in everything; spirits were in the water, the earth, the wind, etc., and the symbols used for worship were usually feminine in form and expression. However, as the ego took control our thinking changed; people not only became more belligerent and dominance-oriented but started to consider God as an external and male entity. We see this personified in the Old Testament's ruthless, controlling, resentful, unforgiving, and jealous God—an image whose qualities would have been incomprehensible to earlier people.

Thus, it was around this time that the ego awoke, disconnected from our inner being, and we began to see ourselves as separate from creation. This again paved the way for our tendency to see the world through the dualistic-oriented mindset, which we are so familiar with. It permeates every aspect of our thinking, and we shall now see how it manifested in the distinction between religion and science.

For these two began as one. When we trace science, we find that its beginnings go back at least 2.500 years to Greece—and to the ancient Greeks it was natural to see science as part of a larger, meta-physical theory of existence. This was an exciting period in human history, for the intellect had evolved to where its analytical capabilities could be put to use. With it, the Greeks made important contributions to the written

---

[8] For more on this development, see KEN WILBER, *UP FROM EDEN*; JEAN GEBSER, *THE EVER-PRESENT ORIGIN*; TERENCE MCKENNA, *FOOD OF THE GODS*.

language and they also developed schools which cultivated the art of rhetoric, thinking, and scientific methods of observation. Personalities like Socrates, Plato, and Aristotle blessed the world with their presence, and their thoughts about life, morality, creation, God, nature, and man's place within this framework—about right and wrong and how it all fit together—was so authoritative and well-systematized that they left a legacy which has influenced philosophical and scientific traditions to our day.

All this happened before organized religion, as we know it, emerged. But religion, in its essence, is our thinking about the spiritual dimension, and these thinkers were so in touch with truth and reason that the worldview conveyed corresponded with the essence of later religions. That is why both Socrates and Plato have been called "Christians before Christ", and they can be counted among the many prophets who have visited earth. I say "many" because there were several before and quite a few since. Prophets, after all, are merely more advanced consciousnesses who come to earth to move way for a bigger plan, but to stick to the topic of science and religion the two have followed each other as one until the 1500s.

By then, however, the surface-consciousness had grown so strong that our play with duality began to take its toll. The ego was becoming increasingly fine-tuned as it distanced itself from the Ground of Being and its cognition had evolved to a point where science and religion were headed for a crossroads[9]. Until then, when it came to matters of primary importance, no one could imagine dividing our search for answers into opposing categories. To the thinking person it had seemed obvious that as the world was put together as one, so would all true understanding reflect an interconnected whole. As Marcus Aurelius, the Roman Emperor and Stoic philosopher, noted nearly 2000 years ago:

---

[9] Despite posterity's distinction, we shall later see how there have always been some individuals who haven't distinguished between the two. Even so, our understanding of history reflects our understanding of ourselves and as we are very dualistic oriented, the gulf between them has become more and more evident over the past 500 years. Today, therefore, we trace the separation back to this period.

"All things are woven together and the common bond is sacred, and scarcely one thing is foreign to another, for they have been arranged together in their places and together make the same ordered Universe. For there is one Universe out of all, one God through all, one substance and one law, one common Reason of all intelligent creatures and one Truth."

As Aurelius continued, therefore, one should "frequently consider the connection of all things in the universe". Wise words. But as the Church grew into a powerhouse with a monopoly on truth, its dogmas withheld progress. It was plain to see that the clergy did not appreciate critical thinking and as the bulk of society's knowledge increased, a growing gulf revealed itself between those who were trying to find the truth and those who believed they already had it.

Hence, unless scientists/philosophers (they were still one) wanted to be burned at the stake, they had to find a way to avoid stepping on the Church's toes. The Frenchman Rene Descartes succeeded in this when he created a philosophy based on the separation of spirit from matter. In doing so, those seeking to understand the world through observation and rational thinking could continue their work, while the clergy could cling to their delusions.

Still, the separation between spirit and matter could not completely appease the Church; one way or another the two were connected, and so the scientists' observations would again and again come to challenge dogmas. The most famous example was the discovery that the earth was not the center of the Universe, as the Church had proclaimed. Already in the 1500s, Copernicus had presented a case explaining why the earth had to be revolving around the sun and not vice versa, and Kepler supported this thesis some 60 years later. The evidence seemed conclusive, but even so Galileo was brought before the Inquisition in 1633 after promoting the idea and forced to recount. In later years, the injustice done was obvious, but it was not until 1992 that the Church acknowledged their mistake.

Until the present day, therefore, we find that the Church has built its power base on violence, threats, arrogance, and ignorance. This was already obvious back then and the men of science did what they could to please the Church. They all believed in a Creator, and from their perspective they were only trying to figure out how God's machinery worked.

When it comes to this question, there have been far more ideas than appropriate to reproduce. However, it only became harder to reconcile dogmas with the complex machinery uncovered by science, and because of the Church's refusal to deal with reality a counterforce emerged.

This was the advocates of Darwin's theory of evolution. In our time most interpret it to mean that life is the result of chance and pure luck: they think that everything has evolved from an accidental mixing of fluids in the Precambrian era and that God is just an idea some people cling onto because they cannot cope with reality. Roughly 50 percent of scientists think of life as established on these terms. The rest are not so sure. But no matter what they personally think it makes less and less difference, for as science has become more specialized its disciples have lost their way by narrowing focus to the details of their respective fields.

So it has become a fundamental assumption that science should only be concerned with the observable; that its area of investigation should be the quantitative and not the qualitative, and that they should leave it to philosophers and theologians to ponder the great questions. These groups have had a couple of thousand years to try and figure it all out, but still they are no closer to answers. The philosophers have only managed to describe how they, through the looking glass of ego-consciousness, view the world, while theologians have been busy discussing Church dogmas as if building on this foundation could lead back to spiritual truth.

Thus, it is small wonder that people are disillusioned and that most of us take it for granted that we will never know the answers to the big questions. It seems as if the world was broken into a thousand pieces and that, as the disciplines of science are becoming more specialized, it only gets more difficult to put the pieces back together. But fortunately, it is not so. On the contrary, the divergent corpus of research, as we shall see, is easy to put together into a coherent whole, and the seemingly chaotic fragmentation only reflects the ego's inability to see itself in a larger context.

4

THE THEORY OF EVOLUTION AND ITS LACK OF CREDIBILITY

"It would be very difficult to explain why the universe should have begun in just this way, except as the act of a God who intended to create beings like us."(23.105)

—*Stephen Hawking, physicist*—

WE HAVE SEEN how the ego's emergence resulted in different paths for science and religion 500 years ago. In the next chapter we shall expand on the development of religion and how it reflects our journey through duality. Before we do, however, we shall become better acquainted with the theory of evolution and look at some of its weaknesses.

We start with this because we live in a time where most are under the impression that theories of evolution and creation are incompatible and that any thinking person swears loyalty to the former. As we shall see, this is wrong, but it is a general feature of our mindset that we like simple answers. Being children of duality, we prefer things in black or white and looking at the status quo it is the most vocal players on each side who have set the standard for the debate. These are people who define themselves in opposition to each other and it is not often they meet to find common ground. Yet, such ground is easy to find, for it is only the most reactionary who believe that one (evolution) excludes the other (a Creator and a meaningful creation).

We shall see more on that. However, let us start with a look at the theory of evolution as interpreted by Neo-Darwinians. This tradition presents itself as the most intransigent and fundamentalist-minded among the scientists, for while some evolutionary theorists have an open mind to the question of a Creator and suppose that evolution may be a goal-oriented and purpose-built process the Neo-Darwinians will hear of no such thing. According to them, life has evolved from the famous mud puddle in the Precambrian Era, and from there we have ended up where we are due to a series of random mutations. In that respect, all life is seen as the result of chance mutations; it has evolved from an initial accidental mixture of molecules through a haphazard process of trial and error and only the most adaptable individuals have survived and passed on their genes. Hence, there is no plan or purpose present—all life is instead only the result of dead matter that has organized itself so that some of us believe it.

There are several weighty arguments that we can draw upon against this interpretation. Most important, however, is that the idea of random mutation and a slow and purposeless evolutionary process neither is supported by the fossil material nor common sense[10]. After all, it takes between 100 and 200 mutations before a species even comes close to reshaping its front legs into functional wings, and none of the many stages in between are useful. It goes without saying that an animal crawling around without functional legs nor wings would have had extremely poor survival capabilities and that the chances of wings arising in this way are microscopic. Adding to the equation, this highly unlikely scenario is supposed to have happened over and over, not only giving birds and insects the ability to aerially navigate but mammals.

Similarly, it is difficult to explain the emergence of complex organs such as eyes, which Darwin admitted:

> "To suppose the eye, with all its inimitable contrivances for
> adjusting the focus to different distances . . . could have
> been formed by natural selection, seems, I confess, absurd
> in the highest degree."(15.36)

Thus, if we give the subject some thought, it seems obvious that the idea of random mutation as the driving force behind evolution is far-

---

[10] For a more thorough elaboration on the improbability of the arguments put forward by the Darwinists see RICHARD MILTON, *THE FACTS OF LIFE: SHATTERING THE MYTHS OF DARWINISM* and ROBERT WESSON, *BEYOND NATURAL SELECTION*.

fetched. We should also keep in mind that all known mutations (Down syndrome, dwarfism etc.) hamper our chances for survival rather than the opposite and that the search in the fossil material for half-developed or dysfunctional species has proved futile. This material, which is enormous, suggests instead that evolution occurs in leaps, as no intermediate forms are found.

Another variable which impugns the idea that life comes down to chance is the fact that the Universe, as we know it, seems to be no more than 14 billion years old. This may seem like a long time and one might think that in a span of so many years something is bound to happen, for as many evolutionary theorists have said: "If we put a monkey in front of a typewriter, he will sooner or later hit up Shakespeare's collected works." The idea is that given enough time, probability suggests blind chance could realize anything, including us, but if we look closer at the time the Universe has had at its disposal we find that evolution has never been idle and that it has moved forward as quickly as possible.

As mentioned, modern science supposes that the Universe began with a Big Bang 14 billion years ago. In this blast the first elements, hydrogen and helium, were created but this was not enough to form life. For that to happen, more complex elements were needed, and so hydrogen and helium (miraculously enough) had to create suns which had to burn out and die before the next stage of development could begin. More advanced molecules were produced by the death of these stars, and as they exploded oxygen, nitrogen, and carbon were ejected into space. All life, as we know it, is carbon based and so it was only then, 8 to 10 billion years after the Big Bang (let us not forget that this is another miracle which science cannot explanation) that planets like earth could form to breed life.

We see from this summary that the earth could not have come into existence much sooner. The oldest rocks are 4 billion years old (some meteorites are 4.5 billion years) and 150 million years later our planet contained microbial forms of life. Since then life has evolved steadily and the process of evolution has advanced at an ever-faster pace.

Thus, based on the timeframe available, it seems more than naive to accuse chance for orchestrating these events. The British astronomer Fred Hoyle estimates that, given the most favorable conditions, the chances for life to occur as the result of chance is in the range of 1 to $10^{40.000}$ and together with F. B. Salisbury, he has estimated that, for chance to succeed, it would take at least 12 billion years to produce one single enzyme. An enzyme is a protein (and proteins are the building blocks of all life), and biologist Lyall Watson describes it thus:

> "A protein is a structure of such gigantic improbability that unguided nature would probably not hit on it given the whole known universe to experiment on for a billion years. The odds against it happening by sheer chance are greater than one in ten-to-the-power-of-eighty, which is a figure larger than the total of electrons in the universe." (116.46)

If we look at a more complicated structure, like a virus, the odds are even more heavily stacked. Paul Davies, a professor of natural philosophy elaborates:

> "It is possible to perform rough calculations of the probability that the endless breakup and reforming of the [Primordial] soup's complex molecules would lead to a small virus after a billion years. Such are the enormous number of different possible chemical combinations that the odds work out at over $10^{2.000\ 000}$ to one against. This mind-numbing number is more than the chances against flipping heads on a coin six million times in a row . . . the spontaneous generation of life by random molecular shuffling is a ludicrously improbable event."(26.118)

Mathematics is not my field of expertise and I have no idea how people calculate these equations. However, speaking of numbers, probability calculations, and the idea that given enough time a monkey could produce Shakespeare's collected works, based on mathematician Warren Weaver's calculations, Saul-Paul Sirag has concluded that one super-fast monkey who presses 10 keys per second would need 20 billion years just to write "to be or not." And as Alan Vaughan says, "if we want the quote finished, then we will have to hire 10 billion monkeys, also typing for 20 billion years, before they could create "to be or not to be?"(112.206)

Consequently, the probability that Neo-Darwinians have got it right is infinitely small. And as we shall see, those who are convinced that life is due to a series of meaningless coincidences are no less in denial of the body of scientific research than their adversaries—those who believe that the world was created in six days and that the earth is 6.000 years old.

Now, it should be added that the Neo-Darwinians are even more Darwinian than Darwin. In their mind, the theory of evolution has evolved into something that he personally would not support, for Darwin considered it quite possible that evolution was the result of intelligent design. He was, after all, an educated theologian and described his position as follows:

> "[When I reflect upon] the impossibility of conceiving this immense and wonderful universe, including man, . . . as the result of blind chance or necessity, . . . I feel compelled to look for a First Cause having an intelligent mind in some degree analogous to that of man and I deserve to be called a theist."(11.84)

This quote may come as a surprise. But if we look into it, virtually none of our great scientists have rejected the idea of an intelligent force—a Creator—being behind the mystery and guiding life forward. The reason for this is that no matter how much we study creation, we find nothing to suggest that we can exclude a Creator from the calculation. On the contrary, the more we study our world and the more we understand of its inherent and infinite complexity, the more obvious it becomes that we are witnessing a miracle that will never allow itself to be reduced to inert matter—and that there is an all-encompassing Intelligence present that is so wonderfully complex that we, with our minds, can hardly grasp its scope. As Einstein put it:

> "Everyone who is seriously involved in the pursuit of science becomes convinced that a Spirit is manifest in the laws of the Universe—a Spirit vastly superior to that of

man, and one in the face of which we, with our modest powers, must feel humble."(92.186)

In fact, it is only because organized religion has put forth so inadequate answers to the mystery of life that scientists can accept the Neo-Darwinian worldview. And had a credible alternative been known, one that could put everything we know about spirit and matter back together into a coherent and meaningful whole, most would have accepted it gladly.

This also applies to the most well-known Neo-Darwinian scientist, biologist Richard Dawkins. For although he has spent several decades being one of the most vocal critics of the concept of God (as presently established), he has this to say:

> "I accept that there may be things far grander and more incomprehensible than we can imagine . . . My mind is open to the most wonderful range of future possibilities, which I cannot even dream about . . . What I am skeptical about is the idea that whatever wonderful revelation does come in the science of the future, it will turn out to be one of the particular historical religions that people happen to have dreamed up. . . . If there is a God, it's going to be a whole lot bigger and whole lot more incomprehensible than anything that any theologian of any religion has ever proposed."(45.140)

I am, of course, totally in agreement with Dawkins. And as we have seen, the "new" theory of existence offers—as he predicted—a concept of God which is far greater, far more complex and wonderful than any organized religion could ever imagine. It is also a more credible, as it unites the body of research from all disciplines into one consistent whole.

Thus, the gulf between modern science and religion is easily overcome. At their core, these two represent only different approaches to empirical knowledge—and there is ultimately only one road leading to a final resolution. The reason for this should be obvious, for as we know the nature of existence *is* Consciousness; the Universe is a multidimensional, living, breathing organism; the outer world is a reflection of the inner world, and the nature of the Universe is the nature of ourselves—*we are one*. The road to understanding therefore goes *through us*, and so it follows logically that the most fundamentalist-oriented people on either side of the science-versus-religion debate are those who live their lives most out of touch with their own inner selves.

That is why merging the two, to them, seems contradictory, for they are so in the grip of duality that the holistic perspective is lost. Even so, this percentage of the population is becoming increasingly marginal, and most people, whether they define themselves as Muslims, atheists, empiricists, reductionists, Neo-Darwinians, Christians, or Satanists, can effortlessly make the leap into a new and more unifying worldview.

This presumes that they are willing to reconsider beliefs and open their minds to new possibilities. But those who are willing to do so will find that we can take the best from each tradition and unite everything in a coherent, meaningful, and unfathomable mosaic—and that we, by doing so, will not only bring rationality back to religion but also the mystery back to science.

We shall later see how the two, in our days, are melting together. Before that, however, we shall take a closer look at how our journey through duality has characterized our quest for spiritual truth.

5

THE PROGRESS OF RELIGION AND THE LOGIC OF FEAR

"One of the main functions of organized religion is to protect people against a direct experience of God." (35.209)

—Carl Gustav Jung, psychologist—

PEOPLE HAVE ALWAYS had their myths about creation and our origins. These legends have always reflected what we believe about ourselves and on this basis, we have organized as a society. The inner and the outer world, as we know, will always mirror each other and we have seen that the earliest humans had a completely different worldview. They saw themselves as a living extension of the environment and knew that they were an integral part of the whole. They therefore lived in more harmonious, equality-oriented societies and had a qualitatively different understanding of time. While we perceive history as a linear process, they experienced it as being cyclical, and as humanity's understanding has always been reflected in its gods, ideas of godhood were essentially different.

Looking back, we can summarize their lives as a more inner-oriented existence (i.e., the outer and the inner world had not yet separated). Consequently, the image of God as an outsider—or male— would have been incomprehensible. After all, the idea of God as a vindictive, jealous, and ruthless old grouch located in Heaven grew forth as a result of the ego-consciousness' secession from the Ground of Being. The Old Testament's punitive God, therefore, reflected the consciousness at the time—and because it was men who ruled, and because they saw mercilessness and vengeance as cherished ideals, this was also the God they worshiped.

We see from this that our idols can be understood as a tribute to contemporary ideals: they reflect what we strive to realize and because people back then were ruthless and self-absorbed, they worshiped a God that was equally full of Himself.

This was then the old Jewish God. On the basis of this image Christianity and Islam appeared and it is no coincidence that they became the great religions of conquest, those who violently endeavored to subjugate the world to rid it of pagans and infidels. As I said, at all times the outer world is a reflection of the inner, and so, because people were so fearful and unsure of their value, they worshipped a God who was just as unsure of Himself—and consequently felt threatened by all other gods.

Truth be told, this feature of religion is still a part of our world even today: There are plenty of people who feel threatened by other truths; who believe that evil is strong and good is weak; who are willing to kill for peace; and who justify war and every other atrocity in the name of God. The reason for this is that most people also today go about their day without a clue of how the world is put together. There are still many who struggle with issues of self-worth; who do not know that their inner life is all there is, and who consequently transfer their inner demons on the environment. That said, this percentage is smaller than it was, and more people are beginning to smarten up. This, again, is because history represents our journey towards the realization of inner potential—and so, as time has moved forward, humanity has gone through a maturation process.

That humanity has been growing in understanding can admittedly be construed as a controversial statement as it most certainly may not look it. We know, among other things, that last century was the bloodiest ever and many people, therefore, will conclude that things are getting worse. If we focus on the bad stuff, this is an understandable, even correct observation. We live in a time of increasing polarity and as the light is growing stronger, the shadow is becoming more noticeable. Even so, if we look at the grand design, we see that humanity, despite its shortcomings, has increased its understanding.

Our idols speak volumes, for looking at them we find that society 2500 years ago was built on values entirely different: Men held all the power and society was a rigid hierarchical structure where compassion, social justice, and forgiveness were more or less unheard of. It was within the framework of this context that people lived their lives and had their experiences. These experiences were transformed into under-standing and as people learned from their misery, so also the quality of the social fabric changed.

500 years later, we find that humanity had evolved sufficiently for idols to be transformed, and with the assistance of prophets like Jesus the image of a more forgiving and loving God grew forth. Obviously, war, oppression, and abuse kept flourishing, the Church itself being responsible for the bulk of it. But even though the institution can be criticized, it has also—in what must be seen as a difficult era in human history—played an important role in maintaining spiritual traditions.

In the grander scheme of things this is clearly seen, for we leave behind a time where the illusion of separation has been so overwhelming that our civilization came close to perish. And that the Church, throughout this time, has presented the spiritual truths in a distorted manner is because a religion can never be better than its followers. The two reflect each other, and as the congregation largely has consisted of fearful, self-absorbed, and petty hypocrites, the law of attraction has given the ignorant masses what they deserved—namely, such leaders who represent the exact same qualities. After all, while they could favorably be revised, the 10 commandments are not that difficult to interpret. And if people only had taken responsibility for their lives—if they had taken their ideals a bit more seriously—it would have been impossible for authorities to do as they have done.

Honestly, the distance between theory and practice has been so great that, to a thinking man, it was obvious that the Church itself never conformed to the message it was born to convey. Jesus, for example, never talked about sin and shame. Instead, he spoke of illusions and awakening and said that *knowing oneself was to know God*. Like any other prophet who has walked the earth, he made it clear that "the kingdom of God is within you": That in the depths of our being we are one with God and, consequently, that if we seek salvation, we must go within and be true to our inner authority—not some self-exalted outside authority like the Church. As he said:

"If you bring forth what is within you, what you bring forth
will save you. [But] if you do not bring forth what is within
you, what you do not bring forth will destroy you."(78.15)

Thus, the last thing Jesus wanted was for us to accept any authority outside ourselves. To do so is *always* the first step on the road to self-destruction and so, no matter how admired he was by the disciples, Jesus never put himself above others. Instead, he practiced and preached the ideals, values, and principles that followed from Wholeness, and by his example—as well as his words—he made it clear that the highest honor and the highest good was to serve creation/others. Consequently, there was nothing about his message that the later Church could cite in support of its behavior and authority. And since men of power always have felt threatened by divine truth, they had to change this simple message—which they did.

The authorities of the Church are not too keen on discussing this. Even so, when it comes to the subject of religion, we should keep in mind that since the earliest of times there have been several models of interpretation. There is much to be said about this, but to make a long story short the most important distinction is found between those who follow the inner-oriented message and those who have advocated a more exterior-oriented version of different religions.

Speaking of early Christianity, the exterior-oriented version is known as the Peter doctrine, the one that the Catholic Church came to represent. When it comes to the inner-oriented tradition, Eliphas Levi and other researchers see it as a continuation of the old mystery schools which at this time, originating from Greece, Tibet, India, and Egypt, made their presence known in the region[11]. It is often referred to as the doctrine of John, because they believe that it was first preached by John the Baptist

---

[11] The following books elaborate on the parallels between early Christianity and pagan/Greek/Indian/Egyptian mystery-traditions: LYNN PICKETT & CLIVE PRINCE, *THE TEMPLAR REVELATION*; J.M. ROBERTSON, *PAGAN CHRISTS*; BURTON L. MACK, *THE LOST GOSPEL: THE BOOK OF Q AND CHRISTIAN ORIGINS*, AND KARL W. LUCKERT, *EGYPTIAN LIGHT AND HEBREW FIRE*.

and that Jesus followed in his footsteps. They also believe that the tradition continued with John the disciple and Mary Magdalene and that it has survived until today as an undercurrent in the Christian faith. Valentin Tomberg summarizes the relationship between the two traditions as follows:

> "Many . . . in France, Germany, England, and elsewhere, promulgate the doctrine of the so-called "two churches": the church of Peter and the church of John, or of the "two epochs"—the epoch of Peter and the epoch of John.   .
> . . This doctrine teaches the end—more of less at hand—of the church of Peter, or above all the papacy which is its visible symbol, and that the spirit of John . . . will replace it. In this way it teaches that the "exoteric" church of Peter will make way for the "esoteric" church of John, which will be that of perfect freedom."(101.226)

Most people have not heard of these two doctrines (or the prophecy), as the Church prefers it that way. Yet, the undercurrent represented by the doctrine of John is very much alive and having made an effort to track it researchers Lynn Pickett and Clive Prince concluded thus:

> "After sifting through the mass of evidence for the existence of a wider John cult, we had to conclude not only that there was such a thing, but also that it has always existed parallel to the Church, keeping its secrets safe.   .
> . . This [secret] was the ancient religion of personal *gnosis*, of *enlightenment*, the spiritual transformation of the individual."(84.349, 350)

After reading this we understand why the Church has kept people in the dark about the existence of this tradition. After all, the doctrine of enlightenment left nothing that leaders could build a power base on, and so they have sought to remove all traces. Already, 200 years after Jesus, Christianity had evolved to the point where certain groups were fighting against others for control of the movement. The most eager were those who understood the least of Jesus' message, for it was only they who had any interest in controlling others and defining their truths. But no matter: these guys (who did not know that the kingdom of God was within) put together a variety of texts which were compatible with their worldview, and thus the New Testament was born in 325.

Since then it has been revised over and over, always in line with the ambitions of power. As a result, a religion was formed where women were marginalized; where the reincarnation concept was declared to be heretical; and where the inner-oriented message was greatly distorted. In other words, anything that threatened the Church's power base had to give way. And a quick glance at history reveals the zeal with which the orthodox persecuted and killed those who did not submit to the dogmas of power.

Reading between the lines, then, a common thread in ecclesiastical history has been authorities' fight against the inner-oriented practice. It was not only the pagan remnants of this tradition that was put down; Christian groups such as the Gnostics, Mandeans, Simonians, Cathars, Dositheans and Templars, not to forget alchemists and every other movement dealing with the mysteries were persecuted. Jesus' words about forgiveness, love, and compassion were evidently forgotten. And in its place a hierarchical, male-dominated, power-hungry structure grew forth—one that did what it could to turn priests into pederasts and its followers (and everyone else) into a subdued, timid flock of sheep.

In order to succeed in this quest, its leaders had to shield people from experiencing God within themselves—or anything else for that matter. They had to create a gulf between man and God, an abyss only the Church could bridge, and by preaching about a God "up there", a God who was separate and fundamentally different, they positioned themselves as intermediaries. Furthermore, they preached about our fall from grace, about sin and our corrupt inner nature, so that they could convey salvation and forgiveness, and they threatened with the eternal torments of hell if we did not submit to the authority of the Church.

By doing so, they made us doubt ourselves enough to ignore the inner-self. If it tried to raise its voice against the shameless absurdities proposed by clergy, cardinals told us to beware, for it could only be Satan playing his tricks—and if we listened to him, we would surely go to hell.

In following this simple recipe, they not only made us accept the authority of the Church, no matter how hypocritical and false, but they established a powerbase that leaders have been very keen to maintain.

The reason is that as every other institution, the Church is primarily concerned with its own survival. In order to ensure this, the Church has collaborated with all kinds of totalitarian regimes against their own people, and so it remains to this day. Its leaders, of course, will never admit to such a thing, for as Jesus was the champion of the poor and oppressed, so too the Church strives to present itself as an advocate of this tradition. Yet, looking back we find that the Church has always taken the side of the aggressors; and whether we are talking about the despotic rulers of the middle-ages, Nazi-Germany, or any other military dictatorship, we find it is the same old story.

That being said, there have always been Christians who have seen this abyss between theory and practice. Like any other organization the Church consists of individuals, and in studying the organizational structure we find an interesting dynamic between those who partake to serve others and those whose primary motivation is power.

This dynamic is no more difficult to spot in the structure of the Church than elsewhere. And even though the overwhelming majority of popes, cardinals, and bishops have been oriented toward the latter, there have always been good Christians around to criticize them. Hildegard of Bingen, John of La Verna, St. Katherine of Sienna, John Tavler, and Martin Luther are former examples. More recent examples are Martin Luther King and Oscar Romero who were both assassinated by agents of the State because of their support of the oppressed[12]. No matter how exceptional, these were not the only—nor the last—of the Christians fighting the good fight. In fact, they are more plentiful than ever as the distance between theory and practice becomes more apparent.

---

[12] According to the official story M. L. King was assassinated by a lone gunman. Still, there is ample evidence that he was killed as a result of a conspiracy involving the U.S. Government. Among other things, this was established by the Circuit Court of Shelby County, Tennessee, when a jury of twelve, in December 1999, after four weeks of testimony and hearing over 70 witnesses, in a unanimous verdict concluded that government agencies, indeed, were involved in his assassination.

What all these "rebels" have in common, whether they lived 1000 years ago or today, is that they have been sufficiently in touch with their inner voice to respect their own conscience rather than their authorities' misdirection. And because of their integrity, they have been feared, censured, and opposed by superiors. One of the many who have experienced this is the Brazilian theologian Leonardo Boff. After repeatedly being condemned by the Vatican for his support for the oppressed, he finally had the privilege of being excommunicated. I say "privilege" because he joined the ranks of some of history's greatest men and women, and as he said of his dealings with the Church: "My personal experience of dealing over the last 20 years with doctrinal power is this: it is cruel and merciless; it forgets nothing; forgives nothing; it exacts a price for everything."(51.225)

That is, unless you are a child molester. Then the tradition of the Church is to look the other way, protect you from harm, and make sure that you are free to continue your calling elsewhere. So far, the Catholic Church has paid more than $3 Billion in legal settlements and other damages related to this issue. Between June 2017 and June 2018 in the United States alone the Catholic Church spent a whopping $301.6 million on costs related to clergy sexual abuse, while in the same 12-month period the church fielded 1,051 new "credible allegations" of sexual abuse of a minor by priests and other clergy. Even more telling, the Survivors Network of those Abused by Priests (SNAP), have filed charges in the International Criminal Court (ICC) against the Catholic Church for crimes against humanity because of its policy on this issue.

Seen from their point of view, its leaders never willfully set out to give the Church a bad name: Like most people they would prefer a better world for all,[13] but as the structure of the Church (and every other

---

[13] There are elements in the Church, as elsewhere, that do not conform to this norm. Indeed, even cardinals suspect that the reversal of morals—satanism—has found a place in high circles. As Fr. Malachi Martin, a Jesuit scholar and Vatican insider, noted: "Most frighteningly for [Pope] John Paul [II], he had come up against the irremovable presence of a malign strength in his own Vatican and in certain bishops' chanceries. It was what knowledgeable Churchmen called the 'superforce.' Rumors, always difficult to verify, tied its installation to the beginning of Pope Paul VI's reign in 1963. Indeed, Paul had alluded somberly to 'the smoke of Satan which has entered

organization) reflects something more than the sum of good intentions, shortsighted priorities tend to win.

To understand this, we must return to the collective consciousness and how it affects society. We shall have more to say about it later, but for now we must take into account that the Church does not exist in a vacuum. If it wants to ensure its existence and increase its influence (which is what all organizations want) it must therefore engage in powerpolitics. It must, in other words, play ball with those conditions contemporary society has to offer and for thousands of years the logic of fear has set the standard, ensuring a social dynamic in which good intentions fall short.

If we remember, the logic of fear manifests with the assumption that the world is a dangerous place. It tells us that good is weak and defenseless while evil is strong and powerful—and consequently, that if we want the good, we must sometimes do evil to achieve our goals. Briefly summarized, it is the mindset which tells us that the end justifies the means, and when we look at the suffering and death we have inflicted throughout history, we find that it started with this assumption.

We shall elaborate on this later, especially in part five. But when it comes to the Church, we see how the logic of fear has affected the organization on the distance between theory and practice; theory being the way the Church *would like* the world to be and the way it *wants* to present itself, and practice being what it actually does. The Catholic Church, for example, (if we exclude some bad apples) only wants to be a force for good—and because it wants to maximize its power to do good, it has, since its inception, aspired to world domination. To realize its goal, it has created a secret fraternity. This is the Jesuits, and it is an open secret that the end-justifies-the-means ideology has been their modus operandi.

---

the Sanctuary'. . . an oblique reference to an enthronement ceremony by Satanists in the Vatican. Besides, the incidence of Satanic pedophilia—rites and practices—was already documented among certain bishops and priests as widely dispersed as Turin, in Italy, and South Carolina, in the United States. The cultic acts of Satanic pedophilia are considered by professionals to be the culmination of the Fallen Archangel's rites." (MARTIN, *THE KEYS OF THIS BLOOD*, p. 632) We shall discuss this bit in part 5, and it is much because of this force—and our willing participance—that immorality abound.

History, after all, speaks for itself. And those who want proof of how a pronounced spiritual organization has availed itself of worldly means to survive, need only look at the Vatican Bank.

For those who have any knowledge of how banks operate, the banking system ranks top among the destructive indecencies troubling civilization, and the Vatican Bank is an example of why. It is one of the shadiest banks the world has ever seen and not only did it collaborate with the Nazis, making a fortune on other people's misery, but it has been implicated in widespread money laundering, murder, corruption, and mafia dealings.

A quick history lesson, then, reveals the distance between theory and practice and how the logic of fear has damaged the Church. When it comes to this logic, it represents a self-perpetuating dynamic; it ensures its own survival in that the disastrous events which follow in its wake seem to confirm what we initially took for granted. Remember that our thoughts are a form of energy which affect the environment. Whereas like attracts like, the more we fear, the more this fear will manifest—and the more it does, the more obvious it will become that our fears were justified to begin with.

In other words, what we believe is what we see: It is a self-fulfilling prophecy, and the more we allow fear to seduce us, the more it will blur our judgment. As an example, we can look at the dynamic between Israelis and Palestinians, for the more convinced they are that the other group wants to see them hurt, the more this fear will manifest in thoughts, words, and actions which create hatred and enmity.

One reason is that in any society there will always be "hawks" and "doves". The hawks, like the fundamentalists, represent that percentage of humanity with the most confused relationship to their inner self. These are the people who, instead of dealing with their fears, project them on to their surroundings, while the doves represent the more perceptive percentage of the population. Hence, they have a more balanced relationship with their environment and they are more tolerant, understanding, and forgiving. In short, they try to treat other people the way they want others to treat them.

It is in the nature of things that the more doves, the more influence they will hold, and the less likelihood conflicts will arise. But the more the logic of fear takes hold of the social fabric, the more hawks there will be, and the more influential their grouping will become. It follows also that the more influence they get, the more society will prioritize defense spending and security measures—and that the more a nation prepares for war, the more threatened and insecure others become.

Hence, the logic of fear leads to a destructive spiral dynamic which slowly escalates—and the more it grows, the more likely someone will start a "preventive" war. The energy laws ensure this result, as a thought will attract a certain answer. The dynamic is the same everywhere; it applies to all areas of society and when it comes to religion, we see it played out on the troubled relationship between Christian and Muslim fundamentalists.

When we are talking about fundamentalism, however, it comes in several forms. To begin with, fundamentalism is a religious response to the corruption and immorality that plague civilization. Fundamentalists see this as a result of a godless and materialistic culture, and so they seek to create a society in which religion permeates every stratum: They want jurisprudence, politics, economics, family structure, and science to rely on a religious foundation—thereof *fundamentalists*.

I must admit that I, like many others, previously thought of fundamentalists in derogatory terms as they often come out as an exceedingly reactionary and intolerant congregation. But from this starting point we see that fundamentalism can take on two forms, one healthy and one less so. After all, it is obvious that moral decay has run rampant and so working for a more decent and humane society is not a bad idea. The problem, therefore, is not the fundamentalists who want a better world and aim to achieve this by embracing the logic of love and setting a good example. The problem, rather, is those who are so affected by the logic of fear that they want to replace the old with a system that is as misanthropic and degenerate as that which they criticize. In the end, a family structure where husband is the undisputed head of the family— and where the wife is subjected to his every whim—is not much better than any other despotic system. And not surprisingly, we see that many fundamentalists have a longing for control which extends well beyond wife and kids.

This control-oriented mindset, however, does rarely reflect ill will, for human nature is inherently good and we all ideally want what is best for everyone. The problem, therefore, is not our intentions. It is that we let the logic of fear inspire our calculations, and looking back we find that all the misery we've inflicted on each other (generally speaking) is the result of good intentions mixed with the end-justifies-the-means ideology.

To say a bit more about the logic of fear, the more immature we are the more likely we are to be attracted. We have already seen how an ignorant affiliation with our inner world results in an ignorant approach to the outside world, and so it is that in any society—whether we are talking about its secular or religious groupings—we find that the most fearsome percentage of the population are those with the most chaotic relationship to their inner world.

These people have not discovered how thoughts create reality and that they can have a more constructive rapport with their environment by looking within. They therefore live their lives on autopilot, taking it for granted that the world "out there" is a sinister and unsavory thing that happens to them. Hence, they *react* to their surroundings instead of *acting* upon them, and the idea that it could be the other way around—that they could consciously create/recreate their own reality—has not yet occurred. Even today, this applies to the majority of the population. Some react more knee-jerk than others. But as long as we do so, we will take part in the aforementioned process where fear plays ball—and as long as we refuse to examine the preconditions of our assumptions, fear will have a power which makes our world smaller.

In the introduction we discussed how all our motivations and thinking is the result of two fundamental forces, fear and love. The first strengthens the perceived distance between us and our surroundings while the other does the opposite, and we see this reflected in the fundamentalists' narrow safe zones: They feel threatened by everything from scantily clad and independent women to gays and otherwise-thinking people—and the narrower their safe-zone, the more intolerant, aggressive, and ruthless they are toward others.

Studying social dynamics from a greater perspective, we find that the logic of fear has always been our greatest problem: It increases the distance between us, creates discord, generates animosity, and even pretends to justify our worst transgressions. For thousands of years, it has influenced the global psyche, and this has always been reflected in society's power- and organizational structure. We have just seen how this mindset counteracts good intentions on two levels: When it comes to the individual, it blurs our judgment; and as it pertains to the collective, it creates a dynamic which encourages the more ruthless, vengeful, and intolerant aspects of our nature. This, in turn, creates favorable career-conditions for that percentage which is *least in control over their own inner-world* and most eager to control the outer world.

We have also seen how the logic of fear not only wreaks havoc on our psyche and the social fabric but that it is at the heart of a dynamic which makes matters worse: It leads to a destructive spiral in which the repercussions of our increasing bitterness, mercilessness, intolerance, and hostility constantly worsen—and this spiral will eventually destroy us if we do not wise up.

It was this dynamic that Martin Luther King observed in his time and opposed by representing its opposite. He understood that "the old law of an eye for an eye leaves everybody blind" and dedicated his life to helping us understand that tolerance, understanding, compassion, and forgiveness were more powerful than their negations. By living his life as a shining example—not only preaching these ideals but practicing them—he inspired millions, and so the American people survived a period where racial issues threatened to tear apart the social fabric.

Gandhi, in his way, did the same. With his capacity to meet the violence and contempt of British colonial rule with peaceful protest and understanding, he inspired enough that India won its independence. And although these two were unique and the logic of fear continues to hold a solid grip on our judgment there is no doubt that we all, in our hearts, want to represent the same ideals as Gandhi and King.

We know each and every one—intuitively if not intellectually—that all values, ideals and principles worth striving for follow from (and lead back to) the Wholeness. And as our innermost nature arises from the Totality, and all we really want is to be complete, it is axiomatic that everything we do which strengthen the illusion of separation must be the result of inept reasoning. *In other words, everything we do that follows from the logic of fear, represents the ignorant ways of an ego that has succumbed to the illusion of separation; which has run amuck in terror and loneliness, and in an attempt to defend itself acts out of desperation because it does not know any better.* But still, even if the outcome is never pretty, we must try to see its helpless behavior in a larger context.

We have already discussed how the ego's emergence was a necessary part of the Universe's/our awakening process and that it in no way was a mishap of nature. The ego *had to be born* if the energy in the Universe /us was to become all-conscious, and so, seen in a larger context, it makes more sense to see the grievance which ensued from its arise as a blessing rather than a curse.

The reason is that without all the painful experiences that followed in the wake of our odyssey from unconsciousness to consciousness and on towards cosmic consciousness, we would never have found our way back of the Whole/ourselves again. It is the sum of all the pain we have endured that teaches us about the suffering of others. This cultivates empathy, and so the suffering and grief we have experienced on our journey has had an important function: Its purpose has been to provide feedback on errors, so that we can correct our ways. Hence, we can see the pain as the Universe's foremost tool of awareness-raising; as God telling us *don't do it!* for without it we would never have learned from our mistakes. As the British author C.S. Lewis wisely said:

> "God whispers to us in our pleasures, speaks to us in our conscience, but shouts in our pains: It's His megaphone to rouse a deaf world."(65.83)

All the emotional pain we have inflicted on ourselves, as well all the hurt we have imposed on each other, has therefore been God's way of telling us that we think or act in violation of our true nature—which is unconditional, all-embracing love—and that we need to change our ways if we want to experience things *as they really are*.

As seen from the cosmic consciousness' perspective, this is the simplest of truths. It is only the ego that struggles with these concepts, but even if we have not yet wised up to the point where we put what follows from the logic of fear behind, we draw closer every day. Our mistakes and their consequences ensure this result, and seen in this context, we can rejoice that the worst is behind. In fact, our journey through dualities will soon be a closed chapter, and we shall now see how this is reflected in the trends within science and religion.

6

FROM AN EXTERIOR-ORIENTED TO AN INTERIOR-ORIENTED RELIGION

"The interior Church was formed immediately after the fall of man, and received from God at first-hand the revelation of the means by which fallen humanity could be again raised to its rights and delivered from its misery. It received the primitive charge of all revelation and mystery; it received the key of true science, both divine and natural.

But when men multiplied, the frailty of man and his weakness necessitated an exterior society which veiled the interior one, and concealed the spirit and the truth in the letter. Because many people were not capable of comprehending great interior truth . . . therefore, interior truths were wrapped in exterior and perceptible ceremonies so that men, by the perception of the outer, which is the symbol of the interior, might by degrees be enabled . . . to approach the interior spiritual truths." (101.228)

—Karl von Eckartshausen, 1795—

WE HAVE SEEN how the ego's emergence made us see ourselves in opposition to everything else and that the notion of a physical world out there (as opposed to the world of idea within) thus was born. Because of this detachment from the Ground of Being, science and religion have been externally oriented for a long time. But no matter how persuasive this distinction between the outer and the inner appears—and no matter how influenced by it the scientific, religious, and philosophical debate has been—this division is an illusion.

As stated many times, these two variables constitute a coherent whole; this coherent whole flows from the inner-world, and so the outer world must at any time be seen as a reflection of humanity's inner self. It follows that the more orderly and harmonious our relationship to our inner world, the more pleasant and peaceful the external world will become. This is not a new insight. As stated, it has been the message of the prophets since the beginning of time, and Jesus himself articulated this fundamental truth when he said:

> "The kingdom is inside of you, and it is outside of you. When you become acquainted with yourselves, then you will be recognized, and you will understand that it is you who are children of the living father. But if you do not become acquainted with yourselves, then you are in poverty, and it is you who are the poverty."(78.178)

Looking back, there have always been people who have attempted to convey this to the rest of the population. The reason why most people have remained in the dark, therefore, is not for these enlightened one's lack of trying, but because the collective consciousness has had such a quality of vibration that the idea itself remained incomprehensible to the common man. For an idea to take proper hold, there must be a resonance between the consciousness of humanity and the idea's quality of vibration, and this is not yet the case. Victor Hugo was quite correct when he said that "nothing is more powerful than an idea whose time has come," but most people have had a vibration which has left the Wholeness-concept without due influence. With the passing of time, however, we have grown in understanding. And we are now nearing that point where the collective consciousness has matured sufficiently for the idea to spread like wildfire.

Thus, we have a mass-awakening coming which is unparalleled in world history. And when people have awakened to the point that they begin to practice the ideals, values, and principles of Wholeness, we shall create a paradise on earth.

As we saw from the quote above, this was what Jesus tried to tell us. History, however, reveals how difficult it was to understand this simple message. By the time of Jesus', humanity had been in the grip of duality for thousands of years, and so his message of "uniting the interior with the exterior" was not easy for people to understand. Even his disciples struggled—and the leaders of the organization that would be erected in his honor were even more lost. That is probably one reason why they failed to include in the New Testament those writings where Jesus preached the inner-oriented message with the clearest voice, for it must be said that no matter how avid reader of the Bible, you will never there find the above-mentioned quote.

The reason is that it is taken from the Gospel of Thomas, one of the Gnostic texts that the Church has tried to remove. These texts, however, are the most interesting material if we want to find out what Jesus' message was, for while the traditional Bible for almost 2000 years has been changed and distorted in keeping with the Church's ambitions it has never been able to do the same with these transcripts. When we read them, therefore, we find a prophet who appeared far more human than the Church would have it—and his message is also far more in keeping with the essence of the "new" theory of existence. For instance, when the disciples asked Jesus when his kingdom would come, this was his answer:

> "When you make the two one [when we see beyond the illusion of separation] and when you make the inside like the outside and the outside like the inside [when we fully come to grips with the fact that our thoughts create our reality], and the above like the below [when the bridge between the inner self and the ego is unblocked and we bring the inner self to the surface] and when you make the male and the female one and the same, so that the male not be male nor the female female [when we merge the masculine and feminine aspects of ourselves perfectly, finding a balance between doing and being, etc.] . . . then you will enter [the Kingdom]."(113.210)

Jesus here sums up what this book uses a couple hundred pages to explain. And even if these insights were removed only to become the learning of a few, they are now coming back. This is having an impact on religion, for the idea of God as an external and remote being, an old man in the sky, never mirrored reality—just our limited understanding. Today, as time has passed, we have matured in our thinking, and so the outer-oriented religion is being replaced by the inner-oriented[14].

In other words, as we smarten up, it is becoming increasingly obvious that the inner world is all there is and that any meaningful relationship with God must be personal, going through ourselves. Helge Hognestad, a Norwegian priest, describes the development:

> "We have reason to believe that humanity is taking part in a journey towards itself, or its Self. We are part of a bigger process where our consciousness slowly has been—and is—evolving. Thus, we come in contact with new areas of our consciousness, and this means that the foundation which upon Christianity builds is deepening.
> ... Cognitively, therefore, we are in a very different place than in the 1500s and 1800s. We are also moving beyond the awareness and understanding which formed our reality in the 1900s. Hence, in religion the focus is moving away from man's sinfulness towards his potentials, from separation from God to communication with God, from God out there to God in here."(55.35,81)

As we see, Hognestad can be counted among the more progressive priests and it should no longer come as a surprise that he has met with resistance from superiors. We have just seen how the logic of fear, through millennia, has been a major player in the formation of the social fabric. Like any other organizational structure, therefore, the Church has been a playground where the most power-hungry and self-absorbed percentage of the population has fought for a place on top. And as the most eager players in this rat-race have been those who were *the least* in

---

¹⁴ For more on inner-oriented Christianity, see Richard Smoley, *Inner Christianity: A Guide to the Esoteric Tradition*. Its essence is also presented in Helen Schucman, *A Course in Miracles*.

touch with the aspirations of Wholeness, the interior-oriented message has been incomprehensible to them. Hence, the majority of bishops and cardinals have felt threatened by esoteric wisdom. And because it undermines the foundation on which the Church has built its power and authority—and because power is so important to those with an unresolved affiliation—these "men of god", to the best of their ability, have fought against the emergence of the inner-oriented religion.

Hognestad, therefore, had to leave the Church in 1984. But even though its leaders prefer the status quo, they cannot much longer resist the changing tides—not if they want their institution to survive. After all, there is nothing that can stop an idea whose time has come, and so, whatever their preferences, they cannot prevent the new paradigm.

This is slowly dawning. And as nothing is more important to the men of power than to preserve whatever influence the institution may have, they do their best to keep up with the times. Consequently, the Church has had to review policies more often than it would have liked. One result of this is the acceptance of gay and women priests, and another is that Hognestad was reinstated in 2000. Yet another sign of the changing tides is former Bishop John Shelby Spong, who has criticized the Church's reactionary attitude. He calls the dogmas that it clings to "nonsense" and "legends", and says that if the Church is to survive, it must undergo a transformation that is "so fundamental that the reformation of the 1500s will pale in comparison."(55.85)

Shelby is not exaggerating, as going from an outer-oriented religion to an inner-oriented, represents a quantum leap in understanding. What happens is that we, at last, have matured to bring our own psyche into the calculation; we finally realize that theology, as psychologist Ludwig Feuerbach pointed out, is a form of anthropology, and that the study of God is a study of ourselves. The new religion, therefore, (if we can call it that) is a fusion of psychology and theology—and from this conflation a discipline "arises" which is as timeless as our oldest wisdom traditions.

We shall elaborate on this shortly. But speaking of organized religion, we find many examples of what it entails when the formerly passive and obedient churchgoer puts her blind faith in dogma aside and goes within, seeking an experience-based spirituality. What happens then is that the more people figure themselves out (i.e., the further they evolve in their self-actualization process) the closer and more personal their relationship with God becomes. And as this relationship evolves, they not only begin to see beyond their consciousness' limited understanding, but they also experience firsthand that the core of all religion is the same.

This applies not only to Judaism, Christianity, and Islam, but all other religions. The only exception is the "religion" that worships separation, namely that of Moloch—or Satanism. The word "religion", however, comes from the Latin *religare* which means to reconnect and bind together with wholeness, and so such an expression of worship cannot be called religion. Satanism is instead the "science" of the Supreme Delusion—it is the cultivation of the illusion of separation taken to its logical conclusion, nothing more and nothing less.

Despite the atrocities that follow in its wake, however, this force also has its place within the framework of a greater context, for it is this "religion"—this aspect of the Universe's/our psyche—which enables our play with duality and provides the Wholeness its virtue. Nonetheless, building as it does on a delusion, it only leads astray, and all other religions are derived from the Wholeness-concept. They therefore symbolize our quest to reemerge from duality, and when we look at the traits between them, we find that they have a common message: They encourage us to hold a non-material focus, to show solidarity with all life, and to live a moral life based on the principles of non-violence, tolerance, self-knowledge, forgiveness, and whatever else follows from Wholeness. In other words: *through know-ledge of self* they offer a path to Oneness, and whether we are talking about a good Muslim, a good Christian, a good Buddhist, a good Indian, or a good humanist, their behavior and way of life is essentially the same and always has been.

Nowadays, more and more people are beginning to understand this and as a result bridges are being built between religions. People like the Dalai Lama have devoted their life to this cause and there are organizations established whose purpose it is to promote dialogue and understanding between different religions[15]. Predictably, there are still

---

[15] Some examples are the Parliament of the World's Religions and the Integral Spiritual Center. For more, see: www.Integraluniversity.org and www.integral spiritualcenter.org.

individuals who abhor such activity as they feel threatened by the faith of others, but the trend is clear: The moderate and unifying forces are gaining ground, and this is also reflected in organizations that have been known to represent reactionary views. The Vatican, for instance, recognized the Eastern religions for their inherent truths and the moral values they contained in 1966, and it has also created an office for dialogue with other religions.

This would have been unthinkable 100 years ago, and as the inner-oriented message becomes more and more widespread the boundaries between the different religions are being chipped away. The inner-oriented religion, however, is not a new phenomenon and we shall now become familiar with its timeless representatives.

7
THE MYSTICS

"The fully formed mystic . . . is the new cultural hero who guides humankind to its maturity. Mystics are heralds of the Interspiritual Age, in which all of humankind's wisdom will be gathered up and shared as in a common tradition."
(109.232)

—Wayne Teasdale—

WE HAVE SEEN how the inner-oriented religion can be traced back long before the emergence of organized religion and although the outer-oriented religion eventually won out a certain percentage of adherents, whether we are talking about Christians, Jews, Muslims, or others, have retained the inner-oriented focus.

These are those who can be called mystics. When it comes to this term it is connected with dissimilar associations. Those who do not know too much about it tend to imagine something dark, secret, and obscure; some creepy club of hooded zealots, perhaps, dealing with cloak and dagger rituals and strange forms of worship. This is, however, entirely wrong. In fact, mystics are nothing more than that percentage of the population who make a determined effort to integrate the larger perspective, that which follows from experiential spirituality. In other words, they aspire to experience their relationship with God to the fullest degree—and they all know enough about the nature of existence to look *inside*, and not outside.

Evelyn Underhill described mysticism as "an expression of the innate tendency of the human spirit towards complete harmony with the transcendental order" and those who have paid attention will know what it means. The transcendental order, of course, is the greater reality. In the deepest sense it is GodForce in its non-fragmented form, and so mystics—through means of self-examination, prayer, contemplation, meditation, or certain drugs—seek to expand consciousness beyond the ego's limited confines to experience those states of awareness that bring them closer to unity with the Absolute.

We have discussed how Hindu mystics see all fragmented existence as the Universe's play with itself. They claim that the Absolute split into fragments so that it could experience an infinity of possibilities instead of one and so that we could experience being less than we are—an illusion that gives way as we, through the self-actualization process, find our way back to the Totality. This was what we summarized as the Universe's exhalation and inhalation process. And to show how this understanding overlaps with the essence of Islam, I shall let the Islamic mystic Seyyed Hossein Nasr elaborate:

> "It can be claimed that according to the Islamic perspective God himself *is* the ultimate environment which surrounds and encompasses man. . . . In reality, man is immersed in the Divine *Muhit* [God's Omnipresence] and is only unaware of it because of his own forgetfulness and negligence, which is the underlying sin of the soul, only to be overcome by remembrance. To remember God is to see him everywhere and to experience His reality as *al-Muhit* [Omnipresent]."(103.120)

That God is everything and that only our limited understanding makes it possible live in ignorance of the larger reality, are just two of the things upon which mystics agree. And because they know that they, by going within, can experience what it means to take part in all that is (to know God directly), they have developed methods aimed at helping transcend ego-consciousness. No matter what religion a mystic belongs to these techniques are congruent and the Jewish mystic Rabbi Eleazar describes one here:

> "Think of yourself as nothing and totally forget yourself as you pray. Only remember that you are praying for the

Divine Presence. You may then enter the universe of thought, a state of consciousness which is beyond time. Everything in this realm is the same—life and death, land and sea . . . but in order to enter this realm you must relinquish your ego and forget all your troubles."(75.104)

This is one way to go about it. And the idea is to get so focused on something (or nothing) that one is "flipped" out of the ordinary range of consciousness[16]. In Hinduism and Buddhism, the traditionally most inner-oriented religions, several schools have evolved whose focus has been to perfect these and other meditative techniques. We should not deride those who look to such authority, as the effort that has gone into developing these techniques is impressive. Nevertheless, the idea is fairly simple, and it is not necessary to spend many years in a monastery or with a spiritual guide to accomplish impressive feats. An example is found in Lord Alfred Tennyson, a British poet from the 1800s. He had plenty dealings with the expanded states and described them thus:

"A kind of waking trance I have frequently had, quite up from boyhood, when I have been all alone. This has often come upon me through *repeating my own name* to myself silently till, all at once, as it were, out of the intensity of the consciousness of individuality, the individuality itself seemed to dissolve and fade away into boundless being; and this [was] not a confused state, but the clearest of the clearest, the surest of the surest, the weirdest of the weirdest, utterly beyond words, where death was an almost laughable impossibility, the loss of personality (if so it were) seeming no extinction, but the only true life."(17.242)

---

[16] This book does not have much to say about meditation or the many helpful meditative techniques. If the reader is interested in the subject, see DAN GOLEMAN, THE MEDITATIVE MIND: THE VARIETIES OF MEDITATION EXPERIENCE, and OSHO, MEDITATION: THE FIRST AND LAST FREEDOM.

These experiences are those to which mystics aspire. However, some find their way out of the ego's domain more easily than others and Tennyson obviously had a knack for it. In fact, there are many people who can attest that, despite many years of concentration and practicing meditation, they have never come close to experiencing such states of consciousness.

This can be a source of frustration. If this is the case, psychoactive substances may be of assistance, for even though they are no guarantee of acquaintance with the Absolute, those who are sufficiently prepared will be richly rewarded. We shall in part four explore the research that has been done on this subject. But it is important to note that although these substances may be helpful, they alone will not take us to a state of permanent enlightenment. The Indian gurus are clear about this. Even so, some still consider them useful being that they can bring insight into the state of an enlightened mind. Neem Karoli Baba, for instance, had this to say:

> "You know, it would be much better to become the saint, rather than to experience his Grace; but having his grace is nice . . . [since] it strengthens your faith in the possibility that such [possibilities] exist."(43.169)

The Indian guru Swami Muktananda told Stanislav Grof the same and he also said that these substances, for the abovementioned reasons, had been used by spiritual traditions in India for millennia. It is also known that many Buddhists find them helpful. According to Jack Kornfeld, most American Buddhist teachers have tried them, but as I have said, they will not provide us with any constant state of enlightenment. Mystic and professor of theology Wayne Teasdale described the situation thus:

> "They can act as a catalyst to profound inner change and facilitate mystical insight, but I do not think they are a substitute for the hard work of transformation through regular spiritual practice, the development of the virtues, and compassionate, loving service to others."(109.229)

Teasdale touches upon an important point, for although all mystics seek to experience oneness with the Absolute (Mystic Union), this is not all they think of. In fact, most have not even had direct experience with the expanded states of consciousness and they are no less mystics for that reason. When all is said and done, then, mysticism is *more* than the direct experience of the Absolute; it also implies an attitude to life which recognizes that the road is as important as destination. Underhill explains:

> "To be a mystic is simply to participate here and now in that real and eternal life; in the fullest, deepest sense which is possible to man. It is to share, as a free and conscious agent . . . in the joyous travail of the universe: Its mighty onward sweep through pain and glory towards its home in God."(111.447)

Hence, if we are to describe the mystics, what separates them from the rest of the population is that they have a conscious relationship to the Mystery; they see life in its eternal context, they have a sense of what it means to take part in this divine play, and they try to live life most fully through their conscious participation. While every one of us is on the road which takes us back to the Source, the mystics are those who have reached the milestone where they have established a certain awareness of the greater reality of which they are part. They have, in other words, fully embarked on the self-actualization process—which is also called the mystical path—and for every step they take, they learn more and more what it means that God, themselves, and the world are One. Shankara, a Hindu mystic from 700 AD, described this insight thus:

> "I am reality without beginning, without equal. I have no part in the illusion of "I" and "you" and "this" and "that". I am Brahman, one without a second, bliss without end, the eternal, unchanging truth. . . . I dwell within all beings as the soul, the pure consciousness, the ground of all phenomena, internal and external. I am both the enjoyer and that which is enjoyed. In the days of my ignorance, I used

to think of these as being separate from myself. Now I know
that I am All."(42.53)

This is the recognition that slowly dawns on all. But unlike most, the mystics have awoken to the miracle that is life, and the more they take it to heart the more they come to grips with the Oneness-concept. When it comes to this, we are not talking intellectual understanding; this understanding encompasses far more, being that a mental restructuring process takes place in which the mind accesses a level of cognition previously out of reach. We shall have more to say about this, but the mystics' path not only brings us out of duality; it also adds *a whole new dimension* to the Here and Now, as it expands and we begin to sense the presence of the eternity of which we are part. In other words, the more we evolve, the deeper into significance, beauty, and sanctity we go, for as we begin to perceive the world from the perspective of the Absolute, we access an emotional and intellectual repertoire previously beyond our reach.

As anyone who has embarked on this quest knows, the first steps are the hardest since they involve a fundamental change in thought pattern. To begin with, we must stop believing in coincidences and instead see everything as a gift sent by God to help us realize inherent potential. This is so contrary to the surface-consciousness' way of thinking that it prevents most from taking this road. After all, most of us have experiences that the ego refuses to appreciate, some scarring us for life, and it is a hard sell to suggest to someone who have been mugged, robbed, and raped that they should see the episode in this light.

This may be an extreme example, but to many it is sadly relevant. My point is that life presents us with many occasions where we take the victim role and very few manage to avoid it consistently. Nevertheless, it becomes easier as we grow, for whenever we accept this role it never helps us overcome our difficulties. Instead, it leads to a helpless state of powerlessness, self-pity, and unravelling; this state only increases our sense of separateness, despair, and loneliness, and not before we decide to take responsibility for the situation can we begin the healing process.

Hence, the further we progress, the more obvious the futility of the victim role presents itself. And the more we mature, the easier we can see how we, in time, grow with every experience—no matter how undesirable it once was. In this way, confidence in the life-process increases, for we begin to understand that our darkest moments come to us so that we can experience, conquer, and heal our greatest fears; and that we, by overcoming them, not just evolve into more than what we were; but that the more we grow, the more also we increase our capacity to grasp the greatest concept of all—unconditional love.

This is the dynamic at the heart the self-actualization process. We shall study it in-depth but speaking of mystics, they have understood that the key to realizing their own (as well as the Universe's) freedom is taking responsibility *for everything* they encounter. No matter what challenges life throws at them, therefore, they strive to represent that which follows from an intimate understanding of the Wholeness—and in doing so, they heal the influence that the logic of fear has had over them and the world at large.

As seen from an immature perspective, this will present itself as ridiculously naive. But the mystics know better than anyone what they are doing as they live their lives with a larger perspective in mind—one that ordinary people do not have the wisdom to consider. For while others live in darkness, bewildered and blind to the Universe's Divine order, they have an enlightened relationship to their environment: They follow a map that not only provides the most of every encounter but, day by day, carries them out of the world of duality, ever closer to the ultimate prize—their Absolute Union with God. Evelyn Underhill describes the process, merging point, and the mystics' role as guides for the rest of us:

> "The mystic act of union, that joyous loss of the transfigured self in God, which is the crown of man's conscious ascent towards the Absolute, is the contribution of the individual to the destiny of the Cosmos. The mystic knows that destiny. It is laid bare to his lucid vision, as our puzzling world of form and color is to normal sight. He is the "hidden child" of the eternal order, an initiate of the secret plan.
>
> Hence, whilst "all creation groaneth and travaileth," slowly moving under the spur of blind desire towards that

consummation in which alone it can have rest, he runs eagerly along the pathway to reality. He is the pioneer of Life on its age-long voyage to the One: and shows us, in his attainment, the meaning and value of that life." (111.447)

8
MYSTICISM AND SCIENCE

"The most beautiful and profound emotion we can experience is the sensation of the mystical. It is the power of all true science."(67.153)

—*Albert Einstein*—

WE HAVE SEEN how the mystics' practice, techniques and worldview overlap, no matter what religion they belong to. The reason is that their discipline makes it possible to transcend the ego's limited perspective and that only then the true nature of reality is revealed.[17] Even so, many people are skeptical of the experiential picture gathered by mystics. They underestimate their discipline as well as their craftsmanship and would object to granting mysticism status as a professional discipline.

They believe that whatever mystics are doing, it is not verifiable. Thus, while they think that it is possible to study biology, physics, and mathematics objectively, they insist that it is impossible to do the same with mysticism. This, however, is wrong. And looking closer we find that this belief is a result of the dualistic worldview we take for granted, not to mention an ego-consciousness refined to the point where it no longer trusts its inner experience.

We shall explore this aspect of the equation in the next chapter. But as science has cultivated the idea of the world as an independent and objective thing-in-itself, our scientists do what they can to rule out inner

---

[17] For more about mystics, see: WAYNE TEASDALE, THE MYSTIC HEART; HUSTON SMITH, FORGOTTEN TRUTH; EVELYN UNDERHILL, MYSTICISM; MAX HEINDEL, THE ROSICRUCIAN COSMO CONCEPTION. Ken Wilber is also great reading (for instance EYE TO EYE, INTEGRAL SPIRITUALITY, UP FROM EDEN, THE EYE OF SPIRIT).

life from their calculations. Seen from such a perspective, it is no wonder that the mystic path presents itself as a meaningless pursuit. Even so, if we accept that the distinction between the outer and the inner is an illusion, it becomes obvious that it is not the mystics quest but the scientific ideal of absolute objectivity that is meaningless. In fact, as consciousness is the nature of everything, we can say that those who go about exploring it—namely the mystics—are the true scientists, and that their experiments (whether in the form of meditative exercises or psychoactive substances) will divulge more about the nature of our Universe than any externally oriented scientific experiment.

Indeed, we just saw Einstein recognize the mystical experience as the source of all true science, and he is not alone. The American philosopher Ken Wilber wrote a book (*Quantum Questions*) on how some of physics' greatest men (Einstein, Heisenberg, Schrödinger, de Broglie, Planck, Bohr, Pauli, Eddington, and Jeans) all were mystics at heart. The French philosopher and Nobel Prize winner Henri Bergson was also influenced by mystics, referring to them as "the vanguard of evolution", and the French paleontologist Pierre Teilhard de Chardin called mysticism "the great science and the great art, the only power capable of synthesizing the riches accumulated by other forms of human activity."(30.47)

When it comes to the great scientists, therefore, science and religion have never been at odds, and mysticism is the discipline that melts them together into what Huxley referred to as the "eternal philosophy". This epithet says a lot about the credibility mysticism holds. And more than anything one can wonder why some are willing to grant philosophy the status of a professional discipline, while excluding mysticism.

As a matter of fact, looking back we find that philosophers have differed on most issues. Despite that, they have become more recognized than the mystics, who among themselves agree on the basics. This may at first seem paradoxical. But in a society where the ego is hailed as king of the hill, it follows that a philosophy fostered by its cognitive faculties will appear more digestible than a philosophy derived from a higher perspective. In other words: in a world of the blind, the half-blind will be king, while the clairvoyant—he/she who sees through the illusion—becomes outcast. Consequently, that philosophers quarrel because they have not seen the world as it really is, whereas mystics agree because they have peeked behind the curtain, passes by unnoticed. This may be expected, but Ken Wilber, a modern philosopher who has studied the mystics, looks at it differently. As he says:

> "So overwhelmingly widespread is the perennial philo-sophy . . . that it is either the single greatest intellectual error ever to appear in human kind's history—an error so colossally widespread as to literally stagger the mind—or it is the single most accurate reflection of reality yet to appear."(119.39)

The assumption that mysticism is a pointless, self-absorbed activity, therefore, should be revised. And instead, we should accept the possibility that the mystics, through their work, have learned how to use their brain/mind in a way that provides access to a worldview that is real but that the rest fail to see.

The reason why people are blind to mystic insight is not that they are stupid. On the contrary, those with the most advanced intellects tend to be the first to rebuff them, simply because their brains are organized in a way that makes the mystical worldview inaccessible. In the next part of the book we shall see that our brain is plastic, constantly being formed and reformed by our thinking. My point here is that the brain is a muscle and that to the degree we spend our time thinking along the lines encouraged by modern science, we will exercise some aspects of the brain/mind at the expense of others. This is a complex process. But to simplify, in looking away from our inner world and putting all emphasis on the outer, we only train the logically oriented, analytical left side of the brain—and in doing so, we miss a lot that would have been obvious to a more balanced mind.

Remember that our thoughts create reality: The inner and the outer reflect each other, and so these people, in their endeavor to see the world through the most impersonal and value-neutral mindset, also end up concluding that they live in an impersonal and value-neutral Universe. Their conclusions, however, only mirror their own beliefs, and for those who take their inner world seriously, the Universe will look completely different. The psychologist Abraham Maslow observes:

"Fact and value have almost always (by intellectuals) been considered to be autonyms and mutually exclusive. But perhaps the opposite is true, for when we examine the most ego-detached, objective, motivationless, passive cognition, we find that it claims to perceive values directly, that values cannot be shorn away from reality and that the most profound perception of "facts" causes the "is" and the "ought" to fuse. In these moments reality is tinged with wonder, awe, admiration and approval i.e., with value."(69.84)

How, then, can the world appear so dramatically different and how can it be that some extremely intelligent people fail to see what is so obvious? The Christian mystics provide an explanation. They describe our view of the world as the result of a process that involves three types of "filters": (1) the eye of flesh, (2) the eye of reason, and (3) the eye of contemplation. All these eyes/filters ideally operate together and supplement each other. By themselves, however, they represent three distinct ways to observe the world, and the first eye is the one prioritized/exercised by empiricists.

Now, "empirical" really means *experiential*, but because these people do not trust their own inner experience (to them it has no validity) they disregard whatever they could learn and focus on the external. They therefore put all emphasis on the five senses; according to them they are the only source of knowledge, and as Wilber describes this approach: "To the extent the mind's eye refuses to rise above the eye of flesh, it produces in philosophy nothing but positivism and in psychology nothing but behaviorism."(120.33)

Positivism is an extreme form of value-neutral science/philosophy. It disregards everything that concerns inner life, while behaviorism is a psychological tradition which reduces man to an organism operating on autopilot out of instinct-based behavior. None of them, in other words, recognizes our inner life in their calculations.

For the more mentally oriented, this way of looking at things falls short and most scientists will agree that the positivists' and the behaviorists' view of the world is too narrow and limited. The people who come with this criticism are those who have integrated the second eye/filter in their outlook. This filter, the eye of reason, is the one prioritized/exercised by rationalists. This group form their conclusions about the world on account of their thinking: they emphasize logical reasoning, conceptual knowledge, and they thrive in the world of ideas. Hence, while the first eye concerns itself solely with the *physical* landscape (what we can measure and weigh), the eye of reason concerns itself with the *mental* landscape.

They are both, in their way, necessary in helping us understand the world and applied properly they result in an acute intellect, capable of great feats. None of them, however, will provide any insight into the *spiritual* landscape. And if we want to access this perspective; if we want to see the greater reality for ourselves, we must make use of the last eye— the eye of contemplation. This is what the mystics do and, seen from this perspective, the Divine order is as obvious as a mathematical formula to the eye of reason, and that the sky is blue to the physical eye. In other words, the eye of contemplation *surpasses and transcends* the eye of reason in the same way that the eye of reason transcends the physical eye. Ken Wilber describes their relationship:

> "The eye of contemplation is to the eye of reason as the eye
> of reason is to the eye of flesh. Just as reason transcends
> flesh, so contemplation transcends reason. Just as reason
> cannot be reduced to, nor derived solely from fleshy
> knowledge, so contemplation cannot be reduced to nor
> derived from reason. Where the eye of reason is
> transempirical, the eye of contemplation is transrational,
> translogical, and transmental."(120.6)

Thus, the higher "up" the ladder we go (i.e.., the more we integrate the third eye in our perspective) the more we can enjoy a worldview in which all variables—physical, mental, and spiritual—are mirrored in the present. Moreover, it follows from this that an optimally functioning human not only will have integrated all three filters, but that he/she also will have balanced them perfectly. This is important, for no matter how brilliant we are, a sharpened intellect will never find its way to spiritual insight—and that is why so many intelligent people see the world as a pointless state of affairs.

We see from this stratification that the further "down" the ladder we are situated, the more compelling the illusion of separation becomes. For an empiricist/positivist, therefore, it will appear obvious that the world out there is an independent and objective size, totally separated from his inner world. For a philosopher, however, one that is oriented towards the world of ideas, the boundaries between the outer and the inner will be more difficult to see—and, indeed, the philosophers offer all manner of possible interpretations. To the mystic, on the other hand, the division will appear as it really is—illusory. It will be obvious that the two, object and subject, are one, and that everything we see is God-Force mirroring, sensing, and playing with itself through the interactions of its individuated portions.

The difference, however, must be directly experienced in order to be understood, for when it comes to the relationship between matter and spirit, words can never bridge the gap that seems so real when the world is seen through the first two filters. We have already seen how the expanded states of consciousness are important tools when it comes to opening the third eye, the one which grants access to the spiritual reality. And we have also seen how the mystics, through long periods of trial and error, have identified those methods that effectively let us experience this reality. Nevertheless, the more we are trapped by the illusion of separation, the sillier and more incomprehensible insights, working methods, and experiments will appear. As such, empiricists will predictably claim that we can only say something sensible about the world as it is seen through the five senses. And since they do not even trust their own inner world, it is only natural that they do not trust that of others. Yet, they should be aware that the mystics build their worldview on the exact same scientific method that empiricists themselves do—it is just that their explorations begin with the inner landscape rather than the external. Other than that, it is all the same.

To explain more fully, let us consider the scientific method. To begin with it involves the gathering of data (observed/experienced events) and trying to work out whichever theory/hypothesis that is most fit to explain them. The data represents the terrain while the theory represents the map—and the more data we have and the better the map corresponds, the better our theory. Now, one can never prove a theory, it can only be corroborated or rebutted. But the more data a theory can explain (i.e., the more terrain the map covers) the stronger its foundation becomes. This is the basis of the scientific method and furthermore the theory must be verifiable. This means that any other skilled practitioner must have the opportunity to examine if map and terrain fit—and the more professionals who concur the better.

The last part of the equation, that the experiment and theory must be verifiable, is a fundamental criterion of science and that is why so many scientists refuse to consider mysticism a professional discipline. They believe that mystical understanding is impossible to verify objectively/scientifically, but this assumption is wrong. Like all other disciplines, the mystics' insights and methods are 100 percent testable, it is just that their theories and experiments are based on *spiritual* data rather than physical[18]. Other than that, everything else is the same. Their meditation practices, for example, have developed over thousands of years as a result of trial-and-error. It takes tremendous discipline to master these techniques but, once proficient, we can amass data that others again can verify. All that is needed is to learn the method and from there we can perform our own experiments and compare them with others.

It is this way, through a long line of professionals' meticulous discipline and devotion to their field, that the inner landscape has been mapped out. And because the map (worldview) of the mystics conforms better to the terrain (both outer and inner) than anything western science has been able to produce, it is also, according to the criteria of science, the best explanation model to date.

Whereas this is as simple as putting two and two together, coming to terms with its implications is exceedingly difficult for those with a brain

---

[18] Remember the aforementioned model in which we saw that three kinds of data exist: physical, mental, and spiritual. The physical data being those accessible to the five senses; the mental being those accessible to the world of ideas (e.g., a mathematical equation); and the spiritual data being those accessible to the enlightened mind.

so programmed that the idea of an inner landscape and spiritual data becomes nonsensical. As we have seen, the evolvement and fine-tuning of the three filters reflects a maturation in the individual and so, as seen from an empiricist's perspective (the bottom rung of the ladder), knowledge accessible at levels above will appear incomprehensible. Therefore, no more than a child can imagine what it means to be an adult, can a positivist or behaviorist imagine how the world is seen from a mystic's perspective.

This, of course, does not mean that the mystic's insights are unattainable. It just means that, if people want to approach this level of understanding, they must dare to leave behind their current worldview; they must recognize that there are levels of understanding that exceeds theirs; they must consider the implications of this insight; and begin to walk the road that the mystic before them have gone.

9

FROM AN EXTERIOR-ORIENTED TO AN INTERIOR-ORIENTED SCIENCE

"The history of science is a history of marriages between ideas which were previously strangers to each other." *(36.41)*

—*Arthur Koestler*—

SO FAR, WE have seen how exterior-oriented religion came into being as a result of the ego's emergence and that now, due to the maturation process we have been going through, this exterior-oriented version is being replaced by the inner-oriented. Furthermore, we have seen how the mystics, the inner-oriented religion's representatives, not only offer understanding that unites all religion but that their perspective is compatible with scientific principles. In the next part we will elaborate more specifically on the findings of modern science and how they can be reconciled with the mystics' worldview. Now we shall take a look at how the evolution of science reflects our maturation process in the same way that religion does.

We have previously seen how the separation between science and religion originated some 500 years ago and how before they were two sides of the same equation. And since the two, in line with the inner-oriented perspective, easily can be reunited, it should come as no surprise that the new science fits together perfectly with the new religion. In fact, looking at the dynamic in a larger context, we find that the two began as one; they became more and more separated as our dualistic mindset emerged, and now, as our journey through duality is nearing its end, we see that the two are becoming more as one. So far, we have followed this trend as it relates to religion. And we shall now not only see how our scientific culture, with its ideal of absolute objectivity, must be seen in light of this journey but how this ideal itself is nonsensical.

9.1 THE IMPOSSIBLE IDEAL OF OBJECTIVITY

"Science has traditionally sought to maintain a value-free attitude. This attitude, of course, is nothing but a prejudice."(32.254)

—David Bohm, physicist—

The science of our day is built on a distinction between the outer and the inner world. It starts from the premise that the exterior is all there is and that our mind is a mirage, a secondary product of the "real" world out there. As a result, scientists do their best to ignore everything that relates to their inner world—their subjectivity. And put simply, the idea is that to the degree they succeed in looking away from this inner reality, they can study the outside world as it actually is.

Nevertheless, the idea of the external as being separate from the interior is completely wrong. It just seems this way because we have not grown wise enough to see beyond the illusion of separation, and when it comes to science we must see the ideal of absolute objectivity as a result of the ego's rise from the Ground of Being. This ideal, therefore, would have been incomprehensible to early humans who had not yet separated the inner from the outer. With the passing of time, however, the ego emerged, and by the 16th century humanity had forgotten what it meant to be part of the whole. It was at this time that the advancement of science gained momentum and it was shaped by an ego at war with the world. We see this in the man-against-nature mindset which has been at the heart of science until today. To a people more in touch with inner reality, this concept would have been absurd, but despite that science's main ambition has been to subjugate nature.

Seen in a larger context, however, this mindset mirrors the ego's narrow understanding. And it follows from the Universe's exhalation and inhalation process that as soon as the ego has saturated itself on the experiential realm made possible by duality, it will return to the Wholeness richer than ever.

Even though a few have taken great strides in terms of this process, we have not yet, as a society, reached the point where this is reflected in the official narrative. One reason is that the status quo, by its very nature, is slow-moving and reactionary. Consequently, while there are individuals within all areas of religion and science who have progressed beyond the old paradigm, our scientific traditions do not yet officially recognize the consciousness-comes-first perspective. To them it's still axiomatic that our consciousness is an epi-phenomenon of matter. Examining this assumption has been too controversial for the establishment even to imagine, and so, instead of reconsidering the dynamic between the outer and inner world, they act as if the external world is all there is.

Hence, the essence of the scientific method has been to ignore anything that the ego cannot measure and weigh. And we see the results of this approach on the reductionistic, empiristic, materialistic, and positivistic interpretation models. These people reduce all life to dead matter: They see through microscopes atoms that become molecules, molecules that become cells, and cells forming organisms—but they do not find *life* anywhere. In their study of these organisms, neither do they find anything that can be termed *qualities* of life, for to begin with there is no life and secondly concepts such as joy, thoughtfulness, morality, and love are nothing more than subjective experiences—confusion factors—that have nothing to do with the world *as it really is*. On the contrary, to them such sensations are nothing but flimsy secondary products of the mechanisms of the brain, attributable to electrochemical activity at the molecular level.

Thus, at the end of the day, everything is inert matter increasing in complexity and the Universe is seen as a machine without value or meaning. Indeed, to philosophers and professionals adhering to this tradition, it is a rule of thumb that as life has no measurable intrinsic value, one cannot conclude from the fact that it exists that it should be preserved. According to them, to do so would be a logical fallacy—and that these people tend to have a pessimistic outlook is hardly surprising.

Still, no matter how eager they are to disregard inner reality, it should be obvious that they cannot succeed. After all, the inner reality is ultimately everything, and so their attitude not only alienates them from their environment; it also alienates these scientists and philosophers from themselves, for as long as they refuse to reconsider fundamental assumptions, they will be lost to a dynamic which ensures an increasingly dysfunctional relationship to the world. They will ignore everything that could help them see beyond their own misconceptions, and this again will shape their brain so that it closes off from such input that could have helped them back on track.

The reason for this is that our feelings are the most important correction mechanism we have. As we shall see, a bad feeling always reflects an unfortunate/mistaken thought pattern (one that does not align with the Wholeness), and only by taking our feelings seriously will we be able to discover and rectify those belief systems that do not correspond with the world as it *really* is. "Rational" scientists, however, discount their feelings because they believe they are contrary and disruptive to reason—that which they worship above all else. Still, reason alone can never help them overcome the illusion of separation which will only appear more and more convincing as long as they are caught in this dynamic. And by ignoring their feelings, they disregard the only clue they have to a way out of the delusion.

Yet, none of these "rationalists" can stick to their worldview without getting tangled in contradictions they themselves cannot talk their way out of. And just like religion, science needs to start taking the human psyche into account. After all, no matter how strenuously science has tried to remove the inner life from its equations, every scientist's work continues to be engrossed by it. The ideal of 100 percent objectivity, therefore, is impossible, being that no matter how soberly and objectively scientists perform their research they will *always* interpret their findings based on their assumptions—i.e., from a *subjective* point of view.

Hence, we can never say anything about the external world without also saying something about the inner, and it is primarily the latter that is done. Our ideas about the world form the basis for all observations; these are qualitative/subjective by nature and can never, no matter how hard we try, be reduced to something quantitative/objective. As Gary Zukav stated "an opinion is a point of view. And the point of view that we can be without a point of view is itself a point of view."

Accordingly, those scientists who reduce life to dead matter and remove all qualitative measures from their calculations cannot do so without first building their argument on a qualitative assessment—thus undermining the very notion on which their premise is based. As Ken Wilber says:

> "If all human experience is ultimately reducible to patterns of electrical and chemical activity within the nervous system and the body . . . then so is that statement itself.
>
> So, in fact, are *all* statements equally biochemical fireworks. But there could then be no question of a true statement versus a false statement, because *all* thoughts are *equally* biochemistry.
>
> . . . If thoughts are indeed ultimately reducible to electrons firing in the nervous system, then there cannot be true thoughts and false thoughts for the simple reason that there are no true electrons versus false electrons. And so, if that statement is the true then it cannot be true."(120.30)

As we see, the ideal of absolute objectivity, of a value-free and non-biased attitude, is not founded on reason. It is a product of unconscious thinking and seen from the larger perspective we find that, just as religion's idea of a God *out there*, it is the result of man's alienation: Since Descartes separated spirit from matter the spirit has more and more disappeared from the scientists' calculations—and the more they have focused on the lifeless matter, the further they have strayed into the illusion of separation.

We now know, however, that this drift mirrors our consciousness' maturation process and that it again is part of a larger plan. We saw in part one that our journey through duality takes place within the framework of a larger context, organized from the "highest level", and we've now reached a point where the pressure of duality is starting to yield.

GodForce, after all, never intended that the ego would be our destruction. And as it now has been allowed to run rampant, seemingly unrestrained for millennia, it is neither possible nor appropriate to hone it further; we have taken this aspect of ourselves (and the worldview that it entails) as far as it can go, and we are now, after experiencing fully what it means to be separated from creation, ready to return to the Whole.

This does not mean that the ego is about be annihilated and that we are heading back to the Whole as nature and the animals experience this concept. Nor does it mean that duality itself is about to disappear, as it is an inherent part of the way things are in our Universe. Life and death, high and low, good and bad, and so on, will therefore (at least for a while) continue to be part of our experience and offer us the dynamic that enables all values as well as life itself in the physical. Even so, the weight of duality's influence will still diminish, for in the same way as the animals pay no heed to it, we, with our expanded awareness, will see beyond. We will, in other words, not lose the self-awareness that the ego has established. Instead, we will bring self-awareness a quantum leap forward so that we naturally see the inner and outer world as one coherent whole without losing ourselves in our surroundings.

It should be evident that this transition is not done overnight. We are talking about a change in the thought pattern which surpasses any-thing humanity has experienced, and when it comes to its implications for society we shall explore these in part six. This change, however, is already well underway. And although the status quo of science, just as organized religion, refuses to accept the new paradigm the foundation upon which both builds has crumbled.

We have already seen how inner-oriented spirituality is emerging to take the place of outer-oriented religion. The same trend is manifesting within science, for just as the 20th century brought forward ancient writings that undermined ecclesiastical authority (the Dead Sea scrolls and the Coptic translations from Nag Hammadi), it brought discoveries that shook established science beyond repair. As we shall see, these findings showed with all clarity that the idea of the outer and inner world as separated does not measure up. And even though most scientists have yet to come to terms with the evidence, it does not change the fact that only ignorance now sustains the old paradigm.

How long this ignorance will prevail is hard to say, as the defenders of the status quo tend to stand their ground long after it has given way beneath them. As Werner Heisenberg, one of the pioneers of quantum physics noted:

> "Once one has experienced the desperation with which clever and conciliatory men of science react to the demand for a change in the thought pattern, one can only be amazed that such revolutions in science have actually been possible at all."(131.211)

Consequently, one should not be surprised that so many, regardless of the evidence, will fight for the old worldview until death. This is the way it has always been, and so old paradigms never really die; they simply fade away as the people holding them die, but that does not stop the inner-oriented science from gaining ground. The "high priests" of objectivity, therefore, represent the old paradigms' last stand and they are so trapped in the grip of duality that the probability of them figuring out the inherent contradiction is slim. According to these scientists, they have soon wrested from inanimate matter its last secret, and they believe it is only a matter of time before they find the answer to the riddle of life in the DNA strand—or our Universe's mystery in the Higgs boson.

Hence, the present situation is not unlike that of the late 1800s. The classical Newtonian worldview had reached its zenith and leading professors advised their students to find something else to do as they figured only a few minor adjustments remained before the mathematical formula for everything was completed. The historical background for this state of affairs was Newton's observations of gravity, which resulted in equations that seemed to predict the movements of matter. Whether objects were large or small they followed Newton's calculations, and after James Maxwell in the 1860s succeeded in bringing light, electricity, and magnetism together in a unified mathematical framework, physics was believed to be closing in on the last formula—the one that would put everything in its proper context.

Back then, atoms were considered the smallest building blocks. As we know, these are the units of which matter is built and the scientists imagined they resembled tiny balls circling each other. In the middle of all atoms a positively charged nucleus was found and around it swirled negatively charged electrons, much like the earth around the sun. These atoms were believed to be moving around in an absolute emptiness of space, and physicists also imagined that the mathematical formulas that predicted the movements of matter represented eternal and immutable laws. The Universe, in other words, appeared as a perpetual motion machine governed by laws that had always been there, and they also assumed that time and space were two fundamentally distinct quantities. The physical realm, it was thought, was a highly predictable machinery. And it was believed that if one knew the right formula, then one would not only be able to explain everything that had ever happened, but also predict all that had not yet transpired.

Things, however, did not pan out the way the scientists expected, and the closest they came to such a supertheory was Einstein's theory of relativity. Accomplished in the early 1900s, it tells us that energy equals mass multiplied by the speed of light squared ($E = MC^2$), which again means that matter and energy are two of a kind (light) and that huge amounts of energy are trapped within the smallest amount of matter.

This theory in many ways completes classical physics, but at the same time it completely rocks the boat. Until then the scientists not only believed that matter bounced around in empty space and that this emptiness represented an absolute zero-point—that it was some sort of sheet on which everything was written; they also believed that gravity was the result of an inherent property of matter, but Einstein turned this on its head. His theory showed that the gravitational force and the electromagnetic field were not really forces *in* time and space, but that they, on the contrary, *generated* time and space. The energy fields, these strange non-physical phenomena, in other words, proved to be *more fundamental* than matter, for they affected matter while they themselves remained impervious. Einstein also proved that space and time were not separate and absolute quantities, existing independently of matter or the observer's perspective. Instead, matter, time, and space turned out to be one continuous, inseparable entity—and light was the overriding variable that tied everything together.

To put it simply, the new physics showed us that time and space coordinates, as physicist Mendel Sachs said, are "only the elements of a language that is used by an observer to describe his environment," (18.166) and that matter itself is but pure energy (light) that is pushed down a slow vibration, i.e., below the speed of light. The implications are enormous, for as a result time and space are not what they appear. To us it looks as if we move *through* space and time, but a better way of looking at it is as if time and space travel through *us*! After all, neither time nor space can be understood as independent of the observer's perspective, and although it seems to us as if yesterday is gone forever and that tomorrow does not exist, they both are equally real and present somewhere out there (or in there).

If this is hard to imagine, just think of space-time (for they are one) as an immense, stretched-out and continuous landscape through which we journey by train: Although we have left the previous station, it nevertheless exists out there, and so it is with space-time. Therefore, even if it seems to us as if time passes on and space stays the same, this is an illusion: We know that we do not wake up to the same day twice, and in the same way we never wake up to the same room. The old room is rather a thing of the past that exists "out there", woven into the space-time fabric—just like a landscape we have left behind.

Briefly summarized, this is the essence of the theory of relativity. Scientists thought until then that there was an absolute zero point, a still-point from which all movement could be measured, but there is not. Instead, everything begins with the observer and the same event is seen differently by two observers. Seen from your perspective, for instance, it seems as if you are sitting quite still reading this book but seen from a spaceman's perspective you are hurtling through space together with planet earth at a tremendous speed. The only constant in all this is the speed of light which never changes. In fact, this overriding variable is *always the same, no matter how fast you are moving and in which direction*. It may sound absurd, but whether you are traveling towards the sun at a rate of one million miles per hour or away from it at the same speed, the light from the sun—seen from your perspective—will be moving towards you at exactly the same velocity, with the speed the light always has.

Hence, Einstein pretty much shook classical physics to its core and beyond. He demonstrated that the concept of objectivity was altogether impossible, for as the astronomer and physicist James Jeans said, his theory shows us

> ". . . that electronic and magnetic forces are not real at all; they are merely mental constructs of our own, resulting from our rather misguided efforts to understand the motions of the particles. It is the same with the Newtonian force of gravitation, and with energy, momentum and other concepts which were introduced to help us understand the activities of the world—all prove to be mere mental constructs, and do not even pass the test of objectivity."(60.323)

9.2 QUANTUM PHYSICS

"The universe will never afterwards be the same. To describe what has happened, one has to cross out that old word "observer" and put in its place the new word "participator". In some strange sense, the Universe is a participatory Universe."(18.141)

—John Wheeler, physicist—

We have just seen how everything in the physical is ultimately attributable to energy fields and that they, in turn, are nothing but mental constructs. In other words, we are closing in on the fact that the *entire Universe is an idea construction*, and although Einstein himself did not follow the implications of his theory through, this has become clearer with time.

The reason for this is that while he was working on his theory of relativity a new discipline arose within physics. This was quantum physics, the study of the Universe's smallest building blocks. It began with the German physicist Max Planck's discovery in 1900 that atoms gave off energy by quanta and not continuously as they should according to classical physics. This meant that the atoms had to consist of even smaller particles and by the 1930s researchers had a certain grasp of its implications.

Among other things, the study of quantum mechanics showed that there was no such thing as matter; that the scientists (subject) and their experiments (object) in fact were one; and that one could never, at this level, predict anything, only infer statistical probabilities. Furthermore, the idea of atoms as tiny balls circling each other proved to be wrong (or at least misleading), because when they looked deeper they found only energy that the scientists, with their attention, turned into particles.

As the world presents itself as a 100 percent solid and continuous quantity and the five senses tell us that we are separate from our surroundings, this might seem absurd. Yet, there is no difference between the outer and the inner, something physicist Erwin Schrödinger confirms:

> "The same elements compose my mind and the world. This situation is the same for every mind and its world, in spite in the unfathomable abundance of "cross-references" between them. The world is given to me only once, not one existing and one perceived. Subject and object are only one. The barrier between them cannot be said to have been broken down as a result of recent experience in the physical sciences, for this barrier does not exist."(124.81)

The reason why there is no difference between the inner and the outer is quite simply that there is no matter that can separate one from the other. If, for example, we picture a tennis ball to be the size of the earth, the atoms would be no bigger than grapes; if we picture the atom to be the size of a 15-story building, its core will be no larger than a grain of salt, and when we watch more closely what we initially perceived as particles are not even real, permanent "stuff". They only appear as particles because they are the object of our attention, but when unobserved they become waves, existing everywhere and nowhere at once. Thus, the

Universe is really a multidimensional sea of energy, and physicist Amit Goswami describes our relationship as follows:

> "The universe exists as a formless potentia in myriad possible branches in the transcendent domain and becomes manifest only when observed by conscious beings." (42.141)

This obviously confuses people because we are caught up in duality. We are so used to thinking of the inner world as opposed to the outer, and matter as a solid continuous quantity, that seeing everything as a coherent whole—and matter as the result of a wave manifesting itself at a frequency—is difficult to reconcile. Many people therefore struggle to understand quantum physics because its findings are so contradictory to the five senses. But if we only stop thinking about the world as formed by matter and instead begin to see it as *a substance of our thinking*, everything will make sense. The physicist Edward E. Close speaks to it thus:

> "We must dispel the wide-spread confusion of objectivity with the current view of physical reality, and deal with new information which indicates that reality exists as a spectrum of substance, ranging from gross matter to energy, to more and more subtle forms, and finally, to the non-physical substance beyond the quantum. The only word we have in the current scientific lexicon that even approximates an appropriate description of this subtle substance is the word consciousness."(21.58)

In other words, to understand how everything is connected, we must turn the most fundamental assumption of established science upside-down. This is an insurmountable task for many. For every physicist who gets it, there are dozens who do not, but Amit Goswami, one of the physicists who do, describes his Eureka experience this way:

> "Physics explains phenomena, but consciousness is not a

phenomenon; instead, all else are phenomena *in* consciousness.

I had vainly been seeking a description of consciousness within science; instead, what I and others have to look for is a description of science within consciousness. We must develop a science compatible with consciousness, our primary experience."(42.215)

The greatest scientists in physics have understood this. They know, to say it with Schrödinger that "the mind is a *singulare tantum*. That is to say, that the overall number of minds is just one,"(124.89) and they know, to say it with Sir Arthur Eddington, that "the world is made of the same fabric as consciousness."(32.250) These two clues is really all we need to understand the nature of our Universe, because when mind itself is without limits; when the sum of all minds are one Boundless Being and consciousness has proven itself to be the nature of all things, it follows that the only limitation is our own understanding.

This is the realization that the leading quantum physicists have come to grips with. James Jeans confirms:

"Today there is a wide measure of agreement which, on the physical side of science, approaches almost to unanimity that the stream of knowledge is heading towards a nonmechanical reality; the universe begins to look more like a great thought than like a great machine. Mind no longer appears as an accidental intruder into the realm of matter; we are beginning to suspect that we ought rather to hail it as the creator and governor of the realm of matter."(124.151)

Although it should be apparent, I will emphasize that even if the Universe is made of mind-stuff it does not mean that you alone create the Universe with your mind: Your world of ideas is part of a much larger dimension of thought, and it is the Creator/Our Common Thought that generates existence. Even so, everything that exists is a fabric of minds, and seen from this perspective the findings of quantum physics become less paradoxical. For instance, the question of where a particle goes when we stop observing it (according to the experiments it becomes a wave, a probability) becomes like asking where an idea resides when our attention is directed elsewhere. It obviously exists out there/in there, but *where* is impossible to answer.

That consciousness is the nature of everything can be difficult to comprehend. But another thing that quantum physics tells us is that everything in the Universe is as connected today as it was before the Big Bang. We may recall that scientists believe the Universe to have come into being as the result of a giant explosion around 14 billion years ago, but it is important to understand that this blast did not happen *in* time and space; instead, it *created* time, space, matter—everything!

Thus, from "nothing" everything came into being. And even though our Universe presents itself as a gigantic, fragmented entity, quantum physics shows us that every particle is still very much connected to every other particle; not only they do form an inter-connected Whole, but each particle is a representation of the totality. In other words, our Universe is essentially *holographic*. A hologram is an image that looks three-dimensional and such images are easily produced with laser technology. The way it works is that the holographic film is composed of a certain number of units with every single one having the entire image imprinted. Each fragment reflecting the whole, therefore, we can divide the image into several pieces; even if we split it down to the smallest fragment every single one will still mirror the whole—and so it is with the Universe.

If we are to understand the Universe, this is important to take into account, for on the one hand it makes it possible for the Universe to reflect our emotions, thoughts, and beliefs back to us individually and en masse and on the other it makes it possible for our minds to affect everything around us.

We shall have more to say about this part of the equation later. But talking of quantum physics, we should be aware that this concept, according to John Stewart Bell's Theorem, is an implicitly proven fact[19]

---

[19] Bell's Theorem proves the non-locality of our Universe. It demonstrates that the Universe is an interconnected, inseparable whole; that whatever affects a particle on one end of the Universe will also *instantly* affect a particle on the other end of it; and that it is no longer possible to talk of *a distance* between two spatially separated

and that a number of experiments have been done which confirm that the particles of the Universe represent an interlinked and inseparable whole. As examples, we can mention experiments done by Clauser and Freedman in 1972, Alain Aspect in 1982, and Nicholas Gisin in 1997. They all show that a change in one particle will affect another immediately—no matter how far they are apart—and it follows that distance, as we perceive it, is an illusion. Instead, everything is *everywhere all the time*, the fabric (mind-stuff) of our Universe being interconnected beyond space-time in a way that makes the idea of locality and separateness nonsensical.

In part four we shall see how "paranormal" phenomena such as telepathy, clairvoyance, and so on, are real. And although many skeptics have denied the existence of such things because they believe it would imply some supernatural and unexplainable property of matter, we see from quantum physics that such things are simple to explain. All it takes is to recognize that the world is made of mind-stuff; that the sum of all minds is one; that the Universe is holographic; and that distance is an illusion—and then the so-called "paranormal" phenomena become quite "normal". Amit Goswami elaborates:

> "It is logical to conclude that psychic phenomena such as distant viewing and out-of-body experiences, are examples of the nonlocal operation of consciousness. Any attempt to dismiss a phenomenon that is not understood merely by explaining it as a hallucination becomes irrelevant when a coherent scientific theory can be applied.
>
> Quantum mechanics undergirds such a theory by providing crucial support for the case of the nonlocality of consciousness; it provides an empirical challenge to the dogma of locality as a universal limiting principle."(42.136)

---

objects. Consequently, many physicists conclude that we must live in a holographic Universe.

10
PHYSICS MEETS MYSTICISM

"We have found that where science has progressed the farthest, the mind has but regained from nature that which the mind has put into nature. We have found a strange footprint on the shores of the unknown. We have devised profound theories, one after another, to account for its origin. At last, we have succeeded in reconstructing the creature that made the footprint. And Lo! It is our own."
(124.74)

—Arthur Eddington, physicist—

IN THE LAST chapter we got to know the world of quantum physics. As we saw, its findings align perfectly with everything we have discussed, and so it seems reasonable to conclude that science itself confirms the mystics' worldview.

Now, this was a crash course into a discipline that one can spend a lifetime exploring and if the reader supposes that this summary must be an outrageous misrepresentation of the science of quantum physics, I recommend several books below[20]. All things considered, I understand if this was mind-blowing material, for the interpretation of quantum physics is a controversial field and as physicist Niels Bohr once said, "those who

---

[20] These books on physics support the consciousness-comes-first perspective: PAUL DAVIES AND JOHN GRIBBIN, *THE MATTER MYTH*; NICK HERBERT, *QUANTUM REALITY*; GARY ZUKAV, *THE DANCING WU LI MASTERS*; AMIT GOSWAMI, *THE SELF-AWARE UNIVERSE*; FRITJOF CAPRA, *THE TAO OF PHYSICS*; MICHAEL TALBOT: *MYSTICISM AND THE NEW PHYSICS*. The last three also compares it to the mystical point of view. For a great introduction into the new paradigm as seen from a physicist's perspective, I recommend EDWARD E. CLOSE, *TRANSCENDENTAL PHYSICS*.

are not shocked when they first come across Quantum theory, cannot possibly have understood it."

Indeed. For one caught in the grip of the old paradigm it requires some serious mental restructuring to become comfortable with a world-view that tells us that there is no past and future, only an eternal now; that consciousness is all that exists; that all minds are one; and that distance and separation is an illusion. Yet, that is the way it is. And the physicists have performed experiments like Wheeler's delayed-choice experiment, confirming that the past is not carved in stone[21] but changes according to our actions in the present. Such enquiry has left physicists perplexed when it comes to its implications, for if the past is not fixed what is? If we cannot infer other than statistical probabilities, is nothing certain? And if the scientist (observer) is such an indispensable part of the experiment (the observed), can we say that our observations create reality? And again, if so, how real is reality?

Our common sense tells us that the Universe would exist regardless of whether we are here to observe its becoming, but quantum physicists are not so sure. John Wheeler, for instance, wrote *Genesis and Observership*, an essay in which he takes the implications of quantum mechanics to their conclusion and speculates if the Big Bang would have taken place if it had not, at a later stage, resulted in us and our observations. No matter how preposterous the idea may appear to our commonsense Wheeler is not alone, for according to the most respected interpretation of quantum physics (the Copenhagen interpretation) this is the most consistent conclusion. Professors Barrow and Tipler elaborate:

> "According to the Copenhagen interpretation, we can regard some restricted properties of distant galaxies, which we now see as they were billions of years ago, as brought into existence now. Perhaps all properties—and hence the entire Universe is brought into existence by observation made at some point in time by conscious beings."(11.470)

---

[21] Other scientists have done experiments that confirm this. We shall see more later.

No matter how absurd the idea may seem to ordinary reason it is, as we can see, taken seriously by physicists. And from their point of view, it seems quite probable that we are not only living in a multi-dimensional holographic Universe but one in which *all probabilities* are realized. Thus, seeing the Universe as a dream that springs into being all places at once is not a bad idea, for it will give us a more truthful under-standing of our experience. After all, the physical is a considerably less solid and continuous quantity than we have suspected. And those who, through adventures in consciousness, have experienced other levels of reality inform us that—as far as they are concerned—the places they visit are just as real.

That we, as a society, have yet to understand that we live in a collectively created dream is not so strange for we know that we, while sleeping, are trapped within the reality of our dreams. And when we take into consideration that a dream is the result of our consciousness changing its frequency of vibration; that everything is consciousness; and that matter, as we see it, is only the result of mind-stuff manifesting at our frequency range, we understand that it is an exercise in futility arguing about which frequency is the most "real". To a dreamer the experience seems totally real because we, while dreaming, forget about the "normal" waking form of consciousness. When we wake up, however, we see that the waking state supersedes and encloses the dream consciousness. This is why we consider it to be more "real"—and because most have no further basis for comparison, people think of it as the absolute measure of reality. Still, those who have experienced the cosmic consciousness will tell us that it transcends and encloses the waking consciousness (just like it surpasses the dream consciousness) and that this form of consciousness is so lucid, so powerful, so profound and fundamental, that the physical world in comparison presents itself as smoke and mirrors.

The findings of quantum physics confirm this idea of a relative, multidimensional reality. To quote the physicist David Bohm, it shows us that "matter is like a small ripple in this tremendous ocean of energy" and that "this implies a reality immensely beyond what we call matter. Matter itself is merely a ripple in this background."(120.136) We have previously seen that the mystics have both experienced and understood this. We have seen how they, through their experiments, have mapped the inner and the outer landscape, merging the two, and how they believe that our world—our Universe—is one of many that are separated by virtue of vibratory frequency. We have also seen that several physicists' worldview overlaps with theirs, as they assume that consciousness is the nature of everything; that matter (as well as time and space) is an illusion; that we live in a multidimensional Universe; and that all is one. As a result of this, Bohm formulated his theory of inner and outer worlds (the implicit and explicit order). That his philosophy resonated with the mystics was no coincidence, for the parallels between their tradition and the new science are so obvious that they could hardly pass by unnoticed. Bohm's scientific quest, therefore, brought him in touch with mystics such as Jiddu Krishnamurti and like other great physicists he was influenced and inspired by the Eastern religions in general and the Upanishads in particular.

That their quest took scientists in this direction was quite natural, for the further they went down the rabbit hole of quantum physics the harder it was to avoid its metaphysical implications. That being said, while they recognized the wisdom in Einstein's words when he pointed out that "science without religion is lame and religion without science is blind", they also emphasized the importance of distinguishing between the two. In their wisdom, they never made the mistake of thinking that their scientific quest would someday present us with the answers to the riddles of life, for they knew its inherent limitations. As Schroedinger said:

> "The scientific picture of the real world around me is very deficient. It gives a lot of factual information, puts all our experience in a magnificent consistent order, but is ghastly silent about all and sundry that is really near to our heart, [the things] that really matters to us. It cannot tell us a word about red and blue, bitter and sweet, physical pain and physical delight; it knows nothing of beautiful and ugly, good or bad, God and eternity. Science sometimes pretends to answer questions in these domains, but the answers are very often so silly that we are not inclined to take them seriously."(124.83)

Nevertheless: The more they reflected on the mysteries of the Universe and the better they understood the implications of their own discipline, the clearer they saw that the two, science and religion, were interrelated aspects of a larger Whole. Thus, Max Planck, the father of quantum physics, pointed to its metaphysical implications in 1944, when he said that "all matter originates and exists only by virtue of a force. . . . We must assume behind this force the existence of a conscious and intelligent Mind. This mind is the matrix of all matter."(14.216)

This fact, that the Universe is a vast Megaintelligence, will become increasingly obvious as we move out of duality. To the mystics and physicists this has only been easier to spot because they—in their own way and through their respective fields—have caught a glimpse of a world "normal" people rarely confront. Through their explorations they have gone eye to eye with the limits of understanding and they have come back humble enough to recognize that we are part of a vibrant dance of energy so extensive and so powerful that we, as seen from our perspective, cannot possible begin to understand its magnitude. All we can do is to try and remember that the larger Whole of which we are a part is *itself a living organism* and that there is a superior intelligence present which interpenetrates everything.

We need only look at snow crystals for a reminder of the exquisite and unfathomable love and affection that GodForce bestows creation. They are, after all, each and every single one a testimony to the care and consideration it puts into its work: We can only marvel at the complexities inherent within its smallest details; we cannot even begin to comprehend the cleverness and intricacy by which the greater picture is woven, and so it is only in our ignorance that we can bring ourselves to doubt its organizing faculties, competence, and mysterious ways.

For those who have seen the world from the cosmic consciousness' perspective, however, there is no longer room for doubt. They have caught a glimpse of the Great Plan; they have seen the world as it looks from the perspective that encompasses All; they have seen the Hand that normally never reveals its presence disclose itself in all things; they have been touched by Divinity; and they are left awestruck by the inexplicable stroke of genius that is our Universe.

For even if they know better than most the inner workings of the world the Mystery is not diminished. Quite the contrary: the more they have seen, the greater the Mystery becomes, and for every step they take on the mystic road they are filled with increasing reverence, humility, and awe for that which they are a part.

Thus, the more we know about the world, the more the miracle of existence reveals itself in all its glory. And even if we have not ourselves seen the world from the cosmic consciousness' perspective (and are therefore blind to that which transcends our understanding), we would do wisely in taking the mystics' insights seriously.

Why should by now be obvious. We have just seen how the practitioners of our most exact science, the physicists, through their experiments have come to the exact same conclusions as the mystics. As their respective fields fit together like hand in glove, we have seen a merging of the eternal philosophy with modern science which reveals the inadequacy of the old paradigm. And when we take into account that a paradigm shift includes stepping away from an inhumane and disempowering worldview, a universe governed by chance and void of meaning, and into a more life-affirming set and setting, good reasons for sticking to the old is hard to find.

PART 3

HOW EVERYTHING IS CONNECTED

11
PSYCHOLOGY

"We are now witnessing a coming together of science, psychology, and spirituality after centuries of ideological and disciplinary fragmentation. Both modern physics and depth psychology are revealing to us a universe in which mind and matter appear intimately related. The very notion of separation seems to be a kind of illusion, and all that we can perceive around us is connected by resonances, both physical and nonphysical, that can make the possibility of universal justice, truth, and love more than just a utopian fantasy." (117.29)

—John E. Mack, professor of psychiatry—

IN PART TWO, we discussed how history reflects our maturation process. We saw that the more the ego grew from the Ground of Being, the more dualistic our worldview became. We saw that the separation between religion and science was a result of this process and that the gap between these two is being bridged as we have reached a point where we can take into consideration the greater picture. We have also seen that, despite the overwhelming pressure of duality, there have always been people around who have seen beyond appearances and that their worldview not only unites all religion but is compatible with the new scientific paradigm.

We shall now have a look at how the science of psychology, biology, and medicine fits together with the framework discussed so far. In part six, we shall add the social sciences to the equation, and that it is possible to weave these disciplines together should no longer come as a surprise. After all, all branches of learning are interrelated and overlap. Theology, for instance, is closely connected with sociology and anthropology, not to mention psychology, which is an integral part of most disciplines. A quick review reveals that mathematics alone stands out, for in all other areas scholars must take their psyche into account. As we are about to elaborate on how the different disciplines of science are associated—and how they connect with mystical insight—it is therefore natural to start with psychology.

To begin with, this field covers a lot of ground. As the *psyche* is Greek for soul, the word *psychology* originally means "the study of the soul." But as the soul has been absent from the calculations for quite some time, we can more properly say that it is the workings of the human (and animal) mind that psychologists aim to identify and under-stand. In other words, their profession is the *study of consciousness*. And although their focus traditionally has been mental illness—and how it can be cured—there are also professionals who concentrate their research on our inherent potential.

Hence, as far as psychology is concerned, it overlaps perfectly with the mystics', and as we shall see, the most perceptive participants are in general agreement. I say "the most perceptive," for most psychologists and psychiatrists have no idea that their profession is compatible with the consciousness-comes-first perspective. The majority of traditions (behavior analysis, psychoanalysis, determinism, nativism, etc.) build on presumptions of scarce validity, for to the degree they differ they argue whether we have become who we are as a result of nature or nurture. In other words, they see our personality as the result of only two variables; our genes (nature) and our environment (nurture), and in no way can they imagine adding a third, the soul.

As a result, none of them come close to describing the nature of our psyche. Some of these researchers, of course, are more correct in their analysis than others, but all are firmly rooted in the old paradigm. They therefore interpret their observations in light of the Darwinian theory of evolution. They continue on a hit-or-miss basis—and the more they miss the point, the more they build their models on the assumption that we are selfish and aggressive by nature; that violence and cruelty is a natural part of human interactions; and that the subconscious is a highly distrustful territory wherein our repressed animal nature lurks.

Now, this is a simplification, as some theories are more levelheaded than others. Nevertheless, it goes without saying that a psychology building on the old paradigm will fail miserably in most endeavors—especially when it comes to helping a troubled mind find relief.

The psychologists themselves are a testimony to this. The state of their own mental health is revealed in statistics showing that more than 60 percent have suffered a clinically significant depression, and their divorce and suicide rates are perhaps the highest among any profession (excluding U.S. soldiers). The list of respected professionals who have killed themselves include Michael J. Mahoney, Paul Federn, Wilhelm Stekel, Bruno Bettelheim, Victor Tausk, Lawrence Kohlberg, and the most influential psychologist of the 20th century, Sigmund Freud. Listening to depressed people whine about their problems all day understandably takes its toll, but would you trust a car mechanic that could not fix his own car to fix yours? You probably would not, and so it seems obvious that, except for prescription medicine, psychiatrists have little to offer.

This is not for their lack of trying. They do their very best with the tools at hand, but it should be obvious that a psychology built on the old paradigm cannot possibly offer relief. As we have seen, our mind creates our reality, and so it follows that a mind-science based on a worldview that is *the reason for all our problems* cannot help us overcome them. Instead, it can only add to our misery, as it only serves to reinforce the faulty beliefs that got us into this mess.

For what good can a psychology do that begins with the premises defined by evolutionary theory? How can it help anyone, when it starts out with the assumption that our fundamental nature is animal nature and that those aspects of the psyche which lie beyond the ego's control are ruled by primitive, aggressive impulses? It should be self-evident that a mind-science that builds on such assumptions is doomed to fail, for not only will it generate a fear of anything that resides outside the ego's domain, but it will also ensure a dysfunctional relationship to our surroundings—one that is built on the logic of fear.

The reason for this disposition is that established psychology got the fundamentals all wrong. As we have seen, our true nature is *godlike* and the ego is the part of our being that is *the least* in touch with the greater reality. To the degree that the ego shuts itself off from that reality, it will be a timid, ignorant, and fearful entity, and so it is of utmost importance that it learns to trust that which transcends it. Instead of encouraging trust, however, western psychology has done the opposite. This has been the source of all our problems, for the ego stands on the shoulders of giants and the greater part of our being understands far better than it how the world is put together. Thus, the subconscious is not the dwelling place of our repressed animalistic behavior. On the contrary, it is a bridge that connects the ego to the greater reality and when the ego suppresses impulses from the inner-self, the natural flow of energy between the two is blocked.

It is this blockage that produces neurosis and psychosis, for all our destructive behaviors are the result of a consciousness which has been so cut off from the Ground of Being that, instead of relying on that which transcends it, the ego goes into a defensive mode and seeks shelter behind barriers of its own making. These barriers are those beliefs and responses which serve to protect us from that which we do not like—i.e., whatever we experience as threatening to our sense of integrity. It is these beliefs and actions that separate our sense of self from the environment. But as we have mentioned many times, this separation is an illusion: instead, we and the environment constitute an energetically whole and it is only the ego's lack of understanding that creates this illusion.

We see from this that the boundaries we define only mirror our own understanding, and the difference between mentally healthy and sick people has to do with how we see ourselves in relation to the environment. In all simplicity, healthy individuals have a constructive relationship with their surroundings, while mentally sick have formed a destructive relationship. Generally speaking, therefore, healthy people have high levels of confidence in themselves and the life process; they experience life as meaningful and feel that they have a high degree of control over their lives. Sick people, however, distrust themselves, their surroundings, and fear the process of life; they are troubled by the logic of fear—and to the extent they are, anxiety and depression follows.

As we can infer from this simple sketch, it is all about attitude. Healthy people feel that they are part of something bigger than themselves; they have a sense of being part of the greater reality and owning a rightful place in the world. This attitude towards life provides them with enough courage and faith to explore the unknown; they are therefore involved in a healthy dynamic—one that steadily increases their sense of well-being and confidence in the life process.

The sick ones, however, are caught in a dynamic which guarantees the opposite result. They feel very much threatened by the unknown and their defensive posture not only fails to protect them but ensures a destructive to-and-fro process that constantly increases their sense of alienation and loneliness. As this dynamic unfolds everything goes from bad to worse; their comfort zones gradually diminish, and as long as they refuse to look within for the answers to their problems, they will project their illness on others.

We have already discussed how repressed impulses, emotions, and aspects do not disappear. Instead, those parts of ourselves that we refuse to acknowledge and take responsibility for are being transferred onto our surroundings, and while Freud missed the point in his focus on the unconscious as a place in which our primitive impulses reside, he had a knack for seeing this mechanism. We shall not go into detail about his psychology, but his understanding of *Ego* and *Id* will suffice. These words are Latin for "I" and "it", but Freud himself never used the Latin expression as he felt it befuddled the message. It was his translators who created these concepts because they wanted his theories to appear more scientific—and in the process also obscured the simple message that the Ego and the Id conveyed.

Seen in the context of our discussion, however, we can see the *Ego* as corresponding to all that we, throughout the life-process, are able to integrate as *ourselves*, while the *Id* represents those elements that we fail to recognize and take responsibility for. The *It*, in other words, represents the alienation of ourselves from the environment—the alienation of the Ego—and as Ken Wilber says, "healthy development converts "I" into "me", unhealthy development coverts "I" into "it"."(122.128)

Hence, when we then take into consideration that "I" really is *all there is* we can see how a healthy development describes the same self-actualization process that the mystics are involved with. Psychological development, therefore, is *the path of the mystics*, and the more we manage to convert the "I" into "me", the more we expand our comfort zones and see the environment as a natural extension of ourselves.

Conversely, it is the opposite with unhealthy development, that which converts "I" into "it". That which we cannot integrate, we will dissociate, and this process promotes an image of self which is rooted in the negative polarity of all things. This image develops as a result of our traumatic experiences and it is the tendency to see ourselves as less than we are that fuels the destructive dynamic between us and environment; *this* is the cause for all anxiety and depression, and a different name psychology uses for those aspects of ourselves which we refuse to acknowledge and take responsibility for is the *Shadow self*. Wilber describes this mechanism thus:

> "Whenever I disown and project my own qualities, they appear "out there" where they frighten me, irritate me, depress me, obsess me. And consequently, in nine out of ten cases, those things in the world that most disturb and upset me about others are actually my own shadow qualities, which are now perceived as "out there"." (122.120)

Does this ring any bells? We all, to different degrees, do this and it is nothing to be ashamed of. What's important is to acknowledge this dynamic in our lives, for only then can we begin to heal instead of shadow-boxing with our issues in a battle we cannot win.

We see examples of how this shadow-forming mechanism works in people who fail to honor their responsibilities. Being born into a culture where moral confusion reigns, people accept a social contract based on lies, deceit, and oppression; they conform to group-thinking, and their personal lives are polluted by unconsciousness. Like their leaders, people will lie, cheat, seek dominion over others; they will be looking for the easy way out and fail to commit to the ideals, values, and principles that follow from Wholeness. Thus, macro and micro reflect each other, and while everyone salutes freedom, few want the responsibility that comes with being an adult. Instead, people will be living on their knees, but as this cannot be consciously acknowledged, they pass this feeling of neglect and betrayal on to their environment. In so doing, it becomes everybody else's fault that that they are depressed, that they drink, that they are having difficulties, and so on.

Control urges and putting self above others is just one result of traumatic life-events. So is uncontrolled anger, hypersensitivity, mistrust, insomnia, and other issues. Stress literally alters the codes of perception, while defense mechanisms such as denial and projection maintain the status quo. The phenomenon is the same whether it takes place on the individual or the collective level; unconsciousness is the price we pay, and when discussing this mechanism, another connection is the enemy images. We will have more to say about them later, but here we see how they arise: It is because we are unsure of ourselves, because we doubt our own self-worth and have other deeply hidden fears, that we, in failing to understand the necessity of looking within and taking responsibility for our issues, transfer them on to others. It seems, then, to us as if our environment is the problem—and not ourselves—and we believe that it is something *out there* that makes us feel scared, nervous, neglected, and threatened. Wilber provides a classic example:

> "You might have seen the recent studies where men who were anti-gay-pornography crusaders, and who had dedicated a large portion of their lives to aggressively fighting homosexual porn, were tested for their levels of sexual arousal when shown photos of gay sexual scenes. The crusaders evidenced substantially more sexual arousal than other males.
>
> In other words, they themselves were attracted to gay sex but, finding that unacceptable in themselves, spent their lives trying to eradicate it in others, while claiming they had no such nasty desires themselves. Yet all they were really doing was projecting their own despised shadows on to others, then scapegoating them."(122.120)

Scapegoating is the tradition of blaming others for problems that we ourselves refuse to look at. At the level of society, this results in wars, persecution, and tyrannical tendencies (normally directed at politically weak groups), while at the personal level it results in destroyed relationships, and as soon as we can come to grips with this mechanism, we will cure the illness of the world. This presupposes that we grow consciously to the point where we take responsibility for those aspects of us which we have hitherto repressed and disowned. But as soon as we can fill those aspects with love, then our personal and collective troubles will be a thing of the past.

This is not only one of the mystics' many insights; it is also acknowledged by leading psychologists, for as Carl Gustav Jung noted "one does not become enlightened by imagining figures of light, but making the darkness conscious."(85.204)

11.1 HUMANISTIC PSYCHOLOGY

"Freud's picture of man was clearly unsuitable, leaving out as it did his aspirations, his realizable hopes, his godlike qualities."(69.12)

—Abraham Maslow, psychologist—

As we have become familiar with the basics of psychology, we can see how the discipline is compatible with mysticism—and this applies particularly to the part of psychology that deals with human potential.

While early psychology in general (and Freud in particular) as a rule studied the sickness of the mind a new movement arose in the mid-1900s that represented a different approach. This was to become known as humanistic psychology and key representatives were people like Carl Gustav Jung, Stanislav Grof, Abraham Maslow, Alan Watts, Huston Smith, Roberto Assagioli, Carl Rogers, Viktor Frankl, Charles Tart, and Alyce and Elmer Green. These professionals had a focus that went further than Freud. The subject of their study was psychologically healthy individuals, and from studying this group they found that the belief in man's corrupt nature was completely wrong. Based on their research, they concluded that psychologically healthy individuals were motivated

171

by values and aspirations that were *essentially different* from the average ego-centered citizen who dabbled with fear-based and self-centered motivations. To say it with Maslow, they understood that "What we call 'normal' in psychology is really a psychopathology of the average, so undramatic and so widely spread that we don't even notice it ordinarily". And that "the study of the authentic person and of authentic living helps to throw this general phoniness, this living by illusion and by fear into a harsh, clear light which reveals it clearly as a sickness, even though widely shared."(69.16)

In other words: by studying the more perceptive percentage of the population, they found that the conclusions of psychology had been based on sick people's worldview—and that because we were born into a society which produced far more pathological than healthy minds, this had escaped them. Because the sick mind had been the object of study, violence, selfishness, conflict, and cruelty were seen as a normal part of human interaction. But now that they had a new standard by which to measure the psyche, they realized that our inner nature was basically good and that the more we were able to cultivate it the better. As Maslow put it: "Human nature is not nearly as bad as it has been thought to be. In fact it can be said that the possibilities of human nature have customarily been sold short."(69.4)

Furthermore, these psychologists believed that what we perceive as corrupt and evil was the result of an upbringing that prevented our true nature to emerge. Consequently, they reasoned that "since [our] inner nature is good or neutral rather than bad, it is best to bring it out and encourage it rather than to suppress it. If it is permitted to guide our life, we grow healthy, fruitful, and happy."(69.4)

In their view, it was only because the natural development of our true nature was suppressed and thwarted that neurosis and psychosis occurred. They believed that the pathological mind grew forth much in the same way as a deficiency disease and that it was the result of basic needs which were not met. Maslow again:

> "It will not occur to anyone to question the statement that
> we "need" . . . vitamin C. I remind you that the evidence
> that we need love is of exactly the same type. . . . Neurosis

seems at its core . . . to be a deficiency disease; it is born out of being deprived of certain needs . . . [and this] produces illness. Most neurosis involves ungratified wishes for safety, for belongingness and identification, for close love relationships and for respect and prestige. When these deficiencies [are] eliminated, sickness tends to disappear."(69.23,21)

Now, unfortunately, we live in a society which is hostile to our innermost needs. We live in a world ruled by the logic of fear and as long as we let it define our personal and collective mindset, we will continue to produce far more sick than healthy minds. We shall look at the societal impact of this logic in part five, while we explore solutions in part six. The point is that these researchers discovered that the human mind is far more than Freud and other psychologists assumed. Through their studies, they found that those who were in touch with their inner-self experienced reality as qualitatively different than the average citizen—and that they could be said to walk the same road as the mystics.

Thus, while Freud and others limited the psyche to include the ego and the subconscious, these pioneers saw clearer and clearer that the subconscious was part of something even bigger. And as this under-standing dawned, they found it necessary to take humanistic psychology one step further—to its logical conclusion. Maslow put it like this:

"I consider Humanistic psychology to be transitional, a preparation for a still "higher". . . psychology. [One that is] transpersonal, transhuman, centred in the cosmos rather than in human needs and interest, going beyond humanness, identity, self actualization and the like."(69.IV)

As we can see, Maslow's vision for psychology is completely in agreement with the mystics. This is no coincidence, for through their research the humanistic psychologists discovered that the traditional understanding of the psyche was too limited. One factor that lead to this conviction was research indicating that consciousness was interlinked, making the idea of the mind as a delimited, independent quantity meaningless. Another factor was that they took seriously research which suggested that consciousness neither began at birth nor disappeared with death. And a third was that they began to emphasize and categorize the expanded states of consciousness—those that other psychologists had dismissed as irrelevant, sickly, or hallucinatory.

These pioneers, in other words, discovered how their discipline was closely related to the mystics. And as it became clear that consciousness could not possibly be limited to the body and the personal sphere, this psychology evolved into *transpersonal* psychology.

12
TRANSPERSONAL PSYCHOLOGY

"The nature and intensity of some of the mainstream scientists' reaction to any form of spirituality in general, and to transpersonal psychology in particular, seems to mirror the fanaticism of religious fundamentalists. Their attitude lacks solid scientific grounding, ignores or distorts all existing evidence, and is impervious to facts of observation and logical arguments. Closer scrutiny reveals that what they present as an image of reality that has been scientifically proven beyond reasonable doubt is a colossus on clay feet supported by a host of meta-physical assumptions."(50.324)

—Stanislav Grof—

The transpersonal field of research is wide. It includes psychology, spiritual experiences, religious studies, neuroscience, and philosophy, and weaves it together as one. Philosopher Michael Washburn therefore calls it transpersonal *theory*, but what we call it is less important. What is important is that psychology, with this, has fused with mysticism and that the spiritual aspect of the psyche finally has been recognized by western psychology.

Now, to be fair, there have been professionals around who took matters of spirit seriously long before the 1960s, when this branch of psychology originated. As we saw in the first part, pioneers such as William James and R.M. Bucke not only took the expanded states of consciousness and the message they conveyed seriously; they also recognized the insights of the eternal philosophy and were attentive to the fact that our current state of awareness represented only an inkling of our potential. As James put it:

> "I have no doubt whatever that most people live, whether physically, intellectually or morally, in a very restricted circle of their potential being . . . much like a man who, out of his whole bodily organism, should get into the habit of using and moving only his little finger. We all have reservoirs of life to draw upon, of which we do not dream."(72.231)

It is also from James' notes that we find the term "transpersonal" used for the first time (1905-1906). As a discipline, however, psychology was at this point well on its way into the dead-end that the theory of evolution was to take it, and because it built on the premise that there was no spiritual side to life—and no godlike potential—any research suggestive of such a thing have been met with disdain until today.

Still, despite their opposition to soul and spirit, even well-established psychologists must admit that the mystics' understanding coincides very much with their own. For example, to those who know a thing or two about religion, the parallels between Buddhism and cognitive psychology are obvious and so are the similarities between developmental psychology and Vedic psychology[22]. Equally, humanistic psychologists like Jung have held that "the Christ-symbol is of the greatest importance for psychology, in so far as it (except for the figure of Buddha) is the most highly developed and differentiated symbol of the self".

Now, many psychologists are unaware of such basic similarities. Nevertheless, more and more are seeing the bigger picture, and as a

---

[22] For more on the parallels between Buddhism and modern psychology see VARELA ET AL., *THE EMBODIED MIND: COGNITIVE SCIENCE AND HUMAN EXPERIENCE*. For more on Vedic psychology and developmental psychology see ALEXANDER ET AL., *HIGHER STAGES OF HUMAN DEVELOPMENT*. For a good introduction to what it entails for the future of psychology when the new theory of existence comes into its own, see WALSH & VAUGHAN (ED.), *BEYOND EGO: TRANSPERSONAL DIMENSIONS IN PSYCHOLOGY*; STANLEY DEAN (ED.), *PSYCHIATRY & MYSTICISM*; AND STANISLAV GROF, *PSYCHOLOGY OF THE FUTURE*. See also STEIN (ED.), *JUNG ON CHRISTIANITY*.

consequence not only the mystics' primary tool, meditation, but also psychedelic drugs are becoming increasingly important in therapeutic practices.

When all is said and done, then, we find that it is only the spiritual aspect of the psyche that traditional psychology refuses to bring into its equation. This is where transpersonal psychologists reject the old paradigm, for as *the Journal of Transpersonal Psychology* defines the discipline, it is "concerned with the study of humanity's highest potential, and with the recognition, understanding, and realization of unitive, spiritual, and transcendent states of consciousness."

The transpersonal psychologists' endeavor therefore, just as the mystics', is to gather all that can be known about our relationship with the world into one coherent system of thought. The field has evolved since the 1960s and leading theorists have their disagreements in terms of the details. Even so, they agree on the fundamentals, and in what follows a summarization shall be presented.

12.1 HUMANITY'S EVOLUTIONARY PROCESS

> *"History is . . . the story of the unfolding of the relationship*
> *between man and the ultimate Whole. Since this wholeness*
> *is contiguous with consciousness itself, we can also say that*
> *history is the unfolding of human consciousness. . . .*
> *History, in this sense, is a slow and torturous path to*
> *transcendence."(123.7)*

—Ken Wilber—

The mission of transpersonal psychologists' is to describe the nature of consciousness. On the one hand, this means that they study awareness as it develops from birth, but in addition they are concerned with the larger picture. Consequently, they look at how our consciousness has evolved from time immemorial to the present day, and from their studies they also try to say something about the road ahead.

When it comes to this subject, we have already described the basics: We have seen how our ego-consciousness originated several thousand years ago; how it has become more and more refined; and how we are about to take our understanding a quantum leap forward. We have also seen how consciousness itself is omnipresent, unbound, and unlimited by our understanding of ourselves, and that the development manifesting in the individual is interlinked with development in the global/collective psyche. We shall now see how this compares with the transpersonal theorists' understanding, and we begin with a look at the overall context into which we are born.

When it comes to the maturation of the collective consciousness, those who have researched it agree with the evolutionary trend outlined thus far. The only point upon which they differ is the number of developmental stages they categorize to describe the process. Jean Gebser, a pioneer, describes in *The Ever-Present Origin* five stages. He calls the first evolutionary stage for the *archaic* (Greek for "beginning") and describes it as "akin, if not identical, to the original state of biblical paradise: a time where the soul is yet dormant, a time of complete non-differentiation of man and the universe." The next stage he refers to is the *magic*: this represents the time period in which man's ego begins to wake up, but where our separation from the environment is not yet clearly defined. At this level, therefore, people think that they can influence others through magic and ritual, for example through wishful thinking, witchcraft, and sorcery. The next stage humanity goes through is the *mythical*. At this point in our evolution, we have established an understanding of us as separate from our surroundings, and Wilber, the leading light of transpersonal psychology, describes the mythical understanding as follows:

> "[Here] I can no longer order the world around as in magic, but God can, if I know how to please God. If I want my personal wishes to be fulfilled, I must make certain pleas or prayers to God, and then God will intervene on my behalf and suspend the laws of nature through miracles."(121.199)

The next phase Gebser describes is the *mental/rational*. At this stage, we have left behind faith in the supernatural and we realize what it means to fully experience ourselves as separate from creation. Wilber describes it thus:

> "[At this level] I realize that the belief in a personal God who caters to my egoistic whims is probably just not true, there isn't any credible evidence for it, and anyway it doesn't reliably work. If I want something from nature—food for example—I'll [therefore] skip the prayers, skip the rituals, skip the human sacrifices, and approach nature itself directly. With hypothetic-deductive reasoning—that is, with science—I'll go directly after what I need. This is a big advance, but it also has its downside. The world starts to look like a meaningless collection of material bits and pieces, with no value, no meaning at all."(121.200)

As we can see, it is at this evolutionary stage we exist as a society today. The next stage Gebser mentions is the *integral*, and it unites all the previous levels in a higher unity. Hence, when we reach this state, we have transcended the worldview that most people today are familiar with and Gebser describes it like this:

> "The undivided, ego-free person . . . no longer sees parts but realizes the "itself", the spiritual form of being of man and world. [He] perceives the whole, the diaphaneity present "before" all origin which suffuses everything. For him there is no longer heaven or hell, this world or the other, ego or world, immanence or transcendence; rather, beyond the magic unity, the mythical complementarity, the mental division and synthesis is the perceptible whole."(40.543)

Gebser's *Ever-Present Origin* was a pioneering study, and many have elaborated on his findings. It varies how many stages they work with and what names they apply but they all describe the same process as

Gebser. To simplify, we can divide the evolutionary process of human consciousness into pre-modern thinking (archaic, magic, mythical), modern thinking (existential, rational, mental) and post-modern thinking (pluralistic, holistic, integral, transpersonal), this progression summarizing our journey through duality.

The transpersonal theorists see this as a purpose-filled and goal-oriented development. Unlike many psychologists, they include spirit in their calculations, and it is obvious that evolution has an objective and that it is the realization of our inner nature. They therefore interpret history as a process used by Spirit to realize itself *through us*, Wilber explaining further:

> "Evolution *is* holistic, because "to evolve" is simply to re-member that which was dis-membered, to unify that which was separated, to re-collect that which was dispersed. Evolution is the re-membering, or putting back together, of that which was separated and alienated during involution [the Universe's out-breath]. And evolution, as a successive remembering or Joining together in higher unity, simply continues until there is *only* Unity and *everything* has been remembered as Spirit by Spirit." (123.305)

As we can see, Wilber describes the same exhalation and inhalation process which we have explored. For the transpersonal theorists—just as the mystics—it follows as a logical consequence of their studies, as it seems self-evident that we, in realizing ourselves, also become more and more what we have always been—Spirit.

As a society, we find ourselves at a point where we are about to take a leap from the mental/rational level and into the integral. As a result, we are confronted with the consequences of the old mindset's thinking. And although the situation may look bleak, the critical state of affairs can be seen as positive being that we, without it, never would have been able to renew ourselves.

Indeed, as the situation evolves it becomes only clearer that the old thinking is leading us towards the precipice. Our choice, therefore, is between annihilation and transcendence, and taking into consideration the nature of our current mindset we need this crisis to wake up. We hate to admit it. Nevertheless, most of us are willing to close our eyes and accept the most horrible forms of systematic abuse, oppression, and exploitation as long as we ourselves have beer in the refrigerator, TV, and other material goods to subdue our spiritual craving. In other words, our sense of responsibility is rather slim. And as helpless little children we prefer the illusions and lies offered by our authorities, rather than dealing with the injury our beliefs and lifestyle has inflicted upon us.

The current crisis, therefore, is an integral part of the transformation process, for without it everything would continue as before. In fact, the worse it gets the better it is, for the more we are confronted with the consequences of those inconvenient truths we refuse to accept, the more likely we are to rise to the challenge; and the sooner we begin to deal seriously with the fundamental problems of our civilization, the sooner the healing process can begin.

As we know, at any given time the collective consciousness reflects the sum of our understanding. Through our upbringing we absorb the norms and worldview of the age in which we live and so we are formed within the framework of a larger context. It is this overall mindset that the German philosopher Hegel called the *Zeitgeist*—the spirit of the age—and simply put we can see ourselves as a sponge which, from the day we are born, begins to soak up the moral codes and worldview that is offered by the collective consciousness.

It goes without saying that this field has a strong impact whether we want it or not and it works positively in that, like a magnet, it pulls/lifts our understanding toward the same level of cognition as the average citizen. It works negatively, however, in that it retards our development once we have reached this level. And those who seek to rise above it will find that for every step they take on their journey towards further self-realization they are being met with an inherent resistance from their surroundings.

Despite that, it is those who refuse to accept the average citizen's level of consciousness who are our guiding lights. They are the ones who see through—and challenge—the delusions and the hypocritical moral codes that the rest uncritically embrace; and they are the ones who, in doing so, add to the social fabric that dynamic which makes it possible for the collective consciousness to rise towards new horizons. In other words, *they are paving the way so that the rest can follow*, and without such people humanity would still have been stuck at the most primitive of all developmental stages.

Our conscious evolution, therefore, can be seen as a result of the dynamic that takes place between individuals. As a result of their interactions and the process that gradually transforms experience into understanding, humanity matures cognitively from day to day, year to year, century to century, and millennium to millennium. And even if we, from the average variable, can say whether we are dealing with an archaic, magic, mythical, rational, or holistic/integral society, it will consist of people who individually exist at various levels. This is easily seen in today's world: Even if a majority can be defined by the mental/rational worldview, a smaller percentage are still influenced by the mythical way of thinking, while some have evolved to the holistic, more advanced mindset.

We shall now take a look at how the maturation process unfolds at the individual's level, as the evolutionary progress we have described for humanity as a whole can be transferred to our own lives: We were born with no clearly defined ego-understanding; when we came into the world we were one with it, and then, as we grew in experience, we built those boundaries that mirrored our understanding. Hence, the way we think about the world today is fundamentally different from the way we saw it when we were young. Looking at our own growth process, there-fore, we find that it is comparable to the evolution that mankind has experienced from time immemorial to the present day; we are a microcosm of the macrocosm, and just as we mature through one lifetime, humanity matures through many.

12.2 THE INDIVIDUAL'S EVOLUTIONARY PROCESS

"When the human ego realizes that its will is a tool, its wisdom ignorance and childishness, its power an infant's groping, its virtue a pretentious impurity, and learns to trust itself to that which transcends it, that is its salvation." (10.66)

—Sri Aurobindo—

In the western tradition, the discipline devoted to our maturation process is called developmental psychology. Traditionally, researchers of this field have assumed that we, by the time we reach our 20s and have integrated the "normal" adult consciousness (that which includes systematic and abstract thinking) were fully cognitively developed. The reason, of course, is that their studies focused on the average citizen and that most of us stagnate at this level. Yet research has also been done on the more evolved percentage of the population, this indicating that the "normal" ego-centered consciousness is only an intermediary state[23] and that there are superior levels of cognition—levels which we would all have evolved to, if we were not born into a sick society.

We have already discussed how our development freezes at this level, which we call normal, as a result of stress growing up. We shall shortly take a closer look at how our brain works, but it basically consists of three layers/parts. The innermost is called the reptilian brain. This is the oldest, most primitive part of the brain; it controls instinct-based behavior, breathing, body temperature, and so on, and its focus is taking care of survival. Outside the reptilian brain, we have something called the limbic system (or mammalian brain). This part manages the emotions and coordinates more complex behavior, and beyond this, closest to the

---

[23] This includes research done by Wilber, Assagioli, Grof, Wade, Graves, Maslow, Washburn, Alexander, Loevinger, Koplowitz, and more.

forehead, we find the latest evolutionary addition, that which we call the neo-cortex or frontal lobe.

This is the most advanced part of the brain, the one that makes it possible to think creatively and to see a situation from new perspectives. At all times, these parts work in unison and each one has its proper place in everyday life, but it is the frontal lobe that distinguishes us from other creatures. Jenny Wade gives us an example of how this construction influences our everyday life:

> "Any single event will be registered and processed by all three small minds at once according to their individual capabilities. For instance, [if] a person is unexpectedly running into his lover lunching with her old flame, [he] is likely to evoke a mixture of responses. The neo-cortical part of the brain will have rationally processed the event and will be struggling to find something socially acceptable to do or say, while the limbic system may be feeling betrayal and anxiety, and the R-complex [reptilian brain] is pushing its innate aggression and territoriality.
>
> No wonder people are often tongue-tied and awkward in such situations; they are having to integrate and sort through constantly changing, conflicting messages *that are all real and valid in their own way.*"(113.70)

I assume that we all recognize something of ourselves in this situation and to what extent we will listen to the voice of the reptilian brain or reason (the frontal lobe) depends on how our brain is organized. Between these parts of the brain runs an intricate network of neural pathways and based on how they are structured our minds will function. Very simply, we can say that the more developed the frontal part of our brain and the better balanced the left and right hemispheres, the wiser and more balanced our relationship to the environment will be.

The problem is that we are born into a competition-oriented society ruled by the logic of fear and that we, through our upbringing, absorb the same mindset and erroneous beliefs that the status quo is built upon. The stress this results in ensures that those neural pathways which are organized around the more primitive part of the brain are developed and strengthened at the expense of the frontal lobes—and so it is that we all end up more or less brain damaged from our childhood years.

The reason for this is that our brains are very much molded into shape by the first five years of our lives: The more stress, anxiety, and uncertainty we experience during this period, the more severe the neurological "wounds" will be, and to a greater or lesser degree we carry these childhood traumas throughout life. In fact, the organization of the neural pathways begins already in the womb. An increasing corpus of evidence suggests that the fetus is not only aware of the mother's thoughts and feelings but directly affected, and so an unhappy and stressed-out expecting mother will already at this point lay the foundation for a less-than-ideal development.

Thus, by the way our brains are molded, we see another example of how the ripple effects generated by the logic of fear expand and how they make sure that we, as individuals and society, become far less than we could have been: Even before we are born, we are affected by the destructive dynamic that a hierarchical and competition-oriented social order ensures, and the negative pressure of the collective consciousness continues to shape our brains through adolescence. Had we known better, we would have done what we could to remedy this situation, for as Joseph Chilton Pearce says:

> "A human nurtured instead of shamed and loved instead of driven by fear develops a different brain and therefore a different mind—he will not act against the wellbeing of another, nor against his larger body, the living earth."(75.)

From this, we see that the self-absorbed, shortsighted, and destructive behavior exhibited by most adults—that which is so common that we confuse it with our true nature—is a byproduct of our culture and can be traced back to emotional wounds inflicted by child-hood experiences.

The reason for this is that the foundation of our emotional apparatus is in place at the age of three. From the way it is set, it will influence later intellectual development, and so the extent to which we will go about the rest of our lives in defense mode or with an open, trusting, and curious mind, depends very much on our experiences those first years. As adults, of course, we can develop quite sophisticated intellects. But nevertheless, we are quite simply put together, for when all is said and done, behind all our big words and highflying aspirations, we find that our basic motivation is to maximize our sense of well-being by maintaining and cultivating our self-image. That is about it. It all starts with our image of ourselves—of who we perceive ourselves to be—and where we go from there has everything to do with how we experience our relationship to the world.

Simply put, we can say that to the degree we have experienced feelings of safety, security, recognition, self-worth, belonging, and control those first three years of our lives, we will build a relationship to the world based on a solid foundation. From there on everything is well prepared for a constructive to-and-fro dynamic between us and our surroundings; a dynamic in which our basic trust in the life-process results in our greeting it with open arms and constantly expanding safety zones. The more we expand our comfort zones, the more we will see ourselves and the world as one cohesive whole—and the more we do this, the more we will see self-interest and public interest as one.

Conversely, to the extent that we the first years of our life experience feelings of hopelessness, shame, insecurity, powerlessness, helplessness, fear, and inadequacy, the opposite will be the case. To the extent that we experience this we will develop a fragile and uncertain self-image and everything is arranged for that dynamic which is built on the logic of fear. Our emotional foundation will provide us with a worldview which tells us that the world is a ruthless, rotten, insensitive, and uncomfortable quantity and so going through life with a defensive posture will seem like the most natural thing. This is how emotionally damaged children end up becoming emotionally damaged adults. And those situations and experiences that a healthy person would think of as positively or neutrally charged will, to them, easily be perceived as threatening—no matter how trivial or hypothetical the threat is.

Now, this is an oversimplified representation of the dynamics involved and reality is more complex being that we, as individuals, come into the world with different baggage. After all, we must bring the reincarnation concept and the soul into the equation. Variables such as previous lives determine how resilient we are in facing contemporary challenges and some spirits are easier broken. Nevertheless, we are all, to some extent, influenced by growth conditions that were less than ideal. It is an inevitable consequence of being born into a society that is ruled by the logic of fear, and all around us we find examples of this.

As a matter of fact, we can see all selfish, deceitful, hypocritical, violent, aggressive, and control-oriented behavior as a symptom of distressed people trying to protect themselves. To the extent that we have known unconditional love, such behaviors would have been alien, and so we are all basically overgrown children who in our everyday lives do what we can to alleviate those traumas carried over from childhood. Just think about it: It is because we fear that we will not be accepted for who we really are that we lie and misrepresent reality. Had we grown up in an environment that offered us unconditional love, we would never have felt the need to present ourselves as something other than ourselves and the idea that so much pain originates from—that we must maintain a facade—would have been foreign.

Correspondingly, if we knew in our hearts that we were good enough *no matter what*, not just all deceitful but also all hypocritical and contemptuous behavior would have disappeared as we would never have felt the need to put ourselves above others. Moreover, if our self-image were built on a 100 percent secure foundation, our safety zones would encompass so much more than they do today, and this would cause all violent behavior to desist. As we shall see in part six, behind all aggression and frustration we find grief and despair, and if we remove the cause of this existential pain (the erroneous belief systems) it is only logical that the symptoms will disappear.

This brief summary already speaks volumes about the beneficial ripple effects reaped by the logic of love. And to all this we can add that secure people also have a basic trust in the life-process; they do not only (more or less) see the environment as an extension of themselves but the more they know about the Universe, the more they understand that it is a blessed place—no matter what happens here. Consequently, they feel no need to control others. Instead, they see it as the most natural thing to help others in their growth process because, to the extent they do, they know that they will also realize *themselves* while at the same time laying the ground for a better functioning society.

We see here how powerful unconditional love is and what a world we will create as soon as we let it rule our reasoning. However, we are all painfully aware that the world is currently no such place. If we want a world governed by this logic therefore, we must create it—and we do this by beginning the healing process. This part of the equation will be dealt with in the last part of the book, but it is important to remember that those deep-felt shortcomings we experience in childhood will pursue us for life if we deny them. If we want to heal our wounds, therefore, the first step is to recognize that we, like everyone else, have our issues, and from there we can begin to untangle our emotional knots by studying our relationship to others.

We should know by now that all those things which we repress will be transferred to our surroundings. And by becoming consciously aware of this mechanism and taking our fears and felt inadequacies seriously, we will be able to trace our thought- and response patterns back to the core issue, which is always some belief system that does not reflect the truth about our inner nature. We have already seen how deep-felt shortcomings influence our adult lives and the bigger our issues are the easier they are to spot. The reason for this is that the more we grieve for something that we did not get enough of when we were young, the more we will chase after it in the environment. This compulsive behavior is our way of compensating: We are constantly trying to catch up on all that we have lost, but no matter how much power we gain over others we will still feel insecure, and no matter how many lovers or admirers we have, we will not feel sufficiently loved and recognized.

Thinking on the matter, it should be obvious why we cannot satisfy the bottomless hunger that the unsatisfied child has instilled in us by chasing after it in our surroundings. In doing so we are fighting the same war against shadows which we have previously discussed, and the only way we can heal our wounds is by going within. Our feelings can always be counted upon to point us in the right direction for *every time we experience a bad feeling* it is trying to tell us something. Hence, if we ask ourselves *why* we feel so small, powerless, and insecure, we will find that our emotions are cries for help and attention from those parts of us that we have not yet accepted and integrated into our personality.

We therefore heal ourselves by taking the little boy/girl inside us seriously. Only then can things get better, because we then begin to fill the darkened rooms within—those aspects of ourselves that we have so long suppressed—with love and light. In doing so we heal our shadow-self, the Ego incorporates the Id, and we emerge as a more complete version of ourselves. We, in other words, become more of that which we actuality are: Our personality (who we think we are) merges with our identity (our true nature) and the "adult" (or traumatized) form of consciousness dissolves into a higher state of being.

This is how we build integrity. This is how we free ourselves from the shackles of our own and society's making. And as we can see, what we have talked about in this chapter is the self-actualization process. The normal adult consciousness is the result of a stagnant growth process and by going within we can resolve that internal chaos which limits us and prevents our inherent potential to materialize. It follows from this that what we have discussed is not only a 101-class in psychology but also in mysticism. In fact, the mystics' way is the one we all must walk if we are to evolve beyond that level of consciousness by which ordinary people operate. Wayne Teasdale, a professor of theology, speaks of it thus:

> "The mystical path is . . . psychologically *integrative*; it unites the unconscious, the conscious, and the superconscious. It also integrates the memory, intellect, will, imagination and emotions with the body and the spirit. Within them, it establishes the harmony of love, compassion, mercy, and kindness—the quieting of the emotions. All this surrenders to something much higher and more ultimate than the human."(109.24)

That percentage of the population which has taken a step forward from the mental/rational worldview have therefore, whether they realize it or not, come to where they are as a result of this path: Because they to a greater degree than others have taken their inner world seriously, they have managed to overcome some of those misconceptions that the average citizen struggles with—and the Universe has rewarded their efforts with access to higher perspectives and deeper insight.

The subject we are now about to discuss may be hard to hear. But from a higher perspective the overwhelming majority of the population are very much lost in the foggy world of illusions offered by the collective consciousness: People here think they are independent and autonomous because they have opinions about many things. Nevertheless, their relationship to the world of thought is so reckless and disorganized that one idea not only contradicts the other, but that they themselves cannot see the contradiction. Thus, they have no problem in presenting themselves as Christians, while in the next breath declaring that they are believers in the death penalty or the Iraq war. Any flaw in their reasoning escapes them, for their thinking is so clouded by culture that they cannot see clearly in any direction.

The reason for this is that their world is not really their own. More properly it can be described as part of an unconscious, collectively shared mass-psychosis, for the collective consciousness field is itself a very diffuse and ambiguous quantity and those who arbitrarily pick ideas without adding two and two together will end up holding beliefs that more perceptive individuals find irreconcilable. We see another example of such confused reasoning in people who claim to be champions of the rule of law and human rights, while they at the same time support the war on drugs and terrorism. If the reader does not immediately see the conflict between these two points of view, there is no need to worry as it will be explained in part five. My point is that most mindsets are the result of so unsystematic and conflicting thinking—of an autopilot function so disorganized and muddled—that the collective consciousness *thinks itself through them*, rather than the reverse.

I declare this not to be rude. I simply state the obvious, because it is imperative that we recognize that the global psyche can confuse and poison our minds just as much as it can be of benefit. History speaks volumes—and as we shall see, it is no less true in our day than it was in Germany in the 1930s and 40s.

If the snippet above presents the average citizen as a relatively comatose being, that does not mean that I in any way disrespect his or her integrity. After all, it is a fact that we are all equally valuable and that we are all equally close to God. But it is also a fact that there are levels of awareness that far exceed the average—and seen in a larger context, it is no exaggeration to say that most people are so far removed from their inherent potential that they have not yet awakened to themselves.

Truth be told, as seen from the cosmic consciousness' perspective, the average citizen's obliviousness cannot be overstated: His reasoning is like a child's as he has not yet found a working map from which to navigate. He is akin to a shipwrecked lost at sea, paddling his life-raft in whatever direction the wind blows, and has not yet learned to navigate by the stars. The average citizen, of course, is not aware of this predicament. To a more evolved being, however, it is obvious, for as Thomas Paine, one of the great minds of the Enlightenment era put it:

> "When a man in a long cause attempts to steer his course by anything else than some polar truth or principle, he is sure to be lost. It is beyond the compass of his capacity to keep all the parts of an argument together, and make them unite in one issue, by any other means than having this guide always in view. Neither memory nor invention will supply the want of it. The former fails him, and the latter betrays him."(80.78)

When such a person is confronted with higher analytical reasoning, he will most likely space out into an incoherent state of mind where logic fails to reach him. No matter how patiently one tries to guide him towards new insight it is destined to fail, for to the degree the higher analytical perspective is discordant with the collective's shared "wisdom", he cannot put two and two together.

The reason for this is that the average person has not yet established a center from which it is possible to step out of the culturally shared delusion. It takes courage and integrity to do so, and he has not yet matured to the point where it is possible to deal with the situation. Thus, the global psyche has such a hold that rather than think for themselves and take responsibility for their life and surroundings, people will leave it to others to define right and wrong and decide what to do.[24] Because most have not found the integrity to stand their moral ground—and because they have not yet established a relationship with the inner-self—they will instead seek shelter in the comfort of group behavior, for as long as they can find belonging in a group, their sense of insignificance and loneliness will be subdued.

Such a person's character will be passive, dependent, insecure, and hypocritical. It is an unarticulated contract between this person and the group that rules out any display of individuality and self-thinking. Thus, he must abide by the group's norms, dogmas, and truisms, and should such individuals begin to question its leadership or its collectively shared wisdom they will quickly find themselves an outcast. The agreement serves both parties in that the group (be it a religious denomination, political party, motorcycle gang, military unit, police force, or secret society) acquires a new member while the individual obtains an identity.

We shall see more to the individual-group dynamic in the last part. However, some 80 percent of the population will obey the authority of another rather than their own, and the only reason why is that their self-image is so poor that they measure their own worth based on what others think. Still, self-actualization in this context is impossible: As long as we are looking outside for truth, verification, and identity, we can never reclaim our inherent integrity, and so those who know better look for these things *within*. Sri Aurobindo spoke to it thus:

> "The individual does not owe his ultimate allegiance either
> to the State which is a machine or the community which is
> a part of life and not the whole of life: his allegiance must
> be to the Truth, the Self, the Spirit, the Divine which is in

---

[24] According to psychologist and moral theorist Lawrence Kohlberg, no more than 10 percent of the population have matured to the point where they are guided by principled universal moral reasoning. His research, in fact, indicated that this estimate was optimistic and that the most evolved form of moral reasoning was even rarer. Furthermore, the average citizen's lack of moral compass is revealed in studies done by psychiatrist Stanley Milgram who, in the 1960s, showed that 65 percent of the subjects were willing to torture another person to death if the order was given by a seemingly authorized person.

him and in all; not to subordinate or lose himself in the mass, but to find and express that truth of being in himself and help the community and humanity in its seeking for its own truth and fullness of being must be his real object of existence."(9.1050)

This is important, for as long as we submit to an authority outside of ourselves, we will contribute to the same dynamic that has been the cause of history's most disastrous events. It is inescapable that without this dynamic neither Nazism nor any other destructive mass-movement could have come into being, and if we want to prevent it from happening again we must stop letting others define our truths. The more evolved have understood this. They therefore refuse to acknowledge any authority but their own—or that of first principles. To more evolved beings, the two become as one; it is the values, ideals, and principles of the Wholeness that guide them and from which they build integrity—and the more they go within for answers, the longer down the mystics' road they wander and the higher levels of consciousness they arrive at.

So it is that our awakening begins the day we take our inner-self seriously and stay true to our conscience rather than an external authority. What happens then, is that we embark on the process that brings our inner nature to the surface. As we know, true individuality comes from within. Hence, by taking responsibility for their journey those involved with this process gradually detach from that world of delusions which clouds the average citizen's judgment—and because they make every effort to "stand in their light" they develop a sense of integrity that others lack.

Consequently, for those on this path, it becomes unthinkable to lie, cheat, manipulate, or intimidate to get their way. They know that nothing will ruin their efforts more than such behavior and instead they endeavor to let all that follows from the logic of love permeate their thinking, speech, and actions. To quote Teasdale, therefore, life for them is "a journey from hypocrisy to sincerity, from self-centeredness to other centeredness and love, from self-deception, ignorance, and illusion to self-honesty, clarity, and truth."(109.106)

If we are to describe this development in terms of that growth process which is represented by the archaic, magic, mythical, mental/rational, and holistic/integral states of consciousness, a simple way to look at it is to compare it with a Russian nesting doll (those layered dolls in which one goes outside and contains the other). Our interpretation of reality corresponds with those limits of understanding that we ourselves have integrated, and we can picture each doll to represent the framework of a worldview.

According to this analogy, the smallest, innermost doll represents us as children. At this level (the archaic), the ego is not yet developed, and so we are part of a worldview in which we and the environment are one. As we grow up, the ego comes forward and for the sake of analogy we can say that doll number two and three (those enclosing/surpassing doll number one) represent the magical and mythical worldview. Most grow through these stages, although many adults are quite influenced by both. This will be that percentage of the population who think in terms of absolute good and evil and who see the world as a struggle between these forces; they believe that "might makes right", and that God is a male entity somewhere who will judge us to eternal perdition if we do not abide by his Book. These people not only need to find someone to look down on so that they can feel good about themselves, but they also worship authority blindly; be it government or church, their leaders are always right, and they will betray and abandon their kids or spouse if the group-consciousness demands such sacrifice.

The people who see the foolishness of this mindset are those who have taken the leap to the rational worldview—doll number four. At this level of cognition the herd-mentality is somewhat less prominent: people therefore, to a greater extent, think for themselves and are keen to find an identity. However, they have not yet matured to the point where they have begun to search within. Consequently, they are still exterior-oriented and show others who they are by their acquirement of material goods such as cars, boats, the right set of clothes, and other status symbols. People at this level also tend to be control-oriented and they are very supportive of the system as long as it serves their own narrowly defined interests/ambitions. Hence, also they are likely to betray friends and family if the group expects such sacrifice, and if they see an advantage they have no problem convincing themselves that the end justifies the means.

At some point, however, people at this stage will have stretched their worldview to its limit. They begin to realize that no matter how much material goods, money, and power they acquire it does nothing to mend or eliminate that fundamental feeling of emptiness generated by such a misdirected, externally-oriented form of "self-realization". One day, in this life or another, they will face the consequences of this recognition and they will move to the next worldview, which in this case corresponds to doll number five.

As we can see, it is at this level of consciousness—the integral/holistic—that people begin to understand what the Wholeness-concept implies; it is only here that they begin to take their ideals seriously, and not before they reach this level will they have an adequately structured relationship with their world to begin to acknowledge the wisdom that their feelings seek to impart. This is, in other words, an important cognitive leap for only when we reach this level can we see ourselves and our surroundings in a larger context and begin the conscious part of the self-realization process. Ken Wilber estimates that around 10 percent of the population have reached this level. The people here are concerned with issues such as solidarity, peace building, social justice, animal and human rights, organic food, and so on. They have a more developed sense of compassion, responsibility, and justice than those at the lower levels; they see no conflict between self-interest and public-interest, and so they contribute to the building of a less hierarchical and competition-oriented society.

The holistic/integral stage, however, only represents the beginning of our journey on the mystics' road, but while there are levels of comprehension which exceed this stage they are less important to categorize. For our purpose, all we need to know is that from this level on we begin to grasp more fully the implications of Wholeness: We constantly push forward and disintegrate the limits of understanding; we see more and more how we and the world are one; we gain access to ever more far-reaching perspectives; and we learn to see beyond the illusion of separation, space, and time. *Thus,* the present is transformed into a qualitatively different quantity; *thus,* the logic of fear loses its hold; *thus,* our confidence in the life process increases; *thus,* a spiral dynamic arises which ensures an ever more personal relationship with God; *thus,* we evolve into something more than we were; and *thus* we become more of that which we have always been, until we arrive at the innermost state of Union and join as One with the Absolute. To quote Wilber:

> "At each point in growth or development, we find a higher-order structure emerges in consciousness. . . . Each successively higher-order structure is more complex, more organized, and more unified—and evolution continues until there is only one Unity, ultimate in all directions, whereupon the force of evolution is exhausted, and there is perfect release in Radiance as the entire World Flux." (119.238)

13
BIOLOGY

"One of the paradoxes of twentieth-century science was that quantum theory ushered in a revolutionary change of perspective in physics revealing the limits of a reductionistic approach, while biology moved in the opposite direction, away from holistic approaches to an extreme reductionism." (97.xxii)

—*Rupert Sheldrake, biologist*—

IN THE PREVIOUS chapter we saw how the logic of fear creates a societal dynamic which negatively influences growth; we saw that it was the cause of mental illness, that it affected us all, and that our current mindset was the result of a stunted growth process.

Of course, that thought patterns play a vital role to mental health is nothing new. Even in conventional medicine this is recognized. When it comes to the question of physical health, however, its adherents have traditionally rejected the possibility that beliefs can have any bearing on the physical body. Building as they do on the matter-comes-first perspective, this is only natural as it would be absurd to think that something non-physical can affect anything physical. Nevertheless, our minds create *all* reality, and we shall now see how the physical body is energetically connected with the environment and how consciousness effects its materialization.

We shall, in other words, examine how the science of biology and medicine is compatible with the mystic perspective. We begin with biology and it should come as no surprise that most biologists have no idea that their discipline can be integrated with the mystics'. Educated as they are within a system which takes for granted that consciousness is an epi-phenomenon of matter, they see the world through the reductionistic[25] and mechanistic eyes of the Neo-Darwinian model of interpretation. They therefore look to the gene pool for the answers to the mystery of life and until recently believed that, as soon as our genome (our total genetic set) was identified, they would have found what they were looking for.

Still, it did not pan out that way. By the year 2000, scientists at the Human Genome Project had completed their mission but they were surprised with the results. Since they already knew that there were more than 100.000 different proteins in the human body, they expected to find more than 100.000 different genes (seeing as the genes produce the proteins) but they found fewer than 25.000. We can appreciate how remarkable this was when we take into consideration that creatures as simple as the ringworm (it consists of 959 cells) and the sea urchin has roughly the same amount and that flowers such as the lily has approximately 30 times more DNA material in its cells than us.

In other words, it became clear that the number of genes could not explain our complexity any more than the number of letters in the alphabet could explain the intricacy of literary history's collected works. Thus, scientists had to revise their ideas about the workings of our DNA—and they also had to deal with some other revelations that the theory of evolution seemed unfit to explain.

To begin with, its fundamental premise is that all life has evolved from one single cell in the primordial soup. If that were the case, one would expect the different species' DNA to mirror those developments that science since then claims to have taken place—and as our DNA is 96 percent identical to the chimpanzee's, some will indeed use it as proof of our lineage back to the apes. As the different species' genome was revealed, however, this linkage became less apparent, for as NOAA scientist David Busbee explains:

---

[25] Reductionism is an approach to the world which presents intricate relationships in a highly simplified (I would say distorted) form. It is a theory based on the belief that living organisms in the end is nothing but the result of electrochemical interactions on the molecular level; that one can explain a complex set of facts/phenomena/ structures by another, simpler set; and that the whole can never be anything more than the sum of its parts.

"It became obvious to us that every human chromosome had a corollary chromosome in the dolphin. . . . We have found that the dolphin genome and the human genome basically are the same. It's just that there's a few chromosomal rearrangements that have changed the way the genetic material is put together."(127.198)

Considering that humans and dolphins belong to different branches on the evolutionary tree this is a mystery to Neo-Darwinians. Even so, as we know, the new theory of existence turns their worldview on its head. According to this theory, consciousness is all there is and what we perceive as matter is the result of the underlying pressure of energy fields. In the chapter on quantum physics, we saw how these fields are nothing but figments of our imagination and that matter therefore, more correctly, can be seen as a temporary/secondary reality resulting from the frequency band on which our consciousness operates. We also saw how we live in a holographic Universe (meaning one in which each fragment is not only interconnected with the Totality but also contains it) and that time and space is an illusion. We shall now see how this understanding of the world is compatible to the body of research found in biology. We shall see how numerous biologists have come to the same conclusions about the world as the mystics[26], and we shall see how life is manifested as seen from this perspective. Hopefully, this will help us understand why the DNA of dolphins is so like ours—but let us first start with us and see how we as multidimensional beings are connected with the environment.

---

[26] For more on this from one of the leading biologist's perspective, see ROBERT LANZA, *BIOCENTRISM: HOW LIFE AND CONSCIOUSNESS ARE THE KEYS TO UNDERSTANDING THE TRUE NATURE OF THE UNIVERSE.*

13.1 AN INTRODUCTION ON HOW SPIRIT CREATES MATTER

"What we regard as ordinary physical matter is simply an idea that occupies a world frame common to all minds. The universe is literally a collective thought, and we have a very powerful say in the reality manifest in our particular sector."(116.331)

—Lyall Watson, biologist—

According to the new paradigm, we and the Universe are one multi-dimensional Being. Only a small portion of our energy manifests as us/matter in our part of the Universe, and just as the physicists know that more than 90 percent of the Universe's energy is invisible to us (they call the remaining energy dark matter because, while it is not present "here", they know it is there) mystics know that only a small part of our energy personality is present on this plane.[27]

We can explain this by looking at it as if we have a physical body, an emotional body, a mental body, and a spiritual body which are part of our energy personality. They are all aspects of one energetically interconnected whole and the main difference is that the physical body is that part of us which is pushed down to the lowest vibratory frequency—and which we therefore consider "real".

To continue with the analogy used in part one (the one in which the earth symbolizes the Universe and our energy-personality was being compared to islands which below the surface were connected to the earth's core) we can see our physical body as that part of us which we see above the surface. Consequently, we tend to confuse it with our entire being, but our emotional, mental, and spiritual body is equally real. The

---

[27] For more on this as seen from the mystics' perspective, see MAX HEINDEL, THE ROSICRUCIAN COSMO CONCEPTION; PARAMAHANSA YOGANANDA, MAN'S ETERNAL QUEST; and SRI AUROBINDO, ON YOGA: THE SYNTHESIS OF YOGA.

only thing that separates them from each other is their vibratory level, one being faster than the other (as measured in Angstrom units).

As we know from science, the higher the frequency, the more highly diversified the information those frequencies carry. Hence, the Higher self has access to a perspective that exceeds ours, as our senses are only concerned with that which exists at the same vibratory frequency as the physical body. In fact, we register only a minute fraction even of that, for out of the electro-magnetic spectrum of waves our eyes only respond to the small range of 0.4 to 0.7 thousandths of millimeters. This is like an infinitesimal percent of the available spectrum and so one should not be surprised that these "higher" aspects cannot be observed by the physical eye. Even so, these "higher" energetic bodies are our connection to the Universe's innermost dimensions. According to the analogy, the spiritual body is that part of us which is closest to the Core and just like an island builds on the foundation of the earth, so the physical body is built on it.

Now it must be said that this is greatly oversimplified. In reality, the spirit is equally present here as elsewhere, it's just that it hides its face in what we think of as dead matter. The point of the analogy is just to give an idea of how we and the cosmos are energetically connected—and from this it should be obvious that everything manifested on this plane is the result of an energy pattern which has its roots in the deeper parts of our greater Being.

Our bodies, in other words, are coming into being as a result of the universal energy that underlie and interpenetrate everything. The way it happens is that the causal energy (our soul) provides the framework for and defines our growth process, for the Universe is so arranged that everything manifested in our system finds its form based on an inherent blueprint. This means that everything in the physical Universe—every seed, cone, nut, egg, and embryo—carries an idea inside which it grows towards and realizes through its own process. Again, remember that time is an illusion. From the higher perspective past, present, and future all exist simultaneously and therefore an acorn is already, in a sense, a full-grown tree and an egg is also a full-grown hen—it is just that the intrinsic energy pattern/potential is not yet (as we see time) fulfilled.

This, of course, is according to the mystics' perspective. But the idea that all creatures have an inherent, fully developed energy pattern which they realize is also found in biology, where it evolved as a result of research done by scientists such as Hans Driesch. In the late 1800s he discovered how, at a very early stage in the growth process, he could split organisms such as sea urchins into several parts and yet each portion would evolve into fully grown, perfectly developed species. This did not fit with the reductionist hypothesis and in the 1940s the American neuroanatomist Harold S. Burr strengthened the holistic theory with his discovery that different seeds and eggs (for instance unfertilized salamander eggs) had an electric field/growth template identical to the one found in mature individuals.

It was already known that life had a unique ability to regenerate. We take for granted that we can take a branch off a tree, plant it, and create a new tree. We also know that our wounds heal and in some animals, like the salamander, the ability to regenerate is even more startling. We can remove its tail and limbs and they will grow back fully functional and the butterfly's metamorphosis from a crawling caterpillar to flying creature is no less impressive.

Now, our consciousness is so subdued that we rarely marvel at the miracles of life. But no matter how spectacular or mundane we find such things the reductionistic worldview is unfit to explain them. Inspired by modern physics therefore, in the 1920s, the idea of *morpho-genetic fields* became popular among certain biologists. As we may recall, it was at this time the superior influence of fields on matter was recognized and some biologists began to think of life as produced by morphogenetic fields. Simply translated, *morphogenetic* means "form-generating" fields— fields that are all-pervading and bring all form into being. Rupert Sheldrake, the leading theorist, describes them thus:

> "[Morphic fields] are self-organizing wholes. . . . They attract the systems under their influence towards characteristic forms and patterns of activity, whose coming-into-being they organize and whose integrity they maintain. . . . Morphic fields contain other morphic fields within them in a nested hierarchy or holarchy."(98.316)

According to biologists like Sheldrake, everything is organized and formed by such fields. The way they see it, there are fields that organize atoms, cells, organs, nervous systems, bone structure, you name it! It's a field for everything that exists and each field is superior and/or subordinate to another field's influence. Thus, this planet's organisms are part of the earth's morphic field; it again is part of the solar system's, which in turn is part of the galaxy's, and so on. These fields do not only regulate the formation of matter and life, but they also affect our ideas and behaviors. Hence, there are informational fields, social fields, behavioral fields, and so on—and for biologists like Sheldrake, there are not any natural laws.

If we think about it, the idea of a law presumes an eternal and unchanging state and this does not compute with our knowledge of the Universe. Instead, these biologists believe that the longer something has been the way it is—the longer, for instance, the boiling point of water has been 100 degrees—the more likely it is that it will continue to be so. As Sheldrake describes it:

> "[This theory] proposes that nature is habitual. All animals and plants draw upon and contribute to a collective memory of their species. Crystals and molecules also follow habits of their kind. Cosmic evolution involves an interplay of habit and creativity."(97.x)

Therefore, just like a habit, the more established, becomes harder for us to break so the same goes for the Universe. But no matter how fixed a pattern is, changes will at some point occur. To us, these habits may seem as laws, as we are born into a Universe that has operated the way it does for a very long time. However, if we ask where the law of gravity was before the Big Bang, we realize that even the most fundamental aspects of existence, at some point, must have come into being.

Consequently, biologists like Sheldrake see the world as in a state of flux. Everything is a creative, ever-changing process of creation and no matter how long things have appeared as they do, one cannot take for granted that it will always be that way. On the contrary, everything is open to change and awaiting the next evolutionary leap.

According to these biologists, what pushes evolution forward is the constantly increasing amount of information generated within the system, for just as the collective consciousness is continually recreated as a result of the dynamics between itself and the individuals involved, so it is with other fields. We have seen how the collective consciousness matures (and thus becomes something more than what it was) on account of our individual and collective experiences. And even if the other fields do not influence individuals with a consciousness exactly like ours, there is a form of awareness present within everything.

To these biologists, therefore, *memory is inherent in nature* and it is the interactions between the parts and the whole that generate change. As a result of this dynamic, an increasing amount of experience is stored within the system; this benefits the entire creation and when the amount of information has reached a certain threshold Consciousness takes its evolution to a higher level of operation.

As we can see, these biologists view life from the consciousness-comes-first perspective and so the Neo-Darwinians have shunned them. For instance, an editorial in the science journal Nature described Sheldrake's *A New Science of Life* as "the best candidate for burning there has been for many years."(97.xxix) Even so, despite their opposition to anything that smacks of a paradigm shift, Sheldrake's work speaks for itself. In his books, he documents several phenomena that the Neo-Darwinians cannot explain and his research supports the new paradigm.

We shall have more to say on people like Sheldrake and supporting research later. The point here was to present a biological interpretation model that fits with everything we have talked about and we shall now take a closer look at how we and the Universe are connected. In keeping with the theory already presented, the mystics claim that the physical body is connected with the deeper parts of our being through the activity of these fields. There are medical doctors who have come to the same conclusions and Dr. Richard Gerber describes this connection thus:

> "The physical body is actually a complex network of interwoven energy fields. The energetic network, which represents the physical/cellular framework, is organized and nourished by "subtle" energetic systems that coordinate

electrophysiologic and hormonal function as well as cellular structure within the physical body. It is primarily from these subtle levels that health and illness originate."(41.43)

The "subtle" energy network Gerber describes consists mainly of the meridian and the chakra system. The meridian is an energy-supply system that supposedly runs through the body. Through this system flows what the Chinese call *Chi*—the life force. Traditional Chinese medicine (acupuncture) is built on this concept, and the idea is that by inserting needles at specific points along the meridian pathways one can dissolve energy blockages causing pain and disease. Western doctors have long been skeptical of the existence of the meridian system because they have not been able to measure it with their instruments, but nevertheless many patients will testify that it has helped them heal problems that Western medicine could not remedy.

On account of this, some will argue that the existence of the meridian system is implicitly proven. And for more scientifically acceptable proof one can point to the research of Dr. Robert O. Becker who demonstrated that our strongest electric fields correspond to the acupuncture points, as well as professors Kim Bong Han, Jean Claude Darras, and Pierre de Vernejoul who have done experiments which seem to confirm its existence[28].

When it comes to the chakra system it is mentioned by virtually every Eastern religious and yogic tradition[29]. It is usually referred to as seven (some reckon more) energy wheels/centers that connect the physical body to the larger part of our energy personality. These energy centers are said to be distributed from the lower end of the spine to the top of the head. According to the mystical tradition, the lower two chakras are related to the physical experience; they have to do with reproduction,

---

[28] By injecting radioisotope liquid into the acupuncture points and tracking its course with high-speed CAT scanners, Darras and Vernejoul concluded that bioelectrical energy is transported along the meridians.

[29] For more on the chakra system see JOHN WHITE (ED.), *KUNDALINI: EVOLUTION AND ENLIGHTENMENT*.

survival instincts, and our attachment to earth. The next three chakras are associated with our personal development; they say something about the command we have over ourselves and our lives, our ability to give and receive love, and our ability to verbalize how we see ourselves and our surroundings. The last two chakras, located at the brow and the top of the head, are of a spiritual nature; they speak about our spiritual connection, our intuition, insight, and clairvoyance—and to the extent that our chakra system functions optimally, it is supposed to bring our inherent potential to the surface.

Each chakra center is an energy wheel that takes energy from a higher form/frequency and channels it down to the physical level. Buddhist and Hindu philosophy have much to say about these energy wheels and a variety of meditation techniques are designed whose purpose it is to balance the chakras and optimize the flow of energy. We have already seen how matter is light that is pushed down to a slow vibration (below the speed of light) and talking about the chakras, we see this reflected in the color of each energy wheel: The first is red, the next is orange, the third is yellow, the fourth is green, the fifth is blue, the sixth is dark blue, and the top is purple—just like the rainbow's colors. And when all these energy wheels are perfectly calibrated, the fusion will result in a white aura, i.e., a white bio-energetic field.

Not many people can see the aura, but some are more perceptive and they can describe the nuances of this light. With something called the AuraMeter and Kirlian photography it is also possible to take a picture and from such images we can deduce the quality of our personal morphogenetic field. In the future, studies of the auric field will most likely be important for the field of medicine, for all bodily ills manifest as a result of an energy imbalance/blockage and we can see this reflected in the aura *before* it results in a physical symptom.

Prevention of disease, therefore, is one reason why people are concerned with their energy wheels and try to influence them through meditation and other cognitive efforts. But as a well-functioning chakra machinery is supposed to be of vital importance to those who want to realize their inner potential, this is an equally important motivation. We have already seen how the normal adult brain is the result of stagnant growth process and that, at this point in our evolution, we are far from our inherent potential. Still, by becoming more aware of our relation-ship to the environment, we can reach levels of consciousness that are unknown. Talking about it earlier, this may already have seemed like a complicated process. Now that we are talking about subtle energies and balancing chakras, it may seem like an even more daunting task, for how can one work with—and balance—energies one cannot even see?

This, I believe, is an unnecessary concern. The balancing of these energies takes care of itself as we begin walking the mystics' way and the calibrating dynamic is as follows: The more we correct our mistaken beliefs and erroneous thought patterns, the more balanced the relationship to our surroundings becomes. The more harmonious the relationship between ourselves and the environment is, the more balanced our energetic machinery will be—and the more balanced this becomes, the more optimally we will make use of the universal energy.

In other words, the one follows the other, and the process takes care of itself as we walk the mystic's path. On the whole then, one can say that it is the same two-way dynamic between us and the bio-energetic field as we previously described between the fragments and the Whole in relation to the morphogenetic fields: Not only will thought patterns more aligned with the Wholeness-concept result in a more harmonious energy field, but the qualitative upgrade of that field will in turn elevate our thinking. There is a beneficial to-and-fro process ensuring that the higher the vibration of one variable, the more advantageous the greater outcome will be.

Physically, we see this dynamic manifest as follows: Each chakra wheel is directly affiliated with one of the body's endocrine glands. These glands control the production of hormones, endorphins, and similar substances and these substances do not only affect the function of our immune system but act upon the fluids/nervous system in the brain. From this we can see how an optimally functioning energetic system affects the body, including the brain, and many consciousness researchers also believe that it can even change our DNA.

We shall have more to say about this DNA upgrade later. But first we need to become better acquainted with DNA itself, so that we know what role it plays in our lives.

13.2 EPIGENETICS

"The latest science leads us to a worldview not unlike that held by the earliest civilizations, in which every material object in nature was thought to possess a spirit." (67.155)

—*Bruce Lipton, professor of biology*—

Simply put, the DNA molecule is a chemical code—an energetic signature—which at any given time reflects who we are. It is estimated that we consist of some 50 trillion cells and in the center of each cell there is a nucleus consisting of 23 pairs of chromosomes. These chromosomes contain our DNA, and we can see this as the place in us where the blueprint for our being is stored.

Looking at the DNA molecule we find an exceedingly long thread, shaped like a spiral staircase. It is this staircase, this double helix, that contains our genes, and a gene is that portion of the DNA strand which is required to make a protein. There are more than 100.000 different proteins in our body and even if we also need some other things to keep it going, like sugar and fat, it is the proteins that build and operate the body's machinery.

In other words, we find in our DNA the instruction manual and manufacturing base for the body's primary constituents. And until recently biologists were in general agreement, believing that the DNA molecule was an all-powerful dictator that told the body what to do and how. They assumed that we were born with one set of genes and that these genes not only governed all aspects of our appearance and functioning but also (to a large extent) our inclinations, aspirations, and thought processes—i.e., our personality.

They were right in so far that our DNA, to some extent, determines the appearance/functioning of our body and that some diseases therefore can be traced back to a genetic defect. Even so, this accounts for no more than 2 percent of our health problems and research indicates that we have greatly overestimated the genes' ability to control our lives. This research shows that our genes, instead, are subordinate to the environment and that we, with our thoughts and behavior, have a great influence on the design/workings of the DNA strand.

In biology, this body of research has given rise to the discipline of epigenetics. *Epi* means "above and beyond" and those involved are working to determine how (and to what degree) the environment affects our genes. When it comes to this study, there is increasing agreement among biologists that the traditional model of interpretation cannot explain the new findings and that radical thinking is needed to make sense of it all. This is where the consciousness-comes-first perspective comes into the equation and we shall now see how it brings together the current body research.

13.2.1 LIVING MATTER

When it comes to the biologists' understanding of the world, it followed naturally from the old paradigm. They thought that matter was dead and that consciousness arose as a result of electrochemical impulses between the brain's various components. From this outset it seemed evident that awareness was created by the brain and that the brain was the body's command center. Furthermore, since everything consisted of cells, it seemed natural to conclude that the cell's nucleus (where the DNA was located) was its "brain"—i.e., the part of the cell that dictated everything else what to do.

The scientists, however, were surprised when, after removing the nucleus, they found that the cells could live on for months. The cells not only continued to eat, breathe, digest, and rid themselves of waste as if nothing had happened, but they could also communicate with other cells and choose the most appropriate pattern of response to external stimuli. In fact, the *only things they could not do* was to reproduce lost and damaged proteins, divide, and create new cells. Thus, it became obvious that the nucleus could not be the brain but had to be the place where the construction manual and manufacturing base was stored. Bruce Lipton, a professor of biology, explains:

"DNA does not control biology, and the nucleus itself is not the brain of the cell. . . . A cell's life is fundamentally controlled by the physical and energetic environment with only a small contribution by its genes. Genes are simply molecular blueprints used in the construction of cells, tissues and organs. The environment serves as a "contractor" who reads and engages those genetic blueprints and is ultimately responsible for the character of a cell's life. It is a single cell's "awareness" of the environment that primarily sets into motion the mechanisms of life."(67.43,xiii)

According to Lipton, "genes are physical memories of an organism's learned experiences." He compares the cell (and therefore the DNA) to a microchip that we, with our behavior, feelings, and thinking continually program and reprogram with different information, but to understand this better, let us take a closer look at our cells.

We already know that within the nucleus we find the chromosomes with the DNA strand. Outside this nucleus, we find a nutritious liquid that represents the cell's internal environment, and this is held in place by a very thin membrane—its surface. There are many different types of cells (skin cells, hair cells, blood cells, bone cells, brain cells, nerve cells, etc.) and they all have specialized tasks. Nerve cells, for instance, is busy keeping tabs on the environment and responding to it is their specialty. As long as they take care of their job other cells can focus on other things and together, they create highly complex organisms.

Thus, a body is the result of an impressive collaboration between cells and proteins running the machinery. As mentioned, there are more than hundred different types of proteins and they are built from 20 different amino acids (we can see the amino acids as the letters and the proteins as the words). The amino acids, for their part, are positively or negatively charged—and so it is that our cells are energy-sensitive organisms. The proteins are found everywhere in the cell (including the membrane) and they act as its sensory- and response apparatus; they read energy fields, sense electromagnetic fluctuations, and react accordingly.

Based on the messages they receive from the environment they will know what to do and then they tell the genes to produce more or less of the requested materials (and not vice versa as previously thought!).

As we can appreciate from this, our DNA is highly responsive to the influence of its environment. It is up to us to decide what kind of stimulus we subject it to, for it is all about vibrations. *Every* thought and emotion have an energy signature that holds a certain vibration, and so does all matter. With thoughts, feelings, beliefs, habits, and behaviors, therefore, we can change the qualitative nature of our energetic environment. If, for example, we are stressed, irritated, frustrated, and our thinking is influenced by the logic of fear, we will create less than optimal working conditions for our cells. The same is also true if we smoke, drink, eat unhealthy foods, or otherwise live in a polluted environment. The more we subject our body to toxicity and heavy metals the worse off we will be, and that's why products such as aluminum-free deodorants and fluoride-free toothpastes are a good idea.

As we live in an age in which virtually everything we encounter, from the carpets we buy to the food we eat, is treated with various toxins and chemicals, the list is not exhaustive. However, we shall not go into detail on this particular issue. Information is provided else-where, and the point here is just to show how the body is associated with the mind/environment—and why bad habits are a bad idea. Based on our energetic vibration we will activate or deactivate different parts of our genome and there is plenty of research available that confirms this fact. Dean Ornish, for example, an American professor of medicine, has shown that by changing diet and lifestyle for 90 days we can also change the activity of more than 500 genes. His research was done on cancer patients and, according to his studies, certain disease preventing genes were up-regulated (turned on) and certain disease promoting genes were down-regulated (turned off).

Another study that has demonstrated molecular changes in DNA was done by researchers from the University of Wisconsin-Madison and the Institute of Biomedical Research in Barcelona, Spain, in 2013. After studying a group of experienced practitioners who partook of mindfulness meditation, they found that genetic changes had taken place and that the new genetic set-up helped participants keep cool under pressure.

In other words, the old idea that we are at the mercy of our genes is proven wrong. Instead, many of our genes are "buttons" we can turn on and off and depending on which ones we have activated we will be healthy or sick. Thus, we cannot blame our genes for the prevalence rates of diseases such as cancer, obesity, alcoholism, and diabetes. The problem can more properly be attributed to our way of life, and there is so much research confirming this link that we shall not elaborate here.

The interesting point about such research is that it shows how lifestyle changes affect our DNA and researchers at the HeartMath Institute in the U.S. have taken this one step further. This institute was established in 1991 and its scientists have performed experiments proving that our mind affects not only the body but its surroundings. In this context, a series of experiments done between 1992 and 1995 are worth a look. The scientists took samples of human DNA, isolated these samples in a beaker, and examined whether it was possible to influence the DNA with thoughts and feelings. Note that the DNA molecule were *physically separate* from the subject and that it therefore, according to the old paradigm, would be mind-boggling if they were able to detect changes. Yet, that is precisely what happened. Gregg Braden elaborates:

> "They performed a series of tests involving up to five people trained in applying coherent emotion. Using special techniques that analyze the DNA both chemically and visually, the researchers could detect any changes that happened. The results were undeniable and the implications were unmistakable. The bottom line: Human emotion changed the shape of the DNA! Without physically touching it or doing anything other than creating precise feelings in their bodies, the participants were able to influence the DNA molecules in the beaker. In the first experiment, which involved only one person, effects were produced by a combination of "directed intention, unconditional love and specific imagery of the DNA molecule." In the words of one of the researchers, "These experiments revealed that different intentions produced different effects on the DNA molecule causing it to either

wind or unwind." Clearly, the implications are beyond anything that's been allowed for in traditional scientific theory until now."(14.52)

We shall have more to say on the research done at the HeartMath Institute later—and if anyone have difficulties understanding how our thoughts can affect DNA *even when* it is separated from us, the answer will be provided. The point here was simply to show that the DNA strand by its very nature is flexible and that it responds to our thoughts and feelings.

Now, as the Neo-Darwinians cannot understand how something nonphysical can influence anything physical, such research has been difficult to accept. Even so, as seen from the consciousness-comes-first perspective, these findings are not surprising. After all, if consciousness is all there is, it is no more difficult to imagine it altering our DNA than reshaping the neural pathways in the brain; *both are the result of consciousness* and so their form and function will naturally be affected by our thoughts. At least to some extent, for we must remember that some conditions, such as Hypophosphatasia and Down syndrome, are caused by a genetic defect—and it will be no less difficult for the affected person to think himself healthy, as it would be for a man to think himself into a woman.

Yet, as consciousness is all there is, we can also see such conditions as a result of the workings of consciousness. Such incurable diseases, however, are produced at a more basic level and should be seen as the result of a choice made by our soul. To understand this, we need to remember that there is no right and wrong for Consciousness; for our soul there is only *experience*—and seen from its perspective a life as mentally retarded (or plagued by disease) is no less informative and unique than the other lives we live. Such lives provide us with access to experiences and perspectives not offered by a normal life and that some conditions are incurable, therefore, does not impugn the consciousness-comes-first perspective.

When we talk about diseases, experiences, and the new existence theory, what is said also applies to non-genetically induced conditions. For although we have some influence over our disease when it comes to such things as cancer, arthritis, multiple sclerosis, and diabetes, we have no guarantee that thought- and lifestyle changes will make us healthy; it will certainly increase our prospects for survival, but illness can occur because of so many variables that to change only some will not guarantee anything.

To say a bit more, we have already seen that according to the new existence theory a disease will always arise as a result of our energy vibration. Seen from this perspective, it is a physical manifestation of an energy imbalance in the non-physical parts of our being (usually in the emotional or mental body), and it becomes "real" because of our failure to correct the imbalance at this level. In energy medicine (the new medical science) these obstructed energy patterns are called *miasms*. Richard Gerber, a doctor of internal medicine, describes the phenomenon thus:

> "Miasms are energetic tendencies which predispose an individual toward manifesting . . . illness. Most miasms are either inherited or acquired during the course of an individual's lifetime. . . . Miasms weaken the natural body defenses in particular areas, creating a tendency toward manifesting different types of illness at a later time. Acquired miasms may be caused by exposure to a variety of noxious agents including bacteria, viruses, toxic chemicals, and even radiation.
>
> . . . Because they can be transmitted from generation to generation, miasms represent an energetic pathway by which events in the life of a parent can be transmitted to their offspring."(41.260)

The energy-personality Gerudas has more to say about these miasms and their transmissive patterns:

> "Miasms are stored in the subtle bodies. . . . Some miasms are passed on to the next generation genetically by inhabiting the molecular level of the physical body, which is the genetic code. A miasm is not necessarily a disease; it

is the potential for disease. Indeed, miasms are crystallized patterns of karma.

. . . Miasms may be dormant in the subtle bodies and aura for long periods of time. They are organized in the subtle bodies, and gradually, through the biomagnetic fields about the physical body, miasms penetrate the molecular level, then the cellular level (individual cells) and finally the physical body. . . . There are three types of miasms, including *planetary*, *inherited* and *acquired* miasms. Planetary miasms are stored in the collective consciousness of the planet and the ethers. They may penetrate the physical body, but are not stored there. Inherited miasms are stored in the cellular memory of individuals. Acquired miasms are acute or infectious diseases or petrochemical toxicity acquired during a given lifetime."(41.262)

As we see, disease can be the result of a disturbance at several levels. The least individual-specific level (yet the most fundamental) is the *planetary*, and examples of such conditions are the plague that struck Europe in the 1300s, as well as mad cow disease, bird flu, SARS, and the current proliferation of cancer. Such diseases are the result of energy imbalances at a deep, non-personal level; they have to do with problems facing us as a civilization, and they mirror environmental conditions and widespread beliefs so incompatible with the collective's well-being that a certain percentage of us necessarily will have to pay.

Disease that has its roots in *inherited* miasms is more "concrete". It can be traced back to conditions in our ancestral history (that our parents, for instance, lived in a radioactive/toxic environment), while disease occurring at the *acquired* level is the most individual-specific—that which most directly can be traced back to our own lifestyle and thinking.

This is the theory. Accordingly, the more individual-specific a disease, the easier it is to heal the energetic imbalance that generates illness. In actuality, however, it's not only hard to separate between the levels but also each individual's likelihood of regaining health. There are many variables one must take into consideration. Every condition is unique to the person concerned and it is impossible to deal satisfactorily with the issue in general terms. If you want to know more about the future of medicine, therefore, I will direct attention to books like Richard Gerber's *Vibrational Medicine*[30] and Finley Eversole (ed.) *Energy Medicine Technologies.*

Now, when it comes to holistic versus traditional medicine, it is a controversial issue. Advocates of the old paradigm warn against New Age clinicians and they take for granted that if traditional medicine cannot help them nothing can. They envision alternative therapists in general to be incompetent and/or unscrupulous snake-oil salesmen and have no faith in their methods. This is perhaps not surprising. For one, they are right to point out that much of the research done on alternative medicine is poorly documented and, secondly, it is easy to explain positive findings with the placebo effect or various other factors.

As seen from the matter-comes-first perspective, this will be the only logical explanation—and yet, despite their mistrust, more and more people put their faith in alternative medicine. The apologists of the old paradigm cannot imagine that this trend builds on an understanding that is superior to theirs. Consequently, they will have to conclude that the growing popularity of alternative medicine reflects an increasing naivety in the general population, but as we shall see this is not the case.

---

[30] Other books I suspect will be important for the future of medicine are ROBERT O. BECKER, *CROSS CURRENTS: THE PERILS OF ELECTROPOLLUTION, THE PROMISE OF ELECTRO-MEDICINE* as well as BECKER AND MARINO, *ELECTROMAGNETISM AND LIFE.* Several hundred scientific studies have been done revealing that "invisible forces" of the electromagnetic spectrum impact every facet of our biological regulation and Becker is well versed in this field of study. Another important book confirming this is BARRY LYNES, *THE RIFE REPORT: THE CANCER CURE THAT WORKED!* By measuring the pulse/frequency of cancer viruses and exposing them to electromagnetic waves of the same pulse/frequency he successfully cured hundreds of cases of cancer in the 1930's. Other important work in this field has been conducted by the German biophysicist Fritz Albert Popp, for more on this check out LYNNE MCTAGGART, *THE FIELD: THE QUEST FOR THE SECRET FORCE OF THE UNIVERSE.*

14

MEDICAL SCIENCE

"The science of medicine is in the unfortunate situation of being built on a truth that does not exist. We have built a model of health and illness, birth and death, around an outmoded conceptual model of how the universe behaves, one which was fundamentally flawed from the beginning. While the physicists have been painfully eliminating the flaws from their own models, we have in medicine ignored those revisions totally."(32.13)

—*Larry Dossey, physician*—

CONVENTIONAL MEDICINE IS built on the assumption of a separation between matter and consciousness and its adherents believe that consciousness has its origins in the electrochemical impulses of the brain. This mechanical way of perception had its glory days from the 1870s to the 1950s but has since been in decline. The reason is that, by this time, more and more people had begun to take into consideration evidence suggesting that mind influences health; this evidence has become more and more prominent and so, from that time on, traditional medicine has moved in the direction of alternative medicine.

In other words, the science of medicine is in the midst of a paradigm shift; officially the old worldview still holds strong, but more and more doctors will agree that a growing body of research does not support the matter-comes-first perspective.

Back in the 1950's, one would be hard pressed to find anyone agreeing that minds could influence matter. Still, the placebo effect and other observations have made this view untenable, and so the dispute today is not whether our thinking influences matter but rather to what extent. For example, all doctors recognize that anorexia is the result of a patient's beliefs (although some think that they will one day find a gene that is responsible for the thoughts that produce this disease) but very few will go as far as to say the same about cancer. As such, they are conflicted when it comes to explaining the cause of disease, and not many doctors would go so far as to say that *all* diseases result from the workings of consciousness.

Despite that, some do—and they are growing in numbers. One of them is Larry Dossey, an American physician who has written 11 books documenting how the consciousness-comes-first perspective applies to medical science. Now, there are many doctors who know that our mind affects our own body but Dossey does not stop there: he shows how our mind can affect the well-being of others!

That we, with our thinking, can affect the health of others may come as a surprise. Taking into consideration all we have talked about, however, it is not that strange and if the idea seems nonsensical it is only because one has not yet put two and two together. Remember that, according to the new theory of existence, Consciousness is all there is and our mind knows no limit; *it's everywhere all the time*, and there is nothing that separates you from me. We have already been introduced to the holographic nature of our Universe and we have also seen how the non-locality principle, according to quantum physics, is a proven reality. In several books Dossey applies this principle to medical science and documents how it can benefit modern medicine.

We shall have more to say about the findings of consciousness research in the next part of the book, but Dossey himself is aware of this research and has no trouble finding documentation in support of his thesis. After 10 years of studying the evidence, he wrote *Healing Words,* and summarizes his findings thus:

> "I probed the scientific literature looking for evidence that prayer works. I found enormous amounts of evidence; over a hundred experiments conducted by adequate scientific methods, many under stringent laboratory conditions, of which more than half showed that prayer brings about significant changes in a variety of living beings."(33.13)

In other words, it is a proven fact that prayer works, and for those who want to know more about the evidence this book is a good place to start. The more than one hundred (131 to be exact) studies to which he refers is done on prayer-based/spiritual healing, and the material was originally collected by psychiatrist Daniel J. Benor and presented in his book *Healing Research*. In addition to this, there is research confirming that we, with our thoughts, have a direct and measurable impact on other organisms. In this case, Dossey refers to 141 experiments collected by psychologist William G. Braud. The focus of these studies is directed toward telepathy and the healing factor is not emphasized, yet they indicate that our thoughts affect everything from bacteria, plants, cells, and animals to other people—and the distance between participants is of no consequence.

As this corpus of research is presented elsewhere, we shall not spend too much time elaborating. I just want to point out that whether we are talking about healing through prayer, clairvoyance, or telepathy it is all a manifestation of the same phenomenon, being that all these "paranormal" occurrences can be explained by the fact that *consciousness is everything and that everything is interconnected with everything all the time. Therefore,* it is possible for us to perceive the actions of others elsewhere; *therefore,* it is possible to mentally influence the wellbeing of others; *therefore,* it is possible to connect with the minds of others no matter the distance; and *therefore* it is possible for all of this to take place even if we are isolated in cages (Faraday cages) where no known forms of electromagnetic energy can connect us with other people.

As we shall see in part four, all of this has been documented. And that such phenomena can occur even when we are shielded from the influence of all known fields is an indirect proof of our consciousness' omnipresent nature and the Universe's holographic structure. Dossey elaborates:

> "[The principle of non-locality suggests that] some aspect
> of ourselves is not confined to points in space and time, thus
> being omnipresent, infinite and eternal. After all, *non-local*
> does not mean "very big" or "very extensive". It suggests

an infinity of time and space, since a limited non-locality would be a contradiction.

In the West, this infinite aspect of the psyche has been referred to as the soul. Empirical evidence of prayer's power, then, is indirect evidence for the soul. It is also evidence of commonality with the Divine—"The divine within us"—since infinity, omnipresence and eternity are qualities we have also attributed to the Absolute."(33.26)

As we can see, Dossey is a doctor who knows how to accept the implications of the consciousness-comes-first perspective. He belongs to that percentage of the medical profession who can think outside the box and has managed to break away from the old paradigm. The vast majority of his colleagues, however, have not. They still find them-selves in that vague area between the old and the new worldview where nothing really makes sense.

This is hardly surprising being that they, through medical school, have been molded by the old paradigm; the reductionistic, mechanical, and materialistic worldview is the one that authorities have constructed from reasoning and it is commonly believed to have consolidated its position in the last couple of hundred years. No wonder, then, that most doctors have more than enough to contend with in trying to understand how our thoughts can affect our own body. Once they understand this, however, it will become more obvious how our mind can affect that of other's—so let us explore how this works.

14.1 THE RELATIONSHIP BETWEEN THOUGHTS AND ILLNESS

"I confidently express the hope and wish that relations between mysticism and medicine would become closer, and that there would be greater understanding and harmony. This harmony would result in great benefits for mystics, for doctors and—most importantly—for poor, suffering humanity." (7.140)

—Roberto Assagioli, psychiatrist—

First and foremost, our mind is a crucial component in the manifestation of any illness. This applies not only to the more obviously mentally produced diseases (anxiety, depression, schizophrenia, anorexia, etc.), but also to every other physical malady—cancer, MS, AIDS, you name it. We shall soon see why some more easily than others fall prey to such diseases but let us first look at the evidence confirming this controversial allegation.

I will use cancer as an example, being that it is a physical disease affecting hundreds of millions. Western medicine has put an enormous effort into finding a cure, and yet the survival rates for most types of cancer are much the same as they were 70 years ago. From this it seems clear that Western medicine has proven ineffective and so it is not very surprising that people, having been diagnosed with cancer, turn to other kinds of treatment. We have already seen the research of Dr. Dean Ornish confirm that, by changing our thought pattern and lifestyle, we can influence the genetic material so that tumor preventing genes are activated while those that accelerate growth become deactivated. Thus, that alternative treatment (other than chemotherapy) has something to offer is obvious, and for those who want to know more about it there are plenty of information on the net and elsewhere.

In any case, I shall not explore the pros and cons of traditional versus alternative forms of treatment. Even if some would argue that alternative treatment has a better effect, there are many who die after having relied on such remedy and this is a serious issue that each person must decide for him/herself. The way I see it, therefore, the only responsible advice to give a person diagnosed with cancer is to carefully review the existing literature with an open mind, especially paying notice to those that have dealt with the condition before. In this regard, I will recommend Massimo Mazzuko's documentary *Cancer: The Forbidden Cures*, and Ken Wilber's book *Grace and Grit*. The former presents several possible cures that have been withheld as a result of the pressure of big pharma, while the latter recounts Ken and his wife's experiences in relation to this sickness. They explore both traditional and alternative therapies and the book is a good introduction to all aspects of living with such a diagnosis.

When it comes to diseases like cancer, we must remember that there can be many reasons why they occur. In addition to thoughts, beliefs, and emotions, other factors involved are lifestyle issues such as food, drinking, and smoking. There are also more external factors involved (such as the conditions we work/live in), and let us not forget the soul's aspirations.

Hence, illness can arise due to a combination of many factors. We have already seen that the discordant energy patterns (miasms) behind it can be located at three levels, from the less to the more individual-specific, but *no matter where the potential for disease comes from* it is always the result of consciousness; it is never the product of random chance and, according to the new existence theory, we can see everything we encounter in life as something we have attracted for three possible reasons. The first has to do with our thought patterns in this life, the second has to do with karmic patterns, and the third reason would be as a challenge/ experience from the Universe/our soul, presented for the purpose of soul growth.

When it comes to the energy laws, these are the primary reasons why any situation occurs. Speaking of the cancer diagnosis, the first reason covers everything that has to do with our thinking in this incarnation; besides our beliefs and the emotions they generate, disease generated at this level can also be a result of the abovementioned lifestyle and environmental conditions. Remember that whether it is mental or physical events, we are talking about different patterns of energy—and that the more we surround ourselves with the lower vibrations, the more we weaken the immune system and increase the probabilities of attracting a host of bodily ills.

As to the second reason, the one having to do with karmic patterns, illness occurring at this level also has its roots in an energy pattern—it is just that it must be seen in a larger context than our present life. We may, for example, be born into the world with a karmic contract saying that we shall experience a serious illness, either to survive or die. We have already seen how this provides us (as well as others) with an opportunity for learning that we otherwise would have missed and there are a million reasons why a soul would choose this experience. Illness manifested at this level, therefore, is similar to the third reason being that the lessons offered is the most important aspect. The only difference is that the reasons for our choice, in this case, can be traced back to something in the past, as a sort of balancing out from the Universe's point of view.

For those with both feet firmly planted in the old paradigm, reasons number two and three will seem improbable and "unscientific". Despite that we shall soon enough see how consciousness research suggests that the karma- and reincarnation concepts are both real. When it comes to past-life experiences, for example, they can be induced through hypnosis, breathing techniques,[31] and psychedelic drugs, and as we shall see later, it is well known that such techniques can heal traumas that traditional psychiatry is unable to deal with.

For now, however, we shall forget about reasons two and three and concentrate on number one. That is to say *an aspect* of it, for we shall leave it as an open question to what extent our environment and lifestyle are the cause of disease. After all, it is well-established that these conditions play an important role for our wellbeing—and that it is for this reason that cancer is so prevalent in our time. That stress and psychological imbalance alone accounts for a relatively small portion of cancer statistics becomes clear when we take into consideration that Germany, in the period between 1940 and 1951, had far fewer incidences

---

[31] Together with his wife Christina, psychiatrist Stanislav Grof has developed one such method (Holotropic breathwork) which has proven remarkably successful in the psychiatric context. For more about it see GROF, *PSYCHOLOGY OF THE FUTURE* and GROF, *THE ADVENTURE OF SELF-DISCOVERY*.

than in the more recent past. Obviously, this period was full of hardship for the Germans, and some believe that it was the almost fat-free diet that did the trick.

Yet, no matter how unfortunate our diet and lifestyle choices may be, some can smoke 40 cigarettes a day their whole life without visibly being affected, while others develop lung cancer relatively quickly. Such differences cannot be explained as predestinated by our gene pool (as we have seen, genes are turned off and on as a result of environ-mental and psychological influence), and so it is in such matters that the impact of our psyche becomes apparent and interesting.

When it comes to this, there is plenty of research documenting the impact of mind and emotion in affecting health and illness. Tony Schwartz, a New York Times journalist and best-selling author, has more to say on this subject. For five years he traveled across the United States doing research on a book; he spoke with doctors, psychiatrists, scientists, as well as other professionals, and having looked at the research suggesting a connection between body and mind, summarized his findings thus:

> "I was struck by at least one unmistakable pattern. Put simply, what is healthy for the mind, emotions, and spirit consistently appears to promote physical health. Conversely, what's unhealthy for the mind, emotions, and spirit tends to make one vulnerable to disease and less able to recover from it successfully. The two emotions most consistently correlated with illness are depression, which leads to hopelessness and isolation; and chronic anger, which is stressful and alienating. The two emotions most associated with physical health are the capacity for love, which prompts feelings of security and intimacy; and hope or faith, which leads to a sense of meaning and resilience. In effect, emotions that encourage more connectedness and awareness appear to be healthy, while those that prompt separation and alienation are unhealthy."(95.199)

When it comes to the association between cancer and the psyche, psychiatrist Lawrence LeShan was a pioneer. In the 1950s, while the idea was still unheard of, he began to examine the relationship between different types of personality and the likelihood of attracting cancer. From his research material, consisting of more than 500 people, he concluded that there was a correlation. Tony Schwartz elaborates:

> "The first pattern LeShan unearthed was the over-whelming majority of cancer patients that had suffered a devastating personal loss in the year before being diagnosed with cancer. These losses ranged from the death of spouse, to losing a job, to having a child leave home for college. Whatever form the loss took, the result was that the patients uniformly felt they'd been robbed of their central reason for living. This led, in turn, to feelings of isolation, worthlessness, despair, and a deep sense of hopelessness about ever again leading a satisfying life. More than three-quarters of the cancer patients whom Le Shan studied had suffered this pattern of loss, versus just 12 present of the healthy control group."(95.202)

Another noticeable characteristic LeShan discovered was that many cancer patients had a tendency to suppress negative emotions; they would not acknowledge issues of fear and anger, and they consistently put the needs of others before their own. About 50 percent of the patients fit this pattern compared to 25 percent in the control group. The trend he discovered was so conspicuous that after studying a personality test done on 28 people (he knew nothing beforehand about their health), he guessed the correct diagnosis on 24 accounts, while three of the people he wrongly diagnosed had other diseases.

Since LeShan's studies scientists have confirmed his findings in relation to a range of diseases. For instance, while LeShan did cancer research, cardiovascular specialists Meyer Friedman and Ray Rosenman studied the connection between heart disease and the psyche and concluded that negative emotions (those that strengthen the feeling of separation) were even more crucial than lifestyle in the development of illness. By this time, Dr. Hans Selye had already shown that stress had a devastating impact not only on our physical but also our mental health, something Dr. Vernon Riley and many others have subsequently confirmed.

To say more about cancer research, in the 60's and 70's, internist D.M. Kissen also found links between the prevalence of cancer and the patients' inability to express feelings. He concluded that the more introverted a person was, the fewer cigarettes he/she could smoke before being diagnosed with cancer. Bernard Fox, another doctor doing similar research, found that depressed men had twice the risk of getting cancer as non-depressed. Other pioneers in this area were oncologist Carl Simonton and psychologist Stephanie Matthews (later Simoton, as she became his wife). In the 60's and 70's, they did a lot of important work, and Stanislav Grof summarizes it thus:

> "They reviewed the medical literature covering different aspects of the relationship between emotional factors and malignancy. According to them, there is general agreement in over two hundred articles which they analyzed that there is a relationship between the two; the question, thus, does not seem to be the existence or nonexistence of such a connection but its degree and practical significance. The personality characteristics of cancer patients and most plausible predisposing factors mentioned by the authors were: (1) great tendency to hold resentment and marked inability to forgive; (2) a tendency toward self-pity; (3) poor ability to develop and maintain meaningful long-term relationships; and (4) a very poor self-image. The Simontons suggested that a life-history pattern of basic rejection might be a possible common denominator behind all these personality characteristics. According to them, this life pattern frequently culminates in the loss of a serious love object six to eighteen months prior to the diagnosis."(47.109)

As you may remember, Grof was not just a psychiatrist but the world's leading LSD researcher. And through his work in LSD therapy, he quickly discovered how Carl and Stephanie Simonton's research matched his own. Grof explains further:

> "Many persons suffering from cancer proved to have a variety of serious psychological conflicts and emotional problems that predated the onset and diagnosis of their physical illness. As a matter of fact, in quite a few instances the nature of these emotional problems was such that it almost suggested an association of a causal nature. ... We saw surprisingly frequent instances of severe guilt, feelings of self-hatred, and autopunitive tendencies that had preceded the clinical manifestation of cancer by years or decades. It was not infrequent that cancer patients in their LSD session saw direct links between such tendencies within themselves and their malignancies." (47.108)

Grof mentions an interesting aspect of LSD research. As the patients, during the LSD session, came into contact with the deeper areas of their personality, they gained access to a perspective in which the connection between the outer and inner world became apparent. These patients, therefore, saw clearly how their inner energetic imbalance eventually manifested in a physical symptom, and this understanding is well-known for those familiar with expanded states of consciousness. Grof has more to say:

> "We frequently found that the area which was affected by primary cancer had been an object of the patients' increased attention for many years prior to the development of the tumor. ... It was not exceptional, for example, to find that a history of severe sexual psycho-traumatization and conflicts about sexuality in women preceded the development of gynecological cancer. Similarly, significant psycho-pathology related to the oral area and

ingestion of food antedated the onset of stomach cancer in
several individuals."(47.109)

Grof wrote this in the mid 70's and since then a growing body of research has confirmed this picture. This research not only shows that thoughts and feelings are important factors behind the emergence of disease, but also that our psyche plays an important role in recovery.

The surgeon Bernie Siegel wrote a book about this where he separates patients into three categories based on personality type. The first category consists of that percentage who on a subconscious level *wants* to be sick; they thrive in the role of victimhood and identify with the disease. It provides them with a sense of self, and they use it not only to gain attention and control over other people but also as an excuse not to deal with more fundamental problematic areas of life. He estimates that between 15 to 20 percent of all patients belong in this category. The next group consists of the vast majority, between 60 and 70 percent of all patients. People in this group are characterized as being naive and uncritical toward authority and so, when it comes to their wellbeing, they put all their faith in the doctor. In short, they accept everything he says, and they themselves take no responsibility for the disease.

The third category consists of 15 to 20 percent of the population, and they are the ones Siegel calls "unusual" and "survivors". Other doctors would call them "difficult" because they are the ones who ask all kinds of questions, who want to know everything about the disease, and who will only agree to a treatment they believe in. Siegel describes them like this:

> "Unusual patients refuse to be victims. They acquire knowledge and are specialists in taking care of themselves. They ask the doctor because they want to understand the treatment and take active part in it. They demand dignity, integrity and control, regardless of the disease."(99.42)

As can be expected, the people in this category have the best survival chances. They are also the most likely to choose alternative therapy—and what is more, they are the ones who manage to see illness as a meaningful experience *regardless* of the outcome. For no matter their choice of treatment, and no matter their mindset, many in this category also end up losing their battle against cancer. Even so, they have that rare ability to see the bigger picture behind their condition, and even if they die, they tend to live longer than their prognosis.

Siegel was introduced to the psyche's impact on matters of health on a seminar held by Carl and Stephanie Simonton in 1978. They were the first Westerners to use visualization techniques in the treatment of cancer (our brain does not know the difference between what we imagine and what we experience) and Siegel has this to say about their results:

> "Of the first 159 patients that were not expected to survive more than a year, 19 percent were completely rid of the cancer, and the disease was in remission in another 22 percent. The people who eventually succumbed did on average live twice as long as their prognosis."(99.37)

Siegel estimates that the survival rate for Simontons' patients was two and a half times higher than for normal patients, those who only used traditional treatment.[32] I say "only", for the better-off patients did not necessarily refrain from chemotherapy. Many of them went through this but they also tried other treatment.

So, what is it that separates the survivors from the rest? This is the big question and no simple answer exists. Nevertheless, it seems clear that the more positively we think and feel, the more we avoid victim roles, and the more we live life from a place of integrity and respect for ourselves and others, the better are our chances. Psychiatrist Wallace C. Ellerbroek has more to say:

> "Personally, I am . . . convinced that anger and depression

---

[32] David Spiegel, a professor of psychiatry at Stanford, has done research confirming the same. He established support groups whose purpose it was to give the patients a sense of acceptance, calm, security, and control in relation to the disease. These patients' survival rates were two times higher than the control group, and even if many died they lived twice as long as the patients in the control group. SEE SPIEGEL, *LIVING BEYOND LIMITS*.

are pathological emotions, and that they are directly responsible for the vast majority of human diseases, including cancer. I have studied more than 57 extremely well-documented so-called "cancer miracles". By cancer miracle I mean that a person does not die when it most certainly and without doubt was expected. At a certain moment in time, these people decided that they didn't want to live with anger and depression the short time they had left, so they changed their attitudes becoming loving, caring, no longer angry, no longer depressed, and able to talk to the people they loved.

Every one of these 57 people showed the same pattern. They completely let go of their depression and their anger by consciously deciding to do so. As they did this, the tumors also began to shrink."(99.213)

I do not know what kind of treatment these patients chose, if any. But Ellerbroek touches upon an important point that medical science cannot explain and that is that solid tumors occasionally withdraw. This has been known to happen even without treatment and in medical terms it is called a spontaneous remission. It is estimated to take place in one out of 80.000 cases, so it is not common—but the important thing is that it occurs.[33]

This phenomenon, after all, remains unexplained as of today, but as seen from the consciousness-comes-first perspective it is no great mystery. The new existence theory tells us that if the momentum for change in the underlying energy is sufficient, any change in matter is possible: And in those cases where the clinical picture does not represent the soul's wish to leave this world behind, but rather is the result of an energy imbalance—a miasm—it follows quite naturally that the physical

---

[33] For an incredible book documenting a miraculous spontaneous remission (as well as the near-death experience) check out ANITA MOORJANI, *DYING TO BE ME*. She was in the final stages of terminal lymphoma when she had a near-death experience, and, after coming back from it, was completely healed within days. Another interesting spontaneous remission and near-death experiencer is Mellen-Thomas Benedict who wrote the *HITCHHIKERS GUIDE TO THE OTHER SIDE: OR WHAT TO DO IF YOU WAKE UP DEAD* about his encounter with death.

symptom will disappear as soon as it is corrected. The same will also be the case when the purpose of disease was a certain experience, for as soon as we have taken its lesson to heart it has played out its role and the road is open to recovery.

That there is a natural explanation behind these apparent miracles does, of course, not in any way diminish their significance. Those who experience them fully know what it means to receive the gift of life, and such spontaneous remissions do not only occur in cancer patients. They have also been documented in advanced stages of MS, when people have recovered literally overnight. For those who want to know more about miraculous healings, I will recommend *Remarkable Recovery* by Carlyle Hirshberg and Marc Barasch, and more evidence for this is found in the archives of The Medical Bureau of Lourdes. Lourdes has not only been a place of pilgrimage since the 1860's but is famous for the many miraculous healings said to occur there. This agency was created in 1883 to confirm or refute such claims. Since 1954, the Bureau has had the most curious cases reviewed by an international committee of physicians/ medical researchers and, so far, 69 cases have been considered so startling that they are called miraculous.

These cases include blind that can see, tumors that disappear, and damaged bone structure that heals. The fact that those on pilgrimage to Lourdes often believe in miracles—and that the recorded phenomenon, quite possible, is more properly attributable to the individuals' *belief* in Lourdes' healing power than anything else—does not change the fact that healing occurs.

Some skeptics might dismiss it as a result of the placebo effect. That, however, explains *nothing* from traditional medicine's point of view, for if there is something medical doctors are at a loss to explain it is the fact that a sugar pill can alleviate or cure diseases, provided that the patient *believes* that the pill contains a healing substance. As seen from the consciousness-comes-first perspective, this is the most natural thing in the world. But for medical science in general it is a troublesome fact because it messes with the premises upon which it is based—and for the pharmaceutical companies it is a serious problem because, to get a drug to market, they must demonstrate that their product works better than a sugar pill.

You might think that this would be a simple matter. But it is not. After a Harvard study in 1955 showed that sugar pills reduce anxiety, depression, and headaches in 35 percent of the subjects, they must show that their drugs have a better effect—which they usually do not. To make it appear so, therefore, they spend a lot of time and money to come up with results that are more favorable. One means at their disposal is that they only publish those studies which speak to their advantage. In addition, they have turned the manipulation of data into a science.

Talking about the placebo effect, however, there is much to suggest that it does not only apply to sugar pills, but to legal drugs and medical science itself. After all, most people have great confidence in Western medicine and see its representatives as omniscient authorities in matters of health. Doctors are aware of this and to strengthen credibility they dress and behave in a certain manner. They know that to the extent they succeed the likelihood that their treatment will work increases, and also pharmaceutical companies know how to take advantage of the placebo effect. Consequently, everything from the color and packaging of their products to their advertising campaigns are designed to maximize this effect, and surveys conducted by psychology professor Irving Kirch suggest that our faith in anxiolytic drugs ensures 80 percent of their effectiveness.

The placebo effect not only applies to pills and doctors, for believe it or not, it even turns out to be an important factor in surgery. A study done by Dr. Bruce Moseley and others in 2002 shows this. Mosley did different types of surgery on patients with osteoarthritis of the knee to figure out exactly what it was that made people better. Bruce Lipton has this to say about the operation and its results:

> "Moseley shaved the damaged cartilage in the knee of one group. For another group, he flushed out the knee joint, removing material thought to be causing the inflammatory effect. Both these constitute standard treatment for arthritic knees. The third group got "fake" surgery. The patient was sedated, Moseley made tree standard incisions and then talked and acted just as he would have during real surgery—he even splashed salt water to simulate the sound of the

knee-washing procedure. After 40 minutes, Moseley sewed up the incisions as if he had done the surgery. All these groups were prescribed the same postoperative care, which included an exercise program.

The results were shocking. Yes, the group who received surgery, as expected, improved. But the placebo group improved just as much as the other two groups!

Despite the fact that there are 650.000 surgeries yearly for arthritic knees, at a cost of about $ 5000 each, the results were clear to Moseley: "My skill as a surgeon had no benefit on these patients. The entire benefit of surgery for osteoarthritis of the knee was the placebo effect." Television news programs graphically illustrated the stunning results. Footage shoved members of the placebo group walking and playing basketball, in short doing things they could not do before the "surgery." The placebo group didn't find out for two years that they had gotten fake surgery. One member of the group, Tim Perez, who had to walk with a cane before the surgery, is now able to play basketball with his grandchildren. He . . . told the Discovery Health Channel: "In this world anything is possible when you put your mind to it. I know that your mind can work miracles."(67.109)

When all is said and done, then, there is not much left of the old medical paradigm's credibility. That is not to say that it has not been helpful. It can take pride in a number of successes, such as penicillin and the eradication of diseases which previously claimed millions of lives. As a result of its advancement, conditions such as diabetes, appendicitis, and many others are no longer deadly, and immunization is credited with cutting infant mortality rates to a fraction of what they once were. It should be noted that there are certain problems with vaccines, including the cover-up of a connection between autism and other associated problems.[34] Even so, while the medical establishment certainly has taken great strides the past century, they can do a lot better as soon as they take the consciousness-comes-first perspective into account.

The day this happens, however, the majority of the pharmaceutical industry and other big-time players with a vested interest in disease will go out of business. Hence, power-political interests are doing their utmost to keep the old worldview in place[35]. This is a problem we shall explore later, but their efforts aside, there is no doubt that a shift to the new paradigm will be entirely positive for all who prioritize health and welfare above short-term profit.

To sum up this chapter, we have seen some evidence suggesting that our mind exerts an influence on our health. And even though we have focused on the relationship between the psyche and cancer, the study of other diseases reveals the same pattern. For instance, when it comes to cardiovascular diseases, Dr. Larry Scherwitz has confirmed that self-centered people are far more likely to develop coronary heart disease than others. And Dr. David McClelland at the University of Boston has shown that the most power-hungry and control-oriented percentage of the population are two and a half times more likely to contract cardiovascular diseases by the time they reach their 50's.

His research also showed that their focus generally weakened their immune system—and this is exactly as can be expected in terms of the new existence theory. According to it, to the extent that we are trapped in the illusion of separation, we will cut ourselves off from the universal energy that gives life to everything. Hence, it follows that to the degree we cultivate the logic of fear, the more we will be open to disease. The psychiatrist Howard C. Cutler has more to say on research confirming this assumption:

---

34 Concerning the MMR vaccine, Rep. Bill Posey have asked the US. Congress to investigate the claims of former CDC researcher and now whistleblower, Dr. Bill Thompson. He claims that research was omitted and destroyed by the CDC to avoid reporting any significant connection in a study. Answers have yet to come forward and the question is why? For more on this, see "Waxxed: From cover up to catastrophe".

35 A good documentary about the medical establishment and how it has fought a cure against cancer can be found in Massimo Mazzucco's *Cancer: The Forbidden Cures.*

"In recent years it's been done a great deal when it comes to documenting the harmful physical effects of anger and hostility. Dozens of studies have shown that these feelings are important causes of disease and premature death. Scientists like Dr. Redford Williams at Duke University has conducted research showing that anger, rage, and hostility is particularly devastating for the cardiovascular system. It is gathered so much evidence on its harmful effects that hostility now is considered a major risk for heart disease—equal or perhaps even greater than common risk factors such as high cholesterol and high blood pressure."(25.258)

As we can see, there is plenty of research supporting the hypothesis of a connection between body and mind. And even though we have emphasized research focusing on the adverse effects of those thought patterns that follow from the logic of fear, there is a corresponding amount of research confirming that thought patterns following from the logic of love have the opposite effect. For example, a number of studies show that people with wholesome social relations are at least twice as likely to survive an illness as those with less developed networks. These studies suggest that the feeling of loneliness is even more destructive to our health than obesity, smoking, drinking, etc.

Another study, demonstrating the importance of good social relations, was done at The Albert Einstein College of Medicine in New York and according to its findings children with cancer had experienced at least twice the amount of hardships as children in the control group. Thus, it is documented that children growing up with poor interpersonal relationships are more prone to cancer, and another study done on 200 Harvard students seem to confirm this connection. This study divided students into two groups based on the environmental conditions they reported growing up, and the students were followed up after a period of forty years. It turned out that 25 percent of those who had reported a healthy/supportive environment had age-related diseases, while in the second group, the one in which students had reported emotional neglect and unsound conditions, 89 percent had contracted such diseases.

To say something about the connection between religious faith and health, we previously saw how believers can experience remarkable healings at Lourdes. Non-believers, of course, can also experience such events. Nevertheless, research confirms that people with a spiritual outlook are not only happier, but more resistant to disease. Psychiatrist Howard Cutler elaborates:

> "There have been done hundreds of scientific studies . . . confirming a connection between religious faith, mortality rates and improved health. One study showed that older, religious women could walk further after a hip surgery than non-believers, and they were also less depressed after surgery. A survey done by Ronna Casar Harris and Mary Amanda Dew at the University of Pittsburgh Medical Center, has shown that religious patients who had undergone a heart transplant had less problems dealing with post-operative medical treatment, and showed better physical and emotional health in the long term. Another study, conducted by Dr. Thomas Oxman and his colleagues at Dartmouth Medical School, showed that fifty-five year old patients who underwent open heart surgery after heart attack or heart valve problems, and who took refuge in their religious faith, were three times more likely to survive than others."(25.314)

There has been too much research on the connection between thoughts and disease to give an idea of how abundantly documented it is. But to sum up a fraction, Dr. Harold Koenig of Duke University, after reviewing more than a thousand studies of the impact of religion on health, said that "Lack of religious involvement has an effect on mortality that is equivalent to forty years of smoking one pack of cigarettes per day."(75.130)

This follows as a natural consequence of the new theory of existence, and we shall now go deeper into the relation between spirit and matter and see how our mind affects our body.

15

THE INTERACTION BETWEEN THE SPIRITUAL AND PHYSICAL BODY

"To see things as parts, as incomplete elements, is a lower analytic knowledge. The Absolute is everywhere; it has to be seen and found everywhere. Every finite is an infinite and has to be known and sensed in its intrinsic infiniteness as well as in its surface finite appearance."(18.486)

—Sri Aurobindo—

AS SOON AS the more perceptive percentage of scientists understood that the psyche had a real and definite impact on our health, the question of *how* became the focus of attention. From the reductionist perspective this was an enigma impossible to solve, but as soon as the scientists started from the other end—that is from the holistic perspective—things began to make sense.

As we saw in chapter 13, it turned out that the answer to the mystery of life did not exist in the DNA strand. It only contained the blueprint and the production manual for maintaining our bodies (i.e., that which the cell's workers, the proteins, uses to hammer out the new parts that are needed) and stimuli from the "outside" was the overriding factor of influence, telling the workers what to do. This environment is best described as an energy field continually being shaped/reshaped by our thoughts and feelings, and we shall soon see how a healthy environment creates health while an unhealthy generates disease. Before we do that, however, we should have an idea of how this field works and the first thing we need to remember is that the fields influences matter, not the other way around.

As we have stated many times, our consciousness is not the result of the brain's electrochemical impulses and this field does not have its origin in the brain. Instead, we can see the brain as an antenna or radio device that takes the frequency signal from this field and reinterprets it into a physical picture. The renowned neurophysiologist Karl Pribram explained it thus:

> "Our brains mathematically construct "concrete reality" by interpreting frequencies from another dimension, a realm of meaningful patterns, a primary reality that transcends time and space. The brain is a hologram, interpreting a holographic universe."(113.14)

Our brain, then, takes the information contained in the energy field and converts it into physical impulses—and so does every cell in the body. We may remember that according to the traditional view, the brain was believed to be the body's control center, but recent research has disproved this myth. This research has shown that to the extent we can point out a control center it is in our heart, as it is here our personal field has its physical origin.

When we think about this, it is perhaps not surprising. The first organ produced in a fetus is its heart and recent heart-brain research shows that while four of the body's nerve centers are located in the head, the fifth is located here. All these nerve centers are closely interconnected and function as a unit but the fifth center, the one science have long neglected, is supposed to have a kind of overall function. Researcher Joseph Chilton Pearce explains:

> "Neurocardiology . . . has discovered in our heart a major brain center that functions in dynamic with the fourfold brain in our head. Outside our conscious awareness, this heart-head dynamic reflects, determines, and affects the very nature of our resulting awareness even as it, in turn, is profoundly affected."(81.4)

We have talked about the nature of fields and their influence. But to refresh, we live in a world where these non-physical, mental quantities govern and underlie the manifestation of all things. These fields are interconnected and there is no separation between them. In the same way that our galaxy has an electromagnetic field emanating from its center, so our solar system has one springing out of the sun, and likewise each planet has its own. Furthermore, all life on the planet has its own field and everything is connected in an ordered and hierarchically structured series of interrelationships. If you have seen pictures of the earth's electromagnetic field you can easily imagine how your own looks, as the only difference is its size. For more information I would recommend a look at the HeartMath Institute's website (www.heartmath.org). But if you can picture having a giant inflatable swim ring around your chest, then at least you will have some idea of how it expands outwards from your body—and our heart is the center. It is estimated that the heart's electromagnetic field is 5000 times more powerful than the brain's, and Pearce has this to say about the dynamic between the two:

> "Brain and body are fashioned to translate from the heart's frequency field the information for building our unique, individual world experience. The brain and body then respond to the resulting perceptual experience and determine or interpret its quality. This qualitative analysis, or emotion, is relayed back to the heart, moment by moment. This influences the heart's own neural field, which responds to the emotional report and relays it to the fields of its origin, subsequently changing those fields, if only on a minuscule level. In response to the brain's reports, the heart also changes its own neural and hormonal signals to the body and the brain, and to the production of that electromagnetic field of information itself. This changed neural, hormonal and electromagnetic action then influences the kind of world we experience. [Thus], we live in an environment of feedback or "mirroring" in which creator and created give rise to each other both within us and outside of us."(81.66)

As we understand from this citation, how we experience the world has everything to do with the signals the brain sends to the heart. The heart can be seen as the main generator of experiential reality as it determines our vibrational interaction with the environment, but the heart itself cannot assess the state of the world. It can only respond to impulses from the brain, and so it becomes obvious why thought patterns matter.

When we go into defensive posture and our thought processes are characterized by the reptilian brain's mode of operation, we will send signals to the heart telling it that we are threatened—no matter what the reality is. This not only impacts our hormone production and generates stress[36], but it also makes the heart's electromagnetic field hold a vibration that creates discord between us and the environment. The opposite, however, will be the case if our brain tells the heart that all is well and that the world is a safe place to be. This will energize our personal field in a positive way, giving it a vibration that generates harmony between us and the environment.

In part six, we shall see what wonders an optimally functioning heart-brain relationship can do. The point is that thoughts and feelings will determine what kind of energy vibration our heart sends out; that this vibration represents a personal code that is entirely our own (our own psychic fingerprint, if you will); and that this unique vibration affects the environment both outside and within.

From what we have talked about, it should be obvious that energy and information are two sides of the same coin, and in *The Biology of Transcendence* Pearce elaborates on the implications. Another book that does the same is Dr. Paul Pearsall's *The Heart's Code*. Pearsall is a psychologist whose area of expertise is the connection between brain, heart, immune system, and our general interpretation of the world. In this book, he presents his findings, and he has this to say about our personal energy signature and its effect on the body:

---

[36] Research has shown that chronic stress not only weakens the body's defenses but can shrink our endocrine glands.

"All cells have energy, and so all cells contain and share
information. All cells store infoenergic memories, and our
heart . . . is the central organ that constantly pulsates info-
energy from, between, and to all other organs and cells.
Because of the heart's code and the cellular memories with
which it deals, every cell in our body becomes a
holographic or complete representation of our energetic
heart."(82.14)

Proof that cells store information and that our heart is greatly
influenced by our personality can be found in the change of character
displayed by some after having a heart transplant. It is not uncommon
that their personality changes after receiving the new heart and in some
cases they also get access to the heart donor's memories. In his book,
Pearsall provides many examples. Among other things, he tells the story
of an eight-year-old girl who received the heart of a ten-year-old girl who
had been murdered. After the operation, the girl began to have dreams
about the murder and the dreams were so accurate that the police, on
account of them, managed to find the killer. It then turned out that
everything she had remembered about the murder—the time, the murder
weapon, killing place, as well as a number of other details—was correct.

For those who want to know more about personality changes
associated with heart transplants I can recommend *A Change of Heart* by
Claire Sylvia, a woman who experienced it firsthand. It shall not be
elaborated on here, as the fact that our cells store information and that
awareness is present in all parts of the body no longer can be said to be a
controversial assertion. Dr. Candace Pert, an American neurobiologist
and former chief of brain chemistry at the National Institute of Mental
Health, confirms:

"We know that the immune system, like the central nervous
system, has a memory and the capacity to learn. Thus, it
could be said that intelligence is located not only in the
brain but in the cells that are distributed throughout the
body, and that the traditional separation of mental
processes, including emotion, from the body is no longer

valid. . . . We may [instead] conclude that the *mind* is in the body, in the same sense that the mind is in the brain, with all that implies."(83.187)

Pert therefore does not separate between mind, brain, and body. She sees it as an integrated and interconnected whole, and in her book *Molecules of Emotion*, she shows how our emotions function as a link between body and mind. The essence of her findings is that every cell in the body has hundreds of thousands of energy-sensitive sensors in the membrane and that the signals these receptors receive from our energy field determine what kind of actions the cell's workers (proteins) will perform.

To explain this very simply, we can see the cell membrane as full of tiny, flexible keyholes and the substances that our body produces (serotonin, dopamine, melatonin, testosterone, oxytocin, etc.) or absorbs from outside (vitamins, drugs, viruses, toxins, food, etc.) as keys that either fit into the keyholes or not. For our body to be influenced by one of these substances *they must find a keyhole that fits*, and whether they will gain entry depends on our energy vibration. This is where our emotions come into play, as the negative emotions create a vibration that makes the cell's keyholes more likely to be linked up with those keys that create imbalance rather than harmony. Remember that our body represents a finely tuned crystalline energy network and that we in this way, through the energy patterns of our mind, can influence the workings of this organism positively or negatively.

We must, of course, take into account that in addition to thoughts and feelings, we are affected by a number of other variables. As we have seen, not only former lives, but the environment of our forefathers as well as our own (both the mental, emotional, and physical environment) plays its part. All of us, therefore, are born with a certain amount of baggage. But besides the environment and the food we eat, what we can influence right here and now is our thoughts and feelings—and based on our preferences, we will strengthen or weaken our resistance to disease by adjusting the vibration of our energy field.

With this summary, we have gained some insight into the workings of our mind and energy field, how together they create our own unique energy-signature, and how the dynamic between the two affects our cell's structure and ability to cooperate. And if we remember that this system of energy functions as a holographic unit, we will have a good grasp on things. As every cell is a reflection of the whole, it should be obvious why a genetic change occurring in one cell will immediately affect the others. And tying this together with the non-locality principle, it becomes apparent why the old attempts of trying to find out *where* in the brain memories and so on are located never succeeded. As we now know, consciousness is paradoxically present everywhere and in no particular place at once, and Pert has this to say about the new science's suggestion of a connection between body, mind, and spirit:

> "As a result from my own and other people's work in the laboratory, we found that . . . we had to consider a system with intelligence diffused throughout, rather than a one-way operation adhering strictly to the laws of cause and effect, as was previously thought when we believed that the brain ruled over all.
>
> So, if the flow of our molecules is not directed by the brain, and the brain is just another nodal point in the network, then we must ask—where does the intelligence, the information that runs our body-mind come from? We know that information has an infinite capability to expand and increase, and that it is beyond time and place, matter and energy. Therefore, it cannot belong to the material world we apprehend with our senses, but must belong to its own realm, one that we can experience as emotion, the mind, the spirit—an *inforealm*! This is the term I prefer, because it has a scientific ring to it, but others mean the same thing when they say field of intelligence, innate intelligence, the wisdom of the body. Still others call it God."(83.310)

If we put two and two together, we see how the research that Pearce, Pearsall, and Pert have summarized fits perfectly with the multi-dimensional energetic structure of the body presented in chapter 13. We saw there that the physical body only represents a small part of our energy personality and that its reality builds on the underlying energy—that which connects us with Universal Center, the "point" that brings together everything. We have, in other words, covered another area in which modern science is consistent with the mystics' understanding. We have seen how the holistic model better explains life's complexity than the reductionistic as whatever manifests comes into being as a result of pressure from underlying fields. We have seen how all life forms have their own energy field; that this field, in turn, is connected to everyone else's through the planet and the Universe's energy field, and how this field's vibration not only determines what kind of reality we create inside but outside. Ashayana Deane expresses the relationship thus:

> "When perceiving your own physical body and the external objects and activity around it, you are seeing the particle content of your own personal morphogenetic field, Earth's morphogenetic field and the Unified field, as they exist within the low to middle frequency bands of 3-D." (28.150)

We have also seen that our DNA is linked to these fields and that there is a holographic concept behind everything which makes a change one place affect everything else. We have seen that these fields are idea-built structures; that they therefore exist in a constant state of flux, and we have discussed how evolution at any time, through them, may take its next quantum leap—provided that the amount of information has reached a certain level. And now that we have been through all this, the time has come to take a look at how our DNA is linked to these fields and what possibilities a more optimally functioning energy field can actualize.

15.1 THE NATURE AND FUNCTION OF DNA

"There is no place where one's body actually ends and no place where it begins."(14.48)

—Dr. Jeffrey Thompson—

At the beginning of chapter 13, we saw how our DNA was strangely similar to the dolphin's and how this finding seemed to undermine the Neo-Darwinists' interpretation of the theory of evolution. According to this interpretation the different species' genome ought to reflect how all life on earth has evolved and branched out since the first cell, but no such logic can be found in the DNA. On the contrary, new research shows that species as diverse as chicken, mice, dogs, and fish all share a DNA structure that is oddly similar—and so it remains to explain *why*.

When it comes to this, David Wilcock does an impressive job with his book *The Source Field Investigations*. He puts forward a well-supported thesis that the DNA is a preliminary product, a manifestation of an energy wave, and this fits perfectly with everything we know. According to the new existence theory, life has not evolved as a result of chance. Instead, the Universe is not only created by life and designed for life: *it is a self-aware, living organism*, and so we can perceive space itself as pregnant with life, bringing it forth where and when conditions are ripe.

We have previously discussed how all matter is light pressed down to a slow vibration and that behind all physical manifestation we find the organizing power of the fields. The DNA molecule, in this sense, can be viewed as an "antenna" that connects us to the transcendent domain. And as all that exists is energy vibrations in one form or another, we can be confident that the DNA itself is a flexible energy wave—a provisional result of the information contained within the fields. We also know that all life is interconnected to everything else and that the energy of GodForce knows no boundaries. It therefore runs like a thread through every life-form's DNA material and this, I believe, explains those similarities between the different species' DNA that the Neo-Darwinists cannot explain.

It follows that we, by changing the energy wave that generates the DNA (we do this by adding new information), not only can transform the appearance of specie specific individuals, but that we can even turn them into a different species! This may seem outlandish. Nonetheless, research has been done that supports this hypothesis. Among other things, Korean scientist Dr. Dzang Kangeng is said to have shown that it is possible to transfer the genetic code from one species to another by influencing energy waves. David Wilcock elaborates:

> "Kangeng placed a duck inside a five-sided, pentagon shaped container, and covered it with a domed mirror roof. Each of the five sides of the container had a hole with a funnel mounted in it—and then each funnel had a pipe that fed into a neighboring room, were there was a pregnant mother hen. For five days, the duck was zapped with a high-frequency electrostatic generator. Amazingly, when the hen laid her eggs, what hatched from them were not baby chicks—they were half duck, half chicken hybrids. Though they came from a chicken's body, they had the typical features of a duck—a flat beak, a longer neck and larger internal organs. . . . After one year the hybrid birds weighed 70 percent more than a normal chicken."(127.206)

Kangeng did his experiment with 500 eggs and 480 of them generated such hybrids. 80 percent of them then had a flat duck-shaped head and 25 percent had webbed feet.

Now, astonishing as it may be, his experiment did not completely transform one species into another. However, Dr. Peter Gariaev, a Russian scientist, apparently did. Wilcock again:

> "Gariaev sent a green nonburning laser through salamander eggs and then redirected the beam into frog eggs. Amazingly, the frog eggs completely transformed into salamander eggs. Though these salamanders hatched from the genetic material of a frog, they lived normal lives—and

could even breed with other salamanders to produce healthy offspring."(127.209)

For those who want to know more about the idea that DNA is the physical component of an energy wave, Wilcock's book is essential reading. It is also one of the best books available on the science behind the new existence theory, as Wilcock goes more deeply into this aspect. When it comes to this bit, the purpose of this book is only to provide an introduction; my focus is that part of the equation which deals with the self-actualization process and when it comes to the DNA molecule, therefore, I will settle for an outline of its workings and how it connects with the energy fields.

We have seen research at the HeartMath Institute demonstrating that our mind has the power to change the shape of the DNA, even when it was contained in an insulated beaker. This research showed that negative emotions made the twisted DNA strand uncoil, while those feelings that were more positive and in harmony with the Wholeness-concept made it coil up further. The former indicates a weakening of the DNA and the latter signifies that it regenerates—and as we remember, the distance between the DNA and the subject plays no role.

We shall now put this finding into context, for there is research to suggest that the ability to store and release light particles (photons) is an essential part of the DNA's function. Among other things, research conducted by the German biophysicist Fritz Albert Popp and Ruth Bernard shows that all living things emit photons[37], and Popp did a series of experiments which confirm that our DNA's ability to absorb and release these light particles are important to health. This research shows that DNA attracts and emits photons in a balanced way when we are in a state of emotional equilibrium. When we are stressed, however, we emit more photons than we attract, this again reducing our DNA's functioning. We can interpret his findings to indicate that when we are stressed, bitter, angry, and so on, we physically drain our body of energy—and that the

---

[37] A photon is a subatomic particle. It differs from other subatomic particles in that it has no mass, in that it always travels at the speed of light, and that it is its own anti-particle.

greater the imbalance becomes between uptake and intake, the easier sickness becomes manifest.

We know from before that energy, information, and consciousness are one and the same and that everything that materializes is created by light/energy. It follows that it should be possible to prove a connection between our thoughts and the behavior of photons and, according to Wilcock, both Eastern and Western scientists have done so:

> "Chinese scientists asked remote viewers with "exceptional vision" to view complex characters from their own alphabet as targets. The characters were placed in a room where no visible light could possibly enter. Very sensitive light-detecting devices were also positioned inside the room. During the times the viewers properly described the target, the numbers of photons in the room surged tremendously—from one hundred to one thousand times above the normal background levels of "virtual photons". This could amount to as many as fifteen thousand individual photons that were released during any one event.
>
> A group of American scientists led by Dr. G. Scott Hubbard attempted to replicate the experiment in 1986. They used a very high-quality photomultiplier tube for sensing light and a 35 millimeter slide of a scene as the target. Their results were excellent. During the time the viewers correctly described the target, pulses of photons consistently appeared—at a level much higher than random chance." (127.76)

As we see, Wilcock claims that a connection between clairvoyance and photons has been discovered and another interesting experiment that should be mentioned was performed by Russian scientists Peter Gariaev and Vladimir Poponin in 1984. First, they removed all the air from a specially designed container. Thus, they created a vacuum and the idea is that the chamber shall be devoid of all content. Nonetheless, subatomic particles pop in and out of reality all the time and the researchers knew that the container would not be completely empty. Their assumption was correct, as they did indeed find photons, popping in and out of reality and scattered about in a non-organized way.

However, something interesting happened when they placed human DNA in the container. What happened was that light particles were drawn toward the DNA strand, accumulating in a helical pattern—just like it! This was a remarkable finding, as there is nothing in the realm of established science that can explain it. But oddly enough, something stranger happened when they removed the DNA from the container as the photons continued to hold this pattern for 30 more days! They called this "the DNA phantom effect" and it was clear to Gariaev and Poponin that they had demonstrated the effect of an energy field of which science knew nothing. Wilcock describes its implications:

> "The DNA Phantom Effect is arguably one of the most significant scientific discoveries in modern history. It shows that the DNA molecule has some bizarre relationship with quantum mechanics that our scientists have not yet discovered in the mainstream world. We now have proof that DNA is interfacing with an unseen, yet-undiscovered energy field that is not electromagnetic, but which obviously can control electromagnetic energy—in this case by storing photons, even when there is no physical molecule there to hold them in place."(127.162)

Wilcock calls this field "the Source Field" and uses a large portion of his book to demonstrate its existence. As the name indicates, Wilcock suspects this to be the organizing field that is superior to all others; it is the one that not only interpenetrates and connects all things, but the one that gives rise to everything that manifests in the Universe. From time immemorial it has been believed that such a field exists. The ancient Greeks called it *the aether* and believed it to be the mysterious fifth element—the one that brought the other four into being. Newton himself was a firm believer in the existence of this field, and even if a famous experiment (the Michelson-Morley experiment[38]) at the end of the 1800s seemed to disprove its existence, Einstein thought that "space without aether is unthinkable."(14.17)

More conservative scholars, however, have for more than 100 years derided those who believe in the aether. Even so, an increasing amount of evidence suggests that they should reconsider their position. We have just seen Gariaev and Poponin's experiment indicate its existence and seen in the context of other research, I will argue that its existence is obvious. After all, the consciousness-comes-first perspective, building as it does on the principles of non-locality and the Universe's holographic structure, presupposes the existence of this field, as the old paradigm cannot explain phenomena such as clairvoyance and telepathy.

This, however, is an issue to be continued in the next part of the book. And we shall now end this section by exploring how the DNA affects our perception of reality—and how its flexible nature is the key to our evolution.

---

[38] It should be noted that E. W. Silvertooth did a similar experiment in 1986 with equipment that was more sensitive than Michelson and Morley's. According to him, this experiment came to the opposite conclusion.

16

EVOLUTION AND OUR
FUTURE POTENTIAL

"The step from man towards Superman is the next approaching achievement in the earth's evolution. There lies our destiny and the liberating key to our aspiring, but troubled and limited human existence—inevitable because it is at once the intention of the inner Spirit and the logic of Nature's process."(8.101)

—Sri Aurobindo—

AS WE HAVE discussed, the DNA reflects the information that the underlying fields bring to the surface. All life-forms are connected with these fields through their DNA and such fields are not fixed entities. Instead, they are in a continuous state of change, constantly developing into something more as the amount of information contained within increases. As this happens, individual life-forms are equally affected, for as the mystics know "the below is a reflection of the above". Hence, as time progresses, we come into contact with more and more advanced levels of understanding and awareness.

Looking back at the history of the Universe, we see this steadily advancing dynamic between the Whole and its parts. It started out as a slow process in which hundreds of millions of years passed and not much happened, but as the Universe had time to act on itself evolution progressed exponentially—and in our days it is approaching fever pitch.

Remember that time, according to the new paradigm, is a mass-movement towards greater levels of value fulfillment and that this process has taken place within perimeters set in advance. We can see the Universe as a bubble constantly being filled with experience, much in the same way as a balloon under the tap is filling with water. In knowing the size and strength of the balloon and how fast the water flows, one can predict the time it will take before the balloon bursts. And in a similar way, God and more advanced constellations of consciousness have always known that evolution, in our time, would make a quantum leap—just as they knew it would 750 million years ago, when single cells began forming multicellular organisms.

The reason is that these primary gestalts of consciousness do not experience time as we do and that they have access to a perspective which, to us, is quite unfathomable: While we can compare ourselves to water molecules inside the balloon—and hence, from our perspective, find it impossible to make sense of much—they find themselves *both inside and outside* the balloon and can view the process as a whole. To them, therefore, the Universe in its entirety is just an episode in the cosmic screenplay—an experiment in consciousness—and because they know the fundamentals upon which it is built, they have always known that the "balloon", in our days, would reach a saturation point which not only made a radical change possible but necessary.

We shall explore this issue more thoroughly in part six. Even so, to say a few words about how major events are organized, scientists have found evidence suggesting that evolution not only advances in leaps and bounds but that these leaps occur regularly and in conjunction with universal cycles. Wilcock has a great deal to say about this subject. And in his book, he shows how paleontologists David Raup and James Sepkoski, after reviewing the fossil material, concluded that evolution the past 250 million years has taken giant strides approximately every 26 million years.

It seems reasonable to suggest that cycles of time are the reason why great changes took place at these intervals and Dr. Richard A. Muller and his colleague Robert Rohde has done research supporting this thesis. They studied the fossil material another 300 million years back, until its very beginnings, and discovered the same pattern as Raup and Sepkoski. The only difference was that the cycles they found were longer, spanning approximately 62 million years. Muller, a physics professor at the Berkeley University of California, believed that astronomical cycles were the reason for the spontaneous evolutionary advances. Wilcock (and I) thinks that he is right, as they seem to match cyclical planetary movements discovered by astronomers.

When we look at the galaxy as a whole, the scientists believe our position to be far out in one of its spiral-formed "arms". These arms are connected to the galactic center, and in a wave-like fashion they move up and down past its mid-plane, going in circle around the center. It is estimated that our arm uses about 250 million years to complete one circle (a galactic year) and that in the course of this action four oscillations above and below the galactic plane take place.

Now there are some differing opinions about this. Our astronomers have not been able to measure out the specifics, and while they believe that it takes approximately 64 million years to complete one up-and-down cycle, they may be a little off. Consequently, Adrian Mellott and Mikhail Medvedev, two professors at the University of Kansas, believe that there may be a connection between this cycle and the 62-million-year cycle revealed in the fossil records.

Wilcock and I agree, but at the same time this wave-like motion around the galactic center does not explain everything. It seems clear that evolution moves cyclically and that everything is well organized. However, there are numerous cycles and just like a field is part of a larger field, so also universal cycles are found in an arranged relationship. This 62-64-million-year cycle, therefore, is only one of several variables that come into play; and just as it contains many minor cycles, so it is part of a greater cycle, which in turn is part of an even greater cycle, and so on.

Speaking of the first 300 million years of the fossil record, it seems clear that leaps in evolution coincide reasonably well with our position relative to the galactic wave-movement, but as evolution speeds up other variables must be included. Looking back at the fossil material in its entirety then, we find that it covers about two galactic years. The first was characterized by an evolutionary upgrade every 62 million years, while the speed of evolution quickened the second galactic year, doubling its drive. It was these cycles Sepkoski and Raup discovered, and as we now approach the end of the second year (or the beginning of the next), we find that evolution is progressing faster than ever before[39]. Approximately 50.000 years ago the most dangerous mammals died out, while something also happened to people that made them bury the dead, make jewelry, and think differently. About 25.000 years ago the Neanderthals also spontaneously disappeared, and since then we have taken part in the evolutionary progress described in part two.

Thus, it would appear that evolution more recently has been under the influence of one of the Universe's smaller cycles, one we call the precession of the equinoxes. This cycle is due to the fact that our planet, as a result of celestial bodies' gravitational influence, is slightly tilting back and forth, revolving like a spinning top around the sun. Because of the earth's cyclic wobbling, the position of the stars shifts in a systematic way, and the discipline of astrology is based on this pattern. It takes approximately 25.800 years for the earth to complete one wobble. Astrology divides it into 12 zodiacs (Sagittarius, Leo, Scorpio, etc.) and based on which zodiac the sun passes through at vernal equinox, one can say which of the twelve ages we find ourselves in. Hence, every age is roughly 2150 years, and in our time, we have just left the Age of Pisces and entered the Age of Aquarius.

Seen from the old paradigm, the idea of coordinated cycles seems absurd, but from the consciousness-comes-first perspective it makes total sense. According to the new worldview, we live in a meaningful and intelligently designed Universe, and so it seems only logical that the creation process follows a plan such as outlined here. When it comes to this, there are cultures who have seen December 21st, 2012, as an important date as we, at this point, would be perfectly aligned with the sun relative to the galactic center. This had not happened in 25.800 years, and because the precession (and astrology) was of utmost importance to former civilizations, it was carefully studied by their astronomers.

---

[39] That evolution has sped up can be seen in humanity's development and according to Dr. John Hawks, in the last 5000 years, we have evolved a hundred times faster than before. This means that people who lived 5000 ago had more in common with the Neanderthals than us. It is assumed that approximately 1800 genes, or about 7 percent of our genome, have changed in this window of time.

Many also believed that great things would happen in the timeframe in which we now find ourselves. To the Mayans it signified the return of Quetzalcoatl, a plumed serpent of great importance, representing the union of spirit and matter. And even if no major changes occurred on this December date, we still live in exciting times. Indeed, there is much to suggest that we are in the midst of the greatest upheaval humanity (as we know it) has experienced, and that our consciousness is undergoing profound change.

What we have discussed so far speaks volumes about this, and we have already seen a few examples of people who have experienced the next step forward. We can see the states of consciousness they describe as precursors for a type of consciousness that has not yet manifested fully. It is, however, coming with ever greater force, and at some point the old consciousness must yield and the global psyche will become qualitatively different.

What happens is that Consciousness will elevate itself to another level, at an order of magnitude currently unheard of. It will organize at a level of complexity, unrestraint, depth, and stability that makes the old consciousness seem puny, infantile, and incoherent. It will be a quantum leap no less majestic than that of the single-celled organisms when they formed multicellular organisms, for in the same way as Consciousness back then had exhausted its possibilities (it could not experience itself at a higher level of complexity without organizing at the multicellular level) it has done the same today. We have taken the illusion of separation to its limit, and for the sake of our personal growth and planetary survival it is essential that a new consciousness comes to the rescue. We must, in other words, learn to think as if *we were the cells and the earth our organism*, and although this understanding may seem impossibly out of reach it will manifest. The reason for this is that as evolution proceeds, we will begin to see ourselves as a part of the Whole quite naturally—and the current crisis is one of the tools that will help bring it about.

All this shall be explored in part six. I just want to make it clear that in seeing ourselves as cells and the Universe/earth as our organism, we will not lose our sense of identity. On the contrary, it will be strengthened considerably—it is just that it will not depend on us defining ourselves in opposition to something, as today.

When it comes to this evolutionary process, it is mirrored in the DNA. Hence, by upgrading consciousness, we will also upgrade our DNA strand. Ashayana Deane has written about this, explaining the process this way:

> "The level of frequencies accreted into the personal morphogenetic field will determine the level of DNA strand assembly you possess. As you pull in more frequency bands from the dimensional Unified Fields, your accretion level rises, more DNA codes assemble and become operational within your DNA strands, and your consciousness and perceptual fields expands."(28.150)

If you want to know more about specifics related to this DNA upgrade, I can recommend Ashayana Deane or the energy personality Kryon (channeled by Lee Carol), as they have written extensively on this issue. For my part, I prefer to speak in more general terms, as the details are still shrouded in uncertainty (or mystery).

The variable that seems certain is that the DNA strand physically will change as we progress in terms of consciousness. I believe what will happen is that those parts of our DNA that is called junk-DNA to a greater extent will be triggered. Our scientists can only make sense of about 3 percent of the DNA, as this tiny percentage produces the building blocks for the body. And I believe that the more we can take the Wholeness-concept into account, the more our junk-DNA will also come into its own, reconnecting us with the deeper parts of our being (and vice versa). Some people also believe that we will evolve from a carbon-based life-form to become a silicone-based. They have their reasons, but it is hard to say and time will tell.

What I can speak of with some authority, however, is the upcoming changes as experienced *through* consciousness. And simply put, the further we progress, the more we will get in touch with those areas of consciousness/ourselves that we are currently blind to. The ego, in other words, will transcend its old borders and we will come into contact with the deeper parts of our being—those we have no access to today. As a result, we will naturally see ourselves and the environment as one cohesive Whole and it will be obvious that we and the Universe are one.

With the deeper understanding, we will access the higher analytical knowledge that is part of the holistic perspective. Reincarnation memories, telepathic powers, and all else that follows from the soul's perspective, therefore, will become available and our understanding of space and time will change. The wiring of the brain will reconfigure, making our consciousness expand in scope. We will literally see the world with new eyes, and we will have access to a cognition and emotional register that is fundamentally different from the present ego.

As already mentioned, this is a process that unfolds gradually, and it has already begun. It is all about walking the mystics' way, and more and more people are doing so. Those with a head start can divulge that as they leave the dualistic perspective behind, they come into contact with a more extensive and cohesive awareness, one in which the boundaries between the inner and outer world are dissolved. Their inner-space deepens as the blockages of the energetic bridge between the soul and the ego evaporate—and the further we progress, the more our sense of empathy expands.

This follows logically from an increased understanding of the values, ideals, and principles that follow from Wholeness. This is the only way of building integrity, and as our consciousness expands to contain all living things, this inner sense (which today is acutely undeveloped) becomes more and more refined, resulting in a deepening sense of understanding, compassion, and solidarity with all life. As we become more in tune with the greater reality, the energy-flow between the ego and the soul becomes optimized, until the two become one. Those involved in the self-actualization process, therefore, will not only remember more of their dreams but they can bring their waking consciousness into the dream world, exploring it consciously. In that respect, the two spheres of reality float together, making the waking world more magical and dreamlike and the dream world more real (and yet, more psychedelic).

Another phenomenon that happens on our walk down Mystic lane is that we access a more direct, immediate, and intuitive form of knowledge and understanding. We become more proficient in the use of our inner senses and the veil that seems to separate past, present, and future, spirit and matter, and so on, fades away. We therefore come into contact with the Wholeness beyond appearances; we see the present from eternity's perspective; we establish an increasingly personal relationship with God, and the deepening bridge between us and Cosmos results in an ever-increasing amount of synchronicities and other magical moments manifested in our presence.

It is quite impossible for the ego to get an idea of the ramifications, implications, and nuances of the information provided above. Nevertheless, it should be obvious that we will create a very different world as more people walk this path.

Forcing consciousness forward is the activity of the Sun. Earth is not the only planet in our solar system going through climate change and according to studies the Sun's magnetic field has increased 230 percent within the 20th century alone. These changes seem connected to the supermassive black hole at the center of the galaxy who looks to be waking up. This year, 2019, astronomers have documented levels of activity and brightness twice what they have seen before, and to say more on the physical process associated with our spiritual awakening, something called the Kundalini-energy has been known to activate in those individuals who are ready for it. All Eastern yoga traditions speak of this energy and it is also known from the mystery schools of ancient Egypt and Greece. The word *Kundalini* is Sanskrit for "coiled energy" and it is described as an energy-potential that is dormant in the human body, resting or coiled up at the base of the spine in a triangular bone called the Sacrum. Different yoga and meditation techniques are supposed to activate this energy, and when it happens the energy flow in the human body is reconfigured at a higher level of functioning.

For those who want to know more about this, Gopi Krishna's books are a good place to start.[40] He lived 45 years with this energy and writes well about the challenges as well as its rewards. I say "challenges" because this power was active in him for some 15 years before it stabilized, and during this time it nearly killed him. His problem was that

---

[40] Another book that summarizes much knowledge of this phenomenon is JOHN WHITE (ED.), *KUNDALINI: EVOLUTION AND ENLIGHTENMENT*.

it was not properly activated at first[41], and as few people have first-hand knowledge of how to deal with this energy, he had to figure it out for himself. In his books, he gives the problematic as well as the beneficial aspects of this energy a fair amount of attention. We shall not go into further detail. I just want to bring this phenomenon to attention, and before we begin exploring the findings of consciousness research, I leave it to Krishna to explain its effect:

> "There has developed in me a new channel of communication, a higher sense. Through this extraordinary and extremely sensitive channel an intelligence, higher than that which I possess, expresses itself. ... When I look within I am lifted beyond the confines of time and space, in tune with a majestic, all-conscious existence, which mocks at fear and laughs at death, compared to which seas and mountains, suns and planets, appear no more than flimsy rack riding across a blazing sky; an existence which is in all and yet absolutely removed from everything, an endless inexpressible wonder that can only be experienced and not described.
>
> ... The transcendental experience has been repeated so often that there is no room for doubt about its validity, and it tallies so clearly with the descriptions left by mystics and yogis as to yield no possibility of mistaking it for any other condition. The experience is genuine beyond question ... [and it exists] as an ever-present possibility ... in all human beings by virtue of the evolutionary process still at work in the race, tending to create a condition of the brain and the nervous system that can enable one to transcend the

---

[41] This energy moves from the base of the spine and is ideally channeled upwards through an energy pathway in the central parasympathetic nervous system called Sushumna. If this energy path is blocked, however, the kundalini energy may rise through two nerve paths (Ida and Pingala) on either side. One is cold and the other hot, and together they balance each other. Krishna's problem was that during a meditation exercise he activated only one of these secondary paths, and the subsequent imbalance almost killed him.

existing boundaries of the mind and acquire a state of consciousness far above that which is the normal heritage of mankind at present." (62.225,226)

PART 4

CONSCIOUSNESS RESEARCH

17
EXTRASENSORY PERCEPTION

"Work in this field is a complete waste of time. . . . There is absolutely no reason to suppose that telepathy is anything more than a charlatan's fantasy."(127.37)

—*Peter Atkins, Professor of chemistry,*
University of Oxford —

LIKE ATKINS ABOVE, most defenders of the old paradigm will deny the existence of that which is incompatible with their worldview. Despite this, research has been done that proves them wrong. I have already presented some of these findings, and we shall now have more to say on this subject. That being said, this section can only begin to explore the evidence base that supports the new paradigm. There are books dedicated to each aspect of this research, and so we shall make do with an overview. If you want to know more about the documentation that supports the consciousness-comes-first perspective, I will therefore recommend Michael Talbot's *The Holographic Universe*. It will give you an idea of the research, and other books worthy of attention are Lynne McTaggart's *The Field*, as well as David Wilcock's *The Source Field Investigations*.

To begin with, one of the central premises of the new paradigm is that all minds are interconnected, and so psychic connections are not only possible but natural. Telepathy and clairvoyance are the most well-known examples. Given that such phenomena do not fit with the matter-comes-first perspective, they have been classified as "paranormal"—and even if skeptics dismiss it as "a charlatan's fantasy", serious research which indicates the opposite has been done, at least since the 1880s.

Then the British Society for Physical Research was established. It soon branched out to the United States, and another pioneering institute was D. B. Rhine's Parapsychology Laboratory at Duke University, which opened its doors in the 1930s.[42] The Soviet Union did not lag behind. Like the Western powers, the communists understood the potential significance of this research, and that mental images could be conveyed from one person to another was confirmed in the 1920s by the Commission for the Study of Mental suggestion.

Now, a lot of this research was for military purposes and much is still classified. Nonetheless, we know that intelligence services on both sides of the Iron Curtain have availed themselves of psychics since at least the beginning of the Cold War[43]. The Americans, for instance, lost one of their planes over enemy territory in the 1970s. It was impossible to locate this plane by conventional means, and President Carter later admitted that the CIA used a clairvoyant to find it. As he said: "She gave some latitude and longitude figures. We focused our satellite cameras on that point and the plane was there."(34.107)

Today, one does not have to look very hard for proof of psychic ability. You need only watch a couple of episodes of TV shows such as *the Psychic Challenge* to discover that pepeople have access to information outside the realm of the five senses. However, considering the manipulative and untruthful nature of our media, I sympathize with those that remain skeptical to televised truths. And for those who are looking for more satisfying sources of information, the research that has been done at places like Stanford Research Institute (SRI) and Princeton Engineering Anomalies Research Facility (PEAR) is worth looking into.

The PEAR laboratory has been researching paranormal phenomena since the 1970s and its scientists have not only shown that people can transmit information and sensations telepathically, but that our minds can even affect machines. That our thoughts may have a measurable

---

[42] Today there are many institutes around the world that focus their efforts on documenting and understanding these phenomena. For an overview of the history of parapsychological research from the earliest of times until the 1990s, see MICHAEL MYRPHY, *THE FUTURE OF THE BODY*.

[43] See LYNNE MCTAGGART, *THE FIELD: THE QUEST FOR THE SECRET FORCE OF THE UNIVERSE;* INGO SWANN, *PENETRATION: THE QUESTION OF EXTRATERRESTRIAL AND HUMAN TELEPATHY;* JOSEPH MCMONEAGLE, *MEMOIRS OF A PSYCHIC SPY: THE REMARKABLE LIFE OF U.S. GOVERNMENT REMOTE VIEWER 001.*

influence on machines may seem farfetched. But in the 1960s Helmut Schmitt, a researcher at the Boeing Aerospace Laboratory, built a so-called Random Event Generator (REG) proving this point, and at PEAR they have taken his work further. Simply stated, a REG is a machine that constantly flips between two variables (for example plus/minus, one/zero, etc.) and which left to itself will produce equal amounts. When we throw a coin into the air, it is a 50-50 probability for heads or tails and these machines work on the same principle. In that respect, they can be described as electronic coin flippers and at PEAR they have done millions of experiments proving that we, with our mind, can influence the machine to produce more of one or the other.

These experiments supply adequate proof that our thoughts have a measurable effect on the environment, but that is not all. Perhaps most interestingly, the PEAR staff have shown that we are not only capable of affecting what the computer is doing, or going to do, but what it has already done! Dr. Larry Dossey elaborates:

> "Can the mind effect past events? To test this possibility, the machine is allowed to run and the results are electronically recorded but not actually observed. Because no one has influenced it, the recorded output should be random [50-50]. But if the operator attempts to influence the REG's output hours or days *after* it has run, and the prerecorded output is *then* examined, it is found to be skewed in the direction of the operator's intent. This suggests that the mind can reach back into the past and influence events that presumably have already happened." (34.73)

Sounds incredible? It is not that strange when we consider that according to the new theory of existence, there is no past or future. According to it, there is only one eternal Now, and from the present we have the power to affect everything that will be and has been[44]. Some

---

[44] Helmut Schmidt and Marilyn Schlitz at the Mind Science Foundation have done similar experiments as the PEAR team, indicating that our mind reaches beyond the present and can change the past. Other research suggestive of the same has been done

skeptics may explain such mind-boggling findings as misinterpretations or manipulations of the research results, but there is nothing to suggest that this is the case. In chapters nine and ten we saw that quantum physicists have done experiments confirming the same, and so I believe experiments like this simply prove to us the timelessness of the present moment—and the power of thought.

If you want to know more about the research at the PEAR lab, I recommend *Margins of Reality*, a most thorough book by Robert Jahn and Brenda Dunne. The research is far more extensive than can be elaborated on here, but to give an idea of its diversity here is an account by Dr. Paul Pearsall who visited the facilities in 1997:

> "It is startling to observe random numbers generated by a machine become less random and move in a positive or negative direction in compliance with the intent of the operator or to hear remarkably accurate descriptions of remote locations by persons sitting hundreds of miles from the location of these scenes. It is also amazing to watch a pendulum's pattern or a computer image altering in accordance with a person's intent, a drum beating a new rhythm in keeping with the rhythm selected by an operator, a robot made to look like a frog summoned to an operator merely by the influence of the subtle energy of the person energetically calling the "frog". The PEAR staff reports that the odds of chance explaining such occurrences are one in a billion."(82.45)

I should mention that not everyone is capable of influencing the REG. The most successful manipulators develop their own technique (it turns out that a loving intention is the most effective), but it is estimated

---

by Dr. Daryl J. Bem, a professor of psychology at Cornell University. His findings show that our consciousness has direct access to events in the future as we, among other things, remember things easier in the present if they will become important for us in the future.

that two out of three—and we are talking ordinary people—can mentally influence the machine.

In addition to the PEAR laboratory, there are others who have conducted similar research. Worth mentioning is the research done by Helmut Schmitt, Marilyn Schlitz, William Baud, Donna Schafer, and Sperry Andrews at the Mind Science Foundation in San Antonio, Texas; the research done by Elmer Green and his staff at the Menninger Clinic in Topeka, Kansas; the research done by Dr. Bernard Grad at the McGill University in Montreal and, not to forget, that done by Dean Radin and others at the Consciousness Research Laboratory at the University of Nevada. Radin collected thousands of scientific studies indicating that telepathy and clairvoyance were real and presented some of this material in *The Conscious Universe: The Scientific Truth of Psychic Phenomena.*

As we can see, there is plenty of academic research available for those who want to know more about "paranormal" phenomena, and even though the skeptics more often than not disagree with the above-mentioned findings, we shall not go into further detail. Our beliefs, after all, create reality, and so no matter how many examples I would give of extrasensory perception it would be impossible to convince an ardent skeptic. Hence, it should suffice to inform that the U.S. Congressional Research Service, in 1981, concluded that:

> "Recent experiments in remote viewing and other studies in parapsychology suggest that there exists an 'interconnectedness' of the human mind with other minds and with matter. This interconnectedness would appear to be functional in nature and amplified by intent and emotion."
> (85.37)

And if this is not good enough confirmation of such phenomena, I will conclude by adding that the CIA, in 1995, undertook a thorough review of the state-sponsored paranormal research which until then had been done at Stanford Research Institute (SRI) and Science Applications International Corporation (SAIC). In this regard, a committee consisting of Nobel laureates and internationally renowned experts in such diverse fields as statistics, psychology, astronomy, and neurophysiology was prepared and Jessica Utts, a professor of statistics at the University of California, concluded thus in her report to the CIA and Congress:

> "Using the standards applied to any other area of science, it is concluded that psychic functioning has been well established. The statistical results of the studies examined are far beyond what is expected by chance. Arguments that the results could be due to methodological flaws in the experiments are soundly refuted. Effects of similar magnitude to those found in government-sponsored research at SRI and SAIC have been replicated at a number of laboratories across the world. Such claims cannot be readily explained by claims of flaws or fraud.
>
> .... It is recommended that future experiments focus on under-standing how this phenomenon works, and how to make it as useful as possible. There is little benefit to continuing experiments designed to offer proof, since there is little more to offer anyone who does not accept the current collection of data."(34.106)

18
HOW MIND INFLUENCES MATTER

"Modern consciousness research reveals that our psyches have no real or absolute boundaries; on the contrary, we are part of an infinite field of consciousness that encompasses all there is—beyond space-time and into realities we have yet to explore."(34.7)

—*Stanislav Grof*—

WE HAVE JUST seen research on paranormal phenomena suggest that telepathy and clairvoyance are real. And those who take the time to consider the evidence will find a massive body of research which confirms that our minds can not only interact with computers and other people but all living things. For example, Dr. Bernard Grad and others have shown that water molecules have memory and that we can influence the quality of water with our thoughts.[45] The biologist Rupert Sheldrake has written books on research that documents the occurrence of telepathy between animals and humans, and Cleve Backster, a pioneering figure in the development of the lie detector, has shown that even plants, bacteria, and cells respond to thoughts. After hooking up a plant to a lie detector, he discovered that it reacted with fear or nervous vibrations when he considered burning it with a match, and he also tried this experiment on other things. David Wilcock, who claim to have witnessed the effects in person, elaborates:

---

[45] Water research is another exciting area that supports the consciousness-comes-first perspective. For those who want to know more about our mind's influence on water molecules and how it affects health, I recommend the following documentaries: (1) *Water: The Great Mystery* and (2) *Water: What We Know is a Drop.*

"Backster also connected yogurt bacteria, ordinary chicken eggs from his refrigerator, and even live human cells to his polygraph—and continued to get stunning results. Consistently, what he found was that every living thing is intimately attuned to its environment. When any stress, suffering or death occurs, all life-forms in the surrounding area have an immediate electrical response—as if they all share the pain."(127.21)

Backster wrote a book called *Primary Perception* on this research and even if it is not taken seriously by the establishment, it fits perfectly with the new theory of existence. Remember the experiments performed at the HeartMath Institute, the ones which showed that the DNA strand reacted to thoughts even when contained in an insulated beaker? Backster did a series of similar experiments with tissue samples and the results were the same: there was no doubt that the cells responded to a person's thoughts, even when separated from the tissue sample by hundreds of miles.

In this context it is worth noting that the effect was immediate, as there was no measurable time span from a subject's change of thought pattern to the cells' reaction. And to add one more piece of information, this was the case even though the tissue samples were shielded from the influence of electromagnetic signals. Another scientist who confirmed that thoughts are connected and affect each other, even when sheltered from this field's influence, is Jacobo Grindberg-Zylberman. And as mentioned, this research indicates that there must exist some field that connects everything with everything, while operating independently of time and space.

Whether we call this field the aether, the source field, or whatever, does not matter—but it is there, connecting us to everything else. We have already seen how hundreds of surveys indicate that we, due to the existence of this field, can affect the well-being of other organisms using only the power of thought. So it is that all healers and psychics make use of their connection to this field and the results can be quite staggering. An example is found in Edgar Cayce, a psychic who worked in the United

States the first half of the 20th century. He was called the sleeping prophet and from his trancelike state he had access to all kinds of information. Cayce is known to have talked more than 24 languages while in this state, and his skills were used in many areas. One was remote healing/ diagnosis, and without knowing more than the patient's name and residence he could with great accuracy (roughly 90 percent) prescribe the correct diagnosis and treatment. Throughout life, Cayce performed more than 22.000 psychic readings. He left behind an archive covering more than 14.000 cases, and today we find some of the same exceptional abilities in people like Caroline Myss.

The neurosurgeon C. Norman Shealy was impressed with her intuitive/clairvoyant abilities and wanted to test them. He therefore began an experiment in which he, over the phone, gave her the name and date of birth of his patients as they visited his office—and nothing more. Shealy and Myss were separated by more than 2000 kilometers, but Caroline would relay a medical diagnosis with 93 percent accuracy.

Their book *The Creation of Health: Merging Medicine with Intuitive Diagnosis* elaborates on their collaboration, but even if few are as skilled as Cayce and Myss, there is nothing that separates them from others. All of us, in other words, have the potential for developing these abilities and there are guidelines on how to succeed. If we ask Myss and other healers/psychics how they best achieve results, they will say that they must relax and center their being. Stress and inner turmoil render this type of work unfeasible and to accomplish their work they must put aside the analytical mind; they must have faith in the intuitive process, stay centered, rely on the inner self, and keep their mind out of that busy mode which we are so familiar with.

We rarely think about it, but we experience at least four different states of consciousness every day: When we are at work or concentrate on a problem to be solved, we are in that state of mind where we have sharpened our analytical and intellectual capabilities. When we relax (listen to music, etc.), our consciousness becomes more fluid and dispersed, and when we relax even more, we fall asleep. We then enter a dreamy state of awareness and experiences at this level can be recalled when we awake. During the night, however, we also go into a state of deep sleep, and the experiences at this level are normally not available to the waking consciousness.[46]

This is the span of consciousness that we are all familiar with, and if we attach a device that measures the electrophysical activity of the brain (an EEG) we can see that each level is characterized by a specific frequency range. The typical alert, sharp, active state of consciousness is dominated by what we call beta waves (13-50 hertz); the wakeful but more relaxed awareness is characterized by alpha waves (13-8 hertz); the dream consciousness is defined by theta waves (4-7 hertz); and that of deep, dreamless sleep consists mainly of what we call delta waves (1-4 hertz).

One hertz is defined as one cycle/wave per second and the higher the frequency, the greater is the number of cycles/waves that pass by per second. It should be mentioned, however, that this is a simplified representation as it is possible to produce several different types of waves. Any frequency can be delivered in a wide array of waveforms, ranging from a rolling sinusoidal pattern, to jagged irregularly shaped sawtooth waves, to waves that are squared off or more rectangular in shape. Each wave is a signature imprint of the workings of consciousness. It is, in other words, a highly complex system of interactions, but it is this spectrum that people working with consciousness are trying to use to their advantage. When we meditate, for example, we are usually between alpha and theta (depending on how deep the meditation), while a person under hypnosis will display more of the theta pattern.

We see from this that as we go from beta- and into the theta- and delta-range, we come more into contact with the unconscious and the deeper parts of our being, which the alert reader might find odd. When we discussed the relationship between the spiritual and the physical body, I stated that the former has a higher vibration than the latter, and here it seems to be the other way around: The lower the hertz-frequency, the

---

[46] As we advance on the mystical path, it will become possible to remember experiences also at this level. Those who claim to know something about this, say that we are then present in the innermost depths of ourselves—the place where we are one with Fullness of being—and that we here find the strength and courage for another day in the physical.

more the illusion of separation gives way. How, then, can this be explained? I was pondering this myself until I read Talbot's *Holographic Universe*, where he mentions the research of Valerie Hunt, a professor of physiological science at UCLA. Talbot explains:

> "The normal frequency range of the electrical activity in the brain is between 0 and 100 cycles per second (cps), with most of the activity occurring between 0 and 30 cps. Muscle frequency goes up to about 225 cps, and the heart goes up to about 225 cps, but this is where electrical activity associated with biological function drops off. In addition to these, Hunt discovered that the electrodes of the electromyograph [a device used to measure the electrical activity in the muscles] could pick up another field of energy radiating from the body, much subtler and smaller in amplitude than the traditionally recognized body electricities but with frequencies that averaged between 100 and 1600 cps, and which sometimes went even higher. Moreover, instead of emanating from the brain, heart, or muscles, the field was strongest in the areas of the body associated with the chakras."(108.175)

The standard devices (EEG, EKG, EMG) were not sophisticated enough to measure this field so Hunt had help from NASA scientists to create a new device for her laboratory, one which would measure frequencies up to 250,000 Hz—a thousand times greater than anything ever used in medical science before that time. The device was called the *AuraMeter*, and it could not only measure the quality of our bioenergic field but also predict and correct future health problems.

For those interested, she wrote a book called *Infinite Mind: Science of the Human Vibrations of Consciousness*. To summarize, however, research showed that the more focused we are on the material world, the more the frequencies of our energy field will drop towards the lower end, closer to the 225 cps of the body's biological frequencies. She also found that psychics with healing abilities tended to work at frequencies between 400 to 800 cps and that people who go into trance and channel information from non-physical entities operate in a narrow band between 800 and 900 cps. She also measured people with even higher frequencies—and the higher their vibration, the further they had walked the mystic's path. Talbot elaborates:

> "People who have frequencies above 900 cps are what Hunt calls mystical personalities. Whereas psychics and trance mediums are often just conduits of information, mystics possess the wisdom to know what to do with the information, says Hunt. They are aware of the cosmic interrelatedness of all things and are in touch with every level of human experience. They are anchored in ordinary reality, but often have both psychic and trance abilities. However, their frequencies also extend way beyond the bands associated with these capabilities. Using [the AuraMeter] Hunt has encountered individuals who have frequencies as high as 200.000 cps in their energy fields. This is intriguing, for mystical traditions have often referred to highly spiritual individuals as possessing a "higher vibration" than normal people."(108.176)

Now, before Hunt's research, we discussed different states of mind as measured by an EEG. The awake, alert state corresponded to the beta pattern and I noted that during meditation we are usually somewhere between alpha and theta, while a person under hypnosis will display a theta pattern. We have previously seen that the physical body/surface consciousness represents only a tiny part of our multidimensional personality. We have seen that illness arises as a result of an energetic imbalance in this greater personality; that this imbalance is often caused by a belief system which is unfortunate (which doesn't reflect the truth), and that by changing the thought pattern, we can correct the imbalance which generated the disease.

That it is possible to think ourselves healthy, however, may be hard to believe. And those willing to experiment with the idea become disillusioned and frustrated when they try to think positively without getting results. In this regard, the above-mentioned frequency spectrum can help us understand *why* it does not work when we think/ concentrate on becoming healthy. Neuroscience estimates that the conscious mind represents no more than five percent of our psyche and that the unconscious mind creates at least 95 percent of our experience. The conscious mind, then, represents only the surface of our personality and new "wind" at this level will not make much difference. After all, if we do not fully believe in the healing powers of the mind, it is obvious that the underlying belief system will ruin our efforts no matter how often we repeat to ourselves that "all is well". Consequently, if we want real and lasting change, we need to go deeper and the more we can affect an adjustment on the deepest level of our psyche, the more successful it will be.

We see from this that mental activity at the beta-range is the one that is *least likely* to help us affect change. At this level we can do a lot of practical things on the surface like homework, repair a car engine, or plan a bank robbery. Even so, if we want to make use of our connection to the energy that interconnects everything—if we, for example, want to see the future, or ensure that our minds have an optimal impact on our own health or others'—we must move away from the concentrated, analytical beta-awareness and into the theta- or delta-range. Biologist Lyall Watson confirms:

> "The conscious mind on its own seems to be incapable of relieving even psychosomatic problems. Nobody ever cured asthma or eczema simply by telling the symptoms to go away. But unconscious action, most easily initiated under hypnosis, has relieved hypertension, peptic ulcers, colitis, hay fever, allergy, psoriasis, warts, shingles and even tuberculosis."(116.188)

Hypnosis is a kind of trance in which we access our subconscious mind. As Watson mentions, there are many examples of diseases that have been cured with hypnosis, but from this state we can also perform other feats. For example, in *The Holographic Universe*, Michael Talbot describes cases where hypnotized subjects have seen through matter. In *How to Make ESP Work for You*, Harold Sherman provides examples of hypnotized subjects who travel out of body and return with accurate descriptions of events elsewhere in the world, and psychiatrists like Dr. Brian Weiss have written books where people under hypnosis not only describe previous lives but experiences in the afterlife.

We shall soon explore evidence in support of the reincarnation concept. But to say a bit more about brain activity, how it is associated with various states of consciousness, and how we can utilize this knowledge, the closer we are to the theta- and delta-range, the more we are able to interact with the Source field. Most healers and clairvoyants operate from theta, and data suggests that the frequency range between waking and dreaming consciousness (between 7-8 Hz) is a trigger point.

We should also take into consideration that our brain is split into two hemispheres, and as the right and left brain normally have different wavelengths it is not only "depth-wise" that frequencies can be manipulated but also "sideways". In other words, the brainwaves of the two hemispheres are usually at odds with each other, and the more they are synchronized the better-functioning we become—and the easier we reach extraordinary states of awareness[47]. When it comes to aligning the two hemispheres, meditation is an effective tool. The brainwaves can also be changed by dancing, breathing, rhythmic drumming, and psychedelic drugs, and there are even helpful scientific methods/ gadgets. Michael Hutchinson has a lot to say about this in his book *Mega Brain*, and one device that should be mentioned was developed by Robert A. Monroe.

Amongst Westerners, Monroe was a true pioneer in the exploration of consciousness. He had the ability to perform out-of-body experiences (OOBEs) at will, and in so doing mapped out the internal terrain.[48] He also created the Monroe Institute, and as a result of the research done by Monroe and his staff, they developed a method that with great certainty

---

[47] For those who want to know more about the brain's electrical activity and the scientific methods available to optimize it, the book *Mega Brain* by Michael Hutchinson is a good start. It is, however, 20 years old and for more recent updates check out www.megabrainworld.com.

[48] Monroe wrote three books about his experiences: *Journeys out of the Body*, *Far Journeys* and *Ultimate Journey*. For an in-depth look at the out-of-body phenomena and the inner terrain the first two is excellent reading.

would help people access different states of consciousness. It was called *Hemi-Sync,* because of the use of sound waves to synchronize the wave-frequency between hemispheres. And since the beginning of the 1970s, many thousands have used this technology to experience OOBEs and other extraordinary states of consciousness. With the Hemi-Sync method, one can bring the waking consciousness into the delta range, and for those who want to know more about this technology Monroe's books or a visit online (www.monroe-inst.com) is a good place to start.

This website also has a lot to say about the Institute's research into extraordinary states of consciousness. And when it comes to this, one of the most interesting findings is that the polarity of our electromagnetic field is reversed when they occur. Hutchinson explains:

> "One of the most striking and important criteria for determining when someone is undergoing a dramatic shift in consciousness, such as having an Out of Body Experience, [is that] the body's polarity, or electro-magnetic field, simply reverses itself. This shift, according to Dave Wallis, former aerospace engineer and now technological director of the institute laboratory, "is like taking out your battery, turning it upside down, and putting it back in. It's mind-boggling!"."(57.196)

Now, many skeptics deny the reality of OOBEs. The phenomenon is incompatible with the matter-comes-first perspective, and so they try to explain it as a result of imagination. Even so, the evidence for its occurrence is so overwhelming that we shall not elaborate on the many instances in which, considering the data, this is the most credible explanation. After all, the possibility of an OOBE follows as a logical consequence of the consciousness-comes-first perspective, and it is not only through hypnosis, psychoactive substances, drumming, meditation, or the Hemi-Sync method that we can experience this phenomenon. As we shall see, it is a documented ingredient of the near-death experience, and it also happens spontaneously. In fact, we travel out of body every night, it is just that few remember the experience. Still, surveys suggest that as many as 25 percent of the population (in the U.S.) remember having had at least one. Usually, these people are convinced that the episode was real and for many it marks the beginning of their spiritual quest. To them, the OOBE provides confirmation that consciousness is far more than traditional culture will admit to, and so wonderful can this experience be that it can turn their old worldview upside down.

Hence, along with cosmic consciousness, the out-of-body journeys are some of the most spectacular examples of the experiences that can be attained by the Hemi-Sync method and various meditation techniques. They are, however, not the only way such methods can improve our life. We have seen that meditation rebuilds and strengthens neural connections in the frontal lobe, and that this in turn makes for a more balanced relationship with the environment. If you want to know more about the benefits of meditation, they are amply documented by Michael Murphy in his *The Future of the Body*. As a summary, it is known to have a positive effect on heart rate, blood pressure, EEG levels, bowel activity, and oxygen uptake. Meditative techniques can also be helpful in preventing/eliminating muscle tension, pain, migraine, depression, anxiety attacks, as well as addiction, while improving awareness, memory, intelligence, mental acuity, compassion, and response ability.

In short, meditation is a unique tool for improving both mental and physical faculties and in helping us cope with the world. Thus, it is becoming increasingly popular in prison rehabilitation programs, sports, and in work with psychiatric patients. There are thousands of studies documenting the effects of meditation in these areas, and an important contributor to this research has been the Transcendental Meditation movement. It teaches simple and effective meditative techniques and has more than three million followers worldwide. The founder is Maharishi Mahesh, an Indian yogi who dedicated his life to making Vedic philosophy, psychology, and meditation practices accessible to Westerners. Maharishi worked under the assumption that properly conducted meditation would not only have a measurable effect on the meditating subjects, but also the environment. To quote sociologists Elaine and Arthur Aron, this was his idea:

> "If a large enough group of people . . . were all drawing on
> the calm, coherence, and wisdom deep within the silent

human mind, then those qualities should prevail in the environment and the right changes, whatever they were, would come about."(39.198)

The idea is, of course, ridiculous as seen from the old perspective. Even so, if the new worldview has any merit, increased inner harmony within a certain percentage of the population should have a measurable effect on the environment. To find out more, experiments have been carried out since the early 70s. Here two of the most dedicated researchers, David Orme-Johnson and Michael Dilbeck, tell us what Maharishi expected and how the body of research corresponds:

"Maharishi predicted a number of years ago that when as few as 1 percent of the population of a society practiced the TM program, a measurable improvement, such as a decrease in crime rate, would occur in the quality of life in that society. This effect has been observed in a number of different studies conducted in populations of various sizes. For example, in one study . . . the crime rate trend in 48 different cities was analyzed over a 12-year period. The 24 experimental cities, defined by having 1 percent of the population practicing the TM program, showed a significant decrease in crime rate trend as compared to 24 control cities randomly selected from matched cities with similar economic, educational, and other demographic characteristics. This decrease in crime rate trend in the "one-percent" cities has been shown to be independent of such factors as police coverage, unemployment, prior crime trend, difference in age composition, and ethnic background."(39.200)

Amazingly, therefore, from the old paradigm's perspective, it seems scientifically proven that increased inner peace in one percent of the population will be reflected in a more harmonious environment. There have been more than 50 experiments confirming the same result. One of them was the International Peace Project in the Middle East, performed in the 1980s by Orme-Johnson and Charles Alexander in collaboration with Israeli scientists. The results were presented in The Journal of Conflict Resolution in 1988 and the number of traffic accidents, terrorist attacks, registered violent crimes, and emergency admissions to hospitals all went down while meditation unfolded.

Other studies have been published in the Journal of Offender Rehabilitation, no. 36 2003. This volume (which can be found at www. tandfonline.com) is devoted to this kind of research, and one of the studies show a 72 percent decrease in terrorism and an average drop of 32 percent in international conflict during the meditation. The results are consistent with other studies and suggest that long-term implementation of group meditation does have a major impact on terrorism, crime rates, and international conflict worldwide.

As we can see, scientific studies have documented the effect of thoughts. This is to be expected as the new existence theory holds that the inner and outer worlds are one. We have already seen this confirmed by plenty of research. Still, there is more material to consider, for not only does our mind affect our surroundings; it is also the other way around. When it comes to this, A. L. Tchijevsky, a Russian professor of Astronomy and Biological Physics, has demonstrated that the sunspot cycle has a definite impact on our evolution. He studied the level of conflict and societal development in 72 countries over a period of 2500 years. He focused on the major trends and found that whenever solar activity was at its maximum 80 percent of the most significant events in our history occurred.

Remember that according to the new worldview, the galaxy itself is a living, breathing entity. It is a vast Mind, a Megacomplex of Consciousness, and the planets are highly evolved consciousnesses. In this greater play, the suns can be seen as the local administrators and coordinators of our evolutionary process, and Tchijevsky's research confirms this perspective as it illustrates how human evolution is influenced by planetary bodies.[49] Now, skeptics scoff at the idea. Nevertheless, astrology builds on this concept, and despite its bad

---

[49] For more on how science is compatible with this perspective, see JAMAL S. SHRAIR, *HELICAL UNIVERSE: THE TRANSFORMATION CYCLE OF OUR HELICAL SOLAR SYSTEM.*

reputation there is research to support it.[50] The planets' influence on our mind has also been established by psychologist Arnold Lieber who found that murder rates rise and fall with the phases of the moon. His findings are compatible with analysis performed by American and British police, revealing an all-around increase in crime on nights when there is a full moon. This kind of research ties in with the work of Dr. Robert Becker, who in collaboration with American psychiatrists demonstrated a correlation between solar flares and admission rates to psychiatric hospitals.

All in all, then, there is evidence that we live in fields within fields of electromagnetic stimulus—a giant sea of consciousness—in which greater and lesser forces exact an influence on each other. And so, as the Norwegian psychiatrist Jan Sunder Halvorsen does, we can safely conclude that "our mind reaches out to the universe, [and that] all living things on this planet, from the initial spark, have been bathed in cosmic electromagnetic fields."(52.80)

Such a connection is further supported by the Global Consciousness Project. Its researchers have shown that Random Number Generators around the globe stop making random noise and instead reveal patterns when events of massive importance take place. One such event was the terrorist attacks of September 11, 2001, and the stress inflicted upon the population could be read off graphs generated by the machines (the anomaly began four hours before the attacks and peaked simultaneously). A similar effect could also be detected by Geo-synchronous Operational Environmental Satellites, a type of satellites that measure changes in the electro-magnetic field. According to them, the collective rise in stress levels made a clear impact on this field on the day of the attacks—and on September 14, while there were ceremonies for peace and brotherhood around the world, they showed equally clear changes in a positive direction.

---

[50] For scientifically acceptable studies of astrology, check out research done by Michel Gauquelin, Suitbert Ertel and Arto Muller. Their work has been reviewed by at least three groups of sceptics and after 50 years Gauquelin's findings still hold firm. In fact, in their book *the Tenacious Mars Effect*, Suitbert Ertel and Kenneth Irving conclude that the scientific evidence is even stronger than he originally found.

To sum it up, we have seen some of the research that indicates a link between the quality of our thoughts and the world "outside", and physicist Claude Swanson[51] describes the ramifications:

> "Our Western culture has taught us that thoughts don't matter. If each one of us goes around each day carrying anger and resentment, the Western belief is that it has no direct effect on the world. As long as we refrain from overt violent action, the present belief is that no harm will be done to others. But in view of the present evidence, this can no longer be maintained. We are truly tied to one and other, and even our thoughts affect one another. James Twyman has led several worldwide synchronized group prayers for peace. Those prayers had measurable effects, and even altered the physics of the quantum background and the level of chaos worldwide for a time [as discovered in the Global Consciousness Project] . . . He observes the following: ". . . conflict in the world is the result of conflict within us. We project that feeling into the world because we are not ready to accept that we are the cause, and therefore the solution, to that conflict. Thus wars have raged in the world since the beginning of time, because we are not ready to deal with the conflict where it really is—within us."(127.241)

---

[51] Dr. Swanson has written two books on the science behind the consciousness-comes-first perspective. See SWANSON, *THE SYNCHRONIZED UNIVERSE: NEW SCIENCE OF THE PARANORMAL,* and SWANSON, *LIFE FORCE: THE SCIENTIFIC BASIS.*

18.1 THE LOGIC OF LOVE

*"Someday, after mastering the winds, the waves, the tides
and gravity, we shall harness for God the energies of love,
and then, for a second time in the history of the world, man
will have discovered fire."(99.198)*

—*Pierre Teilhard de Chardin*—

We have now explored evidence suggesting that we are all connected and
that our minds not only have a measurable impact on ourselves but also
the environment. This brings us back to an important point, for our
thoughts create reality and they are motivated either by the logic of fear
or the logic of love. We have seen how the former adds to the illusion of
separation, creating dissonance between us and others, while the latter
has the opposite effect[52]. The new paradigm tells us that that which we
give energy will increase in scope; it will become more and more
influential, as the law of attraction will return that which we project.

A quick glance at the world provides us with endless examples of
this interaction. The more we cultivate the logic of fear, the more we are
confronted with a reality which confirms that our thought patterns are
well founded and justified. And as the world is nothing more than a
collectively shared dream, the more we let fear take control, every day
the physical landscape becomes more nightmarish.

In the next section, we shall explore the collective damage caused by
the logic of fear. After that, in part six, we shall see how it can be fixed.
The point here is to recall the basic laws that create reality, as whatever
follows from the logic of fear and love has two different vibrations—

---

[52] If you are inclined to doubt the validity of this premise, here is an experiment that
scientifically proves it: Go about your day and consistently follow the logic of fear;
be jealous, bitter, spiteful, hateful, paranoid, and aggressive towards everyone you
meet and see how long it takes before your business falls apart, your friends
disappear, your wife leaves you, and your kids become dysfunctional or suicidal.

vibrations that result in the research just discussed.[53] This is the reason why philosophers of language, like Donald Davidson, hold trust to be a key component of any functioning conversation. Without it communication simply falls apart, and while interactions with the logic of fear makes way for difficult relations the opposite is equally the case. We have already seen how it affects our health and it comes as no surprise that healers, to do their job, make use of the power of love. Richard Gerber, a Doctor of Medicine, has more to say:

> "Over the years, as I have researched healers and healing, I have been impressed by the commonality of loving intent among healers. They work primarily from a position of heart-centered, unconditional love when they work with another living being's energy field. It appears that love may actually be a real energetic force, not merely a catalyst for action, transformation, and healing. Researchers at the Institute of HeartMath, . . . including Glen Rein and Roland McCraty, have discovered a fascinating phenomenon that tends to confirm the concept that love is a real healing energy with measurable physiological effects, even at the DNA level. Rein found that individuals who sat and meditated in a state of love, compassion, and caring actually generated grater coherence in their electrocardiogram (EKG) pattern than those who simply had discordant emotion.
>
> . . . Researchers at the institute . . . are convinced that during times of focused inner love and peace, the heart center sends out a coherent energy pattern to the rest of the body, including the brain. . . . Rein has also found that this

---

[53] For more on the power of love, check out the Institute for Research on Unlimited Love (www.unlimitedloveinstitute.org). This institute seeks to increase awareness of (1) the growing dialogue on unlimited love that is taking place at the interface of new scientific investigations (e.g., in the health sciences, psychology, sociology, neuroscience, physics, and mathematics); (2) insights of the world's great philosophical, spiritual and theological traditions; and (3) inspiring works of love by exemplars across the world.

pattern of increased heart coherence in "loving meditators"
is accompanied by increased salivary IgA, indicating
enhanced immune functioning."(41.527)

IgA is short for immunoglobin-A, an antibody that neutralizes
viruses. Harvard psychologist David McClelland has documented how
compassion increases production of IgA and findings such as these
connect the dots with previously mentioned research. They provide
another example of how positive thoughts/emotions influence the
workings of the body, and in this regard, studies done by Dr. Dolores
Krieger are worth mentioning. In the 70s, she developed a scientifically
based healing practice called Therapeutic Touch. Since then, she has
done several studies which not only confirm that healing has a power (the
results are positive even if the healer is far away and the patient unaware),
but that it effects physical changes in the patients such as increased
hemoglobin production.

Another study which lends credibility to the idea that thoughts have
an impact on others was done by Rosenthal and Jacobsen in 1968. They
IQ-tested classes of schoolchildren and afterwards told their teachers that
some of the children were especially gifted and could be expected to
flourish in the course of the school year. They secretly pointed out these
children and even if the designated students were completely average, at
the end of the school year it turned out that the teachers' expectations had
had a measurable effect. They had far more confidence than before and
compared to the other children they did better on the IQ tests.

A skeptic, of course, can explain such findings with the teachers'
behavior, assuming that they must have given the students favorable
treatment. This is quite possible. However, according to the new
paradigm, when we think negatively about someone, we provide energy
that enhances their negative features and when we think positively, we
provide energy which strengthens their positive traits. This is mirrored
by scientific research, as biologists have found that oxytocin production
increases when people have confidence in us. Oxytocin is a hormone
associated with the ability to trust people (it is a glue for interpersonal
relationships), and the result is a more positive interaction between us
and others.

Now, there are explanation models for the last two examples that are compatible with the old worldview. Taken by themselves, therefore, they do not prove anything, but seen in context of the bigger picture these data fit perfectly with the consciousness-comes-first perspective. We have now got a holistic framework for this research, as we have seen how our mind impacts matter, how it affects the electromagnetic field, and how changes in this field affect us.

Speaking of our connection to this field, one more thing is worth noting. When we talked about brainwaves, I mentioned that the frequency range between alpha and theta (7-8 Hz) was a trigger point that makes interesting things take place. Research suggests that we are more susceptible to telepathy, clairvoyance, and healing energies when we hold this vibration and at the HeartMath Institute they have found that this also applies to the brain waves of the most effective meditators. What we can now add to this equation is that the resonant frequency of the earth's electromagnetic field is attuned to such a loving, meditating state of consciousness. This pulse also holds a vibration between 7 and 8 Hz (7.83 Hz) and it is called the Schumann-resonance because a wave at this frequency acts as a closed waveguide. The limited dimensions of the Earth cause this waveguide to act as a resonant cavity for electro-magnetic waves in the extremely low frequencies (ELF) band, thereby reinforcing and strengthening resonance.

While there are other resonances, this implies that we, when we are filled with love, hold the same vibration as the earth and that we, in a sense, become one with its harmonic frequency. This may explain why significant changes occur in an area where only one percent of the population hold this vibration, as confirmed by the Maharishi effect, and quite a few researchers believe that this harmonic resonance makes it easier for the energies of the non-physical aspects of the Universe/us to connect so that a synergetic effect occurs. Dr. Richard Gerber explains:

> I propose that . . . when healers and patients both resonate
> at the dominant frequency of earth's magnetic field—the
> Schumann resonance—a resonance-frequency window is
> created. This resonance-frequency window allows energy
> from high potential to cascade down the magnetic waterfall

of the planetary field to patients with healers acting as conduits of that energy flow.

. . . As the magnetoelectrical currents flow to patients, their energy fields undergo restructuring and repatterning that ultimately affect biochemical processes at the cellular level. I further hypothesize that healers not only emit subtle magnetic fields that are coherent, but that these healing fields produce coherence in other energy fields around them, both locally and nonlocally. That is, healers may actually increase both local and distant coherence in Earth's magnetic field itself. The power of this organizing effect is proportional to the energy of a given healer and to how many healers might be working together in unison. When healing is done in a group, there is an important amplification effect that is more exponential than arithmetical in nature."(41.529, 530)

We will expand on love's transformative power in part six. However, another interesting feature of this principal background in the electro-magnetic spectrum is that the Schumann resonance has displayed recent spikes which has led more and more to ponder its implications. In the normal mode, the fundamental mode is a standing wave in the Earth–ionosphere cavity with a wavelength equal to the circumference of the Earth. This lowest-frequency (and highest-intensity) mode of the Schumann resonance occurs at a frequency of approximately 4.11 Hz, but this frequency can vary slightly from a variety of factors, such as solar-induced perturbations to the ionosphere, which compresses the upper wall of the closed cavity. The higher resonance modes are spaced at approximately 6.5 Hz intervals, but on January 31, 2017, for the first time in recorded history, the Schumann resonance reached frequencies of 36+ Hz. It was considered an anomaly when in 2014 this frequency rose from its usual 7.83 Hz to somewhere in the 15-25 Hz levels, so a jump from 7.83 Hz to 36+ Hz is a huge deal. At 2am on March, 17th, the readings spiked even further, at 150 Hz, and as Dr. Joe Dispenza noted, "what does this mean to us as inhabitants of Mother Earth"?

According to neuroscience, frequency recordings of 36+ Hz in the human brain are more associated with a stressed nervous system than a relaxed and healthy one, and so Dr. Dispenza wonders whether the rise in frequency have to do with the times we are in. Because our lives are inseparable from the earth, and the earth's frequency is rising, this is highly probable; our consciousness is being stretched to the brink and beyond, but as the energy of the unified field is always moving towards greater degrees of organization and wholeness, Dispenza is part of the movement that sees this as an indication that we on the verge of a great evolutionary jump[54]. Others shall be presented as we continue, but now it is time to delve into the research which shows that consciousness is not a finite quantity, dependent on the body to exist.

As seen, we experience at least four states of consciousness daily, from deep sleep to the more sharpened surface-oriented consciousness. We have also seen how such methods as meditation, hypnosis, drugs, or the *Hemi-Sync* technology can expand our state of consciousness to such a degree that the waking mind is able to explore those areas that are normally outside of its domain. None of this is controversial, as there are explanations for this consistent with the old worldview. However, we have also seen that out-of-body experiences are a natural, albeit controversial, part of the encounter, and that hypnosis and regression therapy grants access to information about previous lives and life after death. None of this is consistent with the old worldview and so many believe stories about OOBEs and reincarnation memories are the result of confused minds, if not outright deceit.

Adherents of this view believe that hypnosis and regression therapy create false memories which the therapist and the patient confuse with reality. As they think in terms of the matter-comes-first perspective, this presents itself as the natural conclusion. Nevertheless, we have seen that the consciousness-comes-first perspective offers a superior explanatory model when it comes to preserving present knowledge in a coherent existence theory. The reincarnation concept and the OOBEs fit like a glove with this, and we shall now explore some of the evidence for such controversial phenomena.

---

[54] For more on his take, see JOE DISPENZA, *BECOMING SUPERNATURAL*

19
THE CONCEPT OF REINCARNATION

"What passes on to the next life is not so much the details as the essence of the scene: . . . What we did not conquer in the past returns again and again, each time with a slightly different face, but basically always the same, until we confront it and untie the old knot. Such is the law of inner progress."(93.111)

—Satprem—

WHEN IT COMES to documenting the reincarnation concept, few have done a better job than Dr. Ian Stevenson, a professor of psychiatry at the University of Virginia. For more than 40 years he traveled the world examining alleged cases of this phenomenon and found over 3000 cases that seemed to confirm its reality. Stevenson concentrated his research on children who had memories and behaviors which substantiated the doctrine and for a serious-minded skeptic his books are a great place to start. The reason is that his research was not only comprehensive but thorough. Anyone with an open mind, therefore, will be impressed with his work and the evidence for reincarnation.

Stevenson interviewed children with a variety of skills, habits, and memories that could be linked to personalities they said to have been in past lives. And as some of the lives recalled were more recent, he would visit the villages and families of the children's previous incarnation to verify their stories. Many of these children remembered specific events from their past life and a good example is found in Suzanne Ghanem, a little girl from Lebanon. Stevenson speaks to it:

"recorded a list of fifty-nine items she had stated about the previous life that she remembered. Her statements included the names of twenty-three members of the family to which she referred and two acquaintances. Moreover, she placed all but one of these persons in their proper relationship to Saada, the woman whose life she remembered."(104.146)

The children did not only have detailed, verifiable memories, but expressed behavior and character that, considering the time and place where they were born, was unnatural. They could have specific fears and preferences linked to a previous life and they sometimes had scars and birthmarks that were consistent with wounds and injuries suffered in past lives. Some also had talents or knowledge stemming from a previous life, and Stevenson even documented a couple of cases where the children spoke a language they had not learned in this life.

Seen in isolation, none of the children's stories can be said to prove the reincarnation phenomenon. Even so, the overall material makes it the most probable explanation—and viewed from the consciousness-comes-first perspective, it is obvious. We then have another piece of data that ties together the bigger picture, and when all is said and done none of our objections are rationally based. Indeed, it is only because authorities want us to believe that it is an unscientific or un-Christian idea that many are uncomfortable considering this phenomenon. But as Voltaire, a leading figure of the Enlightenment Era, stated: "It is no more surprising to be born twice than once." Furthermore, if we broaden our horizons, we find that the doctrine is not only regarded as gospel in Buddhism and Hinduism, but among some Muslim, Jewish, and Christian traditions, as well as most indigenous nations. We find it among the Aborigines in Australia, the Indians in North and Latin America, the Eskimos in the Arctic, and a number of African cultures. It was popular among Greek thinkers such as Socrates and Plato, and a key part of early Christianity until it was declared heretical in 553.

Despite that, belief in reincarnation is becoming increasingly popular in the West, precisely because it offers an interpretation model that matches people's experience and intuitive understanding. All in all, then, historically and generally speaking, the belief in reincarnation is more common than not—and as this book goes to show, there is nothing unscientific about it. It is only because the phenomenon is alien to the ego-consciousness that it may seem so, but if we look at the research that deals with the expanded states, we find that it shows up again and again.

When we discussed hypnosis, I mentioned that Dr. Brian Weiss had written books about his encounters with the phenomenon. Originally, he was a traditional-oriented psychiatrist who could never imagine that one day he would embrace this doctrine. But after meeting Catherine, a patient with mental illnesses no one had been able to explain or cure, his worldview was in for a change. As sessions advanced, he discovered that her phobias and traumas originated in unresolved inner conflict stemming from previous lives, and when she could reexperience traumatic events under hypnosis, her anxiety and depression disappeared. Since then, for more than 30 years and in over 4000 patients, he has studied the phenomenon through hypnosis. This is known as regression therapy, and because it has proven an effective form of treatment it is becoming more and more popular amongst psychiatrists and psychologists.[55]

This kind of treatment is obviously frowned upon by the more skeptically inclined population. Nevertheless, an increasing amount of data supports the reincarnation doctrine. Tens of thousands have tried such therapy, and although they represent a wide range of people their stories are congruent and fit together into an overlapping whole. Their descriptions of the afterlife complement others, and this is the case even if many of the patients originally did not believe in a life after death. A skeptic might argue that this is because of the therapists' expectations. Like other professionals, however, these therapists have a standard and a work ethic they adhere to and they never tell the patient what "should" happen during a regression.

---

[55] For more on this subject, the following books by experienced regression therapists are recommended; JOEL WHITTON, *LIFE BETWEEN LIFE*; HELEN WAMBACH, *LIFE BEFORE LIFE*; MICHAEL NEWTON, *JOURNEY OF SOULS*; MICHAEL NEWTON, *DESTINY OF SOULS*; MICHAEL NEWTON, *LIFE BETWEEN LIVES*; LINDA BACKMAN, *BRINGING YOUR SOUL TO LIGHT*; BRIAN L. WEISS, *MANY LIVES, MANY MASTERS*; GLENN WILLISTON AND JUDITH JOHNSTONE, *DISCOVERING YOUR PAST LIVES*.

Of course, we must not forget that anyone can be mistaken at any time and so we must take into consideration that all the information they individually present can be incorrect. Still, when thousands of people separately describe similar features and elaborate on the same nuances, it is logical to assume that they, under hypnosis, have mapped out what life is like as a soul essence in the inner dimensions.

We have also another reason for taking their descriptions seriously, and that is that their experiential picture is in 100 percent agreement with the one brought back by other travelers in consciousness. Indeed, it seems irrelevant by what means we reach the expanded states. Whether we arrive at them spontaneously or through dance, drumming, breathing exercises, technology such as the Hemi-Sync method, hypnosis, meditation, psychoactive drugs, or a near-death experience, the same thing happens: We are launched out of the limited perspective provided by ordinary awareness and we access a deeper, enlarged aspect of consciousness. And because we and the Universe ultimately are one, through these expanded states, we take part in an experience that appear timeless—even limitless.

All mankind has accumulated of true knowledge about the nature of reality has come through these states of consciousness. They are the source of all religion and were it not for our narrow-minded and limited understanding, the order and divine nature of the Universe would have been obvious to anyone.

We have already summarized the perspective offered by the cosmic consciousness, and we shall now elaborate on this as seen in relation to the research on psychoactive substances.

20
PSYCHOACTIVE SUBSTANCES

"Like almost everyone who has had the veil drawn, I came back a changed man. In the four hours [my psychedelic experience lasted] I learned more about the mind, the brain, and its structures than I did in the preceding fifteen years as a diligent psychologist."(95.30)

—Timothy Leary, professor of psychology—

PSYCHOACTIVE SUBSTANCES INCLUDE several plants and drugs which may expand consciousness to the point where we come into contact with the greater reality. The most renowned are LSD, Peyote cactus (contains mescaline), Ayahuasca (contains DMT), Ibogaine, and various psilocybin-containing mushrooms. Most of these substances are currently prohibited. Good reasons, however, are hard to find and their criminalization should be perceived as a cultural taboo resulting from the narrow safety-zones of a naïve and childlike ego-consciousness, rather than any demonic traits of the substances themselves.

In other words, the prohibition of psychoactive substances highlights our collective alienation from the greater reality. Our fear of these drugs is an irrational product and a consequence of being born into a culture that only recognizes the ego's experiential picture—and so it is befitting that we have chosen to prohibit those substances that can help us overcome this sickness. After all, it speaks volumes about the level of irrational fear in society that we, these past 50 years, have criminalized the use of plants that for at least 10.000 years have been our most important sources of insight. Looking back, various cultures on most continents have had a balanced and constructive relationship with them, but still we are so terrified of these substances that most parents would prefer their children enlisting for war rather than experimenting with "drugs".

Now, I am not saying that these drugs are harmless. They are powerful substances and there are examples of people who have not benefited from their use. Nonetheless, the current hysteria is completely uncalled for, and for a more balanced summary I will let Andrew Weil, an expert physician, explain:

> "In purely medical terms, these may be the safest of all known drugs. Even in huge overdose, psychedelics do not kill, and some take them frequently all their lives without suffering physical damage or dependence. In the right hands, they can bring about dramatic cures of both physical and mental illnesses. Yet these same drugs can cause the most frightening experiences imaginable leaving long lasting psychological scars. . . . In fact the mental effects of psychedelics are completely dependent on set and setting—on who takes them and why, where, and how."(70.383)

These drugs, then, are less harmful to physical health than coffee, alcohol, or tobacco. The potential for dependence is non-existent and they are in no way harmful to the body. They can, however, provide people with an experience so overwhelming that its impact on the surface-consciousness is unfortunate. Even so, this is a rare event. And as we shall see, to the extent that it occurs, it will be due to ignorant usage and our society's backward understanding of the human psyche, rather than inherent properties of the substances.

From the media's coverage, one may get a different impression. However, most people who try these substances are grateful for their experience and its effects have a positive and lasting bearing.[56] Dr.

---

[56] For those who want to know more about these drugs, the following books are recommended: CHRISTOPHER GRAY, *THE ACID DIARIES*; STANISLAV GROF, *REALMS OF THE HUMAN UNCONSCIOUS*; STANISLAV GROF, *LSD: DOORWAY TO THE NUMINOUS*; STANISLAV GROF, *THE COSMIC GAME: EXPLORATIONS OF THE FRONTIERS OF HUMAN CONSCIOUSNESS*; NEAL GOLDSMITH, *PSYCHEDELIC HEALING*; RICK STRASSMAN, *DMT:*

Stanford Unger at the U.S. National Institute of Mental Health has done research on this issue. He estimates that 75 percent of users will experience what is called a full-blown mystical experience and that only a few will experience levels of anxiety or nuisance of any consequence.

This is confirmed by Johns Hopkins Medical University. In 2006, they did an experiment where 36 people were given psilocybin, the active ingredient in magic mushrooms. Over 60 percent of these people reported having a full mystical experience, and although some also experienced fear and anxiety none had subsequent problems. In fact, in a follow-up study 14 months later, the experimental subjects and their families were asked if and to what extent they were still influenced by the experience. 67 percent responded that they considered it to be one of their top five single most important experiences and 17 percent described it as their most valuable experience ever. Moreover, 64 percent said that their quality of life had improved as a result of the experiment ("feeling more creative, self-confident, flexible and optimistic") and 61 percent also said that their behavior had improved as a result with "lasting gains in traits like being more sensitive, tolerant, loving and compassionate". There have also been other studies, such as the Good Friday experiment, and their findings are the same.

The reason why some get so much from these substances, while others lose their wits, is that they influence the fluid-delivery system of the brain, helping us bypass the ego. As we know, our thoughts create all reality. The psychoactive substances merely provide fuel for thought, making it possible for the veil between the ego-consciousness and the larger reality to be rent. We are then taken on a journey into ourselves, a journey that takes us beyond the regular confines of our understanding, and this can be intimidating for those who refuse to let go of old belief systems. Rudolf Gelpke, a Swiss professor of Islamic studies, describes his experience thus:

THE SPIRIT MOLECULE. The more you know about these drugs, the more likely you are to benefit from their potentials, and Christopher Gray's book is a great place to start. It is well-written and informative and will provide a proper perspective on all aspects concerning usage.

"Their effects are such that they lead one beyond the customary (and constraining) coordinate system of space and time, and affords insight into the heaven and hell of one's own self—which can be dangerous to one who is not cut out for that, and hence not prepared."(70.389)

Thus, a taker of these drugs is thrown into a state of consciousness which shows how dreamlike this world really is. And just as we shape our dreams with our mind, those who cannot face their own fears or see past deranged belief systems will create for themselves a nightmarish scenario. This experience can be just as frightening as a nightmare while we are asleep. It is often referred to as a "bad trip" and Huston Smith, a professor of theology who wrote *Forgotten Truth* and *Cleansing the Doors of Perception* after his drug experiences, describes it "like having forty-foot waves crash over you for several hours while you cling desperately to a life raft which may be swept from under you at any moment."(100.27)

When such an episode occurs, however, it is only our own inner reality that is revealed, confronting us with aspects of ourselves that we have long repressed. To stick to Smith's analogy, we take our surface-consciousness on a journey into a multidimensional ocean of existence that is ourselves. Previously, we have seen how our ego is only a small part of our personality, and on this journey, we will meet the rest. It is important, then, that we can let go of the ego's limited understanding and perspective, for it is precisely when we refuse to do so that the situation Smith described occurs. The experience is exactly like life, only more palpable and pronounced. For as long as we refuse to go for the ride, clinging to a fragile and narrowly defined self-image, it will feel as if we cling on to a life raft on stormy seas. This experience, in other words, *tries to teach us something*, and if we let go of prejudiced and wrongful conceptions; if we stop identifying with the life raft and embrace the fact that we are the entire ocean, then it will become a most rewarding encounter.

To begin with, it is only because our ego interprets massive change as death that the experience is perceived as terrible and overwhelming.

But as soon as we let go of fears and arbitrarily defined boundaries, we will experience a catharsis of grand proportions. In LSD therapy, it is called "ego-death", this breakthrough where we transcend the old self and ascend to a state of unity. Words, however, cannot describe this experience. What happens is the most awesome rebirth imaginable; all our misguided notions are corrected, and we become as new, seeing for the first time the Universe as it really is. Instead of seeing ourselves as separate and apart, we find that the Universe and us have always been one. Instead of seeing the Universe as an accidental coming-into-being, it is revealed as a vast webwork of eternal validity, a most Wholesome Order rising towards ever greater levels of value fulfillment. Instead of seeing ourselves at the mercy of chance, we find that evolution has been guided by Spirit, that love is its essence, and that everything has happened as a result of universal law. And instead of feeling lost and alone, we realize with certainty what it means to be a cared for, called for, indelible, and unassailable part of All That Is. It is a transformation that grants access to the Universe's perspective; the present becomes more spacious until it holds all eternity; beauty, divinity, enchantment, sanctity, and significance reveals itself in all things; and the world begins anew as we no longer see ourselves as a purposeless, accidental one-time event, but as a timeless episode in the cosmic screenplay.

In part one, we were introduced to people who had experienced this consciousness. Another example is found in Christopher Mayhew, a British journalist and former Member of Parliament. He describes his LSD experience thus:

> "At regular intervals . . . I would become unaware of my
> surroundings, and enjoy an existence conscious of myself
> in a state of breathless wonderment and complete bliss, for
> a period of time, which—for me—simply did not end at all.
> It did not last for minutes or hours but apparently for years.
> During this period I would be aware of a pervasive bright,
> pure light, like a kind of invisible sunlit snow. For several
> days afterwards, I remembered the afternoon of December
> 2, not as so many hours . . . but as countless years of
> complete bliss."(43.137)

No wonder that this experience makes a permanent impression. We just saw the Johns Hopkins study reveal that 14 months later 61 percent of its subjects were still positively influenced, and the LSD researchers of the 1960s also noted this phenomenon. They called it "psychedelic afterglow" because patients, after encountering new levels of awareness, would remain touched by the greater reality for some time. Christopher Gray, who wrote *the Acid Diaries* about his experiences, had this to say of their therapeutic potential:

> "I don't know anything to compare with the way you can feel after a good trip, when there's been a breakthrough, catharsis, and then everything refigures on a more evolved level. I guess you feel the same sense of being unburdened, of freedom, when there's been a major breakthrough with conventional analysis—but with LSD psychotherapy there's that edge of magic, which seems to be the default setting of psychedelics."(43.66)

These substances, then, can give us the most dreadful *and* the most blissful experiences: If we dare not confront the source of our problems, they may scare the bejesus out of us. But at the same time, if we let go of misconceptions, they pave the way for mystical insight.

It follows that the perceived danger of these substances is closely intertwined with the old existence theory: If we believe consciousness to be the result of the brain's electrophysiological impulses and our subconscious to be a dark and dangerous place where our repressed and animalistic tendencies hide, the former will make any meaningful interpretation of the drug experience impossible, while the latter will make the ego afraid of surrendering to the greater reality. To the extent that these substances can lead to psychological problems, it is therefore a combination of these factors[57]. And if we look at other cultures, such as

---

[57] Dr. Rick Strassman has this to say about adverse effects: "The most comprehensive reviews suggest that in well-screened, prepared, supervised, and followed-up psychiatric patients . . . the incidence of serious adverse reactions is less than 1 percent. It is even lower in 'normal volunteers'. Those most likely to suffer from

the Native Americans of North- and Latin America, we find that ritualistic use of psychoactive substances is not only problem-free but seen as a blessing to the individual and community alike.

After being banned for 40 years, these drugs' therapeutic potential is also increasingly being recognized in our culture. First and foremost, it is their ability to offer new perspectives and to let us access areas of the psyche ordinarily out of reach that makes them so unique tools for psychiatrists. Stanislav Grof, the leading scientist in the field, spoke to it this way:

> "The capacity of LSD and some other psychedelic drugs to exteriorize otherwise invisible phenomena and processes and make them the subject of scientific investigation gives these substances a unique potential as diagnostic instruments and research tools for the exploration of the human mind. It does not seem inappropriate and exaggerated to compare their potential significance for psychiatry and psychology to that of the microscope for medicine or the telescope for astronomy." (49.32)

It may be puzzling to hear professionals speak so enthusiastically of something forbidden. Even so, Grof knows what he is talking about. Prior to their prohibition, he spent more than 12.000 hours with patients in LSD therapy and his research material includes some 5000 subjects.

We shall now examine how this research fits together with everything we have discussed, as the psychoactive substances provide access to the same expanded states of consciousness as those resulting from the use of meditation, hypnosis, and other mind-altering instruments. Since time immemorial they have been important for humanity, and as extensive research was done on these substances from the mid 1950's to the early 1970's, it is important to look into it. In this context, Grof is an important source of information. He has written several books, and in

---

prolonged depression, anxiety, or psychotic reactions to psychedelics are usually those with pre-existing psychiatric disorders."(38.203)

addition to the time he spent with patients in LSD therapy, he has also reviewed the work of other researchers.

At the time LSD researchers began their work Freud's theories was accepted as gospel. As we may recall, this meant that consciousness was seen as a by-product of matter and that our subconscious was an unholy place ruled by repressed primitive tendencies. According to the commonly accepted idea, the ego alone was to be relied upon, and it had to protect itself against those aspects of the psyche outside of its control/domain. Grof himself, like any other psychiatrist in the 1950s, began his career as a convinced Freudian. The more he listened to LSD patients, however, the more he had to rethink his position, for as he observed:

> "All . . . patients . . . undergoing serial LSD sessions sooner or later transcended the psychoanalytic framework [Freud's understanding of the psyche] and spontaneously moved into experimental realms that have been described through millennia as occurring in various schools of the mystical tradition, temple mysteries, and rites of passage in many ancient and pretechnological cultures of the world. The most common as well as the most important of these phenomena were experiences of death and rebirth, followed by feelings of cosmic unity.
>
> [The individuals who had these experiences] independently reported that their attitudes toward dying and their concept of death underwent dramatic changes. . . . [They] often arrived at the conclusion that no real boundaries exist between themselves and the rest of the universe. [Instead] everything appears to be part of a unified field of cosmic energy, and the boundaries of the individual are identical with the boundaries of existence itself. From this perspective the distinction between the ordinary and the sacred disappears, and the individual—who essentially *is* the universe—becomes sacralized. The universe is seen as an ever-unfolding drama of endless adventures in

consciousness, very much in the sense of the Hindu *lila*, or divine play."(47.19,57)

According to Grof, such ego-death experience was beneficial. He described it as the best antidote for suicidal tendencies, and not only did it improve people's mental health but also physical wellbeing.[58]

As the researchers' material increased in scope, the harder it was to ignore the parallels between their findings and the ancient mystery schools. At first, the scientists tried to explain the LSD experience in the context of the old paradigm, which meant as a hallucination. When patients told researchers that they not only could connect telepathically with others but that they could experience directly the consciousness of rocks, plants, animals—even the entire Universe—it was, after all, the only explanation compatible with the old worldview. Nonetheless, as more and more subjects elaborated on the same details, the data simply did not fit with the Freudian model of the psyche and so another model had to be revised.

One reason for this was the increasing amount of data suggesting that phenomena such as telepathy and clairvoyance were real. On many occasions LSD researchers observed it firsthand, and the subjects also revealed knowledge of other things that could not be explained in terms of the old paradigm. They could describe very vividly life in the womb (what they thought and felt, what their parents thought, did, and felt, and so on) and they could tell of incidents that took place long before they were born, such as their grandparents' childhood memories. All in all, they exhibited intimate acquaintance with aspects of experience they under normal conditions could not attain, and the researchers sometimes subsequently confirmed their stories.

In other words, it became clear that our consciousness, from this expanded state of awareness, transcended time and space and that there was no limit to its range. As Grof summed up the scenario:

---

[58] Psychoactive drugs have proven successful in treating post-traumatic stress syndrome, fear of death, and alcohol or drug addiction. They are effective agents in anxiety and pain relief and have been known to cure medical conditions as diverse as anorexia, migraine, tinnitus, and psoriasis (complete healing occurs).

"In an LSD session it is possible to experience the totality of suffering of all the soldiers who have ever died on the battlefields since the beginning of history, the revolutionary fervor of all the communists in the world obsessed by the idea of overthrowing capitalist regimes, or the tenderness of all mothers loving their children and feeling concerned about their well-being. In these experiences one can identify with whole social classes or castes, or the population of an entire country; in an extreme form of group identification, the subject can experience his consciousness expanding to encompass every member of the human race—indeed, all of humanity."(49.180)

"One can [even] transcend the limits of the specifically human experience and tune in to what appears to be the consciousness of animals, plants, or even inanimate objects. In the extremes, it is possible to experience the consciousness of all creation, of the whole planet, or of the entire material universe."(47.56)

Thus, it became clear that the expanded states of consciousness made it possible to experience all forms of existence. They introduced us to a world of experience that was fundamentally different from the human, and those who took part came back certain that consciousness was not the result of matter but rather was the essence of the Universe. To them, the Cosmos had presented itself in all its glory. Consequently, they saw it as an ever more extensive adventure; a perpetual adventure created by Consciousness so that it could explore all imaginable and unimaginable aspects of itself—and from their new perspective, the karma and the reincarnation concept appeared self-evident. As Grof confirms, this was the case even if these concepts previously were seen as a result of deranged thinking:

"These [reincarnation] experiences are not infrequent in advanced psycholytic sessions and occasionally can be observed in a first high-dose psychedelic session. Belief in reincarnation and familiarity with this concept is not a necessary prerequisite for their occurrence. They can be observed in sessions of scientists who previously considered the idea to be an absurd superstition of unsophisticated and uneducated individuals or a primitive cultural delusion shared by certain groups of religious fanatics in India. In several instances, subjects who have not been familiar with this concept had not only past-incarnation experiences but also complex and detailed insights into this area that were strikingly similar to those described in various religious and occult scriptures." (49.174)

Here, we come across another reason why some scientists found the courage to put the Freudian paradigm behind; they did not only test the drug on patients, but themselves. As previously mentioned, it is one thing to hear people talk about the expanded states of consciousness and another to experience them directly. For those who have only seen the world from the surface, it is easy to believe that those who describe them must be confused, mistaking hallucinations for reality. However, having firsthand experience, it is difficult to doubt the power of this elevated state of awareness and most found that they were dealing with a form of consciousness which was more fundamental, more in keeping with the ultimate reality.

Note also that Grof said *advanced* psycholytic sessions. This is another point that strengthened the subjects' credibility, as most needed several sessions before they fully broke through the veil and the inner landscape began to unravel. To the scientists, this was another clue that they dealt with something other than hallucinations. Hallucinations are incoherent expressions of a delusionary nature, but when people had multiple LSD sessions, therapists found that the next session seemed to continue where the previous one left off. In other words, it became clear that they were following the subjects on a deepening journey into their psyche and that these sessions revealed an interconnected and sensibly structured inner landscape.

Karmic patterns were one example of recurring themes that could be followed and resolved from session to session. According to the new existence theory, we live many lives, and we have met many of the people we encounter in this life before. The law of karma ensures that everything is most appropriately arranged for the growth of all things; it guarantees that choices made in one life will affect experiences in another, and so it is that we play key roles, acting our part as seen in relation to a larger karmic pattern. The Universe ensures that we get the most out of every incarnation and seen from the cosmic consciousness' perspective, our lives are intertwined in a grand multidimensional pattern. As seen from the overall perspective, this pattern consists of energy configurations that develop and dissolve through encounters from life to life, and thanks to the organizing force behind everything we evolve into something more than we were. In this respect, the law of karma has nothing to do with punishment. It is a balancing out, a Divine principle ensuring both sanity and orderliness to the Universe. As a result of this law, we attract exactly what we need—and so it is that we find our way back home to Center and the Cosmic Womb.

In the course of serial LSD sessions, people gained insight into these karmic patterns; they charted previous lives, they found out who they had met where, what their relationship had been, and what they could do to resolve knots of inhibited energy between them and others. As they began to untangle the threads—i.e., as they understood the deeper significance of events and were able to let go and forgive—exciting events took place. Not only did it change the patients' feelings and reactions towards himself and his surroundings, but it also affected attitude and behavior in other people. Grof explains:

> "The resolution of a karmic gestalt in an LSD-session can be followed by very beneficial changes in the subject and his interpersonal field. The simplification, clarification, and improvement of interpersonal and situational problems after such a reliving is sometimes dramatic. In some instances, such changes involve circumstances in which the individual was not instrumental in any conceivable material way and which could not, therefore, be directly influenced

by him and his new state of mind. Thus, various specific changes have occurred in the life and behavior of other people who were, according to the subject's description, part of a particular karmic pattern that has been worked through in the LSD-session. Such individuals were not present in the session or aware of it, and sometimes they were not even a part of the subject's immediate life situation; they were at various distant places, and there was no real contact between them and the subject. [Still,] the time of specific changes in their lives coincided exactly with the manifestation, unfolding, and resolution of the karmic pattern in the LSD session. These unusual coincidences observed in LSD work involving past-incarnation experiences seem to indicate that events in the session are part of a broader pattern, the scope of which transcends the energy field of the individual."(49.206)

As Grof experienced more events like these, he began taking the data more seriously and repudiated Freud's psychology. Instead, he moved in the direction of C.G. Jung, a psychologist whose theories were compatible with his findings. According to Jung, the human psyche is an interrelated phenomenon; he saw all minds as interconnected and believed that our conscious mind had its origins in the collective unconscious—an inner landscape from which the outer was formed. He was also gripped by synchronicities, as he felt they revealed a purposeful order to the Universe that could not be explained in terms of cause and effect. He referred to them as "acausal connecting principles", and the concept of *archetypes*, i.e., universal/primordial psychic energies that influenced our thinking, feelings, and actions, was an integral part of his psychology. This fit nicely with the data derived from LSD research, and so Grof began to build on Jung's work to become an important figure in transpersonal psychology.

It is no coincidence that Grof and Jung's ideas about the psyche were congruent. They both had had personal encounters with the expanded states of consciousness, and so it is only natural that their knowledge of the greater reality was reflected in their psychology. For Grof, it was the

LSD experience that helped him understand how the human psyche was part of a deeper layer of universal consciousness, while for Jung it was a near-death experience that made him connect the dots.

21
THE NEAR-DEATH EXPERIENCE

"The near death phenomenon is perhaps the greatest gift to the human family in our time relating to the enormous questions of death and afterlife."(109.231)

—Wayne Teasdale, professor of theology—

WHAT HAPPENS WHEN we die? Is our awareness extinguished when the heart stops beating and the brain's electrophysiological activity ceases, or is there evidence for its continuance?

We shall now look at this, for as medical science has become more efficient large numbers of people have experienced what it means to be clinically dead—and survived. Being "clinically dead" means that there is no measurable pulse or brain activity. According to the matter-comes-first perspective, our consciousness should then no longer exist, and yet, between 20 and 30 percent of those who survive remember having an experience after death. As this is incompatible with the old paradigm, most doctors tend to explain it as hallucinations caused by a confused and oxygen-starved brain. Even so, such experiences have become so common that more doctors and psychiatrists are taking them seriously. Those who do are often scorned by the medical establishment. Nonetheless, thanks to the pioneering efforts of near-death researchers, several studies have been done over the past 50 years suggesting that the phenomenon is real, and we shall now put this research into context.

When it comes to the near-death experience (NDE), investigations have been done going back to the late 1800s. In other words, it is no New-Age phenomenon, (Plato himself described it in his book *the Republic*) and at that time the Swiss mountaineer Albert Hein began collecting evidence. He himself had several NDE's. They made a great impression, and as he began researching the phenomenon, he found 95 percent of the NDE-reporters to be consistent with each other.

Now, death and dying has long been taboo. It is a fact of life that few are comfortable with and during the first half of the 20th century there was no research on this issue. In the 1960s, however, things began to change. Dr. Karlis Otis published a report in 1961, called *Deathbed Observations of Physicians and Nurses*. It was based on the testimony of doctors and nurses who together had witnessed the death of more than 35.000 patients. Sometime after this, together with Dr. Erlendur Haraldsson, Dr. Otis published a book that incorporated even more material. It was called *What They Saw ... At the Hour of Death*, and these doctors concluded that the "evidence strongly suggests life after death more strongly than any alternative hypothesis can explain the data. . . . We feel that the total body of information makes possible a fact-based, rational, and therefore realistic belief in life after death." (77.3)

Psychiatrist Elisabeth Kübler-Ross was another important pioneer. She was known as the "death and dying lady" for her work with children and was said to have gathered some 20.000 accounts of NDEs. She had no doubt that the phenomenon was real and that life continued after death, for as she said:

> "We've talked to blind children who told us about their near-death experiences, and they were not only able to tell us who came into the room first, and who participated in the resuscitation, but they were also able to give us precise details of their clothing, something which one who is blind and the victim of wishful thinking could never have done."(90.97)

Ross never presented the material she had collected in book form, but she wrote the foreword to an important book that came out in 1975. This was Dr. Raymond Moody's *Life after Life*, a book that sold more than 20 million copies and for the first time introduced the phenomenon to the public.

The book, however, was not a perfectly executed scientific study and skeptics were quick to point this out. One of the professionals who found the book hard to digest was Dr. Michael Sabom, a cardiologist. On the other hand, it was an intriguing eye-opener, and so he decided to do further research. In preparing for a lecture, he interviewed some hospital patients and their response was astonishing. As it turned out the patients were both surprised and delighted to be asked about their near-death encounter. They verified and elaborated on Moody's statements, but had not told anyone about their experiences because they feared that the hospital staff and their loved ones would scoff at them.

The response convinced Sabom that this was a topic worthy of further investigation. He decided to write a book that would be more acceptable to scientists than Moody's, and over the next five years he collected a growing corpus of data. It was published in 1982, in a book called *Recollections of Death*, and for a skeptic this is a good start.

Another book that gives us a good introduction is *Life at Death*, published in 1980. It was written by psychology professor Kenneth Ring, another pioneer. Besides founding the International Association for Near Death Studies (IANDS), he also published a terrific book in 1985 called *Heading toward Omega*. This book took NDE research to another level, for while the previous literature sought to document the phenomenon, Dr. Ring here takes it for granted that consciousness continues after death; instead of trying to prove it to skeptics, therefore, he studies *the meaning* of the NDE and its aftereffects. Personally, I think this is the most interesting read because it puts the experience in a meaningful context and concludes thus:

> "Near-death experiences, in my view, represent a brief but powerful thrust into a higher state of consciousness. . . . It is an involuntary and sudden propulsion . . . into a realm of profound spiritual illumination. In this respect, the NDE resembles a full-blown mystical experience and—this is the key—the *effects* of that experience *also resemble those that stem from a mystical experience.* "(87.170)

In other words, Ring believes (as Grof did) that the NDE offers the same kind of mystical experience as LSD or meditation. And just as psychiatrist R.M. Bucke did, he presumes that the increasing number of people in contact with it is a sign that our consciousness is about to take a giant leap forward.

We have already seen what this quantum leap means, and we shall elaborate further in part six. To conclude this part, however, we shall look at how the phenomenon fits in with everything we have said about the nature of consciousness: We shall become acquainted with the experiential picture associated with the NDE and its effect on people.

21.1 THE PHENOMENOLOGY OF THE NEAR-DEATH EXPERIENCE

"God conceals from men the happiness of death so that they may endure life."

—*Marcus Annaeus Lucanus*—

I briefly mentioned that between 20 and 30 percent of those who have come back from death remember their experience afterwards. The NDE, however, is a step-by-step process and only 30 percent of those who remember have had what Ring calls a core experience. This is the most intense form of NDE and the one that is comparable to a full-blown mystical experience. Ring describes it thus:

> "When we come to examine the core of full NDEs we find
> an absolute and undeniable spiritual radiance. This spiritual
> core of the NDE is so awesome and overwhelming that the
> person who experiences it is once and forever thrust into an
> entirely new mode of being. . . . No longer can a person take
> refuge in the comfort of the conventional views and values
> of society. What he has experienced in and retained from
> his NDE has for him a higher and timeless validity."(87.50)

It is the people who have had this core experience that we shall focus on, as they are the ones who have gone all out into this state of consciousness. The remaining percentage did not really break through the veil but also their experiences support the consciousness-comes-first perspective. This milder category's most common description is of the out-of-body experience and variants thereof. People report that they, in connection with an accident, surgery, or the like, had an experience of being sucked out of the body and that they could move around with the power of thought. This has also been known to happen under anesthesia, with people later reporting that they awoke during surgery and found themselves floating near the ceiling. Those who have had this experience tell of an unparalleled clarity of mind: They can describe what the doctors did under the operation and what next of kin in the waiting room talked about and felt—and as Kübler-Ross mentioned, there is also evidence that people who normally are blind and deaf can see and hear in this out of body state.[59]

This is the first stage of the NDE, and those who experience the next usually describe being sucked into a tunnel of light which takes them to an inner world. The journey to this place is often accompanied by heavenly, majestic music and here they are met by loved ones who have been important to them. They also meet "beings of light", "guardians", "angels", or "helpers", and communication is in the form of telepathy. While they are there, they describe existence as timeless, filled with love and relatively free from the illusion of separation. They say that their senses are sharpened, that their inner senses become more prominent, that they become more of themselves ("like going to sleep and waking up in the plural"), that this consciousness gives them immediate insight into the ways of the Universe, and that this form of existence is characterized by ineffable happiness, beauty, significance, and pleasure.

Many also experience life passing before their eyes, giving them a new perspective on things that was unknown on earth. The reason is that they see their life from the perspective of all things, which means that they feel all the pain they have inflicted on others as if they did it to

---

[59] See KENNETH RING, SHARON COOPER, *MIND SIGHT: NEAR DEATH AND OUT OF BODY EXPERIENCES IN THE BLIND*; MICHAEL SABOM, *RECOLLECTIONS OF DEATH*.

themselves and all the joy they gave to others as if they gave it to themselves. This life-review usually takes place in the company of a more evolved soul that is there to help. This entity will come with honest and pertinent criticism, but no matter how self-absorbed and crappy our lives have been we will never be ridiculed or condemned. It goes without saying that we do a lot of stupid things while we are on earth and that we tend to get lost in the illusion of separation. As things are perceived from the higher perspective, this is okay because we are here to experience and to learn—and in any case, as seen from this all-is-one perspective, it would be nonsensical to punish someone for what they have done to themselves.

After all this (or some of this), NDEers are informed that it is not yet their time. They are told that they still have stuff to do on earth and that they must return. They then get sucked out of this inner dimension and wake up in their body.

Briefly summarized, this is a classic NDE. However, it varies more than this summary indicates, and to present a better understanding here are some accounts:

> "I think there was a time I was dead. . . . I think I went from body stuff to body energy for a while and then back again. It's like heaven was not a place you go to but a process you fall back into that makes you remember that you have always been connected with everything and everyone." (82.55)

> "It was a total immersion in light, brightness, warmth, peace, security. . . . It's impossible to describe. Verbally, it cannot be expressed. It's something which becomes you and you become it. I could say "I was peace, I was love". I was the brightness, it was part of me . . . you just know. You're all-knowing and everything is a part of you, it's just so beautiful. I was eternity. It's like I was always there and I will always be there, and that my existence on earth was just a brief instant."(87.54)

"I entered something boundless. It seemed as if I had access to all the knowledge that exists, I could just ask for it and it was there. I had a feeling that "the book of life is open!" But it was more than reading a book, rather it was a sense of spontaneous access to immediate knowledge. I could see how there is a creative power of the universe that creates in patterns, and how it all fit together. I remember thinking: Is this how all things are interconnected? Is life so beautiful?" (74.238)

"That was the most beautiful instant in the whole world when I came out of that body! . . . All I saw was extremely pleasant! I can't imagine anything in the world or out of the world that could anywhere compare. Even the most beautiful moments of life would not compare to what I was experiencing."(92.19)

"When life passes before your eyes, it is said that it's like being in a movie theater and watching your life play out on a large screen. Well, I didn't experience it that way. I re-lived my life as a learning experience. That is, I experienced all my actions. I *was* all of my experiences and actions. I was my life and I was everybody else; people, animals, places, and so on. The times I was an asshole, I experienced being both myself and the guy I was mean to. When I gave a guy some beating, I experienced what it was like to give a beating while at the same time I experienced what it was like to get beat up by myself. I was, in other words, both "executioner" and "victim" at the same time. It was an incredibly powerful, painful, distressing and wonderful experience. I remember thinking of what Jesus had said, that we should love our neighbor as ourselves—which by the way was exactly the same as Confucius had said many years before—and I was painfully aware of the wisdom in these words.

> ". . . At times it was a true hell, but the only judgment was
> myself. I never experienced that someone else was judging
> me or my actions, rather the opposite. In fact, I felt a
> tremendous sense understanding and that all my actions had
> had a purpose, even the ones I reviled.
>
> The experience was also a catharsis. When it was over and
> I had surrendered to it, I was filled with an indescribable
> peace and heavenly calm. I felt forgiven and that I could
> forgive myself. When this life review had passed, I began a
> sort of ascension . . ."(2.162)

This was a tiny fragment of the material that describes the near-death phenomenon. Some of the quotations are excerpts of more elaborate accounts and if you want to learn more about the afterlife experience, check out the already mentioned literature.[60] I also recommend *Journey of Souls* by Michael Newton and *Far Journeys* by Robert Monroe, as they will provide a more thorough understanding.

The reason for this is that the inner world we have described so far is no more than a receiving station for the souls who pass over to the other side. The "other side", however, consists of a layered multidimensional landscape and after we are done at the receiving station, we will journey on to a place whose vibrations are compatible with ours. As we already know, our world of thought has a vibration of its own; the more we can incorporate the Wholeness, the higher we will rise, and the Universe provides a place in the afterlife that reflects our maturity. Hence, it is up to each and every one what kind of experience we will attract after death, and Newton and Monroe bring a better understanding of this multidimensional landscape.

Personally, I think this is a topic worthy of more attention. But my purpose is to show how the NDE ties in with the consciousness-comes-

---

[60] Although this book does not elaborate on more recent research, it continues to this day. The literature I have referred to mostly covers research from the 60s to the 80s, and for an update the work of Pim van Lommel (Dutch cardiologist) and Sam Parnia (assistant Professor of Medicine at the State University of New York) is a good place to start.

first perspective, and from what we have seen so far it fits like a glove: These NDEers have presented a general description of a timeless inner world filled with love, a world that words cannot do justice, and where the illusion of separation is diminished or non-existent. They talk of another kind of consciousness, much more in tune with the greater reality, and those who research this topic will also find that no such place as hell exists. Whether we are talking about the material derived from NDE, regression therapy, or LSD research, I have not seen credible accounts of a place where eternal torment awaits.

I say "credible" because there are a few who claim to have died and gone to hell. But from what I have seen, these stories reflect their own state of mind more than anything else, as these people seem to have created this notion themselves—and then made it their reality.

Remember, the most basic premise of the new theory of existence is that we create reality with our thoughts, and we continue to do so when we die. The only difference between "there" and "here" is that while it may take some time before our thoughts manifest as reality when we are alive it happens instantaneously when we die. In the literature, therefore, I have seen examples of people who do not even realize that they are dead as they refuse to believe in an afterlife. Not recognizing the possibility of life after death, they may think that their body has fallen asleep or stopped functioning. They can spend a lot of time and energy trying to awaken the body, but sooner or later they realize their predicament and move on.

I have also seen examples where people, not believing in a life after death, will wake up to a completely empty existence in the afterlife. There is no light, no darkness, no space, no time; it is only the void of nothingness, and they may exist in this condition for a long "time" before they understand that they themselves have created the situation with their beliefs. There are also ample examples of Christians who are greeted by Jesus at the pearly gates, just as there are Muslims who have met Mohammed or another important authority figure. In all cases, we see how they create their own reality—and that the Universe responds to their belief structure in that manner which, symbolically-speaking, is most appropriate for their growth process.

From what is just said, the afterlife may present itself as a lonely and godforsaken place where we are left to ourselves and at the mercy of our thinking. However, this is not the case. As previously mentioned, there are helpers, mentors, friends, and light-beings available, and they will assist us when the time is ripe. In some cases, it may take some time before they do, but then it is always a matter of some lesson to be learned—just as parents can stand aside and watch their children fumble with a task, waiting for them to figure it out. Understanding how our minds create reality is one of the fundamental lessons we need to learn: It is a bit more obvious in the afterlife, but nonetheless this concept must be grasped before we can move on to higher dimensions.

In the same way that people on earth have the option of going to war if we believe in its usefulness, we are therefore allowed to create our own personal hell in the afterlife if we are convinced of its reality and our own unworthiness. However, "hell" in this sense, is no place of eternal punishment as we relatively quickly wise up and change our thinking. A good example of this is found in the following account. The narrator is "Eddie", a man who worked as a hit man for the mob in New York. He was shot while eating dinner at a restaurant, and here he describes his after-death experience:

> "It happened when I was having dinner at Prolovones. One minute I'm sippin' wine the next sippin' blood. It happened so fast that I didn't get a chance to even get up. I remember hearing my heart beat soundly in my ears. Everything else was a blur. Only my heart beat was clear. I felt sad as it went slower and slow. Finally there was a silence and I felt worse.
>
> I woke up in what I first thought was a hospital. I soon realized that it wasn't. So okay I'm in hell or maybe if I played it right to the Pearly Gates. Where the hell was St.Pete? Beings that I couldn't really understand came into the room. I was asked what I wanted to do? I could reenter the physical or I could atone there. I wasn't sure what the atone business was but I was sure I didn't want to go back to physical. Had enough of that thank you.
>
> I was told that because of all the violence I had perpetrated in the Universe that I must be the one to return balance.

Well, if it meant the Pearly Gates sure. I sat in a chair in the middle of nowhere. I mean there simply wasn't nothing there. Then like a huge movie screen the film started playing. Or maybe not a film. Anyways the next thing I know I'm seeing all the people I blew away. In a very weird moment I felt all of their pain and the pain of all those who loved them. It was horrifying. I screamed for mercy. I screamed for it to stop and was told that I was the creator of it all. I screamed for a chance to fix it and was told that I was in that moment given the chance.

Let me say at the end I understood the folly of my deeds. Whatever you put out there relives itself in you forever. So if you're contemplating evil in any form think again. Your creations are you. And you will have to walk through your gallery when you die."(24.121)

I have also seen other killers describe similar experiences. Stanislav Grof recounts what Ted, one of his patients (who was pronounced clinically dead twice under an operation) said:

"The initial darkness was replaced by brilliant light, and he was able to approach it and fuse with it. The feelings he described on experiencing the light were those of sacredness and deep peace. Yet, simultaneously, he saw a movie on the ceiling, a vivid reenactment of all the bad things he had done in his life. He saw a gallery of all the faces of all the people whom he had killed in the war and all the youngsters he had beaten up as an adolescent hoodlum. He had to suffer the pain and agony of all the people whom he had hurt during his life time. While this was happening he was aware of the presence of God who was watching and judging his life-review."(47.181)

As we can see, none of these murderers describe a location corresponding to Christianity's version of hell. Yet, they experience their own personal hell when they understand that whatever they did to others they did to themselves and their stupidity dawns on them. Hell, in its true sense, is therefore *a state of mind.* It is to experience ourselves as less than we are, and from the larger point of view the devil represents our ignorance of the true nature of things. He embodies our failure to grasp the Wholeness and to incorporate it into our being, for it is only because we fail to see how God could create a world where so much pain exists that we blame the devil for that which makes creation less than perfect.

Even so it is *we*, not the devil, who has created reality. *We* are the ones who with our beliefs have created war, exploitation, oppression, and violence, and if we would but take the Wholeness-concept into consideration and live by its ideals, values, and principles, then the world would be healed and we would experience its glory.

For this to happen, however, we must grow consciously to the point where we are able to take responsibility for what we have created. We must understand that it is our cultivation of the logic of fear, the victim role, and the scapegoating mechanism that has created all our misery, and to the extent we are willing to recognize this fact things will work themselves out. As shall be seen in part six, the laws of the Universe make this a certainty.

21.2 THE NEAR-DEATH EXPERIENCE AND ITS AFTER-EFFECTS

"As near death research has shown, no one who has experienced, even vicariously, what NDErs have can ever again regard death with anything other than a sense of infinite gratitude for its existence."(87.31)

—Kenneth Ring—

So then, what happens when people wake up after a trip to the other side?

It varies, of course, based on their experience. If they wake up not remembering anything it will most likely, if they were religious, shake their faith, while atheists will be strengthened in their convictions. Conversely, the opposite will be the case if they remember their afterlife experience, especially if they have had what we consider to be a core experience. For these individuals there is no doubt that life is just a shadow of a larger—and far more wonderful—reality, and that death is just a transition. They have had firsthand experience with the implications of Wholeness, and this has had a profound effect. Tom, an American soldier who was badly injured in the Vietnam War (he had to amputate a finger and a foot), provides a classic example:

> "After my return I'm in many ways a changed man. What happened to me in that short span of time changed my whole way of thinking and my perspective on life. For the low price of a foot, I received a guarantee for what people can only hope for. If people could look into the keyhole as I did, then our individual, national and global priorities would be radically changed."(2.9)

Just like others who have experienced cosmic unity, the NDEers are deeply grateful, and it changes their perspective on life and death. When it comes to death and dying, they are no longer afraid; instead, they begin to see it as the beginning of a new and exciting adventure, and when it comes to life and living, the Wholeness-concept begins to inform their behavior. Previously they were caught in the illusion of separation and this was reflected in their self-esteem, priorities, and values. However, after having experienced the Universe's divine order, how unconditional love is the essence of its being, and how everything they do to others they do to themselves, they do not return indifferent.

As they have observed the world from the cosmic consciousness' perspective, they understand the connections between all religions, but realize that organized religion promotes a distorted picture of the greater reality. Consequently, whether or not they were religious, their outlook on life becomes more spiritual. Superficial rituals, religious doctrines, formalities, and facades lose appeal, and instead of following the herd their focus becomes building a more personal relationship with God. In other words, their inner development becomes a priority. After having their life flash before their eyes, they know that it is just a "hidden camera" episode. They recognize, therefore, that the only thing that matters is the extent to which they can welcome life's challenges with a smile and in thoughts, words, and action choose that response which follows from the Wholeness rather than the logic of fear.

To the extent they do, they know that it will benefit their spiritual growth and the world at large. This results in people becoming more compassionate, patient, tolerant, and loving. As they have a meaningful context to life, they not only have a brighter outlook, but they are more resilient in times of adversity. Their self-esteem is also improved now that they know who they are. This makes them more courageous and less concerned with what others, more superficial people think. They often feel that their brain works more efficiently than before the NDE, and some reorganization has indeed taken place as they are able to see the world from a higher perspective. As a result, they tend to be more concerned with issues like organic food, animal- and human rights, public welfare, and sustainable development. They are, in short, greater advocates for a better and more just social order than ordinary people, and from the sum of all this we understand why Kenneth Ring—as R.M. Bucke before him—concluded that they represented the vanguard of conscious evolution.

For there is little doubt that change is upon us. One symptom is that the children who come into this world tend to be more evolved than previous generations and another is that an increasing percentage of the adult population begins to understand the folly upon which the status quo is built. We shall shortly look into this. But it is a fact that near-death experiences, together with psychoactive substances, are important factors that help to elevate our thinking. We have not yet reached the critical point where the old mindset must yield to a more holistically oriented but as more people wise up, their collective influence increases exponentially. This book is just one of many that indicates an emerging shift. And as more and more people begin to take the consciousness-comes-first perspective seriously, more and more research confirms its superiority.

John White has studied this consciousness transference some fifty years. Ten years after he had a spontaneous mystical experience, in 1973, he co-founded the Institute of Noetic Science together with Edgar Mitchell, an astronaut who himself had such an experience in a space capsule. Theirs is another institution dedicated to bridging the gap between the old and the new, and White describes the evolutionary trend thus:

> "*Homo Noeticus* is the name I give to the emerging form of humanity. "Noeticus" is a term meaning the study of consciousness, and that activity is a primary characteristic of members of the new breed. Because of their deepened awareness and self-understanding they do not allow the traditionally imposed forms, controls, and institutions of society be barriers to their full development. Their changed psychology is based on expression of feeling, not suppression. The motivation is cooperative and loving, not competitive and aggressive. Their logic is multilevel/ integrated/simultaneous, not linear/sequential/either-or. Their sense of identity is embracing-collective, not isolated-individual. Their psychic abilities are used for benevolent and ethical purposes, not harmful and immoral ones.
>
> The conventional ways of society don't satisfy them. The search for new ways of living and new institutions concern them. They seek a culture founded on higher consciousness, a culture whose institutions are based on love and wisdom, a culture that fulfills the perennial philosophy."(87.256)

PART 5

THE TROUBLE WITH THE WORLD TODAY

22
THE THEORETICAL UNDERPINNINGS OF WESTERN CIVILIZATION

"A culture thinks itself through its myths."

—*G. W. Hegel, German philosopher*—

WE ARE NOW familiar with the main features of the new worldview. In part one we saw that the ordinary type of consciousness was only one of several. We saw that those who have experienced other, more expansive forms claim to have been introduced to a consciousness that reveals the true nature of the Universe. Those who have been fortunate enough to experience these states claim that the Universe is a multidimensional living Being; that consciousness is all that is; that the power of love is the foundation upon which everything is built; that nothing inherently evil exist; and that we and the Universe basically are one.

We spent the rest of part one exploring our relationship to the Universe as it presents itself from the cosmic consciousness and we were also introduced to the idea that this consciousness represents our next evolutionary leap. In part two, we elaborated on how history supports this thesis. We saw how our play with duality made possible an accumulation of experience, how this ensured a growth process towards increasing levels of value fulfillment and understanding, and how we now have matured to see the Wholeness beyond the apparent duality. We saw how trends in science and religion reflected this, and in part three we saw how experiential spirituality could be merged with modern science. In part four, we elaborated on this picture, and in part six we shall see what it entails when we apply this knowledge individually and collectively.

Before we do that, however, we need to know what is wrong with the world, for while millions have incorporated the consciousness-comes-first concept, a majority remain ignorant of its implications.

As a consequence, the logic of fear exerts its undue influence on the global psyche, and we shall now see the result of this. As it stands, few have any idea about the adverse impact the logic of fear has had on our society. It has created a disparity between theory and practice which is not officially recognized, but it is this disparity that we must come to terms with if we are to recover. "Recover" might sound like an exaggeration. Even so, our social order is no less corrupt than that of earlier times, and it is only because most have an unwarranted faith in authority that the distance between theory and practice goes by unseen.

For us to create a better world, however, we need to bridge this distance; for that to happen we need to become fully conscious, and so we shall take a look at the damage done to us by the logic of fear. We do this by examining three problem areas which are closely related. The first is the distance between theory and practice when it comes to our constitutional order, the second is the dynamic that results from the excessive influence of corporations, and the third is the enemy images' characteristics and consequence.

In this chapter we begin by looking at theory. So then, what kind of social order are we part of, according to authorized perceptions?

Through education and the media, we are told that we live in a free and democratic society; we are told that we have a government of the people, by the people, for the people, and that we live in a society governed by the rule of law. Most of us, therefore, take for granted that we are born into a decent society and that modern governments are proud defenders of a freedom-loving tradition which can be traced back to the French and American revolutions.

In the late 1700s these events led to the establishment of some important ruling principles. Until then, nations were ruled by all-powerful kings. These kings claimed their authority from God and below them were nobles, knights, and clergy. People in these groups had privileges, varying according to wealth and power, and below them were ordinary people, having no rights at all. The society, in other words, was a strict hierarchical structure, and most people were at the mercy of their superior's will.

In the late 1700s, however, this system was in for a change. It was an exciting time in Western history. Today, we remember it as the Age of Reason (or the Enlightenment Era), and as people wised up, pressure for reform was building. People would no longer accept strict class distinctions, they were fed up after centuries of increasing exploitation and oppression, and they sought to end their disenfranchised status. Thus, they demanded a certain modicum of dignity and control over their lives and the result was the emergence of human rights, as well as governing doctrines such as the principles of popular sovereignty and separation of powers.

Today, every government with respect for itself (and its people) recognizes these rights and principles and has incorporated them into a Constitution. The first principle, that of popular sovereignty, states that all power emanates from the people. This means that the State has no rights. While the old paradigm put the state on top, making it all-powerful, the new puts it in its rightful place as an organizational body created to assist the people. The State's employees, therefore, are public servants and their sole duty and responsibility is to serve the people. Consequently, the State has no rights in relation to the individual and the people, in turn, have no obligations towards the State. Their only obligation is to is to follow its laws and regulations (which draw legitimacy from the will of the people), but—and this is important—*only insofar as these laws and regulations are in line with certain guidelines as defined by the human rights conventions*.

As we shall see, these conventions' purpose is to define boundaries for the State's rightful exercise of power, and they are the result of a historical lesson we would do well to remember. This lesson is that those who govern have a tendency to adopt laws that aren't necessarily in the interest of the general public. This may be laws whose purpose it is to restrict people's freedom, i.e. laws put in place to gratify the elite's longing for social, political, or economic control. Legislation aimed at particular religious or ethnic minority groups, moral laws that ban homosexuality, as well as other discriminatory practices, are examples. As seen from the perspective of human rights, such laws have no inherent legitimacy as they violate overriding principles upon which society is based, and throughout history the brightest have been keen to point this out. Aristotle, for instance, said 2500 years ago that "even when laws have been written down, they ought not always to remain unaltered."(59.44) Thomas Aquinas said 800 years ago that

> "Human law is law only by virtue of its accordance with
> right reason, and by this means it is clear that it flows from
> Eternal Law. In so far as it deviates from right reason it is
> called an unjust law; and in such a case it is no law at all,
> but rather an assertion of violence."(59.44)

Charles Montesquieu remarked 250 years ago that "there is no crueller tyranny than that which is perpetuated under the shield of law and in the name of justice."(59.15) And another genius, Albert Camus, stated in the mid-1900s that "the law's final justification is the good it does or fails to do in the society of a given place and time."(59.56)

At any given time, then, there have been both just and unjust laws. To put it simply, just laws are those regulations whose function and consequence ensure a social dynamic that is beneficial for individuals and society alike, while the unjust laws are those that violate autonomy rights and inflict a destructive dynamic. It is not always easy to know what kind of law we are dealing with. No matter how inhumane a law is, there will always be people who believe that it is necessary (that without it everything would have been far worse), and no matter how useful it is, there will be some who think it is objectionable. History is full of examples of laws which at one point were accepted as necessary and legitimate, but which later generations regarded as incompatible with a justly ordered society.

That laws have an expiration date might be considered something of a paradox. As we shall see, the legal principles upon which the rule of law is based are both simple and eternal, and so one might think that this was reflected in a nation's laws. This, however, is not the case, and the reason is that we are born into a world where the moral climate is so powerful that it blinds us to the eternal light of these principles. In fact, only the most advanced souls have the integrity to connect with this light, as the delusional waters of culture will muddy most minds, making a principled perspective incomprehensible.

Nonetheless, there have always been people sufficiently perceptive to access this timeless world of ideas. This will be that percentage who have advanced cognitively to the point where they have left behind the troubling mists of the collective consciousness. They are therefore able to see their age in a historical context, and thanks to their commitment the light of these principles is slowly transforming the social fabric, bringing us closer to Utopia[61].

In other words, it is as a result of increasing wisdom that the ideas upon which Eternal Law is built becomes manifest. It is a result of us overcoming the collective unconscious and looking back we see how the laws of the land have progressed, becoming ever more aligned with these principles. Today, most are confident that we have progressed to the point where unjust and discriminatory laws are a thing of the past. Yet nothing does more damage to a society than unjust laws, and wise from injury we know that there may come generations after us who see things differently.

These are the insights that have brought about our legal framework, and if public servants want to ban something they must therefore, before they pass a law, make sure that it is in accordance with the provisions of human rights conventions. These conventions represent the epitome of humanity's maturation process. They guard against darkness and our drift towards unconsciousness, and since the principles upon which they are built became formally recognized, their societal priority and position has become increasingly important. Consequently, they stand above all other laws and if the State wants to be considered a legitimate entity, it must respect the citizens' rights as articulated in the human rights conventions. To the extent that the State fails to do this, it is no longer governed by the rule of law—and if it is no longer a rule of law, it has become a tyranny.

---

[61] We have discussed how the principles of popular sovereignty, limited government and separation of powers grew forth as a result of this process. We shall have more to say on them and other principles not yet mentioned, but for the sake of clarity they are principles of equality, proportionality, autonomy, dignity, non-arbitrariness, and the liberty presumption; together they represent the spirit of the human rights conventions and their letter is derived from them.

Throughout history, we find many examples where special interest groups have become too eager in their pursuit of power and privilege. It is a rule rather than the exception that power is never evenly distributed, and those who have exercise a greater influence on the political process than ordinary people. It is therefore important that the Law of the Land recognizes the problem and aims at keeping would-be usurpers in check. Without such vigilance, there will be a dynamic present where the distance between rulers and subjects increases, until it becomes obvious that the State is no longer a representative of the people but a tool for the ruling class, used to keep the rest of the population in check.

History speaks volumes about this, and that is why we have a legal framework in place that recognizes the problem and means to ensure that rights are protected. This structure is the human rights conventions and their purpose is to protect the individual against unreasonable and arbitrary interference by the government. They say something about the requirements any legislation must meet to be accepted as legitimate; they guarantee a fair trial; and if a defendant argues that natural rights have been violated, he shall have an effective remedy. This means that if you are a Christian, Muslim, or Hindu, living in a country that has forbidden your religion, you are free to violate the law and practice your religion—and then, if you are arrested for doing so, you can use your rights as a defendant to challenge the law.

Every signatory to the UN Conventions recognizes that arbitrary, discriminatory, and disproportional laws have no inherent merit and so, if you tell a judge that the law violates human rights, he/she is obliged to let the issue be determined by an independent, impartial, and competent court. Every defendant must document why he is the victim of a discriminatory, disproportional, and/or arbitrary practice, but if he does—and the court finds that he is right—then everyone is free to practice religion, and the law must be removed.

It is not often that defendants use their right to a fair trial. Few are even aware of its implications, but it is a key aspect of the rule of law and a natural consequence of the principles of popular sovereignty and separation of powers. We have already seen that the first principle implies that a law shall reflect the power of the people (as defined by social contract thinking) and not the government, while the second emphasizes the independence of the courts.

As mentioned, it is because the political process is at risk of being overtaken by prejudice and power-hungry special interests that we have built society on these principles. According to the separation of powers, therefore, the government must be separated into three branches, the legislative, the executive, and the judicial. This separation is a kind of safety valve built into the system, and the idea is that the three branches shall control and balance each other so that an unfortunate centralization of power does not occur.

Despite this division, however, there remains a possibility that one or more factions become so powerful that all three branches end up doing their bidding. History is again full of examples but because we have a free and independent press, we feel assured that such a thing could not happen here. It is the task of this free press to keep an eye on everything and to make sure that we are informed if public officials are crooks—and due to the sensationalist-seeking nature of tabloids, we imagine that they would scream up about gross misconduct.

Now, the way things work, we are under the impression that everything is pretty much ok. Thus, we take it for granted that everything is as it should be with the balance of power; that the interaction between the individual and the State is as it should be; and that benefits and burdens are reasonably divided.

Accordingly, we live our lives under the assumption that we are born into a decent society. We take for granted that our upbringing has left us with an objective and truthful presentation of historical events. We imagine that the primary purpose of our educational system is to sharpen—and not subdue—our minds and that the more educated we are, the more we know about important things. We therefore think that professors, newspaper editors, and other authorities are the ones we must listen to if we want to know something worthwhile. And because these people speak admirably about the norms and values that society is based upon—and only rarely point to a distance between theory and practice—we feel confident that we are part of a social order committed to these ideals. Consequently, we believe that the police apparatus is there to safeguard the community; that the court's prime objective is to ensure the rule of law, and that the multi-party system ensures a political process whereby the rights of citizens are properly looked after and maintained.

How could we not? We are free to vote for the party we please and politicians rely on our trust if they want to succeed. Thus, as politicians from one party disagree with those from the other, while the media keeps an eye on everything, we assume that we would be informed if our civil servants were not worthy of our confidence. We have faith in the integrity of our press and we feel certain that only the citizenry of more remote regions is exposed to censorship and propaganda. In our minds, these "remote regions" would be regimes like North Korea, Russia, China, Venezuela, Cuba, Libya, Syria, Iraq, and Iran, and we shake our heads in disbelief whenever representatives of these countries claim to possess any moral authority by pretending to be supporters of the same norms and values that we adhere to.

As we define ourselves in opposition to such states, this more than stretches credulity. After all, how could there be problems in the world if state representatives everywhere were motivated by the same ethics? Somebody must take the blame for our military expenditures. It would be unpatriotic to question our own leaders, and so we are left with the assumption that leaders of these countries represent the more cynical, corrupt, and self-serving aspects of human nature. To preserve our ideas about Western civilization, therefore, we imagine that leaders of these regions fancy war, terrorism, and environmental degradation if it makes economic or political sense, whereby Western leaders, led by the United States—the free world's beacon for all things good and shiny—do what they can to counteract such rogue influence on world events.

Again, how could we not? That is the story Western politicians and academics, helped by mass media, regurgitate every time they go to war—or participate in "humanitarian" operations, as it is called these days. They tell us that it *only looks* like war because they, unfortunately, must use bombs and armed forces to liberate the population. But they assure us that they bomb them with the best of intentions, so that they one day will be able to enjoy a lifestyle as unique as ours.

According to this worldview, the fact that leaders normally commit to such operations in countries where there is an abundance of natural resources—resources that Western corporations end up controlling—

must be coincidental. If our leaders had other motives than those explicitly stated, it would be a war of aggression, and no matter what they are doing that is not it! A war of aggression, after all, is the most serious crime according to international law and if they had less noble aspirations, they could be held accountable for their actions.

So no! Despite experts on international law who believe that their interventionism more aptly can be termed war crimes than humanitarian operations, our leaders will deny and dismiss such accusations: It is not their fault that Saddam Hussein was an evil despot who threatened the world with weapons of mass destruction. It is not their fault that the Taliban made Afghanistan a haven for terrorists—and that these renegades, from caves in the Afghan mountains, threatened to destroy Western civilization. And it is not their fault that Libya's Gaddafi, or Syria's al-Assad, had to be stopped at all costs. Not at all.

If we ask our leaders, they only did their solemn duty, which was to protect us from these threats. They will say that they acted in the spirit of peace, freedom, democracy, development, Father Christmas, and human rights—and that the lobbyists, bribes, and expectations of war profiteers had nothing to do with it.

To put it bluntly, this summarizes the ideas upon which our social order is built. Nonetheless, it is a quivering facade, one that necessitates vast stretches of unconsciousness, and we shall now look at reality.

23
PRACTICE: A LOOK BEHIND THE FAÇADE

"We have the money, the power, the medical under-standing, the scientific know-how, the Love and the community to produce a kind of human paradise. But we are led by the least amongst us, the least intelligent, the least noble, the least visionary; we're led by the least amongst us, and we do not fight back against the dehumanizing values that are handed down as control icons."

—Terence McKenna—

AS WE HAVE seen, Western countries build their system of government on the freedom-loving tradition that endeavors to give to the individual as much freedom, responsibility, and self-determination as possible. This means that to the extent our personal freedom is to be limited, it must be because compelling societal considerations necessitate state action.

It is this simple principle that is at the heart of the social contract. We, the individuals, have created a government due to the advantages offered by such an arrangement. Before we subjected to the rule of law, the strongest and most powerful ruled as they pleased; there was no reliable mechanism that could settle disputes between individuals, and there was no policing apparatus that could ensure that murderers and other criminals were punished. This injustice created a lot of frustration and so humanity found that a centralized power apparatus, consisting of public servants responsible for law and order, was a better arrangement.

Until then might equaled right. If someone robbed, raped, or killed our loved ones, it was up to us to return the favor, and blood vengeance was the prevailing principle of justice. If, however, the bastard who robbed, raped, or killed our loved ones was stronger or of a higher rank a serious problem arose—for the larger the disparity, the less we could do about it.

As humanity wised up, we realized that such a hierarchical and lawless society had not much to offer. For this reason, we built a state apparatus that had a monopoly on power, which was responsible for law and order, and would ensure the appropriate distribution of benefits and burdens. The idea was that every individual should have equal rights and equal opportunity to use his resources and participate in society; we were to be equal before the law, and the State as an independent and impartial entity should facilitate so that society was running smoothly by leveling the playing field and rooting out unjust and discriminatory practices.

The contract between the individual and the State was formalized in constitutions and human rights conventions. These outlined what the State could and could not do, and as long as its servants did not exceed these limits everything was as it should be. An honest arrangement, in other words, if only theory and practice were one—which it is not.

The reason for this is the impact of the logic of fear, intertwined with the fact that we live in a world with enormous class distinctions. Some people, therefore, have far greater influence on the political process than others, and as long as we let the logic of fear influence our judgment; as long as we go about our days thinking that we live in a world where there is not enough to go around and that what we have will be taken from us if we do not take preventive measures, the result is the social dynamic we know all too well. The privileged, then, will devise cunning plots to ensure and enhance their wealth and power. They will believe that if they do not, others will threaten their position, and so they will think of ruthlessness as their ally, the only trait that can secure a happy life for them and their loved ones.

This survival of the fittest mentality is not reserved for privileged elites. It is just as prevalent at the bottom rung of the social ladder and the behavior that follows in its wake is equally repugnant. It must also be said that everyone is not evenly affected by this logic. Among all classes, we find people who to varying degrees reject it, but like attracts like and those who are most engrossed by it—which is to say the most ruthless, power hungry and self-absorbed population—will find a common bond.

We have already discussed how the more influence it has, the more this logic will generate a dynamic that promotes this type of people's career opportunities. Thus, within society's organizational structure, there will be a rule rather than the exception that the higher up in the social hierarchy, the more overrepresented the people with these traits will be. So it was a 1000 years ago, so it was a 100 years ago, and so it is today. These people, of course, have no real loyalty to each other. To them it is a dog-eat-dog world, and just as they would do to others, they know that their collaborators will betray them if they see a profit. Nevertheless, they are motivated by power and influence, and so it is that networks are built and factions arise.

When we are to account for the gap between theory and practice, this must be acknowledged, for although these factions often disagree internally and fight amongst each other in a game behind the facade that others are not privy to, they must work together to maintain their position and maximize their impact. This is the only way 0,1 percent of the population can control the rest. And if these power groupings get little attention in today's world, it is not because their influence has waned, but because they—as exemplified by the Epstein scandal—through threat and intimidation, have created a global network of control so streamlined and perfected that it boggles the mind.

In the following chapters, we shall investigate this. We shall see how the transnational elite's control grid has evolved, how it operates, and what its purpose really is.

23.1 AN INTRODUCTION TO POWER POLITICS

"Since I entered politics, I have chiefly had men's views confided to me privately. Some of the biggest men in the United States, in the field of commerce and manufacture, are afraid of somebody, are afraid of something. They know that there is a power somewhere so organized, so subtle, so watchful, so interlocked, so complete, so pervasive, that they had better not speak above their breath when they speak in condemnation of it."(129.13)

—Woodrow Wilson, American president, 1913—

When it comes to power-politics, we need to go back a few hundred years to understand current conditions. In the old days, the king and the Church represented the only institutions of power. They both had several tricks op their sleeve that they used to control the populace and if the citizens did not cater to their every whim they were tortured and/or killed. The king and the Church were both dependent on this, for the only way they could increase their power and prestige was to deprive the population of the little they had. To appear legitimate, however, they had to find a way to make the citizenry accept looting and the enemy images were crucial in this ploy.

The Church made use of this tool by threatening with hell and perpetual damnation if people did not submit to its authority. To citizens, this seemed like a terrible way to spend eternity, and luckily for them the Church could offer various indulgences. When it came to matters of the soul, therefore, the more money they gave to the Church, the greater was the possibility that they and their loved ones would escape the torments of hell.

The king, for his part, had to find other pretexts for making the populace part with belongings. People would not accept the increasing weight of burdens if they did not see taxes as necessary and so the king had to present himself as a protector of the people. To do that he needed enemies. Real or imagined was of little importance, for as long as the citizenry believed in a clear and present danger the king could do as he pleased. Thomas Paine, one of the Enlightenment Era's most important philosophers, was a keen observer of these dynamics. He spoke to it thus:

> "War is the common harvest of all those who participate in the division and expenditure of public money, in all countries. It is the art of conquering at home; the object of it is to increase revenue; and as revenue cannot be increased without taxes, a pretence must be made for expenditures. In reviewing the history of . . . Government, its wars and its taxes, a bystander, not blinded by prejudice nor warped by interest, would declare that taxes were not raised to carry on wars, but that wars were raised to carry on taxes."(80.42)

The Church supported the king in his schemes, for although the balance of power was not always harmonious (they were in many ways bitter competitors), they had more to gain by making common cause. Thus, alliances were built, and legislation put in place that served their common interests, while the people as usual had to bear the brunt.

By the 1700s, however, another faction had grown forth, making itself a force to be reckoned with. This was the money lenders. The world of banking as we know it had not yet come into existence. But the king needed money for wars and other expenditures and tax revenues were not always enough. Here, fortune favored the money lenders; they discovered that wars were not only good for business but that the more war, the more their power and influence increased vis-à-vis the king and the Church. It costs a lot to wage a war and usually the winner will be the one with the best access to finances. The kings therefore ended up with huge debts to the money lenders, while these vultures would lend money to both sides if it made financial and strategic sense.

The leading money lenders in the 1700s were the Rothschild family. They originated from Germany, but by the 1800s they played a significant role worldwide in the game of war and peace. Like most in this business they were Jews and as they had been discriminated and persecuted for centuries, they had no loyalty to one nation over another.

Hence, by the 1800s, the money lenders had developed a transnational network which was far more sophisticated than that of any nation state. Their ambition and interests were in opposition to the king and the Church and as the 19ᵗʰ century came to an end, they had won the power struggle. So powerful had they become that matters of war and peace were manipulated with great finesse. In their quest for power, this had been their greatest asset—and it has remained so until today.

Revisionist history, however, has nothing to say on this. According to authorities, there are ideological differences behind the wars we fight, and neither the media nor our education system mentions war profiteers and their influence. Nonetheless, economic interests have been the force behind every war, something the U.S. Navy, in a report to Congress, concluded with:

> "Realistically, all wars have been for economic reasons. [But] to make them politically palatable, ideological issues have always been involved. Any possible future war will undoubtedly conform to historic precedent."(22.408)

This report was submitted to Congress in 1947 and its prediction has held true. The reason why we never hear about this is that the victors write history, and for hundreds of years the war profiteers have been so influential that they have shaped society in their image. If we want to know something worthwhile about politics, therefore, we must look behind the facade. We must dig into the material that concerns history's most taboo topics, and we cannot do so without delving into the world of conspiracy theory.

Now, to most, the word "conspiracy theory" discourages further investigation. Authority will have us believe that conspiracy theorists are a uniform group of mentally unstable people, and when the media discusses the phenomenon (such as regards the assassination of John F. Kennedy or the terror attacks of September 11, 2001) their presentation supports this thesis; the conspiracy theorists appear to be frivolous and incoherent, their message and the evidence isn't properly put forward, and they are opposed by more "rational" researchers who tell us that they have looked into the matter and that it is a waste of time for others to do the same.

These more rational-minded investigators will tell us that Oswald acted alone in killing Kennedy, just as Al Qaeda single-handedly executed the terrorist attacks of 9/11. They refer to the conclusions of the investigation committees that were put together in the wake of these incidents and they claim that the idea itself—that the government could be involved in something so horrendous—falls on its own weight. Their thinking is that Western leaders are motivated by vastly different values than leaders elsewhere. They can therefore sympathize with people who claim that the Russian intelligence apparatus (FSB) was involved in the killing of dissidents such as Litvinenko and Politkovskaya, and that it also was behind a series of bombings; bombings which Chechen terrorists were blamed for and President Putin used as a pretext to launch the war in Chechnya.

It is well-known to anyone who investigates criminal conspiracies that those who stand the most to profit usually are the real culprits. And because the evidence—and power-political realities in Russia—supports this assumption, they can, in this case, agree that two plus two equals four. This simple calculation, however, becomes more difficult when applied to matters at home. These people are under the assumption that our leaders are more ethical than others; they trust that the official separation of powers, overseen by an independent press, represents the real deal; and they therefore believe—despite the evidence—that Oswald and Al Qaeda acted alone.

The logic is that if elements within the government really helped to plan, implement, and cover up these atrocities, it could never, in our type of society, be kept secret. For one, if the conspiracy theorists were right, it would mean that a comprehensive set of accomplices would have infiltrated American institutions like the White House, Congress, Department of Justice, as well as the military and intelligence services. It would mean that these corrupt agents were so numerous, and so well placed, that those who were not part of the plot either did not figure out what had taken place or were sufficiently frightened/disillusioned to keep their mouth shut.

If this were the case, it would mean that the most vital institutions in the United States, including the media, were penetrated and controlled by a group of individuals with an influence so vast—and a behavior so ruthless—that an outright coup had occurred.

Now, to those who know history, it is obvious that no ordinary military coup has taken place in the United States. But in one way or another a force must have been at play that was so organized, so secret, so cunning, and so rich in resources, that it could effectively undermine the country's official organizational structure. In truth, undermine it to such an extent that the Constitution and all the defenses that the Founding Fathers put in place against tyranny were laid waste, and the only thing left was an oversized and thoroughly corrupt police state—a police state ruled by a supranational and control-oriented elite with an agenda no less shady than itself.

I say "supranational", as an organization which could kill presidents and arrange terrorist- and cover-up operations on such a vast scale—and get away with it—also must have a solid grip on society elsewhere. If they had not—and if the body of evidence, as the conspiracy theorists claim, is overwhelming and unambiguous—one would expect that the rest of the world's officials, journalists, and academics would let their voices be heard. But no! As we all know, it has been quiet on that front. Virtually every single politician and leading intellectual have lined up in defense of the War on Terror that the Bush administration launched in the wake of the 9/11 attacks. Despite the fact that this war for more than fifteen years has wreaked havoc upon people's life, safety, and civil rights—and despite the fact that the U.S. Vice President assured us that this was a war that would not end in our lifetime—few have pointed out the retarded logic on which a "war on terror" by necessity must build.

Collectively speaking, if the values we take pride in carry any weight, we could have expected those officials who had the people's interest at heart to have cried out if the premise of this war was a blatant lie. This is as simple as putting two and two together, for even if our politicians and journalists did not take the time to figure it out them-selves, intelligence services would. It is, after all, their job to look into such matters and so, if the conspiracy theorists were right, they would have known about it and alerted the rest of us—except, of course, unless also they were subject to this supranational elite faction's corrupting influence.

It goes without saying that such a notion is difficult to entertain. First, an ordinary citizen will find it difficult to believe that a lie of such gigantic proportions could have survived for so long without authorities having taken issue with it. And secondly, if conspiracy theorists were right, it would put him in a very uncomfortable situation. He would either—as most Germans did under Hitler—have to "forget" all about it because it threatens to expose a reality that is too overwhelming for most to process; alternatively, he must come to terms with it, become an activist for a new and more decent social order, and embark on a quest that no one can predict where ends. The former would imply quietly accepting a social contract based on lies, exploitation, and oppression, and the latter would imply saying goodbye to the comforting life of a well-oiled cog in the social machinery.

We all know that morally the latter would be the right choice, but it comes with a price few are willing to pay. Most people have their hands full taking care of family and pursuing a career within the system; focusing on this, while knowing that the system is infested with a cancerous growth that one day may kill everything they hold dear, is not possible, and so they rely on government-sanctioned truth. Thus, as the Norwegian writer Henrik Ibsen pointed out, the average man depends on a big lie to exist. Accepting reality—and taking responsibility for it—becomes a task much too daunting, and so he ends up willfully unaware of the evidence, while he ridicules or despises those who seek to open his eyes.

Psychologically speaking, *that's why* so few people suffer sleepless nights over the fact that three giant high-rise buildings on September 11th dispersed and collapsed at free-fall speed after mid-sized fires had ravaged a couple of floors. Even if the event was unparalleled in world history, they accept our authorities' assurances that "shit happens". And when conspiracy theorists—or thousands of architects and engineers [62]— tell them that residue of high-grade military explosives has been found in the dust from the towers; that hundreds of human bone fragments have

---

[62] For their take on it see www.ae911truth.org.

been found on the rooftops of nearby skyscrapers; that more than a hundred first responders have described bombs detonating in the basements, the lobby, the elevators, and elsewhere in the buildings; that the explosive force was so great that steel beams weighing up to 50 tons were ejected laterally 500 feet, embedding themselves into neigh-boring buildings; that witnesses, photographs, and satellite images tell of pools of liquid molten metal in the ruins which three months after the attack still held impossibly high temperatures of thousands of degrees centigrade; that the temperatures were so high that even the granite bedrock beneath the World Trade towers melted[63]; that radioactive elements found in the dust samples included uranium, thorium, barium, strontium, yttrium, chromium and lithium among others; and that this evidence clearly proves that there must have been explosives in the buildings that Al Qaeda never could have put there, they simply stop thinking. Instead, like violently abused children, they space out into an incoherent state of mind where logic no longer can reach them. There, they take shelter from reality, seeking refuge in a world of fantasy—and to continue living there, they find it easier to believe that the laws of nature, on this day, were repealed rather than that their leaders are lying.

This "spacing out" is a basic defense mechanism when people are confronted with a reality too horrible to cope with. But problems do not disappear on account of us denying them. On the contrary, they tend to become worse, and if we are to have any hope of survival on this planet we must wake up and face the music.

However, if we are to take responsibility for the situation, we need to know more about it. And we shall now see how a group of autocrats over the past 200 years have undermined the Constitution and corrupted the political process; how they have woven a global network of control, so streamlined and so profound that it baffles the mind; and how they, in

---

[63] As more and more whistleblowers have come forward, an increasing amount of evidence suggests that mini-nukes were used to bring down the towers. For more on this, go to www.veteranstoday.com and look at their 9/11 section. See also *9/11—The Third Truth*, a video interview with Dimitri Khalezov as well as DR. JUDY WOOD, *WHERE DID THE TOWERS GO?* or her video-presentation *Evidence of Breakthrough Energy on 911.*

this way, have distorted beyond all recognition the freedom-loving tradition that our civilization is built upon.

23.2 THE TRANSNATIONAL ELITE AND THEIR ROAD TO POWER

"I see in the near future a crisis approaching that unnerves me and causes me to tremble for the safety of my country; Corporations have been enthroned, an era of corruption in high places will follow, and the money power of the country will endeavour to prolong its reign by working upon the prejudices of the people until the wealth is aggregated in a few hands, and the Republic destroyed." (105.148)

—*Abraham Lincoln, American president*—

The faction that we are examining became a force to be reckoned with in the 18th century. With the growth of the banking system, their power and influence became even more disturbing, and by the early 1800s the leading money lenders toppled and created governments as they saw fit.

Now, as this group has controlled governments, education systems, and media for more than a century, it follows that their influence has gone unnoticed. They have done their utmost to rule from the shadows, but a closer review of history is still revealing. In quotes like the above, we have already seen two American presidents allude to this faction's veiled influence, and as we are to embark on a 101-course in hidden history, we shall follow their road to power.

For now, however, suffice to say that as this faction has exerted a greater influence, their activities have not gone unnoticed. George Washington, the first president, for instance, warned against a secret society group adhering to "the diabolical tenets of the Illuminati" that wished "to separate the people from their government" in a letter written on October 24, 1798. Thomas Jefferson, the third president of the United

States, warned that this group "were more dangerous to the Nation than standing armies," in a letter written on May 28th, 1816. In his autobiography from 1913, Theodore Roosevelt, the 26th President of the United States, warned against this "invisible government that owed no allegiance and acknowledged no responsibility to the people," and said that "to destroy this unholy alliance between corrupt business and corrupt politics is the first task of the statesmanship of the day." In his book *The New Freedom* from 1913, Woodrow Wilson, the 28th President, said that as a result of this group the United States had become "one of the most completely controlled and dominated governments in the civilized world—no longer a government by free opinion, no longer a government by conviction and the vote of the majority, but a government by the opinion and the duress of small groups of dominant men."

In both speeches and articles New York City Mayor John F. Hylan spoke out against this "invisible government, which like a giant octopus sprawls its slimy legs over our cities, states and nation." As he said in a New York Times article on March 26th, 1922, this "little coterie of powerful international bankers virtually run the United States government for their own selfish purposes. They practically control both parties and the majority of the newspapers and magazines in this country. They use the columns of these papers to club into submission or drive out of office public officials who refuse to do the bidding of the powerful corrupt cliques which compose the invisible government. It operates under cover of a self-created screen [and] seizes our executive officers, legislative bodies, schools, courts, newspapers and every agency created for the public protection."

If this little summary does not open to the possibility that such a group exists, probably nothing will. But as Franklin Delano Roosevelt, the 32nd President of the United States, stated in a letter November 21, 1933: "The real truth of the matter is that a financial element in the large centers has owned the government ever since the days of Andrew Jackson." Jackson was president in the 1830s, and while John F. Kennedy, with a speech delivered to the American Newspaper Publishers Association (he was obviously speaking to deaf ears) on April 27th, 1961, was the last president to openly oppose this group, there are many, many others who have spoken against it.

We shall say more on this, as we proceed on this quest to identify the difference between theory and practice. But key to understanding how this group has been able to do what they have done is their control of the central banking system. These banks oversee a nation's monetary system and without control of the monetary supply these people would have done far less damage. Nonetheless, this is the core mechanism from which their control grid operates—and if we wonder who the true rulers are, we need only look behind the facade of this system.

The history of the control-oriented elite and their banking cartel is excellently narrated by G. Edward Griffin in *The Creature of Jekyll Island*. For those further interested this is a good place to start, but to make a long story short, the central banking system is no more than a facade that a few powerful men use to maximize their impact on the world economy. To take the American central bank as an example, it gives the impression of being a public institution (Federal Reserve) but it is owned by a dozen banking families who use their control of U. S. monetary policy to further power-political ambitions.

As the Chairman and the Federal Reserve Board is a front and the men behind them have done their utmost to remain unknown, it is quite a mystery who really controls this institution. However, according to people with behind-the-scenes knowledge, the largest stock owners are Goldman Sachs, Rockefeller, Lehman, Kuhn Loeb, Rothschild, Warburg, Lazard, Israel Moses Seif, and JP Morgan Chase. Behind these names we find a dozen old European and American elite families, and these powerful players decide how much money should be printed, at what interest, who should get it, which government bonds should be purchased, and so on.

The economic system is a so-called debt-based economy, which means that every printed dollar comes with a debt attached. As a result, most of the American people's income tax is spent repaying interests to the Federal Reserve. In addition, as most citizens have a mortgage on their car, house, etc., they also spend a significant part of their savings repaying interests to subordinate banking institutions. Most of these expenses could have been averted if the government were responsible for the nation's monetary policy. And if you wonder why the American people have let a group of international bankers control the nation's monetary supply—as well as profit from it—the explanation is that very few people know how the system works. Their education system is so streamlined with the elite's ambitions that they are only told what the elite wants them to know. And so, although this system of control is quite simple, one can get a PhD in economics and still be clueless about how money is made and who controls its supply.

Thus, a better question might be why public officials have accepted this solution. To answer this question, the system is so rigged that most are unaware of this—and that the majority of those who have a clue are more eager to assist the bankers, rather than safeguard the public.

Despite this, among their ranks, there will always be a few whose loyalty remains to the republic. To these men of integrity, vigilance against threats have been a priority, and so the great heads of state have opposed elite ambition. Both Presidents Lincoln, Garfield, Kennedy, (and now Trump) for instance, defied these forces, spoke out against them, and sought to end their control of the economy. As an interesting side note, they were all assassinated. Trump, of course, remains alive but the media and the Democrats' vendetta leaves no doubt that he has been unduly persecuted for his efforts. Indeed, it is difficult to find a better example of how groupthink and ignorance makes the masses conform to elite propaganda, but another distinguished American politician who has fought against this system is Ron Paul. Since elected to Congress in 1976, he has been a vocal critic of the Federal Reserve; he has written several books exposing its unconstitutional workings, and thanks to such people and their determined efforts, the Feds reign is coming to an end.

After all, the way it works, there are no good reasons to keep this system in place. And looking back, throughout the 19th century, there was a constant tug of war between the politicians that represented the bankers and those representing the people. The right to print money, therefore, went back and forth several times during this period and it was not until 1913 that the bankers finally got their way. It was then the Federal Reserve was created—and this again was another sign of the control-oriented elite's rapidly increasing influence.

If we look back at history, the U.S. in the 1800s was blessed with an exceptionally progressive and idealistic government. The people who came to America fled from the Old World's rigid governance and hierarchical power structure. They were drawn to this continent because of the promise it held for a new beginning and one can say that the United States, at this time, truly was a beacon of hope and freedom. The Declaration of Independence, asserting the rights of the individual, had come into being as a result of common dissatisfaction with the king of England and his schemes of excessive taxation and regulations. The Founders were well-aware that governments of Europe were founded upon tyrannical precepts and wrought a Declaration (and a Constitution) which sought to ensure that the United States would not fall prey to the same corrupting ideology. It held to be self-evident "that all men are created equal, that they are endowed by their Creator with certain unalienable rights, and that among these are Life, Liberty and the pursuit of Happiness". It further stated that "to secure these rights, Governments are instituted among men, deriving their just powers from the consent of the governed", and that "whenever any form of Government becomes destructive of these ends, it is the right of the people to alter or to abolish it, and to institute new Government, laying its foundation on such principles and organizing its powers in such form, as to them shall seem most likely to effect their safety and happiness".

Furthermore, a Constitution was put together building on principles previously discussed. Recognizing the principles of equality, autonomy, proportionality, dignity, and the liberty presumption as a foundation for the rule of law, the Constitution sought to guarantee to the individual as much freedom as possible. Not only that, but to avoid the centralization of power that paralyzed progress and the development of civil rights in Europe, it formalized a separation of powers: Legally, the individual came first, being that power emanated from the people; the state-level came second, with responsibility for law and order and to facilitate for the collective wellbeing; and the federal government, being the furthest removed from the individual, was an entity with limited powers. The Constitution elaborated on these nuances, and by separating the government apparatus into a legislative, executive, and judicial branch, with a free press to monitor it, a system of checks and balances was put in place which—in theory—ensured a government *for* the people, *by* the people, and *with* the people.

Still, despite the Founders' diligence and ambition, the Constitution alone could not defend the American people against the degrading influence of power politics. While the spirit of the Constitution was one with first principles, its letter was open for interpretation, and agents of power put their mind to interpreting rights in the narrowest of frameworks. In doing so, they laid to waste the Ninth Amendment and other articles which reminded of the proper balance of power. Rather than a system of principled law, American law schools began extolling a system of arbitrary law, one much more to the satisfaction of power-hungry elites, and as the 1800s progressed the fabric of society was gradually corrupted.

Not only did Natural Law and society suffer as those who guarded hard-earned freedoms became fewer. The treatment of Blacks, Native Americans, and other out-groups showed that the American Psyche was still defined by cultural baggage/prejudice, and as the continent filled with immigrants so also cities, infrastructure, and industry emerged. With it, an elite grew forth who was no less concerned with power and social control than the European and close ties were forged. The wealthiest American families sent children to schools and universities in England. By marriage, they became part of European elite society and business was booming. In this arrangement the American elite was subordinate to the European network of "Old Money". The European elite, by and large, saw the Americans as an uncultured bunch, while the American elite depended on their cooperation. The Europeans did not only represent an older, more stable and comprehensive power faction; they also had far more capital than the Americans, and so it was that the influence of "Old Europe" continued through this informal power structure, even though the United States had won its independence.

Such power structures exist all over the world. Traditionally, they have been spun from networks involved with the freemasons and other secret societies, and we shall soon have more to say on the historical dimension of their operations and their effects on society. Before we do that, however, we must become a bit more acquainted with this hidden power structure. We shall, in other words, look at the *who, what, why, and how*, before we expand on social dynamics in a historical context.

23.3 THE NETWORK BEHIND FREEMASONRY AND OTHER SHADOWY ORGANIZATIONS

"The governments of the present day have to deal not merely with other governments, with emperors, kings and ministers, but also with the secret societies which have everywhere their unscrupulous agents, and can at the last moment upset all the governments' plans."

—Benjamin Disraeli, British statesman and two-time Prime Minister—

Today's secret societies are part of a tradition that can be followed back hundreds of years, and the Masons themselves trace their organizational structure back to King Solomon. Their historical origins, however, is not topic of exploration. Instead, the purpose of this chapter is to say something about their beliefs and their agenda, as well as to present an overview of their societal influence in the past 300 years. It was at this time the moneylenders began to threaten the Church and the king's power, and there is evidence to suggest that the most prominent secret societies at this time were infiltrated and taken over by a power-faction associated with this group.

Looking back, we find that there have been many different secret societies. Some have been closely associated, while others have kept to themselves. Between them, they have differing historical roots and traditionally they have represented a diversity of interests, goals, and aspirations. With the moneylenders' increased leverage, however, one group became so powerful that it managed to position itself as a spider in the middle of a webwork that interlinked most of these organizations.

The members of this spider faction call themselves the Enlightened ones (Illuminati). There are quite a few myths and conspiracy theories connected with them and many also doubt their existence. Nonetheless, a closer look at history reveals a variety of hints and clues to the power of this grouping and its activities[64]. We have already seen several American presidents describe the power it wields from the shadows, and on the connections to Freemasonry, Svali, a whistleblower and a former Illuminati member, has this to say:

> "The Freemasons and the Illuminati are hand in glove. I don't care if this steps on any toes, it's a fact. The Masonic temple at Alexandria, Virginia . . . is a centre in the Washington DC area for Illuminati scholarship and teaching. I was taken there at intervals for testing, to step up a level, for scholarship, and high ceremonies. The leaders in this Masonic group were also Illuminists. This has been true of every large city I have lived in. The top Freemasons were also top Illuminists.
>
> My maternal grandparents were both high ranking Masons in the city of Pittsburgh . . . and they both were also leaders in the Illuminati in that area. Are all Masons Illuminati? No, especially at the lower levels, I believe they know nothing of the practices that occur in the middle of the night in the larger temples. Many are probably fine businessmen and Christians. But I have never known a 32 degree or above who wasn't Illuminati, and the group helped create Freemasonry as a "front" for their activities."(126.73)

As its members' beliefs, goals, and means are important to take into account if we want to understand what is wrong with the world and why, we shall now look into the influence of this group. When we talk about the secret societies, however, we must keep in mind that most of their members, as Svali pointed out, are socially committed people who do not know much about the leading factions' plans and inclinations. These

---

[64] See for instance MARK DICE, *THE ILLUMINATI: FACTS & FICTION*; ANDREW CARRINGTON HITCHCOCK, *THE SYNAGOGUE OF SATAN; FRITZ SPRINGMEIER, BLOODLINES OF THE ILLUMINATI.*

organizations are highly hierarchical structures and on the lower levels they appear to be idealistic associations where people meet and make contacts. Most Masons, therefore, believe that by supporting their brothers in the lodge, they are helping to make the world a better place—but the reality is somewhat different.

Any indications of this, however, are hard to spot for a person who finds himself in the outer rings, which is to say the lower levels of the organizational structure. Still, to use Freemasonry as an example, it is made clear to him that he undertakes to keep secret everything he learns through his membership in the Lodge and that he will die a gruesome death if he fails to do so. He must also swear absolute obedience to his superiors, and he promises to implement and complete all they ask of him—murder and treason included—no matter the costs to ordinary people and subordinates.

Beyond this, he will not be told anything about his superior's agenda. Not before reaching the 30th degree will it begin to become obvious what kind of organization he is a part of, for while at the lower levels it is presented as a Christian organization, it then becomes clear that its purpose is to undermine all religion and that at the leadership level there are Satanists. It is difficult to say how big this percentage is. For one, there are as many forms of worship concerning this spiritual approach as to that of traditional Christianity, and these nuances aside the inner workings are only known to a few. To simplify, however, the official doctrine at the top is the worshipping of Lucifer, while they see Christianity's god as the bad guy.

This might seem strange. Nonetheless, if we take a look at history it's not that outlandish. After all, we know that the Church throughout history has been a ruthless, hypocritical, power-hungry, and reactionary organization. We have seen how it thwarted the progress of science, and it was no more approving of moneylenders and other entrepreneurs as the social dynamic from the 14th to the 18th century provided for an unprecedented growth of their influence. Just like the philosophers and scientists, this emerging faction were more progressively oriented, and the Church saw them as a threat. Hence, political intrigue followed, and to the Freemasons the Church's (and the French king's) betrayal of the Knights Templar in 1314 is an important part of their lore.

Thus, when we consider the institution of the Church, it is not surprising that some figured that the god in whose name the Church plundered, tortured, and killed had to be the bad guy. As portrayed by the Church, he was a rather vindictive, ruthless, and self-righteous personality, one who saw fleshly desires as sinful, who encouraged ignorance and submission, and punished critical reflection with the eternal torments of hell. Seen as such, it is not surprising that they concluded that the Christian god's enemy, Lucifer, had to be the good guy—and as a result Satanism came to be the "Illuminated" ones' preferred religion.

That being said, we need to take into account that the worship of Lucifer and Satanism in essence is two very different things. It is perfectly possible to venerate Lucifer without being a Satanist, as Lucifer, to most Masons, is no more than a symbol of critical reflection, enlightenment tradition, and rebellion against church dogma[65]. Those who look at it this way can, from this starting point, commence on that spiritual journey which we have described in this book. In practice, however, this rarely happens.

The reason for this is that Freemasonry, as an organization, exposes its members to a dynamic that instead of encouraging self-actualization does the opposite. Just like a military organization, Freemasonry is very hierarchical, and those who wish to rise to the top must abandon critical thinking. It goes without saying that self-actualization in this context is impossible. Instead, the organizational structure becomes a climbing place for the more ruthless, cynical, and thoughtless population, because

---

[65] This is an important point. Many Christian authors (Mark Dice and Fritz Spring-meier included) tend to misunderstand this issue and therefore conclude that Freemasonry as an organization is fully motivated by a satanic and evil ideology. This, however, is wrong. From ancient times Freemasonry, as most other secret societies, has its roots in the same Enlightenment tradition which we have already described—the one which slowly rents the veil, making the individual transcend into godhood, and that was secretly practiced the Templars and other persecuted groups. It seems clear, however, that the principles of this tradition have been lost along the way and that most Masons, therefore, are just as blind to the framework behind this reality as most Christians.

they are the ones whom with the greatest zeal are willing to put aside integrity in exchange for power and privilege.

Hence, although the motto of Masonry is "Liberty, Equality, and Brotherhood," it represents the opposite: it offers neither freedom nor equality and brotherhood only exists if you obey the leadership. In fact, those who think for themselves and act on their integrity are ostracized, even killed, and it is the same mechanisms involved as in any other sick cult. Consequently, Freemasonry does not hold much promise for *real* spiritual development. Instead, to the degree they want to climb to the top, those who are lured in must make a pact with the "devil", and when one under these circumstances meddles with the spiritual Satanism is the natural result.

We shall, however, leave this aspect of their operations aside for now and investigate another fact that reveals itself when one reaches the 30th degree. It then turns out that the leadership follows a plan that has been hundreds of years in the making and where the objective is a new world order where they can consolidate all power and present themselves as liberators (i.e., rulers) of the world.

In other words, they work towards a supranational state where they set the agenda, while distributing resources, benefits, and burdens as they see fit. They see this as a most decent and endearing endeavor, and when the time is ripe and the rulers of the New World Order can openly reveal themselves, they expect to be hailed as saviors.

The reason for this is that they assume that we, by then, will be so disillusioned that the solution they offer will seem as a deliverance from the present system. After all, the nation-state concept has failed to bring about a stable and peaceful world. Instead, it has been the source of an indescribable amount of war, conflict, exploitation and misery as the state machinery internally has functioned as a climbing place for the planet's most selfish and fear-oriented individuals; these have fought among themselves for the most powerful and influential positions, and the last century alone their scheming resulted in more than 200 million dead. R.J. Rummel, a professor of political science, speaks to it thus:

> "During the [last century, at least] 170 million men, women, and children have been shot, beaten, tortured,

knifed, burned, starved, frozen, crushed, or worked to death; burned alive, drowned, hung, bombed, or killed in any other of the myriad ways governments have inflicted death on unarmed, helpless citizens and foreigners. The dead even could conceivably be nearly 360 million people."(37.27)

Rummel only summarizes the suffering governments inflicted on the civilian population, and in addition we can count at least 35 million soldiers who fell for our leaders' external power-political ambitions. When they want something, they will go to war to take it, and so it is that the citizens of the world, until today, have been at the mercy of a power-hungry elite who have set themselves above the laws that they expect others to obey.

We shall look into that later. But to say more about the Masons, it is obvious to them that the current nation-state system is not a working solution. History speaks volumes about it and their solution is a supra-national government which is powerful enough to keep the peace—on their terms. Their stated objective, therefore—that which they try to sell to politicians at the annual Bilderberg meetings[66]—is an arrangement that is somewhat more sophisticated, one where might no longer equals right and a more sustainable development can be realized.

This may not sound too bad, and most politicians have no doubt that their intentions are the best. We should, however, not forget that history's greatest crimes have always been committed with the best of intentions; whether we are talking about Hitler, Mao, Stalin, Churchill, Blair, or Bush, they have all governed under the assumption that the end justifies the means, and this is also the case with the men behind the New World Order: For several centuries, to create an enlightened global autocracy, these fear-mongers have led the way in a game where divide-and-conquer has been their modus operandi. Through cunning and ingenuity, they have devised—and profited from—all the major wars in this period, and this has been essential to their ambition.

---

[66] See DANIEL ESTULIN, *THE TRUE STORY OF THE BILDERBERG GROUP.*

For these social engineers, there is nothing like war and cataclysm. Peaceful societies are by nature stable and those who wish to introduce reforms must convince people that something is wrong with the status quo. War, poverty, and economic recessions, therefore, are not that bad because such calamities provide the kind of dynamic that these elites are looking for. It is only when things go really bad that the masses are motivated to accept the solutions this group has to offer. Hence, the planet's most powerful men have diligently availed themselves of these means to realize their ambitions—and they know that if we are really frightened, we will not only accept their solutions but salute them.

We shall expand on that later. However, the elite behind the New World Order must take their share of responsibility for everything that is wrong with the world. It may seem as if blame is to be put else-where, not least with public officials (for we prefer not to accept our share of responsibility). Nonetheless, we would do well to remember that they are no more than functionaries for the control-oriented elite, puppets subject to the will of more powerful men. Our politicians rarely admit to this, but in 1913 President Woodrow Wilson stated it thus:

> "Suppose you go to Washington and try to get at your Government . . . you will always find that while you are politely listened to, the men really consulted are the men who have the biggest stake—the big bankers, the big manufacturers, the big masters of commerce. . . . The masters of the Government of the United States are the combined capitalists and manufacturers of the United States."(22.187)

Now, this quote is more than hundred years old, and some prefer to believe that things have improved since then. This is not so. As a matter of fact, this elite's control of the political process has been increasing, and there are many who can vouch to that. One is Lindsey Williams, a priest who became friendly with representatives of this group in 1971, when he served as a minister for the big oil companies in Alaska. Among other things, he was present at their Board meetings, and he has this to say on the subject:

"I will never forget the day when I met the elite. I don't know how to stress this enough, because since you've never met them and you've never lived with them, the only thing I can do is to tell you what I lived and saw. I need to say emphatically again to every person: . . . *There positively is a group of people on the face of the world that tell the president what to do; they dictate the Congress what bills to pass; they control the amount of . . . money that you make; they control everything that we do. They have control of the world today, and there positively is such a group of people living on the face of the earth today.*"(70.166)

For those with eyes to see, then, it is difficult to doubt the control-oriented elite's existence and enduring influence[67]. No matter how good intentions politicians might have, therefore, they find themselves in an impossible situation as above them in the system they have the elite's interests and ambitions that they must respect and implement, while below they have a sea of ignorant, short-sighted, and self-absorbed citizens that must be flattered and enticed. Moreover, this population is so helplessly caught in the net of social control that the elite has woven that they do not know up from down: Not only are they educated in institutions so streamlined by the establishment that the gap between theory and practice is difficult to perceive, but they are surrounded by television, books, newspapers, radio, and magazines that fill their heads with exactly what the elite wants.

When it comes to power, a well-oiled propaganda apparatus is this elite's most important tool, for only to the extent that we are filled with ignorance and fear will we voluntarily conform to a social order

---

[67] Now there are "experts" out there who together have written several tons of books on how the conspiracy theorists are ripe with nonsense; they claim that there is no such control-oriented group of elitists above the law and that everything is ok with the world. For those who still believe so—or want irrefutable evidence to the contrary—I recommend General FLETCHER PROUTY: *THE SECRET TEAM*. He was one of President Kennedy's top officials and later wrote this book about his experiences with the transnational elite's power apparatus and operations.

established by war profiteers. It goes without saying that their interests are diametrically opposed to ours—and that we, if we knew better, would vote for those officials who spoke to our cause rather than those who conspire in the logic of fear.

If we did, it would ruin the Satanists' plan completely. No goal can be more worthy than the means used to reach it, and from their means we see that their New World Order is the actualization of everything that follows from the logic of fear. The men behind it have consistently availed themselves of deceit, falsehood, violence, threats, terrorism, and war to reach their goal; they have educated and hypnotized people into applauding hypocritical, ignorant, and inhumane moral codes; and they have elevated the most spineless and corrupt to senior positions. Those who have opposed them have been threatened, killed, or in other ways clubbed into submission, and we have no reason to believe that things will be different when their plans are completed.

It is, after all, gangster mentality all the way with this elite faction, and the only thing that separates them from other criminal organizations is their grip on power. Consequently, we have no reason to believe that their transnational solution entails other than a worldwide police state, a global dominant order where they define appropriate morals and laws. In such a society, some problems would probably disappear. It would, for example, be easier to enact and enforce legislation aimed at limiting environmental damage and fighting crime. But only to a certain level, for the biggest gangsters would be those holding all the power, and although they would be happy to use the law against competing factions and other deviants, they would remain untouched by the justice system.

No matter their claims to the contrary; a world where human rights are respected and people are equal before the law is the last thing these autocrats want. Instead, the optimum condition would be a fascist order where the needs of elite deviants, war profiteers, and Big Business are catered to, and such an arrangement presumes that the ruling elite holds all the power. We are in other words talking about "big brother", that kind of world authors George Orwell and Aldous Huxley warned about with books such as *1984* and *Brave New World*. This is a world where the State relies on an extensive police-, informer-, and propaganda apparatus for its stability, where value systems will be reversed, and the human spirit enchained. Orwell, therefore, was right in picturing our future as "a boot stamping on a human face—forever", as nothing is more threatening to the modern dystopian state than freedom, self-determination, integrity, and reason. For sure, not much to look forward to—but this is the result of the ruling elite's mindset taken to its natural conclusion.

Now, the informal power structure consists of different factions. The interaction and intrigues between them are complex and well-hid, making it difficult to ascertain much. Even so, what we know is that the elites differ and disagree on many things, including means and ends. In other words, there are groups who define themselves in opposition to the ruling elite faction's ambitions and methods and who are working to see a more positive scenario manifest.[68] Some are openly discussing their opposition, while others conspire in secret. That things are quiet on the surface, therefore, does not mean that all our public servants and industrialists are cooperating with the leading elite faction, and current affairs—not least the Epstein case and the scandal surrounding Joe Biden and his corruption—is a testimony that more positively oriented factions are about to gain the upper hand.

When that happens—when the media begins to put those things on the agenda that until now have been hidden, and when it is no longer taboo for academics and policymakers to discuss the reality of power-politics—support for the men behind the New World Order will quickly fade away. We must remember that the network we are talking about has been around for centuries. Very few of its members have chosen to participate voluntarily; instead, they have been born into a family that expects a certain behavior and that they will carry on until the goal is realized. Just like in any other cult, there is an internal dynamic which makes the individual fear the collective's condemnation and contempt. Ordinary people cannot imagine the repressive nature of core moral codes

---

[68] For better insight into the workings of more positive-oriented secret societies and elite factions, see sites such as www.knightstemplarorder.org; www.itnj.org; www.thealliancejournal.org; www.veteranstoday.com. Also watch President Trump "draining the swamp".

and those who have talked tell of an upbringing beyond anything we can comprehend.

I mentioned that the leading faction is swarming with Satanists. They worship Moloch, a Canaanite deity associated in biblical sources with the practice of child sacrifice, and those who have come forth describe a childhood where animals, children, and adults were sexually abused, tortured, and killed in various occult rituals. They claim that cannibalism and other beastly scenarios were part of their lives and that they had to learn to kill at an early age. We shall not go into detail, but they describe an upbringing in a rigid and inhumane structure whose main purpose it is to destroy any connection that children have with inner-self. They are brainwashed to never trust anyone, to despise weakness, to look outside themselves (to their authorities) for answers, to look down on those below them in the hierarchy, and to obey those above them. In short, childhood consists of a series of traumatic events, and their "education" not only results in an amoral worldview fully dissociated from the values, ideals, and principles of the Wholeness, but a motivation for power. They are convinced that there is no way to escape from this group, and so the only means by which they can have a better life is to move up the pecking order.

Now, this may sound outlandish. The evidence, however, is quite overwhelming and for those who have the stomach, books like *Trance-formation of America* (Cathy O'brien), *Access Denied* (Cathy O'brien), *Day Brakes Over Dharamsala* (Janet Thomas), *Paperclip Dolls* (Annie McKenna), *Unshackled* (Kathleen Sullivan), *A Nation Betrayed* (Carol Rutz), *Thanks For the Memories* (Brice Taylor), *Morning Come Quickly*[69] (Wanda Karriker), *Lucifer's Lodge* (William Kennedy), *The New Satanists* (Linda Blood), *Secret Weapons* (Hersha, Griffis, Schwartz), *The Carnival of Life and Death* (James Shelby Downward), *Rabbit Hole* (David Shurter), *Breaking the Circle of Satanic Ritual Abuse* (Daniel Ryder), *Cult and Ritual Abuse* (James Randall Noblitt), and *the Franklin Cover-Up* (John DeCamp) are worth looking into.

---

[69] I note that Karriker's story is fictional. However, she is a psychologist who is highly knowledgeable on the subject and weaves factual information into the text.

If you go online, www.itnj.org and www.endritualabuse.org are a good starting point. The former, the International Tribunal of Natural Justice, put down a commission to study the phenomenon in 2018. Its Chief Counsel was Robert David Steele, a former CIA officer, and he estimates that around 800.000 kids are abused in the U.S. every year, many in such rituals. Hence, although it is a most unpleasant realization, these things are so abundantly documented that nobody should doubt that Satanism is prevalent amongst elites. John DeCamp, a U.S. senator who was introduced to a fraction of the evidence while serving on an investigative committee, has more to say:

> "One of the most potent weapons of the satanists is the inability of the average person to comprehend such hideous events as described.
> . . . A few years ago, if anyone had recounted something like [these] testimonies to me, I would have recommended that they be hauled off to the loony farm. Today, I have no doubt that much—maybe all—of it is true. I have been confronted with documentation of a world I did not know about or believe existed."(29.211)

Thus, although it is difficult to know the extent of the problem, it is real. And if we are to try to understand how adults can expose not only others but even their own children to such atrocities, we must remember that they themselves have been brought up this way—and that they are just as damaged as their children become. Intellectually, adults justify the abuse by the following logic: They think that the world is such a horrible place that to the extent they can harden their children against its cruelty, they will do them a favor. From their own childhood, they have learned that what follows from the logic of love makes them vulnerable and the idea, therefore, is that if they can teach their kids to stand up for themselves (always in opposition to others) and obey the same distorted moral codes as the rest of the group adheres to, they are better off.

We have already mentioned that one incentive is that the higher up in the hierarchy people climb, the less bothered they are by others, and they also learn about a black magic which, according to them, makes them more and more like gods. We are, in other words, speaking "self-actualization" *that builds upon and expands* the illusion of separation. This kind of self-actualization is also possible, as it is based on laws that are quite real. However, as one process is built on the logic of love and the other on fear, the two are diametrically opposed. The former, therefore, unites us more and more with our surroundings, while the latter isolates us. Svali, one of the Illuminati's defectors, has this to say about the grouping's spiritual practice:

> "The Illuminati is a group that practices a form of faith known as "enlightenment". It is Luciferian, and they teach their followers that their roots go back to the ancient mystery schools of Babylon, Egypt, and Celtic druidism. They have taken what they consider the "best" of each . . . and joined them together into a strongly occult discipline. Many groups at the local level worship deities such as "El", "Baal", and "Ashtarte", as well as "Isis" and "Osiris" and "Set". This said, the leadership councils at times scoff at the more "primitive" practices of the . . . lower levels.
>
> I remember when I was on council in San Diego, they called the high priests and priestesses the "slicers and dicers", who kept the "lower levels happy". This is not to offend anyone, it only shows that at the leadership levels, they often believe they are more scientifically and cognitively driven. But they still practice the principles of enlightenment. There are 12 steps to this, also known as "the 12 steps of discipline", and they also teach travelling astral planes, time travel and other metaphysical phenomena.
>
> Do people really do this or is it a drug induced hallucination? I cannot judge. I saw things that I believe cannot be rationally explained when in this group, things that frightened me, but I can only say it could be a combination of cult mind control, drug inductions, hypnosis, and some true demonic activity. How much of

each, I cannot begin to guess. [But] I do know that these people teach and practice evil."(126.72)

Now, one may wonder why some people, despite having a certain awareness of universal law, devote themselves to the self-fulfillment process which follows from the logic of fear rather than love. The answer is that they do not know better. From birth, they are taught to cultivate this logic, and for those trapped by such incentives it seems like the most logical way to survive. As seen from their perspective, it appears obvious that good is weak and powerless while evil is potent and strong. Life has taught them this—and if sufficiently traumatized, for their own survival, anyone will ally with "evil".

I put this in quotes because they do not necessarily see their actions as evil. Remember that these people look at life from a perspective where the implications of the Wholeness are impossible to recognize, and because they are convinced that the world is a terrible place, they cultivate the opposite of compassion, trust, understanding, tolerance, forgiveness, etc. Such qualities make them vulnerable. And because they have been taught to fear the wounds such tendencies can—and will—result in, they embrace what follows from the logic of fear. We must not forget that they have grown up with emotional neglect and physical abuse that most cannot comprehend. Since they were infants, they have been terrorized by their closest relatives. Life has taught them that there is no way to escape the torment, and so it seems that their only defense is taking shelter in the logic of fear.

To the extent they do, they can survive. To continue on, they hide their disappointments deep within, and Satanism therefore is nothing but the name of that spiritual science which follows from the illusion of separation. We have been occupied with the spiritual science that draws towards wholeness, but the Universe is dependent on the interplay between light and darkness for its play. Without darkness, the process we have described as its exhalation and inhalation would not have been possible and so, despite appearances, everything is as it should be. From our perspective, it can, of course, seem a bit too much. Nonetheless, we must be able to choose between dark and light for free will to have any meaning—and the greater the span and the tension between the two, the more beautiful creation becomes as seen from the Ultimate perspective.

I do not mean to romanticize. However, to reach full consciousness, we must accept that the darkness does not exist as portrayed by culture. The devil, in biblical terms, is both real and not, as everything is but a thought, an experience—an emerging subconscious—we must own if the collective is to heal.

Without going into the problem of Evil, which is often the case of poor judgement, we can at the very least accept that nobody is all bad or all good. Whether we are talking about Mother Theresa or Hitler, I believe that in all cases we do our best with the traumas and ideas that we have and that we all aspire to something better. Even so, in human beings, there is a certain attraction towards moral laziness, towards dominance and control. None come untouched by it and, leaving morals aside, the forces of darkness provide pleasure on many terms. Young souls, therefore, fall more easily pray to the reptilian brain, its territorial constraint, proclivity for violence, and push for domination. It has been with us for hundreds of millions of years, and we all have a basement in our psychology that, if unrestrained, can be vile. As we mature, however, we find that in the greater scheme of things there is only one code of honor, and it is to embody the values, ideals and principles connected to Wholeness. Aiming at less will simply be bad for character and the play of fools, even though it is frequently portrayed.

From this lack of perspective, a culture of fear and control has evolved. The Satanists, as we have seen, represent those who willfully endorse anger, threat, and violence to get their will—those who are self-centered, no matter the costs to others. Through sexual energies, ritual, and sacrifice, therefore, they connect with primordial forces who may appear both powerful and frightening.

Whether these entities are a part of our own psyche or outside agents of influence is an interesting question. On the one hand, we know that, from the ultimate perspective, the Universe is a thought thinking itself. Thus, in the final analysis there will always be one. Even so, there are layers of understanding, patterns of interference, and the fragmented perspective provides many options of interpretation. One can, therefore, as many do, see the devil and other demons as agents of outside influence, or we can see these forces as a deeper inheritance within humanity—one that connects us with cosmic potencies. While the former view will frighten and diminish, the latter will empower and expand. It is up to us to choose.

What seems clear is that humans, as we grow in understanding, will encounter these forces. In doing so, we become more than we were, and while those who are guided by Wholeness will manifest more positive potentials those who deal in black magic will connect with negatively polarized entities. They may also, just like lightworkers, to different degrees, embody these forces in the physical, a.k.a. spiritual possession. In any case, as we evolve, we merge with an order of being beyond good and bad as most people understand these values. We tap onto another level of creation. One where the masculine and feminine roam free, uninhibited by fragmented perspectives. And while the darkness, to us, appears as the negative polarity intensified, it is also, as seen from the ultimate perspective, a tossing about in more limitless creation.

The darkness, then, is not the negation of God, for it is a force that knows not only its purpose but its place in the larger play. To personalize this essence is difficult, as is to define its body of being. On one level, it is the taker of innocence, the creator of trauma, and the negation of creation. At another level, however, it is a ghost in the machine, a poltergeist, a universal unconscious, a force that must exist for the ultimate advancement of all. In other words, as seen from the higher perspective, "the devil" performs a humble service.

Being children of duality, we tend to forget this. Nevertheless, there is not only pain and fear but a hidden joy in embracing the darkness. This hidden joy includes the scream of rebellion, enlightened insanity, and imagined omnipotence—pillars of extasy for those without a moral compass. These are just some of the "positive" experiences offered at our level of perception, and from a more evolved entity's perspective, what we perceive as death, trauma, limitation, and destruction, is really a dance of energies, food for thought, processes for growth. Furthermore, as seen from the ultimate perspective, the entire Process is action and potential, wakefulness and forgetfulness—an eternal Self stirring for ages, observing different stages of remembrance.

Within this greater Unconscious force are entities who more or less embody its negative polarity, who feed on despair, finding nourishment by drama and trauma. These entities, however, are not eternally bound within this framework of experience. In fact, also they are a temporary expression of the Light that has forgotten itself, and the closer we get to the core of the multidimensional Universe, the more this forgetfulness evaporates. The Light is, in other words, everything, but in our part of the Universe the illusion of separation weighs so heavily that this secret is well-kept. Here, everything is set so that individual fragments can choose whether to create in the image of light or darkness.

It varies from century to century which of the two are the most influential. The cycles of history are so arranged that everything has its proper place, and we are in a transitional phase as the darkness, after millennia of dominance, has outlived its usefulness and the light is coming back.

Hence, the Wholeness and its implications will become more and more obvious to everyone. And those who have cultivated the logic of fear must either find the courage to embrace the logic of love, or move on to other dimensions where they can continue exploring the dark road. As we shall discuss, just as there are dimensions beyond this where the light has a more powerful presence, so there are dimensions in which forces of darkness prevail. These dimensions, however, have different vibratory levels, and our actions determine whether we move "up" or "down" in this system.

The physical, therefore, is a place where other dimensions not only meet but exercise a certain influence. Our thoughts and feelings can be seen as nourishment for entities in these dimensions, the forces of darkness encouraging and feeding off anxiety, bitterness, hate, etc., while the forces of light encourage and feed off the opposite. Thus, the cartoons where Donald Duck has an angel and a devil sitting on each shoulder comes to mind; they both "whisper" in our ear, and we have a choice whose voice we pay attention to. The more we go in one direction, the more our energy melts together with experiences of either polarity. Even so, we should remember that there are no real boundaries in this World. These other forces, then, represent aspects of ourselves, and to the enlightened mind the forces of darkness are merely guides helping us to see more clearly—and thus heal—those facets of our own being that we have not yet filled with light, love, and understanding.

Again, we come back to the central dynamic involved with the self-actualization process. As we wise up, we become more conscious of this dynamic, and we more consistently begin to represent those thoughts, words, and actions that follow from Wholeness rather than the illusion of separation. We know that to the extent we do the former, we will be considerate and caring and evermore see us and habitat as one. Moreover, to the extent we choose the latter, we will be controlling and egocentric, evermore seeing ourselves in opposition to others.

The Cosmos does not tell us what is best. We are free to experience whatever we want, and it is up to us to choose one or the other. To us, the Universe is seen as a value-neutral place, and because the illusion of separation is so compelling many choose the dark road, endeavoring to get ahead at the expense of others. The earth's time as a playground for these souls, however, has come to an end. And those who insist on continuing this road must go on into dimensions populated by energy personalities with a vibration matching their own.

This means that the next step for them will be a world where they *really* must fight for a place in the sun; there they will experience what might-equals-right fully means, and they get to experience the logic of fear taken to its ultimate conclusion. It goes without saying that these are unpleasant places. Nonetheless, this is the way the Universe is put together, and there is a lot to be learned from going this way. Those who do, however, sooner or later come to understand that they have embarked on a dead end. The premise on which their project is built—that they can overcome Wholeness—is absurd, and those who walk this road will find themselves in an increasingly impossible situation.

It might, of course, take time before this becomes fully recognized. Nonetheless, looking at it from the ultimate perspective, they might as well be trying to win a fight against themselves. They have free will and so they can try, but ultimately it will dawn on them that from the very outset the dark road was self-defeating. Universal law makes sure of it, for if an entity refuses to reorient its energy towards the positive path (if it decides to go the negative way all out) a phenomenon called spiritual entropy occurs. This is the point when the sense of self can no longer be maintained and the soul disintegrates into pure energy.

To put this into context with the multidimensional Universe we have described, we can imagine a Universe of seven dimensions in which we now find ourselves in the third[70]. In this case, the Center is found beyond the seventh dimension and the closer we get, the more of ourselves we become—and the more into Fullness of Being we merge. From this set up, we see that we have a way to go until we reach our ultimate destination and from our place we must choose between the positive or the negative path. The positive leads us all the way to the Center, to Ultimate Unity with All That Is, while the negative takes us no longer than the fifth dimension. This is where its possibilities are exhausted; this is where spiritual entropy is next, and those entities who have advanced to this point must reverse their polarity and embrace the Wholeness if they want to evolve into sixth density and beyond.[71]

We now have an idea of the bigger picture as the drama between polarities plays out. To return to power-politics, however, it is the negative path that ruling elites have chosen. Quite simply, this means that they use fear to control others—and they know that the more we are filled with fear, the more power they have. Later, when we explore the power of enemy images, we shall look at how they use this tool in the service of social control. We shall then discuss how the populace, time and again, are deceived by authorities who fill their heads with misconceptions and

---

[70] The word "dimension" can be a bit misleading. What we are talking about is a series of energy-related reductions from the Center that results in a multilayered Universe—in several planes of experience—and so the word "density levels" might describe this system more accurately.

[71] This cosmo-conception comes from the Law of One Material (channeled by Carla Rueckert). Some, like Ashayana Deane, describe more than seven densities/ dimensions. This might be correct, but the basics are the same. Hence, as the Hindu mystics speak of seven zones of Brahma's egg (of which the Earth represents the outer boundary); as Christian mystics like Rosicrucian's speak of 7 cosmic planes (of which there are 6 above us); as the number 7 is highly significant in other traditions, like Jewish mysticism and eastern/western occultism; and as the research of Dr. Michael Newton and the Law of One material supports this, I have used this as an example.

erroneous assumptions. In this regard, production of enemy images is an effective scheme for controlling the masses, and the elite's propaganda apparatus has been so successful that most prefer to live in a police state rather than a free society where people must take responsibility for themselves.

An example is found in citizens who take politicians seriously when they inform us that we, for our own protection, must give up some freedoms in exchange for a little more security. Only a citizenry scared out of their wits can accept such reasoning. But so fearful have we become that most accept this, leaving it up to the elite to regulate in detail the most intimate aspects of our lives.

In a sense, as seen from the cosmic perspective, this is as it should be. After all, humanity will always get the leaders it deserves, and if people want to live a life on their knees, they must be allowed to do so. Only to the extent humanity actively embraces unconsciousness can the Satanists govern our affairs, and those who have tried know that no one, no matter how enlightened, can force a more enlightened government into being; not even by appealing to the rule of law will it help, for both our leaders and the masses will ignore the call from Higher Law. Nevertheless, there is an alternative to the status quo—and the purpose of this part is to make it clear to people, if they really want to live like sheep, who their shepherds really are.

Thus, I shall say some more about this elite faction and the damage that has been wrought on the social fabric. Svali and others (David Wilcock, FBI's Ted Gunderson, and former Forbes journalist Benjamin Fulford) estimate that this satanic group consist of roughly a million in the U.S. alone, and they worship the logic of fear in a premeditated, systematic manner, often including occult rituals. Sexual abuse of children, mutilation, murder, cannibalism, and blood sacrifice is part of these rituals and former FBI agent Theodore Gunderson estimated, based on three different sources, that between 50 and 60.000 human sacrifices are taking place in the U.S. annually.

Obviously, this is difficult for most to accept, as they are under the assumption that the police, the press, and other authorities would have been aware of this practice and ended it. Yet, the International Tribunal of Natural Justice just did an exposé on this subject, showing that the problem is global. Hence, only willful ignorance now sustains these sinister practices, allowing them to continue. Even the Clinton email scandal revealed that close aides were sacrificing to Moloch and that Hillary herself was into "spirit cooking"—black magic stuff. What people need to understand, therefore, is that these crimes are committed by people at the very top of the social ladder and that they are so far above the law that agencies such as the FBI and Justice Department have covered up their crimes. The cover up of the Hillary Clinton email scandal and the contents found by NYPD on political aide Anthony Weiner's lap top itself speaks volumes. And for those who cannot bring themselves to believe any this, books such as *Why Johnny Can't Come Home* by Noreen Gosch and *The Franklin Cover-up* by John DeCamp are essential reading. Noreen experienced a mothers' worst nightmare when her son was kidnapped by people working for the elite (amongst others, Lt. Col. Michael Aquino, a known Satanist, has been linked to the disappearance) and she discovered that the FBI and the local police suppressed the investigation. When it comes to John DeCamp, he was a senator who, while serving on an investigative committee, experienced the cover-up of another malicious plot. The committee's work began as an investigation of a financial institution in Nebraska, but it soon became clear that Larry King, Chairman of the financial institution, Republican, and an acquaintance of George Bush Sr. (who was vice-president at the time), was involved in a satanic cult.

As the investigation proceeded, the committee uncovered evidence that King was not only into illegal activities such as sexual abuse, drug smuggling, and trafficking of children, but his name was connected to instances of ritualistic abuse and killings. They also found that elites in Nebraska were involved (among others Harold Anderson, owner of the State's largest newspaper, and Robert Wadman, the chief of police), and that George Bush himself, according to several children, had been present when some of the activities took place. Further investigation revealed more details, including the existence of a pedophile ring linked to the White House. It was a case that could have blown the lid of Washington D.C., but despite some commitment from senators, forces more powerful intervened. As DeCamp later said:

"The Justice Department, acting through the FBI and the U. S. Attorney's Office in Omaha, emerges from the record of the Franklin investigations not so much as a party to the cover-up, but as its coordinator.

. . . Though there are no doubt other branches of the government where corruption flourishes, there is no question in my mind that the stench of evil which emanates from Washington, originates in the so-called Department of Justice, particularly in its permanent bureaucracy. . . . In case after notorious case [even] entirely unrelated to Franklin, Justice Department personnel appear as liars, perverts, frame-up artists, and even assassins."(29.293)

The Justice Department's corrupt nature is thoroughly documented in *Human Rising*, my previous book, and we shall not go into detail. Nevertheless, it is because of such cover-up procedures that no one knows the extent of these crimes. Thus, much in the same tradition as the FBI until 1957 denied the existence of organized crime in the United States, so the FBI claims today that there is no organized ritual abuse of children. If we want to know more about such matters, therefore, we must look to others, and former FBI agent Ted Gunderson's estimate that annually some 60.000 ritual sacrifices are taking place in the U.S. should be taken seriously. The reason is that Gunderson spoke with authority on the subject. Before he retired, he had an impressive career in the Bureau. After FBI Director Hoover died, Gunderson was among a handful interviewed for the position as his successor, and later as a private investigator he was involved in a number of such cases.

No matter how unpleasant, therefore, the problem should be openly recognized. Not only is it well documented, but silence on this issue is aiding and abetting perpetrators, leaving innocent children in harm's way. We just discussed how the Franklin investigation threatened to reveal a pedophile ring connected to the White House, and another who can elaborate is Cathy O'Brien. She was sexually abused by her father throughout childhood. When her dad was arrested for selling child pornography, U.S. authorities took action—but rather than punish him, they *bought* her from him. In their eyes, she was just the damaged soul that they were looking for,[72] and so she ended up as a sex slave for the elite, including several presidents.

Her books will provide insight into some of the U.S. Government's dirty dealings, especially in the 1980s, and for those educated in power-politics Cathy knows what she is talking about. As many others, her claims are well-founded and easily verifiable in a court of law. She has even testified before Congress, but despite the help of officials the Justice Department dismissed her case for reasons of national security.[73]

Those who read her book will understand why. For how would it affect society if people learned that former presidents Ford and Reagan abused her sexually, that Dick Cheney repeatedly tortured and raped her, and that George Bush Sr. had sex with her little girl? It goes without saying that if people could wrap their minds around this, they would have lost confidence in not only their representatives but the system itself, and because these guys are part of the Deep State network they are allowed to ravage with impunity.

Other items bear witness to this network's pedophile tendencies and corrupting influence. In 2010, for instance, in what was termed Project Flickr, an investigative committee affiliated with the Immigration and Customs Enforcement service (ICE) linked purchase of child pornography to some 5200 Pentagon employees. Further investigation suddenly came to halt and no new details have come out. As the system protects itself, this was to be expected. Yet, there will always be

---

[72] This was part of a brainwashing project called MK Ultra/Project Monarch, run by the CIA. It is children like Cathy who tend to be captured by this network and used for such purposes. First, because they have no parents to complain to, and secondly because they are so used to the abnormal that it appears normal. In other words, they have no frame of reference with which to compare the insanity of perpetrators, and they are so emotionally battered that it's easy to destroy their self-thinking and self-esteem.

[73] Christine DeNicola and Claudia Mullen have testified before Congress to the same. To the Advisory Committee on Human Radiation Experiments in 1995, they explained in detail how they, as part of the CIA's brainwashing projects, were sexually abused and tortured. Among other things, they named the perpetrators and the institutions where experiments were performed...

individuals who fight for the truth, and Senator Charles Grassley and others continued to push for disclosure.

Predictably, it went nowhere, as conscientious people like these are faced with an almost impossible task in overcoming the complicity and denial represented by top operators. We just saw how congressional researchers of the Franklin investigation, despite their resolve and an overwhelming body of evidence, got nowhere. In fact, former CIA director Bill Colby, a friend of DeCamp, warned him thus:

> "What you have to understand, John, is that sometimes there are forces and events too big, too powerful, with so much at stake for other people or institutions, that you cannot do anything about them, no matter how evil or wrong they are and no matter how dedicated or sincere you are or how much evidence you have. That is simply one of the hard facts of life you have to face. You have done your part. You have tried to expose the evil and wrongdoing. It has hurt you terribly. But it has not killed you up to this point. I am telling you, get out before it does."(29.ix)

As Colby tried to make clear, there is not much a single individual can do to fight the corrupting power that overrides and permeates the system. This is because the unofficial societal structure is stronger than the official. Indeed, the official structure is a secondary product of the real goings-on, and it is only because our attention is channeled towards a facade that we have not yet understood the game being played. Our revisionist history, after all, has nothing to say about the things we have discussed. And so compelling is the facade—and so eager are we to believe in it—that even now, after having got a glimpse behind the scenes, we would like to believe that this talk of conspiracies and secret elite factions is sheer nonsense.

Nonetheless, the body of evidence is overwhelming. And behind history's great events, those who care to look will find traces of this faction's hidden hand. I shall not go into too much detail, but it is not only in connection with the Kennedy assassinations and the terrorist attacks of 9/11 that we see this elite group pulling the strings. Even official history as it pertains to the great revolutions, the World Wars, and the Cold War presents a distorted image as everything having to do with this faction's motives, contribution, and influence is removed from history books.

Thus, the reason why I have named these two episodes is not because they are unique, but because the corpus of evidence is so overwhelming that it fully reveals official history's lack of credibility. When it comes to the study of power-politics, therefore, they provide the best possible starting point, and from there on the reader can delve into other, more obscure events.

I have already said a bit about this when it comes to the terrorist attacks[74], and for those who want to know more about the Kennedy assassinations, the documentary series *Evidence of Revision* is priceless. It puts the killings of John and his brother Robert in a historical context, showing why the official version of history is worth absolutely nothing. Space considerations make further elaboration impossible. But to give nonbelievers something to ponder, E. Howard Hunt, a CIA agent who figured as a suspect in the presidential assassination, has admitted to being involved. On his deathbed in 2007, he gave his version of events and his son, Saint John Hunt, has a tape recording and handwritten confession from his father where he fingers Vice President Lyndon B. Johnson[75] and others. According to Hunt, FBI Director Hoover was a key

---

[74] For more information on the 9/11 attacks see WEBSTER TARPLEY, *911 SYNTHETIC TERROR*; MIKE RUPPERT, *CROSSING THE RUBICON*; PETER DALE SCOTT, *THE ROAD TO 911*; PAUL THOMPSON, *THE TERROR TIMELINE*; and David Ray Griffin's books.

[75] An interesting book in this regard is ROGER STONE, *THE MAN WHO KILLED KENNEDY: THE CASE AGAINST LBJ*. In this book, Stone, a former White House aide who has worked on the presidential campaigns of Nixon, Reagan, and George H. W. Bush, implicates Johnson in nine murders. Among other things, he claims that Nixon once told him that both he and Mr. Johnson badly wanted the presidency but that, unlike Johnson, "I wasn't willing to kill for it." The case against Johnson is presented in the documentary series *Evidence of Revision*. Former Minnesota Governor Jesse Ventura interviews Hunt's son in a documentary on the Kennedy assassination (Conspiracy Theory season 2, episode 5), and for further interested I recommend VENTURA, *THEY KILLED OUR PRESIDENT: 63 REASONS TO BELIEVE THERE WAS A CONSPIRACY TO ASSASSINATE JFK*.

player in the cover-up, and in addition there is circumstantial evidence that links later presidents Nixon, Ford, and Bush Sr. to the assassination.

Now, this might sound outlandish, but not for a student of power-politics. The reason is that for a corrupt system to survive—and for the distance between theory and practice to continue—there must be built-in mechanisms that makes this possible. This is ensured by the system's own force of inertia—that is, by the active and passive resistance it provides those who point to the difference between theory and practice. This mechanism ensures a dynamic where the most spineless and easily corruptible float like a bob to the top, while those who oppose the ruling elite's activities and ambitions are neutralized.

In other words, the people who have the most to hide help each other to conceal the sea of corruption and criminal activity that the system is built upon and dependent on to exist. *That is* why people like Nixon, Ford, Johnson, Bush, Clinton, and Obama (to the elite) are preferred presidential candidates. For one, these candidates were agents of the faction that runs politics—that which includes the Rothchild's, the Rockefellers, and others. Secondly, their willingness to do whatever it took to get ahead was obvious from an early point in their career—and that is all it takes to get to the top.

This probably sounds cynical. But *not one* of our most prominent public servants have built a career on moral qualifications. To use Bush Sr. as an example, he has a record that far surpasses any Mafioso, serial killer, or drug baron. We have already mentioned his involvement with presidential assassination and sexual abuse of children. And although we should be open to the possibility that some of the accusations are false, the evidence would be more than enough to convict you and me. After all, several dozens of people have elaborated on his criminal activities, and in addition to wars of aggression, crimes against humanity, and treason (our leaders' usual crimes), they include murder by proxy, drug trafficking, money laundering, bribery, coercion, and other fraudulent activities. This, again, is according to people with firsthand knowledge. We are talking business associates, ONI, FBI, and other governmental employees, as well as CIA agents/assassins working for him personally, and for those who want to know more I invite you to read *The Bush Crime Family* by Roger Stone and Saint John Hunt.

There are, in other words, more than enough who can testify to our leaders' criminal enterprises, but due to the distance between theory and practice their knowledge has little impact. The elites ensure that the law never extends to them, and as the populace can be counted on to ignore these voices from the wilderness, they have nothing to fear.

The same, however, cannot be said about those public servants who know too much and who challenge the status quo. In a corrupt system, those who speak up against institutionalized violence, injustice, and illegality are the system's sworn enemies—and these people are fair game. As the quote from CIA Director Colby just indicated, they risk their lives if they do not conform to certain expectations, and history is ripe with examples of such unsung heroes' unfortunate end.

When bribery, threats, and other measures cannot bully them back into line, liquidation becomes standard procedure. To use the Franklin cover-up as an example, not only the congressional committee's senior investigator, Gary Caradori, was killed, but also several dozen others died under mysterious circumstances. Furthermore, looking at the Kennedy assassination, more than a hundred people suffered very convenient and mysterious deaths in the aftermath of the incident. And that the same mechanism is currently in effect when it comes to 9/11, is evidenced by the death of Barry Jennings[76].

In the wake of such operations, there are always people who must be silenced for the official version of events to triumph—and those who do not respond to threats are killed or thrown into prison with no chance of a fair trial. As it pertains to the Iraq war, we saw an example of the former when Dr. David Kelly was found dead after having exposed and opposed the Blair government's misrepresentation of intelligence before the invasion. Kelly claimed that it was "sexed up" as a pretext for war, and

---

[76] Jennings was Deputy Director of the New York Housing Authority's Emergency Services Department. As a result of bombs going off, he was trapped in the WTC 7 building on the morning of September 11th but was rescued before it collapsed. While he was in this building, he saw firsthand the damage caused by several bombs (among other things, he saw dead people that officially did not exist) and most probably it was his refusal to keep silent about this that sealed his destiny.

even though the police (as usual) concluded that he had killed himself, there is evidence to suggest he did not.[77]

As examples of the latter—of throwing people in jail—we have Susan Lindauer, Brad Birkenfeld, and many others[78]. In the run-up to the Iraq War, Lindauer was working for the CIA as an intermediary between the Bush administration and Saddam's regime. Not only was she one of several who warned in advance against the terrorist attacks of 9/11, but her negotiations with the Iraqis were highly successful. Indeed, Saddam was so eager to avoid the upcoming invasion that he presented the Americans with a most auspicious deal; he offered favorable oil and reconstruction contracts, promised the weapons inspectors free rein, volunteered to share all his intelligence in the fight against Al Qaeda, and even agreed to democratic reforms.

Nonetheless, nothing could placate the Bush administration's thirst for war. After it began, Lindauer contacted every member of Congress and informed them of the administration's refusal to accept a peaceful solution but because reality put the official version of events to shame, Congress used the Patriot Act against her and threw her in jail. They refused to divulge what crimes she had committed or what kind of evidence they had against her, and their plan was to deny her an effective defense so that she could be drugged down and locked up. In *Extreme Prejudice,* she tells her disturbing tale, but this episode is far from outstanding.

I just mentioned Brad Birkenfeld as another example. He was a Swiss banker that tried to alert the U.S. Government about UBS and HSBC's financing of terrorist groups. He had names, cell phones and numbers connected to 19.000 bank accounts but the U.S. Senate, the intelligence community, and Justice Department did not want him to disclose this information. Consequently, he was gagged and sentenced to 40 months

---

[77] Norman Baker, the British MP who spent a year investigating his death, concluded that he was murdered. For more on why he believes so, check out BAKER, *THE STRANGE DEATH OF DAVID KELLY*.

[78] For some tales, check out JOEL BINNERMAN, *THE CRIMES OF A PRESIDENT: NEW REVELATIONS ON CONSPIRACY AND COVER UP IN THE BUSH AND REAGAN ADMINISTRATIONS*; AL MARTIN. *THE CONSPIRATORS: SECRETS OF AN IRAN CONTRA INSIDER.*

in prison, and I would not have learned of his alarming tale if it were not for another whistleblower he met while in prison. As fate would have it, he met Scott Bennett, a U.S Army Officer who had worked as a terrorist threat finance analyst at U.S. CENTCOM. Bennett, for his part, had taken his job a little too seriously, thinking the point was to eliminate terrorist threats. This was his only crime, but he was put through a sham trial and imprisoned[79]. When he heard Birkenfeld's story, he put two and two together, and it suddenly dawned on him why the system had turned on him when he proved a little too eager. As he said:

> "In the end, when everything was added up, the paper trail seemed to indicate the aiding of the enemy was, in fact, being funded by U.S. taxpayers, was being condoned by the Justice Department, the Intelligence Agencies, President Obama, certain members of Congress, and the defense contractor Booz Allen Hamilton. It seemed we were fighting the enemy like parasites on a host, feeding of it just enough to not completely kill it, just maintain a constant groan of near death. And we were managing the war—and telling our allies to do the same—in a manner which, whether intentionally or not, treated global conflict like a smoldering fire, never allowing it to be completely extinguished in order to preserve just enough flame for the next shift of unionized, government-paid water-bucket bearers."(12.63)

Just like Lindauer, Bennett contacted the media, the Senate, and the Congress, as well as many other agencies, hoping to find an honest soul willing to do his/her job. By now, however, it should come as no surprise that none of these institutions acted on the information, for the status quo is so corrupted that our media and civil servants will cover up anything the elite ask them to.

Hence, as the skeletons in the closet keep piling up, more and more people are being put to death or unjustly imprisoned. In *Human Rising*, I

---

[79] For more about Birkenfeld and Scott Bennett, see BENNETT, *SHELL GAME*.

present firsthand accounts from ex-government employees suggesting that hundreds of people were killed and a thousand unjustly imprisoned in connection with the cover-up of the Iran-Contra affair. Although few remember this incident, it provides an example of how intelligence agencies use the drugs economy to fund their operations. To make a long story short, the Reagan administration, in the 1980s, smuggled tons of cocaine into the United States to fund its war against Nicaragua. After having been ruled by a U.S.-backed dictator for 50 years, the country was ruled by a leftist regime, and because it worked for the good of the population—and not U.S. corporations—President Reagan did what he could to overturn its leadership.

The Congress, however, would not allow this. The war, then, could not be financed through the federal budget and so the drugs economy became the solution. Under the supervision of Vice President Bush, therefore, a covert operation was launched which flew tons of cocaine to the United States and tons of weapons back to the mercenary armies (the Contras, as they were called). "Tons" is no exaggeration, as it is estimated that cocaine imports to the United States doubled in this period (1982-1985).

Both Bush Sr. and later President Bill Clinton were key players in this set-up. Bush had the overall responsibility, overseeing the operation from Washington and making sure that no Federal agencies intervened, while Bill Clinton, then Governor of Arkansas, contributed by making his state a haven for drug trafficking, the training of mercenaries, money laundering, and illegal weapons production. The criminal activities were so widespread that a number of officials, journalists, and police officers became familiar with the operation. Several tried to expose the venture, but Clinton, as head of State, ensured that none of their efforts prevailed.[80]

In other words, in Bill Clinton, we find another example of a man who, after proving his loyalty, was uplifted to the presidency. His path to the top reveals a man willing to do anything for power, and those who

---

[80] MIKALSEN, *HUMAN RISING: THE PROHIBITIONIST PSYCHOSIS AND ITS CONSTITUTIONAL IMPLICATIONS.*

watch it more closely will find that at least 50 of his closest associates have died under suspicious circumstances.[81]

I am not accusing Clinton of orchestrating these deaths. I mention them as an indication of the elite's behind-the-scenes manipulations and the costs that are required to maintain the facade. Such liquidations are by no means unusual, and the system covers them up so that our revisionist history remains silent on the matter.

CIA Director Colby himself, most likely, ended his life as a victim of such an operation. One day he was found drowned, and although the official investigation concluded that his death was a suicide/accident, people who knew him maintain that he was killed[82]. One reason for this is that he grew increasingly discontent with the ruling elite faction. The footnote says more on this, and just before he died Colby was as in touch with Dr. Steven Greer, founder of the Disclosure Project. Since 1993, Greer has helped people understand that we are not alone in the Universe.[83] This Project has gathered more than 500 witnesses who, through their involvement in classified projects, can testify to the fact that the U.S. Government, at least since the late 1940s, has covered up the existence of extraterrestrial life.

Bill Colby was not only aware of this, but he had access to energy technology of extraterrestrial origin and had agreed to give it to Greer. It

---

[81] A documentary elaborating on this is *The Clinton Chronicles: An Investigation into the Alleged Criminal Activities of Bill Clinton.*

[82] One of the people who think so is former Senator John DeCamp. Towards the end of his life, Colby became part of a faction that opposed the one we have discussed here. At the time of his death there was extreme tension between the two being that Colby's faction was planning a thrust that threatened to topple Clinton's presidency and reveal much of the ruling elite faction's unsightly activities. According to Wilcock, besides Colby's death, the episode ended with the death of a dozen admirals, generals, and highly placed officials and a defeat that made White Hats in the government lay low for a few decades. For more on this see David Wilcock's online article *CONFIRMED: U.S. Military Alliance Defeating Federal Reserve* (www.divine cosmos.com).

[83] Greer has written several books on this subject. See GREER, *HIDDEN TRUTH;* GREER, *FORBIDDEN KNOWLEDGE;* AND GREER, *CONTACT: COUNTDOWN TO TRANS-FORMATION.* Another good book is LT. PHILIP CORSO, *THE DAY AFTER ROSWELL.*

is quite possible that this sealed his fate, for there are powerful forces with a vested interest in the status quo that do not want us to know the truth related to this subject. They have therefore gone to great lengths to hide it. Many people have died, and a lot of money has been spent on what must be the greatest cover-up of all times. Despite their efforts, however, there are so many leaks, so much evidence out there, that it cannot be hushed up much longer.

The Disclosure Project is one of several organizations that have made this possible. A look at their website will give an idea about the evidence that speaks to the validity of the phenomenon, and as governments are declassifying more and more UFO-material, I believe this cover-up to be officially abolished within few years.

When that happens, it will create a lot of fuss. For one, it will become undeniable that we are not alone in the Universe, and secondly, it will become obvious to even the most trusting population that the government has lied about the issue for more than half a century. Both require huge psychological reorganization—and as soon as they have come to terms with it, any sane citizen will have to ask what else the government has lied about. Our leaders, then, will try to explain that they have kept this secret because of its implications for national security. They will say that people 50 years ago had not matured psychologically to a point where they would have been able to cope with the truth, and that leaders for that reason chose to keep quiet about it.

There is some truth to this, as it is difficult to predict the extent of chaos that would have resulted if people really knew what was going on. This, therefore, was undeniably one reason for the cover-up, but just as important was the fact that disclosure would have had implications so profound that the elite's web of control would have unraveled. By that time, fossil fuels had cemented its position as our primary source of energy. The machinery of society was not only dependent on oil but it was an important ingredient in manufactured goods such as plastics and synthetic fibers. So it remains today, and the control of oil has been an important device in the elite's power-political toolbox.

People are not aware of this, but the elite's web of control has been built around the importance of oil. For more than a century, this has worked out well, and consequently they oppose any innovation that could make us less dependent on oil.

We see an historical example with the hemp plant. In the 1930s, its many utilities (hemp grew five times faster than trees and could have replaced oil and cotton) threatened to undermine the established order, and so it was effectively outlawed. Similarly, the UFO phenomenon threatens these interests. It makes it clear that there are alternative energy sources and technologies available that are more efficient and environmentally friendly than oil. And because the control-oriented elite do not want to let us in on this little secret, they have not only covered up the UFO phenomenon but sabotaged successful research into alternative energy.

One result is that people involved with this type of research have been bought off or bullied into silence—and if they have not succumbed to such pressure, they have been killed. We just saw that Colby possibly fell into this category and other examples are Dr. Eugene Mallove and Dr. Stefan Marinov. How many more is impossible to say, but free-energy technology does not belong to the distant future. According to people with firsthand knowledge, such technology already exists, and if not for politics it would have been made available[84].

---

[84] According to the Federation of American Scientists, the U.S. patent office had by 2010 suppressed 5135 patents, classifying them as "secret". This technology included solar cells with more than 20 percent efficiency, as well as power systems more than 70 to 80 percent efficient at converting energy. For more information on alternative technology see *Thrive* (www.thrivemovement.com) and *Sirius* (www.siriusdisclosure.com). Check also out The Institute for New Energy at www.padrak.com and www.pureenergysystems.com.

23.4 FURTHER ELABORATION ON POWER-POLITICS

"As we have seen throughout history, fear drives the growth of government. If there is no natural or inadvertent crisis, one is easily created or imagined by those who agitate for the authoritarian state."(79.254)

—Ron Paul, U.S. politician—

We now have some understanding of the men behind the power, what their agenda is, and how they go about pursuing it. From what has been said, it might seem as if this elite faction has such a grip on society that resistance is doomed to fail. The concerns that have been elaborated on, however, is an oversimplified representation and we should not forget that there are other groups who oppose the one considered here.

Neither should we forget that most supporters of the ruling faction do what they do because they (1) do not know any better or (2) because they fear the consequences of resistance. This means that the powerbase of this elite faction is secrecy, ignorance, and fear; if people knew what this faction has done, the majority would see things differently, and if they could oppose it without risking their life, most would have done so.

We saw an example of this in the United States in the early 1800s, when the Masonic order was dealt a major blow. What happened was that Captain William Morgan, a Mason, was killed after writing a book which revealed some of the order's activities. The murder gained widespread publicity, and as a result around 45.000 members quit the order. This represented a majority (some estimate 90 percent) of the American Freemasons, and this, together with the public outrage generated by the attention, put the organization back to such an extent that Masonry was believed to be finished in the U.S.

We must remember that the United States, at that time, represented a new and idealistic project and that it offered its citizens a degree of freedom that the world had not seen before—or after. The Constitution was still held in esteem and the government had not been overtaken by special interests' and their self-serving agenda. All public institutions, therefore, were open to the people; they had access to all official documents; they enjoyed a large degree of personal freedom; and the press was relatively free. As a result, theory and practice was in more ways than today one and the same. With the exception of slaves and Indians, there was a solidarity and equality between the citizens which was new to the world—and the European elite found this disagreeable.[85]

Nothing threatens the status quo more than progress, and as Old Europe was a strict and hierarchical order its elite felt threatened by a government of the people. This elite, therefore, did what they could to sabotage the American project and the Masonic Order was an important tool. In its shadow, the European elite secured for themselves a more powerful influence and so vigilant citizens like Captain Morgan fought against it. He knew that the Order not only opposed Christianity, but the very principles upon which the government was built—and so he spoke out against its activities.

In the wake of his murder, this fact not only became commonly known but it was discovered that the Order's influence by then (1830) had grown so powerful that it threatened to undermine the American project. It became clear that the media and the legal system in some states were already under Masonic control, and there arose a political movement (the Anti-Masonic Party) whose purpose it was to fight its corrupting influence. So successful was this movement that most people believed that Masonry no longer presented a threat to the Republic.

---

[85] While we here are talking about equality, solidarity, and theory and practice as one and the same, remember that we are speaking in relative terms as measured against the standards of that time. In reality, not just other races were oppressed but also most white men and women, and it is estimated that throughout the 1800's only 5 percent of the population had the right to vote and influence the political process. The government was, in other words, still elitist, but as in the past only one percent of the population had an influence on the political process, this was still unheard of to the elite. Taking this into consideration, it may seem like a contradiction in terms when I describe this as a time in history when U.S. citizens enjoyed an exceptional degree of freedom. It is not, for despite many shortcomings (some of which we have improved on today) citizens back then, as we shall see, were far freer to do with their lives as they pleased.

Nonetheless, it continued its activities in secret, and by the time of the Civil War it had become yet again a force to be reckoned with.

To continue the story of how the American freedom loving project was taken over by these forces—and how these forces, until today, have succeeded in turning everything the U.S. originally stood for upside down—we see, with the last half of the 1800s, how the elite's influence become more severe. With the Civil War, the war profiteers won new terrain, and by the late 1800s an elite had emerged which was so powerful that the gap between theory and practice became impossible to ignore.

This was the great age of robber barons and monopolists. Elite families such as Astor, Carnegie, DuPont, Cabot, Rockefeller, Gould, Harriman, Armour, Vanderbilt, Pulitzer, Hearst, Guggenheim, Mellon, and Morgan shared between them most of the continent's acreage, resources, and infrastructure, and it was them—not the people—who controlled the political process. In other words, ideals such as equality before the law, presumption of liberty, and that everyone should have their voices heard (and their rights ensured) had, by this time, become obsolete. Instead, a system of arbitrary law was in place, and from that time, as a result of the elite's increasing power, the legislative branch has designed such laws and regulations as serves their interests; the judiciary has become a vehicle for their aspirations; the media has been incorporated under their control; and the educational system has been formed according to their expectations.

Former economics professor Anthony Sutton studied the dynamics of this period. In *America's Secret Establishment,* he describes the influence of this elite faction:

> "The Order has set up or penetrated just about every significant research, policy, opinion-making organization in the United States, in addition to the church, business, law, government and politics. Not all at the same time, but persistently and consistently enough to dominate the direction of American society. The evolution of American society is not, and has not been for a century, a voluntary development reflecting individual opinion, ideas, and decisions at the grass roots. On the contrary, the broad

direction has been created artificially and simulated by the Order."(31.88)

This U.S. elite was subordinate to the European. For instance, the most powerful banker in the U.S. was J.P. Morgan, but he owed his position to the European Rothschild family. With Morgan as a front man the Rothschilds gained greater influence over American finance and industry, and so to speak of an American and European elite is misleading. They see themselves as supranational and have common interests that know no borders.

In all this, we should not forget that it is the big corporations the elite hide behind. Previously, their ownership was concentrated, and individual families had a most personal relationship to their companies. Rockefeller was big on oil, Hearst on newspapers, DuPont on gunpowder and synthetic fibers, Morgan on finance, Carnegie on steel, and so on. They all had their own areas which they dominated, but during the first half of the 20th century this changed. There was too much risk involved in betting on one horse and so they began to spread risk and finances. Thus, one company no longer represents the family business. Instead, the most powerful elitists have streamlined and spread their influence over the greatest possible portion of the overall market; they do not sit on individual mounds as before but have shares in each other's companies and seats on each other's Board of Directors.

We shall soon expand on this. But to continue our timeline, the men behind the power—or the corporate structure—had so much influence by the 1900s that the government was run according to their interests and aspirations. They had already divided the market between them, and they had become so big that it could no longer sustain their growth. The financial crises of 1874-79 and 1893-94 were symptomatic of their plight; as growth conditions became more limited, these crises thinned out the ranks and only the largest players were left standing.

Consequently, to be able to expand, they had to find new markets and more resources, and the government became more imperialistic. In this way, the Masters of Commerce used the U.S. military machine to take control of external markets and resources. They already had their plantations and mining operations in Latin America and now they subjugated Cuba, Puerto Rico, Guam, Hawaii, and the Philippines. The European colonial powers were still ahead elsewhere in the world. The British Empire, however, had reached its zenith and when the Second World War ended the U.S. government took over the reins of world exploitation. After having fought two world wars, Europeans were exhausted to the point where they were struggling to get back on their feet. This meant that they had to give imperialist ambitions a break and so the United States increased its power and hegemony.

According to conspiracy theorists, both world wars were stage-managed by the elite and created as useful tools for realizing their New World Order. We shall not go into detail but evidence abounds that they financed both sides, that their involvement was covered up, and that the function and consequence of these wars was a societal dynamic in their favor.[86] For one, they provided a smokescreen for the theft of the world's gold reserves[87]; (2) they impaired the power of nation states; (3) they arranged for hundreds of billions in profits for the war profiteers; and (4) the elites' maneuvering ensured that they would control the peace negotiations and direct the conditions upon which postwar development would depend.

The result was a more supranational world, one where the war profiteers were more powerful than ever. The U.S. Government was not only under their control, but the entire U.S. economy was on war footing and it was imperative to keep it that way. The defense budget after the Second World War was around $13 billion. This was nothing compared

---

[86] In 1945 the Treasury Department revealed to congress that United Steel produced the following percentages of war munitions for the Nazis: Pig iron 50.8%; Pipe & tubes 45.5%; Universal plate 41.4%; Galvanised sheet 38.5%; Heavy plate 36%; Explosives 35%; Wire 22.1%. Prescott Bush was Hitler's banker in this business and more than 300 American corporations had armed Germany during the war; Rockefeller's Standard Oil provided fuel, IBM provided services for the concentration camps, DuPont synthetic rubber, etc., etc. For more on the U.S. elite and their involvement with the Nazis, check out GLEN YEADON & JOHN HAWKINS, *THE NAZI HYDRA IN FASCIST AMERICA*; ROGER STONE, *THE BUSH CRIME FAMILY*; EDWIN BLACK, *NAZI NEXUS: AMERICA'S CORPORATE CONNECTIONS TO HITLER'S HOLOCAUST*.

[87] See David Wilcock's articles *Financial Tyranny*; *Trillion Dollar Lawsuit*, and the like.

to today's $700 billion, but the military-industrial complex had arisen as an influential player and it was hell-bent on maintaining its position. To do so it needed enemies, and so the power elite in the Soviet Union became an important ally.

Now, this might come as a surprise. Even so, we must remember that neither the U.S. nor the Soviet state apparatus offered its citizens any real freedom or equality before the law. The ruling elites, of course, hailed such ideals, just as they swore that the purpose of an empowered government was to serve the people. Nonetheless, neither the Eastern nor the Western elite had any interest in pursuing a policy that mirrored the values they officially embraced. Instead, leaders' foremost priority was themselves, and because they feared that policies which took these ideals seriously would mean the loss of privilege, this was the last thing they wanted.

In other words, to the elite, theory and practice was diametrically opposed, impossible to reconcile. What both elite factions wanted was a government ruled from the top-down rather than bottom-up, and to achieve this they needed an enemy image, one that represented every-thing they were not. If they had this they could, with some credibility, tell the people that in times like these they needed a strong government to protect them against the nation's enemies. The problem, however, was that after the defeat of Hitler, Western and Eastern elites had no credible threat against which they could mobilize the nation; without it they could not realize their power-political ambitions, and so the Cold War became the solution.

By painting the citizenry a picture of the other form of government as Evil Incarnated, the elite not only found a way to present themselves as protectors of people, but they found a pretext for dealing with that percentage of the population who saw through this charade. As long as they had a compelling enemy image, they could not only blame the enemy for everything that went wrong, but they could accuse regime critics for siding with the enemy—and that's exactly what they did.

As citizens of the West, we are aware of how the rulers of the East Bloc used the enemy images to neutralize opposition. We are, after all, born into a system that teaches us to see the terror and hypocrisy behind such actions but not those of our own leaders. Consequently, we believe that we are freer than others and that our leaders are more decent—but as we have seen, this is not entirely so. Our public debate *only seems* free and prosperous because it is less obviously censored; we can freely associate, we can discuss politics, and our journalists have no official party line to which they owe fidelity.

Nonetheless, censorship is no less prevalent in our part of the world. It is less palpable—that is why we feel so free—but the degree of self-censorship is extensive. That most citizens cannot bring themselves to put two and two together if it is contrary to accepted wisdom is one thing. Another is the propaganda machinery of CNN, BBC, the New York Times, and other major news outlets; their mission, as proven over and over, is to present a façade the masses can believe in, and if the individual journalist himself does not limit his curiosity to "acceptable" issues, his editor will quickly clamp down on aberrant behavior. The same applies to any ordinary citizen. And he who writes an article attempting to deal with current taboos will discover that the trustees of the public discourse do not want anything in print that deals with the distance between theory and practice. Hence, we are free to think and to say what we want, but as soon as we try to make ourselves heard, we will find that the public debate refuses to accommodate those who question the premises upon which the system is based.

The examples are many. I, for one, after having written several articles questioning the constitutional parameters of the wars on drugs and terror, have been denied a voice in Norwegian, American, British, and Danish newspapers at least 30 times. The editors make it clear that these are issues of no interest—and every journalist who has tried to shed some light on the facts surrounding these deceptive and inhumane campaigns are faced with a similar response. As Benjamin Fulford, Forbes magazine's former Asia-pacific bureau chief, said:

> "I already knew [the media] was controlled, but I didn't know how thoroughly it was controlled until I had press conferences about 9/11 and presented the evidence. I had the New York Times correspondent telling me that he would be fired if he wrote about this."(125.17)

Hence, our social order is not as decent and enlightened as we like to think. When it comes to basics, its foundation is built on a web of lies and institutionalized corruption, and because the supporters of the status quo refuse to acknowledge this they focus on theory.

A look at the media and academia's willful ignorance on social issues of fundamental importance for the past 100 years serves as an indication: Every time our leaders go to war, they are believed when they say that they do this for the sake of all things good and holy, and no journalist or academician with respect for him/herself (or his/her leaders) doubts their motivations or points to the war profiteers behind-the-scenes influence. Instead, they take it for granted that their leaders are truthful servants, and in their eagerness to interpret even the most unambiguous lies as a well-intentioned (though perhaps misguided) response, they contribute to upholding the distance between theory and practice.

The outcome of our collective neglect is that no matter how easy it is to see that our leaders have been pushing wars of aggression and fronting criminal conspiracies, they have never been held accountable. Just as 100 years ago "experts" looked back on the history of the British Empire and sought to explain its slaughter and exploitations with the best of intentions, so they will explain the history of the American Empire today. The only thing new is that whereas in the old days they justified the atrocities and oppression with it being the white man's burden to civilize savages, they now explain U.S. imperialistic policies as a fight for our values. In other words, *then as now* the "experts" are in league with the criminals, and *then as now* the masses are too bewildered by the elite's propaganda to figure out what is going on.

According to conventional history, the CIA's mind control and assassination plots, drug dealing, arms sales, coup d'états, and other interventions during the Cold War were intended to combat the Communist threat. And when Western "experts" comment on the matter, they still highlight the domino theory (that if one country went communist, all others would follow) as an explanatory model for the roughly 50 U.S. instigated wars and regime changes in this period. Thus, we are deluded into thinking that the United States government's support for right-wing military regimes and dictators all over the world—which was extensive—was an unintended consequence of its struggle for a better world, but the truth is otherwise. What we call the Cold War was a cleverly manipulated facade, arranged by the war profiteers, and that the elite on both sides worked together to keep it going is confirmed by many insiders. Al Martin, a retired U.S. Navy Lt. Commander and former officer in the Office of Naval Intelligence, speaks to it thus:

> "The hardliners in the Russian military saw [peace] as a tremendous threat. So there became commonality between hardline interests in both the United States and the Soviet Union to preserve the status quo. The status quo of the cold war was very good for business, and it was very good for maintenance of old power structures and cabals. Those who had benefited from it on both sides didn't want to give it up."(70.245)

That the elite played both sides while the official U.S. and Soviet Union were bitter enemies, may, as I said, come as a surprise. But for the elite the Communist ideology was just as good as the Capitalist. That is, *in actuality* both ideologies were abhorred, as a government where all men/women were equal and the common good prevailed was seen as equally disgusting as one where the principles of the Enlightenment Era were respected and securing individual freedom as well as free enterprise was top priority. What the elite wanted was the opposite of this. While the Eastern and the Western systems of government both played on the values, ideals and principles that follow from Wholeness, merely focusing on different aspects, the elite thought otherwise. They had no need for a government of the people, building from ground up on principled reasoning. They would rather have a strong government that they could control, manipulate, and use to their own ends—and luckily for them, the collective will to unconsciousness was so profound that that is what they got.

Both the Soviet and U.S. state apparatus was, after all, formed in the image of the upper class. Both catered to monopolistic aspirations and both satisfied equally their hunger for more wealth, power, and control. For the men behind the power, therefore, it did not matter which flag the ship of state sailed under as long as they were at the helm, shaping the course. This was no less the case in the Soviet Union as in the United States, and for further information *None Dare Call It Conspiracy* (Gary Allen), *The Creature from Jekyll Island* (G. Edward Griffin), *Western Technology and Soviet Economic Development 1917-1930* (Anthony Sutton), *Major Jordan's Diaries* (George Racey Jordan), *New World Order* (William T. Still), *The Synagogue of Satan* (Andrew Carrington Hitchcock), and *Red Cocaine* (Joseph D. Douglass) are a place to start.

Books like these reveal that the transnational elite offered vital support to the communists before, under, and after the Bolshevik revolution in 1917. They describe how the West provided communist regimes with not only financial support but the technology, resources, and expertise to keep their project up and running so that their interests, in turn, were well looked after by the Soviet state apparatus. Stalin himself acknowledged that at least two thirds of all the major industries in the USSR were built with U.S. aid and support; the communists could even thank the U.S. elite for their nuclear capabilities, and their collaboration was so extensive that the Western bankers had secret meetings with their communist colleagues in Prague on a weekly basis. Those defectors who would talk about this, like General Jan Seina, were taken care of by Western intelligence, and their stories were never recounted by the Western media.

Speaking of the intelligence services, it is their responsibility to weave the unofficial power structure seamlessly together with the official narrative and ensure that the gap between theory and practice gets as little attention as possible. The way the system is put together, the elite's representatives are positioned wherever it makes sense strategically; they hold key positions in the media, publishing houses, police, courts, military, church, and corporate structure, as well as elsewhere in public administration—and the secret services ensure that this structure is coordinated into a more or less well-oiled machinery.

If we look at the intelligence services, therefore, we touch upon another area in which the distance between theory and practice is uncovered. Officially these organizations are created to protect the respective interest of nation states. In other words, it is the citizens' wellbeing they are supposed to defend, but reality is another as they are controlled by a cast of characters whose loyalty is to the ruling elite. It is them, not the people, they are accountable to and James Casbolt, a former agent of British intelligence, has more to say:

> "As intelligence insiders know MI 5 and MI 6 control many of the other intelligence agencies in the world (CIA, MOSSAD, etc) in a vast web of intrigue and corruption that has its global powerbase in the City of London. . . . My experience was that the distinctions of these groups became blurred until in the end we were all one international group working together for the same goals. We were puppets who had our strings pulled by global puppet masters based in the City of London. Most levels of the intelligence agencies are not loyal to the people of the country they are based in and see themselves as `super national´. [For instance] the CIA operates under orders from British intelligence and was created by British intelligence in 1947. The CIA today is still loyal to the international bankers based in the City of London and the global elite aristocratic families like the Rotschild's and Windsor's."(70.173)

Although secret services have done their utmost to shape the social fabric in line with the elite's objectives, the gap between theory and practice has been so great that covering it up has presented a series of problems. The current Epstein-predicament, where Mossad has been running a pedophile-island to corrupt officials and other influencers, provides a valuable example. The facts are already in the open and the attempted cover up of this affair can only succeed to the extent that the public wants to remain in ignorance.

So also with more and more scandals surrounding the democratic party, Hillary, Obama, and Biden: Evidence for treason is plentiful, but with the exception of a few outlets Big Media keeps blaming the Trump administration for what others have done. It is quite impressive to witness the psychosis that plays out, but historically this is not new. Another occasion when covering up the distance between theory and practice became a problem was when the enemy image of communism, in the 1950s and 60s, wreaked such havoc on the American psyche that the fear of internal enemies threatened to expose the elite's double-dealings. FBI Director Hoover, for instance, investigated some 5 million public employees in his pursuit of communist sympathizers and those who failed to unreservedly praise the U.S. Government as a shining beacon of all things great and beautiful were fired.

Such purges at the lower levels were unproblematic for the elite. However, communist hunters such as Nixon and McCarthy were not content persecuting movie stars, lower officials, and labor unions, and investigative committees such as the House Committee on Un-American Activities threatened to also expose some of the bigger game. It looked bad for a while. David Chambers, Time magazines' senior editor and a former member of the U.S. Communist party, under oath named Harry Dexter White and Alger Hiss as belonging to the upper echelons of the communist party. White was a senior U.S. Treasury department official whom as the leading U.S. delegate had dominated the Bretton Woods conference and imposed his vision of post-war financial institutions on the world, while Hiss was the president for the Carnegie Endowment for International Peace, a major tax-exempt foundation. It did not help that Rowan Gaither, the President of the Ford Foundation, in December 1953 confessed to Norman Dodd, the Research Director of the US House of Representatives' Reece Commission, that the objective of all the major tax-exempt foundations was "to alter life in the United States so as to make possible a comfortable merger with the Soviet Union".

While all this was going on, the elite's henchmen were cleaning up the mess. Dexter White died mysteriously three days after he had testified for the House Committee, and a series of murders ensured that Hiss got off the hook.[88] Hence, the elite managed to keep their facade. And until this day they have by intimidation, propaganda, lies, bribery, and murder filled the collective psyche with so much fear and ignorance that most people have yet to discover theory from practice.

Nonetheless, if not for the production of enemy images, we would have seen through the web of lies our authorities have woven. Without enemy images, the elite's project would have fallen on its own weight,

---

[88] See Henry Makow, *Our Leaders Hold a Gun to Our Heads* at http://www.savethe males.ca/ 090702.html.

and so, as the Cold War came to an end, it was of paramount importance that they had a new threat as leverage. Here, terrorism came to the rescue. And by blowing up an initially modest social problem to hysterical proportions, they found the perfect enemy image for fulfilling their New World Order.

Just like communism, this enemy image was so flexible that the elite could define it on their own terms. Objectively speaking, "terrorism" can be defined as the use of violence and/or threats to intimidate or coerce, especially for political purposes. Strictly speaking, this includes the bulk of our governments' activities in matters of criminal and foreign policy, but our officials will admit to no such thing. To our leaders, the beauty of power is that it provides them with the opportunity to define problems and interpret phenomena—and this is a privilege that they use to their advantage. Consequently, they label as "terrorism" that which *they* consider threatening and subversive, while their own actions, no matter how frightful, count merely as protective measures.

We shall look more into enemy images and how they are used later. But to make a long story short, the elite has used the wars against communism and terrorism as an excuse to realize their own political ambitions. Firstly, they could not tell us that they wished to invade another country simply because they hungered for its natural resources or because they wanted a more corporate-friendly regime in power. Secondly, without these enemy images, they could not have trampled the Bill of Rights as we would not have accepted a legal framework which undermines everything civilization is supposed to be.

Looking at the bigger picture, evermore comprehensive legislation has been implemented to deal with the alleged threat behind the enemy images. In 1917 the Espionage Act was enacted; in 1918 it was extended as the Sedition Act, and its purpose was to quell any anti-government criticism. It made it illegal to utter, print, write or publish any disloyal, profane, or abusive language about the U.S. government, the Constitution, or the military, and was used against those who responded to the gap between theory and practice. Eugene Debs, the Socialist Party's presidential candidate, for example, was sentenced to 10 years for his opposition to the war profiteers, and Victor Berger, the Party's founder, was sentenced to 20 years for speaking out against the war.

Many other Socialist leaders were arrested under the Espionage Act, and the Party effectively destroyed. The censorship also rooted out any truthful media reporting, as magazines like *The Masses* were outlawed after pointing to Wall Street's role in the First World War.

During this period, as a result of the elite's manipulation, the social fabric became more streamlined according to their wishes; values were reversed and soon there were no need for draconian legislation to control the people and the media. After elimination of the Socialist Party, "Republican" and "Democrat" defined the American psyche; people took pride identifying with one or the other, and since these political parties were both (to quote Patrick J. Buchanan, a senior advisor to three Presidents) "nothing but two wings on the same bird of prey", everything was arranged for a dynamic in the elite's favor. As Professor Sutton already mentioned, the media had by that time become a mouthpiece of the elite and the education system had been corrupted. Thus, opposition against bankers and industrialists was doomed to fail as unpopular truths were not allowed to prosper.

This is how the facade grew strong, while reality became harder to see. And it was not before the internet that the elite's monopoly on information and reality interpretation finally ended. With it, the gap between theory and practice again became visible, and the elite realized that if they should have any hope of finishing their New World Order, they had to get their end game up and running.

Hence, the terrorist attacks of September 11, 2001. By orchestrating this attack, the elite had the pretext they needed to launch their War on Terror, and despite the evidence—and the U.S. Vice President's promise that this was a war that would not end in our lifetime—there were few objections. Neither academics, journalists, nor politicians pointed out the absurdity of a perpetual war for perpetual peace, much less the evidence suggesting that the U.S. state apparatus was involved. That the Bush administration, two months before the terrorist attacks, told Pakistan's foreign minister that they would attack Afghanistan in October didn't puzzle; that the same administration had failed to act on the warnings from a number of different foreign intelligence agencies as well as U.S. officials, didn't seem suspicious; that senior FBI officials like Dave Frasca sabotaged investigations that could have stopped the attacks didn't seem to register; that Frasca, along with other high-level officials that failed their duties or were conspicuously absent on this day, afterwards were rewarded with promotions didn't seem the least bit curious; and that the Patriot Act, the legislation that subsequently formalized the police state, was drafted before the attacks, didn't raise their alarms.

This, along with hundreds—if not thousands—of other bits of data indicative of something more than a few well-financed cavemen was carefully ignored. Instead, leading academics and journalists hailed the new enemy image as the defining threat of our time, and even the U.S. President's declaration that "if we weren't with the Administration we were with the terrorists" could not make them see the writing on the wall. Instead, they dug their heads in the sand, dumbed down the debate to the point where a 10-year-old could see through their rhetoric, and refused to admit the obvious; that this so-called War on Terror, in fact, was a war against our civil rights in general and those who opposed the New World Order in particular.

Now, 17 years later, this war still wreaks havoc because of our authorities' spinelessness. Even though most of those involved with the 9/11-Commission have renounced its conclusions—and several have admitted that it was a cover-up—our leaders have no wish to rethink this crusade. On the contrary, they appear to be happy the way things are, and their first priority seems to be keeping the enemy image intact.

Considering that most of them by now—in action, if not words— have proved their loyalty to war profiteers, it would be naive to expect otherwise. Nonetheless, even though the truth lives a wretched life, it will always survive a lie. And despite the truth being a taboo topic, some officials are trying to steer us in a different direction. The media gives these officials little attention. Even so, they are fighting an epic battle, doing their best to enlighten a dumbed down citizenry. Indeed, if the public overcomes media bias, they will find that the White House has never been a greater force for good. Trump, for all his flaws, has done more to resurrect the Constitution from the bureaucracy and corruption of the Deep State than any other president. He has also alluded to the deception of the two towers, pointing out that fire never could have brought those buildings down. It will be exciting to see how his battle with the web of corruption unfolds, but another official that has fought longer is Ron Paul, a recently retired U.S. Congressman. He put it this way:

> "The war on terror is no more a true war than . . . [the war on] drugs. It's a mere metaphor to provide fear and intimidate people into sacrificing their liberties. I have actually heard a member of Congress say it's all justified because "the people are too stupid to take care of themselves.""(79.94)

For decades, Rep. Paul has tried to help the American people come to their senses and for his efforts he shall be remembered as one of the great champions of our time. He is one of very few politicians who see our day and age in a historical context and has worked diligently to save the Constitution from the control-oriented elite's attack. The elite's minions being more plentiful, better financed, and more popular with the media, however, Paul and his ilk have fought a losing battle—until the Trump Administration came into power.

There is reason to believe that this Administration is the result of a collaboration between forces that are sick of the Satanist plot to overthrow wholesome values. That is the only proper name for an agenda that seeks to undo the implications of First Principles, and patriots have long objected to the rise of a despotic government. Due to the lobbyism of fear-oriented corporations, jurists of the positivist tradition, and adopted legislation such as the Patriot Act and the National Defense Authorization Act, a legal framework has been established which makes any conscientious citizen fair game. As long as they define you as a threat, you can be imprisoned indefinitely without a right of access to case documents, without a right to know what you are suspected of, without a right to know about the witnesses or evidence against you, and without a right to have the case tried before a court.

This is bad enough, but it is not even the worst. Since 2010, the U.S. government has officially claimed the right to kill anyone, anywhere, and anytime, if its lackeys consider the "target" a threat—and again, no charge, trial, or judgment is required.

Now, this is nothing new. As we have already seen, the U.S. Justice Department, since its very inception, has been so corrupt that you risk a guilty verdict regardless of the evidence. And as we have seen, the men behind the power have reserved for themselves the right to kill anyone, anytime, anywhere long before 2010. The only thing new, therefore, is that while they formerly tried to hide it, they are now openly admitting it to the world.

The fall of the American Republic is furthermore evidenced by the media and congressional response. Whereas there was media outcry and Congressional hearings in the 1970s, when it was discovered that the CIA was involved in assassination attempts, illegal wiretapping, and other abuse of power, by 2010 the media and Congress had become so gutless that no one raised an eyebrow at the admission of extra-judicial executions of American (and other) citizens.

The Congress' genuflection before despotism was no sudden affair. Looking closer, as the 20th century unfolded, power became more and more centralized, and this process has now gone so far that the executive branch can do pretty much as it pleases. Every time the elite want something done, therefore, they get the President to sign one of his Executive Orders—and from there, they do what they want. Thus, an increasing part of the decision-making process takes place by means of such orders, and that the system has much to hide is seen by its increasingly extensive secrecy. While citizens throughout most of the 19th century had access to all government documents, Bill Clinton, during his eight years as president, classified 5.8 million documents. This was unprecedented but surpassed by George Bush who six years into his presidency had classified more than 20 million documents—far more than he publicized.

It is also worth noting that while the secrecy stamp previously applied for a period of 15 years, it now holds indefinitely. All this is in blatant violation of the ideas that the American society was built upon. But because those defenses the Founders put in place are vestiges of an era long lost, no public servant fears accountability for aiding and abetting the elitist and criminal U.S. Government. To call it "criminal" is not an exaggeration. We have already seen enough examples of its aberrant behavior, and most of the wars instigated since World War II have not only been a violation of the Constitution but International Law. Staale Eskeland, a professor of law, confirms:

> "With the post-World War international criminal tribunals and the UN Charter a solid legal foundation was laid down for the future. However, it turned out that the States, and especially the superpowers, to a large extent did not respect International Law and its prohibition against military action. In the subsequent years, the use of military force became an ordinary part of the political theater. ... The use of power led to wars such as the Korean War (1953-1956), Vietnam War (1959-1975), . . . the war between the U.S. and Afghanistan (2001-present) and the war between the U.S. and Iraq (2003-present). These wars . . . started with a crime of aggression. In their wake followed genocide, crimes against humanity, war crimes, torture, and terror."(37.291)

As we see, there is not much left of the rule of law as defined by the Constitution and International Law. The supporters of the status quo, of course, will deny this as they have a legal framework in place which, as they see it, gives them a green light for everything we have discussed. Nonetheless, the proper rule of law belongs to a bygone era, and those who examine the legislation that the U.S. Government points to in its defense will find that it is basically the same as that used by the Nazis. In both cases, the liberty presumption is reversed, principled law does not apply, and the State reserves the right to go to war to preserve its idea of peace—and as long as it is considered necessary for reasons of "national security", any convention or bill of rights created to protect our civil/human rights must yield.

People, therefore, can only hope that the elite and their lackeys regard them as exemplary citizens. If they are considered a problem, they find themselves in a tight spot, and it is important to emphasize that you do not have to be an advocate for violent revolution to be designated as a threat. All you need to do is oppose the system's foundation (that is, the ruling elite's grip on power) and over a million Americans are now listed as potential terrorists, while the State monitors and infiltrates everything from environmental movements to civil rights organizations.

This speaks volumes of where they put the bar, as they designate anyone responding to the gap between theory and practice as the enemy.

This, again, is as to be expected from a system so corrupt as the one we have described. And now that we have an overview of the gap between theory and practice, it is time to investigate the difficulties associated with the corporations' control of the political process. For what exactly is the problem with the ideology underpinning the status quo? We may have established that the United States is a wolf in sheep's clothing, but perhaps this is just as well? I mean, there are so many other corrupt regimes, so many power-hungry psychopaths, that maybe the status quo is the least of evils? Perhaps we need this wolf to look after us, to protect our way of life, our form of government, and Western values at all costs?

It may be some who think along these lines. And because we live in a world where the prevailing ideology is so powerful, so thoroughly established that the fundamental problems associated with the status quo tend to pass by unnoticed, we shall expand on its implications.

24

THE PROBLEM OF CORPORATE INTERESTS AND THEIR INFLUENCE

"Unpopular ideas can be suppressed without the use of force, and a good education is an effective means to reach this result."(19.175)

—*Noam Chomsky*—

IN THE PREVIOUS chapter, we saw that the Western world is controlled by a shadowy elite faction. The big corporations are its representatives and looking back we see how the political process has been formed according to their expectations. This means that their ambition has been the magnetic north, that which sets the standard and defines the evolution of policy, and that the quest for expansion and profits has been behind our leaders' policies and imperial ambitions.

Politicians, however, could not admit as much and instead used the enemy images as a pretext for their actions. Hence, every time the CIA toppled a regime or the U.S. military invaded a country, we were told that they had to protect us against the communist or terrorist threat. Not only that, but officials and leading experts were careful to explain that such operations were always done with the best of intentions. They argued that they were necessary to make the world safe for Western values and interests, and the documents that threatened to reveal too much were kept secret for reasons of "national security". We were supposed to believe that the former implied all things wholesome, and what the latter meant . . . well, let us just say that our leaders preferred that we did not busy our heads with such matters. We should leave it to our authority figures— those who knew better—to run the world on our behalf and otherwise be content with the fact that we, the citizens of the West, were on the side of good, something our designated enemies surely were not.

Briefly summarized, that is the way things have been until today. But theory and practice are two different things, and when our leaders talked about our values, interests, and safety it was the values, interests, and security of the Masters of Commerce they meant to protect.

What we, in this context, should consider is that their values and interests are diametrically opposed to those of ordinary people. After all, the most important thing for corporate owners is to ensure shareholders' profit. Unless there is a bigger game being played, one where corporations are set up to provide cover for more nefarious activities, this is their primary objective. Rising stocks being equal a competitive company, they must ensure the greatest possible profit margins, and this means that they are looking for the most promising conditions for exploitation: they want to take as much as they can from the Whole and give as little as they can in return.

We see from this that captains of industry, to increase their stock price, need access to (and control over) natural resources. They want to control and exploit these resources with a minimum of expenditure, and they seek out the cheapest possible labor for extracting resources, refining them, turning them into products, and selling them. This is what a good business model is all about, and to ensure the best terms for exploitation, they need a corporate friendly regime. This means that they are looking for a regime that will ensure access to cheap resources and manpower, while simultaneously offering the kind of taxes, laws, and regulations that are most advantageous.

The titans of industry focus their efforts on accommodating such regimes; they will bribe, murder, and terrorize to keep such regimes in power, for to the extent they do business will flourish. History says all about it. The communist ideology, which made a name for itself by scapegoating the moneyed classes, did inspire revolution for a reason and looking into this matter the pressure on the political process manifests in three stages. First and foremost, they shape policy through lobbyists and other well-paid professionals. Through these efforts, they make politicians accept their point of view, and if advisory efforts, threats, and bribery at this level do not bring about desired results the pressure increases. What happens next is that the intelligence services come into play. They use whatever tools they have at their disposal to make officials cooperate and if blackmail, propaganda operations, and assassinations are not sufficient, the elite will play their last card. What happens at this point is that the U.S. military goes into action—and the result is always regime change in line with their ambitions.

I mention the U.S. military specifically, for although the elite is transnational and all governments obey them, the U.S. government is their greatest asset. From the late 1800s until today, in more than a hundred instances, it has forced upon other nations its version of an ideal governance—and the ideal form of government is a fascist regime.

As we are raised to believe that fascism died with Hitler's Germany and Mussolini's Italy, this may seem odd. Even so, fascism's defining characteristic is not that of a dictator; instead, its essential characteristic is a strong, militarized government controlled by corporations, something Mussolini alluded to when he said that "Fascism should rather be called corporatism, because it is the merger of state and corporate power".

This is why American elitists like Andrew Mellon, J.P. Morgan, Irenee du Pont, John D. Rockefeller, Henry Ford, Prescott Bush, and William R. Hearst were staunch supporters of Hitler—and *this is why* some of these families tried to stage a fascist coup against President Roosevelt in 1934. The soul of fascism, therefore, is revealed in any government which puts the interests of big business above the people. The way politics work, their interests are entirely opposed, and so such states will always be authoritarian, anti-liberal entities governed by a centralized and overextensive police-apparatus. There must be a mechanism in place that can subdue rebellion when exploitation becomes too severe, preventing people from seeing that the State is an oversized control apparatus tailored to protect the ruling class. Such states, therefore, are dependent on propaganda and the production of enemy images to veil the distance between theory and practice—and from what we have said, it should be obvious that fascism is not dead.

In fact, an unbiased observer will find that the ideology has never been more triumphant, and that the United States is its stronghold. History has never seen a government so corrupted by Big Business. And because fascism and imperialism go hand in hand, this superpower has used its might to make the world conform to the corporations' needs and expectations.

This should be uncontroversial as there are many can confirm this. I could mention General Smedley Butler, a military man who not only sabotaged the elite's fascist coup against Roosevelt by testifying to Congress, but wrote *War is a Racket* about his work as mercenary for the corporations; John Perkins, a man who wrote *Confessions of an Economic Hitman* on his career as a financial mercenary for the same forces; and William Blum, a former employee of the State Department, who wrote *Killing Hope*, a review of the CIA and the U.S. military's interventions on behalf of these conglomerates. In his book, Blum documents at least 50 such episodes throughout the Cold War, and Philip Agee, a former CIA agent, describes the CIA's role this way:

> "The difficult admission is that I became . . . one of [capitalism's] secret policemen. The CIA, after all, is nothing more than the secret police of American capitalism, plugging up leaks in the political dam day and night so that shareholders of US companies operating in poor countries can continue enjoying the rip-off. The key to CIA success is the 2 or 3 percent of the population in poor countries that get most of the cream. . . . These privileged minorities . . . lead back to, and are identified with, the interests of the rich and powerful who control the US.
>
> . . . What [the CIA's operations] really comes down to is the protection of the capitalists back in America, their property and their privileges. US national security, as preached by US leaders, is the security of the capitalist class in the US, not the security of the rest of the people— certainly not the security of the poor except by way of reinforcing poverty. It is from the class interests in the US that our insurgency programs flow, together with that most fundamental of American foreign policy principles: that any government, no matter how bad, is better than a . . . government of workers, peasants and ordinary people." (1.558,562)

Other CIA agents, such as John Stockwell, have confirmed this. In 1988, he estimated that at least 6 million people had been killed in what he described as the CIA's then 40-years war against the people of the Third World. The true figure, however, is even higher as Stockwell, in summarizing the death toll, only counted the most obvious examples. Adding to this, we must take into consideration that the 50 invasions mentioned—and which Blum elaborates on in *Killing Hope*—constitute only a fraction of their actions.

The real extent of the CIA's activities is unknown as secrecy is an essential part of its business. Yet we know from research undertaken by the U.S. Congress in 1975 (the Church Committee) that the CIA, during the preceding 14 years, had executed some 900 major and 3.000 minor operations worldwide. If we extrapolate this number, we can assume (if this level of activity is unchanging) that the organization has performed roughly 5.000 major and 15.000 minor operations from its inception in 1947 until today.

The damage these operations have done to individuals across the world is inconceivable. The damage done to the social fabric, however, is even worse, for their common bond has been the ambition to defeat every indication of a government that puts the needs and aspirations of citizens before Big Business. That the organization has succeeded is self-evident. And the corporations have now molded our minds to the point where few see the problem or can even imagine an alternative. Nevertheless, we would do well to reflect on this. The driving force behind corporations is the idea of perpetual growth, and this is not only an absurd but dangerous notion.

After all, we do live on a planet. This means that we have limited resources and room for expansion, and the good old days when big companies could grow naturally are gone. Continuing reluctance to take this into consideration is an integral part of today's structural problem, and we shall look at the societal dynamic associated with fascism.

24.1 THE DYNAMIC BETWEEN CORPORATIONS AND SOCIETY

"People who know too much are likely to rebel. Both the exploited and the exploiter are impelled to regard knowledge as incompatible with being a good, nice, well-adjusted slave. In such a situation knowledge is dangerous, quite dangerous."(69.62)

—Abraham Maslow, psychologist—

We live in a competitive society and this is easily seen in our economic system. The premise upon which it is based is that competition is good because it provides stable prices and a certain quality of goods.

That it could be different is rarely pondered and few question this thesis. Most believe that we, by nature, are cynical and selfish beings, and it follows that a more co-operative venture is impossible to realize. The Communists tried it and we know how that went. By force, they took the ownership of business away from capitalists and left it to the State to manage their affairs. The effect was not a classless and just society. The only result of this experiment was that they replaced an upper class of capitalists with an upper class of bureaucrats—and that the system was run with less efficacy.

The reason for this was that individuals were no longer sufficiently motivated to do their best. The earth they toiled over, or the factory where they worked, no longer belonged to people who craved efficiency but to the collective; those who rose to the top were not the best and the brightest, but spineless yet cunning psychopaths, and because few felt that they had a vested interest in this scheme motivation disappeared. This experiment, in other words, demonstrated that self-interest was stronger than public interest—and because people cared more for themselves than the common good, the entire project failed.

Thus, communism seemed to confirm that the only viable option was the Western and that society would prosper to the extent that people were left alone. That, at least, was the argument made by those with the sharpest elbows, those who would rise to the top in such a system. Not only would they prosper, but they lobbied politicians for policies that consolidated their position and so we have arrived at this point. But how are we doing? What has the pursuit of self-interest done, and can we say that our system has proven its excellence?

Taking a look around, the answer is evident. Even so, to bring our predicament to light, we should examine history and we begin with the industrial revolution. With this revolution a new social dynamic was born. New machinery, inventions, and methods of production created another social class, the working class, and assisted by steam engines, electricity, telephone lines, etc., Western civilization conquered the world. The population increased rapidly, and more and more settled in cities or emigrated to novel places. Whereas the world was shrinking, it was still rich with plenty and there was no lack of resources to plunder and land to conquer.

As a result of this revolution, the British Empire, by the end of the 19th century, stretched around the world. The colonial powers, however, had divided the world and even in America, this vast continent, space was no longer plentiful. This continent had functioned as a pressure valve as it provided an opportunity for those who were not satisfied with life elsewhere. It was an incredibly rich country and as the sun set on the British Empire, the glory days of the United States were just begun.

As the 1800s ended, this enormous continent had been "civilized". What valuable land the natives possessed had been taken, their culture wiped out, and as the West was won cities arose. With the emerging townships, railways and infrastructure followed. Massive projects were initiated, and capital was needed. The money lenders were happy to assist—and while the focus of contractors and engineers was to build a new society, the financiers' only interest was to profit and control.

We have seen how the elite conquered the American continent. We spoke briefly of the unparalleled growth in this period; of how the dynamics between supply and demand ensured the emergence of a class of extremely influential men; of how these men had a vested interest in collaboration; and of how the end of the 1800s, therefore, became known as the age of robber barons and monopolists. Together these people cornered the market, set up cartels, foundations, and trusts, and made it impossible for newcomers to take on their position. Through the network of secret societies, they were so powerful that they controlled the political process, and through a collective effort they set out to form society in their image.

What we should know is that although tycoons like Harriman, Carnegie, du Pont, and Vanderbilt had enormous influence, the financial elite was a class of its own. Without access to capital, industrialists could not expand or upgrade their business, and so the bankers came out on top; they decided who should prosper or go out of business, and they never lent money without securing something in return. Historian Hugh Brogan elaborates:

> "In return for their assistance the New York banks usually exacted drastic reorganization, heavy fees and seats on the board for themselves or their representatives. The leader in this movement was the House of Morgan . . . Between 1893 and 1913 . . . its chief was behind all the moves to stabilize operations and promote mergers in the railroads, in shipping, in the new electricity industry, in the telegraph, in telephones, as well as in steel. J. P. Morgan was the spider in a vast web of interlocking directorships (741 of them in 112 corporations) and as during the same period Standard Oil was steadily extending its influence, by the end of the first decade of the twentieth century it was almost the case that all the leading American capitalists were associates either of Morgan or of Rockefeller."(16.401)

According to revisionist history, since then, the leading elitist's influence has been in decline. Evidence, however, abounds that the main difference between now and then is that their power has become less obvious. To understand how this came about, we must consider the creation of the Federal Reserve in 1913. Its official purpose was to give back to the American people control over the U.S. economy. Even so, the whole thing was a sham, as it was the same financiers who agitated for the formation of the bank who took control of it, thus consolidating position as the most powerful men in the world.

The official reason behind their effort was that before 1913, what is known as the business cycle was fluctuating unrestrained, ruling all aspects of the market. This cycle of ebb and flow—of boom and bust—is equally alive today but then it was operating unhindered, leaving not only common people but the elite vulnerable to its ups and downs. The way our economic system functions, this cycle is an integral part of its essence. As the system is built on the idea of exponential growth, it can be compared to a bubble that constantly needs to increase in scope. As long as there is a good feedback dynamic between supply and demand, this bubble will constantly expand and all is well; people earn more and buy more, manufacturers are producing more and selling more, and banks lend more and earn more. At some point, however, something will happen that makes money scarce. The bubble can no longer be inflated, and we enter a recession.

This is how it has been for hundreds of years, and in the 1800s there were a handful of such recessions. That they can be manipulated by the moneylenders, those who decide how much money they will put into the system or retract from it, is lost on most people, but President James A. Garfield knew better. As he said in 1881:

> "Whoever controls the volume of money in our country is absolute master of all industry and commerce . . . and when you realize that the entire system is very easily controlled, one way or another, by a few powerful men at the top, you will not have to be told how periods of inflation and depression originate."(54.48)

Garfield, of course, was assassinated a few weeks later. To continue our story, however, there were recessions in 1873, 1893, and 1907. Considering this, the financiers presented a central bank as the solution, as it was supposed to regulate the market and put an end to recessions. The problem, however, was that the market's most powerful players were tasked to regulate. Control of the central bank gave them a variety of new tools, including the printing of money, manipulation of interest rates, as well as all the other instruments a lender of last resort needed to create monetary policy.

Aside from the fact that the fox was left with the responsibility of guarding the henhouse—and that the most powerful players got to decide who should get what and when—another problem with this arrangement was that the business cycle's natural regulation of markets no longer took place. Before 1913, when the bubble had become too large and a natural correction was needed, recession kicked in and rooted out the least viable businesses. In 1873, 1893, and 1907, for example, a lot of banks went bankrupt as they were too greedy and had gambled too much money on investments that did not pay off. For the people who lost their savings, this was unfortunate, but it was a necessary adjustment, the way things worked.

With the creation of the central bank, however, natural adjustments no longer took place. Instead, it became possible to ignore reality and to artificially inflate the financial bubble to ever greater proportions. In this way smaller collapses, or what one might call natural adjustments, were avoided. Even so, it is not possible to keep a bubble inflated by artificial figures and false expectations alone, and one day reality comes knocking. Thus, came the great depression of 1929, as the stock market had reached insane proportions; at one point it was not possible to ignore structural problems and the greatest recession Americans had seen set in. From this market crash it was evident (for those who would see) that the central bank was part of the problem rather than a solution. Nonetheless, the men behind it have continued their manipulations until today, and as a result our economic system is in a worse condition than ever.

We saw an indication with the 2008 financial crisis, as it came about as a result of central bankers' monetary policy the past 30 years. I oversimplify, for we are all part of the problem and it has taken more than 30 years to become what it is. Even so, it is not possible to explain the 2008 crisis without pointing to the U.S. central bank as it represents the hub of a centralized and interconnected network that controls some 80 percent of the world's wealth.

We get an idea of the structure of this network when we look at a study done at the Swiss Federal Institute of Technology in Zurich. Under the leadership of James Glattfelder, researchers used supercomputers and chaos theory to map out the implications of Orbis 2007, a database covering 37 million corporations and individual investors. What they found was that 80 percent of all the money that was made filtered back to the Fed through interlocking directorates, consisting of the world's most powerful corporations. These corporations, 737 of them, were ten times more powerful than suggested by their wealth, and by crunching the numbers Glattfelder's team narrowed them down to a super-entity consisting of 147 companies. 75 percent were financial institutions, the most powerful being Barclays Bank, J.P. Morgan Chase, Merrill Lynch, Bank of New York, Deutsche Bank, Goldman Sachs, HSBC, Citigroup, and so on.

The men behind these banks are all shareholders in each other's companies and part of a pattern so intertwined that any real extinction, except for brands, is difficult to find. Thus, the term "super-entity", and behind it we find the men who effectively rule the world.

They are the ones who tell our officials what to do—and that they are motivated by self-interest was revealed by the 2008-crisis. The reader may recall that banks then, large and small, were struggling with liquidity. Despite clever schemes, it was no longer possible to conceal the sea of red numbers that threatened to drown them and our officials were told to fix it. After successfully having spent the last 30 years lobbying to remove any regulation that limited their growth, the banks now argued that they had become so big that if they failed the economy would follow. They therefore made it clear to public officials that we, the citizens, had to pay their bills so that bankers could continue their fun and games. Treasury Secretary Henry Paulson warned Congress that if this were not done, martial law would be next. He handed Congress a bailout bill of over $700 billion and hard pressed the representatives conceded to his demands.

Now, these $700 billion, as we shall see, was only a fraction of the total amount given to the banks. Nonetheless, what should be taken into consideration is that Paulson himself, along with other corrupt officials, was instrumental in creating the crisis. As a civil servant, he had not only removed the regulations that banks wanted gone; he was former CEO of Goldman Sachs, a bank receiving more than $60 billion from his bailout plan.[89] Again, we see the fox guarding the henhouse—and as icing on the cake, he denied AIG the right to sue Goldman for the financial losses its fraudulent transactions had caused the insurance company.

The word "fraudulent" is not hyperbole. Among other dirty deeds, Goldman's investors sold securities to pension funds, knowing full well that they were worth zero. The basis of this scheme was (1) sorting out those securities that were garbage and then (2) selling to unsuspecting customers after having bribed credit rating companies to inflate ratings. While they did this, they bet *against* the same securities on the stock exchange—and so it was that Goldman earned billions while others lost their pension. Goldman was not alone in concocting such schemes: J.P. Morgan and Merrill Lynch did the same, and the punishment they got was—at most—a slap on the wrist.

One should think that a better example of the wicked morality these banks abide by would be hard to find. This, however, is not the worst, for when Congress (for the first time in the history of the central bank) was allowed access to behind-the-scenes transactions, they found that from December 2007 to June 2010 the Fed had given away $26 trillion. Admittedly, $10 trillion were disguised as currency swaps, but this was money the Fed had secretly created and distributed amongst its friends.

We are talking about a sum so astronomical that the brain cannot comprehend it—26 million *million* U.S. dollars—and the recipients were the usual suspects, first and foremost Goldman Sachs, Citigroup, Bank of America, J.P. Morgan Chase, Barclays, Morgan Stanley, Deutsche Bank, and Royal Bank of Scotland.

Thanks to this avalanche of money (that the Federal Reserve creates from nothing), these banks have done exceedingly well. Their profits and bonuses are larger than ever, but this does not mean that the crisis is over. Except for fictitiously elevated stock prizes, the only effect this money has had is diluting the economy; it has increased the collective debt level and made it possible for the bubble that should have burst in 2008 to grow on to even more bizarre proportions.

---

[89] $6.8 billion of these $60 billion were paid as bonuses to Goldman executives. It is also worth noting that in addition to Paulson, ten more Goldman employees were put in charge of the Bush administration's financial policies.

Like a heroin junkie welcomes his next shot, no matter its price, so this influx of money was welcomed at the stock exchange. It was, however, nothing more than a temporary fix, one for which a price will be exacted. One problem is that even if this money is not directly taken from one place—the Fed creates them out of nothing—the total sum of money in circulation increases all the time, and this makes each dollar less worth. This is called inflation. And although U.S. citizens have some way to go before they reach those conditions that prevailed in Germany in the 1920s, when people had to carry a wheelbarrow of money to afford a loaf of bread, they are no strangers to the detrimental effects of their central bank's monetary policy.

Now, the repercussions of this monetary influx have not manifested. But the printing presses have been running nonstop for some time, and we see an indication of their consequences in that while Americans in the early 1980s were working an average of 1700 hours per year, they are now working 1900 hours. In other words, they are working *200 more hours every year*, but they are worse off. Another indication is that Americans' real income has been in decline since the 1960s and while they in 1980, as measured per capita, had roughly $15.000 in U.S. household debt per person, this debt burden has increased to more than $50.000.

Still, it is about to become worse, as the central banks are printing money at an increasing rate. Ridiculously, this is their solution to the mounting debt levels that we succumb to, for on a collective basis we have reached beyond our means. The U.S. national debt alone has increased by $13 trillion since the beginning of the 1980s. As the U.S. Government are forced to raise its debt ceiling again and again, the probability that this debt will ever be repaid is looking increasingly dim, and more and more European states are in the same situation.

As a matter of fact, if we look closely, we are stuck in the same situation that developing countries the last 40 years have become so familiar with; hoping to promote economic growth and improve social conditions, our officials accept the agreements offered by the banks, but these are so unfavorable that the state can never repay its debt. This is a strategy that banks have deliberately used against developing countries since they won their independence.[90] It makes it impossible for a country to break free from exploitation, for the debt is used as leverage ensuring that the country is taken over by Western corporations.

Hence, although we are enslaved by debt, nothing is wrong with the system as seen from the banks' perspective. Once we owe them money, we are in their pockets—right where they want us—and then we are caught in the rat race, obliged to conform to their expectations while working hard to take care of our next interest payment. Sometimes they push us too far and we are unable to comply with our obligations. When it happens to ordinary people, the bank is just as happy; the loan is backed up by what we own, and so the bank will take our house, car, and other valuables to continue exploitations elsewhere.

For the bank, however, it becomes a problem when big borrowers such as a country can no longer manage its debts. If the debt level is sufficient, the bank is forced to negotiate as the debtor must not become too discouraged and declare bankruptcy. If that happens, the bank finds itself in a lot of trouble and so it will make every effort to renegotiate a working agreement. Thus, as the debt burden becomes too great, such renegotiation of debt will surely take place. The point, as always, is to keep the debtor afloat—but barely—so that the bank can continue its extortion.

Even so, the size of the debt has now become so enormous that it is unlikely to be a solution to anything. As banks worldwide have a vested interest in this debt and the stock market depends on it, such action will have disastrous consequences and it is doubtful that we can patch things together without pushing the restart button. As the system currently operates, I should add "fortunately", for we would be better off if we began anew. Currently, the game is rigged in the banks' favor, and if we look closer it is a giant pyramid scheme designed to do exactly what it does—transfer assets from the people below to those at the top.

History itself speaks volumes: Every recession has been a milking mechanism which extracts to the biggest banks whatever assets ordinary

---

[90] See JOHN PERKINS, *CONFESSIONS OF AN ECONOMIC HITMAN*.

people and lesser financial actors possess[91]. As a result, the ten largest banks control more than 80 percent of all assets owned by American banks. Thus, whatever can be put a price tag on in our materialistic society is gathered in the hands of an increasingly powerful elite—and the bigger their corporations, the more invulnerable they become.

Their power has long since reached a point where they define the rules. And when they tell us that they are too big to fail, they expect us to pay their bills so they can maintain their lifestyle and bonuses. No matter how outrageous this is, our leaders accept it without too much objections, for the political process is no friend of the little man.

To the contrary, the game is so rigged that higher-ups have a vested interest in the status quo. We just saw an example in Treasury Secretary Paulson of how the bankers pretend to be public servants, and his case is not unique. On the contrary, it is the rule rather than the exception, as key players move about in an endless circle between academia, private industry, and government agencies. In fact, no matter where we look, it is the same group who operates the controls. At one moment they are in the boardroom of a corporation, the other they occupy a professorate at a prestigious university, and the next they are found posing as civil servants—if not, for the occasion, they front as ambassadors in the UN or elsewhere.

Proof that they are working for the good of each other—and not the people—is found everywhere, not least in the growing gap between rich and poor.[92] Elitist objections aside, this social dynamic is not the result of people growing lazier, while a minority are becoming ever more

---

[91] The 2008 crisis provides an example: Summarizing the assets owned by the world's 1,500 largest banks, we find that while the 10 largest banks in 2008 controlled 18 percent, the following year they controlled 26 percent.

[92] While America's wealthiest 1 percent earned 10 percent of the total income in 1982, they now rake in more than 25 percent. They own more values than 95 percent of the population combined, and they have increased their salaries 275 percent since 1980. Crunching the numbers further, however, we find that most of the one percenters' income has not changed much and that it is the richest point-zero-zero-one percenters (0.001) and so on that has reaped the profits. Hence, according to Forbes/CNBC the 400 richest Americans are now worth a combined $2 trillion, more than the net worth of half of all Americans.

diligent. Rather, it is the natural outcome of a political process which prioritizes the needs and expectations of a few, mixed with the fact that equal and fair access to the system's representatives has become a thing of the past.

It is not easy to reverse this trend, for how can the average citizen expect to have his voice heard when some 33.000 registered lobbyists are working to influence the political process? The financial sector alone has more than 3.000 lobbyists. This means that they outnumber members of Congress five to one, and between 1998 and 2008 they spent over $5 billion greasing the wheels of Washington D.C. Another powerful grouping is the pharmaceutical industry, with 1.300 registered lobbyists. They spent at least $1 billion wheeling and dealing in the same period. No doubt, these moneys are well spent, for the politicians, in turn, enact such laws and regulations that Big Business want. That is obvious to anyone who does not refuse to see, and so it takes a well-paid professor at one of the prestigious universities to find this straight-forward.

For according to economists like Martin Feldstein at Harvard this is no problem. According to experts like him everything is as it should be, and details such as bank regulations and constraints on their lobbying efforts are rejected as nonsense.

That people like him are paid consultants for the banks—and often sit on their board of directors—probably has something to do with their philosophy. Even so, if you want to know why these people think that everything is simply perfect, they will answer that the market knows best and that the less we interfere with the affairs of Big Business, the more likely executives will manage their business most appropriately—which is to say for the good of all. The idea is that the less taxes, the better it is, and they explain this with the trickle-down effect. Put simply, it means that the more prosperity rains upon those at the top, the better off we are, for when they buy palaces, limousines, jets, golf courses, racehorses, and Caribbean islands, ordinary people also stand to profit. After all, someone must serve them, drive their limousines, fly their aircrafts, trim their golf courses, and pick up the dung from their fine-breed horses. And because this is our job, it is amazing for everybody that the elite's bribes work their magic on politicians.

In short, this is the argument they are trying to sell. But no matter how awesome they envision a government with the corporations, by the corporations, and for the corporations, the premise upon which it is built—the idea of ever-expanding growth—is killing us.

One reason for this is that the good old days when the corporations could grow naturally are long gone. And as they are trying to ignore indications of this, it is at our expense that profit margins are being maintained. The fact that human exploitation is an essential part of their profit machinery is, of course, something the elite do not want us to think about. Nonetheless, for their stocks to rise, we must (1) work harder for less wages or (2) spend more of our money on their products—and so it is that the only value we have is that of producers or consumers. That is it! And when markets are saturated and we can no longer buy more cell phones, TVs, washing machines, or cars, corporations must either find new markets or increase efficiency.

The latter usually involves firing as many workers as possible and making those who still have a job toil harder. At one point, however, it is not possible to maximize profits through cuts in expenditure and the companies, to satisfy their shareholders, must purchase or merge with other profitable enterprises. This may generate growth, but mergers are not unproblematic. It is far easier for a smaller corporation to double its earnings—and the larger the corporation, the harder to maintain growth.

This simple math translated to a historical context shows that, by the 1960s, the biggest companies were struggling. They had outgrown the Western market and to maintain growth the elite had to conquer new markets, consolidate, or cut costs. Temporarily, they solved this problem by moving production to those areas where conditions were most ripe for exploitation[93]. Thus, export production zones came into being, where the

---

[93] As a result, some 40 million American jobs have either been closed down or moved overseas. In other words, good jobs with decent wages have become scarcer, and to uphold the dynamics of supply and demand between east and west (someone has to buy everything that is produced) the elite has organized for us so that we get to borrow more and more of their printed money. Therefore, to maintain our lifestyle, we have become increasingly indebted, and this is another sign of the times that it is all about to unravel.

planet's poorest people "volunteered" to work long hours for nickels and dimes under the most primitive and hazardous conditions.

This made additional growth possible, at least for a few decades. It was, however, no lasting solution, for even in those areas of the world production costs could not be reduced beyond a certain point, and soon the western market was saturated with cheap goods. It is this problem the Masters of Commerce are now facing, and it has put us in a tight spot. Not only because we are about to drown in an avalanche of debt, but because we, with our lifestyle and consumption of resources, already have brought the planet to its knees.

Now, for arguments sake, if we forget that survival is dependent on sustainable development; that we cannot continue living indefinitely on borrowed money; and that there are no resources left that can withstand a plunder at such a rate and such a scale that further expansion entails, a short-term solution would be to look for new markets. Much of the population in Asia, Latin America, and Africa are still missing out on the Western lifestyle and, hypothetically speaking, corporations could concentrate on this market. However, for these people to afford those things we take for granted their standards of living must improve. This means that their salaries must be increased—and this is a big no-no for the elite. They have the current conditions, so ripe for exploitation, to thank for their success and if they were forced to upgrade the working conditions in the mines of Africa or offer Chinese laborers anywhere near decent wages, this would wipe out their profit margins.

Theoretically, of course, CEOs could repair some of the damage by lowering their multimillion-dollar salaries and eliminating extra bonuses. Moderation, however, is not one of their virtues. They are as unlikely to think in these terms as their shareholders are to be motivated by anything other than short-term profits, and as long as the "greed is good" mindset rules supreme, only one solution remains—tightening the grip on Western citizens.

As we can see, the situation is desperate, for if they cannot batter the world's poor into further submission, they need to make us lower our expectations; we must accept lower wages, longer hours, more social and economic inequality, and so on. Now, this has already been the name of the game for centuries, but the elites know they must tread carefully. As citizens of the West, we are well-accustomed to a lifestyle on borrowed wings, and we are not too fond of being pushed around. Children as we are of a civilization built on centuries of exploitation, murder, and oppression elsewhere, we take it for granted that it is the natural order of things—and that it will forever remain so.

In our hearts, of course, we have always known that the medal has another side. But as long as our lifestyle has improved, we have cared little for human or environmental costs. On the contrary, we have been blinded by the glittering façade of fascism; as long as others paid the price, we were only too happy to let the Masters of Commerce go about their business, and neither their wars of aggression nor our politicians' shameless lies upset us.

The beauty of fascism, however, is that it is insatiable and so it will eventually eat its own. We have long felt the impact of its appetite, for while it feeds on the poor and other outgroups, the more it grows, the more ravenous and indiscriminate it becomes—and we are watching the end game, as it devours the remnants of our constitutional heritage.

Besides everything we have discussed, another warning that we are reaching fever pitch is the dominance interests' increasing influence. We know that corporations rely on growth to survive and this promotes a societal dynamic that ultimately benefits them. The reason is that at some point it will become harder to generate growth in the regular markets. There is a limit to how many toasters, computers, and cell phones we need, and when the elite is no longer able to manipulate us into buying things that are good for us, they begin to speculate in things that are bad.

As indicated by tabloids, nothing sells like fear. This is not lost on the elite, and to generate demand they make use of simple recipes such as playing on insecurities and focusing on enemy images. These images are manipulated in different ways. We have mentioned how they use the threat of terrorism to scare us, and by facilitating for the emergence of this enemy image they have not only succeeded in taking away our civil liberties but they have earned billions in the process. Since 9/11, few stocks have provided better value than the military-industrial complex. Between 2002 and 2008 the hundred largest arms companies increased with an average of 37 percent, and the bigger the corporation, the more massive their profits. Lockheed Martin's stocks, for instance, increased by 145 percent between 2003 and 2007, and another indication of the profits involved are found looking at defense expenditures. After the end of the Cold War they gradually declined, but the War on Terror reversed this trend. As a result of this "eternal war for peace," the world now spends about $1.5 trillion on such folly. This is 50 percent more than before 9/11, and the U.S. alone counts for more than half of the world's total expenditures. Thus, the enemy images represent a most profitable market; while Clinton's outgoing defense budget was $385 (in present day dollars), by 2012 the national defense cost $700 billion, much thanks to the ruling elite, as they have no moral qualms against manipulating a perceived threat to increase their influence and revenue.

We shall soon expand on this. But to say more about the financial aspect of the enemy images, they are most welcome sources for profit. The reason is that while ordinary markets have an inherently limited growth potential, the security-, war-, and domination industry does not obey the same rules. Instead, this market's potential is proportional to the logic of fear's influence on society, and the United States is an example of the destructive dynamics that follow in its wake.

All things considered, it is because of these forces' influence that the U.S. economy has become a war economy, dependent on enemy images and a perpetual warfare. Looking at the bigger picture, we find that after the crash of 1929, it was not until the Second World War that the U.S. economy got back on its feet and since then the influence of the military-industrial complex has multiplied. President Eisenhower cautioned against its "acquisition of unwarranted influence" in his farewell address to the nation in 1961. He warned that "the potential for the disastrous rise of misplaced power exists and will persist", but his call could not rouse the American people. Thus, its cancerous influence could spread, and any alert student of history knows the result. As Ron Paul summarized the current situation:

> "The United States is . . . quite possibly the most aggressive, extended, and expansionist [empire] in the history of the world. . . . [It is] an empire which requires perpetual war and preparation for war, [and it] is incompatible with a free society."(79.84,88)

It goes without saying that the U.S. war economy is a huge problem for the rest of the world. There is always an enemy image that must be maintained, a regime that must be changed, and a country that must be bombed to keep going. Nonetheless, it is also a serious problem for Americans as the war economy not only destroys the healthy aspects of their economy, but also promotes an internal dynamic which serves no one—except the war profiteers' shortsighted interests.

We see an example of the former in that warfare is expensive. By now the war in Afghanistan and Iraq has cost U.S. taxpayers well over one trillion dollars, and although it has a positive effect on the GDP every time the U.S. military bombs a bridge, a dam, a funeral, or a wedding in Iraq, this is bad business for most Americans. They are the ones who must pay for the elite's fun and games, and even though this violation of international law in Iraq or elsewhere equals Christmas for war profiteers, society is slowly being stripped of moral and financial resources.

That taxes are not enough to feed the war machine, is seen in the fact that the U.S. national debt increased by 50 percent during the Bush administration. Despite the dollar's privileged position, however, this debt cannot be increased in perpetuity. Sooner or later, cuts must be made, and it is the people that take the brunt. This is how the system works, for even though politicians, at some point, will have to reduce defense expenditures (which claim $1.2 trillion of a federal budget of $3.7 trillion), their masters will ensure that those with an agenda of fear wins out.

Hence, even though politicians could have balanced the budget by lowering the corporations' expectations, it is the citizens that must pay: they are the ones who must endure more taxes, who must bear the burden of rising inflation, who must work harder for less pay, who must deal with increasing unemployment and worsening work conditions, and end up with poorer health services and educational opportunities.

This is the price they must pay for being subjected to a political process which cater to the elite's needs and expectations. And because such an economy can only survive in an equally sick society, the men behind the power have a vested interest in dumbing down the populace. After all, only a most befuddled citizenry will accept a social contract on such terms. If they could think, they would have seen through the smoke and mirrors that the elite has put in place; they would have seen the distance between theory and practice for what it is, and they would not have been dazzled by the selection of pre-purchased candidates for President that the elite has authorized.

We have already discussed how fascism, to keep its wheels turning, depends on enemy images in addition to an extensive propaganda apparatus that emphasizes theory while disregarding practice.[94] As long as this is in place, the system will be able to hide its true colors a little longer. But no matter what, the monster of fascism cannot hide its face indefinitely. To survive, it must also feed on its own, and whereas this feature becomes increasingly prominent as it grows, it has an inherent drive towards tightening its grip on the population.

We have already seen how the American people, as a result, now find themselves naked, stripped of all their God-given rights, before the monstrosity they call a government. If their "public servants" regard them as a threat, they are fair game—and we see the degree of social control this State on steroids feels entitled to by looking at the prison population. Looking at this, we find that the U.S. criminal justice system at any given time has around 2.3 million citizens locked up in prisons and a total of 7 million under its control. That is more than three percent of the adult population and colored people are overrepresented. They are six times as likely to serve time, and as a result 10 percent of all black men between 30-34 years are imprisoned. No country in the world can compare, and even China with its 1.3 million prisoners pales in comparison.

We see from these figures which state is really the most totalitarian, for adjusted for population the U.S. Government incarcerates around seven times more citizens than the Chinese. To some extent these numbers can be explained by the class divisions in the United States, for

---

[94] We see the effect of this propaganda apparatus on surveys revealing that some 50 percent of Americans in 2004 believed Saddam's regime was directly involved in the planning, execution, and financing of the 9/11 terrorist attacks; that some 50 percent in 2006 believed that weapons of mass destruction were found in Iraq (and that around 40 percent still believe it); that about 50 percent still believe in the government's version of events on 9/11; and that approximately 50 percent of those surveyed did not even know that a third building, WTC-7, also collapsed that day.

its well-known that the bigger the difference between rich and poor, the greater also the percentage of the imprisoned population.

This, however, does not fully explain things. Looking at statistics, the prison population showed little variance from World War II until the 1980s. In this period, the United States had roughly 100 prisoners per 100.000 inhabitants—a normal level if we compare with other Western countries. Throughout the 1980s, however, the prison population doubled, and the curve has continued to rise until today, where we find some 700 prisoners per 100.000 inhabitants.

We know from before that it was in the beginning of the 1980s, with the Reagan administration, that social inequality in America really gained momentum and so, to some degree, the rise in prison population can be explained by the social dynamic that followed in its wake. Even so, this social dynamic should be studied more carefully, for looking at the statistics we find that they do not reflect an increase in real crime. In fact, crime statistics reveal that *actual* crime—that which includes victims— declined 25 percent from 1988 to 2008. Thus, the explanation for the escalating prison population is not that Americans plunder, rob, rape, and kill each other at an alarmingly increasing rate, but that criminal justice policy is being aligned with the control-oriented elite's ambitions. Americans, therefore, serve longer sentences for evermore petty crimes. It is not difficult finding people imprisoned for blameless behavior and a major reason for the rise in prison population is the drug laws. Since the early 1980s, they have become increasingly severe and many people believe that this is a good thing. They assume that these laws are in place to protect society and that violators pose a threat. This assumption, however, is not entirely correct but shall be examined after we have become better acquainted with the enemy images' importance to rulers.

25

ENEMY IMAGES, THEIR OVERALL FUNCTION AND CONSEQUENCE

"[Before I discovered it myself,] respected professional contacts in Washington D.C. and other knowledgeable citizens had told me for some time that, like Pogo has said, "We have met the enemy and he is us". That our enemy is not wearing communist uniforms in Southeast Asia, but rather, was dressed in three piece suits in our nation's capital."(46.13)

—James "Bo" Gritz[95]—

WE HAVE ALREADY become acquainted with enemy images. We have seen how the elite used the war against communism as a pretext for most of their coup d'états and warfare in the 20th century, and we have seen how the War on Terror took over after it expired. Thanks to these enemy images the elite have had the pretext they needed to realize their political ambitions in places like Latin America, Asia, Middle East, and Africa. But as we have seen, neither Europe nor the United States have escaped unscathed from the dynamic that followed in their wake. After all, the elite had to convince citizens that the threat was not only real but so substantial that, besides the most grotesque acts of warfare, it justified restrictions on our civil rights.

---

[95] Gritz, one of America's most decorated soldiers, wrote a book after discovering that a CIA faction affiliated with George Bush Sr. controlled most of the world's drug trade. He tried to stop this but was met with great resistance from superiors. See GRITZ, *A NATION BETRAYED*. See also MIKALSEN, *HUMAN RISING*.

What we shall do now is examine the two enemy images that have been the elite's greatest assets in demolishing our catalogue of rights. The first, as we already know, is the threat of terrorism, while other is the threat of drugs. That "drugs" is an unwarranted enemy image may come as a surprise. Even so, not only do these enemy images depend upon misconceptions, but their societal function and consequence are identical; they are both short-sighted, mendacious, and misanthropic campaigns promoted by the elite to facilitate an increasing control grid. In truth, they are the pillars upon which fascism in our time depends, and we shall now elaborate on this controversial claim, starting with terrorism.

25.1 THE WAR ON TERROR

"We need to go back to the beginning and not just simply and blindly trust the U.S. Government's explanation and the indirect information provided by them. There were too many victims, so I think we need to start again from the beginning. We need to ask who the real victims of this "war on terror" really are. I think the citizens of the world are its victims. . . . We need to look at the evidence and ask ourselves what the war on terror really is."

—Yukihisa Fujita, representative of Japan's Democratic Party, in a parliament hearing January 11, 2008—

Terrorism is no new phenomenon. Throughout history, it has been the most effective weapon of war against a superior adversary and a certain percentage of the population has always seen it as a legitimate strategy. In fact, there is evidence to suggest that while our media is more focused than ever, the phenomenon is no more prevalent than before.

We shall have more to say on this shortly, but to begin with any discussion of terrorism should recognize that, at its most basic level, terrorism takes on two forms. The first is the one media focuses upon. This is the kind of terrorism where individuals become so overwhelmed by circumstances and the logic of fear that they, in accordance with the end-justifies-the-means ideology, retaliate violently. The second form of terrorism is the one that the State itself is engaged in. This type of terrorism includes those instances where operators of the state use unjust force against civilians. War, persecution of minorities, ethnic cleansing, discriminatory and disproportional laws, arbitrary detention and prosecution, as well as other human rights violations, are just some of its manifestations. The State, of course, will not call it terrorism, but there is no doubt that the State is the perpetrator.

Speaking of state-sponsored terrorism, however, another category must be considered. This is terrorism instigated by government, but where agents of state put the blame on others. Such operations provide the State with opportunities and a freedom of action which it otherwise would not have had and so this type of terrorism is more common than we presume. Whether the State wants to go to war or to tighten its grip on populations, it must first convince us that it is doing so for the public good, and to do so our leaders have initiated several terrorist operations.

Keep in mind that the full truth, in these instances, is never exposed as the State will use all its might to cover up its involvement. As time goes by, however, secrets tend to surface, and we saw the ugly face of state-sponsored terrorism revealed in a series of bombings that took place on the European continent from 1956 to 1990 (Operation Gladio). Western intelligence, financed by the CIA, then used right-wing groups to carry out a series of bombings and assassinations which were blamed on communists. The purpose was to demonize the European left-wing, so that only such governments as approved by the CIA came into power—a mission they accomplished.

The U.S. propaganda machine, for its part, was so powerful that Americans did not need this type of "evidence" to be convinced that the communist threat was real. As they believed in the integrity of U.S. institutions, they depended on CIA to protect them from the red hordes, and so they accepted the Korean War, the Vietnam War, and the CIA's dealings in Latin America, Africa, and elsewhere as legitimate defensive measures. Ignorance aside, Americans owe it to President Kennedy that the CIA did not launch any major terrorist operations on U.S. soil during this period: We know today that the military, to have a pretext for war against Cuba, presented plans for a series of such attacks (Operation Northwoods) but that Kennedy refused.

In the 1990s, however, the fear of external enemies began to wane. The Soviet threat was overcome, and new enemy images had to take its place. We saw the result of this in the bombing of the World Trade Center in 1993 and Oklahoma's Murrah-building in 1995. Although there is evidence to suggest that U.S. intelligence, in both cases, were involved, the WTC attack generated a fear of external enemies (Muslim terrorists) while the latter increased the fear of internal enemies (right-wing militias).

As a result of such operations, new regulations were put in place, but the enemy image of terrorism had not become sufficiently powerful to justify the elite's ambitions. For that to happen something even more frightening had to occur, something so traumatic that we would accept a War on Terror. Hence, the 9/11 attacks. Despite a collective refusal to deal with this wound, half the world's population doubt the official version. Even so, as this summary makes clear, this is not the first time governments have sacrificed citizens as a pretext for war.

In this regard, the 9/11 terrorist attacks are not even the most recent examples of state-sponsored terrorism. On the morning of July 7, 2005, four bombs went off in London which were blamed on local Muslims, but there is enough to suggest that intelligence services were involved[96]. Circumstantial evidence is a BBC-interview from the same morning in which Peter Power, former anti-terrorism investigator in Scotland Yard and at that time Managing Director of Visor Consultants, had this to say:

> "At half past nine this morning we were actually running an exercise for a company of over a thousand people in London *based on simultaneous bombs going off precisely at the railway stations where it happened this morning*, so I still have the hairs on the back of my neck standing up right now."

---

[96] See Nick Kellerstrom, *Terror on the Tube: Behind the Veil of 7/7*; Daniel Obachike, *The 4th Bomb: inside London's Terror Storm*. For a documentary, see 7/7 Ripple Effect, part 1 and 2.

As Power would not reveal more details and Prime Minister Blair decided that no investigative committee should be appointed, we have no further information on these exercises. Nonetheless, similar exercises took place on 9/11 and they are helpful covers whenever agents of mischief plan and implement real-time events. We shall not elaborate, but chances are near-zero that a scenario "just happens" to go from exercise to real-time like this.

To say more on the War on Terror, those with a better-than-average memory will remember that the Bush administration was not the first to declare a war on this scourge. In fact, in 1980, when President Reagan came to power, he declared that his chief priority would be to combat communist-backed terrorist organizations. Not surprisingly, he meant those liberation movements who fought against fascist oppression and exploitation. Hence, in addition to FARC in Colombia, Zapatistas in Mexico, and Sandinistas in Nicaragua, Nelson Mandela and other ANC-members were targeted for elimination in South Africa.

I say "not surprisingly", because anyone with a grasp on history knows that Big Business defines policy, and so it's the modus operandi of government to label such movements as "communist" or "terrorist" regardless of reality. As the Brazilian Archbishop Dom Helder Camara described the predicament: "When I give food to the poor, they call me a saint. When I ask why they are poor, they call me a Communist."

Throughout the 20th century, therefore, the United States has been a consistent supporter of fascist dictatorships. The U.S. have trained their mercenaries and police forces, armed them, and helped to suppress every popular uprising. The Americans have done all this under the pretext of fighting communism, but as Noam Chomsky put it: "The fear of Communism was always a total fraud. We know that and we have known it for years from the declassified internal record."(19.73)

In keeping with this pattern, Reagan singled out Libyan President Muammar Gaddafi as the administration's top threat. He was the perfect villain: not only a leading opponent of the former colonial powers' continued domination and exploitation but a fan of violent revolution. Just like Al Qaeda today, therefore, Gaddafi was a symbol of everything that threatened the hegemony of the Western/fascist ideology—and according to Reagan, it was Soviet, Eastern European, North Korean, and Cuban authorities that enabled this despot to thrive.

As always, however, reality was another. And as usual it was the CIA that gave Gaddafi the equipment and expertise to supply left-wing terrorists around the world and continue operations. Besides providing him with 21 tons of C4, the world's most formidable non-nuclear explosive, and missiles that could shoot down airliners, the CIA also supplied him with the mercenaries, aircraft, and weapons to invade neighboring countries[97]. To put it simply, U.S. intelligence, assisted by MOSSAD, made it possible for him to do as he did—just as they, over the following decades, have done the same for Al Qaeda and ISIS.

Those who remember the 1980s may recall that the Russians, at this time, invaded Afghanistan and Al Qaeda was the living remains of the mercenaries that the CIA organized and trained to fight the occupiers. The revisionist version of history is that the CIA's links to Al Qaeda ended after the war. Even so, the relationship not only continued until 9/11 but, most probably, persists until this day. Those who want to know more about the relationship between terrorists and intelligence services should check out books such as Webster Tarpley, *911 Synthetic Terror* and Mike Ruppert, *Crossing the Rubicon*. As it pertains to governments' behind-the-scenes operations, however, what we need to know is that the production of enemy images is an important aspect—and that if it wasn't for Western intelligence, there would be no Al Qaeda or ISIS.

We would do well to remember this now that the latter is becoming an increasing "threat" in the Middle East. As media and public officials are clamoring for war, we should keep in mind that this motley crew of bandits have been trained and armed by CIA and MOSSAD—and that their finances could have been cut by 2007, if leaders had wanted to[98].

We could go on and on, elaborating on the consistent pattern of penetration of opposition groups. Whether we are talking about the anarchist movement at the beginning of the 20th century; anti-colonial

---

[97] See JONATHAN KWITNY, *THE CRIMES OF PATRIOTS*; PETER MAAS, *MANHUNT*.

[98] As elaborated on by Scott Bennett, Swiss banker Brad Birkenfeld then tried to give the Americans 19.000 bank accounts connected to this and other networks but was thrown in jail for his efforts. See BENNETT, *SHELL GAME*.

nationalist groups in Africa, Latin America, Middle East, and Asia; the Black Power movement in the United States; IRA in Ireland; the anti-war movement; or Al Qaeda and other Islamic movements today, they have always been targets for infiltration—and the most vocal agitators for violence have usually been agents of government. In this way, they hope to turn non-violent organizations into terrorist organizations; in this way, they hope to provoke an escalation of hostilities; and in this way, they manufacture the enemy images upon which they thrive.

Anyone familiar with the history of the IRA, for instance, knows that at the leadership level the organization was filled with informants; that British intelligence was aware of planned terrorist operations but let them happen; and that several operations were carried out by British double agents. This pattern is no less present in Iraq today, and so no one should have been surprised when Iraqi police arrested two members of the British Special Forces dressed up as Arabs in a car loaded with explosives in Basra 2005. It is the height of ignorance to believe that the CIA, MOSSAD, and MI6 have not been involved in bombings in Iraq; that they haven't manipulated the Shia and Sunni community into a position of mutual distrust; and that they haven't prepared the ground for civil war. The British were experts in this art of covert warfare hundreds of years ago; they built their Empire on the divide-and-conquer strategy, and it is still the elite's greatest weapon against the people of the world.

25.2 THE DYNAMIC WHICH CREATES TERRORISM

"You see, the danger is not a single politician with ill intent. Or even a group of them. The most dangerous thing any nation faces is a citizenry capable of trusting a liar to lead them."(6.42)

—Andy Andrews, American author—

Now that we have discussed those terrorist actions our governments are directly responsible for, we shall elaborate on that threat for which they are indirectly responsible.

As already mentioned, sometimes intelligence agencies do not have to do the job themselves. They know that whenever a government or occupying force exposes a people to continuous oppression and degradation a certain percentage will become enraged and fight back violently. It is people like this who account for much of the terror in places like Iraq and the Israeli occupied territories. But no matter how apparent this cause-and-effect is, our leaders have refused to recognize a connection between their actions and such acts of desperation.

This is hardly surprising as an honest look at the situation must involve a healthy dose of self-criticism. Occupiers and aggressors, however, aren't too keen on imagining other persons' perspective; they are too busy justifying their own actions, and so American and Israeli leaders never ask themselves the key question: *what makes a mother of five become a suicide bomber?*

Despite their reluctance to look at this cause-and-effect relationship, the truth is obvious for anyone who cares to look, and Robert Pape, a researcher at the University of Chicago, conducted a study which puts any doubt to rest. After examining 2200 terrorist attacks, he concluded that: "We have lots of evidence now that when you put the foreign military presence in, it triggers suicide terrorism campaigns . . . and when the foreign forces leave, it takes away almost 100 percent of the terrorist campaign."(79.288)

This is so obvious that one must be a premeditated moron not to get it. Nonetheless, our leaders will have us believe that it is because they hate our freedoms that people around the world blow themselves up.

It is a sad testimony to the sorry state of our judgment that a large segment of the population accepts this explanation, but the elite's propaganda has clouded our thinking so that simple logic escapes us. Instead, just as the most spoiled brats, we believe that we can have the playground for ourselves; that we can throw sand on all the other kids; that we can beat them, spit on them, and take their belongings without our behavior ever backfiring. And when someone sooner or later throws sand our way, we become perplexed, begin to cry, and expect our authorities to give them a good whopping.

It is a great mystery to us why the Iraqis, Palestinians, and Afghans make all this fuss; why they cannot simply behave and be thankful for the leaders, lifestyle, and terms of exploitation offered. To use the Iraqis as an example, we believe that we have freed them from a diabolical monster's reign of terror, and so we cannot imagine why Western forces are not welcome. Had we thought about it, we would probably have known better. After all, it is no more than 70 years ago that Europeans were living under occupation and we still salute those who fought against the invading forces. Why, then, is it so difficult to see the Iraqi's point of view?

Most likely it is because we believe that we, by definition, are on the side of good while those we fight are bad. That is how experts in the media analyze things. They tell us that Saddam was an unpredictable, cynical dictator who not only subjugated his own people but repeatedly invaded neighboring countries and spread fear in the region. They refer to the war against Iran, the gassing of the Kurds, and the invasion of Kuwait as examples. And the way they tell their story it does not seem implausible that our leaders, after looking at all this, had to take responsibility and remove him from power. After all, (again according to our authorities) he was not only an avid supporter of Al Qaeda; he was developing weapons of mass destruction, and his contempt for international law threatened not just the region—but the West itself.

If we accept our authorities' version of history, then, Operation Iraqi Freedom, as the invasion was called, does not stand out as a too outrageous militarist adventure. Nonetheless, we should know better than to believe them at their word, and those who dig a little deeper will find that truth is different.

It turns out then that yes, Saddam was a despot who did a lot of nasty stuff: he attacked Iran and started a war that cost hundreds of thousands of lives, he acquired chemical weapons and used them as he saw fit, and he also invaded Kuwait. All this is true. But what our authorities forget to tell us is that *he did all this with the Western elite's blessing*. Since the 1960s, he had been an important asset to the Western intelligence services' hidden warfare in the region and, until 1990, he remained one of their most cherished allies. He attacked Iran with Western weaponry and our wholehearted support, and even the gassing of the Kurds, which earned him his reputation, was supported by the Reagan administration. Not only did it block any effective protest by Congress in the wake of the episode, but it was Western leaders who supplied him with chemical weapons.

To our politicians, of course, this is water under the bridge; their selective memory has made them forget all about it and revisionist historians have helped them bury these events in the dust of oblivion. Nonetheless, if we wonder who sold Saddam chemical weapons, we need look no further than Mark Thatcher, son of Margaret Thatcher, who was British Prime Minister during the same period[99].

Now, we all know that Western powers' amiable relationship with Saddam ended after his invasion of Kuwait in 1990. Even so, be aware that Saddam, before taking action, consulted with the Americans on this issue and that April Glaspie, U.S. ambassador to Iraq, assured him that it was okay. The green light from the U.S. embassy, however, turned out to be a ruse, giving the first Bush administration a pretext for going to war.

Exactly why Saddam, with this invasion, became more valuable to the Americans as an enemy is hard to say. What we know is that the official reasons for going to war was pure stage play, and that leaves a secret agenda. When it comes to this, it is always the matter of *who*

---

[99] For more on this, as well as the West's arms dealing to both sides during the Iran-Iraq war, see ARI BEN MENASHE, *PROFITS OF WAR*. As a former MOSSAD agent, he had ringside view to these events and has written an excellent book on the subject.

benefits, and we should begin with President Bush, a man with much to hide. He knew that there is nothing like a good war for diverting attention from more pressing and incriminating personal matters and the collapse of the nation's savings and loans was in the nation's headlines. Neil Bush, son of the President, were in serious trouble that threatened to expose the father, and this alone would make Bush thirsty for war. In addition to this, Israeli dissatisfaction made Saddam an easy scapegoat, and so did the United States' constant search for enemies. The Cold War had just ended and as the military-industrial complex needed another justification for its existence, Saddam must have been the ideal villain. As a dictator, he had become increasingly self-confident. He was never too eager to please and when he nationalized the oil industry, thus obstructing Big Oil's ambitions for the country, powerful forces conspired against him.

To the elite, messing with oil revenues is one of the major deadly sins. History is ripe with examples and one need not look further than the origin for the U.S. Government's quarrel with neighboring Iran. The problems between the two countries began in 1953, when Iran's democratically elected leader nationalized the oil industry, and it was not long before the oil companies, through a CIA orchestrated coup, put a more cooperative leader into power. This was the Shah, a dictator who ruled the country on behalf of David Rockefeller and his clan for 25 years.

The discontent generated by his violent and corrupt regime resulted in a revolution and the coming to power of the Iranian theocracy in 1979. Since then the two countries have been bitter enemies: Iranians portray the U.S. as the Great Satan and the Americans return the favor by picturing Iran as the greatest obstacle to world peace. The U.S. Congress is pretty much bought and controlled by Israeli lobbyists and influential forces want to give the Israelis a green light to bomb the country and start a major war.

All this, of course, could have been avoided if (1) the Iranians had allowed the Western corporations to plunder their natural resources—or (2) if the United States had other ambitions than to conquer the world on behalf of the corporations. At the time being, however, the status quo is what it is, and so the media keeps painting Iran as the defining threat of our time.

I am not contesting that Iran's theocracy is a reactionary and misanthropic government. Even so, one must be addlebrained to buy the elite's propaganda, as the Iranian regime has never had any imperialist ambitions. Unlike the United States Government, this regime has never started a war, and if left alone the theocracy does not constitute much of a problem—except for Iran's more progressive population and the West's control-oriented elite.

It is the latter that makes Iran so reviled, for its anti-democratic and arbitrary system of government has absolutely nothing to do with the West's problematic relationship with the country. The only reason why politicians and media pundits spend so much time and effort trying to demonize Iran, therefore, is that their corporate masters are unhappy with the terms of exploitation and the same is true worldwide. Consequently, whether we are talking about North Korea, Venezuela, Cuba, or Iran, the negative attention is always related to this—and the human rights situation in these countries have absolutely nothing to do with it.

Not surprisingly, this is another taboo topic, but we need only look at Saudi Arabia: This government is no less reactionary, repressive, and misanthropic than the countries just mentioned, but because it offers Americans oil contracts and military bases this does not matter. Indeed, if the conditions are acceptable for control-oriented elites, not even the fact that most hijackers involved in the 9/11 attacks came from this country becomes a point of controversy.

No doubt, a less cooperative country would have been bombed, if the connection between the State and the financing of terrorists was as obvious as in this case. But as already mentioned, the point of the War on Terror is not really to put an end to terrorism. After all, even our leaders know that we cannot fight a strategy—which is all "terrorism" is—with bombs. Instead, the whole point of this war is to have a pretext to intervene anywhere the elite sees fit, and the most recent Iraq war provides a perfect example.

For Saddam did not have any connections to Al Qaeda. The Blair- and the Bush administration, it is true, tried to make it appear so—just as they tried to convince us that he had weapons of mass destruction. Nonetheless, in both cases, it was obvious that their pretexts for war was a pack of self-serving and shameless lies—lies that were designed to serve their puppeteers' expectations[100].

Now we, the citizens of the West, are so blinded by propaganda that we hardly understand our predicament. We exclude the war profiteers' influence on the political process from our calculations, and we are happy to accept assurances that it was to defend our values and spread democracy that our military intervened. Even so, Iraqis are not as easily fooled. They live in a country where reality is more difficult to hide, and they know full well that we could not care less about their well-being. History has taught them all about it—and if the population had forgotten the horrors of British colonial rule, Americans have made it refreshingly clear.

For although Saddam Hussein was cruel towards real and imagined enemies, at least oil revenues benefited the nation. Thanks to these moneys, the Iraqis had some of the region's best educational opportunities and health services. Iraq, for example, was the second country in the world to perform heart transplants and the nation was doing good. Besides a flourishing sheep- and chicken industry, the country produced enough wheat, rice, fruits, and vegetables to feed its own citizens, and the industrial sector exported textiles, steel, cement, oil, and leather products.

All in all, then, Iraqis were well-off; they had low infant mortality, high average life expectancy, and an effective governance—but all that changed in the early 1990s, after Bush Sr. had bombed Saddam out of Kuwait. What happened was that Western powers, led by the U.S., adopted a series of sanctions. These sanctions not only destroyed Iraq's agricultural and industrial business but made the life of ordinary citizens a miserable ordeal. They were now cut off from the world community, and this resulted in a complete lack of essential items like medication and components to run basic machinery. So terrible was the result that Denis Halliday, who was tasked by the UN to oversee the sanctions, called it a "genocide" and resigned. According to his assessment, sanctions targeted

---

[100] See SUSAN LINDAUER, *EXTREME PREJUDICE*. As an intermediary between Saddam's regime and the Bush administration before the war, she had a ringside view to the real goings-on, and this book tells the true story.

civilians and more than a million Iraqis, half of them children, had died as a direct consequence. Halliday was not alone in this assessment and two years later Hans von Sponeck, his successor at the UN, resigned. He also protested that the sanctions were in violation of the UN's conventions against genocide.

The Americans, for their part, argued that sanctions were necessary to weaken Saddam's regime and Madeleine Albright, the U.S. Secretary of State, assured the world that the suffering and death inflicted on the Iraqi people "was well worth it".

As the stated purpose of the sanctions was to weaken Saddam, this assertion did not make much sense. On the contrary, to those in touch with reality, it seemed clear that the sanctions only served to strengthen his position, for so devastating were their effects that the entire middle class—and thus all real opposition—disappeared. As a result of the sanctions, the average family had just 12 U.S. cents a month to live by: Hence, Iraqis' key concern became the day-to-day struggle for survival, and they directed their anger at the Americans rather than Saddam's regime.

Consequently, despite these sanctions ravaging the country, killing some 1.7 million people (one million children), they only helped Saddam affirm his grip on power. And even though the tragedy of the Iraqi people hardly registered in the West, it by no means eluded the Iraqis. They had first-hand knowledge of how their country was laid to waste and they all had loved ones who died as a result of the sanctions. To them, Western leaders' assurance that this was something we did to help them embrace our values was only adding insult to injury—and the worst was yet to come.

By 2000 it was becoming obvious, even to our leaders, that the sanctions were ineffective at toppling Saddam. Stronger measures were needed and the result was Operation Iraqi Freedom, the most privatized war ever[101]. This operation made things even worse for the Iraqis. What was left of infrastructure, electricity, sewage, and water treatment plants were decimated, and besides the unspeakable terror and frustration which

---

[101] Halliburton, the company Dick Cheney ran before he became Vice President, alone received some $40 billion worth of contracts.

the bombing and subsequent occupation inflicted on the already traumatized population, at least another million died.

In other words, even a deafblind Iraqi could not fail to see that we, the people of the West, do not care about the Iraqi people's wellbeing as long as war profiteers get their way. And so, if we are serious about reducing terrorism, the first thing we need to do is take a hard look at ourselves. If we do, we find that in acting with a minimum of decency, not only will state-sponsored terror campaigns vaporize, but we will put an end to the outcome of our aberrant behavior—namely the hopelessness and despair that makes oppressed people blow themselves up.

25.3 ENEMY IMAGES AND US

"How fortunate for leaders that men do not think. Make the lie big, make it simple, keep saying it, and eventually they will believe it." (6.32)

—Adolf Hitler—

That we could eliminate terrorism simply by treating others the way we would have them treat us may be a difficult recognition. To consider this possibility we must stop seeing ourselves as victims and instead take our share of responsibility. This is difficult, as doing so requires a certain degree of maturity and capacity for self-reflection: We must put aside our preconceived ideas about good and evil—including the idea that we are always the good guys—and we must look within so that we stop projecting our personal fears on our interpretation of the world.

Another reason is the power of enemy images, for when an enemy image is imprinted and we are convinced of its reality, it is difficult to look at the preconditions of our assumptions. Again, history, as well as present-day conditions, tell us all about it: Whether people have been afraid of witches, savages, Jews, Blacks, communists, gays, Muslims, drugs, or terrorism, they have felt so assured about the danger of the enemy that nothing could convince them otherwise. They have in all cases seen the threat as so overwhelming that they have accepted the end-justifies-the-means logic—and so, fully convinced of the merits of their crusade, they have committed the worst atrocities imaginable.

It is irrelevant what enemy image we discuss as the dynamics are exactly the same: Racists do not want to deprive colored people of their right to equal justice because they consider themselves petty or mean but because they believe that it is necessary to ensure the survival of all things good (i.e., the race/culture with which they identify); the Nazis did not exterminate Jews, gays, gypsies, and the mentally retarded because they saw themselves as evil, but because their idea of a perfect society was so ensnaring that they thought ridding the world of "those of lesser worth" was the proper thing to do; prohibitionists do not persecute drug users because they like to harass people, but because they believe illicit drugs to be such a threat that they are willing to do just about anything to realize their ideal of a drug-free society; and last but not least, the majority of Western citizens are so convinced of the terrorists' hatred against all things good and decent that they are willing to fight a preventive war against potential enemies in the hope that one day this great evil will be uprooted. No matter what enemy image we are talking about the destructive mechanisms following in their wake are always the same. Hence, the more we fear an enemy image, the more we will believe that everything good and decent is threatened by it—and the more ruthless we will become in our quest to eliminate the problem once and for all.

It should be obvious from this that modern racists (in most cases) do not like to be compared to Nazis; that homophobes do not appreciate being equaled to racists; and that prohibitionists will deny the parallels between their crusade and former mass movements like the Inquisition or the Nazi's. They are all so convinced of the reality of their enemy image that they believe they are on the side of good, and so the suggestion that there could be compelling parallels between their project and the Nazi ideology is nonsensical. After all, the victors write history: We are taught that the Nazis represented the purest form of evil, and so it would seem as comparing night and day.

Now, I am not saying that the Nazi movement was not unique. Never had a state, with such zeal, focused its resources on ridding society of unwanted elements. Yet, the difference is only a matter of degrees and if the prohibitionists believed as firmly in the danger of drugs as the Nazi's believed in the danger of Jews, they would have escalated their persecution of the illicit drug users to the same level.

We shall discuss this controversial issue and the parallels between prohibitionists and Nazis shortly. My point here is to emphasize that *no matter what grouping* we are dealing with, they are all sure of the threat, and so they rarely bother to examine the preconditions behind their assumptions. Had they done that, however, they would in all cases have discovered that they were wrong—and that they have been suckered into this position by an ego on unsteady ground. When it comes to the enemy image of terrorism, we have already seen some indication of this. And if we take a closer look, we find that our leaders' actions do not only account for most of the terrorist attacks, but that our fear of falling prey to such an event is greatly exaggerated.

For what is the likelihood that terrorism will strike us? If we look at the statistics of the Department of Homeland Security, we find that on a worldwide basis 55.661 people were killed in such attacks between 1968 and 2008. Considering that this does not include the terrorism that the U.S. war machine itself is engaged in this may sound like a lot. But we must remember that these are the figures as the U.S. Government defines terrorism and that they include attacks on U.S. troops in places like Iraq and Afghanistan. We must also take into account that 39.281 of these people died *after* the Americans declared war on terror and that 27.867 died in Iraq and Afghanistan. Thus, we find that *not only did the vast majority of terrorism-related deaths in this 40-year period take place in the wake of the Americans' War on Terror, but that most occurred in those countries the United States invaded.*

This alone speaks volumes about what a retarded concept a War on Terror really is. If we, however, ignore this piece of evidence and focus our attention on the figures related to terrorist attacks in the Western world (Australia, New Zealand, United States, and Europe), we find that 5.019 people died in this 40-year period. We should remember that 4.000 of these deaths resulted from government-sponsored terrorism. Nonetheless, whether intelligence services or confused individuals are involved, it is still terrorism and assuming that this number is real, we find that an average of 125 people were killed annually.

It should be obvious, then, that our fear of terrorism is exaggerated, especially when we consider that every year some 15.000 Americans are shot and killed by ordinary people and that they are 9 times more likely to be killed by a cop than a terrorist. To put the fear of terrorism in its proper context Americans are more likely to die as a result of lightning strikes, snake bites, natural disasters, collisions with deer, or peanuts. Even so, authorities will try to convince us that this is a threat to our civilization. Greatly helped by the media, they do what they can to instill in us the fear of terrorism and their propaganda obviously has an effect. In the wake of 9/11, more than half of all Americans lived in fear that they or their loved ones would become the next victim, and this level remained until 2006. Today, the perceived threat is less prevalent, but about 40 percent of the Western population still fear an imminent attack.

When we take into account that more Americans have drowned in their own toilets since 9/11, the irrational nature of this fear is evident. Even so, Western leaders continue to focus on the terrorist threat as our civilization's greatest concern. The reason, of course, is that they have a secret agenda and that for their New World Order to be realized our fear of terrorists must be maintained. Nevertheless, it should be clear who our real problem is, for while "ordinary" terrorists in the past 100 years have killed less than 50.000 people, our leaders have murdered more than 200.000.000! Hence, as it is said: War is when the government tells you who the enemy is; Revolution is when you figure it out for yourself.

However, this obvious fact—that our leaders are the greatest threat we face—is lost on most. As the enemy images have a power that cannot be rationally justified, people also stop thinking logically as soon as we are caught in their grip. Convinced of the terrorists' hatred towards all things good and decent, therefore, most citizens are under the illusion that our leaders want what is best for us—and from there on defense mechanisms keep reality at bay.

Proof of this is found in the childlike naivety many expose towards authority. Not in their wildest dreams can people imagine that elites have an agenda of their own, and so when told that they must give up some freedoms in exchange for security—or that our leaders must go to preemptive war to protect the peace—they accept. Being under the spell of a carefully crafted enemy image, the average citizen is unable to question their motives or see the absurdity of their logic. And because the enemy image is a product of the logic of fear, and like attracts like, the reasoning that follows in its wake manifests that which we fear the most.

After all, he who sees enemies everywhere will behave in a way that makes him find enemies everywhere, and so the enemy images' ever-widening repercussions tear society apart. The proof is in the pudding, for looking at the post-9/11 world we see how the fear of terrorism has spread its poison: to the extent that we have accepted this enemy image, so also distrust, vengefulness, intolerance, ruthlessness, and contempt has grown at the expense of these fear-oriented responses' opposites—and this, in turn, has had terrible consequences.

The War on Terror is only the most obvious example as it illustrates how a sick mind generates obnoxious behavior. It is not without reason that 90 percent of the population in Arab countries see the U.S. and Israel as the greatest threat to their security, while only 10 percent mention Iran—and it is not without reason that Iranian leaders are eager to acquire nuclear weapons. By now they have seen how these states have no respect for international law; they have seen how they time and again topple governments and make life miserable for the people of the Middle East, and the theocracy knows full well that having an atomic bomb is their greatest protection against U.S./Israeli aggression.

As using such a bomb, however, would equal self-destruction, it should be obvious that the last thing they would do—if they ever had such a bomb—would be to use it against another country. Nonetheless, this scenario is so frightening to Israeli leaders that they will not under any circumstances allow Iran to become a nuclear power. That it is inconsistent to keep this right for themselves while denying it to others does not even cross their mind, for so long have our leaders applied one standard for themselves and another for everyone else that the inherent hypocrisy of their position goes by unnoticed.

To take Israel as an example, we see how its leaders threaten with war and whatnot every time Iran and the Arab countries fail to comply with a UN resolution, while they themselves have made a mockery of international law since its very inception. We also see it in their use of language as they consistently define Palestinian actions as "terrorism", while their own are referred to as "anti-terrorism".

Most probably they are themselves so caught up in the deranged thinking produced by enemy images that they do not even see the discrepancy. This is the only natural conclusion, for had they been serious about their values they would have been grateful if somebody pointed out to them the mismatch between words and reality. However, as self-examination is out of the question, constructive criticism is not welcomed. Instead, as soon as their conduct in the occupied territories is questioned, their first line of defense is the role of the victim; they start talking about the persecution of Jews, call their opponent an anti-Semite, and imply that the criticism is malignly motivated.

They do not mind that the word anti-Semite, as used in this context, is utterly meaningless[102]. How could they? Israeli leaders stopped making sense long ago when the power of enemy images first took control of their reasoning. Since then they have been raised to see themselves as God's chosen people, to consider Palestinians and everyone else as beings of lesser worth, and to believe that others hate them for their "unique" status. It is no surprise that accepting apartheid, occupation, and an intelligence service that is deeply immoral comes with the territory. The life of Shimon Peres, Ariel Sharon, and Benjamin Netanyahu—just to mention a few Israeli leaders—speaks volumes of the extent to which the system elevates individuals with no intention of solving the problems between Israel and the Arab nations. To the contrary, being locked in groupthink, Israeli politicians see themselves as just and righteous no matter what, while the citizenry remains too weak to give effect to any other political ambition than that of thugs. Their leaders' only objective, therefore, in using this word is to help them claim the moral high-ground, the idea being that anyone who disagrees with the Israeli Government's policies is also against the Jews' right to exist—and consequently in league with the Nazis.

Even though this strategy has been effective, we shall not spend time elaborating on the absurdity of its reasoning. Simply put, the matter falls

---

[102] The word *Semite* refers to the Semitic-speaking peoples of the Near East and northern Africa. This includes Arabs as well as Jews.

on its own weight and no thinking person can take it seriously. Talking about the similarities between Nazism and modern-day movements, however, what I *will* focus on is the common ground shared by Nazis and prohibitionists. In the beginning of this chapter, I said that there were not only compelling parallels between the two, but that the only relevant difference was the power of the enemy images.

This is a serious allegation. As the ideology of prohibition currently holds great sway, it is only natural that some will object to it—so let us explore the issue.

25.4 PROHIBITIONISTS AND NAZIS

"Where did this policy come from? Unfortunately, I have conducted an inquiry into this, and I am convinced that drug prohibition came [into being] for reasons of racism, empire building, and ignorance."

—James P. Gray, Judge of the Superior Court in Orange County, California—

The time has come to investigate the most powerful enemy image of our day, the one which conceivably has impaired our judgment the most and done the greatest damage to the social fabric. In the next chapter we shall have a look at the ideology of drug prohibition, the outrageous premises upon which it is based, and the unfortunate consequences that have followed in its wake. What we shall do now, however, is explore *the enemy image* of drugs; we shall look at it in a historical context and see how it is that prohibitionists can be said to equal the Nazis.

As already noted, I am aware of the controversial nature of such an endeavor. Raised as we are to see Nazism as the embodiment of human wickedness and drug prohibition as a worthwhile endeavor, we are used to seeing the two as night and day. Nonetheless, even though it is not my intention to trivialize Nazism, it was ignorance—not evil—behind its popularity. To think of the Nazis as exceptionally evil, therefore, is impractical, even dangerous. Bernt Hagtvet, a professor of political science, explains:

> "To dismiss Nazism as an ideology of the bullies, as a result of the ignorant masses ferocity—this is dangerous oversimplification. Doing so distances us from Nazism, making it seem remote and non-threatening. At the same time, through this reduction, we immunize ourselves against the ominous thought that the light from this racist brutality may not be limited to the period between the two World Wars. What if it can afflict everyone, anytime, anywhere (but take on new and different forms)? To think of Nazism as so deviant and morbid that it cannot be taken seriously as an ideological impulse—this is to deny those sources of totalitarian fervor that may exist in today's world."(51.121)

Thus, if we want to avoid the pitfalls that have entrapped previous generations, we must not only look at today's ideologies in a historical context but we must stop demonizing the Nazis. We must take an honest look at what made people accept the atrocities that followed in the wake of the ideology—and we have to see if there could be parallels to our time that should be taken seriously, even if they become evident where we least expect it.

This is the only way we can learn from history, for the Nazis did not commit atrocities because they were more evil-minded. If we want to understand the alluring nature of Nazism, therefore, we need to look elsewhere for answers. And when we do, we find that the Germans, at this time, were born into a moral climate that shaped their worldview to such a degree that they would come to see Nazism as a solution to their problems. Bernt Hagtvet explains why:

> "Nazism was not an appeal to brutality and torture. Nazism was primarily an appeal to idealism, patriotism, self-sacrifice, solidarity, pride, and wholesomeness. And . . . precisely because it appealed to all things good and decent,

the Nazis had no inhibitions against using mass violence as a means to an end. The violence was rational and authorized by the state, not personal and selfishly motivated."(51.120)

Now, as we shall compare this ideology to that of drug prohibition, please note that there is nothing said here that cannot also be said about the latter. As we have yet to elaborate on the destructive societal effects generated by prohibition, further parallels are difficult to spot. However, as we shall see, also this ideology satisfies every requirement to be defined as a crime against humanity—and please note that experts in the field have referred to it as "a totalitarian solution"(70.27) and "a vehicle for fascism."(70.97)

Again, it is not my intention to mock prohibitionists or to trivialize Nazi brutality. I only want to explain more parallels because in doing so we have a unique opportunity to learn something about ourselves, our time, and the enemy images' influence. When it comes to this, we have already mentioned the collective consciousness; how it provides us with fundamental assumptions, and how it shapes us. This field, as we may recall, represents the sum of all experience gathered by humanity. Thus, it is a world-of-ideas in development; humanity constantly learns from its mistakes and as we can look back on Nazism as one of the most repugnant ideologies produced, we like to believe that we would have had the integrity to speak out against this ideology.

Nonetheless, most of us would have failed in this endeavor and we would have done exactly as most Germans. As we saw in the chapter on psychology, the collective consciousness has a powerful grip on our judgment and only a small percentage has matured to overcome the confusion. Developmental psychologists estimate that some 80 percent belongs to the category whose judgment is easily clouded by the sway of this field. This includes those people with a thinking so impaired that they will leave it to others to define right and wrong, who will believe any lie as long as it is government-sanctioned, and who will take the delusions of authority and make them their own. To put it differently: *"the Nazi" denotes a cognitive level of understanding*; at some point in our life we have all existed at this level, but as we mature some evolve and stop letting group expectations determine our behavior.

It is evident from this that the majority of the population—had they been born into the same moral climate as the Germans did; had they grown up with the same enemy images; and had they been subjected to the same dynamics between the individual and the State—would have become Nazis themselves. No matter how uncomfortable we are thinking about it, this is an undeniable fact—and it is also an undeniable fact that the supporters of prohibition belong in this category.

A closer look at the parallels between the two ideologies reveals why. To begin with, the ideologies of Nazism and Prohibitionism were encouraged by government officials because they make it possible to increase the State's sphere of influence vis-à-vis the individual. Thomas Szasz, a professor of psychiatry, sums up the basis for their popularity thus:

> "The first law of political dynamics is that the ruler's basic aim is always the same, namely, to deprive the ruled of liberty. The only thing that varies from time to time is the justification for the deprivation, namely, whether it is religious, political, economic, or medical. Thus *protectionism* always plays a prepotent role in the government's regulating the affairs of men."(106.155)

Such ideologies, therefore, are quickly embraced by those officials who have no other ambition than to serve the system. And as few politicians have the integrity to criticize or cross the party line, this includes the vast majority. We shall explore the dynamics between rulers and subjects later but as any student of organizational theory knows, all bureaucracies seek to expand their influence. Systemwise, therefore, there will be an internal mechanism which sees to it that those civil servants whose primary concern it is to help this force feed itself (by enlarging his department or organization's power and budgets vis-à-vis competing agencies and the population) will get promoted.

To do this, nothing works better than a problem they can fix or an enemy image they can fight. The solution, however, must always be more money and power to the bureaucracy, and so ideologies such as Nazism and Prohibitionism offer exactly what they want. Not only do they inspire belief in a powerful state as the purveyor of core values, but because these ideologies also promote a societal dynamic that cultivates spinelessness, mercilessness, and irresponsibility among individuals (and thus facilitate for the emergence of a strong State), public officials tend to welcome them.

Furthermore, that drug prohibition and Nazism offer the same adverse societal dynamics is revealed by the reliance on inflated enemy images. Without such aid the Nazi-movement would never have been able to unite and gather strength. The Nazi Party consisted of a left and a right wing and had it not been for the threat that Jews and other sub-humans were commonly believed to represent the movement would have lost its momentum. What made the Nazi ideology so alluring, therefore, was that it embodied a systematized longing for purity; it blamed the Jews for everything, painted a glorious picture of a possible future, and convinced the German people that the Nazi party was the solution. *That is why it was so successful*—and because people were convinced that these "subhumans" were a problem that had to be dealt with, they accepted the way they were treated.

As we can conclude from this, the same applies to prohibition. The movement is a cross-political endeavor, one in which the left and the right find common cause in the belief that we need to combat the evil of drugs. In their minds, the enemy image has such destructive power that survival seems to depend on their fighting spirit. And because the lure of a drug-free society is so strong that they accept the end-justifies-the-means ideology, they ignore the human costs of their crusade. To the extent they are willing to acknowledge negative repercussions, they see this as a price worth paying—and, like the Nazis, they are so convinced of the righteousness of their quest that they refuse to consider basics.

This is the enemy images' power. And no matter how gracious we are towards other people, they make us scornful, intolerant, and ruthless towards the grouping whose persecution they aim to vindicate. Thus, to the degree a prohibitionist is enthralled by enemy images, it seems no less obvious that he is within his rights in pursuing drug dealers than it did to a Nazi when he arrested Jews, sending them off to concentration camps. As it is in the service of all things good, the prohibitionist never really reflects upon his actions—and if anyone tries to tell him that what he is doing is wrong, that he violates the human rights of drug users (or traffickers) when he persecutes them for their involvement with drugs, he will scoff and discount it, thinking they are halfwits.

Indeed, that drug law violators are protected by the same human right conventions as everyone else—and that they shall enjoy protection against discriminatory, disproportional, and arbitrary practices—is an idea so entirely alien that it has not even occurred. And should anyone tell him that, from the perspective of the Constitution, the War on Drugs meets the requirements of a crime against humanity, he will—if possible—understand even less.

After all, "drugs", to him, denotes a threat so overwhelmingly real that nothing can convince him otherwise. No matter how unambiguous the evidence, he will not see it, as the capacity for self-examination is as rare as it was among the Nazis. He will therefore close his mind to any possibility that the activists for drug legalization may be right. If two plus two equals an argument against prohibition, he simply spaces out into an incoherent state of mind where reason no longer can touch him. Thus, that prohibition has proven to be a useless tool in the pursuit of a drug-free society and that less invasive means, like a health-oriented approach, have proven more apt to reduce drug-related harms is lost on him. Likewise, the meaningless separation between licit and illicit drugs is ignored. Under no circumstances can he imagine a world where drugs (just like Jews) have a natural and rightful place, for in his mind they undermine the very fabric of society.

Consequently, convinced of the importance of a drug-free society— and equally frustrated that we are further from this ideal than ever—he will argue that an *escalation* of the war on drugs is needed. Hence, to save society, a prohibitionist wants to increase the penalties for involvement with drugs, intensify the law-and-order approach, and make sure that society takes a clearer stand against drug use. This is the only solution he sees fit. And the possibility that drugs could pose a lesser threat than he presupposes is out of the question. To a prohibitionist, even to insinuate such nonsense would be immoral and to encourage abuse, for to him there is no normal or acceptable use of these drugs. On the contrary, to him, *all use equals abuse* and nothing positive has ever come from them.

That most drug users—just like alcohol drinkers—appreciate these drugs and that 90 percent have experienced no serious dependency or problems associated with their usage, is a fact that is most inconvenient. He therefore ignores it and takes refuge in the delusion that anyone advancing such claims must be either a fool, liar, or another victim of these substances sinister influence.

Furthermore, presupposing that he holds the moral high ground by virtue of position alone, this backward and ignorant approach does not even bother him. Quite the opposite, just like a Nazi, the prohibitionist imagines that those who challenge his presumptions must be in league with the enemy—and that those who have a less hysterical approach are traitors. It is of critical importance that everybody shares his fears and accepts the threat level as defined by prohibitionists. Just like a Nazi, he relies on a moral panic to sell his message, and because a more nuanced debate would result in "mixed messages" this is strongly opposed. In fact, if he had his way, any objections to the prohibitionist ideology would be banned, for he is firmly convinced that if the law-and-order approach were intensified the perfect society would one day be realized.

As the shining ideal of a drug-free society blinds his reasoning, the prohibitionist does not concern himself with how this would come about and what kind of society an escalation of the drug war would result in. Nonetheless, no end is more glorious than the means used. And when we look at the prohibitionist's means, they are no less terrifying than the Nazi's. In practice, they both advocate a system of thought where no objections to their ideology are allowed. They want a world where the State (they) have a monopoly on the truth and where people uncritically submit to its zero-tolerance vision and propaganda. Only in such a world could their ideology thrive—and to the extent that prohibition has prevailed, it is precisely due to such conditions.

Thus, when prohibitionists talk about "clear signals" and "greater moral courage", this is what they really mean. Even so, no matter how outraged, no matter how all-powerful their propaganda apparatus, and no matter how much fear and prejudice they add to the global psyche, there will always be a certain percentage of the population who will not be swayed. These people will continue their experiments with mind-altering substances, and to weed out these disruptives they rely on the law-and-order apparatus.

That enhanced penalties, ever-increasing budgets, and a more all-powerful police apparatus have not made a dent in the supply and demand of illicit drugs may be a troublesome fact, but not enough to make a prohibitionist rethink his crusade. Like everything else that does not fit with his distorted worldview he ignores it and presses ahead under the assumption that if we only intensify the approach, then one day the dream of a drug-free community will become a reality.

It should be noted that an exaggerated control apparatus is not the only instrument a prohibitionist makes use of against the population. Just like the propaganda apparatus, this is part of a larger totalitarian package and ultimately the success of this project depends on our willingness to inform on each other. Without this, the prohibitionists will never be able to realize the drug free society, and so they make an effort of cultivating a rat mentality within the populace. The propaganda apparatus, therefore, informs us that we are doing friends and family a favor by giving them up to the authorities, because "only by doing so can we help them understand the unfortunate effects of their drug use".

This is, briefly summarized, the prohibitionist's recipe for a perfect world. He ignores that it only has brought us closer to hell, just as he closes his eyes to the fact that his continued persecution of outgroups presupposes a blatant disregard of their human rights. Even so, as freedom will be devoid of meaning in this ideal society, it is clear to the more perceptive percentage that to the degree the prohibitionist gets his way not only will drug users be subjected to the whims of an all-powerful State's control apparatus—but also the rest of the population. I mean, not even high-security prisons with their frequent use of searches, surveillance, drug-sniffing dogs, cavity examinations, and collections of urine samples are drug-free.

This alone says quite a lot about where we are headed if we do not, as a society, think further—and as we can see from this little summary, the prohibitionists and the Nazis' mindset is basically the same. They both feed off the logic of fear, and minus time and place the only relevant difference is the respective enemy images—and, of course, that prohibitionists have not yet taken their project to its natural conclusion.

Considering that European and American states only imprison drug law violators, this is an important distinction. They do not exterminate them as the Nazis would have done and so, granted, they are more humane. Even so, the difference is inconsequential. Firstly, it is only because the most passionate supporters of prohibition have not yet got their way that they, in most cases, only imprison drug law violators. After all, in more than 30 countries, there is a death-penalty for involvement with drugs and if the most zealous legislators had their way, it would not have been better here. Examples of this are found in Al Edwards, a Texas politician who proposed to cut off a finger for every drug conviction received, not to mention William Bennett, the man in charge of America's Drug War in the 1980s, who admitted that he would have "no moral qualms about beheading convicted drug dealers".

We shall not elaborate on the delusions which form the basis for such calculations. Suffice to say that they are extensive, that they mirror our collective refusal to accept/respect constitutional values, ideals, and principles, and that drug prohibition is merely another expression of the scapegoating phenomenon which has followed us through history. The Nazi crusade, just as the Inquisition, was an example of the same phenomenon, and this mechanism is behind all unjust persecution. When it comes to drug prohibition, we see the level of unconsciousness in Nancy Reagan, when she as First Lady accused drug users of being complicit in murder. This notion is widely shared by prohibitionists and we saw another example when Antonio Maria Costa, as head of the UN's Office for Drugs and Crime (UNODC), levied the same accusations against singer Amy Winehouse.

Now, it is difficult to see how it is reasonable to blame drugs or drug users for the unfortunate consequences that have followed in the wake of prohibition. For a prohibitionist, however, this is the most natural thing, and for this thinking to make sense, they turn the model of supply and demand on its head. Thus, they no longer see drug users as adult customers in search of a product and drug dealers as those who provide them with the substance of their choice—agents of autonomy. Instead, seeing drugs as the active and responsible agent, they imagine these substances to have some kind of demonic influence. This demonic influence supposedly turns the users into brain-dead zombies—drug fiends unable to think further than their next fix—and while the drug user becomes a victim of sinister forces' influence, the drug dealer becomes the "pusher"—the cynical profiteer who lures them into a life of crime, debasement, and misery.

This is how prohibitionists justify their crusade, this is what makes them so cruel and intolerant, and the result of this logic taken to its ultimate conclusion was summarized by Daryl Gates, Los Angeles' chief of police, when he said that "casual drug users should be taken out and shot. We are in a war and drug use is treason."(59.269)

Most police officers would probably prefer that their leaders, when speaking in an official capacity, would refrain from putting it so bluntly. Nonetheless, if politicians enacted a law ordering the police to execute drug law violators, you can bet your money that most "peace officers" would have obliged. After all, history leaves no doubt about their faith in authority and the professional pride with which they carry out *whatever* order and enforce *whatever* law, no matter its merits. As a result, the police have always been a totalitarian State's most terrible weapon against its population. When the Nazis, for example, occupied Europe, there was no social grouping who to a greater extent embraced the Nazi ideology, and a look at current events reveals that little has changed.

Considering that the police, as a government agency, thrives the most in a police state this should come as no surprise. And the average policeman's will to power (and inability to critically reflect upon the consequences of his actions) makes it hard to disagree with author Joseph Conrad when he concluded that "the terrorist and the policeman both came from the same basket." That the police, therefore, constantly agitate for an escalation of the drug war is to be expected. Instead, the enemy images' disruptive influence on our powers of thought is better exemplified by the fact that they make even priests think along the same lines. Rev. Jesse Jackson, an American civil rights leader who received the Presidential Medal of Freedom for his work for social justice, said it thus:

> "Since the flow of drugs into the U.S. is an act of terrorism,
> antiterrorist policies must be applied. . . . If someone is
> transmitting the death agent to Americans, that person

should face wartime consequences. The line must be drawn."(106.113)

"Wartime consequences", of course, means execution and Jackson is not the only prohibitionist drawing parallels between the use of illicit drugs and terrorism. In the aftermath of the 9/11 attacks it became quite common and one of the results was the introduction of the Victory Act in 2003. For the reason that drug users, involved as they are with the drugs economy, help finance large-scale terrorist operations, this bill classified the possession of any amount of drugs as a terrorist offence. If this seems a bit harsh, remember that prohibitionists always reason backwards. In their mind it is not prohibition that is to blame for the black economy but drug users; they disregard the fact that drug use, through most of history, have been viewed as a voluntarily activity—an activity reasonable people may freely pursue. Instead, they see it as the embodiment of evil—and so, as this bill proposed, they see nothing wrong in prosecuting drug users as terrorists and drug dealers as "narco-terrorist kingpins".

Fortunately, this bill did not make it through Congress. Nonetheless, powerful forces are constantly working to coordinate and intensify the campaigns against drugs and terrorism—and as this summary shows, there is no doubt that an escalation of the War on Drugs could have increased its destructive effects to the point where it equaled Nazism.

Regarding further parallels, we must take into consideration that few Nazis realized what they were a part of. Just like the prohibitionists, they believed that ridding society of unwanted elements was an altogether decent ambition and only a tiny percentage knew how bad the persecuted groups were treated. While history has not been kind to the Germans, we must not forget the power of state propaganda, and the concentration camps were presented as effective rehabilitation camps where problematic elements got what they deserved. It is difficult to say to what extent the citizens would have objected if they knew what was really going on. Even so, one can safely assume that the vast majority, just like today, would have chosen deliberately to remain in ignorance.

One reason for this is that Nazism, just as prohibition, dehumanized the persecuted groups to such an extent that the rest of the populace were unmoved by their fate. This is another fact we do not like to admit, but the average citizen is no less indifferent to the drug users' catalogue of rights than the Germans were to Jews. The effect of the enemy images, then, must take some of the blame. More salient, however, is our lack of personal responsibility as it was mental lethargy in the first place that made it possible for the enemy image to seduce us.

Indeed, when it comes to Consciousness, another word to describe its essence could be *response-ability*; from atoms, to molecules, to minerals, to plants, to animals, to humans, we see the evolution of consciousness characterized by an increasing ability to respond to changes in the environment. The words "responsibility" and "response-ability" reflect on each other and so we see that the more evolved a person becomes, the greater his response-ability *and* his sense of responsibility. As most people, however, have not advanced very far in terms of self-actualization, we find that their sense of responsibility is somewhat lacking. They have not yet built a base of integrity sufficient to connect with the values, ideals, and principles that follow from the Wholeness. Nor have they freed themselves from the childish trait of accepting authority blindly. For this reason, they subscribe to the values of society's most dominant group, and it is psychology 101 that to those in the thralls of group-thinking, it has always been easier to disregard the emergence of totalitarianism than to resist the unconscious forces at play. Hence, as knowledge equals responsibility, most people close their eyes to their leaders' lies and behavior.

Psychologically, then, the Germans "ignorance" is understandable. And in taking a look at this period, we find that people elsewhere were no less indifferent to the fate of the persecuted groups. To take Norway, my country of origin, there are few records of people speaking up when the police arrested over 700 Jews, sending them off to concentration camps, and the same happened all over Europe. We can try to flatter ourselves. Even so, there is little to suggest that we have learned much since then. Just as previous generations, by and large, accepted the American genocide in Vietnam in the 1960s and 70s, we accept military actions in Iraq, Libya, Syria, and Afghanistan—and no matter how blatant our leaders' lies, there is nothing to suggest that we have any intention of holding them accountable.

All things considered therefore, from decade to decade, humanity demonstrate the same ill-fated apathy towards the suffering of others. In fact, living in an age where information is more accessible than ever before, our willful ignorance is even more inexcusable than that of Germans living under Hitler: If our leaders tell us that we live in a state governed by the rule of law, few will look beyond the facade, and not even our academics—those who really should have known better—react to the gap between theory and practice. Instead, just like the judges, bureaucrats, and lawyers of Nazi Germany, they ally with the ruling elite; they shiver and shy away from the light of truth, and as long as the State is sufficiently powerful to imprison or kill off any meaningful opposition, they have no interest in protecting the integrity of their profession or society at large.

Now, this generalization might seem unfair. After all, there is a strong undercurrent, one that is represented by the anti-war movement, 9/11 movement, Occupy Wall Street movement, the Q-movement, drug policy reform activists, environmental activists, and so on. This fact notwithstanding, the Nazis were not so different from you and me, and our tacit acceptance of criminal campaigns such as the wars on drugs and terrorism makes it impossible to claim moral superiority.

If we have any ambition to learn from history, we would do well to recognize this. Indeed, as our societal dynamic is becoming more and more like the one that put the Nazis in power, we live in an age where history seems to repeat itself. Just as the Germans in the 1920s, we live in an age where systemic failures become more apparent; inflation is spreading, unemployment is increasing, the debt-level is rising, class distinctions are growing, the middle class is threatened, the political process is increasingly being influenced by fear, and the state becomes more powerful. As this process continues, it becomes more and more obvious that the "responsible" political parties fail to reverse the trend— and the more people feel cheated by politicians, the more fertile ground for the emergence of extremist alternatives.

In times like this, the search for scapegoats increases and there is never a shortage of politicians who will cater to this whim. Sensing an easy rise to power, they will blame immigrants, single mothers, welfare clients, criminals, poor people, rich people, terrorists, drugs, or Muslims for everything that is wrong with the world—and the more frustrated people become, the more they will accept their reasoning.

Unfortunately, collectively we are still too immature to take responsibility for our misfortunes. As a society, we have yet to understand the necessity of abiding by first principles for successful organization and we continue our unconscious drift guided by totalitarian premises. As a result, in the coming years, we are likely to witness a strengthening of enemy images, and a sign of the times is that right-wing organizations, Islamic extremists, and other fanatics are gaining ground. The fact that systemic failures become more apparent, however, is not a bad thing in and of itself. Seen from the larger perspective, it is an indication that the old has exhausted its possibilities, and the situation will continue to deteriorate until we wise up and organize at a more evolved level.

In the next part of the book, we shall see how we can reverse the current situation for the good of all. Before we do that, however, we shall end this section with a look at the enemy image that so terrifies prohibitionists.

26
THE WAR ON "DRUGS" AND CIVIL LIBERTIES

"War has been declared on drugs. If war is to be declared on something, one would first hope that two conditions would be satisfied. First, the enemy should be clearly identified. Second, the special significance of the enemy should be demonstrated. Unfortunately, neither condition is satisfied by the war on drugs." (56.20)

—Douglas Husak, professor of law—

THE TIME HAS come for a look at consciousness-altering substances and how the War on Drugs has been a war on civil liberties. As indicated above, I put the term in quotes, because as Professor Husak points out, the categorization of drugs is vague, making no sense.

For our purposes, however, we shall disregard that the term itself is meaningless[103]. Instead, we shall accept that "drugs" (or narcotics) is a generic term for a set of substances, some of which we regulate and some of which we criminalize. Accepting this premise, what can we say about the fact that some are prohibited?

As Husak pointed out above, we should expect that our leaders can demonstrate good reasons for doing so. They spend vast sums trying to rid the world of this plague and they see it as so important that they leave it to the law-and-order apparatus to hunt down those associated with these substances. In fact, together with terrorism, our leaders have made the fight against drugs their top priority, and so the basis for this war effort,

---

[103] See DOUGLAS HUSAK, *LEGALIZE THIS: THE CASE FOR DECRIMINALIZING DRUGS*

namely the legal framework and the classification of the illicit drugs, should be possible to justify.

After all, according to our authorities, we live in a decent, rationally based, even enlightened society. Indeed, if we ask them, they will insist that our society is protected by the rule of law, which means that to criminalize a group of people and throw them in jail the State must demonstrate good reasons. As regards the classification of illicit drugs, therefore, we must not only assume that it reflects their danger; we must also assume that there is a rational distinction between them and legal drugs; and furthermore, when it comes to the legislation itself, we should expect it to be compatible with the provisions of human rights law. This is what we should expect from a criminal justice approach that has cost trillions of dollars, that has encouraged intolerance and contempt, that has cost hundreds of thousands of lives, that has imprisoned many millions, that has spread disease, and that has affected our privacy to such a degree.

Even so, as Professor Husak and many others have demonstrated, none of these presumptions are correct. First, a closer look reveals that the classification system in no way reflects the potential for harm. Second, it shows that the distinction between legal and illegal drugs is culturally and not rationally determined. And third, it turns out that the legislation has not only made matters worse but that it, in fact, violates basic human rights law.

Although this might be construed as sensational and controversial claims, it is nothing of the sort to the experts in the field. For them, it is plain as day that drug prohibition has been an unmitigated disaster—and that our politicians, for whatever reasons, refuse to correct the situation. David Nutt, a professor of neuropsychopharmacology and former head of the British Government's advisory body for drug policy (ACMD), confirms:

> "[I am] critical of the "war on drugs", not just because this set of policies has caused enormous damage to millions of people around the world, but also because the evidence of the harm it has been causing hasn't led to a change of approach."(76.7)

We shall now take a closer look at the irrational and biased basis for drug policy, as well as its fundamental incompatibility with human rights law. Due to restrictions on space I refer to *Human Rising*, my previous book, for a full analysis. Nonetheless, the following presents the gist of it.

26.1 HOW PROHIBITION CAME INTO BEING

"Prohibition goes beyond the bounds of reason in that it attempts to control a man's appetite by legislation and makes crimes out of things that are not crimes. A prohibition law strikes a blow at the very principles upon which our government was founded." (44.122)

—Abraham Lincoln, American president—

World powers have pledged themselves to a drug policy centered on prohibition and the historical basis for this is the UN Single Convention adopted in 1961. The roots of prohibition, however, extend further as we have a history of criminalizing substances that were culturally suspect. Looking back, therefore, not only alcohol and tobacco, but also coffee, tea, and chocolate have been categorized as illicit substances.

When it comes to modern prohibition, it was in the United States that the drug laws first came into being. Americans adopted a set of laws targeting opium/heroin and cocaine in 1914 and cannabis in 1937. According to historians, there was a moral panic behind this legislation and prohibitionists had to sensationalize a negligible problem to have it passed. Not only that, but the criminalization was racially motivated.[104] Drug historian David F. Musto summarizes:

> "The most passionate support for legal prohibition of narcotics has been associated with fear of a given drug's effect on a specific minority. Certain drugs were dreaded because they seemed to undermine essential social restrictions which kept these groups under control: cocaine was supposed to enable blacks to withstand bullets which would kill normal persons and to stimulate sexual assault. Fear that smoking opium facilitated sexual contact between Chinese and white Americans was also a factor in its total prohibition. [Mexicans] in the southwest were believed to be incited to violence by smoking marijuana. . . . In each instance, use of a particular drug was attributed to an identifiable and threatening minority group."(73.245)

In those days, the prohibition movement was more powerful in the United States than elsewhere. Yet, even though the 1914 and 1937 legislation resulted in the criminalization of these substances (and their users), this was not the explicitly stated intention. In fact, the original purpose of these laws was to regulate the *sale and production*, not to prohibit, as that would have been unacceptable—even unconstitutional. As Lincoln's quote above suggests, throughout the 1800s, enlightened minds were watchful and suspicious of any attempt made by the government to infringe on their liberties. And as the very idea of a drug law presupposes that we grant to the State a right to regulate in detail the most intimate area of our lives—our own consciousness—it would not only have been regarded as an absurdity by intellectuals such as the Founding Fathers, John Stuart Mill, Lysander Spooner, and Abraham Lincoln, but the populace at large.

---

[104] See DORIS MARIE PROVINE, *UNEQUAL UNDER LAW*; DAVID F. MUSTO, *THE AMERICAN DISEASE*; ROBINSON & SHERLEN, *LIES, DAMN LIES AND DRUGWAR STATISTICS*; JACK HERER, *THE EMPEROR WEARS NO CLOTHES*; MIKALSEN, *HUMAN RISING*.

Now, few could have imagined that later generations would look at things so very differently. However, to prevent such intellectual and moral decay, the Constitution limited the federal government's power to enact a prohibition law. It was for this reason that Congress had to adopt a constitutional amendment (the 18th) before imposing a prohibition on alcohol in 1920. No such thing was ever done in the case of drugs. Nonetheless, as voices of reason were subdued, prohibitionists ensured that no proper legislative or judicial review took place. Instead, they were free to interpret the 1914 and 1937 legislation as they saw fit, and this paved the way for more invasive and aggressive legal practices. To justify escalating persecutions, they hyped up the dangers of drugs—and so the bona fides of the drug laws were taken for granted.

While the propaganda machine worked its wonders, printing falsehoods and appealing to the fear of the unknown, prohibitionists agitated for a supranational legal framework. International consensus, however, was difficult to obtain and not before the post-World War period did the Americans wield enough power.

Then, after the war, the legal framework materialized in the 1961 Single Convention. According to its authors, the evil of drugs posed an acute threat, and to protect "the health and welfare of mankind" a law-and-order approach was agreed upon. This was believed to result in a drug-free world by 1986 and to validate this endeavor, the substances were categorized according to their presumed danger. As prohibitionists knew next to nothing about these drugs, cannabis and coca leaves were put in Schedule 1, along with heroin and cocaine. Henceforth, all non-medical use of these substances was forbidden—and as they had no medical utility which could not be substituted by the pharmacological industry's patented products, this meant *all* use.

This is the situation as it remains today. The only thing new is the adoption of the 1971 and 1988 conventions, which include even more substances among those prohibited—and despite an increasing body of evidence to its lack of legitimacy, prohibitionists have managed to avoid debate.

"The key problem is the total illogicality of the current list of controlled drugs, and their classification within the list; this problem is so great as to render the list scientifically "arbitrary" and therefore impossible to defend on other than political grounds—not good if one truly desires an evidence based strategy."(70.34)

*—Richard Brunstrom, North Wales'
Chief of Police—*

Current policies, as Brunstrom indicates, cannot be rationally defended. They have come into being as a result of U.S. pressure and neither the situation as it relates to science, human rights, nor any other meaningful indicator has been considered. On the contrary, prohibitionists ensured that their fundamental premises were never challenged—and that it has remained so until this day.

The American delegation to the UN, for example, was led by Harry Anslinger. Married to the niece of Andrew Mellon, one of the world's most powerful men, he had run the Federal Bureau of Narcotics (FBN) for 30 years when the Single Convention was adopted. Among his early achievements was the U.S. Marijuana Tax Act of 1937. Just like the Single Convention, it was the result of a corrupt political process, and it remains to this day a Rosetta Stone for those who wish to understand how the criminalization of cannabis came into being.

The reason for this is that the hearings were recorded and that they reveal a remarkable distortion of the evidence. Before the hearings, few congressmen had even heard about "marijuana" but as Harry Anslinger was the much-respected chief of police, they accepted his word when he described the drug as worse than heroin. To the extent politicians knew anything about marijuana, it was from the propaganda of the tabloids and the narcotics police. This propaganda told people that "prolonged use of marijuana frequently develops a delirious rage which sometimes leads to high crimes, such as assault and murder." And as Anslinger could divulge to his audience that "in many cases one cigarette might develop a homicidal mania" and that "all the experts agree that the continued use leads to insanity," it seemed reasonable to regulate sale of the plant. Thus, the bill went through Congress, and people had to have a stamp of approval from the state to sell cannabis. This stamp did not cost more than a dollar, but as the U.S. Government refused to provide approvals, the result was a prohibition.

Described by drug historians as "a classic example of bureaucratic overkill,"(73.235) the Marijuana Tax Act not only resembled the style of previous prohibitionist achievements but was indicative of things to come. As we have seen, Anslinger took his crusade to the UN—and as principled thinking was eclipsed by the power of exaggerated enemy images, the curious case of how the international drug control system came into being is explained. In respect to cannabis, Mark Leinwand pointed to the absurdity of the classification system in 1968:

> "[Cannabis] does not belong—and, objectively, never did belong—in the provisions of a treaty whose stated purpose is to prevent "addiction to narcotic drugs". The inclusion of cannabis . . . was a mistake based on erroneous scientific and medical information generally available to the delegates when the treaty was drafted."(13.285)

The issue of cannabis, however, is part of a bigger picture that testifies to the entire drug control system's lack of legitimacy. Besides the erroneous classification of substances, drug policy researchers point out that substances such as tobacco and alcohol are not included. As these drugs comparatively come out worse than illegal ones, this is weighty criticism. Even so, more salient is the accusation that prohibitionist assumptions have never been proven correct and that the relationship to the human rights conventions has never been considered.

Whereas the situation was unclear sixty years ago, when the Single Convention was enacted, evidence has since been mounting. Today, it has become so overwhelming that most scholars agree that the system has failed and that the costs of pursuing prohibition are unjustifiable. Drug policy experts Room, Fisher, Hall, Lenton, and Reuter, for instance, reviewed the situation in 2010, concluding thus:

"By an accident of history, cannabis was included in the
international drug control regime. . . . [Now], fifty years
after the adoption of an unequivocal international
prohibition, we face a very different world. The set of
international rules and norms which were adopted then
have not proven effective in the modern world, and they
have adverse consequences for those who get caught up in
their provisions. . . . There is a clear need for change, and
yet the international drug control system seems increasingly
paralyzed and immobile."(89.145,150)

As we shall see, the criticism directed towards cannabis can be
applied to the other classified substances. Indeed, the system is entirely
backwards, as we have legalized the most harmful drugs while we have
criminalized the use of less problematic ones.

Taking into consideration that most people believe we are born into
a rational society, i.e., a world where politics mirror an evidence-based
reflection of serious deliberations, this may be difficult to comprehend.
Our culture, after all, has a relaxed attitude towards such drugs as tobacco
and alcohol, while it has a particularly hysterical relationship towards
prohibited substances. Assuming that our leaders know what they are
doing, therefore, we take it for granted that the illicit substances must be
far more dangerous than legal ones. Evidence to the contrary, however,
abounds, for as drug scholar David Nutt says:

"Each year, tobacco kills 5 million people across the world,
while alcohol kills 1.5 million. By comparison, illicit drugs
kill around 200 000 people between them. Even taking into
account the much smaller populations who use these drugs,
in many cases they are considerably less deadly."(76.280)

A study by the British medical journal Lancet has more to say on this
subject. And after looking at the number of users per drug-related death
in Britain, it concluded with the following ranking list: Tobacco (87 users
per death); Street Methadone (111 users per death); Benzo-

diazepines/Valium (246 users per death); Heroin (428 users per death); Solvents (545 users per death); Alcohol (1000 users per death); Cocaine (3644 users per death); Amphetamine (12.285 users per death); Ecstasy (18.518 users per death). Drugs like cannabis, LSD, ketamine, and khat are missing from this list even though quite popular. The reason is that the numbers of deaths associated with their use are too few to count.

Granted, there are more that can be said about this ranking list, one criticism being that it only refers to British patterns of use. Nonetheless, tobacco is by far the leading death-agent, and while the licit drugs combined kill about 155.000 Britons, the illicit drugs together kill roughly 1000 a year.

Now, we just saw Nutt attribute some 200.000 deaths worldwide to the illicit drugs. Even if it is less than the 300.000 deaths attributed to legal prescription drugs in the U.S. alone, this is quite a lot. We shall have more to say about this issue later. Already here, however, the reader should be aware that most of these deaths do not reflect the inherent danger of illicit substances. Indeed, *prohibition itself is responsible for the majority*, as these deaths can be attributed to its unfortunate repercussions.

Not surprisingly, that licit drugs are worse than the ones we have criminalized and that prohibition kills many more people than the illicit drugs, is something our leaders are doing their very best to obscure. As the credibility of their quest depends on there being a meaningful distinction between the two categories, government-funded research tends to ignore this issue. In fact, speaking of the factual accuracy associated with the separation of legal and illegal drugs, the only government that has pointed to its inherent absurdity is Holland. This is no coincidence. As the country, since the beginning of the 80s, has had a much more progressive drug policy than the rest of the world, its government does not have the same interest in polishing the facade of prohibition. Thus, when the Dutch Department of Health compared licit and illicit drugs on a scale of harms, most found it embarrassing that the legal drugs were rated as worse than most illegal.

Despite the evidence, this is still a taboo topic in other countries. For example, when David Nutt, by virtue of his position as the British Government's chief counsel on drug policy, encouraged a more rational debate, politicians tried to muzzle him. And when, despite this censorship, Nutt publicly stated that alcohol was more dangerous than cannabis and that horse riding—the British elite's favorite sport—was more dangerous than the use of ecstasy, they fired him. Professor Nutt commented on the matter thus:

> "As long as our politicians refuse to consider framework other than prohibition and criminalization, then science and evidence will be considered dangerous, and those who champion it will be sidelined and even sacked."(76.7)

In the wake of this episode, Nutt got funds from private benefactors to start an independent institute for drugs research. The result was the Independent Scientific Committee of Drugs (ISCD), and its scientists have presented astonishing findings. Among other things, they have conducted an analysis of the problems associated with the 20 most popular drugs. And after considering their hazards on the basis of 16 criteria of harm (of which 100 represents the maximum potential for harm), they ended up with the following ranking list: alcohol (72), heroin (55), crack (54), meth-amphetamine (33), cocaine (27), tobacco (26), amphetamine (23), cannabis (20), GHB (19), benzodiazepines (15), ketamine (15), methadone (14), mephedrone (13), butane (11), anabolic steroids (10), ecstasy (9), khat (9), LSD (7), buprenorphine (7), and psychoactive mushrooms (6). (76.43)

If we look at this list, there is a big difference between its findings and common preconceptions. To most, it is inconceivable that alcohol can be rated more harmful than crack and heroin and that substances like LSD and ecstasy are rated as having the least potential for harm. Even so, it is our own prejudices that play a trick on us and not this list. In fact, the most significant criticism levied against it is that illicit drugs are presented as worse than they are, as most of the harms should be blamed on prohibition. For instance, ISCD include the environmental and health consequences of spraying coca bushes with toxic pesticides as part of the harm associated with cocaine, and they count the overdoses, lifestyle, and diseases associated with the criminalization of heroin—even the situation in Afghanistan—as a part of the problem with heroin.

If drugs were legalized, however, most of these problems would disappear. In fact, methadone is generally considered as being more harmful to the body and having a greater potential for addiction than heroin. As we can see, methadone is rated with 14 points, and so it is reasonable to assume that legalized heroin would have been among the least harmful substances.

Now, as this flies in the face of commonly embraced truisms, many people will be outraged. Nonetheless, our fear of illicit drugs remains greatly exaggerated. To us, "drugs", "narcotics", and "addiction" are among our most negatively charged words, and many believe that if kids tried cannabis, cocaine, or heroin, they would most likely become addicted and devote themselves to a life of crime and misery. However, even if heroin's potential for addiction is great (about the same as tobacco), the idea that illicit drugs could hold some sort of demonic power is false. Instead, popularity should be attributed to their positive effects; most people use them because they enjoy their properties, and their drug use is no more problematic than other people's alcohol use.

Now, I am not saying that all drug use is good. We know that the more we use drugs, the greater the potential for harm, and quite a few develop unfortunate relationships. Thus, even if roughly 90 percent of drug users avoid this[105] (just as a similar percentage of alcohol users), my point is not to encourage drug use. All I encourage is a less hysterical approach, as the myths of addiction can only diminish our sense of personal responsibility.

In all this, remember that addictive behavior is not reserved for drugs. Everything that stimulates us, enriching our life, can become a burden. This applies to eating, playing video games, watching TV, shopping, gambling, working out, social media activity, as well as sex, money, and power, as an unbalanced relationship affects our brain in the same way as drug abuse. Our body, for instance, produces natural opiates (endorphins and dopamine) when we exercise or eat chocolate. Whatever

---

[105] For instance, as explained by media and politicians, crack cocaine is instantly addictive, turning users into junkies in record-time. Even so, according to the U.S. National Survey on Drug Use and Health, just 3 percent of Americans who have tried this reputedly irresistible and inescapable drug have smoked it in the last month.

the addiction, the same biological and psychological processes are involved—and so our culture arbitrarily marks drug users for persecution, seeing this addiction (even regular use) as particularly immoral.

I shall not say too much on this widely shared belief. Even so, we have already discussed the scapegoating phenomenon as the engine behind all unjust persecution and it is the true reason why drug law violators remain detested. For psychological reasons, humanity has had a drive towards mob-mentality and the Drug War is nothing but the modern expression of our unwillingness to confront our own fears. This is seen when prohibitionists discuss policy: while they want us to believe that drug use is immoral, they reason one way on illegal drugs and another on legal drugs. Immorality, in other words, is not a result of habit but of legislation. Accepting this, only the demonization of drugs and drug users can help prohibitionists avoid the most immediate contradictions: They must paint the fiend so horrible that their purge becomes a glorious endeavor, and they must ignore the implications of human rights conventions.

This is the recipe for prohibitionism. Unconsciousness is its engine. We are stuck at a level of policy where prohibitionists define the terms and intelligent minds must be ignored to maintain the illusion of a just and necessary venture. Hence, to maintain the moral panic that ensures survival of state machinations, we have officials who keep advancing dysfunctional policies; who appeal to totalitarian premises to satisfy halfwits and sadists; and who refuse to think beyond accepted truisms. They will have us believe that "drug use is immoral because it is illegal and that it is illegal because it is immoral". They can only pray that we accept the premise upon which their logic is based—that all laws, by definition, are moral. Even so, excepting prohibitionists, not many people will argue from such a position. After all, history provides us with plenty of examples of laws that were not moral, and there are good reasons why an increasing number put the drug laws in the same category.

By the end of this chapter it will become more obvious why, as the irrational distinction between licit and illicit substances is not the main problem with prohibition. Indeed, also every other premise of this ideology is demonstrably false,[106] and of greater importance is that that arbitrary separation leads to arbitrary persecution—and that the latter means a violation of human rights law.

Living in times of moral panic, only a minority have the wits to put two and two together. In the discipline of law, however, since drug prohibition began, there has been strong principled opposition coming from natural law scholars who say that prohibitionists cannot claim the right to decide over another person's consciousness. Lawyers of this tradition do not acknowledge the prohibitionists' twisting the law of supply and demand into one of victim and aggressor, and they do not accept the idea that all illicit drug use equals abuse. Instead, they see the fundamental separation between misuse and medical use as an over-simplification and they argue that it cannot be justified rationally. They therefore believe that the State should reserve its use of punishment to those "crimes" that involve real victims, and that it has no more right to refuse drugs to people who want it (recreational use) as opposed to those who need it (medical use).

Except for natural law scholars, however, such reasoning is rare among professionals. Even academics are children of time and being born into a society that has forgotten what freedom is and what the social contract entails, most thinking is so muddied that the implications of human rights principles are difficult to perceive. All too often, therefore, academics accept prohibitionist calculations and they rarely point out that their entire project is built on flawed premises. Nonetheless, the most clairvoyant, those who connect with first principles, can still put two and two together. Psychiatry professor Thomas Szasz is one, and he describes one of many inconsistencies in prohibitionist reasoning:

> "The modern . . . zeitgeist [is] our seemingly limitless fear of *and* faith in drugs. The fear explains our timidity toward opiates; the faith, our belief that the habitual use of one narcotic (heroin) is a disease, which can be successfully treated with another narcotic (methadone). Grounded in

---

[106] See for instance TED GOLDBERG, *DEMYSTIFYING DRUGS: A PSYCHOSOCIAL PERSPECTIVE*; NUTT, *DRUGS: WITHOUT THE HOT AIR*; MIKALSEN, *HUMAN RISING*.

pharmacomythology, not pharmacology, these fears and faiths cannot be dispelled by common sense or medical experience. Instead, we live according to the old adage *Credo quia absurdum est* (I believe it because it is absurd), which we find comforting because the credo lifts the burden of responsibility for our bad habits from our shoulders. Using one narcotic to cure the addict by taking another narcotic authenticates the doctor's expertise about habit-forming and habit-curing drugs, legitimizes them as pharmacological miracle workers, and makes them steadily more indispensable as the suppliers of *new* controlled substances."(106.136)

The current drug-treatment regime is one example of the confused thinking generated by prohibition. Unfortunately, stupid laws make stupid people and after being brainwashed by this ideology even more "moderate" professionals think it appropriate to force upon drug users their idea of treatment. The reason is that our authorities will not acknowledge that any legitimate or unproblematic use of these drugs exists. According to them, all users have a drug problem, and the only question is whether they should be dealt with by the prison system or the health system.

It speaks volumes about the sorry state of the debate that this is the question most professionals focus on. And by what right they impose upon people one or the other has so far been a non-issue. Despite this, it should be obvious that we can never have rational/evidence-based drug policies before we confront the most perceptive reform activists.

As we live in an age in which few accept an argumentation that begins with our fundamental and moral right to decide over our own body and mind, however, I shall lower the bar and present an argument against prohibition that all can agree upon. After all, there are plenty of objections and when we have gained some insight into the pros and cons of drug policy, it will be much easier to see why people have a right to use drugs. What I shall do, therefore, is review the evidence, and from there we shall see how the prohibition paradigm compares to our catalogue of rights as articulated in human rights conventions.

Now, we have already seen that some criticism revolves around the classification system and the irrational distinction between licit and illicit substances. Proceeding from this, another objection is that prohibition has not had the effect hoped for; that less invasive measures are better suited at dealing with the alleged problem, and that prohibitionists refuse to take this into consideration.

This is important for human rights reasoning. To elaborate, the signatories of the Single Convention envisioned a drug-free world within the next 25 years. The fact that prohibition, however, in this period, failed to achieve the desired result did nothing to discourage the UN bureaucrats. In 1998, after looking into the matter, they promised more of the same and assured that reinforced efforts would result in a drug-free world within the next ten years. When 2008 came and we were further from a drug-free world than ever, one might think that there would have been a willingness to reconsider—but no. As author Upton Sinclair noted, "it is difficult for a man to understand something when his salary depends upon his not understanding it", and the drug warriors predictably denied all signs of failure, promising more of the same.

The next revision was planned for 2019. Even so, the disastrous consequences of prohibition were becoming more obvious and pressure from Latin American countries ensured that a General Assembly special session on drugs was prepared in 2016. Needless to say, prohibitionists were not happy. More and more people were noticing a discrepancy between the UN human rights conventions and the drug control conventions and the call for drug policies based within the human rights paradigm were becoming increasingly difficult to ignore. As a solution to this problem, world leaders embraced the superiority of the human rights paradigm; they solemnly declared their allegiance to the principles of human rights but refused to consider whether the prohibition paradigm was compatible with basic principles.

Thus, also this time prohibitionists directed the outcome, and the same thing happened again in 2019. While politicians and bureaucrats, at this meeting, accepted that drug prohibition had had serious side-effects, they took for granted that the prohibition paradigm was basically sound and the only improvement was a more flexible regime. This was in response to the growing trend among nations to see (1) the drug user as in need of help rather than punishment and (2) a regulation of the drug trade as a more sensible approach than a continued prohibition. Currently, this insight is leading to changes at policy-level, but politicians are still reluctant to consider the right with which they persecute violators. Consequently, while the prohibition paradigm is no longer unanimously embraced, its adherents, at the very least, have been free to continue the persecution of drug law violators unchecked by the rule of law.

We shall have more to say on this, but as their crusade is about to hit the ground burning world leaders have a huge explanatory problem on their hands. In fact, since the drug laws were put in place, the arrogance and ignorance with which officials have pressed on has become so obvious that the European Coalition for Just and Effective Drug Policies (ENCOD), in an open letter to the UN Commission on Narcotic Drugs (CND), in 2012 accused the bureaucrats of "criminal negligence in the management of the global drug problem."

ENCOD claimed that the systemic refusal to confront the evidence had reached a point where world leaders personally should be held accountable for all the suffering, death, violence, and disease that prohibition had inflicted on humanity. This may sound harsh but remember that ENCOD and other NGOs have tried for years to help better drug policies into being. Bureaucrats in the UN and elsewhere, however, have consistently refused to engage in any debate that questions basic premises. Already 25 years ago, this pattern of denial had become sufficiently evident that Peter Cohen, then director of the Amsterdam Drug Research Project, referred to the UN bodies as "Ivory towers developing a stone-age ideology"(70.97), while psychiatrist Frederik Polak, ENCODs president, had this to say:

> "It is not difficult to understand why governments don't want an open and informed debate about drug policy. They cannot be unaware that the probable outcome of that debate will be that the prohibition must be abolished and replaced by a regulatory system. And they don't like to admit that they are responsible for what has been called the most harmful public policy in the last century."(130.3)

Prohibitionists, of course, object to their ideology being derided as "the most harmful public policy in the last century". The way they see it their law-and-order approach is what prevents the world from going to hell, but if we take a look at this assumption we find that it is based on another faulty premise. To begin with, there is evidence that the degree of criminalization has minimal impact on the supply and demand of drugs. In the Netherlands, for example, cannabis products have been legally available for more than 40 years, yet the Dutch have a lower per capita use than most neighbors—and far lower than the United States, the leading proponent of the War on Drugs.

In other words, there is nothing to suggest that it would be the end of the world if not for prohibition. As a matter of fact, as drugs today are cheaper, of better quality, and more available than before, while drug use at the same time is more widespread, evidence abounds that it has failed in reducing their supply and demand. And as the sole reason for prohibition was to reduce—even annihilate—the use and production of drugs, this speaks volumes about the failure of the drug war. This, however, is not the worst, for not only has it proven a useless means to an end; it has made matters worse for both users and society at large.

The list of unfortunate repercussions is long. It would take several books to elaborate, but most apparent are the adverse consequences prohibition has had for the drug law violators and their families. As a result of this legislation many millions of nonviolent citizens have been imprisoned. This again ensures an unfortunate societal dynamic, and Espen Schaanning, a Norwegian professor, recaps some implications:

> "Among other things, imprisonment separates the prisoner
> from his loved ones and other positive influences on his life.
> He loses his job, he misses out on education and learning,
> he is exposed to suicidal thoughts and mental illness, he sets
> off on a delinquent career and becomes vengeful against
> society; he becomes lonely, stigmatized, institutionalized,
> marginalized, isolated, submissive, alienated, disoriented
> and powerless; he experiences despair, anxiety disorders,
> grief, frustration, deficiency, and cultural poverty; he is
> bereft of self-determination, property, prospects for

development, and the opportunity to use certain goods or services; unwanted contacts is forced upon him, his personal integrity is threatened or impaired—all this and more."(94.117)

Schaanning only cites the immediate consequences of incarceration. In addition, we must include the destructive dynamic that is played out between prisoner and society, for not only does the prisoner represent an economic, social, and moral burden while incarcerated; at some point (usually), he is destined to return to the world—and the longer the time served, the less likelihood of becoming a functional citizen.

Furthermore, we must not forget the impact on friends and family. Psychologically speaking, house searches, interrogation, arrests, and so on, are perceived as a stressful violation of privacy, and the incarceration of a loved one may be as disastrous to those left behind as the person who is locked up. Typically, to those on the outside, imprisonment is experienced as a social, economic, and personal disaster, and the stress associated with it—anxiety, depression, grief, shame, stigma, trauma, despair, and so on—leads to divorce, bitterness, and other discordant interpersonal relations.

In addition to these issues discussed, there are other unfortunate consequences stemming from criminalization. As drug users are at the mercy of an illegal market, prohibition forces them into contact with the underworld. This again puts them in a highly disadvantaged situation. Firstly, as there is no law-and-order apparatus to solve disputes when they occur, the market is defined by a dynamic which ensures that the most ruthless and cynical percentage of the population comes out on top. Outsiders cannot possibly imagine how easy it is to mess up in this business, and if you end up owing the wrong person money you find yourself in an extremely uncomfortable situation. There are plenty of imbeciles willing to torture you and your family for a few dollars and contact with this market has cost hundreds of thousands of people their lives. In Latin America alone, it is estimated that 150.000 are killed every year as a result of the drugs economy. And while drug war-related violence has reached epidemic proportions in these countries, things are not much better in the United States and elsewhere.

Besides the ordeal that befalls innocent bystanders, we find even more examples of the misfortune suffered by people involved with the illicit market. Those unable to meet the demands of ruthless participants will quickly find themselves forced into heavier, more serious crime or prostitution—and this is just one of the many stressful effects of prohibition on drug users. Indeed, they find themselves caught between a rock and a hard place, and on the other side they have the drug law enforcers. These crusaders make their life a living hell, for they are the people who with professional pride and great zeal spy on them, tap their phones, open their mail, ransack their houses, demonize them, stigmatize them, terrorize them, confiscate their valuables, destroy their belongings, force them into rehabilitation, threaten them, jail them, perform cavity examinations on them, destroy their education and work possibilities, fine them, beat them, shoot at them, kill them, take their children from them, and deprive them of their civil rights.

We shall soon see how all this represents a grave violation of the human rights conventions, but this is not all. Prohibition also ensures that users do not have access to quality-assured drugs, which means that they never really know what they are consuming. It is well-known among drug researchers that this is a major problem and that many drug-related deaths could have been avoided under a legal regime. In Norway, for instance, doctors estimate that a health-oriented approach would have reduced the number of overdose-deaths by 90 percent. Internationally, remember that Nutt estimated some 200.000 drug-related fatalities each year. Heroin contributes to well over half (roughly 70 percent), and all things considered we could easily have reduced this number by at least 80 percent if we had legalized drugs.

Thus, it is undeniable that prohibition kills, and a more humane regime would also remove much drug-related disease. To take heroin users, they are at risk of attracting diseases such as HIV and hepatitis B and C. If we ignore sub-Saharan Africa, about a third of world's HIV-infections are due to shared needles and this could have been avoided if it were not for prohibition. In fact, a regulated regime would ensure an entirely different social dynamic than that caused by the drug war. For as psychiatry professor Thomas Szasz says:

"Although the prohibitionists stubbornly deny it, drug controls foster precisely those moral values and personal behaviours that we mistakenly attribute to drugs. It is not drugs but drug prohibitionists that lead to drug use that is uninformed, irresponsible, self-indulgent, and personally and socially destructive."(106.149)

We need only look at the situation related to heroin and other opiates a hundred years ago to confirm this. Back then the patterns of use were completely different and few problems followed in its wake. In fact, as long as the users got their fix, they were well-functioning citizens; they worked hard, took care of their children, were in good health, and lived long lives. Consequently, their problem today is not primarily heroin, but the lifestyle forced upon them by prohibition.

Now, more could be said about this and how the criminalization of drugs has forced upon us a dynamic that has increased the problems associated with drug use. For one, the first victim in war is truth. For more than 50 years drug war propaganda has encouraged ignorance and fear and the moral panic that prohibition relies on has made serious information about substances difficult to obtain. Those not deterred by this propaganda will quickly discover that the "information" they were raised to believe in does not reflect reality. From there on they must find out for themselves the pros and cons of drug use and this, no doubt, has had an adverse effect on patterns of use.

It is also clear that the forbidden-fruit effect attracts young people to experiment with these substances and that the irrational distinction between licit and illicit drugs is confusing. Not only does it result in a false impression of the risks associated with alcohol and tobacco but it blurs the difference between the illicit drugs. It is, after all, a huge difference between cannabis and heroin, yet prohibition ensures that those who experiment with one easily come into contact with the other.

It was the perceived importance of separating the markets for "hard" and "soft" drugs that made Holland regulate the sale of cannabis products. Because of this (and an overall drug policy that is largely health-oriented) the Dutch have very few problematic heroin users and some of Europe's lowest overdose figures. As already noted, the use of heroin is not itself problematic; used correctly the only physical ailment associated with its use is itching and constipation, and alcohol is a far more harmful drug to both users and society.

We saw this reflected by ISCD's ranking list. And talking about drug policy, we should keep in mind that alcohol, historically, has always been considered the worst drug. A good example is found in the fact that until the 20th century opium was frequently used and that its use was considered unproblematic. At the height of the Roman Empire, some 20 percent of its tax revenues derived from its trade, and yet there is not a single word for "opium addict" in Latin. Still, it has six words for "alcohol abuse", and this should tell us about our exaggerated fear of the drug.

Obviously, it must be taken into account that heroin is a stronger drug than opium, just like cocaine is a stronger drug than coca leaves. In the case of coca leaves, use has a long tradition in different indigenous cultures and this has also been unproblematic. In fact, we can compare the Amerindians' use of coca leaves with our use of coffee—if we ignore the fact that coffee is a *more* harmful drug.

Looking into the matter, then, we have no reason to believe that the widespread use of opium and coca leaves (should it occur) would be a problem. And as we have legalized alcohol, the worst of all drugs, current drug policies have the unfortunate effect of encouraging its use rather than less harmful alternatives.

In addition, another consequence of prohibition is that it promotes the use of stronger drugs like cocaine and heroin instead of milder varieties. Smugglers want to earn as much as possible trafficking as little as possible and because smuggling one kilo of heroin or cocaine makes more sense than smuggling one kilo of opium or coca leaves, prohibition ensures that the former is everywhere while the latter is impossible to come by.

Everything mentioned is a consequence of prohibition dynamics. Hence, looking at alcohol prohibition in the 1920s, wine and beer became less commonplace while hard liquor was readily available. Even if the total consumption of alcohol declined, therefore, people drank more of the hard stuff—and because they did not have access to quality-controlled products, prohibition ensured a fivefold increase in alcohol-related death and disease.

Furthermore, criminalization resulted in the rise of organized crime. And while having to buy their goods from gangsters who sometimes sold them poisonous drink first and foremost was the users' problem, the underground economy became society's predicament. As historian Hugh Brogan noted:

> "The price of official righteousness always comes high and in case of alcohol prohibition some $2 billion worth of business was transferred from brewers and bar-keepers to bootleggers and gangsters who worked in close co-operation with the policemen and politicians they corrupted. Blackmail, protection rackets and gangland murders became all too common and no one was punished."(16.518)

As prohibition never had much effect on the supply and demand, it was nothing but a politician's gift to organized crime. And as the rise of organized crime necessarily must reflect a corresponding corruption of the institutions created to protect society and the rule of law this had disastrous side-effects. After all, only gangsters and war profiteers stood to profit from the criminalization; every year prohibition was in effect their influence on the social fabric increased—and the more it did, the more these two forces became one.

The difference between alcohol prohibition and drug prohibition, therefore, boils down to this: that the damage done to users and society by the former was nothing compared to latter. For one, alcohol prohibition was a limited national effort which lasted a mere decade before politicians put an end to their divisive policies. Drug prohibition, however, is a worldwide endeavor which has been given free and expansive reign for more than 50 years. While the former put $2 billion worth of business into the hands of gangsters, the latter provided them with the control of a market worth $500 billion. In fact, next to weapons and oil, the drug economy is the world's biggest; every year we put another $500 billion into the coffers of the world's greatest criminal enterprise, and these monies' corruptive influence has been so vast that it has become impossible to separate leaders from gangsters.

Now, as the power-political dimension is unknown to most, this is a controversial assertion. Even though experts on drug policy agree that the drugs economy has had a destabilizing effect on Afghanistan and Latin American countries' system of government, we like to think that the elite in more stable "democracies" refuse to co-operate with gangsters. Thus, we take it for granted that our leaders have a more idealistic ambition than to profit from prohibition, and we find it hard to consider that it could be exactly what it presents itself to be—a cynical power-strategic act of genius.

Even so, nothing is as it seems. While our authorities present the world in black and white, it is a blur of grays, and the black and white economy is seamlessly interwoven. As documented in *Human Rising*, the major banks launder about $500 billion annually and so important is the drugs economy that they depend upon this injection of capital. Furthermore, bankers are not the only ones to be corrupted by this economy. There are plenty of business owners, police officers, judges, lawyers, bureaucrats, and politicians who profit from prohibition. And even if our civil servants rarely will admit to this problem, there is no doubt that the drug war has had a disastrous effect. Speaking of corruption, its effects on society are so adverse that the Council of Europe, in its *Criminal Law Convention on Corruption*, summarized it thus: "corruption threatens the rule of law, democracy and human rights, undermines good governance, fairness and social justice, distorts competition, hinders economic development and endangers the stability of democratic institutions and the moral foundations of society."

In other words, ridding society of this evil should be a much bigger priority than the elimination of drugs. And as the drugs economy is the most corruptive force, the first thing we should do is to regulate this trade. *Only* by doing so can we reverse organized crime's devastating impact on the political process; *only* by doing so can we safeguard and maintain the integrity of the rule of law; *only* by doing so can we protect drug users and the rest of society from the side-effects of prohibition; and *only* by doing so can we protect the ideas, values, and principles that our society is founded upon. In fact, as events proceed from bad to worse, the survival of civilization depends on us regulating this trade—but our leaders refuse to act.

Although it is unfathomable, a major reason for their stalling is that prohibition has corrupted society to the point where it has become an indispensable part of the elite's play for power. Not only has it made possible a net of social control that people would not otherwise have accepted, but it has made it possible to fund shady operations and terrorist networks worldwide—stuff that that the elite cannot finance through official budgets. For these reasons, the intelligence services, led by the CIA, have cooperated and/or competed for the control of the drug market. I refer to *Human Rising* for an elaboration on how U.S. intervention in Southeast Asia in the 1960s and 70s was motivated by the need to streamline and centralize the control of this market. The same applies to the war in Afghanistan today, and this book gives voice to many police officers, politicians, and military/intelligence officials who can attest to this.

Hence, although its corrupting consequence is rarely mentioned, this is one of the most important reasons why we should end prohibition. Drug users' rights, of course, is no less important. But everything is interconnected—and because the drug law's impact has been so destructive, it also violates the rest of the population's catalogue of rights. Simply stated, this means that the incompatibility with human rights law is so severe that the drug law represents gross human rights violations and a crime against humanity ("a widespread or systematic attack directed against the civilian population"). As mentioned, it is only gangsters and war profiteers who have benefited from this prohibition— and for the rest it has been an absolute disaster. The most clairvoyant have pointed it out for decades, and Thomas Szasz spoke to it thus 22 years ago:

> "Doctors, lawyers, and politicians started the War on Drugs and continue to wage it, and . . . they are its real beneficiaries. In contrast, the drug war's ostensible beneficiaries—the poor, the uneducated, the young, the old, and the sick—are its actual victims."(106.157)

Even so, politicians continue to deny reality. They keep up the act of embracing the premises of drug prohibition, while ignoring the evidence that speaks to its inherent flaws.

Scholars troubled by this moral confusion explain it as a mix of institutionalized ignorance and a fear of speaking out against the party line—a lack of integrity, in short. 80 percent of British politicians, for example, admit that the War on Drugs has failed, but only a few have the guts to fight for evidence-based drug policies. There is a reason for this as, traditionally speaking, those with the courage to question basic premises have not fared so well. It is the same in every country: prohibitionists have held evidence-based policies at bay by claiming the moral high-ground, and as they have been sufficiently powerful to destroy those who disagree others have kept silent.

This is the traditional explanation for their lack of moral courage: The moral panic is simply too great for integrity to matter, and until the people begin to wise up, politicians will cater to their destructive whims. Nonetheless, for those who add the power-political dimension, the taboo on drug policy is also because those who govern have a vested interest in maintaining prohibition *regardless* of its costs to society.

To us, this should be obvious as we have already seen how the political process is controlled by war profiteers. In addition, history speaks volumes about our authorities' lack of moral compass; in the main, politicians are guided by short-sighted interests and selfish power-political ambitions, and so the system's force of inertia sees to it that prohibition is maintained. As organizational theory reminds us, our bureaucracies' primary objective is to increase their own influence as much as possible vis-à-vis other competing agencies and the population at large. Evidence-based drug policies threaten the budgets and position of powerful groupings, and so those who are employed by the police, courts, customs, prison industry, health department, ministry of justice, and so on, tend to favor prohibition regardless of its merits.

They have done so for over 50 years. There is nothing to suggest that they will be motivated by reason, long-term thinking, or concerns about the common good any time soon. For that the collective psychosis is simply too great, and so—if we are to put an end to the destructive dynamic these forces inflict upon the social fabric—there is only one thing to do: We must make drug policies a human rights issue.

27

THE DRUG LAW AND HUMAN RIGHTS LAW

"Ignorance, neglect, or contempt of human rights, are the sole causes of public misfortunes and corruptions of Government."

—Declaration of the Rights of Man and Citizen, 1789—

TRADITIONALLY, TO THINK of drug policy in terms of human rights has been a non-issue. Most people take it for granted that those who put together the UN drug control conventions knew what they were doing and that lawyers and other professionals in retrospect would have had sufficient respect for themselves and their discipline to let us know if there was a problem between the drug laws and human right law.

This belief notwithstanding, a look at the relationship reveals that our drug laws are fundamentally incompatible with our rights as defined by the human rights conventions.

As this discrepancy is seen easily by anyone knowledgeable on the subject matter, one might wonder why our authorities have ignored it. Looking back at history, however, this is perhaps not so strange. We find then that our leaders have supported many dimwitted and inhumane laws and that it rarely has occurred to them that it might have been the law that was the problem—and not those who were in breach of it. Racial laws, religious laws, and laws affecting lesbians, gays, and so on, are just some examples of laws that have been incompatible with the principles of human rights law. This is commonly accepted today, even though most people took these laws for granted only decades ago—and as we shall see, the situation is exactly the same with the drug laws.

Now, it was only after the Second World War, with the formation of the UN, that the issue of human rights was taken seriously by our governments. The concept, however, is not new and our human rights conventions are really the result of Enlightenment Era thinking. The French Declaration of the Rights of Man and Citizen, referred to above, mirrored this trend. It was the first of its kind, and as "ignorance, neglect, or contempt of human rights was believed to be the sole cause of public calamities and corruptions of government", a declaration was put together which reminded the government of its duties. Thus, the purpose of the first human rights declaration was to establish "the natural, unalienable, and sacred rights of man". It defined a standard the state had to abide by to be considered legitimate and, based upon simple and incontestable principles, formulated articles whereby grievances could be addressed.

Later human rights conventions elaborate on this thinking. The gist of this reasoning is that all people are born equal; that we all share the right to life, liberty, and the pursuit of happiness, and that we all share the same rights and obligations. Furthermore, the State shall guarantee the protection of rights. As we saw earlier, it shall serve the public/the greater good and ensure that no group of privileged few infringes on the rights of others. It shall ensure the most appropriate distribution of benefits and burdens, and to the extent that our freedoms are limited it must be due to compelling social considerations. Our laws, then, shall be a mutual protection against injustice. And, as Rawls's first principle of justice holds, each person is to have an equal right to the most extensive liberty compatible with a similar liberty for others.

In short, this is the essence of the social contract, and in this equation the State is a non-entity. It has no rights of its own: it is a service apparatus constructed for the purpose of securing our catalogue of rights and ensuring that the machinery of society functions optimally—that is all. The slogan of the French Revolution (and the Freemasons) "Liberty, Equality, and Fraternity" sums up the essence of the modern project, and it is a result of this thinking that human rights conventions have come into being.

As mentioned, the articles set forth are the result of principles, first and foremost those of autonomy, equality, dignity, proportionality, and the liberty presumption. To put it simply, the purpose of human rights conventions is to promote these principles so that their light can shine forth as we mature towards greater levels of understanding. These principles overlap and sustain each other. Autonomy is the name of the game, a presumption of liberty the rule, and while the equality principle invalidates discriminatory laws and practices, the test of proportionality defines criteria that laws must follow to be compatible with our human rights heritage.

We shall now see how the drug laws are in violation of these principles.

27.1 THE EQUALITY PRINCIPLE AND THE DRUG LAW

"Law and order are always and everywhere the law and order that protect the established hierarchy."(59.23)

—Herbert Marcuse, sociologist—

The Equality principle prohibits all unjust discriminatory practices. As the perceptive reader have already deduced, drug laws are in violation of this principle because there is no rational distinction between legal and illegal drugs and because a health-oriented approach, in all cases, is the most appropriate. We have already elaborated on this part of the equation. And looking at the distinction between the two categories, the only reason why some substances are lawful while others are prohibited is that influential power-political players want it so.

In other words, we are dealing with a cultural distinction. This again means that the credibility of current policies is built upon prejudiced conceptions—and that the situation is strikingly similar to the one which "legitimized" Jim Crow laws. Back then, the white ruling class felt threatened by other races: Blacks were seen as less reliable, more primitive, and more prone to mischief, and so race-specific laws were enacted to keep them in place. Without this legislation, the ruling class argued that civilization would perish, that all things good and decent would crumble, and that the culture of society would give way to uncultured and inferior people. Thus, there was a moral panic behind race laws and along with pseudo-scientific research, this panic served as justification.

Looking at the drug laws, the situation is exactly the same. We have separated drugs into classes of black and white and while the former is associated with culture and positive experiences, the latter represent the opposite. That only the minorities' drugs of choice were prohibited—and that it happened in times of social crisis between them and whites—highlight the parallels.

Drug policy scholars are aware of these similarities and see the drug laws as a continuation of race laws. The fact that law enforcement specifically targets non-whites only confirms this impression; while drug use is equally popular among blacks and whites, blacks are four times as likely to be arrested and six times as likely to go to jail for drug law violations, and there is no doubt that law enforcement efforts are disproportionately focused on the lower classes. Books like Doris Marie Provine's *Unequal under Law* attest to this. And even if authorities declare that this is not their intention, we have no good reason to believe them. After all, President Nixon, the man who started the War on Drugs, emphasized to his closest advisors that "the whole problem was the blacks, and that the key was to devise a system that recognizes this while not appearing to."(70.60)

We already know that by hyping the enemy image of "drugs", Nixon and others not only found a way to make themselves look good but an excuse to subject an entire population to the elite's law and order apparatus. Hence, looking at the evidence, it is difficult to escape the conclusion that ignorance, racism, empire building, and class warfare were the real reasons for the War on Drugs. The proof is in the pudding, as the drug law's social function and consequence—and our leaders' refusal to make amends—speaks for itself.

We shall not, however, elaborate on how drug legislation has been a tool for social control. Here, our focus is its problem as measured against the principle of equality and adding two and two together there can be no doubt that modern drug policies represent a discriminatory practice. After all, no thinking person would accept the same policies for alcohol and tobacco. When it comes to protecting alcohol drinkers from undue interference the European Court of Human Rights, in Litwa v. Poland, looked into the matter. And while the Court decided that the State was allowed to intervene if the intoxication posed a danger to the person or others, it found that 6.5 hours of forceful detention was a disproportionate infringement. The judges, therefore, ruled in favor of the applicant, agreeing that the detention was unlawful and that the proper thing to do would have been to drive Litwa home.

From this verdict, we see how different alcohol drinkers and drug users are treated. When it comes to alcohol, we seek to ensure the most appropriate balance between the rights of the individual and the protection of society. When it comes to drug users, however, this basic parameter of justice seems objectionable. Instead, as evidenced by the last hundred years, the State is free to demonize and persecute drug users at will as international bodies like the European Court of Human Rights will do nothing to ensure that their rights are protected. In fact, in today's world, you will have great difficulty even finding a human rights organization willing to speak up; so powerful is the enemy image of drugs that users, while constituting between five and twenty percent of the population, remain without the protection of human rights.

The unlawful persecution of drug users, however, is not the worst. As a result of drug warriors' success in framing the dynamic of supply and demand into one of victim and aggressor, this is peanuts compared to what is being done to those involved with the drugs economy. The smugness and zeal with which prohibitionists demonize this group, outbidding each other with demands for tougher sentences, would be sickening to a population more rationally inclined. Nevertheless, so damaging is the enemy image to our reasoning that those involved in the drug trade are seen as scum of the earth.

Politicians, police officers, judges, prosecutors, and anyone else involved with their persecution, therefore, do not think twice about promoting tougher penalties than they would give to murderers and rapists. The viciousness and manifest absurdity of such penalties is lost on them, for according to a prohibitionist's logic their involvement in the drug economy generates millions of "victims". Thus, they continue to promote strict sentencing, even the death penalty, while ignoring the faulty premises of their presumptions.

Had they looked more closely, however, they would have found that it is precisely the same supply and demand mechanisms involved with the illicit drugs as with others. Accepting this, it would have become embarrassingly clear that the drug law violators, those evil and cynical dealers in death, were in fact no more cynical and depraved than anyone involved with the supply chain of alcohol or tobacco. And that they just as well, therefore, could have supported criminal policies that put people like this (farmers, brewers, truck drivers, salesmen, barkeepers, and—most likely—themselves) behind bars for the longest possible amount of time.

Not only that, but they would realize that the idea being discussed seriously among more "progressive" activists—to decriminalize use but prohibit the sale and production of these substances—is no less absurd. Such thinking is merely the result of scapegoatism. It is the result of our need to justify the morality of prohibition, to whitewash the atrocities that is being done in its name, and without a habit of reasoning from totalitarian principles the fallacy would be plain as day. More shall be said on this in the next chapter. Even so, if the use of a substance is legal it is a contradiction in terms to criminalize its sale, for as Lysander Spooner, a 19th century legal theorist, noted: "The seller is, at most, merely an accomplice of the drinker [drug user]. And it is a rule of law, as well as reason, that if the principal in any act is not punishable, the accomplice cannot be."(102.11)

Thus, to decriminalize use while maintaining prohibition falls on its own weight. Firstly, because the legal reasoning behind this trend accepts that drug users are autonomous individuals, not mere victims of sinister forces. Accepting this premise, they not only have a right to use their drugs of choice, but to obtain these drugs without exposing themselves to the dangers of being involved with the underworld. Moreover, they have a right to a regulated market because prohibition makes matters worse in so many ways—not only for the drug user but everybody else. We are familiar with the unfortunate side-effects of drug prohibition. We have established that, except from gangsters and war profiteers, we are all better off without it—and this brings us to the principle of proportionality.

27.2 THE PROPORTIONALITY PRINCIPLE AND THE DRUG LAW

"Bad laws are the worst sort of tyranny."(59.47)

—Edmund Burke, British politician
and philosopher, 1780—

This principle limits the government's legitimate intervention in our lives. As we may remember, society is built on the premise that the individual is to have as much freedom, responsibility, and self-determination as possible. The human rights conventions, therefore, declare that to the extent the State can limit our freedoms, it must be because "just requirements of morality, public order and the general welfare in a democratic society" necessitate such action. Without going into detail, this means that for the drug law to be in compliance with human rights law, it must (1) be suitable to achieve the desired end, which is a drug-free world; (2) its interference must be proportionate to the identified aim; and (3) it must strike a fair balance between the rights of the individual and the interests of the community.

The law, then, must be no more repressive or severe than necessary for the general welfare. And as virtually all experts on drug policy agree that (1) drug prohibition can never achieve its goal of a drug free world; (2) that there are less invasive means available, more fit to minimize the harms caused by drug use; and (3) that the harms associated with prohibition outweigh the harms produced by drug use, it follows that our drug laws are incompatible with the proportionality principle.

Now, there is a lot more that could be said about this. We could elaborate on the liberty presumption, how it was reversed when the drug laws came into being, and the strict criteria that constitutional law demands for maintaining this reversal. We could discuss the avalanche of documentation showing that the drug laws no longer can be justified from such an "enemy at the gates" perspective, how the debate therefore has gone from this extreme to one of social justice and tolerance—and why human rights is the solution to the sins of our fathers. For an in-depth view, my previous books *Human Rising, To Right a Wrong,* and *To End a War* goes along way, and so does the website of the Alliance for Rights-Oriented Drug Policies (www.arodpolicies.org). Due to space considerations, the point has been sufficiently made, and while this little summary may not leave the reader fully convinced about the merits of the legalization argument, this is less important. What is vital is to understand (1) that the principles of proportionality, equality, autonomy, dignity, and the liberty presumption are entwined; (2) that they put the burden of evidence on the advocates of prohibition; (3) that any human rights analysis must begin with these principles; and (4) that advocates for legalization have informed the Council of Europe, the United Nations, and individual nations why we consider the drug law to be a human rights violator.

No matter how strongly our leaders favor prohibition, therefore, these institutions are obliged to let the issue be reviewed properly. This means that it should be left to an impartial, independent, and competent tribunal to determine if the drug law violates human rights law. And for prohibition to be found compatible with human rights commitments, its defendants must answer the following questions:[107]

- Whereas all comparisons of the problems associated with legal and illegal drugs (such as those made by EMCDDA, ISCD, and the Dutch Ministry of Health) demonstrate that the legal ones are more harmful to users' health and more destructive to us as a society: How will you defend the present policies? How can you, without building your drug policy on a discriminatory practice—and thus violate the principle of equality—argue in favor of a health-oriented approach toward alcohol users and a continued criminalization of cannabis users?

---

[107] The following questions use cannabis as an example. The case for the other drugs must be specified differently, but the same line of reasoning apply.

- Whereas it is the same supply and demand factors involved when it comes to the licit and illicit drugs, and whereas the different groups of drugs also have the same varying patterns of use associated with them: How will you justify the persecution and the demonization of the drug law violators? What sort of crimes against his fellowmen has a cannabis producer, transporter or seller committed that an alcohol producer, transporter, or seller has not?

- Whereas most drug policy researchers are in agreement that the drug laws have had worse consequences for society in general and users in particular than the drug use itself would have had; and whereas more and more organizations and commissions publish reports that confirm the same: How will you, from the growing evidence base which suggests that the cure (drug law) is worse than the disease (drug use) defend current policies as measured against the principle of proportionality?

- Whereas a majority of drug policy experts agree that there was a moral panic behind the outlawing of cannabis; whereas drug policy experts acknowledge that its current classification makes no sense; whereas scholarly works such as James Ostrowski's *Answering the Critics of Drug Legalization,* Douglas Husak's *Drugs and Rights,* and David A.J. Richards' *Sex, Drugs, Death, and the Law* have refuted the traditional arguments in favor of criminalization; whereas an independent, impartial, and competent tribunal (the Cannabis-tribunal in the Hague, 2008) has already qualified the prohibitionist argument as "based on fallacies" and "absolutely worthless", and whereas the drug laws thus seem to build their credibility on a series of faulty premises: Considering the fact that the enemy image of marijuana has proven vastly exaggerated; considering that the separation between the licit and illicit substances has proven an arbitrary divide; considering that that the evidence is increasingly clear that the drug laws have failed in reducing their supply and demand; considering that American, as well as European decriminalization experiments have shown a health-oriented approach to be more successful in dealing with the harms caused by drug use; considering that the cure has proven worse than the disease to the degree that the harms caused by prohibition now have become so enormous that they threaten to undermine the fabric of our society; considering that paternalistic and moralistic arguments have failed, and considering that you can no longer justify prohibition on the basis that (1) it suppresses different types of crime, (2) that it protects our youth and the wellbeing of society, (3) that drug abuse has substantial economic and social costs, (4) that marijuana use is intrinsically immoral and degrading in nature, (5) that its use is self-destructive, dangerous and may cause a variety of harms, including physical injury, addiction and death, (6) that it is a gateway drug, (7) that its use is not a victimless crime since it causes harm to others, and (8) that we do not know the consequences of legalization:[108] *All this considered, what compelling reasons can there be for prohibition, and in what way are its means tailored towards its explicitly stated ends?*

The supporters of the status quo may feel confident that all is well and that no further thinking along these lines is necessary. Nonetheless, *only by answering these questions can they stand their ground*; only by doing so can they verify that current drug policies are compatible with the human rights conventions; only by doing so can they reassure the world's 300 million drug users that their rights are respected; and only by doing so can the State present itself as an adherent to the rule of law.

It is that simple. Any meaningful discussion on drug policy, therefore, begins with these questions. For the rule of law to mean anything, the drug law must defend its status according to the demands of the human rights conventions, and should the prohibitionists fail to answer these questions the drug control conventions must yield.

Now, so far, prohibitionists have been so powerful that they could do as they please, regardless of reason or the relationship to human rights. Only time can tell when this situation will change. But to say what it means the day they take human rights law seriously, the legal principles

---

[108] Further documentation for all these claims can be found in MIKALSEN, *TO END A WAR: A SHORT HISTORY OF HUMAN RIGHTS, THE RULE OF LAW, AND HOW DRUG PROHIBITION VIOLATES THE BILL OF RIGHTS.*

presented here are related to another, namely the principle of arbitrariness. Legal systems prohibit arbitrary detention, and this means that if prohibitionists cannot defend the status quo, then the drug laws shall not only be removed but the millions imprisoned for violating them shall also be freed!

No doubt, this will be a bitter pill for prohibitionists to swallow. Maybe it helps to remember, then, that the drug law enforcers have committed a far more serious crime against their fellowmen than violators. After all, principles such as autonomy, proportionality, equality, and the liberty presumption define the perimeters of the rule of law. And while the violators merely have made a product available, the enforcers have done so much worse, persecuting people for their choice in the most ruthless manner. Prohibitionists should also not forget that they have been followers of a policy so dysfunctional and inhumane that it deserves a place among history's great crimes against humanity. Thus, as prohibition draws to an end, rather than anger and bitterness from their side, a show of humility would be more appropriate.

Prohibitionist-minded officials should also remember their duties as civil servants. We are living in times of moral panic and if they have failed to act after having been made aware of our drug policies' destructive workings, they should not only be held criminally negligent but responsible for aiding and abetting in crimes against humanity.

This, again, is difficult for prohibitionists to comprehend. They are so used to seeing themselves as defenders of the ultimate good that they have no idea that they can be held responsible for the misery and death that has followed in the wake of their crusade. Nonetheless, as the failures of prohibition become more obvious, it is becoming harder and harder to maintain ignorant policies. Hence, the winds of change are blowing across the drug political landscape, and the question is no longer *if* the current regime will end—but *when*.

The longer the time span between now and then, the worse the prohibitionists' explanatory problem will be. Its leading representatives, therefore, would do wisely to leave their imagined high-ground behind, address the criticism levied against the status quo, and give the rights-oriented debate the attention it deserves.

28
SUMMARY OF STATUS

"No government is, or can be, committed to freedom. Only people can be. Government, by its very nature, has a vested interest in enlarging its freedom of action, thereby necessarily reducing the freedom of individuals." (106.14)

—Thomas Szasz—

IN THIS PART we have discussed theory and practice. While politicians claim to be humble servants of the common good, we have seen that the state apparatus, more properly, function as a vehicle for the ambition of a diversity of factions. We have seen that the ruling elite, while giving lip-service to principles of fairness, justice, democracy, freedom, good governance, and the rule of law, have no real interest in such things and that our politicians, in their eagerness to please, have made lies, deceit, and hypocrisy their livelihood.

As a result, today, the state apparatus is no less a machinery of oppression than it was 500 years ago. In fact, the government has never been more powerful, and an unmistakable warning is the expanding regulatory regime; public officials claim dominion over evermore of our daily lives, while they themselves operate more and more behind closed doors. Despite promises to the contrary, they hide behind a thickening veil of secrecy, and the disharmony between the power of the State and the individual—and between theory and practice—is evidenced by the fact that a citizen will find it a punishable offence if he is caught lying to a public official, while they themselves spin an ever more elaborate net of deceit and corruption without fear of consequences.

This disparity and this dynamic have been such a constant in our lives that we hardly react to it. However, a shocking example of the problems associated with a State on steroids was found in its wars on terror and drugs. We saw how the credibility of these wars is built on lies and exaggerated enemy images; how our leaders, despite these campaigns' social function and consequence (and the faulty premises of their reasoning) actively promote both; and how these wars neither fight "terror" nor "drugs" but the people's God-given rights.

Now, the reader might disagree. I have presented a series of claims that skeptics tend to dismiss, and although I have tried to summarize the most relevant features of our development, I have not *proved* anything. I have only offered my interpretation of power-politics and supported my analysis with books that the reader can look into on his/her own. That is all. On the other hand, this is all I can do. And even if I had spent 1000 more pages elaborating on specifics, the argument would have been no more convincing to a mind already closed to the notion that these ideas are worth further investigation.

This is understandable, for if the information presented here is new, it is also shocking—even potentially traumatizing. If this is the case, I hope comfort can be found in reading part six. Nonetheless, whereas knowledge is empowering, it is a most demanding exercise to readjust to a worldview so contrary to the one we are brought up to believe in. A certain percentage of my readers, therefore, will prefer to forget this snippet of history as soon as possible. This will be up to the reader to decide but for those willing to think outside the box, you now have the basics of power-politics.

That being said, I am *not* an impartial and objective observer in the sense many academics purport to be. To me—and anyone who knows about the Light—these are dark days, and if this is the best we can do, I would rather see civilization crash and burn. That is the well-deserved way of all societies that fail to honor the call of first principles, and nothing would please me more than to see the people revolt against the corrupt regimes that govern in their name.

That said, it goes without saying that I would rather see a non-violent revolution than a violent one and that I would rather see a fresh, new, and improved civilization burst into being than the old one turned to dust. In fact, the two—non-violent revolution and renewal—are closely related, and in part six we shall elaborate on their relationship as well as the road ahead. Hence, the point is not to encourage defeatism or violence. It is just, if there was any doubt, to emphasize a position on the matter. And because I define myself in opposition to the status quo and have a vested interest in the renewal, the reader may want to take this into consideration.

Now that this is clear, I should also bring another matter to your attention. This is the fact that even if I cannot possibly prove all I have said on power-politics, I can at least prove that Norway, as of today, is a police state. And because Norway's post-constitutional status is closely related to everything we have talked about, we shall conclude this summary by seeing how Norwegian officials, to protect the wars on terror and drugs from proper review, have put aside the rule of law.

28.1 HOW NORWAY BECAME A POLICE STATE

> *"Injustice anywhere is a threat to justice everywhere."*
> *(59.18)*
>
> —*Martin Luther King*—

That the Norwegian people are subjected to the whims of a police state may come as a surprise. Internationally, to those blinded by the facade, Norway is known for the Nobel Peace Prize, its peace negotiating efforts, its stable democracy, and its respect for human rights.

When it comes to brand building, beyond fjords and exceptional nature, this is the image Norwegians are trying to sell. Through decades, we have worked hard to promote human rights worldwide, and so most would assume that respecting the conventions has been a priority for Norwegian officials at home. This, however, is not the case. As we shall see, the Norwegian state-apparatus has fundamentally failed its people, as well as its obligations towards human rights law. And as a result of civil servants' denial of responsibility, Norwegians are no longer ruled by law but a police state engaging in crimes against humanity.

To fully understand these allegations, we need to go back in time, and the story begins 15 years ago with me trying to stop the War on Terror after reading Mike Ruppert's *Crossing the Rubicon*. This book, written by a former police officer, leaves no doubt that shadowy elements within the U.S. government, the so-called Deep State, ensured that the terrorist attacks of 9/11 and their cover-up unfolded as planned. I had spent years researching power-politics, but this was shocking. Having some trust in the decency of the status quo, I had discounted the notion of state-sponsored terrorism before, and not until reading this book could I believe that such a lie could endure unchallenged. The evidence, however, was overwhelming. I therefore bought 100 copies of this book and besides the Prime Minister, contacted politicians, journalists, and academics. They all got a copy, and as the evidence was unambiguous, I thought that it would be the beginning of the end for our involvement with the War on Terror.

As it turned out, however, it was not so easy. None of the people I contacted seemed to care and it became apparent that if change were to be effected it would have to be by other means. By this time, I had some understanding of the distance between theory and practice, and the more I learned, the more obvious the parallels between the wars on terror and drugs became. Hence, as politicians, academics, and journalists shied away from societal responsibilities, I resolved to up the ante. This meant that I decided to take advantage of opportunities offered by the legal system.

As you may remember, in chapter 22 we talked about the right to a fair trial and judicial review. It is further detailed in the human rights conventions (such as ECHR Article 6 and 13) but, simply stated, means we can use our rights as a defendant to challenge the law. Although few are aware of it, it's an accepted consequence of the principles of popular sovereignty and separation of powers. Thus, it is a fundamental part of our justice system. Citizens in all civilized countries can make use of it, and so important is this principle that Johs Andenæs, Norway's most celebrated jurist, described it as "essential to the rule of law" and "one of the most significant contributions to civilization." (70.558) He was not exaggerating. Our right to challenge the law is the system's safety valve when all else fails and if government officials deny this right, they have effectively robbed us of our most effective defense against the police state.

It follows that if the State aspires to protect the rule of law—and its own reputation—its officials must respect this right to an effective remedy. It is not often people make use of it, but we saw an example in 2010, when the Norwegian Shipowners Association protested the legality of a new tax act. According to the shipowners, it was a violation of their economic rights, and after looking into the matter the Supreme Court agreed.

It was this right to a fair trial and an effective remedy that I recognized as an opportunity to end not only the War on Terror but the War on Drugs. As the parallels between these campaigns were obvious, I would avail myself of the doctrine of Necessity and violate the drug laws.[109] I had already, by more conventional means, tried to force politicians into acting. But as the distance between theory and practice had rendered these efforts futile, I now saw the justice system as the last option. By claiming rights as a defendant, I intended to force the police and the courts to accept the evidence, thereby facilitating for a process that would put an end to these crimes. This is not just a citizen's right. More properly, it is a duty, for as the preamble to the UN human rights conventions holds: "the individual, having duties to other individuals and to the community to which he belongs, is under a responsibility to strive for the promotion and observance of the rights recognized in the present Covenant."

All things considered, then, the violation of the drug laws was a win-win situation. I already saw the system as rotten. Nothing could make me accept a social contract based on lies, exploitation, and injustice; this had resulted in marginal respect for the law to begin with, and as the state

---

[109] In claiming this right, a defendant argues that it was necessary to commit a crime in order to remedy a greater evil. Thus, as the impact of the wars on terror and drugs was sufficiently destructive to categorize them as crimes against humanity—and as I, by violating the drug laws, would have a right to present the evidence needed to prove it—I would argue that I had no choice but to break the law to put an end to these campaigns.

machinery's force of inertia ensured that its disciples would never willingly take into consideration evidence that undermined the authority of state, Mario Savo's words rang louder in my mind. As this great freedom fighter of the 1960's cried out at Berkeley: *"There comes a time when the operation of the machine becomes so odious, makes you so sick at heart, that you can't take part, you can't even tacitly take part, and you've got to put your bodies on the gears and upon the wheels, upon the levers, upon all the apparatus, and you've got to make it stop. And you've got to indicate to the people who run it, to the people who own it, that unless you're free, the machine will be prevented from working at all!"*

As it was unthinkable to be a cog in this machinery, my ambition was to put words into action. Hence, if Norwegian officials would not listen to reason, my mind was set on becoming the biggest possible rock in their machinery—and by involving myself in the drug market I found the perfect opportunity. On one hand, I could use profits to support activists and forces fighting for the renewal of society. And on the other, when the law intervened, my rights as a defendant would provide a shortcut to the heart of the system—a shortcut that, I imagined, would strike a blow to these campaigns and the corrupt machinery that depended on them for survival.

As events progressed, the second option manifested quickly. In 2006, I was charged by the police for helping to build a cannabis farm, thereby enabling my odyssey to the heart of the system. Thus, I wrote my first book, *Freedom Forever*, wherein I summarized an argument to end the War on Terror and the War on Drugs. In 2008, I delivered 10 copies to the police, along with a letter and two other books. One (*Crossing the Rubicon*) was written by a cop and the other by a judge[110]; together they summarized the picture I needed to convey, and since that day the Norwegian police had all they needed to come to terms with these atrocities.

To establish a better foothold, I also wrote letters to the Prosecutor General and the Minister of Justice. These letters impressed upon them the seriousness of the situation, while providing these powers with an

---

[110] JAMES P GRAY, *WHY OUR DRUG LAWS HAVE FAILED AND WHAT WE CAN DO ABOUT IT: A JUDICIAL INDICTMENT OF THE WAR ON DRUGS*

opportunity to prove their qualities. I never heard from the Minister of Justice, not until several years later. The Prosecutor General, however, who already had a reputation for opposing human rights law, did respond. Even so, instead of seizing upon this opportunity, he argued that the human rights conventions did not apply to drug law offenders. To summarize his response, he ignored all the evidence presented and maintained that if a law had made it through parliament then everything was ok. He carefully avoided to comment on graver concerns and, although he did not specify any valid counterarguments to the legal reasoning, decided that the right to a fair trial and effective remedy, when it came to drug law violators, was non-existent.

Now, this was 10 years ago, and things have gone from bad to worse for the rule of law. The police have not only refused to confront the evidence, but together with the Department of Justice they are so eager to ignore the rights-oriented debate that they have declined to prosecute me for involvement with some two metric tons of cannabis-related crimes. When it comes to this participation in the drug market, I have sent letters to the police and Justice Department in which I have offered to explain my role more fully. The only condition put forward is that they support the right to a fair trial, i.e., an opportunity to demonstrate how the drug law violates first principles. Even so, instead of accepting this offer, representatives of the state have met this proposal with a silence that speaks for itself, making it clear that the rule of law is not taken seriously.

To those unaware of the distance between theory and practice, this is difficult to fathom. Not only does the Department of Justice have a responsibility to ensure the integrity of the law, but it is the duty of the police to enforce the law and to protect society from such perils as documented. Consequently, my offer would have been a much-appreciated gift to both—if only theory and practice were one and the same. This, however, is not the case, and so these officials' response becomes just another reminder of their loyalty to practice as opposed to theory.

I say, "another reminder", for even if the Norwegian system of government might be less corrupted than others, it is not difficult to find examples of how the State is governed by an elite above the law. As these institutions are designed to protect the interests of the elite, there-fore, we see time and again that the police and justice systems ensure the proliferation of arbitrary law.[111] This is the only structure of law that can maintain a distance between theory and practice, and the Norwegian justice system speaks volumes about it.

To summarize these proceedings, every level of the justice system, all the way up to the Supreme Court, denied an opportunity to prove the allegations directed against the State. Even though I had completed another book, *Human Rising*, which documented serious state crimes and incompatibility between drug prohibition and constitutional law, the Supreme Court had no intention of abiding by primary obligations. The UN Human Rights Committee, in 2008, not only compelled courts to present reasons for denying an appeal but held that failure constitutes a violation of the right to a fair trial. The Supreme Court had previously recognized the importance of providing due process and yet, when it came to the persecution of drug law violators, the judges ignored the human rights argument without any attempt at justification.

Concerned citizens may want to ask these judges *why they ignored the relevance of human rights by resorting to unlawful practices*. Their response, however, can only provide fuel for controversy as they, just before denying drug law violators an effective remedy, accepted the shipowners' right to the same. No wonder, then, that they will go to extremes to ensure that this question is never satisfactorily answered[112].

---

[111] Two examples should be mentioned, the Lillehammer incidence in 1973 and the Scandinavian Star affair in 1990. In the first, Israeli intelligence agents acting on erroneous information murdered an innocent man in the town of Lillehammer. The Norwegian Justice system being a farce, however, the MOSSAD agents were not punished, and the leader of the operation, Mike Harari, travelled on to Latin America to become General Noriega's right-hand man and a major player in the Israeli intelligence's drug operations in the region (more on this in *Human Rising*). The second, the Scandinavian Star incident, was one of the world's worst ferry disasters. A fire killed 159 people onboard—and even though private investigators have gathered evidence that it was an insurance scam that went wrong, the Norwegian police, thanks to the Prosecutor General and his minions, have refused to investigate properly.

[112] We saw an example at the Supreme Court. As the Court would not discuss the relationship between human rights and the drug law, my lawyer, John Christian

The idea they are trying to convey is that the Judiciary provides a barrier against unsavory state measures. The principle of equality before the law, therefore, is the very basis for the rule of law in Norway as elsewhere, and yet this principle is now an undeniable sham being that the Supreme Court has proven more concerned about protecting the wallet of shipowners than in protecting the fundamental rights of ordinary people to be free from persecution.

Hence, the past must one day catch up with the Norwegian system of justice. And when it does, the argument that will be delivered in these judges' defense is the same that can be heard every time a society comes to grips with state-ordained campaigns of oppression. Just as Germany's judges after the Second World War, they will claim that the system had indoctrinated thinking to the point where it short-circuited when asked to contemplate the distance between theory and practice. They will say that the drug law was too much of a given to question and that it was difficult even to consider the possibility that it was a crime against humanity.

Nonetheless, after the Second World War, the Nuremberg-principle has made it impossible to claim innocence on these grounds. Today, even policemen, politicians, and judges are responsible for their actions, and the fact that persecuting drug law violators conforms with systemic expectations are of no consequence. As a result of a few judges' disregard for constitutional law, several thousand Norwegians have died needlessly, many more thousands have been imprisoned, and hundreds of thousands remain persecuted for no good reason. Worst of all, this is just a fraction of the unfortunate consequences generated by their abuse of power, for without this neglect of duty the lives of drug users would have improved both nationally and internationally.

Thus, there is a reason why constitutional law frowns upon the impunity with which public officials disrespect human rights. Throughout history, the greatest crimes have been perpetrated by those who follow orders, and as a direct result of the Court's failure to comply with constitutional obligations every Norwegian policeman, prosecutor,

---

Elden, asked judges to explain why they refused to do so in their judgment. The Court's only response was a murderous glance which made it perfectly clear that the idea was frowned upon and that his request would not be satisfied.

customs officer, prison employee, and so on, are now part of a criminal conspiracy: Every day they enforce the drug law, they are effectively aiding and abetting crimes against humanity, and so these judges have not only put themselves and the drug law violators in a most unfortunate situation but other enforcers.

Now, I am not arguing that these people should be held collectively responsible and jailed. As we shall see in part six, one ambition with this book is to help a crime-free society into being: By integrating the lessons learned in part one, two, three, and four we can reform criminal policies to the point where prisons are no longer needed, and so I do not want to see drug law enforcers behind bars. I say this only to explain the gravity of the situation, for since the Supreme Court, knowing full well the implications of their actions, denied to the drug law violators an effective remedy, Norway has been a police state and 35 percent of the prison population are political prisoners.

Our leaders, of course, will not grant drug law violators this status. The way they see it, the term only applies to dissidents lounging in prisons elsewhere—in Russia, Iran, Syria, and other places they define themselves in opposition to. And "police states", as far as they are concerned, only exist in the more obscure regions of the world. Even so, we find ourselves in a situation where (1) 30 to 40 percent of prisoners are held for disrespecting a law that can be shown to be a violation of basic human rights; and (2) where politicians and courts, to keep the law in place, for ten years have set aside the rule of law.

Hence, Norwegian drug law prisoners are by every meaningful definition *political prisoners*. This was the ill-fated situation forced upon Norwegians by the Court's decision. And even if its judges, at some point, will have to make amends, it will not happen because of the system's inherent respect for the rule of law, the people, or the ideals to which officials pay lip-service. To the contrary, the day they redeem themselves it will be a matter of necessity. It will be an unfortunate event, regretfully brought about by social progress to the point where it is no longer possible to uphold a system of drug prohibition.

This might sound cynical, but *power knows no morality and never abdicates willingly*. History proves it, for every time authority has yielded its powers and given the people a greater degree of freedom it has been because of necessity. The idea has been to give a little in order not to lose everything—and that is it.

After all, our institutions are climbing places for that percentage of the population which is the most eager to play along with the game. Its rules are quite simple: follow the path of least resistance, speculate in fear, and let the system's force of inertia work its magic. To the degree this is done, the status quo will not only be preserved but their power and authority will increase vis-à-vis other competing agencies and the population at large. The Norwegian justice system is no different. And so, even if those responsible will later pretend that it was a glitch, an anomaly and a terrible mistake that the rule of law somehow was put aside, truth is otherwise.

Taking the dynamics of system theory into consideration, it is more likely that these judges—as the politicians, the police, and the Justice Department before them—not only knew what they were doing, but *that they did exactly what they were expected to do*[113]. Not from the perspective of constitutional obligations, of course. However, we know that the state represents the elite and not the people, and so "separation of powers", "a defendant's right to a fair trial", "a court of law established in accordance with principles of reliability, impartiality, adversariality, equality, fairness, justice, proportionality", and so on, are but slogans the operators exploit to legitimize practice. Rulers love these words as they make them all warm and fuzzy inside. Nevertheless, no matter how much lip-service they pay to expressing these ideals, anyone remotely familiar with the criminal justice system knows that it is a charade.

While there is a liberty presumption in the Constitution and this puts the burden of evidence on the state, the fact of the matter is that disputes between the individual and the state are usually settled in favor of the latter. The exceptions are, as we saw an example of with the shipowners, those times when the government does not properly play along with elite aspirations. When the Norwegian government wanted them to pay taxes built up from 1996 until 2007 (when tax rules were changed and

---

[113] An indication is that the Appeals Court judge, shortly after denying to the drug law violators a right to have the legality of the law reviewed, was rewarded with a seat in the Supreme Court.

shipowners could operate with virtually no tax liability), the justice system ruled against the state. Even so, for the rest of us there is never "equality of arms", "equality before law", or "innocent until proven guilty". Stuff like this belongs to the imaginative world that system representatives like to write books about, whereas in reality justice is dispersed accordingly: The lower a defendant's social status, the more the burden of evidence is turned against him; the more likely he is to go to prison; and the stricter his sentencing.

This fundamental trait permeates every country's legal system. Not because of a malfunction—or any other variable that operators may point to—but due to its very design. The real purpose of the justice system, after all, is to provide a legal outlet for the scapegoating mechanism. History leaves no doubt about it and this explains both (1) why elites have introduced a system of arbitrary law and (2) why the populace has accepted the injustice that follows in its wake. It is to be expected, then, that the system is horrible to outgroups. And as population control is the true purpose of our system of law, this also explains why the wars on terror and drugs—the elite's sacred cows—have avoided critical review. If it were not for these campaigns, the population control that the elite works so hard to maintain would have lost legitimacy. In its place a less fear-driven social dynamic would have grown forth and this would have been bad for war profiteers and their social engineers.

Cynical as it may seem, I believe this is the reason why public officials assist in the cover-up of presidential assassinations, terror operations, or wars of aggression. They do not have the integrity to look where the system does not want anything found and so they keep ignoring reality. This is also the psychological mechanism that keeps protecting the drug law and why the judges at the Norwegian Supreme Court (and later, the European Court of Human Rights) refused to do their job. For it must be made clear: *It was not up to the judges to let their instincts determine whether drug prohibition was consistent with human rights. As the argument had been made that the law was in violation of human rights—and as evidence that supported the allegation was presented—it was their duty, nothing less, to let the issue be determined by an independent, impartial, and competent court.*

It should be emphasized that the Norwegian Supreme Court did not act alone in obstructing justice. After the system had denied justice to violators, the Alliance for Rights-Oriented Drug Policies (AROD) was created to enlighten politicians and citizens on the importance of rights-oriented drug policies and this organization contacted civil servants across the board to stop unjust persecution. As it was up to the State to present good reasons for the status quo, AROD presented five questions that had to be answered by those responsible for policy, but every department failed to respond—and has continued to do so until this day.

Without going into too much detail, the Parliament's Health- and Justice committees, several Prime Ministers, Justice Ministers (I think there were five, actually), Health Ministers, as well as other politicians, departments and officials have been instructed on their duties. Even so, the drug laws have corrupted society to such an extent that Norwegian officials collectively have failed their obligations to human rights.

The rights-oriented debate has not only been silenced by civil servants. In Norway moral panic is so conditioned that most of the organizations in the area of drug policy have sided with the system, effectively barring violators an opportunity for justice. Even among intellectuals the charade is evident, as AROD has contacted professors from a wide diversity of fields and few care to respond with a defense of drug users or the prohibition law. Instead, they can be found on TV and other media appearances where they keep talking about "justice", "the rule of law", and so on, as if everything is ok. Hence, the hold that the collective psyche has on these souls is plain to see—and not one journalist thinks it is worth mentioning that Norway, as the nation celebrates 200-years of constitutional law, is reduced to a police state, actively engaged in two major crimes against humanity.

Internationally, things are not much better. To resolve this issue, a complaint was filed to the European Court of Human Rights in 2010, asking judges to review the legality of the drug laws. As the issue concerned the rights of more than 40 million Europeans, it was the most important case the Court ever accepted, and one should expect it to be treated accordingly. Still, the Court proved more eager to protect the Norwegian State (and the drug laws) from the serious allegations than its own reputation. In a single judge setting, the Court dismissed the matter for reasons of incompetence. Considering that the European Convention states that drug users are entitled to have the issue decided by *a competent court*, this decision would be comical if not for its implications. AROD, therefore, asked the president of the Court and the Secretary General to intervene but both washed their hands of this decision, leaving drug law violators hanging.

As far as the European Court of Human Rights goes, that was it. On one hand, not much productive happened but on the other the actions of the Court spoke volumes. Perhaps, then, in the long run, something good will come of this decision as the Court has shirked its obligations towards the rule of law to the point where all credibility as a promoter and protector of human rights is lost. Instead, the Court has shown its true colors and to this day remains an instrument of oppressors.

These may be harsh words. However, by any objective standard they describe the situation neatly, and as more and more constitutional courts (Alaska, Mexico, Colombia, Georgia, South Africa) invalidate the persecution of drug users, the European Court—and the nation of Norway—should rethink its position. After all, at the Council of Europe and elsewhere there is increasing commitment to policies embedded in the human rights paradigm. There is also a recognition that the status quo is incompatible with human rights concerns and its drug policy arm, the Pompidou Group, encourages member states to undertake further investigations. This is a sign that the rights-oriented debate is growing upon us and that the drug control conventions—and the drug laws—one day will be consigned to the rubbish heap of history.

In the meantime, not only the European Court, the COE, the UN, and the state of Norway, but also all other states continue to reach far beneath their potential, and we shall now look at the blueprint for a more positive future.

PART 6

THE ROAD AHEAD

29
INTRODUCTION

"What, then, is the rightful limit to the sovereignty of the individual over himself? Where does the authority of society begin? How much of human life should be assigned to individuality, and how much to society? . . . [These are] questions seldom stated, and hardly ever discussed, in general terms, but which profoundly influences the practical controversies of the age by its latent presence, and is likely soon to make itself recognized as the vital question of the future." (71.109,5)

—John Stuart Mill, 1859—

WE HAVE DISCUSSED how the logic of fear has led to a gap between theory and practice. Hence, not much is left of the freedom-loving tradition that we pledge allegiance to. Its basic premise is that the government shall be a tool utilized to preserve the interests of the individual and society at large. As a society, however, is nothing but the sum of its parts, the whole idea is to give to each individual as much freedom, responsibility and self-determination as possible. All laws and regulations are to be measured against this fundamental principle, but as we have seen there are activities that cannot be justified within this framework.

The War on Terror and the War on Drugs are the most obvious examples. Even so, these campaigns are no more than a sign of the times and looking at the larger picture, we find that a persistent variable has been the increasingly oppressive and omnipresent intervention of government in what was previously recognized as the individual's sphere of influence. Thus, while we remain constitutionally bound to perimeters of right reason—to steer our ships of State by the lights of those values, principles, and ideals that follow from the Wholeness—mankind has forgot about the connection between freedom and responsibility, subjecting society to a mighty spell of unconsciousness.

Looking back, this dynamic could not have unfolded without some serious social engineering skills. A more levelheaded population would have reacted to the evermore extensive regulation of everyday life. They would not have fought wars built on lies and deception, and they would not so easily have given up previously recognized rights and freedoms. Instead, they would have acted upon their natural inclination to cooperate and thrive and, knowing this, control-oriented elites have facilitated for a dynamic which made us more docile and powerless.

When it comes to this, fear is the weapon and enemy images are encouraged to subvert thinking. Looking at history, no sane person can trust government to know the difference between right and wrong. Even so, we have become so habituated to the behavior of our leaders and their constant meddling in our lives that we hardly know how to react. Not only that, but so effective has the elite manufactured consent that the most important question: where the line should be drawn between the individual and the government's sphere of influence? has remained a non-issue.

That is, *superficially* it is often enough discussed, as politicians will say that they take it into consideration every time they pass a new law and further expand their position of power. Even so, a *principled* public debate on the issue has remained virtually nonexistent—and the reason is that we have drifted so far from the principles of the Social Contract that it would be impossible for officials to justify decisions in this manner. As Forrest McDonald, an expert on the U.S. Constitution said:

> "The Government [today] interferes on a level in ordinary
> people's lives in a way they [the Founding Fathers] would
> have regarded as the most vicious form of tyranny

imaginable. George the Third[114] and all of his ministers could not have imagined a government this big, this intrusive."(106.25)

Our leaders do what they can to avoid that we notice or react to this widening gap between theory and practice. On the one hand, they fill us with fear so that they can present their system of government as a protective and well-intentioned entity and on the other they blind us with talk of shining ideals. The idea is to feed us a steady diet of lies and illusions; it is to dazzle with appearances so that we do not recognize—and react to—the fact that the state apparatus, rather than being a mere provider of services, is what it always has been: an instrument whose primary function is to dominate populations on behalf of control-oriented elites.

Be that as it may, people are increasingly waking up to recognize the reality behind power-political schemes, enemy images, and divide-and-conquer techniques. This again is a result of the times, for as we have discussed the wheeling and dealing of corrupt government agents and elites are part of a much greater game called the Universe's grand play and we are now in a period of transition in which the darkness is retiring after having dominated for thousands of years.

Remember that from the cosmic consciousness' perspective, the darkness is a necessary tool for growth. The darkness is not only the Light that has forgot about itself; it is also a means to its own remembering, and now that it has played out its role we can—as the presence of light increases—expect to see ever more of that which was hidden come out in the open. As a result, those who cling to the old—those who are used to getting their way with threats, manipulation, and intrigue—can expect a difficult time, for along with the increased consciousness-raising a dynamic will unfold which is the opposite of the one that has prevailed.

---

[114] George the Third was the British king whose taxes and laws were so intolerable that Americans claimed their dependence. To the Founding Fathers, his government was synonymous with all they detested, thus inspiring the American Revolution, the Declaration of Independence, and the U.S. Constitution.

The reason for this is that the dynamic unfolding between the individual and society is a variable in constant flux—and what changes it is our level of consciousness. I explain this more fully in *To Right a Wrong*,[115] a book that explains how the evolution of consciousness affects systems of law and politics. The gist of it is simple, for while the psychology of love paves the way for enlightened minds and societies, the psychology of fear preserves and generates trauma which leads to totalitarian government. To social engineers, therefore, the powers of love and fear are prime determiners. And while oppressive societies are defined by unconsciousness—and, to survive, encourage deception and fear—we find that freedom loving, healthy societies arise naturally whenever a population has matured sufficiently to deal with the implications of Wholeness.

In other words, it was only confused thinking and a bewildered relationship to our inner reality which made possible the dynamic of escalating state power and hypocrisy. This becomes clear when we remember that the external world reflects humanity's inner world. According to the new existence theory, therefore, we will get exactly the kind of leaders we deserve—and it is precisely because we have ignored the inner reality (which is also the greater reality) that we have ended up in dire straits.

Indeed, on the scales of constitutional reasoning, autonomy and tyranny is not only opposed, but as the inner and the outer world mirror each other, *we must first look at ourselves* if we want to see leaders acting less fear-oriented, self-righteous, deceitful, and corrupt. We must build integrity at the individual level by standing firm with those values, ideals, and principles that follow from the Wholeness, as to the extent we reject these qualities in ourselves we will have public officials who do the same.

While controversial, this is self-evident. Integrity-building at the Nation level presupposes a people who care sufficiently about right and wrong to hold accountable those who abuse the authority of state, and a citizenry capable of taking responsibility would never have succumbed to an apparatus so eager to govern at their expense. Collectively speaking,

---

[115] MIKALSEN, *TO RIGHT A WRONG: A TRANSPERSONAL FRAMEWORK FOR CONSTITUTIONAL CONSTRUCTION*

therefore, the current gap between theory and practice reflects the average citizen's ability to deceive himself. It is a testimony to our neglect of first principles, and to the extent that we get our act together the distance will also disappear.

To understand this better, perhaps we should remember Francois de La Rochefoucauld's quip that "hypocrisy is the homage that vice pays to virtue." Even though we do not always act honorably, we know in our hearts the difference between right and wrong, and looking at those instances where we act against our better judgment (meaning a course of action which contradicts the ideals, values, and principles that follow from Wholeness) we find that it is not really a reflection of evil. Rather, when all is said and done, it boils down to the logic of fear's influence. It is the result of deranged thinking coming from an ego that is transfixed by trauma—and when we take into consideration that "theory" mirrors what we know is right, while "practice" reflects what we, for various reasons, choose to do, it is easy to see that this logic is ultimately the problem.

The logic of fear, however, is merely the result of delusional beliefs. Had we known better, we would have seen the dynamic it brings about, and we would have stopped projecting inner fears onto the environment only to fight their shadow in a battle that we cannot win. Be that as it may, it takes a certain degree of maturity before we are able to understand the relationship between the inner and the outer world. It takes a while before we seek truthfulness, and as humanity is still in adolescence we have not yet taken this lesson to heart. All we can see in the news is a testimony to this. Nonetheless, *only by going within* can the impact of the logic of fear be reduced—and to the extent that we collectively rise to the challenge, we will not only see theory and practice become one, but our leaders will represent the best of humanity instead of the worst.

As it stands though, honest and astute politicians have little chance of effecting change. The reason is that the body politic reflects the average citizen's values and understanding—and because most people tend to be rather short-sighted and self-absorbed, the political apparatus responds in kind. Thus, politicians who demonstrate courage by going into/recognizing the gap between theory and practice will be opposed by indignant peers. Lacking themselves enough integrity to oppose the mindless ramblings of mass-culture, the latter will retaliate against anything that threatens the illusion they have spun—and this is why the public debate about important matters remains absent. The system's force of inertia ensures that integrity is punished wherever it is found, and the result is systems of arbitrary law and politics. On those grounds, nothing functional can ever be built. Only lies can maintain the status quo and Psychiatrist Wilhelm Reich summarized the result:

> "It is in the nature of a political party that it does not orient itself in terms of truth, but in terms of illusions, which usually corresponds to the irrational structure of the masses. Scientific truths merely interfere with the party politician's habit of wriggling himself out of difficulties with the help of illusions."(86.210)

This was the situation a 1000 years ago. This was the situation a 100 years ago. And this the situation today. And so, we should not be surprised that most politicians support wars on terror and drugs, even if every thinking person knows that these campaigns' intellectual, legal, and moral credibility is non-existent.

Now, thankfully, the mismanagement and abuse of authority has never gone entirely unnoticed. At any given time, a certain percentage has seen through political deceit, and had not a majority been functioning at the same level of cognition which inspired Nazism the despotic inclinations of rulers would have been arrested. Even so, psychologically speaking, when it comes to humans, there is not much that separates the most astute from the most impeded and only a minimal upgrade of the global psyche will lead to changes which will have huge repercussions.

After all, our leaders' lies have never been very convincing. And the elites have only been able to do what they have done because most people remained willfully ignorant. Now that the light is coming back, however, the fog of illusions is lifting. It evaporates like dew to the sun and as this process takes place the distance between theory and practice is not only becoming more difficult to hide but harder not to notice.

In the days to come, therefore, the authority of government will suffer. The credibility of its representatives as suppliers of truth will expire and people will be forced to think for themselves. It goes without saying that this will be fatal for those devoted to practice rather than theory, for the dam of fear and ignorance which has blinded us from seeing the greater reality will burst and the upheaval that is becoming ever more pressing will register in full force.

Even if things seem quiet on the surface, this process has already begun. And the momentum for change is building rapidly as it becomes increasingly obvious that the old way of thinking has exhausted its possibilities. In fact, we live in the midst of times long foretold: We are about to witness the process of evolution's most amazing quantum leap, humanity's crowning achievement, and although the force of renewal has yet to reach fever pitch nothing can stop this prophecy. In this final part of the book, we shall see what it entails for society when the new existence theory becomes recognized. The reader can hardly imagine the world that is set to arise from the ashes of the old, for as the psychologist Abraham Maslow said:

> "When the philosophy of man changes, then everything changes. Not only the philosophy of politics, of economics, of ethics and values, of interpersonal relations and of history itself, but also the philosophy of education, of psychotherapy and of personal growth, the theory of how to help men become what they can and deeply need to become. We are now in the middle of such a change in the conception of man's capacities, potentialities and goals. A new vision is emerging of the possibilities of man and of his destiny, and its implications are many, not only for our conceptions of education, but also for science, politics, literature, economics, religion, and even our conceptions of the non-human world."(69.189)

As Maslow makes clear, the new existence theory is bound to affect how we organize all areas of society. Its implications are profound and to the extent we take them seriously, we will create a paradise on earth.

The reason for this is that none of the problems we are faced with are purely political, economic, or social. If we look more closely, we will find that they are truly spiritual, for in all cases they lead back to a mindset that organized religion and the Neo-Darwinist theory of evolution has brought to bear. We have already discussed how none of them make it possible to see ourselves as the sacred, indelible, and invaluable fragments of Godhood that we are. To the extent we believe in established science we will see ourselves as insignificant, short-lived, and worthless beings brought forth by a haphazard Universe devoid of meaning, while to the extent we adhere to the dogmas of religion we will think that we are sinful, depraved, and unworthy creatures subject to the will of a punitive, petty, and vindictive God.

These fundamental assumptions are not only wrong but harmful. In fact, if we are looking for the root of much evil, we need look no further as most of our stupidities have been the result of one or the other. Unfortunately, both these belief systems still carry a great influence on the social fabric. Those with a vested interest in the status quo will defend their convictions fiercely and no matter how adverse the consequences they will not question basic premises. It is a strange affliction indeed. But no matter how limited, disastrous, erroneous or disempowering our belief systems are—and no matter how good news it would be to discover that we were wrong—we often have great difficulty in letting go.

In a sense, then, we are all addicted to our beliefs and the more ingrained our thinking the harder it is to break an addiction. To many, the ways of the old have such a hold that no reasoning or evidence to the contrary can convince them otherwise. Thus, it will take time before a paradigm shift of the magnitude that we are aiming at can be completed. As seen from the consciousness-comes-first perspective, the belief systems that result from the theory of evolution and organized religion can be understood as viruses in the collective consciousness. There they roam about doing their damage. But while it will take some time before society has managed to recuperate none of these dribblings of unconsciousness will survive the passing of time.

Historically speaking, the time allotted has run out. They have both played their role. And since the new existence theory puts them both to shame the supporters of the status quo will find that, to the extent they grasp for the old, they will lose both credibility and terrain. As Jesus himself said, "By their fruits ye shall know them." And when we look at the damage that the Church, with its persecution of pagans and other dissidents, and the State—with its loyalty to the control-oriented elite—has inflicted on the social fabric, it is obvious what kind of institutions we are dealing with.

Hence, none of them can expect to remain untouched by the winds of change. The new way of society will mirror those values, ideals, and principles that follow from Wholeness; our current society does not, and as the task of building a better, more humane/sane world becomes a priority our authorities, whether they be religious or secular, will find that they must adapt or perish.

We shall now learn more about the coming change and what it entails for how we organize as a society.

30
THE DYNAMICS BETWEEN THE INDIVIDUAL AND THE STATE

"There will never be a really free and enlightened State, until the State comes to recognize the individual as a higher and independent power, from which all of its own power and authority are derived, and treats him accordingly.

I please myself with imagining a State at last which can afford to be just to all men, and to treat the individual with respect as a neighbour; which even would not think it inconsistent with its own repose, if a few were to live aloof from it, not meddling with it, nor embraced by it, who fulfilled all the duties of neighbours and fellow men. A State which bore this kind of fruit, and suffered it to drop as fast as it ripened, would prepare the way for a still more perfect and glorious State, which also I have imagined, but not yet anywhere seen." (110.41)

—Henry David Thoreau, 1849—

THE READER MAY remember from chapter one that Thoreau was one of the people R.M. Bucke discussed as a representative of the new consciousness. This quote indicates why, as Thoreau's vision will come to pass when the new existence theory has worked its wonders.

Remember that the founding principle of the Social Contract, as recognized by constitutional law, is that the state apparatus shall be a service agency which ensures that the machinery of society functions optimally—and that is it. The fact that the State has grown out of proportion and is now messing with our lives in a way that would have been unthinkable to the visionaries of the Enlightenment does nothing to change this basic premise: As we have seen, the dynamics that have unfolded between the individual and the State is a result of increasingly crippled thinking, and it is time to reverse the trend.

"Increasingly crippled thinking" might be harsh. Even so, the State and the individual's sphere of influence must be seen as two opposing poles, for to the extent that one expands the other will be reduced. A more vigilant citizenry, therefore, would have stood its ground against attempts to increase the State's influence. Recognizing that freedom comes with responsibility, attentive citizens would have been a barrier against tyranny—and so, to the degree that the State has grown, it must mirror an increasingly pitiable demeanor. However, now that the light is returning, a consciousness-raising process takes place. This means that no matter how much public officials talk about "freedom" and "human rights", celebrating this as if the fight for these ideals was truly spearheaded by government, the equation above will become increasingly obvious. As it does, people will begin to see the State as a wolf in sheep's clothing: We will understand that the State cannot possibly be a champion of freedom or civil rights because the State, by virtue of its very nature, has a vested interest in increasing its sphere of influence—which it can only do at the expense of ours.

In other words, *only individuals can be freedom fighters and human rights defenders*. And that the State, despite insurances to the contrary, represents the greatest possible threat to our liberty is not only revealed by history but current conditions. After all, if the concept of freedom is to have any meaning, it must be a measure of the power we have to do with our lives and property as we please. Only to the degree that this is actualized will the constitutionally established right to life, liberty, and the pursuit of happiness be of any consequence and we have never been more enslaved.

A look at current conditions leaves no doubt about it. Not only has the justice system of America put more men behind bars than any nation in previous centuries; as we have seen, even the citizens of Norway, one of the most stable democracies, are openly being subjected to absolutist government and things are not much better elsewhere.

Indeed, worldwide, if a drug user, drug dealer, or prostitute should attempt to claim autonomy rights, it is easy to predict that government agents will set aside the rule of law rather than let the citizenry seek protection in human rights conventions. Civil servants across the board have become so habituated to ignoring first principles that they hardly consider the implications, and we are hard pressed to find a government that does not treat its whistleblowers and human rights defenders as if they were terrorists.[116] Just look at how governments have treated Julian Assange, Chelsea Manning, or Edward Snowden. Worse yet, look at what the American political machine did to Senator Huey Pierce Long Jr., President John F. Kennedy, Rev. Martin Luther King, Seth Rich, and many others: They were murdered for their efforts to oppose or expose the emerging Deep State monstrosity.

Even so, the fact that governments have gone rouge is not all bad. For one, these giant beasts of the collective unconscious were never tame to begin with. They were always the tools of oppressors, the chains to our slavery, and it took some serious indoctrination to ensure loyalty to a system that preached wholesome values while practicing the opposite.[117] Not only must integrity be shunned; our value-system must be reversed, and it requires a great deal of painful, fear-induced energy to ensure the furtherance of this plot. Even more, it demands a steady state of insentience, of forgetfulness, one where society embraces madness over reason. Today, it is this spur that keeps us going, and having lulled ourselves into a sleep of timeless magnitude it takes more than a whisper to wake up.

Thus, we can see our leaders' behavior as a negative catalyst for change. After all, it is clear that events need be taken to an extreme before the average citizen wakes up from the illusion that "authority" knows better than him how to regulate his own private affairs. Our officials'

---

[116] Human rights activists in the Middle East, Africa, Latin America, Russia, China, and elsewhere in Asia are executed by their governments on a regular basis and it also happens in Europe and the United States, even if the media ignores it.

[117] The pride with which mothers and fathers throughout history have sent young boys to fight and die in the service of totalitarian agendas is just one of many indications that we are victims of a satanic plot, for it is in the reversal of values that the darkness remains hidden.

eagerness to protect us, however, have proven so misguided that this awareness is rapidly dawning, and so the war on drugs and terrorism can be seen as an IQ-test that people must pass to merit successful living. The reasoning and the lies that support these campaigns simply do not add up and people are now awakening to the horror show of a government on steroids—one run by powerful special interests and officials who have forgotten their place within the greater scheme of things.

As this recognition dawns, it is becoming increasingly clear that, as John Stuart Mill said, "there is a limit to the legitimate interference of the collective opinion with individual independence: and to find that limit, and maintain it against encroachment, is as indispensable to a good condition of human affairs, as protection against political despotism."(71.10) And when this issue becomes a concern and people begin to reflect on the nature of this limit, it also becomes clear that the issue must be discussed on principled grounds.

This understanding is as old as civilization. And because all true knowledge is timeless, anyone who thinks seriously about the issue will conclude that the principle most apt to protect the interests of the individual and society is that *the State shall limit its intervention to those instances where it is a matter of individual or collective self-defense.*

Now, as we know, this principle summarizes the basis for the Social Contract, and we find it reflected in our constitutions and human rights conventions. In other words, *it is a principle beyond dispute*: Even the disciples of the police state will agree with it—and that is precisely the problem. We know by now that no matter how totalitarian a state becomes its officials will argue that its actions are for the good of all and in defense against some perceived threat. Thus, this principle is useless, unless we include the liberty presumption and agree with Mill that:

> "The only purpose for which power can be rightfully exercised over any member of a civilized community, against his will, is to prevent harm to others. His own good, either physical or moral, is not a sufficient warrant. He cannot rightfully be compelled to do or forbear because it will be better for him to do so, because it will make him happier, because, in the opinion of others, to do so would

be wise, or even right. These are good reasons for remonstrating with him, or reasoning with him . . . but not for compelling him, or visiting him with any evil in case he does otherwise. To justify that, the conduct from which it is desired to deter him, must be calculated to produce evil to someone else. The only part of the conduct of any one, for which he is amenable to society, is that which concerns others. In the part which merely constitutes himself, his independence is, of right, absolute. Over himself, over his own body and mind, the individual is sovereign."(71.17)

Now, that is more like it. And even if some will oppose a principle that so clearly limits the State's right to intervene in our daily lives, objections fall flat. After all, no matter how altruistically motivated they purport to be, the essence of their argument is not only that they (1) know better than others their own good, but (2) that they have a right to force upon others their opinion with the violence of law—and those who embrace such reasoning should not be allowed to govern in our affairs.

History speaks volumes about the kind of regimes this thinking generates. And although it is quite true that we rarely make the best decisions as measured against a hypothetical ideal; that most of us would be better off if we drank less, spent less time watching TV, playing videogames, surfing the internet for porn, and instead exercised more, ate more healthy foods, cared more for others, and so on, we should be mindful of the pitfalls of enacting laws aimed at regulating behavior.

As a matter of fact, as most of the misfortunes that have afflicted humanity are the result of such thinking, the proportionality principle forbids it. This principle renders any "cure that is worse than the disease" incompatible with constitutional law. And as history leaves no doubt that whatever "errors we are likely to commit against advice and warning", as Mill said, are "far outweighed by the evil of allowing others to constrain our actions for what they deem to be our own good", it follows that the individual's freedom to do with his/her own mind, body, and property what he/she wills must be *absolute*.

It is a simple as adding two and two together. Not even the fact that alcohol and drug abuse can be said to affect others legitimizes legal intervention, for as Mill pointed out: "Mankind are greater gainers by suffering each other to live as seems good to themselves, than by compelling each to live as seems good to the rest."(71.21)

Consequently, even if politicians tend to think that their actions are necessary, the concept of freedom will only be meaningful to the degree that we hold true to this ground. The liberty presumption dictates that weighty reasons must be presented to infringe upon the freedom of individuals—and while the task of balancing the right to liberty against society's right to protection may be somewhat less precise (and more difficult) than Mill's principle conveys, the proportionality analysis that has been developed by constitutional courts echoes this understanding.

Thus, even though the modern system of human rights has arisen as a result of the need for legal scholars to tidy out some equations, John Stuart Mill was a reminder of the spirit that moved the founders. They were, after all, representatives of Freedom and as any prophet before him Mill defended the individual against the dangers of collectivism.[118] He did not need the Nazi movement to know that tyranny hid beneath its tempting allure, for also he knew that autonomy and tyranny was perpetually opposed and that utopian societies could only arise out of integrity building. He therefore predicted that to the extent we recoiled from this principle Western civilization would fail, for as he said, "such tyranny, penetrating deep into the details of life, enslaves the soul itself."

That he was right is plain to see. Since Mill wrote this in 1859, agents of State have slowly repressed autonomy rights, thus enslaving populations. On behalf of corporations, gangsters, and war profiteers, social engineers have streamlined society—and as we have seen, their interests are diametrically opposed to ours.

Not only do they thrive on fear, but control-oriented elites must keep human self-confidence at an absolute minimum. This is their first order of business, for only to the degree that this is done will people accept their message that we need their brands to be happy, that we need their protection to be safe, and that we need their wisdom to get by. Quite simply, those in authority are trying to sell us the idea *that we are nothing*

---

[118] See MIKALSEN, *HUMAN RISING* (2019) for more on how the morality of the prophets and the founders were one and the same.

without them, and it follows from this equation that true individuality—meaning originality, self-knowledge, integrity, sense of responsibility, etc.—is not what they want to encourage.

The elites' engineers know a thing or two about population control and they understand that to the extent we are in touch with our inner-Self we will see through their lies and deceptions. Hence, they divert attention from the self-actualization process. Instead, they try to inspire "actualization" in the context of military service, the buying of brand clothes, or a career in the system. In other words, they do everything to ensure that we remain as comatose as practically possible—and that we look anywhere but to ourselves for answers.

It is obvious, however, that no good can come of this. A society is nothing more than the sum of its individuals and because individuality is synonymous with *inner development*, society can only prosper to the extent that we allow it to flourish. This is uncontroversial and Mill expressed it this way:

> "The worth of a State, in the long run, is the worth of the individuals composing it; and a State which postpones the interests of their mental expansion and elevation, to have a little more of administrative skill, or that semblance of it which practice gives, in the details of business; a State which dwarfs its men, in order that they may be more docile instruments in its hands even for beneficial purposes—will find that with small men no great thing can really be accomplished; and that the perfection of machinery to which it has sacrificed everything, will in the end avail to nothing, for want of the vital power which, in order that the machine might work more smoothly, it has preferred to banish."(71.168)

As we can see, we are talking timeless truth. Only the building of integrity—of representing the ideals, values, and principles that follow from the Wholeness—can realize inherent potentials, individually and en masse. If we are to lift ourselves as a civilization out of the darkness of unconsciousness that surrounds us, therefore, we must be the change we want to see, and the engineering of a system built on the new existence theory implies nothing more than putting the discernment of our great thinkers to good use.

Indeed, if we do our research, we will find that they have all, to the extent that they have been in touch with the greater reality, agreed on the gist of it. From Tacitus in ancient Rome who said that "The more corrupt the state, the more numerous its laws"; to Spinoza, 1700 years later, who said that "the true purpose of the state is in fact freedom"; to Hegel who said, in the early 19th century, that "this march of freedom is what the World Spirit wants, as it seeks to realize itself"; to Bjornson who 50 years later said "That evil must be good and wrong must be right when the government demands it—this is the enemy"; and so on, and so on. The key to integrity building and to higher reasoning has always been to represent the ideals, values, and principles that follow from the Wholeness. If we commit to this, we will overcome the trauma (the limited and deranged thinking) that comes with being born into lesser-ordered societies, and our most advanced thinkers are those who have penetrated the collective unconscious, the mass-culture of our day, to see the greater reality beyond.

This is how they have brought society forward. By holding up a mirror and showing contemporary humans their foolish ways, they have shaken ill-conceived preconvictions and allowed for a greater truth to emerge. In literature, physics, religion, mind sciences, politics, and other arenas these frontrunners have challenged the old. And to the extent that they have excelled they have all known that the individual is the alpha and omega; that we are born free and equal, with the right to pursue our happiness; that we have the same right to self-determination over our lives and property—be it our body, thoughts, or possessions; and that the power of love is the force that brings us forward, helping us realize inherent potentials.

However, they have also known that individuals, unfortunately, do not always behave respectably and that we sometimes violate the right of others to the same liberties as ours. Thus, they have understood that the State, with its monopoly of force, is a necessary arrangement for the safeguarding of rights and ensuring the welfare of society.

All this has been plain as day. Even so, logic dictates that the state apparatus can never be better than that allowed for by the quality of the national psyche. And while we have matured to the point where we, at least, recognize wholesome values and government principles, it is easy to see that mankind remains an immature entity consisting of individuals who all too often see self-interest and public interest as two opposing variables. Not only that, but it has been a constant feature of our civilization-building that the state apparatus, as a result of us living in a divided society, ends up being a tool for a minority's oppression of the majority. More astute thinkers, therefore, have seen the distance between theory and practice, aware that the state apparatus, instead of functioning as it was supposed to, has been an arena for power seekers and special interests whose priority has been self-enrichment.

Nevertheless, while this has been the way of the world, the great thinkers, sages, and prophets have perceived in mankind a higher calling. An inner knowing has produced a certainty that the ideals, values, and principles behind our social order must be more than mere weightless formalities and naive notions that rulers could exploit to divert attention. This inner knowing resulted in the conviction that these ideals, on the contrary, were *far more real* than anything the physical system could contain. For while what we see around us is no more than a temporary expression of humanity's trials and errors, the idea-gestalt from which such principles as equality, proportionality, autonomy, and the liberty presumption are derived mirror a larger, more timeless and fundamental reality.

As a matter of fact, they originate from the Wholeness; they reflect the sum of all that is, and these idea-shapes are even more primary to our existence than archetypes of the psyche, or elements of earth, water, and fire. Together they make up that emergency relief package which God has instilled in all soul fragments so that, guided by their light, we can again realize ourselves as all that is. As the stars above us, therefore, these values, ideals, and principles carry within a promise of something more and they have a reality that far exceeds anything the physical system can muster. Because they have their origin in a World infinitely greater than temporary reality, their light produces a shadow even in the smallest of minds; they are something elevated, something humanity can strive for and reach for—and to the extent that we honor their implications, they offer a roadmap.

That the vast majority have ignored this roadmap changes nothing. These ideals are infinitely more powerful than matter, time, and space, and even if we should erase life as we know it, it would no more impair their reality than that of Spirit. There is in fact nothing humans can do to upset the balance of the Cosmos at the deeper levels. Just as Spirit veils itself in the world of matter, so Wholeness hides in diversity—and no matter how blind we are to the greater reality, the Universe's exhalation and inhalation process continues unperturbed.

The realization of Spirit through matter and Wholeness through the pressure of duality, therefore, is an intrinsic part of a prophecy that the Universe's divine order will see fulfilled. And no matter how blind we may be to the greater reality, its inherent power will ensure that humanity—and the Universe—matures into something more.

Lucky for us, it cannot be helped. Whatever we decide to do, we grow richer in experience and no matter how ignorant our thoughts and actions, experience is transformed into understanding. As mentioned, a characteristic of consciousness is *response-ability*. Our maturity level is determined by this capability and just as the most dimwitted, after experiencing fire burn, will stop touching its flame we will all—sooner or later—bring the Wholeness into our calculations. Evidently, it takes some time before humanity en masse has wised up to realize the importance of our constitutional heritage. Even so, despite our failures, experience is amassed into understanding in the global psyche and it follows that a greater and greater percentage are unwilling to compromise their ideals.

Looking back at history, we see this process clearly. The evolution of our justice system is an exact mirror of this process, and *this is why* ideas of legitimacy come and go.

We discussed in chapter 22 how the principles of law are both simple and eternal. As individuals, however, we are blinded from their light by the cultural and moral climate and so it is that these principles are only gradually (re)discovered. To take the principle of equality as an example, it has been part of our legal system since at least Cicero and Roman law. Even if it has yet to be fully realized, its ideal has always inspired our brightest minds and they, in turn, have moved society in a direction closer to its proximity. Thus, legal history documents how this principle has made its influence known—and that the more humanity has matured, the more its light has been allowed to shine through, allowing for more wholesome societies. The establishment of human right conventions was an important milestone in this regard. And we have now matured to the point where this principle can be realized to its fullest extent, letting go of old and disserving prejudices.

Not only must drug users, prostitutes, and others be included into society but the scapegoating phenomenon in all forms must be wiped out if we are to build integrity at the nation level. It can only be obliterated by a collective effort to choose consciousness above unconsciousness and if we want to know where the bodies are buried, we need only look at society's taboos. They are a sure indication where reason is not allowed, and the War on Terror and the War on Drugs are cases in point.

There is nothing more destructive to the social fiber than mass-movements gone wrong and the enemy images are always behind, blinding us to our ill-begotten ways. In taking a greater view on history, however, we find that a primary reason for our failure to manifest a more perfect society has been our dualistic thinking. We have been accustomed to thinking in terms of good and evil, life and death, self-interest and public interest, science and religion, matter and spirit, body and mind, emotion and reason, subject and object—in short, in black and white and of us and the world as two different things.

This thinking has generated a distance between theory and practice, for while theory reflects the Wholeness, practice is a result of dualistic thinking. Nevertheless, such a mindset is only the outcome of our ignorance of the greater reality; it is the result of inferior analytic reasoning and seen from a larger perspective, the contradictions inherent in the dualistic point of view are overcome by reasoning from an ever more unified Whole. Hence, as seen from an enlightened mind's perspective, the futility of dualistic thinking appears plain[119]. And even

---

[119] The dualistic mind sees the world from a fragmented perspective; it only sees the pieces of a jigsaw puzzle, while the enlightened mind sees the entire puzzle. To the dualistic mind, therefore, it seems impossible to judge whether a blue piece signifies water or air—or something else. To the enlightened mind, however, it is plain as day

if the jump to a more holistic perspective may seem like a leap of fate, it is no such thing. In fact, it is the logical result of a more organized and higher-functioning mind—it is the snake that bites its tail, allowing for ever more solid ground.

It is this—the bridging of apparent duality—that is the essence of self-actualization. To the extent that we can reconcile contradictions, we reach a deeper understanding, and the result is a form of consciousness that increasingly makes us one with the Universe. We have already seen how spirit and matter, life and death, science and religion, body and mind, emotion and reason, subject and object, etc. are all part of a greater Whole and we have also seen that there is no genuine evil—only ignorance of our true nature and the greater reality. It is this ignorance that makes us receptive to the influence of the logic of fear, and when we know that this has caused all our problems, we also know how we can redeem ourselves.

We shall have more to say on this. However, to discuss the implications for society as more and more are seeing beyond duality, current practice will become a thing of the past.

One reason for this is that freedom and responsibility are closely entwined. Despots can only come to power in a society where the collective psyche is defined by unconsciousness—where it has proven so corrupted by the logic of fear and thoughtlessness that the citizenry do not care about right and wrong but entrust to their leaders the responsibility for their destiny. As Wilhelm Reich correctly described fascism, it is therefore "in its pure form the sum total of all the *irrational*

---

as it sees the hidden pattern behind appearances. To the dualistic mind the higher analytical reasoning will appear as guesswork, but it is none of the kind. It is just a matter of knowing different variables, calibrating them against the impact of first principles, and putting two and two together. To use another analogy: while the dualistic mind, from its flat-earth perspective, thinks going east, west, north, and south leads to different directions, the enlightened mind sees the globe, knowing the outcome of every direction. In terms of the political map the situation is similar: while the dualistic mind thinks in terms of right-wing and left-wing policies, the enlightened mind only sees sensible/life-affirming/ humane policies vis-à-vis nonsensical/life-degrading/ inhumane policies. It will know that the separation has nothing to do with republicans or democrats, communist or capitalist ideology, etc., but with love-oriented and fear-oriented politics.

reactions of the average human character." (86.xiv) We could say the same of any other popular mass-movement of the 20th century, for whether we are speaking of capitalism, socialism, or any other ideology that put the power of state above the individual, it thrived on unconsciousness—which provides fertile ground for scapegoating and totalitarianism.

This equation never fails, for as knowledge and self-actualization increase the burden of responsibility, which they dread, fearful people want none of it. Instead of looking inside, therefore, they seek outside for a leader, a strong personality who symbolizes what they feel lacking internally—a person they hope will rescue them and protect them from themselves. As soon as such a character appears, they will submit to his authority and like sheep they will be guided in whatever direction their shepherd goes. It does not matter if it bears to the left or right of the ideological spectrum. The important thing is that such people will always be subjected to a powerful state—and that this state, in turn, will be occupied by officials who in their own way are as short-sighted and influenced by the logic of fear as the general population.

In hindsight, of course, when things have gone terribly wrong and the event is to be explained, the population, true to their character, will put the blame on their leaders. Even so, it is no less absurd to blame Hitler for the atrocities of the Second World War, or Stalin for the failures of Communism, than it is to blame our leaders for the wars on terror and drugs. In any case, the responsibility is equally ours, for as Reich noted on the communist revolution:

> "The Russian Revolution encountered an obstacle of which
> it had no knowledge and which was therefore shrouded in
> illusions. The obstacle was man's human structure. . . . It
> would be absurd to set the blame to Stalin or anyone else.
> Stalin was only an instrument of circumstances."(86.260)

Whatever the shortcomings of Communism, we should not forget that it began with good intentions. Its theorists (Marx, Engels, and Lenin) envisioned a more decent alternative to Capitalism's exploitation and oppression and their idea was to return to the people the control of their lives and property (labor). When they talked about the "dictatorship of the proletariat", therefore, they never envisioned a bureaucratic dictatorship that was as devastating to the individual as the industrialists' rule. Not at all. The idea was that the people, for a while, should hold the reins of power so that the bankers and the traditional network of exploiters were not able to regroup and reconsolidate power.

This dictatorship, however, was not supposed to last. It was only a temporary solution that the theorists saw as a necessary evil to achieve their goal which was a classless, harmonious society free of exploiters. Thus, freedom and equality for all was the idea—and because this ideal society, when accomplished, would need a minimum of government they imagined that the State would eventually disappear.

As we know, this did not come to pass, and the simple reason for this was man's primitive state of consciousness. As long as this variable is what it is, it does not matter what ideology our leaders (or we) adhere to. Whether the politicians define themselves as capitalists, communists, or socialists (for they dare not call themselves fascists) their governance will be just as dismal, as the logic of fear will wreak havoc with all good intentions. For one, people in general will see self-interest in opposition to public interest. To the degree they do, theory and practice will become different realities, for we will have a class-divided society where people ally with cohorts to ensure the most advantageous position at the expense of competing groups. We will, in other words, end up in the same old game where the poor want to overthrow the rich, the rich want to exploit and oppress the poor, and the State will be an instrument of the ruling class.

It goes without saying that this is a game in which we are all losers. The poor, most obviously, but also the rich, for although the privileged classes seem to come out on top, they live in fear that one day they will not. The dynamics between the haves and the have-nots ensures that the distance between the two increases and like clockwork history shows us what happens when the oppressed become so desperate that the state apparatus is no longer able to protect the ruling classes. Then, the revolution finally arrives. But the only result is that the previously oppressed become the new oppressors—and the game begins anew. Hence, nothing is really changed, and that is why the only effective revolution humanity will ever have is a revolution *of thought*.

This is what we are facing. Again, we have reached a crisis point where the old has played out its role; something has got to give, and to the extent that we respect the implications of the new existence theory we will have a revolution where *we all* come out on top. After all, it follows as a logical consequence of the new worldview that there is only one here: Every time we use violence against others, therefore, we use violence against ourselves; every time we oppress others, we oppress ourselves; every time we violate the integrity of another person we violate our own, and so on.

In other words, only the old consciousness' limited understanding prevented us from experiencing oneness. And now that consciousness has matured to the point where we can bring a greater reality into the equation, a major barrier is broken. We know now that death is an illusion. We know that consciousness at the moment of "death" goes from one state of being to another and that we are an integral part of an energy pattern that spans across innumerable horizons, reaching beyond the surface of space-time and to the very heart of Intelligent Infinity. We also know that Divine Order rules and that the law of karma ensures that victim and aggressor never meet by chance. Instead, such encounters are part of a greater design and the laws of the Universe guarantee that its fragments not only get what they deserve—which means what they need to grow in understanding—but that everyone's growth, happiness, and blissful consummation in the long run is guaranteed. Hence, from this new perspective, it should be simple enough to understand why respecting the principle of equality and other people's integrity it is a good idea. It should be easy to access the wisdom of all higher reasoning—that which follows from the Wholeness—and to translate it into practice should not be too difficult.

It is true that progress is stalled by appearances. We live on the brink of extinction and our social and political problems are profound but we would do well to remember that *all experiences are important* and that *all of God's fragments are of equal importance and value.* We live many lives and we need each other so that we can get a taste of all the experiences offered by the play of duality. We have all been male and female, black and white, rich and poor, victims and aggressors, ostracized and praised, cowardly and courageous. And no matter how exemplary our behavior may be in this life, we have a previous record that includes the most heinous atrocities.

Knowing this, it should be simple to look at things differently. In fact, we have the best possible blueprint for the way forward, as it should be easy to forget old grievances, forgive each other, and prepare the ground for a new dynamic. We all know the Biblical proverb "do onto others as you would have them do onto you." It is quite obvious really, even if it proved difficult for the old consciousness to understand why. From the new perspective, however, it is only all too apparent, for the non-dual self-awareness knows that all fragmentation is an illusion and that all that exists is the Whole who experiences different aspects of its being. We can therefore add "because they are you" to the old proverb— and to the degree we succeed, an entirely new world will come into being.

Now, it may seem unlikely that this new dynamic/understanding will take precedence anytime soon. However, more and more are getting it, and as this percentage increases it will become progressively difficult to stay in power for those who continue to see their well-being in opposition to the collective. As the new existence theory becomes recognized, this thinking will be seen as the sickness it really is. And because we have built a bridge over the idea of self-interest and public interest as two opposing things—and because this idea has been the cause of all our misery—we shall find that as the new paradigm gains momentum, the healing process begins.

31

THE ROAD TO A MORE PERFECT SOCIETY

"The scientific method has not yet come to practical application in politics, economics, culture, the educational system, and the military." (51.240)

—Andrei Sakharov—

THE SCIENTIFIC METHOD implies a thorough analysis of data, theories, and views and it presupposes an unprejudiced and open discussion. From this point of departure, we should arrive at conclusions based on facts, not assumptions, but as the Russian Nobel Prize winner Sakharov makes clear: When it comes to how we organize as a society, no such thing has taken place. The reason why should be obvious, for the interests of government and the individual are fundamentally opposed and the ruling elite has had different aspirations than the establishment of an enlightened society. In the abovementioned areas, therefore—and Sakharov could have added the Church and the judicial system—the "might makes right" principle has been the dominant philosophy; and as the fabric of society has been shaped according to the demands of those with a perceived interest in power, principled thinking at a more wholesome level have yet to take effect.

Time has come to remedy this state of affairs. And in the following chapter we shall see how the new existence theory will inform society. The details, of course, will manifest with time but even if it is impossible to foresee every detail, it is easy to predict major trends. We have already seen how the dynamics between the individual and the state is a variable in constant change and that what effects this change is our level of consciousness. The essence of this dynamic is a correlation between responsibility and freedom: the more we mature, the more we will not only take responsibility for our own lives, but the freer and more utopian society becomes.

As we have seen, the old consciousness is like a child's compared to the new. That is why corrupt leaders have been able to do what they have done, for just as children need adults to define boundaries so also immature adults want authorities who do the same. They will do anything to be free from the burden of responsible living and the less developed their cognitive faculties, the more naïve their faith in authority. As our mental reach increases, however, we reclaim our power and we no longer accept autocratic interference.

It is that simple. The more we mature, the less use (and tolerance) we will have for self-exalted authorities; instead, the individual will begin to obey his/her own inner-authority, and this means that most of today's institutions will perish. There will be some time before we have evolved to the point where politics, economics, Church, and State is a thing of the past, but this will be the end-result of our consciousness-raising process.

The idea of living in this type of society, if we can imagine it, might seem frightening. Living in a time so different, this is easy to understand, for we appear to be threatened by a scourge of destructive forces. Even so, we are not that far away from the point where integrity can be built on a nation level. Historically, we are at a key turning point, for it is only now that society has matured to the point where we can utilize the new existence theory en masse and organize according to more wholesome perimeters.

Until today, we have functioned more or less on autopilot and in our interactions, we have staggered around as blind in foreign lands. We have stumbled into the same traps over and over and it is only now, after the dualistic worldview has reached its conclusion, that it begins to dawn on us how inadequate our thinking has been. It is also only now, in our time, that the body of research and knowledge presented here is becoming more generally known. In other words, it is only now beginning to dawn who we really are, how our mind shapes reality, and to what extent the logic of fear and false beliefs have ruined good intentions. And as we are coming to terms with this realization, it will not be too long before we correct our ways.

After all, it is plain to see that the old has exhausted its possibilities and that the sooner we bring something new to the table the better it is. The world we have built—the one based on ideas of eternal expansion, competition, control, hierarchy, military power, and self-fulfillment through material goods and superficial status symbols—has proven to be an inhumane and self-defeating phenomenon. It has become a machine of double standards and reversed values and looking at the status quo, we see how a sick society creates sick people. In the UK, for example, doctors estimate that ten percent of all children between ages 5 and 16 are mentally ill; in the United States, 6 percent of all children are diagnosed with ADHD and 10 percent of children aged 3 to 17 are said to have moderate to major behavioral and emotional problems. Similar numbers are found elsewhere, and adults fare no better. In their book *The Spirit Level*, professors Wilkinson and Pickett estimate that one out of four Americans either have a psychosis, neurosis, or is addicted to a drug. 25 percent reported to have been mentally ill in the past year, and a quarter of these cases were described as severe.

This clinical picture is a symptom of being born into a sick society. And the root cause of all this suffering is the belief systems established by the theory of evolution and organized religion. Because of these ideologies, people find no meaning in life and they cannot accept (or see) themselves as the precious, unique, and indispensable expressions of GodForce that they truly are. Instead, they cling to arbitrary and unwholesome moral codes, which again pollutes their sense of self. This is good business not only for war profiteers, religious cults, human traffickers, and agents of big government but also the pharmaceutical industry. In 2003 alone U.S. citizens spent $100 billion on drugs that are supposed to remedy such disorders. We have already discussed the powerful influence of this industry on the political process: It is easier to diagnose than to cure, and because profit margins decide policy—and because the discipline of psychiatry has no model to offer that can help these people with the cause of their depression or anxiety—they are put on a diet of antidepressants and other medications.

Hence, as a society, we have become habituated to seeing these issues as medical rather than existential problems. This treatment of symptoms, however, is only good for Big Pharma's stock prices and it should be obvious that if we continue to mistake symptom for cause, we cannot hope to recover. Instead, if we want to improve things, we must confront the root of all this anxiety and self-doubt—which again means that we must take seriously the research indicating that it is society and not primarily these individuals that has gone wrong. As a matter of fact, when all is said and done, it is the culture of greed and materialism that tears society apart—and not crime or drug use, as our politicians claim. The latter are merely symptoms of the former; they mirror the self-alienation that our social order brings about, and only in accepting this can we address the problem and effect some real changes.

After all, the society in which we live provides the most vital determinant for mental health. In a balanced and well-adjusted community, the logic of love will prevail, and class distinctions will be marginal or non-existent. Not only will holistic thinking be present, but there will be a constructive dynamic that strengthens the confidence, tolerance, and sense of community among individuals. The reason for this is that we all want approval; we tend to measure our value from the feedback of others and the feeling of self-worth in such a society will not come from narcissistic behavior but from the extent to which we contribute to the common welfare. If we want the admiration of others, therefore, we must cultivate qualities of gratefulness, empathy, tolerance, compassion, and other collaborative skills. To the degree that this is done, we will be examples to others—and, as we can imagine, this is a to-and-fro process between the individual and society from which everyone benefits.

Not so, however, in dysfunctional, competitive, and hierarchically modelled societies like the United States in particular and the modern world in general. In these types of societies, more dominant and selfish behavior has been rewarded. To most, the measure of success is social status and because most unwholesome qualities are needed to reach the top objectionable behavior runs rampant. As identity and morality is fundamentally entwined, this explains the cognitive dissonance that comes with being called for higher service, for while the ideational foundation of our constitutional heritage is anchored in principles of reason, which again connects to the values and ideals that follow from the Wholeness, people more often than not ignore their implications. We need only study drug policy to see how this unfolds—and it unfolds not merely because leaders are psychologically inclined to reject the responsibility that comes with office, but because they, like the rest, have lost their moral compass.

It does not take a genius to understand that this prepares the ground for a different societal dynamic than that intended by the Founders and all around us we see the result. We live in a society ruled by the logic of fear: a world where cynicism, hopelessness, distrust, and superficial ideals have an unhealthy grip on populations and where our moral compass and integrity is under constant attack by mass-culture. To the extent that these movements are driven by fear, they will divert us from realizing our potential, the Spirit of Freedom, and instead it will encourage half-witted and unconscious living. We will be subjected to perverted value systems, and we need not look hard to see how lost we are. Our culture celebrates the ideals of youth, beauty, power, and money, and we tend to measure our worth based on the extent to which we have more or less of any of the above. Consequently, we all share a deep-felt sense of inadequacy, and our way of life is exerting a toll that many succumb to.

It is the nature of things that it generates a great deal of stress to live under such conditions. When all is said and done, "get rich or die trying" isn't a very encouraging philosophy on which to build a life, and no matter how enthusiastically we pursue superficial ideals we can "shop until we drop" without ever satisfying a deeper yearning for meaning. The suicide rates, the population's deplorable mental and physical health, the drug misuse, the violence, and crime statistics are all symptoms of this. None of these are controversial assertions and to the extent we remedy the psychological pressure brought about by culture, the abovementioned symptoms will disappear. We shall soon discuss its implications for criminal policy but as to health issues, Wilkinson and Pickett has this to say:

> "It is now almost universally accepted amongst scholars
> and practitioners of public health that the most important

determinants of health are social and economic circumstances. Geoffrey Rose, who is one of the most highly influential and respected epidemiologists of the twentieth century, said 'medicine and politics cannot and should not be kept apart.' Our growing understanding of how human health and wellbeing are so deeply affected by social structure inevitably pushes science into politics." (128.277)

There are also behavioral scientists who can tell us that violence is not a natural way to solve problems. One of them, psychiatrist Howard Cuttler, speaks to it thus:

"Over the past two or three decades, there have been literally hundreds of scientific studies indicating that aggression is not essentially innate and that violent behavior is influenced by a variety of biological, social, situational, and environmental factors. . . . There's nothing in our neurophysiology that compels us to act violently. In examining the subject of basic human nature, most researchers in the field currently feel that fundamentally we have the potential to develop into gentle, caring people or violent, aggressive people; the impulse that gets emphasized is largely a matter of training."(25.42)

Hence, whether we become violent depends on upbringing and the kind of society we are born into. Researchers point out that people with dysfunctional and violent behavior have experienced a great deal of violence, ridicule, and humiliation throughout childhood. They believe this is the reason for their behavior and that violence, to the aggressor, is never irrational but a defensive measure—a desperate attempt to save face. This ties in with everything we have discussed about the human psyche, for even if in many ways we are different, we have the same basic make-up and we share the same needs and wants, desires and longings.

When it comes to this, the trait that decides the dynamic between us and others is our safety zones. As discussed in chapter 11, different people have different safety zones and those with a difficult childhood usually end up with fragile self-images and narrow safety zones. The narrower these safety zones, the easier we feel threatened—and when we do, the response depends on our self-esteem and self-awareness. Sometimes we manage to keep our calm; we meet the perceived threat with dignity and understanding and avert an escalation. Other times we respond with defense mechanisms such as arrogance, irony, or mockery, or we may react with irritation, anger, or violence. All these tools are available responses. It depends on the perceived threat, as well as our personal make-up, which alternative we choose but the lower our self-image, the greater the perceived threat and the quicker we are to react with the most extreme means—violence.

James Gilligan, a psychiatrist who heads the Center for the Study of Violence, is more informed on this topic than most. He studied the issue for more than 30 years in prisons and mental institutions, and after extensive research on the most violent population has found a common denominator. As he says:

> "[Acts of violence are] attempts to ward off or eliminate the feeling of shame and humiliation—a feeling that is painful, and can even be intolerable and overwhelming—and replace it with its opposite, the feeling of pride." (128.133)

Gilligan contends that every violent episode follows this recipe. Consequently, even if aggressors cannot shy away from responsibility, it follows that *as a society* we all share the blame for the prevalence of violent behavior. It is, after all, clear that healthy, well-functioning citizens would never act out in such a way and that the type of society that we are born into—a society where superficial values, class divisions and false beliefs generate fragile egos; where politicians and mass-media hail war and violence as manly and legitimate problem solving; and where competitiveness is cultivated to a degree where we end up distrustful and alienated from one another—is a perfect recipe for dysfunctional behavior.

This applies not only to violence, as our culture is to blame for all antisocial behavior. For example, there is nothing that generates crime like depression, frustration, and low self-esteem, and when we add a social order where hypocritical and distorted moral codes are encouraged, we only reap what we sow.

Our authorities, of course, will beg to differ. But just as children notice whenever parents say one thing and do another—and just as they imitate practice, not theory—so populations follow authorities. Thus, our sense of responsibility depends on the society that we are born into. If the system encourages wholesome values and reflects those values in its being it is easy for the individual to obey the moral code of society. It comes naturally whenever there is resonance between soul and environment. However, as long as our system institutionalizes and promotes large-scale violence and exploitation; as long as selfishness, dishonesty, hypocrisy, and psychopathic behavior is the way to the top; and as long as the unscrupulous dealings of those in power rob people of their self-esteem and essential basis for existence, it doesn't matter how much leaders encourage temperance, frugality, self-sacrifice and good morals.

To begin with, proper morals—those following from the ideals, values, and principles of Wholeness—have been so despoiled by culture that they are hardly recognized. They are not only frowned upon by agents of government but duly neglected by all who have succumbed to the demands of the status quo. They are that which must be ignored for this state of affairs to continue—and considering that only the naive is taken in by the facade, one should not be surprised to find that a certain percentage of the population follow their leaders' example.

Hence, in the same way as a society will have the politicians it deserves, it will also get the crime it deserves. According to the new existence theory, *healthy human beings want to contribute positively*; they know that to the degree this is done, they will also actualize themselves, and they understand that what they do to others they do to themselves. Consequently, only a disillusioned individual, ignorant of the greater reality, will commit robbery and other crimes-for-profit, and only a deeply troubled individual will torment and/or kill others. This follows as simple as two plus two. The inner world is always a mirror of the outer and so no one should be surprised if a person who himself does not know or feel love fails to exhibit this connection towards others. It goes without saying that a person without respect for himself will fail to respect his neighbor, but that none of us came into the world so damaged. All wrongdoers, therefore, somehow along the way have lost faith in themselves and society. They have given in to despair—and *that is why* they end up committing misdeeds.

Discussing the topic of crime, please note that we are talking about offenses that involve transgressions committed against someone else's person or property. As we know, there are many criminal laws that can be broken which do not constitute a felony in these terms. The drug laws being a prime example, the violation of such laws has nothing to do with dysfunctional and anti-social behavior. In fact, one can argue the opposite, for as the American civil rights activist Martin Luther King wrote from prison "there are two types of laws: just and unjust. One has not only a legal but a moral responsibility to obey just laws. Conversely, one has a moral responsibility to disobey unjust laws." (63.196)

The unjust laws are the result of a corrupt political process. They are the laws whose function keep people in chains rather than help society prosper—and despite that leaders will always invoke the best of intentions, there must be something else behind the comprehensive legislation to which we are being subjected. Indeed, if we look closer, we find that society has always had a knack of blaming isolated groups for problems that are a collective responsibility. This is what has been referred to as the scapegoating phenomenon, which arises from our inability to integrate experience and put responsibility where it belongs. Historically, it is this predisposition that has troubled mankind and psychologically speaking it can be construed as the antithesis to the vision of the founders, that of an enlightened realm.

We know that the founders connected responsibility and freedom but that this burden of freedom is too much for most to bear. Rather than a world where autonomy is praised and encouraged, therefore, people will prefer a social contract based on deceit and oppression. They will be living way below the standard that responsible individuals must confront, and as this cannot be accepted the scapegoating phenomenon provides the illusion of purification by the creation of a vilified outgroup. In persecuting this group, the citizenry becomes convinced of their own moral superiority, for they have identified the problem with the world and attained a moral standard that puts them beyond reproach. Thus, they can continue life, feeling ok, while ignoring the inconvenient fact that they are living on their knees.

The importance of the scapegoating mechanism, then, can hardly be overestimated. It has been the generator of much human suffering and René Girard, the French philosopher, not only described how prohibitions derive from this phenomenon, but considers it to be the very foundation of cultural life. He claims that "Natural man became civilized, not through some sort of rational deliberation embodied in a social contract, (as it was fashionable to think among 18th century philosophers) but rather, through the repetition of the scapegoat mechanism."[120]

His perception is keen. As it is powered by projection and denial, this mechanism relies upon unconsciousness to survive, and to the extent that it is present society will be retarded from reaching the destination set out by the founders. Rather than the bliss of utopian societies, we will then experience a hellish circle where the psychology of fear runs amuck, and modern academics have written shelves on this topic. We can find them in any library, describing the social dynamics of Pol Pot's Cambodia, Mao's China, Stalin's Soviet Union, and Hitler's Germany and how they drove otherwise law-abiding citizens to commit mass-atrocities. Yet, as a society, we have failed to see the parallels to our time and the greatest social experiment the world has ever known.

Even so, if society is to heal, we must focus towards eliminating this tendency in all shape and forms. And when it comes to mass movements gone wrong, the destructive potential of drug prohibition is second to none. We have seen how this campaign is incompatible with first principles and while our leaders continue to see illicit drugs as the root of all evil, claiming that criminalization is needed to protect the weakest among us, it is precisely they who are the hardest stricken.

We summarized earlier the retarded reasoning behind prohibitionist policy. But even if we discussed the irrational separation between licit and illicit drugs, pointing out that it was the same supply and demand mechanisms involved and that the different groups of drugs also had the same varying patterns of use, it is nonetheless a fact that some (roughly

---

[120] http://www.iep.utm.edu/girard/#H3

10 percent) develop a problematic relationship to their drug of choice. It is on this basis that politicians justify policy. To them, drug prohibition is solidarity in practice, but the idea is entirely misguided. Psychologist Karen Haldis Leira explains why, for "drug abuse is not the cause of a problem. Rather, it is a symptom that represents the user's attempt to *solve* his problem, which in turn strengthens the problem instead of solving it."(64.25)

Competent researchers, therefore, agree that to criminalize these people for their choice in drugs is not a good idea. We have already given some reasons why, and another reason is that drug abusers—those ten percent whom politicians want to help—are already struggling with a poor self-image. For instance, it is estimated that 50 percent of opiate addicts use drugs to alleviate trauma which goes back to childhood. These are the people who are *least likely* to be deterred by prohibition; they will do just about anything to get their next fix, and current drug policy only succeeds in making everything worse for them.

In a sense, this is also the intention, as a central premise behind prohibitionist reasoning is to stress drug users—they want to persecute, harass, and condemn them to the full extent for their choice of drugs in the hope that they will surrender and leave their drug-using days behind. In other words, the idea behind drug prohibition is exactly the same as that of parenting in older days—the harder you punish unruly children, the faster they will submit to authority. We have with good reasons abandoned such thinking in terms of parenting. Nonetheless, because of the scapegoating phenomenon, it continues in respect to drug users— even if it should be obvious that such an approach only makes matters worse for everybody involved.

The heart of the problem is that current policy sends a clear message to users that society looks down on them because of their choice in drugs and that they, because of this choice, are considered social outcasts. This approach not only exacerbates the underlying problem (as it guarantees that the addicts' self-esteem will deteriorate further), but it provides fertile ground for a dynamic that strips the drug users for resources and hampers their way back to society.

Whether drug users know how to behave or not, the prohibitionists' policies constantly remind them that they are enemies of the State, too low on the social ladder to be entitled to even the most basic human rights. And whether it is police harassment or ordinary people's scorn, they are on a daily basis being subjected to a feed-back process that generates *a lot of* frustration. This frustration represents a certain amount of negatively-charged energy, and it will either have to be expressed externally or internally[121]. It will not disappear by itself and to the degree that users absorb and internalize its effects, the result will be a weakened self-image. The weaker the perception of self, the more they will be bothered by feelings of worthlessness and shame; they will see themselves as other people see them, and the only way to ward off some of this pain is to externalize the frustration. To the extent they do, they will return the negatively charged energy to society. This in turn leads to antisocial and problematic behavior—behavior that ordinary people believe to be a result of drugs, but rather should be seen as a consequence of prohibition.

Had we thought about it—or had we listened to the experts—we would have known better. Among drug policy researchers and addiction therapists it has been accepted wisdom for more than 40 years that only to the extent that they "strengthen the abuser's self-confidence and courage, while weakening his self-loathing and resignation,"(64.13) can they help him out of the destructive cycle.

In other words, if politicians had any sympathy for these people—if their talk about "solidarity with users," and so on, had a ring of truth—they would have listened to the experts. This, however, they have not been willing to do. In fact, they have worked *against* evidence-based drug policies since day one, and so it should be clear that *politicians themselves are to blame* for the problems their drug policies have the stated aim to prevent. Not only must they accept their share of responsibility for all the deaths-by-overdose and all the suffering associated with drug abuse, but also for the power of organized crime. Thanks to our politicians a market worth roughly $500 billion a year is controlled by gangsters and terrorists. The OAS estimates that 150.000 people die every year as a direct result of this in Latin America alone; it

---

[121] Note that racist, homophobic, as well as other hostile, infantile and prejudiced attitudes generate exactly the same dynamics.

is a vicious circle of violence, and the disastrous consequences of the corruption that has followed in the wake of organized crime is quite unimaginable.

We have already discussed much of this. And if we would just wise up and remove the drug law, not only would all "drug crime" disappear but we would eliminate all the *real crime* that has followed in the wake of prohibition. Violence, kidnapping, murder, theft, burglary, robbery— all this would decrease dramatically. Not only that, but we could create a society *entirely free of crime* if we would address the major social and economic inequalities of the world. Together with the delusional beliefs generated by the theory of evolution and organized religion, these are the generator our misfortunes; the former is a result of the latter, and as soon as we confront these issues the general level of health and quality of life will improve considerably.

For those who want to know more Richard Wilkinson and Kate Pickett's *The Spirit Level: Why Equality is Better for Everyone* is good reading. To make a long story short, however, it is now proven that the most effective way to cure societal ills is to reduce the gap between rich and poor. These professors do not have much to say on the root-cause of this gap, namely the mistaken beliefs on which we build our worldview, but after taking into consideration a massive corpus of research they conclude that "reducing inequality is the best way of improving the quality of the social environment, and so the real quality of life, for all of us . . . [and] this includes the better off."(128.29)

In other words, evidence from the social sciences is conclusive that we all—*even the richest 1 percent*—will have everything to gain from a more equality-oriented society. Adding the new existence theory to the equation it should be self-evident why, and so it should be relatively easy to create a better world—*if we want.*

As simple as it is, however, it takes a certain modicum of awareness before we understand this. Promoting war as a natural state of affairs, our culture has us stuck in childish ways, and we have not yet matured to the point where society can translate into practice the insights offered by experts. Because ignorance and the logic of fear still have a hold on the global psyche, short-term thinking sets the standard of the day and we have not only politicians who speculate in counterproductive ways, attempting to carve out a career by appearing "tough on drugs and crime", but a public that rewards such behavior.

Nevertheless, it should be obvious that once a sufficient percentage stop applauding, we will get politicians who listen to reason and who refuse to pursue policies that only make matters worse.

When it comes to crime control, we should always remember that the purpose of law is not to limit but to free; it is to protect autonomy individually and en masse, and while current systems of arbitrary justice fail to preserve this basic principle of law, it is well known among criminologists, psychologists, and other professionals that prisons are counterproductive and that to the extent we use other options we will be better off. *Why* should by now be evident, for just as drug policy targets underdogs and strips them of resources, it is the same with our penal system: Imprisonment tends to weaken an already fragile self-image, it increases the inmate's hatred of society, isolates him from constructive influences, and reinforces the negative dynamics between individual and society. The American psychiatrist James Gilligan sums it up by saying that "the most effective way to turn a non-violent person into a violent one is to send him to prison." 128.154)

So why do we spend so much resources on making matters worse? If we look at the rationale for the use of prisons, imprisonment shall (1) be society's punishment/retribution for crimes committed; (2) it shall protect society from dangerous individuals; (3) it shall rehabilitate these individuals, making them better-functioning citizens; and (4) it shall have a preventive effect, making it less attractive for potential criminals to commit crimes. We now know, however, as Wilkinson and Pickett says, that "a prison is not particularly effective for either deterrence or rehabilitation" and that "a society must only be willing to maintain a high rate (and high cost) of imprisonment for reasons unrelated to effectiveness."(128.155) Hence, justifications three and four cannot account for our penal policy. As only a small percent of the incarcerated population poses a threat to society, the second rationale also fails to explain the current use of incarceration. It is simply dimwitted to pretend otherwise, and since an argument for criminalization will hardly ever be built on the premise that the perpetrator deserves punishment, there must be other reasons behind criminal policy.

To explain our use of prisons, therefore, we must look at the unofficial reasons. Prime among them are the utility of the scapegoating mechanism for nation building and many criminologists know better than to believe the nonsense that is produced to justify the status quo. According to the American criminologist John Irwin, for instance, the real reasons behind the use of prisons are (1) class control, the desire of the ruling elite to keep us on a tight leash; (2) the compulsion to provide simple "solutions" to more complex problems that leaders refuse to address, such as class distinctions and an oppressive societal structure; and (3) the elite's dependency on enemy images—their need to define a threat so that we will see them as our protectors.

As we can see, these are the exact same reasons already pointed at— and these reasons, which politicians will never admit to, are *really* shaping criminal policy.

Our use of prisons, in other words, is just another example of the logic of fear. For this reason, it should be no surprise that this entire area of policy reveals the difference between theory and practice, but that practice is destructive is well-known. Most employees of the prison system, for instance, know that imprisonment constitutes a significant social, economic, physical, and psychological burden and that the harder they punish an inmate the less likely they are to successfully rehabilitate him.

Although all countries have a backward penal system, some adapt to the consequences of this realization better than others. The collective consciousness is no uniform entity and there are regions on the planet where the logic of fear holds less sway. We know by now that to the extent its influence increases, we will be dealing with an ailing society, and so it is only natural that the sickest societies will be those with the most revolting criminal policies. Russian author Fyodor Dostoevsky hinted as much when he wrote that "the degree of civilization in a society can be judged by entering its prisons." In fact, when it comes to determining how evolved a society is, criminal policy is an ideal yardstick—and the more repressive the former, the more retarded the latter.

It follows that countries with class differences will not only struggle with more crime but that they will also have more laws and stricter punishment; they will not only subject a larger percentage of the population to the penal system, but they will put people away for longer periods of time and for evermore petty crimes.

The reason is that the greater the distance between poor and rich, the more powerful the control apparatus will be—and the stronger this is, the less criminal policy will be swayed by reason. Instead, society will be subjected to a dynamic that constantly makes matters worse for everyone except the war profiteers. Just as Orwell described, there will be a dynamic where the dominance industry will have a vested interest in increasing its position, it will cultivate enemy images and lobbyists will push for more and more draconian legislation. Always seeking the path of least resistance, politicians will go out of their way to be seen as tough on crime; and the people will be so blinded by the enemy images, so terrified of becoming the next victim of crime, that they will support such politicians.

It is to be expected that the more this dynamic unfolds, the more a fertile ground is created for a rise in crime. And as long as the logic of fear prevails, more and more behavior will be criminalized, increasingly draconian laws will be adopted, and more and more money will be diverted from the welfare- and education sector into the law-and-order sector until the police state becomes an undeniable reality.

It is this dynamic we have seen unfold in the United States, for it is no coincidence that the nation with the greatest differences between its citizens is also the one with the highest percentage of the population under the criminal justice system's control. More than 7 million people are currently subjected to it—and it is also no accident that Americans have the most privatized prison system. The incarceration of people is one of the most profitable businesses in the United States; the two biggest corporations earned over $3 billion in 2013, and it is also the fastest growing industry.

The problem with this development becomes evident when we take into account that the past 30 years there have been a five-fold increase in the prison population. As seen, this reflects no actual increase in real crime (that with victims). Rather, it is the result of an increasingly repressive law-and-order approach, which is reflected in the fact that the U.S. Government in 1982 spent $35 billion of taxpayers' money on its criminal justice system while in 2006 it spent $214 billion. We have already seen several examples indicating how unhealthy this trend is. To elaborate, however, from 1984 to 1999 21 new prisons were built in California alone, whereas in the same period only one university was built. 360 people in 2004 served life-sentences for shoplifting in same state, and the United States spends close to $600 billion on incarcerating its population.

While the cost of incarceration is high for government, the cost is even higher for African Americans. Remember that a fundamental trait of our justice systems is that the lower a person's social status, the less evidence is needed for his conviction and the more severely he will be punished. Nationwide, therefore, blacks are more than 6 times as likely to end up in jail, even if whites commit just as much crime. The result of this policy is that the United States (adjusted for population) enslaves about 7 times as many black citizens as South Africa did under apartheid; that one in three African-American males between 20 and 30 years are subordinate to the penal system; that the United States have more black men in prison than in universities; that African-Americans without a high school diploma are more likely to go to jail than to find a job; that one in every fifteen black men are incarcerated—and that one in three can expect to be in their lifetime.

As a matter of fact, according to project Muse, 25 percent of African Americans who grew up in the past three decades have had at least one parent locked up during their childhood. This means that the family is split up and subjected to all the dynamics elaborated on in chapter 26. The social, economic, and psychological burden of this incarceration rate means that current criminal justice policy traps people in poverty. It makes life so much harder and ensures an enduring disadvantage for the people at the very bottom of American society. In addition, many States also revoke their voting rights, and it is estimated that some four million African American males have lost their right to vote.

The United States, in other words, represents the perfect example of everything that is wrong with Western civilization; everything we can observe of adverse mechanisms at work elsewhere is there unfolding with unparalleled clarity. After all, the political process is so corrupted by corporate interests that the aspirations of Big Business are constantly being prioritized at the expense of the population. On top of that, the logic of fear holds such sway that the dominance industry is the most influential enterprise, and the result is an increasingly fragmented and divided society where more and more people become outcasts.

So big and so powerful is the U.S. Government—and so colossal is the system's force of inertia—that most individuals are overwhelmed by a sense of powerlessness. Since its inception, the government has increasingly strengthened its position by promoting to power the most faithful servants and thanks to these system-zombies a moral climate has been created that is well-fitting of a police state.

There will always be criminologists, sociologists, jurists, political scientists, and economists willing to defend the will of Power at all costs and we see the result in a society alarmingly similar to a vision of George Orwell: The individual's catalogue of rights is practically wiped out, and as a testimony to the general sense of helplessness we find that 97 percent of those in contact with the criminal justice system go for a plea deal. Guilty or not, their lawyers—who care about money and little else— advise them to do so, as they hopefully then might reap whatever goodwill the system has.

The client, for his part, may do well to accept this advice, for the legal system is so corrupt that even its most conscientious servants have forgotten about basic principles of law. This is the price of unconsciousness. Being born into a culture where only systems of arbitrary law can satisfy the ambitions of power, the link between law and morality—which is so important to the integrity of legal systems— is outright opposed, while such notions as equality before the law, the presumption of innocence, the presumption of liberty, the adversarial principle, the principle of proportionality, the doctrine of substantive due process, and the jury nullification principle have been emptied of content to a point where they are rendered meaningless. Even so, only psychological defense mechanisms like projection and denial can contain the status quo. Only they can stop a conscious reckoning, and were it not for the collective psychosis that has become so pervasive—the one that makes the gap between theory and practice impossible to see, contemplate, or discuss—the problems with the current state of affairs would have been plain.

The way things work, however, people pretend that this distance doesn't exist. To the extent that they fear the responsibility that comes with knowledge, they will rather have their leaders' lies than the truth, and to preserve their sense of self they will join the state in attacking those who try to open their eyes. The annoyance and the contempt with which the 9/11 and anti-war movements are met is a sure sign of this. And in all places where they demonstrate or hand out their fliers, they will encounter the anger of people who believe that patriotism means being loyal to the ruling elite.

These "patriots" (as they like to call themselves) see everything as black or white. They believe that the State, by definition, represents all that is good and their worldview is so misguided that they imagine that those who for various reasons dislike, criticize, or hate the state do so because they are against democracy, freedom, human rights, or whatever officials of government claim to represent. This seems like a natural conclusion, for they cannot imagine that their leaders' words and actions are very different—and that it is practice, not theory, people react to.

Nevertheless, it is a fragile facade they struggle to preserve. And the government's practice, as well as these patriots' response patterns, is nothing more than a clue of how powerful the collective unconscious is and how its quality has affected nations.

Again, just look at the United States and how timid and incapable its impact has made Americans. It goes without saying that a people who were serious about the ideals they take so much pride in would not have tolerated that 50 million citizens live below the poverty line. Nor would they have accepted the constant empowering of Government at their expense, or the persecution of whistleblowers—those officials who have the integrity to remind people of the gap between theory and practice. The U.S. Government, however, is not only at war with informers. With the War on Drugs and the War on Terrorism, it is at war with its people, and a people who believed in themselves and the values they claim to represent would not have accepted such campaigns. Being built on totalitarian premises, they can only infringe freedoms, and sentient beings would never have consented to a criminal justice policy which incarcerates millions of non-violent citizens nor foreign policies that invade other countries to satisfy the needs and wants of war profiteers.

Indeed, if the American people had represented the ideals, values, and principles of their founding documents, they would not only object to these most troubling affairs but they would have a justice system that protected autonomy rights and the liberty presumption. They would have a government responsive to their needs, and there would be a spirit of companionship which truly made America great.

Be that as it may, because integrity-building at the nation-level presupposes a certain degree of integrity in the population, the founders' vision has not come to pass. The Spirit of Freedom is clearly brewing, but at least half the population is seriously asleep. We have already seen how unconsciousness and powerpolitics influence the status quo. And to say more on the extent to which the former has influenced the American psyche, it goes without saying that a people who had more confidence in themselves or the values they hail would never have intervened in other countries' internal affairs or felt so threatened by other truths and lifestyles. If it were not for the distance between theory and practice, they would not even have been bothered when people in Iran, Iraq, or elsewhere burn an American flag—and if they were truly confident of their own worth, they would not have had such a desperate need to put themselves above all others. But still, there it is. They salute their flag as if it were an emblem for all that is worth fighting for, they frantically hail themselves as the world's greatest nation—and so threatened do they feel by their surroundings that they spend as much money on defense as the rest of the world combined.

If we study the American psyche all this makes perfect sense, for as long as Americans refuse to take responsibility for their problems it is only natural that a people so paralyzed by the system's force of inertia will let off steam by taking their frustration out on others. Blaming communists, terrorists—or whatever their leaders point to as the source of their problems—is therefore what one can expect from a collection of individuals so crushed beneath the boot heel of a totalitarian state. And as long as most Americans remain too ignorant to look inside for the real reason for their felt weakness and helplessness, they will continue to project the shadow of their own psyche on their environment. Powerless people, after all, will always want to compensate by trying to gain power over others—and this is why American "patriots" (and their military machine) think and act as they do.

Now, I want to make it perfectly clear that we have used the United States as an example only because the dynamics unfolding between the State and the individual are exceptionally notable, but things are not much better elsewhere. As we have seen, even the peace-loving nation of Norway has given in to police-state tactics, and worldwide (with the exception of a few pockets of indigenous communities) the influence of the logic of fear is so powerful that we choose leaders who continue to make problems worse. The American people's problem, therefore, is also everybody else's. But even if this is the status today, it does not take much to improve our ways. A rapidly increasing percentage of the population already knows better and if we choose to see the deplorable state as a negative catalyst for change, it becomes clear that things are perfectly prepared for our next evolutionary leap.

In the greater scheme, consciousness has now been groomed to a point where we can draw upon the lessons of social engineering. Human rights commitments are becoming more pronounced and the only way to reach the Sustainable Development Goals (SDGs) set by the UN before 2030 is to build on First Principles. Seen in this context, the United States is an interesting country. With the Trump Administration, we see almost a civil war unfolding as the Deep State tries to defend its systemic outreach. Even so, it appears to be a losing battle and that everything is set for the Russiagate and 2020-election scandal. Never before in the history of the United States has a coup such as this been attempted and after the Italian government recently fired 6 heads of intelligence, we can expect that John Brennan, the former CIA Director, is next. It was he and a handful for FBI agents that tried to cover up for Hillary and her crimes by taking down the President, and with the Q-movement we see an outlet for revolutionary fervor.

There is already solid indication that much is happening behind the scenes. The President, assisted by Judicial Watch and other watchdogs, may bring Hillary and others down for treason and we see a window of opportunity for serious change. At the very least, grave crimes have already been exposed. Patrick Byrne, former CEO of Overstock, has gone public telling the story of how he helped the FBI catch Hillary Clinton receiving $18 million in bribes, and the China and Ukraine corruption cases show that Biden, the recently "elected" President, belongs behind bars. The Democrats' attempt to cover it up is just pathetic, and the more zealous these bureaucracies are in their defense of the status quo, the more they reveal their true colors and the more a fertile ground is created for antifascist movements.

Consequently, although the citizens of the United States in many ways are worse off, they will probably reclaim their sovereignty sooner than the rest of the world. Indeed, a Public Policy Polling survey released in April 2013 revealed that "28 percent of American voters believe a secretive power elite with a globalist agenda is conspiring to eventually rule the world through an authoritarian world government, or New World Order." More recently, an NBC/Wall Street Journal poll showed that 60 percent of Americans would favor an all-inclusive congressional overhaul—that is *fire every single* congressional representative, if they could. The American people are, in other words, waking up to power-political realities. Polls like this would be unheard of almost anywhere else and so chances are that the citizens of the United States, as they did 200 years ago, will rise to the occasion again in a not-too-distant future.

It should also be noted that the power faction behind such events as the Kennedy assassination and the 9/11 attacks, who use the War on Terror and the War on Drugs to consolidate power, long has been opposed by other factions. Media has little to say about the goings-on behind the façade. However, even in the offices of government integrity builds and according to several insiders more constructive factions have gained an upper hand. If this is correct, clearly this will have major consequences also for the rest of the world. The United States' influence is immense and so, if the dam that has kept the old in place bursts, we can expect changes to manifest quickly on a global scale.

Only time will tell what the future holds. Nonetheless, the math should be simple as the supporters of the status quo can only offer more of the same; and they will—if we let them—continue to speculate in the logic of fear until the world is in ruins. Ron Paul, one of the politicians who has led the movement for change, summarizes the current state of affairs:

"I certainly agree that ever so often, after long periods of apathy, when the people, driven by the architects of fear, have plunged into dependency, agitators have their day. That which had been ignored and scorned bursts forward with sudden credibility and offers an alternative to the failed ideas that bred and nourished tyrannical government.

Though great agitators for liberty in past centuries have struggled to keep the spirit alive, the climate looks quite healthy for significant and fruitful social and political changes to come out of hibernation. We all need to become agitators for liberty, else we end up in a permanent state of slavery."(79.264)

His voice is one of many. A tidal wave of change is building. And when we take into account that the new existence theory implies that there are no coincidences; that the Universe is a Superintelligent organism and that the evolution of history is the result of an inherent blueprint; that there is a plan that seeks to be realized—a prophecy that is to be fulfilled—and that the main evolutionary trends are coordinated by forces far more powerful than us; that the earth has functioned as a school where less advanced consciousnesses have incarnated to experience a variety of conditions and learn to use their consciousness in more constructive ways; that there are themes behind the dramas that unfold, and that every century offers a unique environment for learning; that our voyage through time, therefore, presents us with challenges we have to face and overcome; and that the issue humanity is currently exploring is precisely the one we have summarized here—the one that deals with the dynamics between the individual and the State and our emancipation from false authorities—it follows that everything is as it should be. It follows from this that we are part of an ingeniously put together project; that we are guided by Divinity—by Destiny—and that we find ourselves here today because we have chosen to be here, because we are mature and brave enough to be here, and *because we have everything we need within to see to it that our trials are overcome*. We shall have more to say on this in the last chapter. It is intimately connected with inner development, and for now we stick to exploring how our maturation process will affect us as a society.

To explain a thing or two about the nature of unconsciousness and its impact on society, we have only digressed into a rant on its visible tentacles. Yet, these problems and childish attitudes are becoming increasingly difficult to ignore and as roughly 30 previous cultures and civilizations have independently looked forward to this time as an age when the spirit and matter shall become one—a time when humanity, again, will see itself as one with the world and build a reality on the Wholeness-concept, we can see prophecy unfolding. As the Hopi Indians say, therefore, "we are the ones we have been waiting for." And even though we have a massive restructuring ahead, the Force of Foreverness is on our side and has organized everything for humanity's next leap forward.

As we have seen, the defenders of the status quo have played their last hand; with the new existence theory, we hold all the aces and can safely call their bluff. There is more than enough research indicating that all our problems can be solved as soon as we build on principled reasoning, and it should not be too hard to change our ways. I mean, we know better than to leave pedophiles with the responsibility for our children. We also know better than to let pyromaniacs become firefighters, just as we know better than to let incompetent and retarded people build planes, bridges, dams, and skyscrapers; we leave this stuff to educated engineers, and so it should not be too long before we fire from office those civil servants who abide by the logic of fear.

Politics and governance, after all, is a professional discipline. Even if it does not look it, it is the art of designing the most well-functioning social machinery, and just as we leave the responsibility for building and maintaining our infrastructure to accomplished engineers, it is time that we leave the task of social engineering to those who can guide by principled reasoning. We know that the logic of fear is at the root of all our problems. Hence, it should be a walk in the park to correct our mistakes, for as the French physicist and Nobel Prize winner Louis de Broglie said:

"If we wish to give philosophic expression to the profound connection between thought and action in all fields of human endeavour . . . we shall undoubtedly have to seek its sources in the unfathomable depths of the human soul. Perhaps philosophers might call it "Love" in a very general sense—that force which directs all our actions, which is the source of all our delights and pursuits. Indissolubly linked with thought and with action, love is their common mainspring and, hence, their common bond. The engineers of the future have an essential part to play in cementing this bond."(60.290)

It follows as self-evident that, to the degree we accept and act on this insight, we will turn things around and see the healing process unfold. Building on the ideals, values, and principles that follow from Wholeness, we have all the tools needed to reshape our reality, and we shall now see how the renewal will manifest in a new and better world.

32
SOCIAL ENGINEERING FOR THE FUTURE

"In our society, love and knowledge still do not have the power at their disposal to regulate human existence. In fact, these great forces of the positive principle of life are not conscious of their enormity, their indispensability, their overwhelming importance for social existence. It is for this reason that human society today ... still finds itself on the brink of the abyss."(86.xvi)

—Wilhelm Reich—

WE HAVE SEEN how to create a world without war, poverty, crime, abuse, inequality, exploitation, and oppression. To the extent that we bring the new existence theory into the equation all this will disappear, and we shall now explore what it entails when it comes into its own. The main features have been elucidated upon as the correlation between responsibility and freedom is the fundamental variable from which everything follows. Our sense of responsibility reflects our level of consciousness and, as the light is increasing, people not only become more conscientious, but they see themselves and the environment as one.

This is the essence of the dynamic that we look forward to, and on this basis the most amazing things will happen. For the first time in history, humanity will take the Wholeness-concept and its implications seriously. We will understand that we are all unique, precious beings; that we are an integral part of a greater, immortal, Divine Being, and as a consequence we will evolve from a hierarchically-oriented society towards an equality-oriented; from a control-oriented society towards a freedom-oriented; and from a competition-oriented society towards a cooperative-oriented.

The major trends, therefore, are easy to predict. They follow as a logical consequence of enhanced cognitive faculties, as the status quo is the result of flawed and incoherent reasoning. After all, the argument in favor of our economic system is that competition is good because it stabilizes prices and ensures a certain standard of quality; the argument in favor of a powerful State is that control is good because it prevents abuse of freedoms; and the best argument the ruling class can muster in their defense is that "hierarchal social structuring is good because it allows us (who know best) to govern as we do."

For thinking people, however, none of this is convincing. And we can say that cooperation is better because it makes things free and allows us to prosper; that freedom is better because it is the natural, life-affirming state; and that equality is better, not only because it provides for a more optimal dynamic, enhancing the quality of life for everybody but because we are sentient beings, endowed by the Maker with equal worth, and no person is truly free who is subordinate to a more privileged person's authority.

Now, there will be some time before humanity has matured to the point where the new existence theory and its implications are fully understood. Thus, it will take a while before transgressions such as murder, rape, and theft belong to the past. There will also be some time before we are so accommodatingly inspired that everything we need is freely available. Likewise, it will be some time before we have matured to the point where we refuse to submit to the authority of others—just as it will take a while before first principles will be fully ingrained in the fabric of society.

Consequently, for the near future, we will need a government to administer our affairs. Nonetheless, we have no use for the kind of officials we are familiar with. And as soon as we take the new existence theory seriously, we will ensure that more perceptive and honorable civil servants are elected to office. These will know their place within the framework of the larger scheme of things; their motivation will be to serve rather than to dominate; because principled reasoning will be their forte, they will not be manipulated by special interests and short-term thinking and they will have no need to empower themselves at the expense of others. The Wholeness-concept and its implications will be embedded in their reasoning and this will ensure a political process that is compatible with the new worldview. Consequently, officials will want to encourage our individuality rather than suppress it, they will inspire rather than disempower, and they will want to foster our sense of responsibility rather than discourage it.

In other words, this type of officials will *actively strive to reverse* the dynamics that have unfolded between the individual and the State. They will know that everything begins with the individual; that we are born with the best of intentions and something uniquely our own; that our soul's objective is to honor the Totality and contribute to the good of all things by exercising autonomy and letting uniqueness flourish; and, therefore, that to the extent we as a society are able to cultivate inherent potential, the better off we are.

Hence, governments will have welfare procedures that strengthen family ties, providing mother, father, and children with enough time. As we have seen, stress disfigures our brains and stunts our growth and so, rather than encouraging enemy images and playing on our fears, they will do the opposite; they will endeavor to make us feel as safe, secure, and cared for as possible (while not interfering with autonomy rights), and they will change much related to the educational system.

Building as it does on an outdated and backwards understanding, this should come as no surprise. The way it works, we fill our children with "facts" of a delusional nature; they are presented with the ruling class' (the victors') version of events and they are credited on the extent to which they accept and copy this information. Thus, put in the bluntest of terms, the function of our educational system is to discourage self-thinking and distinctiveness—and instead of inspiring curiosity, individuality, and critical thinking it tends to mold young people into a narrowly defined box. The purpose of this is to rework their brains, to shape their thinking so that they will adapt to the gears of a backwards machinery. "School" is an assembly-line where students are at no point rewarded for being critical of authority and its selective interpretation of events. In effect, you must become a professor before you are allowed to think for yourself; by then it's normally too late, and the result is paradoxical: the longer people have been schooled, the more narrow-minded they become.

There are, of course, exceptions. But broadly speaking the longer they endure this system, the more they are streamlined and the more rigid their belief systems become until students find themselves in a mental straitjacket provided by academic training. Examples abound, as most economists do not know how the monetary system works; most doctors do not know how our mind affects health; most psychologists do not add soul to the psyche; most political scientists do not understand power-politics; most priests know nothing about spirit; and most jurists care no more for the integrity of their profession than those in Hitler's Germany.

Common sense, in other words, is not so common. In all areas we are dealing with professionals who do not know how to penetrate the essence of their discipline—and if their understanding is arrested by more cogent reasoning, many would sooner stop thinking than broaden horizons.

A more perspicuous educational system would not be generating such rigidity in belief. And the sooner we get the new existence theory into the schools, the sooner we can prosper. Any sensible curriculum must accept its implications and in his book *Conversations With God (book 2)* Neale Donald Walsch suggests the following topics: (1) understanding power, (2) peaceful conflict resolution, (3) elements of loving relationships, (4) personhood and self-creation, (5) body, mind and spirit: how they function, (6) engaging creativity, (7) celebrating self, valuing others, (8) joyous sexual expression, (9) fairness, (10) tolerance, (11) diversities and similarities, (12) ethical economics, (13) creative consciousness and mind power, (14) awareness and wakefulness, (15) honesty and responsibility, (16) visibility and transparency, (17) science and spirituality.

In the future, courses such as these will likely be taught at schools, and the sooner the better.

Now, it is not just primary schools that are in for a change. Higher educational facilities are also mired in the misleading worldview that the traditional interpretation of the theory of evolution adds up to, and most disciplines are in for a massive overhaul. When this is done, astronomers will no longer see the Universe as a lifeless and pointless entity; psychologists will no longer disregard the soul from their calculations;

biologists will no longer see life as a result of coincidences and inert matter; theologians will no longer accept the dogmas of organized religion; political scientists will no accede to the tenets of realpolitik, seeing war and conflict as a natural state of inter-governmental affairs; doctors of medicine will no longer see bodily ills as detached from belief systems; and last but not least, the practice of law will no longer be a rogue profession.

Most jurists, of course, will deny that they make a living detached from moral considerations. Nevertheless, history leaves no doubt that behind every dictator and totalitarian regime there was and will always be a clique of lawyers who tailor legislation. It does not matter how immoral a government's misconduct; jurists have always been there to "legitimize" abhorrent actions. Thus, as we must acknowledge jurists of the arbitrary law tradition as the providers of legitimacy to immoral regimes, it is no exaggeration to speak of their discipline as a bandit's profession. In fact, it is *the ultimate* bandit profession, for as legal theorist Lysander Spooner noted it is a "science" that originated "in the desires of one class of persons to plunder and enslave others, and to hold them as property."

This is a secret that has remained hidden in plain sight. For obvious reasons it is not taught in law school but looking back all governments trace their origin back to a band of robbers who joined forces to plunder, control, and subjugate the rest of the population. The formation of governments was the natural result of their ambition and the making of laws their method for keeping the people in subjugation. Even though servants of the status quo come and go, this system of oppression remains intact to this day, and this is why the practice of law remains devoid of moral and intellectual integrity.

This, however, must come to an end. The integrity of the profession depends upon a connection between morality and law, and those jurists who aspire to represent the *ideal of justice* rather than rulers' arbitrary, self-serving idea must see to it that their discipline becomes compatible with the new paradigm. *Only in doing so* will they be able to present an aura of respectability, *only then* can their discipline claim credibility, and *only then* can it be called a true science.

To those wondering what this means, it is quite simple, as law is the science of how justice is served and peace kept/restored.[122] It is all about protection of autonomy rights, and while we take for granted that judges are the proper dispensers of justice, a *fully evolved* society would have had the wits to realize that our sense of justice is, at best, distorted and leave it to God to see justice done. At least, it would be sufficiently wise to take the bigger picture into consideration. We have already seen how the Universe, through the law of karma, the law of one, and the law of attraction, ensures that we get what we deserve—and that justice will always be done, no matter what we may think.

As a society, however, we have not yet reached that point where most people are aware of the greater reality, much less have established an intimate connection. We seldom look bigger on events than what happens between birth and death and, seen from that perspective, it is impossible to understand that the greatest punishment a wrongdoer can receive is the crime committed. Even so, no matter how horrible our transgressions, we can never evade consequences. In part four we saw that when we die, we become one with the greater reality; we realize that everything we, from our narrow perspective, assumed we did to another we did to ourselves. As this recognition dawns, it is up to us how we choose to atone. Even so, we can never evade responsibility for our transgressions—and, as we see things clearer from the afterlife perspective, we would not want to if we could.

As humanity matures, we will gradually face up to this recognition. And just as the idea of justice took a quantum leap when we left behind the principle of blood vengeance to let government punish the offender, in the same way we will stop relying on imprisonment and leave it to the Universe to "punish" the wrongdoer.

As a society, however, we have not yet matured to the point where this is feasible. And because the legal system will always reflect our maturity it is impossible to put together a system of justice that is so far advanced. Legal systems, after all, are not only limited by cultural boundaries among the intellectual elite. To operate satisfactorily, they must appeal to the average citizen's sense of justice, and so we return to

---

[122] See also Lysander Spooner, *Natural Law, or the Science of Justice*.

the basic premise; that the science of jurisprudence is to ensure that justice is served so that people can coexist peacefully. And because the State, in theory, should ensure a smooth-running social machinery by securing a right to life, liberty, and the pursuit of happiness but in practice has an inherent tendency to expand its position at their expense, it is of paramount importance that the practitioners of law recognize this tendency and draw a principled line between the two.

This is well-known amongst jurists and because many have good intentions, we have the human rights conventions. These conventions, which most states to this day have sought to nullify in practical terms, are the result of the most perceptive lawyers' reasoning and labor. Thus, they endeavor to draw the line between the State and the individual's sphere of influence where it is most appropriate—as measured by the proponents of individual freedom *not* the disciples of the police state. Yet, the conventions have not been very successful. And the reason is that they (1) are vague on where this limit shall be drawn, and (2) that the bodies who oversee the conventions pretty much have left it to the State to draw the line where agents of power see fit.

This issue, however, is easily remedied. We have already seen what Mill and the tradition of natural law has to say on the matter and by drawing a distinction between vices and crimes we solve this problem.

Now, as a society we have lost our way to such an extent that the distinction between the two has long been forgotten. Even so, it is quite simple, as *vices are those acts that we do to ourselves and our property, while crimes are what we do to other people and their property—against their will.* This is an especially important distinction, for while the definition of crimes is simple and clear-cut (i.e., murder, rape, violence, theft, robbery, arson) an attempt to define vices brings us into murkier territory.

In the simplest of terms, of course, a vice is the opposite of a virtue. We like to think that we know the difference but if we contemplate, we find that one man's vice may well be another man's virtue and that it becomes difficult to tell the two apart. As an example, let us see drug use, gambling, sex, gluttony, sloth, and so on, as vices, while we see modesty, graciousness, meekness, abstinence, and so on, as virtues. It may look straight, but things are not so simple.

If we look more closely, all we can say about virtues is that they are those habits that over time make us happier, healthier, and better people, while vices are those habits that do the opposite. Ostensibly then, the only reasonable distinction between the two has to do with patterns of behavior—nothing more. For this reason, drug use, sex, abstinence, and everything else we voluntarily expose ourselves to may just as well be called a virtue as a vice—and when a vice becomes a virtue, and vice versa, is not possible to speak of with certainty.

Also consider, while we may learn from others the most valuable lessons are always those we experience directly. Hence, we must find out ourselves what makes us happy or miserable, what works and what is not for us. This trial-and-error process is what life is all about. It is the most complex of human endeavors—and because there are as many different opinions about the relationship between vices and virtues as there are people, no one can determine this for others. As Lysander Spooner says on the subject:

> "If, then, it become so difficult, so nearly impossible, in most cases, to determine what is, and what is not vice; and especially if it be so difficult, in nearly all cases, to determine where virtue ends and vice begins; and if these questions, which no one can really and truly determine for anybody but himself, are not to be left free and open for experiment by all, each person is deprived of the highest of all his rights as a human being, to wit: his right to inquire, investigate, reason, try experiments, judge, and ascertain for himself, what is, *to him*, virtue, and what is, *to him*, vice; in other words: what, on the whole, conduces to *his* happiness, and what, on the whole, tends to *his* unhappiness. If this great right is not to be left free and open to all, then each man's whole right, as a reasoning human being, to "liberty and the pursuit of happiness", is denied him."(102.2)

We see from this how absurd it is when politicians discuss among themselves what to prohibit and what to offer as opportunities for growth.

And we also see why it is so important that we clarify the distinction between vices and crimes. For those who want to explore the issue, Lysander Spooner's *Vices Are Not Crimes* is basic reading. He wrote this vindication of moral liberty in the mid-1800s and as the infantilization of society has run rampant since, it is more important than ever that we reflect on this issue. In fact, our freedom depends on it, for as Spooner describes the distinction between criminalizing vices and crimes:

> "The object aimed at in the punishment of *crimes* is to secure, to each and every man alike, the fullest liberty he can possibly have—consistently with the equal rights of others—to pursue his own happiness, under the guidance of his own judgment, and by the use of his own property. On the other hand, the object aimed at in the punishment of *vices* is to *deprive* every man of his natural right and liberty to pursue his own happiness, under the guidance of his own judgment, and by the use of his own property.
>
> These two objects, then, are directly opposed to each other. They are as directly opposed to each other as are light and darkness, as truth and falsehood, or as liberty and slavery. They are utterly incompatible with each other; and to suppose the two to be embraced in one and the same government is an absurdity, an impossibility. It is to suppose the objects of a government to be to commit crimes, and to prevent crimes; to destroy individual liberty, and to secure individual liberty."(102.5)

This is as simple as putting two and two together. The doctrine that people cannot be punished for that which they voluntarily commit against their own person and property is at the heart of Natural Law, and not before legal systems abide by its commands can the discipline of law be regarded as anything but a bandit's occupation. Its directions are most apt to draw a line between the State and the individual's respective sphere of influence—and once this is in place the judiciary has a solid foundation.

As we are discussing the future of our legal system, we should never forget that the wars on terror and drugs must be dealt with. These campaigns represent everything that is wrong with our current thinking and they have no place in a decent society. Furthermore, we must also investigate all other areas in which the logic of fear has shaped the social fabric. Criminal policy is an important area in this regard. And because the belief in prisons as a good idea is a delusion that only makes matters worse, we should abandon it as soon as possible.

Considering the messed-up state, there will be some time before we have a crime-free society. Even so, I have lived among outlaws for 30 years and except for some poor lifestyle-choices they are no worse than most law-abiding people. Their criminal codes are often a result of a great dissatisfaction with society; they tend to see the status quo as a hypocritical and immoral quantity, and because they see no point in being part of what they intuitively recognize as a collectively shared sickness they prefer a life outside the traditionally accepted boundaries. There, they may experience solidarity and a sense of belonging that they have not found elsewhere. Even opportunities for heroism can be found in divesting of society's codes. Like law enforcement or the military, therefore, the criminal lifestyle has a certain appeal, and a moral ground is found in the idea of "the other". As we have seen, if people fail to connect with the implications of those values, ideals, and principles that follow from Wholeness, they will find a moral ground by defining themselves in opposition to something. It may be criminals, terrorists, or society; the important thing is that it allows for a moral/cognitive dissonance to prevail—and so it is that many criminals rob, steal, and lie, while they may also be solid friends, fathers, and family members.

Now, obviously I am talking about the more astute percentage of outlaws. Morally, you find the same diversity on the outskirts of society as elsewhere and there are those who are less developed. These people do not have the same integrity and the same moral resources, and their behavior is more noticeably dysfunctional. Even so, I have spent several years in a high-security prison and society would be better served if at least 90 percent were back with their families. Drug law violators for sure. However, when it comes to murderers, they are usually normal people who for some reason end up in a terrible situation. Rapists tend to be more difficult, and there are some—let us say two percent of the prison population—with a behavior so problematic that others rightfully avoid them. Nonetheless, no one is born evil. Instead, "monsters" are created by the world[123] and there are plenty of examples that they, with help, can become "normal" again. As the American psychiatrist Karl Menninger said in 1966:

> "Do I believe that there is an effective treatment for offenders, and that they can change? Yes, definitely... The secret to success in any program is to replace a punitive attitude with a therapeutic approach."(4.41)

I am convinced that he is right. Indeed, because of the scapegoating phenomenon, criminal justice is that area of policy which has been *the least* affected by reason and the sooner we take this insight seriously, the more rapidly we will have a safe and healthy society. After all, we are talking about people who have succumbed to the illusion of separation. For various reasons, they have gone lost, but they can be rehabilitated if we rebuild their faith in humanity/themselves. It is here the Wholeness-perspective comes to the rescue, for to the extent we can give these people a life-affirming and meaningful context they will abandon mischievous ways. Meditation and psychedelic therapy have proven effective on inmates for this reason. So have proper legal frameworks, for they are integral to the moral direction of society—and let us not forget the importance of love.

Everything is a mirror, and to the extent society resonates with its vibration we will find that crime seizes to exist. Not only would murders, violence, and rape end (because the framework for the build-up of anxiety and despair would be gone), but it would be impossible for bank robbers to live as local heroes if society were decently ordered. In a more perfect world, moral codes like "honesty among thieves", "no snitching", and such would only ring too hollow for anyone to seek out a career on these

---

[123] This does not mean that I excuse their actions or that the Universe won't hold them responsible for their activities. It is important, however, that we mature to the point where we recognize that we as a culture and society also share a responsibility for an individual's dysfunctional behavior. We must see it as a part of a greater pattern of energy, *then* the healing process can begin.

terms and rather than violate the right of others to life, liberty, and the pursuit of happiness people would seek out ways to contribute to the welfare of their fellowmen. It is that simple.

Another important area is the military. For obvious reasons, this institution has been hailed by authorities as an altogether decent one. Nevertheless, if we look closer, the soldier and the criminal's moral codes are not only related but equally retarded; they are both based on affiliation with one group and they only make sense as far as this group is defined in contrast to others. Such codes of conduct, however, are essentially worthless for the simple reason that they do not include all people.[124]

Moreover, while many other social groups share a belief in hollow moral codes, few can compare with the military's brainwashing procedures and inhumane structure. We are dealing with a hierarchical structure where young boys are indoctrinated into believing that they, by annihilating themselves (i.e., their inner voice) and submitting to authority, will become more than they were. Our leaders' exploitation of their naïveté aside, this idea is all backwards. As we have seen, it is only by cultivating our inner voice that we can become more than we already are, and what the military does is transform potentially self-thinking young people into brain dead zombies.

Now, fortunately, this is an oversimplification. The human spirit is not as easily broken as generals would like, and no matter how elaborate their brainwashing procedures they cannot fully silence the voice within. That is why there will always be deserters and people like Bradley Manning and Edward Snowden; people whose conscience rulers loathe and fear and who must be broken by other means, like the justice system. People like this, however, are a great minority, and the vengeance with which they are pursued confirms the system's inherent dislike for integrity.

---

[124] Being children of duality, it has been difficult to understand that moral codes which fail to include everybody are self-defeating. Many people, therefore, take pride in adhering to them (racists, Nazis, prohibitionists, and certain religious people are cases in point); they all claim the moral high-ground, but it doesn't make much sense to present yourself as a moral person when the consequences of your position is a misfortune to others, who have done no harm.

As integrity, in fact, is its enemy number one, it follows that the army's organizational structure is diametrically opposed to the new existence theory. The only way to transform thinking people into system-zombies ready to kill is by destroying what they have of self-esteem and respect for human dignity. Only to the degree this is done will generals succeed in building an efficient war machine, and the sooner we put an end to this organizational structure the better.

For one, the laws of the Universe make sure that the more we prepare for war, the more likely we are to have it. Like all organizations relying on enemy images, the military tend to encourage their growth—and the more these images are nourished, the greater the impact of the logic of fear will be and the more certain are conflicts to arise. Furthermore, war is not only a terrible ordeal for the population of the invaded countries. What we train soldiers to do is incompatible with their true nature; it is a violation of their very essence and no matter how "successfully" they are brainwashed into becoming killing machines, the training and the combat experience does tremendous damage. These are wounds they are not only likely to carry throughout their lives but beyond. As we saw in the chapter on the near-death experience, it does not matter if we commit atrocities and murders in service to self, the mafia, or the State. Such misdeeds always create a karmic bond between victim and perpetrator—and the Universe makes sure that imbalances are recalibrated.

We are, in other words, always responsible for our actions. And although servants of the state hand out medals of Honor, telling veterans that they are heroes for contributing to peace and that everything is all right, the soul knows better. It only resonates with that with follows from Wholeness, and the fact that most soldiers do what they can to suppress their inner voice and to numb and erase their inner pain with drugs changes nothing. In truth, the more they ignore this festering wound the worse symptoms become, for as long as they refuse to look at the root of their problems their dreams and everyday life will remind them that something is wrong.

We know by now that frustration always takes its toll and that distressed individuals will either torment others or themselves. Violent, disruptive, and other dysfunctional behaviors are examples of the former, while self-harm, alcoholism, and suicide are examples of the latter. And just as more U.S. soldiers killed themselves after the Vietnam War than those who died fighting, so the soldiers who die on the battlefield in Iraq and Afghanistan are few compared to the veterans who commit suicide back home.

The government's treatment after they have lost their value to the dictates of war profiteers is probably a contributing factor. It does not help that what they have fought for is revealed to be a cruel and indecent fraud. When all is said and done, however, we are discussing two sides of the same coin and we will do each other a huge favor by removing the source of so much despair and frustration—the tendency to put the interests of profit and power above those of humanity.

We now have a general sense of what the future will bring. And the main feature is that in all areas of society we will endeavor to mitigate the harms caused by the logic of fear. We will therefore elect "doves" and not "hawks" to positions of power and the end-justifies-the-means ideology will be recognized as ill-founded and intolerable for nation building. That some structure which corresponds to the military will be in place is for sure. But we have matured to a point where the idea of war and violence as legitimate problem solving will be history. Until today, the reasoning of the old mindset has flourished and so the threat of mutual destruction has been the most effective guarantee for peace between powers. The "peace", in other words, has been static warfare but as the Wholeness makes its presence known this will change.

Another changing matter is peacekeeping operations. When we take the power of thought seriously, this will take on a new meaning, for instead of superior weaponry peacekeepers of the future will rely on meditative practices. We have already seen how trained meditators, through collective effort, can lessen the impact of the logic of fear on specified areas. As we saw in part four, this will reduce the level of stress and aggression and allow for a more productive dynamic.

When it comes to organized religion, its days are clearly numbered. The power base of the Church is bound to evaporate as soon as people know better than to hand over to priests the responsibility of their salvation. And because we know that God is not an old man in the sky but instead is Everything That Is—and that we, if we want to build a personal relationship to God, must listen within—the Church and its dogmas have outlived their usefulness.

Consequently, as we take responsibility for our spiritual growth organized religion will disappear and other sectors that will have less impact are health services. These will outlast the Church, as doctors and hospitals will remain indispensable. But in much the same way as we have given responsibility of our salvation to priests, we have handed to doctors the responsibility for health. In this respect, one was no smarter than the other for every time we give power away, we become a little more enslaved.

As seen, any grouping we exalt to a position of authority will abuse its position. This is nothing individuals aim at consciously, but we all like to feel important and to the extent that we leave it to authorities to save the world/ourselves, there will be a dynamic which tilts power towards authority. We see therefore, the past hundred years, that the medical profession has become more powerful. Until the 1900s, people were responsible for their own health. If they were sick, they self-medicated, and the idea that the State should punish them for exercising autonomy rights would have been difficult to take seriously. Even so, that is the way it went—and I will leave it to the reader to ponder whether it was all accidental that the State ended up criminalizing the use of traditionally recognized medicinal plants such as cannabis, opium, and coca.

Now, this is history. But to look forward, the new existence theory will ensure that we reclaim power over our own bodies. The supremacy of consciousness makes it clear that individuals can affect their physical condition by changing thought patterns and behaviors. And it goes without saying that this recognition—along with the fact that we are about to reclaim our right to self-medication—will leave matters of health much more in our own hands.

It is certainly time. The way things work profit margins shape policy, and even though an increasing portion of the budget is spent on health services (15 percent in the U.S.), mental and physical health is constantly deteriorating. As we better understand the implications of the new existence theory, this trend will be reversed. As already discussed, our problem is that we have addressed symptoms rather than cause, and that we have set into motion dangerous mechanisms by letting those who profit from disease design health policies—in much the same way as we have let those who profit from crime inform criminal policy. Soon, we will not only understand the foolishness of propagating war and misery to enhance profits, but we will address this problem. When we do, we will create a world rich with plenty, for the funds released when we cut spending in health-, law and order-, and military budgets, will be spent far more wisely elsewhere.

Furthermore, the new existence theory will change our relation to nature. Not only does it provide a new perspective on human dignity, but on the value of Life in general. And when respect for Life in all its forms becomes the foundation of civilization building, it follows that we will not only stop cruel experiments on animals but that we will stop eating them. Like everything else, this will be a gradual transition. And before we arrive at this stage, the main feature will be a movement away from largescale assembly-line ventures towards more dignified, wholesome, and organic operations.

Consequently, the age of extensive breeding farms, where animals live horrible lives before they are slaughtered, will become a thing of the past. Energy laws inform us that the poorer an animal's quality of life, the worse off we are. Not only is our moral constitution reduced; bodies are also impaired, for the more stressful an animal's life, the more the quality of meat is debased.

Everything we have summarized is closely related. And the more our sense of empathy and responsibility evolves, the better off we will be. It is our current thinking that has created today's problems; it is the illusion of separation and our ignorance of the greater reality that got us into this mess and the more we build on First principles the sooner we will redeem our ways.

To the degree we remember who we are, therefore, we will stop poisoning the planet and ourselves; we will treat the earth and others as we would like others to treat us, and an era of sustainable development will commence. Technology that has been kept under wraps will make this much easier. There is nothing like free energy and advanced technology to speed up progress, and finally it will become clear that we are not alone in the Universe.

Instead, it will be revealed that we have always been surrounded by curious eyes. It will be seen that aliens are not the monsters Hollywood has presented, but (by and large) high-spirited and constructively oriented individuals who are more than happy to welcome us into the Galaxy's greater community.

In fact, that they have not yet done it is nobody's fault but our own. It takes a certain level of consciousness before we are qualified to take this step and until now earth has functioned as a "greenhouse" where larger forces have sown the seeds and organized for our growth process. These forces have prepared cycles of light and darkness and ensured balance; thereby, through the pressure of duality, they have created the conditions for our growth so that we could evolve into something more. We have now, however, matured to see beyond appearances; the implications of Wholeness are within our reach—and as we make this leap, we shall once more see our place.

33
THE MERGER OF US AND ENVIRONMENT

"The idea of limit, of the impossible begins to grow a little shadowy and it appears instead that whatever man constantly wills, he must in the end be able to do; for the consciousness in the race eventually finds the means. It is not in the individual that this omnipotence expresses itself, but in the collective will of mankind that works out with the individual as a means. And yet when we look more deeply, it is not any conscious will of the collectivity, but a superconscious Might that uses the individual as a center and a means, the collectivity as a condition and field. (9.15) . . . But what after all, behind appearance, is this seeming mystery? We can see that it is the Consciousness which had lost itself returning to itself, emerging out of its giant self-forgetfulness, slowly, painfully, as a Life that is would-be sentient, to be more than sentient, to be again divinely self-conscious, free, infinite, immortal." (93.291)

—Sri Aurobindo—

WE NOW HAVE an idea of where the future will take us. However, the progress of society cannot go faster than our maturation process allows and so it depends on our inner development how the outer will come to pass.

This inner development is key to everything, and we shall now see what we can expect in this area. We have already become familiar with the main features as we, through the self-actualization process, will transcend duality and access increasingly higher levels of understanding until we finally become one with our surroundings. We will encounter a new type of consciousness, the cosmic, and as seen in part one this is so qualitatively different that those who have not experienced it cannot imagine the implications. Even so, I shall try to explain what the future holds for our inner world. We shall see how we all, in our own way, can aid in the renewal and we shall see how the collective consciousness is in for a most amazing transformation.

First, what we need to understand is that we are talking about two variables. And while the cosmic consciousness for millennia has been available as a potential to those who have been able to reach for it, it is in the cards that humanity as a whole, at a future date, will partake in its delight. This is the natural—and logical—next step in our evolution, and that it has not happened yet is due to the impact of fear on the collective consciousness.

One way of looking at it is to imagine this greater consciousness as a watery-like vibratory liquid that surrounds us. By virtue of its nature, darkness/fear has a low or slow (heavy) vibration, and because of its presence its effect is similar to a backpack full of bricks in water; as long as we carry this load, we will be drawn to the bottom, and because we have walked around in this condition for millennia, we have forgotten what it means to breathe fresh air.

Taking into consideration, however, that dualities do not reflect the true nature of things, it should be obvious that this is not our natural habitat. As seen, the dualistic worldview is a backdrop consciousness uses to experience itself as less than everything and darkness/fear is a necessary part of the Cosmic Play—the process of exhalation and inhalation. To think of the darkness/fear as an enemy or evil, therefore, is nonsensical. The Universe is far more ingeniously put together than we can imagine. It is a self-regulating, self-organizing, self-aware, and supercoherent structure which aims at levels of perfection far beyond our comprehension and pushed forward by the pressure of duality its fragments ascend towards increasingly elevated levels of awareness and understanding.

Thus, the passage of time perfects creation. And as the Hand-that-moves-all-things ensures that we constantly encounter what we need for growth purposes, we not only advance cognitively but out of duality. As this process evolves darkness is transformed to light; its weight and influence declines as the fragments become more self-aware, more able to hold and integrate the Wholeness. Hence, Society proceeds towards a tipping point and when enough love has replaced fear, we will have changed the qualitative pressure of the collective consciousness so that a breakthrough can occur.

Remember that the logic of love has a vibration that is qualitatively different from fear. Its vibration is faster or higher (lighter), and when the presence of light has become sufficiently strong, we will experience a breakpoint where the waters of old is breached and we reach the surface. The water analogy, however, can only take us so far, for the difference between the old and the new consciousness will be far more remarkable. It will be like the fabric of the world has been turned inside out, so extensive is this transformation, and we will have taken a leap into a whole new world—one where we, through our eyes, no longer look at the world but *into ourselves*.

In other words, we are talking about much more than a paradigm shift. We are talking about a *dimensional* shift, and in retrospect it will seem strange that we could live in ignorance so blind to the nature of things. From this new perspective, we will not only recognize our connectedness but we will *feel* it in our bodies. It will feel as if our cells become hyperlinked—as if they are bathed in light, supercharged, and connected to all there is—and the present moment becomes so radiant, so awe-inspiring, so penetrated by the quality of love that the air we breathe today will feel like a poisoned atmosphere.

I know this because I am among the millions who have had a taste of cosmic consciousness. And even though this may seem dubious, such a state will not only remind us what it means to draw fresh air and be one with All That Is; from this perspective, we see how light and darkness are interrelated, how the Light is constantly reaching beyond itself, how the web and fibers of the physical are increasingly saturated, and that a breakthrough is approaching when it will have the momentum to turn the world inside out.

When it will happen, I have no idea. For one, time is not experienced in the usual way from this state of awareness and perhaps the process needs more time than it appears. The threshold, then, could manifest over a longer period and it could be more gradual than instant. I no longer care for guesses, but previously I have noted between 5 and 50 years as an optimistic estimate. What I do know is that my first composed affiliation[125] with the cosmic consciousness was January 2009; that since then I have had some 20 peak-experiences, and that the underlying pressure has become more potent.

Now, a skeptic can dismiss this as delusions. I fully understand, but as regards the timeframe several travelers in consciousness (Terence McKenna, David Wilcock, David Pinchbeck) have come back with the same impression and others have spoken in more general terms.

There is also scientific evidence that points towards a confirmation of the dynamics just described. As we saw in part three, some biologists believe that everything physical is materialized/given shape as a result of underlying fields. One of them is Rupert Sheldrake, and he has done experiments which indicate that all experiences gathered by individual fragments (humans, animals, plants, minerals, molecules, and so on) enrich these fields; that they are being saturated by increasing amounts of information; that the more replete they are, the easier it becomes for individual fragments on a collective basis to draw upon information—and that all under a field's influence will spontaneously benefit when a certain permeation is reached. In other words, the same dynamic that appears so obvious as seen from the cosmic consciousness.

Another biologist who has researched this issue is Lyall Watson, and in *Lifetide* he offers an example of the same dynamics at play. What happened was that Japanese researchers, after observing Macacafuscata monkeys for 30 years, discovered something amazing. These monkeys were living on a cluster of islands and there was no way for monkeys on one island to communicate with those on another. As a part of their study, the researchers put food stations on the islands. At these stations the

---

[125] There are different levels/intensities of the cosmic consciousness and I had had a certain taste of it before 2009. It was then, however, that some kind of barrier was breached, and it stabilized on what (to me) seems like a most flawless and complete (though a bit intense) evolutionary next step.

monkeys had access to potatoes, but they were full of sand, etc. and the apes weren't interested.

Then something happened. A young monkey on the island of Koshima brought the potatoes to the river and washed them. He taught his mother and his mates to do the same, and they in turn showed the trick to others. Watson further explains:

> "By 1958, all the juveniles were washing dirty food, but the only adults over five years old to do so were the ones who learned by direct imitation from their children.
>
> Then something extraordinary took place. The details up to this point in the study are clear, but one has to gather the rest of the story from personal anecdotes and bits of folklore amongst primate researchers, because most of them are still not sure what happened. And those who do suspect the truth are reluctant to publish it for fear of ridicule. So I am forced to improvise the details, but as near as I can tell, this is what happened.
>
> In the autumn of that year an unspecified number of monkeys on Koshima were washing sweet potatoes in the sea . . . let us for arguments sake say that the number were ninety-nine and that at eleven o'clock on a Tuesday morning, one further convert was added to the fold in the usual way. But the addition of the hundredth monkey apparently carried the number across some sort of threshold, pushing it through a kind of critical mass, because by that evening almost everyone in the colony was doing it. Not only that, but the habit seems to have jumped natural barriers and to have appeared spontaneously . . . in colonies on other islands and on the mainland.
>
> . . . The relevance of this anecdote is that it suggests there may be mechanisms in evolution other than those governed by ordinary natural selection. I feel that there is such a thing as the hundredth monkey phenomenon and that it might account for the way in which . . . ideas and fashions spread through our culture. It may be that when enough of us hold

something to be true, it becomes true for everyone."
(116.157)

Although this example is not sufficiently documented to satisfy skeptics there are other researchers, like Sheldrake, whose research confirms this phenomenon. The 100'th monkey effect, therefore, I believe is real and another interesting person whose work ties in nicely is Ilya Prigogine, a Belgian physical chemist who received the Nobel Prize in 1977 for work on dissipative structures. A dissipative structure is an open physical/chemical/biological system that exists in a condition of non-equilibrium. An "open system" means a system that interacts with its environment (which in principle implies all systems) and his research indicates that a self-aware and self-organizing intelligence is inherent in the cosmos. The reason is that these systems are constantly exchanging information with their surroundings; they are in other words dynamic structures, not static, and Prigogine found that the influx of energy (information) could generate a non-linear formation in the structure, creating order out of chaos.

Looking at history, this can explain how evolution has organized at higher and higher levels of complexity, ensuring a more fine-tuned and perfected Creation. It appears that the Universe calibrates all variables, and then, when an imbalance becomes unbearable and a new direction is crucial, something amazing happens and everything is re-organized at a higher, more evolved level. Thus, a new balance, a new order, is created. This order will continue to operate until the status quo has exhausted its possibilities—and then, as a change of ways becomes more pressing, the Universe repeats the process.

Today there are other scientists who will attest to this, but Prigogine was a trailblazer whose work built a bridge between physics and other sciences. Holistically oriented scientists were inspired by his thinking and when it comes to the evolution of man, this dynamic is not only described by cognitive- and transpersonal psychologists but well known among organizational-, chaos-, and system theorists. It is, in other words, observed by anyone who knows to look for it and this should bring us some comfort. After all, there can be no doubt that our system is out of balance; across all areas we see a host of problems converging and the imbalance has reached critical proportions. Hence, many people have lost all hope and think that we are beyond salvation. If we refuse to rise to the occasion, they will indeed be proven right, but perhaps things are not as hopeless as they seem. In fact, *perhaps everything is as it should be* and that the Universe, as it has done before, will take advantage of a seemingly impossible situation and bring life a quantum leap forward.

I am, of course, not implying that everything will fix itself and that we should carry our insanity onwards until its logical conclusion. I am saying that I believe everything is properly arranged; that the precedent of history indicates that the Universe has a plan and a solution—and that *we can be part of this solution* if we choose to wise up.

Delusions or not, it is this guided evolutionary process that seems so obvious from the cosmic consciousness' perspective. And while the timeframe is difficult to pinpoint, the way forward is the same whether it takes 5 or 5.000 years. The timeframe, therefore, should be of less concern; in the final analysis it all depends on the condition of our inner world and so it is up to each and every one to decide when—and if—we get to experience this quantum leap.

As previously established, the collective consciousness must be of a certain quality for that to happen. We know now that the Universe is made of the fabric of thought and that we, through our world of ideas, partake in its design. We also know that thoughts represent negatively or positively charged energy and that the logic of fear and love are the opposites that generate this play of energy. Throughout the book, we have seen plenty of documentation, and so it should be simple to decide what kind of future we want to create.

Now, I write under the assumption that most readers would agree that it is a bad idea to continue to reward those officials who hail the logic of fear with positions of power, only to let them lead us to certain destruction. I prefer to think that most would rather see a new, improved version of the world shine forth, and we shall conclude this book by elaborating on this possible way forward.

As it pertains to this, it does not matter whether we exist at the top or the bottom rung of the social ladder. Priority number one must be to minimize the logic of fear's influence on the collective consciousness, and as we all contribute to the current state of affairs, we all have an equally important job to do in our everyday lives. After all, through our interaction with the environment, we are constantly offered a choice if we want to make things better or worse. Whether we think about it or not, we cannot fail to do one or the other, and to the extent we reject the logic of fear in our everyday lives we will not only contribute to the purification process; we will also create a better life for ourselves and make it easier for others to do the same.

To begin with, we are part of a larger energy pattern. Each of us is admittedly on our own unique journey through the Universe and we meet on earth just for a fleeting moment. However, even if we represent our own little universe while we are here, we are an integral part of a highly interconnected unit. Hence, while there is, in the final analysis, only One the interaction between us and environment takes place on two levels— the individual and collective. As pertains to the former, we have the freedom to create our own reality through our thought process and to the degree that we are faithful to those ideals that follow from the Wholeness, we will not just wander the mystic's way, but we will also have a vibration that makes us immune to the logic of fear.

Quite simply, by virtue of our existence, we are connected to a positively or negatively charged energy network: To the extent that our inner world is a product of love or fear, we will be hooked up to one or the other, and because the two are essentially different it should be possible to be part of only the positively charged grid. If we succeed at this task, we will constantly keep the greater reality in mind; we will see Godhead revealed in everything and never experience boredom, despair, bitterness, hopelessness, jealousy, or vengefulness. As long as we can hold this vibration everything will be seen in a Divine light and we can live surrounded by war and disease without becoming directly affected.

This, however, is exceedingly difficult as the illusion of separation is so compelling that it takes a true master to consistently see the world from this perspective. Therefore, like everyone else, we live our life connected to an energy grid that is *both* positively and negatively charged. Hence, none of us are immune to the logic of fear, and the result is that we live our lives surrounded by the same frustration factors as the rest of the population.

It is the nature of things that the more the global psyche is mired in lower vibrations, the more uncomfortable our everyday lives will be: We become more vulnerable to violence, threats, contempt, ridicule, envy, and so on, and because this represents negatively charged energy it will not just simply disappear. We saw earlier how frustration takes its toll and how this energy will do its damage either by us absorbing or passing it on to others. We are all familiar with this. In fact, most of us experience on an everyday basis that things do not work out as planned, that we are not accepted for who we are, or that others are insensitive to our needs. It may be our boss that is unfair, friends that are tactless, acquaintances that are rude, or a partner that irritates. And what do we do? Do we bury our grudge or explode in anger?

Obviously, it depends on the situation. But every little annoyance leaves its mark, no matter how quiet we are, and as a pressure builds, we will sooner or later have a fit. Maybe not directed at our boss—because then we get fired—but surely someone, and most likely someone close.

If we look more closely, we can see that this negatively charged energy constitutes a certain mass. It has a measurable weight as reflected in the status quo and its pressure on the collective consciousness acts like sand in cosmic gears. There can be no doubt that the Wholeness represents a huge energy machinery and that we are all cogs. And while that which follows from love works like oil in this system and ensures that it operates smoothly, negatively charged energy does the opposite. It creates friction between gears, it creates imbalance and disharmony, and it poisons relations.

Now, while uncomfortable, we know that this negatively charged energy is indispensable to the Whole. As we have seen, without it, the divine play would not have been possible and the energy laws/ GodForce ensure that the light and dark are most appropriately balanced. Even if this is easy to forget, we must remember that the illusion of separation is a means to an end. Inherent in the laws of the Universe is the work towards inner-potential and so the Totality, in its infinite wisdom, ensures that everything progresses towards a harmonious "endpoint" through a perfecting principle.

Until today, humanity has been unaware of this process. Our consciousness has been so subdued that we have functioned on autopilot and the greater play behind our joys and sorrows has been unknown. When someone has hurt us, therefore, our knee-jerk response has been to put them on our list of enemies; we have not only rejoiced in their adversity but wanted to avenge the injustice. To forgive those who have wounded us the most deeply has somehow conflicted with our sense of justice. This has told us that it is only right that they should suffer, for we have suffered and it seems only fair that they should know the pain they have inflicted.

Hence, to this day, *eye-for-an-eye* has been the prevailing justice, but when we examine events from the larger perspective this calculation looks somewhat different. We see then that what we do to others we do to ourselves, and although the ego—this lonely, fearful, insecure, and most underdeveloped aspect of us—may find it difficult to understand, whatever we project onto the world *always* returns. It is only because a certain amount of time is likely to pass that this observation is lost. Even so, a situation (and a life) is always a minor part of a larger energy pattern and this is seen from the expanded states of consciousness.

From this perspective, we can see the river of time stretching from "beginning" to "end". We see it as one enormous totality, and while we from the ego's perspective exist as water molecules in this river, unaware of the greater reality of which we are part, everything becomes clear from the cosmic perspective. Whereas this river of time, to us, appears as a chaotic and pointless drift where we arbitrarily bump into other water molecules, we see then that this river forms a meaningful whole; we see that intelligent design interpenetrates everything and that it is never a coincidence which molecules meet and where; and last but not least, we discover that not only is there a reason why each and every molecule is located exactly where it is, but that—in the final analysis—*each and every one of us is the entire river*. In other words, we see how our lives from Alpha to Omega are intertwined in the most intricate and appropriate manner, how no experiences—no matter how horrible—have been for nothing, and how fragments and the Wholeness mutually enrich each other.

When we bring this into the equation forgiveness becomes easier, for we recognize that no matter how mischievous or inconsiderate people are their actions will come back to haunt them. The Universe ensures that everything will be balanced. And so, if we want to steer clear of the same pitfalls, we would do well to forgive others their stupidity. *Only* in doing so can we avoid entangling ourselves—and reinforce—those pathways which over time results in more of the same, both for us and others.

It follows, after all, from the optics of the Universe that the old eye-for-an-eye mentality not only makes life miserable for others. As long as we abide by this doctrine, we will carry formerly felt injustices into the present—and by reliving this sensed injustice in the present, we strengthen the same pathways that originated the problem. Remember that everything that manifests is energy which has become so powerful that it results in word or action. Every thought has a certain vibration and by feeding these lower-vibrational pathways everything remains the same and we will never be free to create/experience something new. The only momentum that can free us from this wheel is forgiveness, and Joseph Chilton Pearce describes it thus:

> "Forgiveness is a state of mind, a way to live in the present moment, which means to allow each instant to pass without carrying negative elements of it over to the new. . . . In one of the Gnostic gospels Jesus reportedly said "behold, I make all things new." Through forgiveness, intelligence can do the same, making things new moment by moment. Through leaving behind our history in which fire burned, we discover that it doesn't have to in our present moment."(81.212)

The perceptive reader may have deduced that the ability to accept reality as it is—to welcome the world with an open mind and resist the temptation to label and judge everything according to the ego's limited understanding—is closely related to forgiveness and unconditional love. Hence, now that we have matured to the point where we are able to integrate the greater reality, these concepts are our greatest allies. *Nothing* has the power to heal old wounds like an accepting, loving, and forgiving approach to life, and to the extent we manage to hold this focus the negative energy that for so long has poisoned our minds and interpersonal relationships will disappear.

This, then, is the work we can all do in our everyday lives. We constantly encounter situations where we see the manifested result of negative energy; and when we do, we have a choice whether to react on autopilot and let the lower energies take control or to stay calm and answer with a response that follows the logic of love. If we choose the latter, we will discover that there are no limits to the wonders we can do, for by meeting unpleasantness such as anger, contempt, despair, and jealousy with understanding, patience, tolerance, and a smile, the law of resonance[126] will melt away the negative energy, bringing a new dynamic into play.

From the ego's perspective this is easy to forget. Nonetheless, this is the true alchemy. As most will remember, the alchemists of old were known for their endeavor to turn lead into gold. This, however, was a figure of speech for the process that has always been the essence of the mystery traditions. It illustrated the art of transforming lower-ordered energies into higher-ordered outcomes—i.e., of turning the negative into positive—and it takes a lot of determination and practice to master this skill. When all is said and done, it is the most profound quest, for it is the art of purifying the soul. It is the science of transforming matter into spirit, the discipline of being dedicated to a work which aims to realize inherent potential, and we all know how hard it is to go through life with a perspective that looks bigger on things than the ego.

The ego, after all, considers itself to be king of the hill. It believes that its opinions, truths, and perspectives reflect the real nature of things and to see itself as a tiny part of a much larger pattern of energy—and the practice of acceptance, forgiveness, and unconditional love as a worthy endeavor—is not its forte. The great mystic Aurobindo depicted the ego's resistance to its role as a cog in the greater machinery thus:

> "The divine working is not the working which the egoistic
> mind desires or approves; for it uses error in order to arrive
> at truth, suffering in order to arrive at bliss, imperfection in
> order to arrive at perfection."(10.71)

---

[126] A higher vibration is superior to a lower. Therefore, as the lower is uplifted and transformed, the law of resonance ensures that the higher vibration will prevail.

As a consequence, when life does not work out according to plan and the ego's hopes and ambitions fail, we are caught up in the gridwork of low-frequency pathways; we get depressed, frustrated, disappointed, and angry; we feel unfairly treated, and we get lost in the victim role. We forget to see the opportunities for growth that *any* situation offers—and the result is that we let the environment take control of us instead of vice versa. In doing so, however, we only give away the power we have over our lives. Had we known better, therefore, we would have seen everything the Universe sent our way as an energy wave; we cannot avoid it, and so the choice is whether to ride or succumb.

The choice, in other words, should be simple. Despite that, most are so ego-driven that it can take many years, even lifetimes, until we are willing to see a situation from a different perspective. It speaks volumes about the ego's limited mental faculties that we would go through years of hell rather than reconsider our position, but so it is: while the ego is more than happy to take credit for everything that turns out all right, it will go out of its way to deny responsibility for misfortunes. Even so, laws of the Universe ensure that our misery will continue until we have learned our lessons. And the more rigid our delusions (i.e., the more we judge from the ego's perspective), the stronger measures the Universe will employ to elevate our thinking.

Thus, we achieve nothing (other than the experience of pain, grief, loneliness, despair, and hopelessness) by refusing to acknowledge the greater reality. As a matter of fact, things will not improve until we recognize our creation and accept responsibility, and this is what the wisest have understood. That said, even these people may be troubled and dismayed. But they have a basic trust in the life-process that most others lack and because they are more open to integrating the greater reality, they are more flexible. Hence, they free themselves relatively quickly from the low-frequency energy grid; every time they fall, they see an opportunity to learn about themselves, and each time they rise they become more than they were.

This is how they build a personal relationship with God. They are not only learning to trust that which is greater than their comprehension; they are also reaping the rewards from this trust, and as a result the logic of fear becomes an ever-diminishing influence in their life.

When all is said and done, this is what sets them apart. No matter how terrible things may seem to the ego, they take comfort in the notion that everything, despite appearances, is ok with the world. Many of them have not even become acquainted with the cosmic consciousness—they could even live in ignorance of the basics of the new existence theory—and yet they have a confidence in the process of life that others find wanting.[127] Without such a confidence, however, our quality of life will not only suffer but our personal development will be arrested. We will carry a fear which in all areas retards growth, and we see it result in the anxiety, depression, and mental disorders that are so common.

If we want out of this vicious circle, the first thing we need to do is recognize that our thoughts are just that; they are our *ideas* about the world and not necessarily a correct observation. From there, we should recognize that just as our thoughts do not necessarily reflect the truth, so also with feelings. Even so, while thoughts can give rise to the most outrageous misconceptions without ever giving us a clue to their delusive nature, feelings are far more reliable. The reason is that they are not only a result of thoughts, but they are the perfect correction mechanism when it comes to mapping out our relation to the greater reality; they are our bridge to the inner self, a compass which indicates the extent to which the ego's perspective is consistent with the greater reality—namely, the soul's perspective.

One way of looking at it we all have our window to the world: Ideally, this window should be transparent, both the inner and the outer world mirroring the greater reality. However, as we are born and raised in a world where the illusion of separation is so convincing, our window becomes clouded with erroneous belief systems until it provides a distorted outlook. It is here our feelings come to the rescue, for *behind every bad feeling there is always a belief system that is incompatible with*

---

[127] It is to be noted here that such an acceptance of the life process does not mean that one allows transgressions or fails to react to injustice. It simply means that one acts from a position of strength; that one does not react from a place of negativity, despair, and fear, but rather from a more positive impulse for change.

the truth. Following this logic, we find that the feeling of loss only hurts because we think we can lose something; that the feeling of betrayal only hurts because we fear that our integrity can be violated; that the feeling of loneliness only hurts because we think we are separate; that the feeling of inadequacy only hurts because we fear that we are not good enough; that the feeling of despair only occurs because we do not know that we are divinely protected, and so on.

Now, most of us have no idea of how our relationship with the world is seen from the cosmic consciousness' perspective. We have never known unconditional love; we have never seen how it is the very foundation upon which everything is built; and we have never seen the Divine Play for what it is. As a result, it seems obvious to us that loss, betrayal, separateness, and shortcomings are threats to our existence. Our pettiness, therefore, reflects the degree of *felt* littleness, our cynicism the degree of *felt* hopelessness, and our need for control the degree of *felt* powerlessness. It is not easy being human. Danger appears to lurk everywhere, and these are just some of the defenses we put in place to protect ourselves. Having never seen beyond the confines of our limited understanding, it is small wonder that we have fallen victim to such beliefs. And yet, all of this is a systematized delusion. They are beliefs generated by the illusion of separation and part of the game, those lies we are here to see through.

Once we recognize that our thoughts do not necessarily reflect the real state of affairs and that our emotions are a compass that reveals the lies we have spun, however, we have made a quantum leap in terms of consciousness. We then begin to unravel the thread that leads out of duality and the illusion of separation loses more and more of its persuasive powers.

Despite this, our way back to Source is long and thorny. There is a big difference between understanding something intellectually and to acknowledge it fully, and many of our beliefs are so deep-rooted that we are not even consciously aware. We must therefore face opposition time and again, for as we deal with unpleasant experiences, we clarify one by one those misconceptions we have taken to heart.

It is here our enemies and the dark forces come in handy. Thanks to them we encounter situations that constantly confront us with our fears, they remind us of our deeply felt vulnerability, inadequacy, insecurity, and loneliness—in short, all those falsehoods we have fallen victim of—and in so doing, they ensure the dynamics needed for our growth. Remember that when all is said and done, we are Unconditional Love. This is our true nature, our essence, before we were draped in forgetfulness, and when the self-actualization process is completed we will not only see the world from a perspective that recognizes this, but we will see *all that is, was, and ever will be* as ourselves.

Most have a hard time grasping this enlightened perspective. Nonetheless, our feelings seek to remind us of this greater reality; they point in its direction, pushing us ever further into new territory. Like shoes we have outgrown they hurt because they limit, because they define what we are not. Thus, they serve as a reminder that *we must learn to see beyond who we think we are in order to realize who we truly are.*

We can therefore thank God, as well as our enemies, for the agony, grief, loss, treachery, and hardships. Without the chaos of emotion this generates (individually as well as collectively), we would have buried our fears so deep that they never would have been acknowledged. There, they would have wreaked havoc and manipulated us from a darkness so overwhelming and terrible that we never ever voluntarily would have confronted them. On the contrary, we would rather, at any cost, have walked the surface, willfully ignorant of what was hiding in the depths—and we would never have been able to heal and become whole again.

That is why things happen the way they do: As long as we build an image on misconceptions incompatible with our/the Universe's innermost nature, *we must perish in the ruins of our being*, for only then can we rebuild a new, more secure foundation—a foundation which will lead to new insight, new knowledge of who we really are. It follows that true wisdom is hard won. It requires all and must be earned. This is, however, also its reward. And as soon as we have grown wise, we will see that the most painful lessons were not only the most important but the most precious.

This is true both on the individual level as well as the collective. When we look more closely, then, we see that everything is as it should be; it is *good* that the police state becomes more and more all-powerful, it is *good* that fascism increasingly eats its own children, it is *good* that lifestyle diseases, anxiety, and depression becomes more widespread, it is *good* that crime flourishes, and it is *good* that war and terrorist acts abound. The world, obviously, would have been a better place without this horror, but these events are no more than symptoms to remind us of what is wrong with the world.

A more perceptive populace, therefore, would have had the wits to note the message; they would have learned the lesson being taught and they would have followed this horror to its source—namely our limited, short-sighted, and selfish ways of thinking. So far, however, taking responsibility for our creation does not seem like an option, and so the Universe will have to speak louder to its children. Consequently, both on a personal and collective level, we will be increasingly confronted with the consequences of our actions until (1) we perish in a hell of our creation or (2) address our issues. Whatever happens, we will get what we deserve, for as Satprem says:

> "There is not a single perversion, a single shame in the
> world that does not have some root in us, not a single death
> in which we are not an accomplice. We are all guilty and
> involved, no one is saved unless everyone is saved." (93.332)

Even if we could accept that we have our share of responsibility for the condition of the world, this is another truth that sits uncomfortably. After all, it seems obvious that a woman being raped by fourteen men in India, stoned to death in Iran, or on death-row in the United States for a crime she did not commit, is innocently being wronged. On a certain level this is true, as seen in isolation she has done nothing to deserve this punishment. Seen from the cosmic consciousness' perspective, however, this incident is a part of a greater energy pattern; we see how reincarnation and karmic relationships must be taken into account and how this is not only true on a personal and collective level, but that *the collective and personal level in the final analysis is one*. Remember that when the river of time is revealed in its totality, we see each and every life-form as intertwined. The individual becomes the Whole, just like the cells in our body become us; it is all one greater organism which grows evermore sentient, and horrible events such as those above are a necessary part of this process.

Seen from the greater perspective, then, we are "all guilty and involved" as Satprem said, for when the individual's reincarnation and karmic patterns are added to the equation, we see that there *is a reason* why people choose a certain time and place for their experiences. These reasons, of course, are as many as there are people in the world, but just as each century affords opportunities for growth, so does each culture. No one, in other words, would choose to be born as a woman in places like Afghanistan, Saudi-Arabia, etc., if it were not for good reasons. This does not vindicate those who transgress upon their autonomy rights, but as to the horrible events that are happening *none of them* would have taken place if earlier generations (or this one) had had the wits and the courage to represent those ideals, values, and principles that follow from Wholeness.

Thus, everything is as it should be with the world; *it is exactly as we have created it* and if we want to see a better tomorrow, we can help by taking responsibility for our creation. To the degree we do, we will find that the Universe is on our side. Its inherent drive is ever nudging us forward, rooting for our success, and so it is true, as the old proverb says, that if we can face it God can fix it.

Hence, when all is said and done, we are ideally positioned to help the world heal. *We are exactly who and where we should be*, and to the extent that we embrace life—to the extent we joyfully accept it as the miracle it is—we will not only prepare for our own growth process, but we will help others do the same. Any doubt reflects the ego's limited comprehension for this moment, here and now, is as perfect as it can be. It is a gift from the Universe, perfectly tailored to our process, and every inclination to oppose it and wish we were elsewhere mirrors a yearning to escape responsibility. It represents the cog that fights the machinery— and it is because most of the population give in to this urge that the machinery does not function more optimally.

Just think about it! If current affairs, as measured against the ego's would-be-ideal, is weighted and found wanting we will—if we refuse to embrace the status quo and take responsibility for our creation—begin to look for scapegoats. It will be the drugs' fault that youth misbehave, the boss's fault that we are miserable at work, the wife's fault that we drink, and the devil's, politicians', or terrorists' fault that there is war; in all areas, we will put responsibility for how we feel on others. Our happiness, however, is no one's responsibility but our own, and we cannot function optimally before we understand this.

The fact that primarily we need to take responsibility for ourselves, that we must prioritize our own well-being and let others do the same, might sound selfish. It may even be construed as being inconsistent with everything we have said about becoming an integral part of a larger Whole—but it is not. It is simply a prerequisite for the establishment of healthy relationships, for we cannot serve the Whole by shortchanging ourselves. Having said that, neither does the Whole benefit from us prioritizing ourselves at the expense of others, and the trick is to find a balance.

When it comes to this, there is a great deal of calibration that needs to be done before we begin to approach something close to an optimal balance. But if examples of perfection are hard to find, we see all around examples of those unhealthy energy patterns that develop when we become dependent on the energy of others to feel good. We will then either (1) become an energy vampire who in dealings with others ensures that they at all times have to give more and more ground for the friendship/relationship to work. *Or* (2) we will find ourselves on the other side of the equation and assume the role of the self-sacrificing party, the one who constantly must disregard his or her integrity and needs to satisfy the "vampire's" expectations.

It goes without saying that nothing healthy can be built on such a foundation. The energy imbalance will be amplified until we are dealing with a rather obvious victim-offender dynamic, and it will not improve until one or the other sees the pattern clearly enough to do something about it. In both instances, however, the problem is the same. It is that neither one nor the other feels good enough about themselves; that they fail to go within and look for the root of their felt littleness; and that they instead seek to remedy it in their dealings with the world.

Not before they understand this—and accept responsibility—will a new, more life-affirming pattern emerge. Even so, it is possible to give without giving up oneself, just as it is possible to be loving and supportive without becoming another person's crutch. To the extent that we stand in our light, therefore, we will facilitate for more constructive dynamics. We will be helpful while also preserving our integrity—and to find the most optimal balance sums up the self-actualization process.

Everything, then, boils down to this. Any decent student of first principles knows that we cannot be at peace with others until we find peace with ourselves, and the sooner we take our inner world seriously, the faster a better and more harmonious world manifests.

We have become familiar with the features of this process that brings us closer to the ultimate consummation, merger with Intelligent Infinity. As seen, it is the science of establishing the most beneficial balance between us and the world; it is about every day, all the time, through thought, words, and action, to try and represent the ideals that follow from Wholeness, and it is about being present in the moment to the utmost degree.

As simple it may sound, mastering this project is the most difficult of all human endeavor. Not only is the mystic road not for novices, but to the new in class it will not even present itself as an alternative. It is only when consciousness has matured to the point where we see beyond our delusions—beyond the realm of the five senses—that it begins to make sense and so, historically, only a minor percentage has been occupied with its call.

In keeping with the growing presence of Light, however, this is about to change. To go into detail is difficult, as the mystic road is long and represents a range of conscious states and cognition levels. Nonetheless, several hundred million have already matured to the point where they have begun this journey. Few have come very far. But as seen in part three, around 10 percent of the population have reached the point in their development (the holistic/integral level) where they begin to connect with the bigger picture; they are coming to grips with the understanding that the exterior is less important than the interior; that they must obey themselves rather than others, and with this recognition they have taken their first step on the path that leads out of duality.

Now, the first steps are the most difficult. We must unlearn much that culture has instilled, and it takes several years before we become proficient at seeing events in the context of the greater reality. The more adept we become, however, the more humble, flexible, and translucent the ego also becomes—and the more it aligns with the greater reality. Thus, as we evolve, it becomes easier to accept life, to see a meaning in everything that happens, and even our troubles are seen in a more divine light.

We will, of course, waver in the beginning and fall into the traps offered by encounters with lower energies. That is part of the process. It is not easy going through life with the greater perspective in mind, and I personally stumble and fall on an everyday basis. Even so, intentions have an infinite organizing power. And as we will always want to be better humans—more tolerant, understanding, patient, and so on—this ensures that we become more proficient. One step at a time, we learn to practice unconditional love. We find that it is inseparable from the Wholeness-concept; that the more we understand one the more we understand the other; and that the more we evolve, the more we will not only see the Divine in the world but in ourselves. As the illusion of separation is lifting, we also see more and more of ourselves in everyone and everything we meet. Thus, we continually expand our presence. We find that the more love we can contain the more we are able to embrace everything; the more we can embrace, the more understanding will grow upon us—and the greater our understanding the more fully we merge with Wholeness, penetrating ever deeper into the mystery of Being.

As a result, not only is our presence in the NOW increasing but the NOW itself changes presence, stretches towards infinity, and becomes more spacious. This is important, for the traditional consciousness is a stranger even to the present. It looks at everything from an extremely superficial and short-term perspective; it sees itself in opposition to the world, it feels threatened by much and due to its self-absorbed nature, its protectiveness, and unstructured relationship to the world, we are seldom present in our own life. Life, after all, is Here and Now, but the present is of little interest to the ego. It tends to see it as a less-than-satisfactory and imperfect state and would rather busy itself pondering the joys and sorrows of the past, as well as its hopes and fears of the future.

The further down the mystics' way, the more this changes, for it is only because the old consciousness fails to take into account the greater energy pattern of which the present is only a tiny part that it appears less than optimal. As we learn to see the pattern as a whole, however, we will learn to see the perfection and Wholeness behind the seemingly unfinished—the present. We will begin to perceive it as the Totality, an awakening Satprem describes as follows:

> "When we emerge from our second and enter the Totality, everything changes and we see perfection in the making. This world is not finished, it is *becoming*, it is a progressive conquest of the Divine by the Divine for the Divine, so as to *become the endless more that we must be.*"(93.170)

As we follow the mystics' road, then, we are gradually integrating the greater reality—and as this is done, we not only become one with eternity but the present. We find that Here and Now is the key to everything; and that it is by being *absolutely* present in this moment that the Gates of Eternity will open, allowing the perfection of *the Present* to be revealed. This is the oldest trick in the book. Meditators and seekers of enlightenment have known this for millennia for only in becoming one with the moment can they take part in the cosmic consciousness.

That is, at least, my experience. And to say a little more on this consciousness, it seems that to bring it forth we must silence the waters of the surface-consciousness. It is hard to describe such a process, but the trick seems to be to exert as little effort as possible; every thought is a ripple on the surface of this ocean of consciousness and that is why one must still the mind. Practicing being present in that state of awareness which exists *before* a thought becomes manifest is one way to do this; it is only the thought that separates us from our surroundings, and so the longer we can maintain this state before we start thinking, the more we will experience becoming one with the fabric of the Universe.

Now, I myself am not the authority I pretend to be. I have never successfully managed to hold this focus for too long before a thought enters the mind and, except for some occasions related to sleep, I have used psychedelic substances to become one with the "ocean". The process, however, seems much the same; to the degree that the mind is stilled in meditation, there is a sense that the different layers of the personality—the physical, emotional, mental, and spiritual—are recalibrated into one coherent structure. Extrapolating from experiences with sleep and psychedelics, it is as if our deeper element is nearing the surface, and when at some point the inner world is adjusted to the right frequency it becomes aligned with the vibration of the world. This allows for an energetic bridge, and so a more coherent superstructure is formed where the Universe is turned inside out, and we become one with everything.

That is how it feels. And when I say, "one with everything", we are not speaking about theoretical insight, an intellectual understanding of the Wholeness arrived at by the mental faculties of the ego. Instead it is a *quantum* leap in consciousness; it is as if the organism becomes calibrated with the Universe, as if everything falls into its proper place and a new consciousness takes over. We are speaking of a dimensional shift in consciousness, a change of perspective that is more dramatic than one moment seeing the world from the perspective of a leaf and in the next from that of the entire forest—which is possible from some states of consciousness. To me, it seems to be another level of Being, *a level where one literally becomes the Universe.*

Perhaps this sounds farfetched but, in the context of everything we have discussed, I believe it is evolution's next leap. Looking back, we see how consciousness from time to time takes a leap beyond itself; that it from "nothing" created matter, that it from matter created unicellular organisms, that it from unicellular organisms created multicellular organisms, that it from these organisms created the mind—and this is simply the next logical step. It is *the completion* of the process, for as mentioned the human being is a bridge that the Universe uses to realize itself. The Universe could never do it at the plants', or the animals' type of consciousness. It had to create self-awareness; this had to be refined and taken to its logical conclusion, for only through the play of duality could it mature and prepare for the next cognitive leap—the Great Remembering and reemergence with Totality.

This is what happens here. We can see the Universe as an organism in much the same manner as us, and so this leap can be compared to our relationship with our cells. For also cells are living organisms: As seen, they breathe, eat, communicate, dispose of waste, collaborate, exchange functions, and adapt to change. In a way, they are their own agents, and just as about 50 trillion cells unite to become us, all fragmented existence unites to become the Universe. The entire creation, however, is the Force of Foreverness at play, sensing itself and experimenting with itself at different levels of complexity, and just as it took existence a quantum leap forward when it advanced from the unicellular organisms' level to ours, so—in this case—it does again.

Indeed, the relation (and connection) between us and the Universe is, as measured by degree, pretty much the same as between our cells and us—and this explains what I mean when I say that we "become the Universe". We change perspective from ours' to the Universe's, and this change is so one of a kind, so exciting and profound that it is truly ineffable.

It is unclear if this will become our everyday consciousness. That is, at some point, it probably will be. But it could be that the upgrade of the collective consciousness, at first, will be of a less overpowering character. The most intense experiences of this consciousness are so staggering that it is difficult to imagine how the world would operate if everyone were to connect with it full-time. Drawing upon my own experiences, the first few times I connected with this awareness it was impossible to do anything other than sit or lie down, and only after having interacted on a number of occasions could I walk around.

This may seem strange. But the full-blown cosmic consciousness is so consuming that what happens here, in the "real" world, on the one hand can be experienced as alien, distant, uninteresting, or irrelevant, and on the other so peculiar, so amazing and mind-boggling that one becomes too lost in detail to function by any normal standard. The Veil is rent, and we experience what Mircea Eliade called "a complete rupture of the mundane plane". We become one with an understanding that is immediate, an otherworldly intelligence that is both simple and infinite. This is not necessarily to say that we become more intelligent as measured by mass-culture, for as Arthur Klepps, a psychiatrist with experience from LSD, said in 1966:

> "If I were to give you an IQ test and during the
> administration one of the walls of the room opened up
> giving you a vision of the blazing glories of the central

galactic suns, and at the same time your childhood began to unreel before your inner eye like a three-dimensional colour movie, you would not do very well on the test." (76.257)

As seen from the perspective of cosmic consciousness, the former can be experienced as no less intimate and real than the latter. There is no more "me" and "you", "this" and "that"; it is all one manifesting at different levels, and so the inner life of the central galactic suns is just as accessible as own inner life when we were toddlers.

It goes without saying, therefore, that experience with this form of consciousness is needed before we can function "normally". It must be tamed or integrated before it can be controlled, and this can be easier said than done. My experience has been limited to between three or four hours at a time, and while I now can socialize or go shopping in this state, I do not recommend driving. It might be that all it takes is more practice. As it stands, however, I believe that it would be too much for most if this were to become our everyday consciousness. It is so considerable that we can experience more within hours than we would in a lifetime. In order to process and integrate this encounter, it seems necessary that normal consciousness returns, allowing some time to pass until the next experience. That is how this consciousness has been introduced to humanity. And because the Universe is so impeccably put together, I expect the coming upgrade of the global psyche to be less intense—at least at first.

Hence, we return to the point already mentioned: we are dealing with two variables—the collective and the individual. When it comes to the latter, I think that the cosmic consciousness will be accessible on occasions. It will remain what psychologists call a "peak experience", for while it may represent the fulfillment of evolution in the physical, we have yet to reach a point where it can become an enduring constant. It will therefore, for a little longer, be located just out of reach. It will be the reward that lies in wait, the carrot for those who dare reach for it.

The recipe is given. We know now that the more we take our inner world seriously and the more we take responsibility for our relationship to world, the more we disentangle blockages on the bridge that connects us to the Inner Universe—and the more we do, the more we pave way for this new consciousness. On the collective level, then, an upgrade will manifest in an enduring constant, qualitatively and fundamentally different from today's, as soon as a certain modicum of fear is washed away and there is enough "oil the machinery" for the world to become a more optimally functioning, superconductive unit.

There is always a certain force needed to start an engine, and so it is with this upgrade. To trigger the hyperlink-feature that puts the entire system in "Love Overdrive", therefore, the influence of fear must withdraw—and then the most amazing things will happen. As Richard Gerber describes this process:

> "If we can produce a ripple effect of healing energy upon
> the waters of humanity's collective unconscious, it will be
> carried by the flowing stream of Earth's magnetic field and
> grid work systems. Thus, we may be able to build a rising
> tide of driving harmonic resonance and coherence. An
> energetic tidal wave of healing energy, fuelled by the power
> of unconditional love, might transform our planet in a way
> that could only have been dreamt about in past
> times."(41.532)

We now have a rough sketch of what the future will bring for our consciousness. Seen in a historical perspective, we can expect this transformation to take place relatively soon. Our evolution, after all, is a testimony to the ingenuity with which GodForce knows how to balance all variables in that manner which ensures the most advantageous outcome. As a result, the cosmos, with the passing of time, has become an increasingly coordinated unit and we are now witnessing the old consciousness play out, fertilizing the ground for a new paradigm to emerge victorious.

The planet's—and our—survival depends on it. In all endeavors, the old consciousness has demonstrated the futility of our ways and the emergence of the new consciousness is essential to continued existence. Hence, it is no coincidence that the cosmic consciousness is spreading its wings, preparing for flight. Instead, as seen from the consciousness-comes-first perspective, it is a most natural progression and we have now matured sufficiently to put its insights into practice.

We have, in other words, a most exciting time ahead. *Never before* has the world—as we know it—been faced with a transformation like this and *never before* have we had an existence theory which involves such good news. The illusion of separation notwithstanding, we know now that the world is our collectively shared dream—and that we, with the power of thought, can create any reality we want.

Draped in forgetfulness, we have long lost our way in this dream. The weight of duality has almost crushed us, and the logic of fear has clouded our thinking to such an extent that we have created a keen nightmare. Nonetheless, being alive today is the most privileged position in history and a change of attitude, a change of perspective—a change *in awareness*—is all that is required to transform the dynamic between us and habitat. It is as simple as that and we only need to wake up to this realization, visualize another dream, and a new, more constructive vision of what we are—of *who* we are—will manifest.

All things considered, then, redeeming ourselves should be a simple matter. We know now that we and the Universe are one and that we are a sacrosanct and inviolable part of the Whole. After all, as seen from the greater perspective, nothing is limited, perishable, inadequate, or of lesser value. Concepts such as these are misconceptions arising from our inability to see the greater reality. And even though society has not yet come to terms with the implications of Wholeness, we have all the information we need to piece together how everything connects to everything. We have seen science give credence to mystical insight; how it confirms that consciousness is the essence of all things; that boundaries are illusory; and that things only appear separate because of our limited understanding. We also know that time is not linear, but a Totality that comes into being everywhere at once—and that *we all are everything all the time*. Thus, there is only *One*, but we study ourselves from an infinitude of perspectives so that we can see and experience every possible angle of existence.

It is only our surface-consciousness' narrow perspective that makes this recognition difficult. But it appears clearly from the expanded states of consciousness and Erwin Schrödinger, one of the great pioneers of quantum physics, described our relationship to time and totality as follows:

> "Inconceivable as it seems to ordinary reason, you—and all other conscious beings as such—are all in all. Hence this life of yours which you are living is not merely a piece of the entire existence, but it is, in a certain sense, the *whole*; only this whole is not so constituted that it can be surveyed in one single glance. This, as we know, is what the Brahmins expressed in that sacred, mystic formula which is yet really so simple and so clear: *Tat tvam asi*, this is you. Or, again, in such words as "I am in the east and in the west, I am below and above, I am this whole world."
>
> Thus, you can throw yourself flat on the ground, stretched out upon Mother Earth, with the certain conviction that you are one with her and she with you. You are as firmly established, as invulnerable, as she—indeed a thousand times firmer and more invulnerable. As surely as she will engulf you tomorrow, so surely she will bring you forth anew to new striving and suffering. And not merely, "some day": now, today, every day she is bringing you forth, not *once*, but thousands upon thousands of times, just as everyday she engulfs you a thousand times over. For eternally and always there is only now, one and the same now; the present is the only thing that has no end."(124.98)

A mystic could not have said it better. The Wholeness, eternity, and the present, after all, is one and the same—us—and through the process of self-actualization we gain access to a widening perspective which allows us to see it all the more clearly. As Aurobindo, one of the great mystics, described this process:

> "We know the divine and become the divine, because we are that already in our secret nature. All teaching is a revealing, all becoming is an unfolding. Self-attainment is

the secret; self-knowledge and increasing consciousness are
the means and the process."(10.60)

It is significant that finally, after billions of years, we have accrued
the wisdom to understand the bigger picture and see ourselves in this
context. Behind we have a long journey of distress, despair, loneliness,
and all else that followed from the illusion of separation, but when all is
said and done we shall find that it was worth it.

As the illusion of separation has left behind an incalculable amount
of pain some may feel less convinced. I, however, can only speak for
myself, and having seen the Universe from the cosmic consciousness'
perspective I would say that *only a taste* of this mystical experience
seems worth all the effort, all the difficulty and distress, associated with
our journey through duality.

Now, I believe the Universe is put together so that, from the standpoint of eternity, we can have as much cosmic consciousness as we would
like. Nevertheless, at some point, we will grow tired of even the bliss of
existence that perfect harmony with everything in the Innermost
Sanctuaries has to offer; we will feel like experiencing other sensations
than God's all-consuming, all-embracing love; and we will find our way
back to the physical, forget everything we know, everything we truly are,
so that we once more can recreate and rediscover ourselves as all there is
surrounded by the hardships of life in duality.

For as seen from the larger perspective, it is not so bad. Not only does
forgetfulness make the divine play possible; not only does duality offer
experience, qualities, and wisdom that we otherwise could not have
known; not only does our reduced being allow for a *re*cognition and
*re*membering we otherwise would have missed; not only does it make
possible all values; not only does it provide the ideals that follow from
Wholeness with weight and magnitude; not only does it allow us to be
what we couldn't otherwise have been: As seen from the greater view, it
is all those things we take so for granted on earth that draws us to this
place.

Being in human body and experiencing the world through the lens of
its consciousness, senses, and emotional register is a unique and superbly
enriching experience for the soul. Becoming acquainted with itself in this

form; the experience of childhood, adolescence, adulthood, and old age; of being man, woman, brother, sister, mother, father, grandmother, friend, lover and enemy; of getting to explore nature, bond with animals, marvel at the mystery, and despair over issues related to impermanence, inadequacy, and loneliness is the ultimate ride. Having to breathe to function, eat to keep the organism operating, fight to survive; all this is immensely interesting to the soul. It simply loves the infinity of experiences life has to offer; to enjoy the seasons and the weather, the wind against skin, the warmth of the sun; to sense the smells, tastes, touches, sounds, and inebriations; to be uplifted by hope, companionship, joy and other delights; to be swept away by desire, anger, fear, and love; to be subjected to the weight of gravity, vulnerability, delusion, and sorrow—*all this* is a source of unrivalled gratification and amusement. *Everything*, the good as well as the bad, are staggeringly good reasons to be here.

All things considered, then, we find that no matter how hard life on earth may be, it is actually quite grand; it is a truly amazing adventure—and no matter how horrible it may appear, the Force of Foreverness will make sure that everything works out in the end. Its hidden hand has guided us this far, trough all our trials and tribulations, and now that the worst is behind us we can look forward to a time that will be essentially different.

We are about to enter that Golden Age which has been foretold, and this age will be as bright as the past was dark. What this means will be up to time—and us—to tell, for even if there have been Utopian ages before they are never alike. The only thing they have in common is the overall picture; the illusion of separation gives way, consciousness is upgraded, the fog of fear and mistrust disappears, and the implications of Wholeness, first principles, and the Universe's/our glorious nature are exposed. The transition is huge, for we go from an age of virtually *zero* knowledge about reality to one with *complete* knowledge; the fullness of Being will come into its own and the Hand that moves everything—the one that never showed itself to the old consciousness—will reveal itself in all things.

It is written in the fabric of time that this age shall come to pass. It is the purposeful fulfillment of physical existence—the embodiment of the

Divine—for it is not only we who are lost with a desire to be found and complete; even the Universe feels that way, and that is precisely what will happen. We therefore all await the Great Revelation, that hour when the veil is rent, when GodForce is revealed in all things and we shall see clearly. We all await the Great Awakening, that hour when forgetfulness withdraws and the fragments remember themselves as all that is. We all await the Great Reunion, the hour when all that was lost will be found; when all that was separated will be full and complete; and when the Miracle, through unveiled and direct presence, will be even grander and more profound than before. We all await this Great Transformation, the hour when the Spirit will uncloak itself in matter and our cells start to glow; when we will feel the Universe breathing through every fiber of our Being; and when we will be filled with an overwhelming appreciation of what it means to be the Mystery, that the Mystery is us, and that we have always been ONE. We all await this Radiant Hour when our roots in Eternity will emerge in the open; when we will feel the Universe's timeless reality interpenetrate and pervade our being; when we will see everything that ever was, is, and will be as us; and when we will realize that our voyage through time is our journey *through ourselves.*

At this hour, we will understand completely what it means to be the Universe's road to remembrance, its striving towards perfection; we will see that *total self-awareness* is the clue to everything (as without it there can be no completion) and that we are the means to this end.[128]

That we will get to experience this hour is for certain. As seen from the greater reality it has already occurred, for there is no time and the only reason why we have not yet experienced this transformation is that the collective psyche remains enthralled by unconsciousness. It need not be long, however, for as Aurobindo noted, "If earth calls and the Supreme answers, the hour can be even be now for that immense and glorious transformation."(8.105) And when this hour strikes, we will finally

---

[128] Reason dictates that without the principle of enlightenment, there can only be the blind leading the blind, and so we are continually being hammered on the anvil of time until salvation is found in the ideals, values, and principles of Wholeness. As we merge with this Wholeness, however, we see that this river of time was the Universe sensing itself, awakening to itself, getting to know itself, and slowly remembering itself—and that this is the secret behind this magnificent odyssey through All That Is.

understand the full implications of the eternal truth so beautifully immortalized by T.S. Eliot:

"WE SHALL NOT CEASE FROM EXPLORATION
AND THE END OF ALL OUR EXPLORING
WILL BE TO ARRIVE WHERE WE STARTED
AND KNOW THE PLACE FOR THE FIRST TIME."

AFTERWORD

WE HAVE SUMMARIZED the implications of Wholeness and how everything connects to everything as seen from the consciousness-comes-first perspective. I understand if this book is not capable of satisfying every reader's curiosity or skepticism. This, of course, was not its purpose. Its purpose was to sketch a framework for the new existence theory, present some evidence, and elaborate on its connotations for individuals and society.

It is in the cards, therefore, that this roadmap is not only incomplete but that educated minds will find glitches and room for improvement. In a sense, it can be compared to the 17th century's maps of the world, and it will be the task of professionals to improve upon its flaws. That said, the book is a good starting point for more thorough explorations. And when it comes to this, I recommend some basic books:

- Neale Donald Walsch, *Conversations with God* (Book 1, 2, 3). These are easy-to-read books that will provide the reader with a good introduction to most aspects related to the new existential theory and the self-actualization process.

- The following books by Jane Roberts: *Seth Speaks*, *The Nature of Personal Reality*, and *The Individual and the Nature of Mass Events*. These books present us with the energy-personality Seth's view on the world. Channeling this entity, Jane Roberts and her husband left behind a huge legacy, and for those who want to dig deeper into the nature of reality they are vastly informative. The first book presents a general introduction, the second elaborates on our personal relationship with the world, while the third has more to say on the greater picture and the role of the individual as seen in a social context. For social engineers and other professionals who want to read more, they should check out Aurobindo's trilogy *The Human Cycle, The Ideal of Human Unity, and War and Self-determination*

- *A Course in Miracles*: This is the inner-oriented Christianity's new "bible", and a good book on the self-actualization process.

I would like to make it clear that the abovementioned books, except Aurobindo, are "channeled" material. This means that non-physical entities make use of a medium (the author) to present their message. While they are worth a read, many people will prefer less controversial literature, and for those who want more traditional and down-to-earth authors the following books are a great introduction:

- (1) Tony Schwartz, *What Really Matters: Searching for Wisdom in America*; (2) Michael Talbot, *The Holographic Universe*; (3) Lynne McTaggart, *The Field: The Quest for the Secret Force of the Universe*; and (4) David Wilcock, *The Source Field Investigations*. These books are more scientific in their approach. The first is easy to read and entertaining; the second is a classic and one of the most impressive books I have read in terms of consciousness research; the third is another classic, elaborating further on consciousness research and the science behind the new paradigm; the fourth is Wilcock's masterpiece and it will take the reader through the science behind the consciousness-comes-first perspective. If these books cannot make a skeptic change his/her mind, nothing will.

- For those who want to know more about psychedelic drugs, their history, effects, and potential as aides in self-actualization Christopher Gray, *The Acid Diaries* is great. Also this book is highly entertaining, well written, and easy-to-read.

- And last but not least, for wisdom-seekers who want to know more about mysticism, transpersonal psychology, and how the inner and the outer world connects, Ken Wilber's books are required reading.

SHOUT OUTS!!

This book was originally written in a high-security prison in 2011-14. It was reedited in 2019, but superficially, and this means that the work is defined by challenges that had to be overcome (inadequate access to internet, computer, professionals, bookstores, etc.). Whether the result is satisfactory is for others to decide, but I will thank the following people for being there during prison days:

- Lisbeth Livsdatter Mikalsen, my mother: For life and for helping with a thousand favors these years in prison. You have been my closest friend and benefactor throughout a difficult period of life.

- Stian and Ewa Simonsen: For your encouragement and all you have invested of time and resources in helping see this project through.

- Jan Erik Enerud: For your dedication to this project and for many good conversations these prison years.

- Enrico Marcus Quarto: For keeping it real behind bars of steel and for helping proofread this book. Also, thanks to Ekene Amaechi and David Bullen for helping out.

- Reidun and Asbjørn Mikalsen, my grandparents: For your contribution to my life, for helping economically, and for your visits to prison.

- Moreover, I would like to thank the following people for helping me keep the faith in humanity these prison years: Kim Andre Hagen, Cathrine Burud, Nina Jansen, David Emberland, Sjur Kolstad, Anne Kristine Bohinen, Anne Knudtsen, Denis Pados, Sondre Mikalsen, Silje Mikalsen, Svein Mikalsen, Marie

Grinder, Trond Grinder, Thea Kathrin Grinder, Anett Grinder, Magnus Grinder, Elin Marie Tveter, Astrid Amor, Petter Nyhagen, Simen Våreid, Espen Sørli, Åsil Rønning, Ylva Drage, Hilde Andersen, Anthony Strand, Øystein Bjor, Geir Jevnsveen, Andreas Ribe, Hans Petter Wold, David Toska, Patrick Kihle, Daniel de Linde, Bjørnar Jensen, Diego Hobber, Wiggo Norum, Daniel Mortensen, Tudor Istrate, Odd Gjøen, Nils Christie, and Frederik Polak.

- Ellen Caroline Brenger, my soulmate, for being there and making the last six months of prison—and thereafter—a journey like none. I Love you.

- And last but not least, the reader: For lending me your time and for keeping me company through these pages.

LIST OF REFERENCES

1. Agee, Philip, *Inside the Company: A CIA Diary* (Stonehill 1975).
2. Amundsen, Rune, *Livets Speil* (Kolofon 2006).
3. Andenæs, Johs, *Alminnelig Strafferett* (Universitetsforlaget 2004).
4. Andenæs, Johs, Straffen Som Problem (Exil 1994).
5. Andenæs, Mads. Bjørge, Erik, *Menneskerettene og Oss* (Universitetsforlaget 2012).
6. Andrews, Andy, *How Do You Kill 11 Million People* (Thomas Nelson 2010).
7. Assagioli, Roberto, *Transpersonal Development* (Aquarian Press 1993).
8. Aurobindo, Sri, *The Hour of God* (Lotus Press 2009).
9. Aurobindo, Sri, *The Life Divine* (Pondicherry 1970).
10. Aurobindo, Sri, *On Yoga: The Synthesis of Yoga* (Pondicherry 1957).
11. Barrow, John. Tipler, Frank, *The Antropic Cosmological Principle* (Oxford University Press 1996).
12. Bennett, Scott, *Shell Game* (2013) (online book)
13. Bewley-Taylor, David R., *International Drug Control: Consensus Fractured* (Cambridge University Press 2012).
14. Braden, Gregg, *The Divine Matrix: Bridging Time, Space, Miracles, and Belief* (HayHouse 2007).
15. Braden, Gregg, *The God Code* (HayHouse 2010).
16. Brogan, Hugh, *Longman History of the United States of America* (1987).
17. Bucke, R. M., *Cosmic Consciousness: A Study in the Evolution of the Human Mind* (University Books 1961).
18. Capra, Fritjof, *The Tao of Physics: An Exploration of the Parallels Between Modern Physics and Eastern Mysticism* (Shambala 2010).
19. Chomsky, Noam, *Power and Terror: Conflict, Hegemony, and the Rule of Force* (Pluto Press 2011).
20. Chopra, Deepak, *Livet Etter Døden* (CappelenDamm 2008).
21. Close, Edward R., *Transcendental Physics* (toExcel Press 2000).
22. Colby, Gerard, *Du Pont Dynasty: Behind the Nylon Curtain* (Lyle Stuart 1984).
23. Collins, Francis S., *The Language of God: A Scientist Presents Evidence for Belief* (Gate, Centage 2007).
24. Crawford, April, *Parting Notes: A Connection With the Afterlife* (First Books 2002).

25. Cutler, Howard C. Lama, Dalai, *The Art of Happiness; a Handbook for Living* (Hodder & Stoughton 1999).

26. Davies, Paul, *The Cosmic Blueprint: New Discoveries in Nature's Creative Ability to Order the Universe* (Templeton Foundation Press 2004).

27. Dean, Stanley R. (ed.), *Psychiatry & Mysticism* (Nelson-Hall 1979).

28. Deane, Ashayana, *Voyagers: The Secrets of Amenti* (Wildflower Press 2009).

29. DeCamp, John, *The Franklin Cover-Up* (AWT. Inc 1992).

30. DeChardin, Teilhard, *Letters From a Traveller* (Fontana Books 1975).

31. Dice, Mark, *Illuminati: Facts and Fiction* (The Resitance 2009).

32. Dossey, Larry, *Legevidenskabens Krise: Universet og Menneskets Sunnhed—Det Banebrydende Paradigma* (Borgen 1984).

33. Dossey, Larry, *Ord Som Helbreder: Om Bønnens Kraft i Lys av Moderne Medisin* (Grøndahl Dryer 1996).

34. Dossey, Larry, *Reinventing Medicine: Beyond Mind-Body to a New Era of Healing* (Harper Collins 1999).

35. Dyer, Wayne W., *Åndens Energi: Gir Løsningen på Alle Dine Problemer* (Hilt og Hansteen 2003).

36. Eckhoff, Torstein. Sundby, Nils Kristian, *Rettssystemer* (Tano 1991).

37. Eskeland, Ståle, *De Mest Alvorlige Forbrytelser* (CappelenDamm 2011).

38. Forte, Robert (ed.), *Entheogens and the Future of Religion* (Park Street Press 2012).

39. Gackenbach, Jayne. Bosweld, Jane, *Control Your Dreams* (Harper & Row 1989).

40. Gebser, Jean, *The Ever Present Origin* (Ohio University Press 1997).

41. Gerber, Richard, *Vibrational Medicine* (Bear & Co 2001).

42. Goswami, Amit, *The Self-Aware Universe: How Consciousness Creates the Material World* (Simon & Schuster 1993).

43. Gray, Christopher, *The Acid Diaries: A Psychonaut's Guide to the History and Use of LSD* (Park Street Press 2010).

44. Gray, James P., *Why Our Drug Laws Have Failed and What We Can Do About It: A Judicial Indictment of the War on Drugs* (Temple University Press 2001).

45. Grinde, Bjørn, *Gud: En Vitenskapelig Oppdatering* (Flux Forlag 2008).

46. Gritz, James Bo, *A Nation Betrayed* (Lazarus Publishing Company 1989).

47. Grof, Stanislav. Halifax, Joan, *The Human Encounter With Death* (E. P. Dutton 1977).

48. Grof, Stanislav, *Psychology of the Future* (Suny Press 2000).

49. Grof, Stanislav, *Realms of the Human Unconscious: Observations From LSD Research* (Souvenir Press 1979).

50. Grof, Stanislav, *When the Impossible Happens* (Soundstrue 2006).

51. Hagtvet, Bernt, *Ideologienes Århundre: En Personlig Vandring i det 20. Århundrets Politiske Idehistorie* (Dreyer 2010).

52. Halvorsen, Jan Sunder, *Mennesket: Maskin Eller Mysterium? Naturvitenskapen Møter Mystikken* (Flux Forlag 2010)

53. Hegel. G. W., *The Philosophy of History* (Dover Publications 1956).

54. Hichcock, Andrew Carrington, *The Synagogue of Satan* (online book)

55. Hognestad, Helge, *Gud i Mennesket: Ny tid—Ny Kristendom* (Flux Forlag 2006)

56. Husak, Douglas, *Drugs and Rights* (Cambridge University Press 1992).

57. Huchinson, Michael, *MegaBrain: New Tools and Techniques For Brain Growth and Mind Expansion* (Ballantine 1996).

58. Høstmælingen, Njål, *Hva Er Menneskerettigheter?* (Universitetsforlaget 2010).

59. Irving, Ronald, *The Law Is a Ass* (Duckworth Overlook 2010).

60. Jahn, Robert G. Dunne, Brenda J., *Margins of Reality: The Role of Consciousness in the Physical World* (Harcourt Brace, Jovanovich 1987).

61. James, William, *The Varieties of Religious Experience* (Barnes & Noble 2004).

62. Krishna, Gopi, *Kundalini: The Evolutionary Energy in Man* (Shambala 1997).

63. Langer, Ellen. Alexander, Charles, *Higher Stages of Human Development: Perspectives on Adult Growth* (Oxford University Press 1990).

64. Leira, Haldis Karen, *Det Gode Nærvær: Kulturens Psykologiske Betydning* (Fagbokforlaget 2009).

65. Lewis, C. S., *The Problem of Pain* (New York MacMillan 1962).

66. Lilly, John C., *The Center of the Cyclone: An Autobiography of Inner Space* (Julian Press 1972).

67. Lipton, Bruce H., *The Biology of Belief: Unleashing the Power of Consciousness, Matter and Miracles* (HayHouse 2010).

68. Magee, Brian, *Filosofi: Tenkningens Historie Gjennom 2500 år* (CappelenDamm 2010).

69. Maslow, Abraham, *Toward a Psychology of Being* (Van Nostrand Reinhold 1982).

70. Mikalsen, Roar, *Human Rising: Et Oppgjør Med Narkotikalovgivningens Manglende Troverdighet* (Kolofon 2010).

71. Mill, John Stuart, *On Liberty (Penguin Books 2010)*.

72. Murphy, Michael, *The Future of the Body: Explorations Into the Further Evolution of Human Nature* (Tarcher 1992).

73. Musto, David, *The American Disease: Origins of Narcotic Control* (Yale University Press 1973).

74. Myskja, Audun, *Kunsten å Dø: Livet Før og Etter Døden i et Nytt Lys* (J. M. Stenersen forlag 2012).

75. Newberg, Andrew, et al., *Why God Won't Go Away: Brain Science and the Biology of Belief* (Ballantine 2001).

76. Nutt, David, *Drugs—Without the Hot Air: Minimising the Harms of Legal and Illegal Drugs* (UIT Cambridge 2012).

77. Osis, Karlis. Haraldson, Erlendur, *What They Saw... at the Hour of Death* (Avon Books 1977).

78. Pagels, Elaine, *De Gnostiske Evangelier* (Lille Måne forlag 2007).

79. Paul, Ron, *Liberty Defined* (Grand Central 2011).

80. Payne, Thomas, *Rights of Man* (WordsWorth 1996).

81. Pearce, Joseph Chilton, *The Biology of Transcendence: A Blueprint of the Human Spirit* (Park Street press2002).

82. Pearsall, Paul, *The Heart's Code: Tapping the Wisdom and Power of Our Heart Energy* (Broadway books 1998).

83. Pert, Candace B., *Molecules of Emotion: Why You Feel the Way You Feel* (Pocket Books 1999).

84. Pickett, Lynn. Prince, Clive, *The Templar Revelation: Secret guardians of the True identity of Christ* (Touchstone 1988).

85. Pinchbeck, Daniel, *2012: the Return of Quetzalcoatl* (Penguin 2006).

86. Reich, Wilhelm, *The Mass Psychology of Fascism* (Ferrar, Straus & Giroux 1970).

87. Ring, Kenneth, *Heading Toward Omega: In Search of the Meaning of the Near-Death Experience* (Quill, William, Morrow 1985).

88. Roberts, Jane, *The Seth Material* (Buccaneer Books 1970).

89. Room, Robin, et al., *Cannabis Policy: Moving Beyond Stalemate* (Oxford University Press 2010).

90. Ross, Elisabeth Kübler, *Døden Er Livsviktig: Om Livet, Døden, og Livet Etter Døden* (Damm 2005).

91. Russel, Peter, *The Global Brain: Speculations on the Evolutionary Leap of Planetary Consciousness* (J. P. Tarcher 1983).

92. Sabom, Michael B., *Recollections of Death* (Harper & Row 1982).

93. Satprem, *Sri Aurobindo or the Adventure of Consciousness* (Manipal Press 2008).

94. Schanning, Espen, *Den Tilsiktede Smerten: En Blindflekk i Norsk Kriminalpolitikk* (Unipub 2009).

95. Schwartz, Tony, *What Really Matters: Searching for Wisdom in America* (Bantam 1996).

96. Sheldrake, Rupert, et al. *Chaos, Creativity and Cosmic Consciousness* (Park Street Press 2001).

97. Sheldrake, Rupert, *Morphic Resonance: The Nature of Formative Causation* (Park Street Press 2009).

98. Sheldrake Rupert, *The Presence of the Past: Morphic Resonance and the Habits of Nature* (Park Street press 1995).

99. Siegel, Bernie S., *Love, Medicine and Miracles* (Random House 1999)

100. Smith, Huston, *Cleansing the Doors of Perception: The Religious Significance of Entheogenic Plants and Chemicals* (Tarcher/Putnam 2000)

101. Smoley, Richard, *Inner Christianity: A Guide to the Esoteric Tradition* (Shambala 2002).

102. Spooner, Lysander, *Vices are Not Crimes* (Nettartikkel).

103. Steinberg, Leif, *The Islamization of Science* (Novapress 1996)

104. Stevenson, Ian, *Children Who Remember Previous Lives: A Question of Reincarnation* (The University of Virginia 1987).

105. Still, William T., *New World Order: The Ancient Plan of Secret Societies* (Huntington House Publishers 1990).

106. Szasz, Thomas, *Our Right to Drugs: The Case for a Free Market* (Praeger 1992).

107. Talbot, Michael, *Mysticism and the New Physics* (Routledge & Kegan 1981).

108. Talbot, Michael, *The Holographic Universe* (Harper Perennial 2011)

109. Teasdale, Wayne, *The Mystic Heart: Discovering a Universal Spirituality in the World's Religions* (New World Library 1999).

110. Thoreau, Henry David, *Civil Disobedience* (Penguin Books 1984).

111. Underhill, Evelyn, *Mysticism: A Study in the nature and Development of Man's Spiritual Consciousness* (Methuen & Co 1962).

112. Vaughan, Alan, *Incredible Coincidence: The Baffling World of Synchronicity* (J. B. Lippincott 1979).

113. Wade, Jenny, *Changes of Mind: A Holonomic Theory of the Evolution of Consciousness* (State university of New York Press 1996).

114. Walsch, Neale Donald, *Himmelske samtaler: En Uvanlig Dialog, Bok 1* (CappelenDamm 2010).

115. Walsh, Roger N. & Vaughan, Frances (ed.), *Beyond Ego: Transpersonal Dimensions in Psychology* (J.P. Tarcher 1980).

116. Watson, Lyall, *Lifetide: A Biology of the Unconscious* (Hodder & Stoughton 1979).

117. Weiss, Brian, *Samme Sjel, Mange Liv: Om Den Healende Kraften i Fremtidige Liv* (N. W. Damm & Søn 2006).

118. White, John (ed.), *Kundalini: Evolution and Enlightenment* (Paragon House 1990).

119. Wilber, Ken, *The Eye of Spirit: An Integral Vision For a World Gone Slightly Mad* (Shambala 1998).

120. Wilber, Ken, *Eye to Eye: The Quest For the New Paradigm* (Shambala 1996).

121. Wilber, Ken, *Grace and Grit: Spirituality and Healing in the Life and Death of Treya Killam Wilber* (Gateway 2001).

122. Wilber, Ken, *Integral Spirituality: A Startling New Role For Religion in the Modern and Postmodern World* (Integral Books 2006).

123. Wilber, Ken, *Up From Eden: A Transpersonal View of Human Evolution* (New Science Library 1986).

124. Wilber, Ken, *Quantum Questions: Mystical Writings of the World's Greatest Physicists* (Shambala 2001).

125. Wilcock, David, *Confirmed: The Trillion Dollar Lawsuit That Could End Financial Tyranny* (online article).

126. Wilcock, David, *Financial Tyranny* (online article).

127. Wilcock, David, *The Source Field Investigations: The Hidden Science and Lost Civilizations Behind the 2012 Prophecies* (Dutton 2011).

128. Wilkinson, Richard. Pickett, Kate, *The Spirit Level: Why Equality Is Better For Everyone* (Penguin 2010).

129. Wilson, Woodrow, *The New Freedom* (1913, online book)

130. www.encod.org: *ENCODs statement to the CND session*

131. Zukav, Gary, *The Dancing Wu Li Masters: An Overview of the New Physics* (Morrow & Co 1979).

132. Zukav, Gary. Francis, Linda, *Sjelens sinn* (N.W. Damm & Søn 2005).

Roar Mikalsen is the author of six books which are changing the world one at a time. His authorship covers a large area ranging from cosmology, mysticism, self-help, and consciousness research to power politics, human rights, drug policy, constitutional interpretation, and social engineering. He is the founder of the Alliance for Rights-Oriented Drug Policies (AROD), an organization which addresses drug policy reform from a perspective of human rights law and a nominee of two prestigious human rights awards (Vaclav Havel and Martin Ennals).

A platform for his work is Life Liberty Productions, a publishing house and consulting agency dedicated to the Spirit of Freedom. You will find books that are embraced by professionals and have the potential to bring humanity one step further on the online store lifelibertybooks.com

9 788826 923214